Advanced Image Processing Techniques and Applications

N. Suresh Kumar
VIT University, India

Arun Kumar Sangaiah
VIT University, India

M. Arun
VIT University, India

S. Anand
VIT University, India

A volume in the Advances in Computational
Intelligence and Robotics (ACIR) Book Series

www.igi-global.com

Published in the United States of America by
    IGI Global
    Information Science Reference (an imprint of IGI Global)
    701 E. Chocolate Avenue
    Hershey PA, USA 17033
    Tel: 717-533-8845
    Fax: 717-533-8661
    E-mail: cust@igi-global.com
    Web site: http://www.igi-global.com

Library of Congress Cataloging-in-Publication Data

Names: Kumar, N. Suresh, 1979- editor. | Sangaiah, Arun Kumar, 1981- editor.
  | Arun, M., 1979- editor. | Anand, S. (Engineer), editor.
Title: Advanced image processing techniques and applications / N. Suresh
  Kumar, Arun Kumar Sangaiah, M. Arun, and S. Anand, editors.
Description: Hershey, PA : Information Science Reference, 2017. | Includes
  bibliographical references.
Identifiers: LCCN 2016054395| ISBN 9781522520535 (hardcover) | ISBN
  9781522520542 (ebook)
Subjects: LCSH: Image processing--Industrial applications--Handbooks,
  manuals, etc.
Classification: LCC TA1637 .H363 2017 | DDC 006.6--dc23 LC record available at https://lccn.loc.gov/2016054395

This book is published in the IGI Global book series Advances in Computational Intelligence and Robotics (ACIR) (ISSN: 2327-0411; eISSN: 2327-042X)

British Cataloguing in Publication Data
A Cataloguing in Publication record for this book is available from the British Library.

For electronic access to this publication, please contact: eresources@igi-global.com.

Advances in Computational Intelligence and Robotics (ACIR) Book Series

Ivan Giannoccaro
University of Salento, Italy

ISSN:2327-0411
EISSN:2327-042X

MISSION

While intelligence is traditionally a term applied to humans and human cognition, technology has progressed in such a way to allow for the development of intelligent systems able to simulate many human traits. With this new era of simulated and artificial intelligence, much research is needed in order to continue to advance the field and also to evaluate the ethical and societal concerns of the existence of artificial life and machine learning.

The **Advances in Computational Intelligence and Robotics (ACIR) Book Series** encourages scholarly discourse on all topics pertaining to evolutionary computing, artificial life, computational intelligence, machine learning, and robotics. ACIR presents the latest research being conducted on diverse topics in intelligence technologies with the goal of advancing knowledge and applications in this rapidly evolving field.

COVERAGE

- Pattern Recognition
- Algorithmic Learning
- Adaptive and Complex Systems
- Computer Vision
- Artificial Life
- Artificial Intelligence
- Evolutionary Computing
- Brain Simulation
- Intelligent control
- Agent technologies

IGI Global is currently accepting manuscripts for publication within this series. To submit a proposal for a volume in this series, please contact our Acquisition Editors at Acquisitions@igi-global.com or visit: http://www.igi-global.com/publish/.

Titles in this Series

For a list of additional titles in this series, please visit: www.igi-global.com

Advanced Research on Biologically Inspired Cognitive Architectures
Jordi Vallverdú (Universitat Autònoma de Barcelona, Spain) Manuel Mazzara (Innopolis University, Russia) Max Talanov (Kazan Federal University, Russia) Salvatore Distefano (University of Messina, Italy & Kazan Federal University, Russia) and Robert Lowe (University of Gothenburg, Sweden & University of Skövde, Sweden)
Information Science Reference • copyright 2017 • 297pp • H/C (ISBN: 9781522519478) • US $195.00 (our price)

Theoretical and Practical Advancements for Fuzzy System Integration
Deng-Feng Li (Fuzhou University, China)
Information Science Reference • copyright 2017 • 415pp • H/C (ISBN: 9781522518488) • US $200.00 (our price)

Multi-Agent-Based Simulations Applied to Biological and Environmental Systems
Diana Francisca Adamatti (Universidade Federal do Rio Grande, Brazil)
Information Science Reference • copyright 2017 • 406pp • H/C (ISBN: 9781522517566) • US $205.00 (our price)

Strategic Imperatives and Core Competencies in the Era of Robotics and Artificial Intelligence
Roman Batko (Jagiellonian University, Poland) and Anna Szopa (Jagiellonian University, Poland)
Business Science Reference • copyright 2017 • 302pp • H/C (ISBN: 9781522516569) • US $185.00 (our price)

Emerging Research on Applied Fuzzy Sets and Intuitionistic Fuzzy Matrices
Amal Kumar Adak (Jafuly Deshpran High School, India) Debashree Manna (Damda Jr. High School, India) and Monoranjan Bhowmik (Vidyasagar Teacher's Training College, India)
Information Science Reference • copyright 2017 • 375pp • H/C (ISBN: 9781522509141) • US $205.00 (our price)

Multi-Core Computer Vision and Image Processing for Intelligent Applications
Mohan S. (Al Yamamah University, Saudi Arabia) and Vani V. (Al Yamamah University, Saudi Arabia)
Information Science Reference • copyright 2017 • 292pp • H/C (ISBN: 9781522508892) • US $210.00 (our price)

Developing and Applying Optoelectronics in Machine Vision
Oleg Sergiyenko (Autonomous University of Baja California, Mexico) and Julio C. Rodriguez-Quiñonez (Autonomous University of Baja California, Mexico)
Information Science Reference • copyright 2017 • 341pp • H/C (ISBN: 9781522506324) • US $205.00 (our price)

Pattern Recognition and Classification in Time Series Data
Eva Volna (University of Ostrava, Czech Republic) Martin Kotyrba (University of Ostrava, Czech Republic) and Michal Janosek (University of Ostrava, Czech Republic)
Information Science Reference • copyright 2017 • 282pp • H/C (ISBN: 9781522505655) • US $185.00 (our price)

www.igi-global.com

701 E. Chocolate Ave., Hershey, PA 17033
Order online at www.igi-global.com or call 717-533-8845 x100
To place a standing order for titles released in this series, contact: cust@igi-global.com
Mon-Fri 8:00 am - 5:00 pm (est) or fax 24 hours a day 717-533-8661

Table of Contents

Detailed Table of Contents

Chapter 1
Ezhilmaran D, VIT University, India
Adhiyaman M, VIT University, India

Fuzzy set theory originates to a great extent of interest among the researchers in past decades. It is a key tool to handle the imperfect of information in the diverse field. Typically, it plays a very important role in image processing and found the significant development in many active areas such as pattern recognition, neural network, medical imaging, etc. The use of fuzzy set theory is to tackle uncertainty in the form of membership functions when there is an image gray levels or information is lost. This chapter concerns the preliminaries of fuzzy, intuitionistic fuzzy, type-2 fuzzy and intuitionistic type-2 fuzzy set theory and its application in the fingerprint image; furthermore, the contrast enhancement and edge detection are carried out for that with the assistance of fuzzy set theory. It is useful to the students who want to self-study. This chapter composed just to address that issue.

Chapter 2
Prabhakar C. J., Kuvempu University, India

In this chapter, we present an overview of text information extraction from images/video. This chapter starts with an introduction to computer vision and its applications, which is followed by an introduction to text information extraction from images/video. We describe various forms of text, challenges and steps involved in text information extraction process. The literature review of techniques for text information extraction from images/video is presented. Finally, our approach for extraction of scene text information from images is presented.

Chapter 3

Chantana Chantrapornchai, Kasetsart University, Thailand
Jitdumrong Preechasuk, Silpakorn University, Thailand

Steganography is one of the techniques used to communicate secret data through the cover media such as images, videos, audio, texts etc. In this work, we consider the algorithms of steganography based on DCT and wavelet transform. The aspects of media quality after hiding the information in the digital media are considered. Particularly, we compare the performance of the prototype algorithms, representing the DCT and wavelet-based image steganography algorithms respectively, using the PSNR, capacity, robustness and accuracy aspects. For video steganography, with various wavelet transforms, we compare the quality of the derived information, when frames are dropped and the effects of payload is studied. The application of using such steganography algorithm which can embed multiple messages, each of which requires a separate key is proposed. The application can estimate the capacity used and capacity remains for the given cover image and texts.

Chapter 4

Alex Noel Joseph Raj, VIT University, India
Vijayalakshmi G. V. Mahesh, VIT University, India

This chapter presents an analysis on Zernike Moments from the class of orthogonal moments which are invariant to rotation, translation and scaling. The chapter initially focuses on the review of Zernike moments as 1D, 2D and 3D based on their dimension and later investigates on the construction, characteristics of Zernike Moments and their invariants, which can be used as a shape descriptor to capture global and detailed information from the data based on their order to provide outstanding performance in various applications of image processing. Further the chapter also presents an application of 2D Zernike Moments features for plant species recognition and classification using supervised learning techniques. The performance of the learned models was evaluated with True Positive Rate, True Rejection ratio, False Acceptance Rate, False Rejection Ratio and Receiver Operating Characteristics. The simulation results indicate that the Zernike moments with its invariants was successful in recognising and classifying the images with least FAR and significant TRR.

Chapter 5

Shantharajah S. P., VIT University, India
Ramkumar T, VIT University, India
Balakrishnan N, Sona College of Technology, India

Image enhancement is a quantifying criterion for sharpening and enhancing image quality, where many techniques are empirical with interactive procedures to obtain précised results. The proposed Intensity Histogram Equalization (IHE) approach conquers the noise defects that has a preprocessor to remove noise and enhances image contrast, providing ways to improve the intensity of the image. The preprocessor has the mask production, enlightenment equalization and color normalization for efficient processing of the images which generates a binary image by labeling pixels, overcomes the non-uniform illumination of image and classifies color capacity, respectively. The distinct and discrete mapping function calculates the histogram values and improves the contrast of the image. The performance of IHE is based on noise removal ratio, reliability rate, false positive error measure, Max-Flow Computational Complexity Measure with NDRA and Variation HOD. As the outcome, the different levels of contrast have been significantly improved when evaluated against with the existing systems.

Chapter 6

Kuppusamy Krishnamoorthy, Alagappa University, India
Mahalakshmi Jeyabalu, Alagappa University, India

Security of images in transmission medium is most prime issue found in literature. Encryption of images is a way to secure it from unauthorized access. The authors in this chapter insist on the encryption of images via block ciphers. Block ciphers works simultaneously as well as on chunks. In this chapter, an encryption method using improved cipher block chaining is proposed to encrypt RGB color images. For every encryption methodology, key generation process is the most important phase. The authors proposed sub-optimal key generation algorithm and this nature inspired optimization technique reveals complex keys, remains very useful for decision making in dynamic environment. Key generation is crafted as complex with this mathematical model that overcomes the predicament key problem exists in existing methods and upgrades quality of encryption. Results of the proposed algorithm show the efficiency and its resistance against various cryptanalytic attacks.

Chapter 7

Mangayarkarasi Ramaiah, VIT University, India
Bimal Kumar Ray, VIT University, India

This chapter presents a technique which uses the sum of height square as a measure to define the deflection associated with a pseudo high curvature points on the digital planar curve. The proposed technique iteratively removes the pseudo high curvature points whose deflection is minimal, and recalculates the deflection associated with its neighbouring pseudo high curvature points. The experimental results of the proposed technique are compared with recent state of the art iterative point elimination methods. The comparative results show that the proposed technique produces the output polygon in a better way than others for most of the input digital curve.

Chapter 8

Shape Determination of Aspired Foreign Body on Pediatric Radiography Images Using Rule-Based Approach 170

Vasumathy M, VIT University, India
Mythili Thirugnanam, VIT University, India

Foreign body aspiration (FBA) is a common problem among pediatric population that requires early diagnosis and prompt successful management. Conventionally the radiography image inspection processes are carried out manually by the experts of medical field. Recently automated systems are developed to improve the quality of the radiography images but none of the work carried out especially to determine the characteristics of the foreign bodies in pediatric foreign body aspired radiography images. The proposed approach focuses on characterizing the foreign body shape using sixteen various geometric and edge features. The shapes are determined by using fuzzy logical connectives formed by logically connecting two or more extracted information and a binary decision tree. More than 100 X-Ray radiography images are used to obtained the experimental research. The method proved that the results are more accurate in determining the foreign body shapes as circle, polygon, sharp and irregular automatically with less time.

Chapter 9

Evaluation of Image Detection and Description Algorithms for Application in Monocular SLAM 182

Claudio Urrea, Universidad de Santiago de Chile, Chile
Gabriel Solar, Universidad de Santiago de Chile, Chile

The results of new experiments on the detection and description of images for an EKF-SLAM monocular application are employed in order to obtain a dispersed set of features without related data association problems. By means of different detectors/descriptors, the number of features observed and the ability to observe the same feature in various captures is evaluated. To this end, a monocular vision system independent of the EKF-SLAM system is designed and implemented using the MatLab software. This new system allows for—in addition to image capture—the detection and description of features as well as the association of data between images, thus serving as a priori information to avoid incorrect associations between the obtained features and the map of an EKF-SLAM system. Additionally, it enables the evaluation and comparison of the precision, consistency and convergence of various algorithms.

Chapter 10

Diophantine Equations for Enhanced Security in Watermarking Scheme for Image Authentication 205

Padma T, Sona College of Technology, India
Jayashree Nair, AIMS Institutes, India

Hard mathematical problems having no polynomial time algorithms to determine a solution are seemly in design of secure cryptosystems. The proposed watermarking system used number theoretic concepts of the hard higher order Diophantine equations for image content authentication scheme with three major phases such as 1) Formation of Diophantine equation; 2) Generation and embedding of dual Watermarks; and 3) Image content authentication and verification of integrity. Quality of the watermarked images, robustness to compression and security are bench-marked with two peer schemes which used dual watermarks.

Chapter 11

Claudio Urrea, Universidad de Santiago de Chile, Chile
Alex Yau, Universidad de Santiago de Chile, Chile

The design, construction and programming of a mobile robot controlled by means of artificial vision, capable of recognizing, grabbing and moving specific objects in a completely autonomous way is presented, together with the conceptual and theoretical-practical grounds for the work. A mechanically robust robot is built and a system is designed, allowing the mobility of two sensors jointly, i.e., artificial vision camera and distance sensor. This makes it possible to improve the range of artificial vision, over approximately 180°, achieving precise positioning of the mobile robot. The artificial vision camera, CMUCam 2, provides the mobile robot with great autonomy thanks to its excellent interaction with its surrounding world. Having a mobile robot like this will allow interesting developments to be made in various areas of mobile robotics.

Chapter 12

Chitra Anil Dhawale, P. R. Pote College of Engineering and Management, India

Biometric Systems provide improved security over traditional electronic access control methods such as RFID tags, electronic keypads and some mechanical locks. The user's authorized card or password pin can be lost or stolen. In order for the biometrics to be ultra-secure and to provide more-than-average accuracy, more than one form of biometric identification is required. Hence the need arises for the use of multimodal biometrics. This uses a combination of different biometric recognition technologies. This chapter begins with the basic idea of Biometrics, Biometrics System with its components, Working and proceeds with the need of Multimodal Biometrics with the emphasis on review of various multimodal systems based on fusion ways and fusion level of various features. The last section of this chapter describes various multimodal Biometric Systems.

Chapter 13

Jeyabharathi D, Anna University Regional Campus – Tirunelveli, India
Dejey D, Anna University Regional Campus – Tirunelveli, India

Developing universal methods for background subtraction and object tracking is one of the critical and hardest challenges in many video processing and computer-vision applications. To achieve superior foreground detection quality across unconstrained scenarios, a novel Two Layer Rotational Symmetry Dynamic Texture (RSDT) model is proposed, which avoids illumination variations by using two layers of spatio temporal patches. Spatio temporal patches describe both motion and appearance parameters in a video sequence. The concept of key frame is used to avoid redundant samples. Auto Regressive Integrated Moving Average model (ARIMA) estimates the statistical parameters from the subspace. Uniform Local Derivative Pattern (LDP) acts as a feature for tracking objects in a video. Extensive experimental evaluations on a wide range of benchmark datasets validate the efficiency of RSDT compared to Center Symmetric Spatio Temporal Local Ternary Pattern (CS-STLTP) for unconstrained video analytics.

The sensing power of traditional camera networks for efficiently addressing the critical tasks in the process of cluster – based target tracking of human, such as measurement integration, inclusion/exclusion in the cluster and cluster head rotation. The Wireless Camera Networks efficiently uses distribution friendly representation and methods in which every node contributes to the computation in each mechanism without the requirement of any prior knowledge of the rest of the nodes. These mechanisms and methods are integrated in two different distributed schemas so that it can be implemented in the same mean time without taking into the consideration of cluster size. Thus, the experimental evaluation shows that the proposed schemes and mechanisms drastically reduce the energy consumption and computational burden with respect to the existing methodology.

Digital data transmitted over the insecure communication can be prone to attacks. Intruders try various attacks to unauthorized access of the confidential information. The Steganography is such as security system that provide the protection to the images, text and other type of data digitally transferred through the data communication network. This chapter elaborates the basics of Digital Image Steganographic techniques from ancient era to digital edge, types of images used for the steganography, payload used for the steganography, various attacks and different algorithms that can provide the information security. The performance analysis of the various Digital Image Steganographic algorithms are discussed. The current applications and their necessities are discussed in this chapter.

This is the survey for finding vegetation, deforestation of earth images from various related papers from different authors. This survey deals with remote sensing and normalized difference vegetation index with various techniques. We survey almost 100 theoretical and empirical contributions in the current decade related to image processing, NDVI generation by using various new techniques. We also discuss significant challenges involved in the adaptation of existing image processing techniques to generation NDVI systems that can be useful in the real world. The resolution of remote sensing images increases every day, raising the level of detail and the heterogeneity of the scenes. Most of the existing geographic information systems classification tools have used the same methods for years. With these new high resolution images, basic classification methods do not provide satisfactory results.

Chapter 17

Enthusiasm for accuracy farming practices and advances is becoming quickly all through the agrarian world. The accuracy farming can make utilization of the current methods, for example, GPS (Global Positioning System) innovation, GIS (Geographical Information System) innovation, RS (Remote Sensing) innovation and ES (Expert System) innovation et cetera, with a specific end goal to separate the agribusiness specialized measures among plots to acquire the better peripheral advantage of economy and environment. The study demonstrates to those generally accepted methods to utilize GIS (Geography Information System), Data mining and Web innovations in the rural master choice framework. This security with mass storage is satisfied by using GIS cloud server. This chapter discuss with an Integrated Geographic Information System with ES using Cloud Computing.

Foreword

When I was invited to write a foreword for this book, *Advanced Image Processing Techniques and Applications*, I was very happy to note the variety of applications in Image processing techniques. This book is a significant collection of 19 chapters covering image, video Processing and cloud based processing, as well as their applications in emerged in the recent decades. This book provides an excellent platform to review various areas of Image processing in depth, and caters for the needs of both beginners to the field and seasoned researchers and practitioners. The rapid growth and advances in a wide variety of applications of Image and video techniques are documented in this book, such as fuzzy, genetic algorithms, and optimization techniques, which are focused in different types of images like Hyper spectral images.

To my knowledge, this is the first attempt of its kind, providing an intensive and in-depth coverage of the key subjects in the fields Advanced Image processing techniques and applications. This book is an invaluable, topical, and timely source of knowledge in the field, which serves nicely as a major text book for several courses at both undergraduate and post graduate levels. It is also a key reference for scientists, professionals, researchers, and academicians, who are interested in new challenges, theories, practice and advanced applications of the specific areas mentioned above.

I am happy to commend the editors and authors on their accomplishment, and to inform the readers that they are looking at a major piece in the development of image processing and its engineering applications. This book is a main step in this field's maturation and will serve to unify, advance, and challenge the scientific community in many important ways.

Karanjeet Singh Kahlon
Guru Nanak Dev University, India

Preface

Image processing is used to process the images based on the requirement by using the signal processing techniques. The signal processing techniques is organized with mathematical operations, for which input is an image or video frame. The response of the processing unit may be either an image or set of parameters / characteristics related to the input image. Basically, image processing is dealing with two dimensional signals. In that, classifications of image parameters / characteristics are using the standard signal processing techniques. The three dimensional image processing has lot of applications in real time like computer vision, where the z-axis being time / frequency. Generally, image processing refers to digital, optical and analog input signal processing.

The digital image processing is dealing with computer simulations based on the mathematical algorithms. Based on the mathematical algorithms, the parameters / characteristics of the images can be studied / enhanced. The digital image processing techniques widely used to study the medical images and satellite images. By using the advanced digital image processing techniques, now researchers can predict the crop growth, cancer cells and material defects. The cancer cell detection in early stage is possible using optical microscopy imaging.

NEED FOR A BOOK ON THE PROPOSED TOPICS

The advanced image processing techniques are widely used in computer vision and control, by processing the two and three dimensional images as input. The three dimensional image processing is widely used to control the robotic movements and machine processing. The robot can move even non-planar surfaces by analyzing the two / three dimensional images. The fast responses with high accuracy of the robotic functions are achieved by using the advanced feedback processing units with digital image processing systems. Today, image processing and recognition has broad scope due to the requirement and gap in the scientific visualization. In materials science, generally X-ray and UV are used to evaluate the structure without disturbing it. In the bio-medical field, even today the working mechanism of the advanced imaging techniques are based on the ionizing radiation like X-rays, UV rays, etc. The ionizing radiations will affect the adjacent tissues as well as organs.

Now, researchers are interested to work with terahertz imaging techniques, because it has lot of merits and opportunities like non-ionizing radiation, unlicensed spectrum and high spatial resolution. In the electromagnetic spectrum, the terahertz waves lies from 0.1 THz - 10 THz (wavelengths of 3 mm to about 1 μm). The designs of THz transreceivers are under research, due to its system complexity and miniaturization. The THz imaging is playing interesting role in nano-biology, weapon and hazardous materials detections. In 1995, Bell laboratories developed a first terahertz imaging systems based on the terahertz time domain spectroscopy. In which, the terahertz waveforms are down converted in to kilohertz frequency range. The short wavelength terahertz pulses enhanced the spatial resolution. The non-ionizing radiation opened the new research opportunities in the field of bio-medical imaging as well as radiology. The broadband terahertz pulses can be generated using photoconductive antennas. The terahertz time domain systems and coherent detectors are required to detect the terahertz pulses. The continuous wave terahertz systems are less expensive than terahertz time domain systems. Now, the terahertz imaging systems are used in airports to detect the hidden weapons / materials in the form of solids / powder. Even today, terahertz systems can differentiate the explosive materials, by studying the materials absorption.

ORGANIZATION OF THE BOOK

The book is organized into 17 chapters. A brief description of each chapter is given as follows:

Chapter 1: This chapter concerns the preliminaries of fuzzy, intuitionistic fuzzy, type-2 fuzzy and intuitionistic type-2 fuzzy set theory and its application in the fingerprint image; furthermore, the contrast enhancement and edge detection are carried out for that with the assistance of fuzzy set theory. It is useful to the students who want to self-study. This chapter composed just to address that issue.

Chapter 2: This chapter starts with an introduction to computer vision and its applications, which is followed by an introduction to text information extraction from images/video.

Chapter 3: This chapter deals with steganography algorithm which can embed multiple messages, each of which requires a separate key is proposed. The application can estimate the capacity used and capacity remains for the given cover image and texts

Chapter 4: This chapter presents an analysis on Zernike Moments from the class of orthogonal moments which are invariant to rotation, translation and scaling. The chapter initially focuses on the review of Zernike moments as 1D, 2D and 3D based on their dimension and later investigates on the construction, characteristics of Zernike Moments and their invariants, which can be used as a shape descriptor to capture global and detailed information from the data based on their order to provide outstanding performance in various applications of image processing

Chapter 5: This chapter deals distinct and discrete mapping function calculates the histogram values and improves the contrast of the image. The performance of IHE is based on noise removal ratio, reliability rate, false positive error measure, Max-Flow Computational Complexity Measure with NDRA and Variation HOD. As the outcome, the different levels of contrast have been significantly improved when evaluated against with the existing systems.

Chapter 6: In this chapter, authors have proposed sub-optimal key generation algorithm and this nature inspired optimization technique reveals complex keys, remains very useful for decision making in dynamic environment. Key generation is crafted as complex with this mathematical model that overcomes the predicament key problem exists in existing methods and upgrades quality of encryption. Results of the proposed algorithm show the efficiency and its resistance against various cryptanalytic attacks.

Chapter 7: This chapter presents a technique which uses the sum of height square as a measure to define the deflection associated with a pseudo high curvature points on the digital planar curve. The proposed technique iteratively removes the pseudo high curvature points whose deflection is minimal, and recalculates the deflection associated with its neighboring pseudo high curvature points.

Chapter 8: This chapter presents Foreign body aspiration (FBA) is a common problem among pediatric population that requires early diagnosis and prompt successful management. Conventionally the radiography image inspection processes are carried out manually by the experts of medical field.

Chapter 9: The results of new experiments on the detection and description of images for an EKF-SLAM monocular application are employed in order to obtain a dispersed set of features without related data association problems.

Chapter 10: Hard mathematical problems having no polynomial time algorithms to determine a solution are seemly in design of secure cryptosystems. The proposed watermarking system used number theoretic concepts of the hard higher order Diophantine equations for image content authentication scheme.

Chapter 11: The design, construction and programming of a mobile robot controlled by means of artificial vision, capable of recognizing, grabbing and moving specific objects in a completely autonomous way is presented in this chapter, together with the conceptual and theoretical-practical grounds for the work.

Chapter 12: This chapter begins with the basic idea of Biometrics, Biometrics System with its components, working and proceeds with the need of Multimodal Biometrics with the emphasis on review of various multimodal systems based on fusion ways and fusion level of various features. The last section of this chapter describes various multimodal Biometric Systems.

Chapter 13: This chapter illustrates the Extensive experimental evaluations on a wide range of benchmark datasets validate the efficiency of RSDT compared to Center Symmetric Spatio Temporal Local Ternary Pattern (CS-STLTP) for unconstrained video analytics.

Chapter 14: These mechanisms and methods are integrated in two different distributed schemas so that it can be implemented in the same mean time without taking into the consideration of cluster size. Thus, the experimental evaluation shows that the proposed schemes and mechanisms drastically reduce the energy consumption and computational burden with respect to the existing methodology.

Chapter 15: This chapter elaborates the basics of Digital Image Steganography techniques from ancient era to digital edge, types of images used for the steganography, payload used for the steganography, various attacks and different algorithms that can provide the information security.

Chapter 16: This chapter describes the survey for finding vegetation, deforestation of earth images from various related papers from different authors. This survey deals with remote sensing and normalized difference vegetation index with various techniques.

Chapter 17: This chapter discussed with an Integrated Geographic Information System with Expert Systems using Cloud Computing.

AUDIENCE

The intended audiences of this book are scientists, professionals, researchers, and academicians, who deal with the new challenges and advances in the specific areas mentioned above. Designers and developers of applications in these fields can learn from other experts and colleagues through studying this book.

Many universities have started to offer courses on Image Processing, Techniques and applications on the graduate/post graduate level in information technology and management disciplines. This book starts with an introduction to image Processing and applications, hence suitable for university level courses as well as research scholars. Major contributions of chapters are expected from leading researchers, industry practitioners, and implementers. Their insightful discussions and knowledge, based on references and research work, will lead to an excellent book and a great knowledge source.

N. Suresh Kumar
VIT University, India

Arun Kumar Sangaiah
VIT University, India

M. Arun
VIT University, India

S. Anand
VIT University, India

Acknowledgment

We would like to express our sincere gratitude to all the contributors, who have submitted their high-quality chapters, and to the experts for their supports in providing insightful review comments and suggestions on time.

N. Suresh Kumar
VIT University, India

Arun Kumar Sangaiah
VIT University, India

M. Arun
VIT University, India

S. Anand
VIT University, India

Chapter 1
Fuzzy Approaches and Analysis in Image Processing

Ezhilmaran D
VIT University, India

Adhiyaman M
VIT University, India

ABSTRACT

Fuzzy set theory originates to a great extent of interest among the researchers in past decades. It is a key tool to handle the imperfect of information in the diverse field. Typically, it plays a very important role in image processing and found the significant development in many active areas such as pattern recognition, neural network, medical imaging, etc. The use of fuzzy set theory is to tackle uncertainty in the form of membership functions when there is an image gray levels or information is lost. This chapter concerns the preliminaries of fuzzy, intuitionistic fuzzy, type-2 fuzzy and intuitionistic type-2 fuzzy set theory and its application in the fingerprint image; furthermore, the contrast enhancement and edge detection are carried out for that with the assistance of fuzzy set theory. It is useful to the students who want to self-study. This chapter composed just to address that issue.

INTRODUCTION

In 1965, Zadeh defined the notion of fuzzy set theory. It deals with degree of membership function. Later in 1985, Atanassov introduced the perception of intuitionistic fuzzy set theory which deals with degree of membership and non-membership function. He discussed the degree of non-membership function is equal to 1 minus degree of membership function, which is not always true, but there may be some hesitation degree will occur in the membership function. Likewise, it begins a vital role in image processing, for example, image enhancement, morphological image, edge detection and so on.

Physical attributes and behavior are the parameters for identifying a person in biometric security. The biometric traits, for example, face, gait, ear, odor fingerprint, hand geometry, iris, retina, hand vein, facial thermogram, signature, voice print, and keystroke dynamics which are exceptionally suitable for human acknowledgment because of their singularity, integrality and consistency (Maltoni, Maio, Jain, &

DOI: 10.4018/978-1-5225-2053-5.ch001

Prabhakar, 2009). Among all biometric traits, fingerprints have the elevated amount of dependability and widely used by criminological specialists as a part of criminal examinations (Figure 1). Fingerprints are fully fledged at around seven months of fetus development and finger ridge configuration don't change duration the life of an individual except due to the accident such as wounds and cuts on the finger. Even for twins, it has never changed (Babler, 1991). Fingerprint patterns are shaped in the epidermis on the fingertip. The ridge orientation map and frequency map, pores, incipient ridges, singular points, dots and minutiae are the features of the fingerprints. Minutiae points are strictly defined by the ridge ending and bifurcation points. Fingerprint image have contained three types of patterns like Arch, Loop and Whorl and have nine- types of classifications, namely, arch, tent arch right loop, left loop, double loop, right pocket loop, left pocket loop, whorl, and mixed figure (Jain, Flynn, & Ross, 2007).

Image enhancement is required before handling any image. It assumes a principal part in image handling where human specialists make vital choices in view of image data. It is utilized to restore an image that has decayed or to improve certain elements of an image. The purpose behind image improvement is to change an image to another structure that is more suitable for further handling. To recognize the crime person, fingerprint examiner should have a decent knowledge of the images. Fingerprint images are poorly illuminated and hardly visible and many regions and boundaries are ambiguous in nature. Along these lines, if the quality of the image is enhanced, handling might get to be less demanding. Consequently, fingerprint image enhancement is extremely important. In an enhanced image, it becomes easier for forensic departments to identify the crime individuals. Image enhancement partitioned into contrast enhancement and edge enhancement.

The motivation behind contrast enhancement is to build the general visual differentiation of the image, which the human eye can envision unmistakably, to be more qualified for further examination. It is useful when the intensity of important regions of images such as fingerprint image, latent fingerprint image and it turns out be exceptionally hard to make out the structure with the human eye. Contrast enhancement and edge enhancement are utilized to expand the region of low intensity and unclear edges respectively. The histogram equalization is the most used crisp method of image enhancement among the gray-level transformation and modification. Clearly, fingerprint images are less in quality and contain uncertainties, so crisp may not improve the image appropriately. The mathematical tools are needed to overcome with such kind of vague images, for example, fuzzy set theory and some advanced fuzzy set theories such as intuitionistic fuzzy set and type-2 fuzzy set. It considers some more uncertainties are used to obtain better quality images comparable than fuzzy set.

One of the image processing techniques is called edge detection which is used to find the boundaries of objects inside the images. It works by recognition discontinuities in brightness, color, texture, etc. Edge identification techniques simplify the analysis of the image by decreasing the information to be prepared. Edge strength is computed by taking the gradient value of the image when there is a sharp change in the pixel values. A good edge detecting operator needs to act at any desirable scale and detect all the edges properly because edges might exhibit in many directions. The most widely recognition problem in edge detection is the occurrence of the of noise in the image. This problem leads to find the false edges. There are numerous ways to deal with edge detection. The edge strength is calculated by using first order derivative methods and operators (Roberts, Sobel, Prewitt, canny, etc.), second order derivative methods, Laplacian of Gaussian and difference of Gaussian. Laplacian of Gaussian produces continuous closed boundaries, being the zero set of the implicit function. However, since it is a second derivative operator, it is extremely noise sensitive. According to the surrounding pixels the image is

Figure 1. Example of fingerprint images

(a)   (b)   (c)

decided which is an edge pixel or a noise pixel. Smoothing is necessary to remove the noise present in the image and Gaussian smoothing is the most common method used for smoothing.

There are many excellent textbooks on image processing. however, this chapter is useful for undergraduate and graduate students in universities worldwide. It is extremely useful for teachers, scientists, engineers, and all those who are interested in the fuzzy set theory of image processing.

BACKGROUND

Intuitionistic fuzzy enhancement was suggested by Vlachos and Sergiadis, (2007), where they used intuitionistic fuzzy entropy. Enhancement using type-2 fuzzy set is also suggested by Ensafi and Tizhoosh, (2005). Wu, Shi, and Govindaraju, (2004) have described an Anisotropic Filter (AF) and Directional Median Filter (DMF) for fingerprint image enhancement purposes. DMF is used to join the broken fingerprint ridges, fill out the holes, smooth irregular ridges and remove some annoying small artifacts between ridges. Discrete Wavelet Transform (DWT) and Singular Value Decomposition (SVD) has been proposed by Bennet and Perumal, (2011) for image enhancement. Image normalization and Gabor filter techniques are used to enhance the fingerprint image according to Kim, Kim, and Park, (2002). First, they have used the adaptive normalization, which is based on block processing, so input image is partitioned into sub-block with KxL size and Region of Interest (ROI) of the image is acquired. Second, taking a two parameter form of Gabor filter for enhancing the finger print image. The authors have proved with a novel filter design method for fingerprint image enhancement. They are inspired by the Traditional Gabor filter (TGF) which is called the Modified Gabor filter (MGF). The modification of the TGF can make the MGF more accurate in preserving the fingerprint image topography. A new scheme of adaptive parameter selection for the MGF is discussed. This scheme leads to the image-independent advantage in the MGF (Yang, Liu, & Jiang, 2002).

The fingerprint image enhancement is carried by Mao, Zhu, and Jiang, (2010) with the help of Gabor filter. A robust against gradient deviation technique provides us to estimate the orientation and frequencies of a fingerprint in a local region. It allows effective Gabor filtering for fingerprint ridge and valley pattern enhancement (Karimi-Ashtiani & Kuo, 2008). The integration of Anisotropic Filter (AF) and Directional Median Filter (DMF) techniques were used for fingerprint image enhancement which is discussed by Wu et al. (2004). The non-stationary directional Fourier domain filtering enhancement technique is introduced by Sherlock, Monro, and Millard, (1994). Greenberg, Aladjem, Kogan, and Dimitrov (2000) explained the different types of filters for fingerprint image enhancement such as local histogram equalization, Wiener filtering, image binarization and a unique anisotropic filter. Jayaram,

Narayana, and Vetrivel (2011) proposed a fuzzy inference system based contrast enhancement of gray level images. The fuzzy based fingerprints enhancement method which is used to reduce the noise free image from the original image for further processing (Selvi & George, 2013). Tamalika Chaira, (2013) and Bansal, Arora, Gaur, Sehgal, and Bedi, (2009) has used the soft computing technique such as type-2 fuzzy set for medical and fingerprint image enhancement. Tamalika Chaira and Ray, (2014) disclosed a novel technique to create fuzzy edges in medical images using type-2 fuzzy set theory. It has taking into account the calculation of minimum and maximum values of the intensity levels of the image in a 3×3-pixel neighborhood to form two image matrices with maximum and minimum values.

There are many common edge detection methods are used in image processing such as Prewitt, Sobel, Roberts, canny and as well as others (Gonzalez & Wintz, 1977). An edge detection approach based on fuzzy if-then rules is presented by Tao, Thompson, and Taur, (1993). It avoids the difficulties of selecting parameter values in most of the edge detectors method. Tamalika Chaira and Ray, (2003) have proposed a new image thresholding method using fuzzy divergence and gamma distribution. It used for determining the membership function of the pixel of the image. A fuzzy edge detection method based on learning fuzzy edges by the method of fuzzy categorization and classification (Ho & Ohnishi, 1995). Gomez Lopera, Ilhami, Escamilla, Aroza, and Roldán, (1999) used divergence of gray level histogram obtained by sliding window over an image for edge detection. Biswas and Sil, (2012) explained an algorithm based on the concept of type-2 fuzzy sets to handle uncertainties that automatically selects the threshold values needed to segment the gradient image using classical Canny's edge detection algorithm. An edge-detection method is carried out based on the morphological gradient technique and generalized type-2 fuzzy logic (Melin, Gonzalez, Castro, Mendoza, & Castillo, 2014). The theory of alpha planes is used to implement generalized type-2 fuzzy logic for edge detection. Aborisade, (2011) has developed a fuzzy logic based edge detection technique in digital images. Yoon, Feng, and Jain, (2011) have proposed an algorithm for latent fingerprint image enhancement which only requires minimum margin in ROI and singular points to promote the automatic matching accuracy. Later, they have planned to use manually marked ROI and singular points for latent fingerprint enhancement (Yoon, Liu, & Jain, 2015). Further in 2013, they have introduced the algorithm for Fingerprint Image Quality (LFIQ), which is used for latent fingerprint exemplar and crime investigation (Yoon, Cao, Liu, & Jain, 2013). Karimi-Ashtiani and Kuo, (2008) have presented a robust method for latent fingerprint image segmentation and enhancement which is tested with more than 10 images for experimental and obtained reasonable results. Cao, Liu, and Jain, (2014) have approached a dictionary-based method for automatic latent segmentation and enhancement in the direction of the objective of accomplishing "lights-out" latent ID frameworks. Feng, Zhou, Member, and Jain, (2013) have proposed a novel fingerprint orientation field estimation algorithm based on prior knowledge of fingerprint structure. The area of intuitionistic type-2 fuzzy set in image processing is beginning to develop the concept.

Preliminaries of Fuzzy Concepts

The concept of fuzzy set theory is defined by Zadeh in 1965. It has a vital role in various filed of image processing in past decades. Images are considered to be fuzzy for their grey levels or information lost while mapping and so fuzzy set theory is used, which considers uncertainty in the form of the membership function. Fuzzy logic is an effective tool for handling the ambiguity and uncertainty of real world systems. (Sivanandam et al., 2007). The database of a rule-based system may contain imperfect information which is inherent in the description of the rules given by the expert. This information may be incomplete, imprecise, fragmentary, not fully reliable, vague, contradictory or deficient in some other ways. Nowadays, we can handle much of this imperfection of information using fuzzy logic in many active areas, such as remote sensing, medical imaging, video surveillance, clustering, pattern recognition, neural network and so on.

Fuzzy Set

Typically, the fuzzy set theory indicates the membership functions which contain the closed interval range [0, 1]. The degree of membership function denoted as a fuzzy set A by μ_A. It can be represented as follows

$$A = \left\{ (x, \mu_A(x), \nu_A(x)) \mid x \in X \right\}$$

where $\mu_A(x) : X \to [0,1]$. (Zadeh, 1965)

Type-2 Fuzzy Set

Type-2 fuzzy set is helpful in circumstance where the membership values are such that it is hard to concur with accurate membership values. This is due to the way that some uncertainty might exhibit fit as a fiddle or different parameters. Type-2 fuzzy set accounts this uncertainty by considering another level of opportunity for better representation of instability where the membership functions are themselves fuzzy. Type-2 fuzzy set considers some more uncertainty in the form of membership function (Lee, 2006). It can be written as follows,

$$A_{Type-2} = \left\{ x, \widehat{\mu}_A(x) \mid x \in X \right\},$$

where $\widehat{\mu}_A(x)$ type-2 membership function. It includes the upper and lower of membership functions.

$$\mu^{upper} = [\mu(x)]^{\alpha}$$

$$\mu^{lower} = [\mu(x)]^{1/\alpha},$$

where $\alpha \in [0,1]$.

The membership function on an element $x \in X$ with the necessary condition

$$A_{Type-2} = \left\{ x, \mu_U(x), \mu_L(x) \mid x \in X \right\}$$

$$\mu_L(x) < \mu(x) < \mu_U(x), \mu \in [0,1].$$

Footprint of Uncertainty

The membership function of a general type-2 fuzzy set $\tilde{A}$ is three-dimensional, where the third dimension is the value of the membership function at each point on its two dimensional domain that is called its Footprint of Uncertainty.

Operations on Fuzzy Set

Fuzzy complement, Fuzzy intersection and Fuzzy union are the standard fuzzy operations.

1. **Fuzzy Complement:** A complement of a fuzzy set A is specified by a function $c : [0,1] \rightarrow [0,1]$ which assign a value $c(\mu_A(x))$ to each membership degree $\mu_A(x)$. Axioms:

    a. $c(0) = 1$ and $c(1) = 0$ (boundary conditions).
    b. For all $a,b \in [0,1]$, if $a \leq b$, then $c(a) \geq c(b)$ (monotonicity), $c1$ and $c2$ are called axiomatic skeleton for fuzzy complements.
    c. c is a continuous function.
    d. c is involutive, i.e., $c(c(a)) = a$, for each $a \in [0,1]$.

2. **Fuzzy Intersection:** The union of two fuzzy sets A and B is specified by a function of the form $i : [0,1] \times [0,1] \rightarrow [0,1]$. Formally, $\mu_{A \cap B}(x) = \mu[\mu_A(x), \mu_B(x)]$. Axioms:

    For all $a,b,d \in [0,1]$

    a. $i(a,1) = 1$. (boundary condition)
    b. $b \leq d$ implies $i(a,b) \leq i(a,d)$. (monotonicity)
    c. $i(a,b) = i(b,a)$. (commutativity)
    d. $i(a,i(b,d)) = i(i(a,b),d)$. (associativity)

    Axioms a and b are called axiomatic skeleton for fuzzy unions. If the sets are crisp, i becomes the classical intersection.

    e. i is a continuous function. (continuity)
    f. $i(a,a) \geq a$. (superidempotency)
    g. $a_1 < a_2 \ \& \ b_1 < b_2 \rightarrow i(a_1,b_1) < u(a_2,b_2)$ (strict monotonicity)

3. **Fuzzy Union:** The union of two fuzzy sets A and B is specified by a function of the form $u : [0,1] \times [0,1] \rightarrow [0,1]$. Formally, $\mu_{A \cup B}(x) = \mu[\mu_A(x), \mu_B(x)]$. Axioms:

    For all $a,b,d \in [0,1]$

    a. $u(a,0) = a$. (boundary condition)
    b. $b \leq d$ implies $u(a,b) \leq u(a,d)$. (monotonicity)
    c. $u(a,b) = u(b,a)$. (commutativity)
    d. $u(a,u(b,d)) = u(u(a,b),d)$. (associativity)

    Axioms a and b are called axiomatic skeleton for fuzzy unions. They differ from the axiomatic of fuzzy intersection only in boundary condition. For crisp sets, u behaves like classical union.

    e. u is a continuous function. (continuity)
    f. $u(a,a) \geq a$. (superidempotency)
    g. $a_1 < a_2 \ \& \ b_1 < b_2 \rightarrow u(a_1,b_1) < u(a_2,b_2)$ (strict monotonicity)

Fuzzy t Norm

The mapping $T : [0,1] \times [0,1] \to [0,1]$ is triangular norm (T-norm) if satisfies the properties

- **Symmetry:** $T(x,y) = T(y,x), \forall x,y \in [0,1]$
- **Associativity:** $T(T(x,y),z) = T(x,T(y,z)), \forall x,y,z \in [0,1]$
- **Monotonicity:** $T(x_1,y_1) \leq T(y_1,x_1), if\ x_1 \leq x_2\ and\ y_1 \leq y_2$
- **One Identity:** $T(x,1) = x, T(x,0) = 0 \forall x \in [0,1]$

Fuzzy t Co-Norm

The mapping $T : [0,1] \times [0,1] \to [0,1]$ is triangular co-norm (T-co-norm) if satisfies the properties

- **Symmetry:** $T(x,y) = T(y,x), \forall x,y \in [0,1]$
- **Associativity:** $T(T(x,y),z) = T(x,T(y,z)), \forall x,y,z \in [0,1]$
- **Monotonicity:** $T(x_1,y_1) \leq T(y_1,x_1), if\ x_1 \leq x_2\ and\ y_1 \leq y_2$
- **One Identity:** $T(x,1) = 1, T(x,0) = 0 \forall x \in [0,1]$

Fuzzy Entropy

A real function $e : F \to \mathbb{R}^+$ is called an entropy on F, if e has the following properties:

1. $e(D) = 0, \forall D \in P(X)$
2. $e\left(\left[\frac{1}{2}\right]\right) = \max_{A \in F} e(A)$
3. If A^* is a sharpened version of A, then $e(A^*) \leq e(A)$
4. $e(A^c) = e(A), \forall A \in F$

Distance Measure

A real function of $d : F^2 \to \mathbb{R}^+$ is called distance measure, if d satisfies the following properties

1. $d(A,B) = d(B,A), \forall A,B \in F$
2. $d(A,A) = 0, \forall A \in F$
3. $d(D,D^c) = \max_{A,B \in F} d(A,B), \forall D \in P(X)$
4. $\forall A,B,C \in F, if\ A \subset B \subset C$, then $d(A,B) \leq d(A,C)\ and\ d(B,C) \leq d(A,C)$, where $F(X)$ is the class of fuzzy set of X and $P(X)$ is the class of crisp set of X.

Fuzzy Similarity

A real function of $s : F^2 \to \mathbb{R}^+$ is called a distance measure, if s satisfies the following properties

1. $s(A,B) = s(B,A), \forall A, B \in F$
2. $s(D,D^c) = 0, \forall D \in P(X)$
3. $s(C,C) = \max_{A,B \in F} s(A,B), \forall C \in F$
4. $\forall A, B, C \in F, if\, A \subset B \subset C$, then $s(A,B) \leq s(A,C)$ and $s(B,C) \leq s(A,C)$, where $F(X)$ is the class of fuzzy set of X and $P(X)$ is the class of crisp set of X.

If we normalize e, d, s, we can ensure

$$0 \leq e(A) \leq 1, 0 \leq d(A,B) \leq 1, 0 \leq s(A,B) \leq 1,$$

for $A, B \in F$. The relation between d and s is $d = 1 - s$. The fuzzy entropy defined as $e(A) = s(A,A^c)$, where, $e(A) = 1 - d(A,A^c)$ is called the fuzzy entropy. Where 'e' represents the entropy, 'd' represents the distance and 's' represents the similarity (Szmidt & Kacprzyk, 2001).

Fuzzy Divergence

For fuzzy sets *A, B,* the fuzzy divergence between A and B is

$$D_E(A,B) = I(A,B) + I(B,A)$$
$$= \sum_i \left(2 - \left(1 - \mu_A(x_i) + \mu_B(x_i)\right)e^{\mu_A(x_i)-\mu_B(x_i)} - 1 - \mu_B(x_i) + \mu_A(x_i)\right)e^{\mu_B(x_i)-\mu_A(x_i)}$$

Intuitionistic Fuzzy Set

Intuitionistic fuzzy set theory was introduced by Atanassov, (1986) which includes two functions such as degree of membership and non-membership functions respectively. The degree of non-membership function denoted as an intuitionistic fuzzy set A by ν_A. It can be mathematically represented as follows

$$A = \left\{(x, \mu_A(x), \nu_A(x)) \mid x \in X\right\};$$

where $\mu_A(x), \nu_A(x) : X \to [0,1]$. $\pi_A(x) = 1 - \mu_A(x) - \nu_A(x)$ is the representation of the third parameter which is called the hesitation degree.

Intuitionistic Type-2 Fuzzy Set

A IT2FS denoted by $\widetilde{A}$, which is characteristic by Intuitionistic type-2 fuzzy membership function $(\mu_{\widetilde{A}}(x,u), \nu_{\widetilde{A}}(x,u))$ where $x \in X$ and $u \in J_x \subseteq [0,1]$, i.e.,

$$\widetilde{A} = \left\{(x,u), \mu_{\widetilde{A}}(x,u), \nu_{\widetilde{A}}(x,u) \mid \forall x \in X, \forall u \in J_x \subseteq [0,1]\right\}$$

in which $0 \leq \mu_{\tilde{A}}(x, u), \nu_{\tilde{A}}(x, u) \leq 1$.

Operation of Intuitionistic Fuzzy Sets

If *A* and *B* are two IFSs of the set *E*, then

1. $A \subset B \, iff \, \forall x \in E, \left[\mu_A(x) \leq \mu_B(x) \, and \, \nu_A(x) \geq \nu_B(x) \right]$

2. $A \subset B \, iff \, B \subset A$,

3. $A = B, iff \, \forall x \in E, \left[\mu_A(x) = \mu_B(x) \, and \, \nu_A(x) = \nu_B(x) \right]$,

4. $\overline{A} = \left\{ \left\langle x, \nu_A(x), \mu_A(x) \right\rangle \mid x \in E \right\}$,

5. $A \cap B = \left\{ \left\langle x, \min(\mu_A(x), \mu_B(x)), \max(\nu_A(x), \nu_B(x)) \right\rangle \mid x \in E \right\}$,

6. $A \cup B = \left\{ \left\langle x, \max(\mu_A(x), \mu_B(x)), \min(\nu_A(x), \nu_B(x)) \right\rangle \mid x \in E \right\}$,

7. $A + B = \left\{ \left\langle x, \mu_A(x) + \mu_B(x) - \mu_A(x) \cdot \mu_B(x), (\nu_A(x).\nu_B(x)) \right\rangle \mid x \in E \right\}$,

8. $A \cdot B = \left\{ \left\langle x, \mu_A(x) \cdot \mu_B(x), \nu_A(x) + \nu_B(x) - \nu_A(x) \cdot \nu_B(x), \right\rangle \mid x \in E \right\}$,

9. $\square A = \left\{ \left\langle x, \mu_A(x), 1 - \mu_A(x) \right\rangle \mid x \in E \right\}$,

10. $\Diamond A = \left\{ \left\langle x, 1 - \nu_A(x), \nu_A(x) \right\rangle \mid x \in E \right\}$.

Intuitionistic Fuzzy Distance Measure

$X = \{x_1, x_2, \ldots, x_n\}$. The hamming distance between two IFSs *A* and *B* is defined by

$$d_H(A, B) = \sum_{i=1}^{N} \frac{\left| \mu_A(x_i) - \mu_B(x_i) \right| + \left| \nu_A(x_i) - \nu_B(x_i) \right|}{2}$$

Clearly, $0 \leq d_H(A, B) \leq N$. The euclidean distance between two IFSs *A* and *B* is defined by

$$d_E(A, B) = \left[\sum_{i=1}^{n} \frac{\left[\mu_A(x_i) - \mu_B(x_i) \right]^2 + \left[\nu_A(x_i) - \nu_B(x_i) \right]^2}{2} \right]^{1/2}$$

Divergence Measure for Intuitionistic Fuzzy Sets

Let *X* be a universe, and let *IFSs(X)* denotes the set of all intuitionistic fuzzy set on *X*. A map

$$D_{IF} : IFSs(X) \times IFSs(X) \to \mathbb{R}$$

is a divergence measure for intuitionistic fuzzy sets if for every $A, B \in IFSs(X)$ it fulfills the following properties

1. $D_{IF}(A, B) = D_{IF}(B, A)$.
2. $D_{IF}(A, A) = 0$.
3. $D_{IF}(A \cap C, B \cap C) \leq D_{IF}(A, B), \forall C \in IFSs(X)$.
4. $D_{IF}(A \cup C, B \cup C) \leq D_{IF}(A, B), \forall C \in IFSs(X)$.

Intuitionistic Fuzzy Entropy

Let *I* be a fuzzy set defined in the universe of discourse *X*. intuitionistic fuzzy entropy is given as follows

$$E(I) = \frac{1}{n} \sum_{i=1}^{n} \frac{\min\left(\mu_I(x_i), \nu_I(x_i)\right) + \pi_I(x_i)}{\max\left(\mu_I(x_i), \nu_I(x_i)\right) + \pi_I(x_i)}$$

IMAGE CONTRAST ENHANCEMENT

The major idea of image enhancement is to create another image in such a way that, it uncovers data for investigation more than the first image. it is utilized to increase the contrast of the image by making the dark pixels darker and bright pixel brighter. As the images, especially the fingerprint image are poorly illuminated and hardly visible. So, contrast enhancement is required to increase the ridge and valley structure for more clear. Image enhancement also termed as a pre-processing. The pre-processing is categories into two processes which are Binarization and Thinning. The aim of pre-processing is a change of the image that upgrades a few elements important for further handling. Gray scale image is reformed into binary image which is labeled as binarization. This means each pixel is stored as a single bit i.e. 0 or 1. The usability of image thinning is reducing the darkness of ridge lines. It is used in matching process because better image quality is required.

Contrast Improvement Using an Intensification Operator

The intensification operator used to modify the membership function. It initially chooses the membership function and finds the membership values of the pixel of an images. Then it is find out the transformation of the membership values which are above default values (0.5) to much higher values and membership values which are lower than default values to much lower values are carried out in a non-linear fashion to obtain a good contrast in an image. The contrast intensifier (INT) operation is written as

$$\mu'_{mn} = \begin{cases} 2 \cdot [\mu_{mn}]^2 & 0 \leq \mu_{mm} \leq 0.5 \\ 1 - 2 \cdot [1 - \mu_{mn}]^2 & 0.5 \leq \mu_{mm} \leq 1 \end{cases}$$

After completion of the process, the inverse function is utilized to convert the modified membership values into spatial domain. This is named as NINT operator which uses Gaussian membership function in membership function generation (Hanmandlu, 2003).

Contrast Improvement Using Fuzzy Histogram Hyperbolization

The concept of histogram hyperbolization and fuzzy histogram hyperbolization is given by Tizhoosh and Fochem (1995). Due to the nonlinear human brightness perception, this algorithm modifies the membership values of the gray levels into logarithmic function. The procedure for histogram hyperbolization is as follows.

Initially the shape of membership function is selected based on the user's requirement. The Membership values $\mu(g_{mn})$ (where g_{mn} are the gray levels of an image) are calculated using the membership function. The fuzzifier beta (β which is a linguistic hedge) is set in such a way that it modifies the user's membership function. Hedges can be very bright, very very bright, medium bright, and so on, and the selection is made on the basis of image quality (Melin et al., 2014; Sonka et al., 2001; Zadeh, 1972). The value of beta can be in the range of $\beta \in [0.5, 2]$.

If $\beta = 0.5$, the operation is dilation and if $\beta = 2$, the operation is concentration. If the image considered is a low-intensity image, then the fuzzifier β after operating on the membership values will produce slightly bright or quite bright images.

Then new gray levels using linguistic hedges are generated using the following equation:

$$g'_{mn} = \left(\frac{L-1}{e^{-1}-1} \right) \cdot \left[e^{-\mu(g_{mn})^{\beta}} - 1 \right]$$

where L is the maximum grey level of an image.

Contrast Enhancement Using Fuzzy If–Then Rules

Image quality can be improved by utilizing human understanding, which is very subjective in nature. According to the observer judge the image will be different. Fuzzy rule–based approach

is such a method that incorporates human intuitions that are nonlinear in nature. As it is difficult to define a precise or crisp condition under which enhancement is applied, a fuzzy set theoretic approach is a good approach to this solution. A set of conditions are defined on a pixel for image enhancement and these conditions will form the antecedent part of the IF–THEN rules. The conditions are related to the pixel gray level and also to the pixel neighborhood (if required). Fuzzy rule–based systems make soft decisions on each condition, then aggregate the decisions made, and finally make decisions based on aggregation. Russo and Ramponi, (1994) and Russo (1999) proposed rule-based operators for image smoothing and sharpening. Choi and Krishnapuram, (1997) suggested three types of filters based on fuzzy rules that are used in image enhancement. Hassanien and Badr, (2003) used a comparative study on a mammogram image using contrast intensification method, hyperbolization and IF-THEN rules to highlight the important features of the image. A typical rule in a traditional rule-based system is If (Condition) Then (Action). A very simple fuzzy rule–based algorithm is depicted. Initially the maximum and minimum gray levels are initialized and mid gray level is calculated. Then fuzzification of gray levels or the membership values are calculated for the dark, gray, and bright regions. A simple inference mechanism that modifies the membership function is used as follows:

- If image is dark then black,
- If image is gray then gray,
- If image is bright then white.

Finally, the enhanced output is computed by defuzzifying all the three regions i.e., dark, gray, and bright regions. Defuzzification is done by using the inverse of the fuzzification.

Locally Adaptive Contrast Enhancement Filters

Apart from global enhancement, locally adaptive enhancement algorithm selects an $m \times n$ neighborhood of a pixel and moves the center of this area (window) from pixel to pixel and at each location enhancement the algorithm is applied. Local contrast enhancement increases the performance of enhancement procedure. As the images have variable and different gray levels, global histogram treats all regions of an image equally and thus yields poor local contrast enhancement. For fingerprint images, especially, where the image is of poor contrast and low quality, locally adaptive enhancement works well. In locally adaptive enhancement method as described, the image is divided into sub blocks, and enhancement algorithms are applied for each sunblock. In this method, the minimum and maximum gray levels are computed that may lead to noise, thereby affecting the membership values. This can be improved by increasing the number of sub blocks.

Contrast Enhancement Using Fuzzy Expected Value

The following steps are needed for Contrast enhancement using fuzzy expected value:

Step 1: Calculate the image histogram.
Step 2: Determine the fuzzy expected value (FEV).
Step 3: Calculate the distance of gray-levels from FEV:

$$D_{mn} = \sqrt{\left| (FEV)^2 - (g_{mn})^2 \right|} \ .$$

Step 4: Generate new gray-levels:

$$
\begin{aligned}
\overline{g}_{mn} &= \max(0, FEV - D_{mn}) && \textit{if } g_{mn} < FEV \\
\overline{g}_{mn} &= \min(L - 1, FEV + D_{mn}) && \textit{if } g_{mn} > FEV \\
FEV && && \textit{otherwise}
\end{aligned}
\ .
$$

Fuzzy Filters

Fuzzy filters provide promising results in image-processing tasks that cope with some drawbacks of classical filters. Fuzzy filter is capable of dealing with vague and uncertain information. Sometimes, it is required to recover a heavily noise corrupted images where a lot of uncertainties are present and in this case, fuzzy set theory is very useful. Each pixel in the image is represented by a membership function and different types of fuzzy rules that considers the neighborhood information or other information to eliminate noise, are used. Fuzzy filters are very robust in the sense that the classical filter removes the noise with blurry edges but fuzzy filters perform both the edge preservation and smoothing. Images and fuzzy set can be modeled in a similar way. Fuzzy set in a universe of X is a mapping from X to a unit interval [0,1], that is, every element x of X is associated with a membership degree. Similarly, in the normalized image where the image pixels ranging from {0, 1, 2..., 255} are normalized by 255, the values obtained are in the interval [0, 1]. Thus, it is a mapping from the image G to [0, 1]. In this way, the image is considered as a fuzzy set and thus fuzzy filters are designed. Noise reduction is an important area for image preprocessing. Besides classical filters, there are lots of fuzzy filters in the literature. Images can be corrupted with impulse noise, Gaussian noise, or both. Depending on the type of noise, filters can be used. The fuzzy filters are categorized into two subclasses: (a) fuzzy-classical filters and (b) fuzzy filters.

Here, we listed out the various types of fuzzy filters

1. **Fuzzy-Classical Filters:**
   a. Fuzzy median filter,
   b. Fuzzy impulse noise detection and reduction method,
   c. Fuzzy weighted mean filter,
   d. Weighted Fuzzy Mean Filter (WFM),
   e. First Adaptive Weighted Fuzzy Mean Filter (AWFM),
   f. Fuzzy decision–directed filter,
   g. Fuzzy multilevel median filter,
   h. Multipass fuzzy filter.
2. **Fuzzy Filters:**
   a. Gaussian Noise Reduction Filter (GOA),
   b. Histogram Adaptive Filter (HAF),
   c. Iterative Fuzzy Control–Based Filter (IFCF),
   d. Smoothing Fuzzy Control–Based Filter (SFCF),
   e. Fuzzy Inference Rule by Else-Action Filter (FIRE).

Fuzzy Image Contrast Enhancement

Contrast is a property that is based on human perception. An approximate definition of contrast is

$$C = \frac{(A - B)}{(A + B)}$$

Figure 2. Fuzzy image enhancement

where A and B are the mean grey levels of the two regions where the contrast is calculated. Contrast enhancement is applied to the images where the contrast between the object and the background is very low, that is, when the objects are not properly differentiable from the background. In this case, contrast enhancement should be such that darker regions should appear darker and lighter regions should appear lighter, but no contrast enhancement is required when the contrast of the image is better. Fuzzy image contrast enhancement is based on grey-level mapping from a crisp (grey) plane into a fuzzy plane using a certain membership transformation (Figure 2). Based on a user-defined threshold, T, the contrast is stretched in such a way that the grey levels below the threshold T are reduced and the grey levels above the threshold T are increased in a non-linear fashion. This stretching operation induces saturation at both ends (grey levels) (Acharya & Ray, 2005). The idea may be extended for multiple thresholds where different regions are stretched in a different fashion depending on the quality of an image. Fuzzy contrast enhancement initially assigns membership values $\mu(x)$ that may be triangular, Gaussian, gamma, etc., to know the degree of brightness or darkness of the pixels in an image. Then a transformation function is applied on the membership values to generate new membership values of the pixels in the image. Finally, an inverse transformation is applied on the new membership values for transforming back the membership values to a spatial domain.

Algorithmically, it can be expressed as

$$\mu'(x) = \psi(\mu(x)), \; x' = f^{-1}(\mu'(x))$$

where, $(\mu(x))$ is the membership function. $\psi(\mu(x))$ is the transformation of $(\mu(x))$ and $\mu'(x)$.

Type-2 Fuzzy Method for Image Contrast Enhancement

Type-2 fuzzy set considers the membership function in ordinary fuzzy set as fuzzy or vague, and so the membership function lies in an interval range with upper and lower membership levels. Thus, type-2 fuzzy set represents the uncertainty in a different and better way than type-1 fuzzy set, and so better enhancement results may be expected.

The following formula is used to fuzzified the original image

$$\mu_A^{fuz}(g_{ij}) = \frac{g_{ij} - g_{min}}{g_{max} - g_{min}}$$

where g is the gray level of the image ranges from 0 to L-1. g_{max} and g_{min} are the maximum and minimum values of the image.

The Hamacher T-co norm is used to develop the new membership function that considers both the upper and lower functions

$$\mu^{type-2}(g_{ij}) = \frac{\mu^{upper} + \mu^{lower} + (\lambda - 2)\mu^{upper} \cdot \mu^{lower}}{1 - (1 - \lambda)\mu^{upper}\mu^{lower}}$$

$\mu^{upper}(g_{ij})$ and $\mu^{lower}(g_{ij})$ are the upper and lower membership function of the type-2 fuzzy set respectively, $\lambda = im\_avg$, where im_avg is the average value of the pixels in the image. The parameter α is usually determined heuristically to satisfy the requirement $0 \leq \alpha \leq 1$.

Intuitionistic Fuzzy Method for Image Contrast Enhancement

IF methods are used for image enhancement as it considers two uncertainties: the membership and non-membership degrees as compared to one uncertainty in a fuzzy set.

The membership and non-membership function is calculated for each window using Takagi-Sugeno-Kang (TSK) type intuitionistic fuzzy set (IFS) generator.

The TSK type IFS generator is followed as (Bustince, Kacprzyk, & Mohedano, 2000)

$$K(\mu(g)) = \frac{(1 - \mu(g))}{(1 + \lambda\mu(g))}, \lambda > 0;$$

where $K(1) = 0, K(0) = 1$.

The non-membership function is derived by using Sugeno type intuitionistic fuzzy generator

$$\nu_A^{win}(g_{ij}) = \frac{1 - \mu_A^{fuz}(g_{ij})}{1 + \lambda\mu_A^{fuz}(g_{ij})}$$

The TSK-IFS become as:

$$A_\lambda^{IFS} = \left\{ x, \mu_A(g_{ij}), \frac{1 - \mu_A(g_{ij})}{1 + \lambda \cdot \mu_A(g_{ij})} \mid g_{ij} \in A \right\}$$

For all windows, the hesitation degree can be mathematically written as follows,

$$\pi_A(g_{ij}) = 1 - \mu_A^{fuz}(g_{ij}) - \nu_A^{win}(g_{ij})$$

In this experiment $\lambda = 1$ is utilized to maintain the quality of the image because on raising the λ value, the enhanced image will be worsening. At the same time, as λ increases, the Sugeno generator will decrease thereby the non-membership value will decrease and the hesitation degree will increase.

The average value of the enhanced features is considered in each window. As has been discussed in definition due to hesitation degree, membership values lie in an interval range, so, the modified membership value is written as:

$$\mu_A^{mod}(g_{ij}) = \mu_A^{fuz}(g_{ij}) - mean\_window * \pi_A(g_{ij})$$

Example 1

In Figure 3 and Figure 4 that will illustrate the effect of crisp method, fuzzy method, intuitionistic fuzzy method, type-2 fuzzy method, intuitionistic type-2 fuzzy method on fingerprint images.

IMAGE EDGE DETECTION

Edges are significant local changes in the image and are important features for analyzing images. Edges typically occur on the boundary between two different regions in an image. Edge detection is frequently the first step in recovering information from images. Due to its importance, edge detection continues to be an active research area. Most of the shape information of an image is enclosed in edges. So first we detect these edges in an image and by using filters and then by enhancing those areas of image which contains edges, sharpness of the image will increase and image will become clearer.

Figure 3. (a) Original image (b) crisp method (c) fuzzy method (d) intuitionistic fuzzy method (e) type-2 fuzzy method (f) intuitionistic type-2 fuzzy method

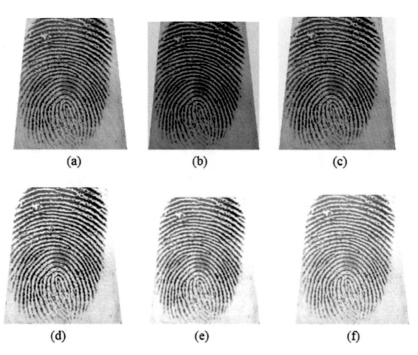

Figure 4. (a) Original image (b) crisp method (c) fuzzy method (d) intuitionistic fuzzy method (e) type-2 fuzzy method (f) intuitionistic type-2 fuzzy method

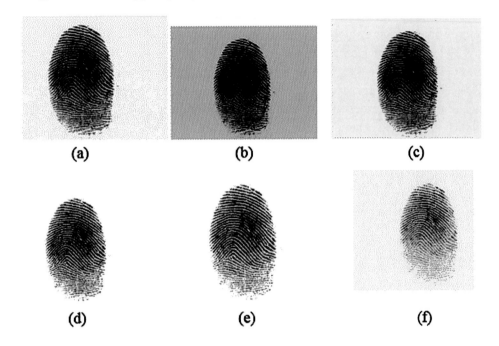

Threshold Based Method

When an edge strength is computed using any of the methods such as Canny and Prewitt, thresholding is required to know the existence of edges. Threshold selection is crucial. If the threshold is low, many unwanted edges and irrelevant features are detected, and if the threshold is high, the image will have many missed or fragmented edges. If the edge thresholding is applied to the gradient magnitude image, the resulting edges will be thick and so some type of edge-thinning post-processing is required. A good edge detection method uses a smoothing parameter to remove any noise and, depending on the type of image smoothing parameter, is adjusted to minimize the unwanted noise, and the thresholding parameter is adjusted so that well-formed edges are produced.

A commonly used approach to compute the appropriate thresholds is thresholding using hysteresis that is used in Canny's edge detector. It uses initially a smoothing parameter to remove the noise. Gradient image is computed, and then non-maximal suppression is used, which is an edge thinning technique. A search is carried out to see if the gradient magnitude is the local maxima in the gradient direction. It keeps only those pixels on the edges which have high magnitude. Finally, hysteresis thresholding is done where unwanted edges are removed. If a simple threshold is used, many important edges are removed. In hysteresis thresholding, two thresholds are used. Initially, to find the start of an edge, an upper threshold is used. Then, following the image pixel by pixel, a path is traced whenever the edge strength is above the lower threshold and stops when the value falls below the lower threshold. In this method, the edges are linked and continuous. But still a problem lies in selecting the threshold parameter.

Boundary Method

Boundary methods mainly follow the gradient features of the spatial positions of an image for segmenting the structures of an image. A global shape measure is used when the whole boundary is considered (Chakraborty, 1996). The first approach to boundary method for edge detection is the use of parameterized templates called rubber masks. But the most popular method of detecting whole boundary, is the snakes by Kass, Witkin, and Terzopoulos (1988). Kass developed a novel technique called snake for image segmentation that had excelled more conventional techniques. Kass (1988) proposed the concept of a snake, which is an active contour model which is "an energy minimizing spline guided by external constraint forces and influenced by image forces that pull it toward features such as lines and edges."

Hough Transforms Method

It is another way of finding the boundaries of an image. If an image consists of objects with known shapes and sizes such as squares, circles, rectangles, etc., segmentation procedure may be viewed as a problem of finding this object within an image. One possible way is to move masks of exact shapes and sizes over the image and find the correlation or match between the image and the mask. But this specified mask might differ from the objects present in the image. Hough transform is an effective feature extraction method that can solve the problem. The basic idea of this technique is to find curves like straight lines, polynomials, circles, etc., in a suitable parameter space. It was originally used for parameterizable shapes like curves, but was extended later to include general shapes (Ballard & Brown, 1982). Maxima in Hough space signify possible shape features. The advantage of this method is that it is insensitive to gaps and noise and the drawback is the computational requirement that goes up with an increase in the number of parameters.

Fuzzy Methods

Fuzzy edge detection is an approach to edge detection that considers the image to be fuzzy. In most of the images where edges are not clearly defined, edges are broken, vague or blurred, making edge detection very difficult. Especially fingerprint images are poorly illuminated and hardly visible, edge detection becomes very crucial because improper selection of edges may lead to incorrect the recognition process. In those cases, fuzzy set theory is very useful, which considers vagueness in the edges. It takes into account the vagueness and ambiguity present in an image in the form of a membership function, and then the edges are detected. Edges may be detected using FEDGEs that use some fuzzy templates or fuzzy reasoning that uses some linguistic variables.

Fuzzy Sobel Edge Detection

This method is suggested by El-Khamy, Lotfy, and El-Yamany (2000). Sobel method uses two 3×3 masks that calculate the gradient in two directions, which are convolved with the image. Edges are detected using a threshold defined by the user. In the fuzzy Sobel method, the image is divided into two regions: high- and low-gradient regions. If the pixels are having a high difference in the grey level with respect to the neighbourhood, then the pixels are in the fuzzy edge region, and if the pixels are having a low difference in the grey level with respect to the neighbourhood, then the pixels are in the fuzzy smooth region. The boundaries of the two regions are determined from the four threshold values in the difference histogram. The difference histogram is formed by finding the maximum difference in the grey value of each pixel in all eight directions. The gradient of the input image is initially obtained using the Sobel operator. The final edge image is obtained after using simple fuzzy rules that consider the gradient of the image obtained from the Sobel operator.

Entropy Based Edge Detection

This method was introduced by El-Khamy, Ghaleb, and El-Yamany (2002). In this method, entropy is used to find the threshold of a gradient image. Initially, a gradient image is formed using the Sobel operator and then normalized. Then probability partition of the normalized gradient image is then computed using probabilistic distribution in order to partition the image into two regions: edge and smooth regions. The two fuzzy partitions are characterized by the trapezoidal membership function, and the partitions follow a probabilistic distribution. The membership function represents the conditional probability that a pixel is classified into two regions. Then the entropy is used to calculate the threshold. The threshold partitions the image into two regions – edge region and smooth region – which are determined by minimizing the entropy.

Type-2 Fuzzy Edge Detection

The fuzzy edge image can also be obtained using type-2 fuzzy set where the membership function in an ordinary fuzzy set is considered as fuzzy. The image is initially normalized to obtain the values in the range [0,1]. For each pixel, a 3×3 neighbourhood is selected and minimum and maximum values are noted. This is done for all the pixels. This way, two image matrices are obtained with maximum and minimum values of the pixel in a 3×3 window. As the image is itself fuzzy, the maximum and minimum values are also fuzzy, so for each image matrices, type-2 levels are computed.

The upper and lower membership functions for the maximum value image are written as

$$\mu_{\max}^{\text{upper}} = [\mu_{\max}(x)]^{\alpha}$$

$$\mu_{\max}^{lower} = [\mu_{\max}(x)]^{1/0.75}$$

Likewise, the upper and lower membership functions of the minimum valued image matrix are computed.

Fuzzy divergence between the upper and lower levels of the maximum value is computed as

$$Div(\mu_{\max}^{upper}, \mu_{\max}^{lower}) = 2 - (1 - \mu_{\max}^{upper} + \mu_{\max}^{lower}) \cdot e^{\mu_{\max}^{upper} - \mu_{\max}^{lower}} - 1(1 - \mu_{\max}^{lower} + \mu_{\max}^{upper}) \cdot e^{\mu_{\max}^{lower} - \mu_{\max}^{upper}}$$

Likewise, the divergence between the upper and lower levels of the minimum value is computed as

$$Div(\mu_{\min}^{upper}, \mu_{\min}^{lower}) = 2 - (1 - \mu_{\min}^{upper} + \mu_{\min}^{lower}) \cdot e^{\mu_{\min}^{upper} - \mu_{\min}^{lower}} - 1(1 - \mu_{\min}^{lower} + \mu_{\min}^{upper}) \cdot e^{\mu_{\min}^{lower} - \mu_{\min}^{upper}}$$

Then the difference between the two divergences – min_divergence and max_divergence – is computed. The difference image obtained is the edge image. In doing so, each pixel is associated with different membership degrees corresponding to its interval length (divergence between the maximum and minimum matrices).

Intuitionistic Fuzzy Edge Detection

In this method, the membership and non-membership degrees are considered in a fuzzy image. That means it considers more uncertainties. Edge detection in fingerprint images is considered to perform well as fingerprint images contain unclear regions/boundaries.

Template–Based Edge Detection

This method is an extension of fuzzy divergence–based edge detector (Chaira, 2004). For edge detection, a set of 16 fuzzy templates, each of size 3×3, representing the edge profiles of different types are used.

$$
\begin{bmatrix} 0 & y & x \\ 0 & y & x \\ 0 & y & x \end{bmatrix}
\begin{bmatrix} x & x & x \\ 0 & 0 & 0 \\ y & y & y \end{bmatrix}
\begin{bmatrix} x & x & y \\ x & y & 0 \\ y & 0 & 0 \end{bmatrix}
\begin{bmatrix} y & y & y \\ 0 & 0 & 0 \\ x & x & x \end{bmatrix}
\begin{bmatrix} y & x & x \\ 0 & y & x \\ 0 & 0 & y \end{bmatrix}
\begin{bmatrix} y & x & 0 \\ y & x & 0 \\ y & x & 0 \end{bmatrix}
\begin{bmatrix} x & 0 & y \\ x & 0 & y \\ x & 0 & y \end{bmatrix}
\begin{bmatrix} 0 & 0 & 0 \\ y & y & y \\ x & x & x \end{bmatrix}
$$

$$
\begin{bmatrix} x & x & x \\ y & y & y \\ 0 & 0 & 0 \end{bmatrix}
\begin{bmatrix} x & y & 0 \\ x & y & 0 \\ x & y & 0 \end{bmatrix}
\begin{bmatrix} 0 & 0 & 0 \\ x & x & x \\ y & y & y \end{bmatrix}
\begin{bmatrix} 0 & x & y \\ 0 & x & y \\ 0 & x & y \end{bmatrix}
\begin{bmatrix} y & y & y \\ x & x & x \\ 0 & 0 & 0 \end{bmatrix}
\begin{bmatrix} y & 0 & x \\ y & 0 & x \\ y & 0 & x \end{bmatrix}
\begin{bmatrix} y & 0 & 0 \\ x & b & 0 \\ x & x & y \end{bmatrix}
\begin{bmatrix} 0 & 0 & y \\ 0 & y & x \\ y & x & x \end{bmatrix}
$$

Set of 16, 3×3 Template

For edge detection, a set of 16 fuzzy templates (Figure 5) each of size 3x3 representing the edge profiles of different types has been used. The choice of templates is crucial which reflects the types and direction of edges. The templates are the examples of the edges, which are also the images. x, y and 0 represent the pixels of the edge templates, where the values of x and y have been chosen by trial and error method. It is to be noted that, the size of the template should be less than that of an image. The center of each template is placed at each pixel position (i, j) over a normalized image. The IT2FD measure at each pixel position (i, j) in the image, where the template was centered, IT2FD (i, j) is calculated between the image window (same size as that of the template) and the template using the max–min relationship, as given below:

$$
IT2FD(i, j) = \max_N \left[\min_r (IT2FD(\widetilde{A}, \widetilde{B}) \right]
$$

where, N = number of templates, r = number of elements in the square template.

The IT2FD ($\widetilde{A},\widetilde{B}$) is calculated by finding the IT2FD between each of the elements (x_{ij}, u_{ij}) and (y_{ij}, u_{ij}) of image window $\widetilde{A}$ and of template $\widetilde{B}$ is given as

$$IT2FD((x_{ij}, u_{ij}),(y_{ij}, u_{ij})) = (2 - [(1 - \mu_{\widetilde{A}}(x_{ij}, u_{ij}) + \mu_{\widetilde{B}}(y_{ij}, u_{ij})]\exp\{\mu_{\widetilde{A}}(x_{ij}, u_{ij}) - \mu_{\widetilde{B}}(y_{ij}, u_{ij})\}$$
$$-(1 - \mu_{\widetilde{B}}(y_{ij}, u_{ij}) + \mu_{\widetilde{A}}(x_{ij}, u_{ij})\exp\{\mu_{\widetilde{B}}(y_{ij}, u_{ij}) - \mu_{\widetilde{A}}(x_{ij}, u_{ij})\} + (2 - [1 - (\mu_{\widetilde{A}}(x_{ij}, u_{ij}) - \mu_{\widetilde{B}}(y_{ij}, u_{ij}))$$
$$+(\pi_{\widetilde{B}}(y_{ij}, u_{ij}) - \pi_{\widetilde{A}}(x_{ij}, u_{ij}))]\exp\{\pi_{\widetilde{A}}(x_{ij}, u_{ij}) - \pi_{\widetilde{B}}(y_{ij}, u_{ij}) - ((\pi_{\widetilde{B}}(y_{ij}, u_{ij}) - \pi_{\widetilde{A}}(x_{ij}, u_{ij}))\}$$
$$-[1 - (\pi_{\widetilde{B}}(y_{ij}, u_{ij}) - \pi_{\widetilde{A}}(x_{ij}, u_{ij})) + (\mu_{\widetilde{A}}(x_{ij}, u_{ij}) - \mu_{\widetilde{B}}(y_{ij}, u_{ij}))]\exp\{\pi_{\widetilde{B}}(y_{ij}, u_{ij}) - \pi_{\widetilde{A}}(x_{ij}, u_{ij})$$
$$-(\mu_{\widetilde{A}}(x_{ij}, u_{ij}) - \mu_{\widetilde{B}}(y_{ij}, u_{ij}))\}$$

The IT2FD $((x_{ij}, u_{ij}),(y_{ij}, u_{ij}))$ is the IT2FD between each element in the template (y_{ij}, u_{ij}) and those in image window (x_{ij}, u_{ij}). IT2FD (i, j) is calculated for all pixel positions of the image. Finally, IT2FD matrix, the same size as that of image is formed with values of IT2FD (i, j) at each point of the matrix. This IT2FD matrix is threshold and thinned to get an edge-detected image.

Intuitionistic Type-2 Fuzzy Divergence Edge Detection

Let

$$\widetilde{A} = \left\{ ((x, u), \mu_{\widetilde{A}}(x, u), \nu_{\widetilde{A}}(x, u)) \mid \forall x \in X, \forall u \in J_x \subseteq [0,1] \right\}$$

and

$$\widetilde{B} = \left\{ ((x, u), \mu_{\widetilde{B}}(x, u), \nu_{\widetilde{B}}(x, u)) \mid \forall x \in X, \forall u \in J_x \subseteq [0,1] \right\}$$

be two intuitionistic type-2 fuzzy set. Considering the hesitation degree, the range of the membership degree of the two intuitionistic type-2 fuzzy set $\widetilde{A}$ and $\widetilde{B}$ may be represented as

$$\left\{ \mu_{\widetilde{A}}(x, u), (\mu_{\widetilde{A}}(x, u) + \pi_{\widetilde{A}}(x, u)) \right\}, \left\{ \mu_{\widetilde{B}}(x, u), (\mu_{\widetilde{B}}(x, u) + \pi_{\widetilde{B}}(x, u)) \right\}.$$

The distance measure has been proposed here taking into account the hesitation degree.

In an image of size $M \times M$ with L distinct gray levels having probabilities $p_0, p_1, ..., p_{L-1}$, the exponential entropy is defined as $H = \sum_{i=0}^{L-1} p_i e^{1-p_i}$.

In fuzzy information circumstance, based on the definition the type-2 fuzzy entropy of an image $\widetilde{A}$ of size $M \times M$ is defined as follows

$$H(\widetilde{A}) = \frac{1}{n(\sqrt{e}-1)} \sum_{i=0}^{M-1}\sum_{i=0}^{M-1} \begin{bmatrix} (\mu_{\widetilde{A}}(x_{ij},u_{ij})\exp\{(1-\mu_{\widetilde{A}}(x_{ij},u_{ij})\} \\ +(1-(\mu_{\widetilde{A}}(x_{ij},u_{ij})\exp\{1-\mu_{\widetilde{A}}(x_{ij},u_{ij})\}-1) \end{bmatrix}$$

where,

$$n = M^2, i,j = 0,1,2,3,.....,M-1$$

and $\mu_{\widetilde{A}}(x_{ij},u_{ij})$ is the membership degree of the $(i,j)^{th}$ pixels (x_{ij},u_{ij}) in the image $\widetilde{A}$.

For two images $\widetilde{A}$ and $\widetilde{B}$, at the $(i,j)^{th}$ pixels, the amount of information between the membership degree of images $\widetilde{A}$ and $\widetilde{B}$ is given as follows,

- Due to $m_1(\widetilde{A})$ and $m_1(\widetilde{B})$, i.e., $\mu_{\widetilde{A}}(x_{ij},u_{ij})$ and $\mu_{\widetilde{B}}(y_{ij},u_{ij})$ of the $(i,j)^{th}$ pixels:
$$\exp\left\{\mu_{\widetilde{A}}(x_{ij},u_{ij}) - \mu_{\widetilde{B}}(y_{ij},u_{ij})\right\}$$

- Due to $m_2(\widetilde{A})$ and $m_2(\widetilde{B})$, i.e., $\mu_{\widetilde{A}}(x_{ij},u_{ij}) + \pi_{\widetilde{A}}(x_{ij},u_{ij})$ and $\mu_{\widetilde{B}}(y_{ij},u_{ij}) + \pi_{\widetilde{B}}(y_{ij},u_{ij})$ of the $(i,j)^{th}$ pixels:

$$\exp\{\mu_{\widetilde{A}}(x_{ij},u_{ij}) + \pi_{\widetilde{A}}(x_{ij},u_{ij})\} / \exp\{\mu_{\widetilde{B}}(y_{ij},u_{ij}) + \pi_{\widetilde{B}}(y_{ij},u_{ij})\}.$$

Corresponding to the type-2 fuzzy entropy, the fuzzy divergence between images $\widetilde{A}$ and $\widetilde{B}$ due to $m_1(\widetilde{A})$ and $m_1(\widetilde{B})$ may be given as

$$D_1(\widetilde{A},\widetilde{B}) = \sum_i\sum_j (1-(1-\mu_{\widetilde{A}}(x_{ij},u_{ij}))\exp\{\mu_{\widetilde{A}}(x_{ij},u_{ij}) - \mu_{\widetilde{B}}(y_{ij},u_{ij})\}$$
$$-\mu_{\widetilde{A}}(x_{ij},u_{ij})\exp\{\mu_{\widetilde{B}}(y_{ij},u_{ij}) - \mu_{\widetilde{A}}(x_{ij},u_{ij})\}$$

Similarly, the divergence of $\widetilde{B}$ against $\widetilde{A}$ is

$$D_1(\widetilde{B},\widetilde{A}) = \sum_i\sum_j (1-(1-\mu_{\widetilde{B}}(y_{ij},u_{ij}))\exp\{\mu_{\widetilde{B}}(y_{ij},u_{ij}) - \mu_{\widetilde{A}}(x_{ij},u_{ij})\}$$
$$-\mu_{\widetilde{B}}(y_{ij},u_{ij})\exp\{\mu_{\widetilde{A}}(x_{ij},u_{ij}) - \mu_{\widetilde{B}}(y_{ij},u_{ij})\}$$

Corresponding to the type -2 fuzzy entropy, the fuzzy divergence between images $\widetilde{A}$ and $\widetilde{B}$ due to $m_1(\widetilde{A})$ and $m_1(\widetilde{B})$ may be given as

$$D_2(\widetilde{A},\widetilde{B}) = \sum_i\sum_j (1-(1-\mu_{\widetilde{A}}(x_{ij},u_{ij}) + \pi_{\widetilde{A}}(x_{ij},u_{ij}))\exp\begin{bmatrix}(\mu_{\widetilde{A}}(x_{ij},u_{ij}) + \pi_{\widetilde{A}}(x_{ij},u_{ij})) \\ -(\mu_{\widetilde{B}}(y_{ij},u_{ij}) + \pi_{\widetilde{B}}(y_{ij},u_{ij}))\end{bmatrix}$$
$$-(\mu_{\widetilde{A}}(x_{ij},u_{ij}) + \pi_{\widetilde{A}}(x_{ij},u_{ij}))\exp\left\{(\mu_{\widetilde{B}}(y_{ij},u_{ij}) + \pi_{\widetilde{B}}(y_{ij},u_{ij})) - (\mu_{\widetilde{A}}(x_{ij},u_{ij}) + \pi_{\widetilde{A}}(x_{ij},u_{ij}))\right\}$$

Similarly, the divergence of $\widetilde{B}$ against $\widetilde{A}$ is

$$
D_2(\widetilde{B}, \widetilde{A}) = \sum_i \sum_j (1 - (1 - \mu_{\widetilde{B}}(y_{ij}, u_{ij}) + \pi_{\widetilde{B}}(y_{ij}, u_{ij})) \exp\left\{ \begin{matrix} (\mu_{\widetilde{B}}(y_{ij}, u_{ij}) + \pi_{\widetilde{B}}(y_{ij}, u_{ij})) \\ -(\mu_{\widetilde{A}}(x_{ij}, u_{ij}) + \pi_{\widetilde{A}}(x_{ij}, u_{ij})) \end{matrix} \right\}
$$
$$
-(\mu_{\widetilde{B}}(y_{ij}, u_{ij}) + \pi_{\widetilde{B}}(y_{ij}, u_{ij}) \exp\left\{ (\mu_{\widetilde{A}}(x_{ij}, u_{ij}) + \pi_{\widetilde{A}}(x_{ij}, u_{ij})) - \mu_{\widetilde{B}}(y_{ij}, u_{ij}) + \pi_{\widetilde{B}}(y_{ij}, u_{ij}) \right\}
$$

The total divergence between the pixels (x_{ij}, u_{ij}) and (y_{ij}, u_{ij}) of the images $\widetilde{A}$ and $\widetilde{B}$ due to $m_1(\widetilde{A})$ and $m_1(\widetilde{B})$ is

$$
Div\text{-}m_1(\widetilde{A}, \widetilde{B}) = D_1(\widetilde{A}, \widetilde{B}) + D_1(\widetilde{B}, \widetilde{A})
$$
$$
= \sum_i \sum_j 2 - (1 - \mu_{\widetilde{A}}(x_{ij}, u_{ij}) + \mu_{\widetilde{B}}(y_{ij}, u_{ij}) \exp\{\mu_{\widetilde{A}}(x_{ij}, u_{ij}) - \mu_{\widetilde{B}}(y_{ij}, u_{ij})\}
$$
$$
-(1 - \mu_{\widetilde{B}}(y_{ij}, u_{ij}) + \mu_{\widetilde{A}}(x_{ij}, u_{ij}) \exp\{\mu_{\widetilde{B}}(y_{ij}, u_{ij}) - \mu_{\widetilde{A}}(x_{ij}, u_{ij})\}
$$

The total divergence between the pixels (x_{ij}, u_{ij}) and (y_{ij}, u_{ij}) of the images $\widetilde{A}$ and $\widetilde{B}$ due to $m_1(\widetilde{A})$ and $m_1(\widetilde{B})$ is

$$
Div\text{-}m_2(\widetilde{A}, \widetilde{B}) = D_2(\widetilde{A}, \widetilde{B}) + D_2(\widetilde{B}, \widetilde{A})
$$
$$
= \sum_i \sum_j 2 - \begin{bmatrix} 1 - \mu_{\widetilde{A}}(x_{ij}, u_{ij}) - \mu_{\widetilde{B}}(y_{ij}, u_{ij})) \\ +(\pi_{\widetilde{B}}(y_{ij}, u_{ij}) - \pi_{\widetilde{A}}(x_{ij}, u_{ij})) \end{bmatrix} \exp\left\{ \begin{matrix} \mu_{\widetilde{A}}(x_{ij}, u_{ij}) - \mu_{\widetilde{B}}(y_{ij}, v_{ij}) \\ -((\pi_{\widetilde{B}}(y_{ij}, u_{ij}) - \pi_{\widetilde{A}}(x_{ij}, u_{ij})) \end{matrix} \right\}
$$
$$
- \begin{bmatrix} 1 - (\pi_{\widetilde{B}}(y_{ij}, u_{ij}) - \pi_{\widetilde{A}}(x_{ij}, u_{ij})) \\ +(\mu_{\widetilde{A}}(x_{ij}, u_{ij}) - \mu_{\widetilde{B}}(y_{ij}, u_{ij})) \end{bmatrix} \exp\left\{ \begin{matrix} \pi_{\widetilde{B}}(y_{ij}, u_{ij}) - \pi_{\widetilde{A}}(x_{ij}, u_{ij}) \\ -(\mu_{\widetilde{A}}(x_{ij}, u_{ij}) - \mu_{\widetilde{B}}(y_{ij}, u_{ij})) \end{matrix} \right\}
$$

Thus, the overall IT2FD between the image $\widetilde{A}$ and $\widetilde{B}$ is defined as follows,

$$
IT2FD(\widetilde{A}, \widetilde{B}) = Div - m_1(\widetilde{A}, \widetilde{B}) + Div - m_2(\widetilde{A}, \widetilde{B})
$$
$$
= \sum_i \sum_j 2 - (1 - \mu_{\widetilde{A}}(x_{ij}, u_{ij}) + \mu_{\widetilde{B}}(y_{ij}, u_{ij}) \exp\left\{ \mu_{\widetilde{A}}(x_{ij}, u_{ij}) - \mu_{\widetilde{B}}(y_{ij}, u_{ij}) \right\}
$$
$$
- \left(1 - \mu_{\widetilde{B}}(y_{ij}, u_{ij}) + \mu_{\widetilde{A}}(x_{ij}, u_{ij}) \exp\left\{ \mu_{\widetilde{B}}(y_{ij}, u_{ij}) - \mu_{\widetilde{A}}(x_{ij}, u_{ij}) \right\} \right)
$$
$$
+ \left(2 - \begin{bmatrix} 1 - (\mu_{\widetilde{A}}(x_{ij}, u_{ij}) - \mu_{\widetilde{B}}(y_{ij}, u_{ij})) \\ +(\pi_{\widetilde{B}}(y_{ij}, u_{ij}) - \pi_{\widetilde{A}}(x_{ij}, u_{ij})) \end{bmatrix} \exp\left\{ \begin{matrix} \mu_{\widetilde{A}}(x_{ij}, u_{ij}) - \mu_{\widetilde{B}}(y_{ij}, u_{ij}) \\ -((\pi_{\widetilde{B}}(y_{ij}, u_{ij}) - \pi_{\widetilde{A}}(x_{ij}, u_{ij})) \end{matrix} \right\} \right)
$$
$$
- \begin{bmatrix} 1 - (\pi_{\widetilde{B}}(y_{ij}, u_{ij}) - \pi_{\widetilde{A}}(x_{ij}, u_{ij})) \\ +(\mu_{\widetilde{A}}(x_{ij}, u_{ij}) - \mu_{\widetilde{B}}(y_{ij}, u_{ij})) \end{bmatrix} \exp\left\{ \begin{matrix} \pi_{\widetilde{B}}(y_{ij}, u_{ij}) - \pi_{\widetilde{A}}(x_{ij}, u_{ij}) \\ -(\mu_{\widetilde{A}}(x_{ij}, u_{ij}) - \mu_{\widetilde{B}}(y_{ij}, u_{ij})) \end{matrix} \right\}
$$

Figure 5. a) Fingerprint original image b) edge detected image using canny method c) edge detected image using Sobel method d) edge detected image using proposed method

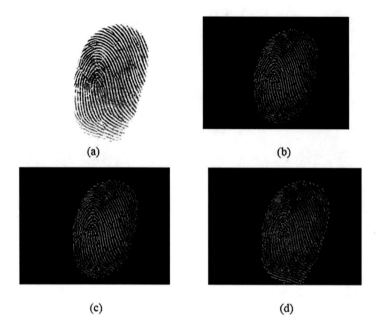

(a)

(b)

(c)

(d)

Example 2

Figure 5, Figure 6, Figure 7 and Figure 8 will illustrate the effect of Canny method, Sobel method, Prewitt method and Intuitionistic type-2 fuzzy divergence method on fingerprint images.

ISSUES AND CHALLENGES OF BIOMETRICS

1. The real grand challenge of biometrics is to create, develop, and commercialize systems that address all the needs for biometrics, provide all of the potential benefits, and exhibits all of the desirable properties:
   a. Works for everyone,
   b. 100% accurate in all conditions,
   c. Doesn't degrade with time,
   d. Easy to enroll,
   e. Transparent (not cumbersome or inconvenient),
   f. Inexpensive,
   g. Works anywhere, in all environments.
2. Problems that involve fundamental issues related to design of recognition systems.
3. Problems that are specific to applications that will use biometric recognition.
4. Techniques to shield a biometric system from adversarial attacks/threats and provide assurances on user privacy.
5. Techniques to assess usability of a biometric system and estimate the return on investment.

Figure 6. a) Fingerprint original image b) edge detected image using Sobel image c) edge detected image using Prewitt method d) edge detected image using proposed method

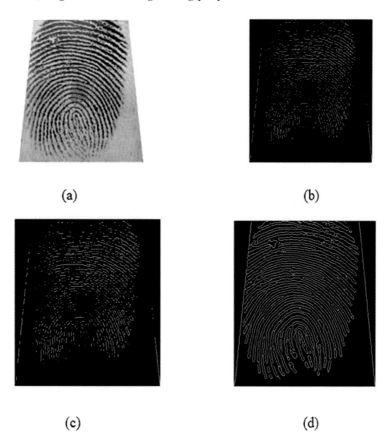

(a)   (b)

(c)   (d)

IMPLEMENTATION USING MATLAB

A MATLAB code for image enhancement and edge detection is given which will be beneficial to the readers to implement the method.

Intuitionistic Type-2 Fuzzy Set for Contrast Enhancement Using Hamacher t-Co-Norm

Pseudo code:

Input: Fingerprint Image.
Output: Fingerprint Contrast Enhancement Image.
1. Specify the input image with dimension.
2. Gray scale image converted into binary image.
3. Calculate $\mu_A^{fuz}(g_{ij}) = \dfrac{g_{ij} - g_{min}}{g_{max} - g_{min}}$.

4. Find the mean of the image.
5. Upper membership level.
6. Lower membership level.
7. Calculate $\mu^{type-2}(g_{ij}) = \dfrac{\mu^{upper} + \mu^{lower} + (\lambda - 2)\mu^{upper}.\mu^{lower}}{1 - (1 - \lambda)\mu^{upper}\mu^{lower}}$.
8. Apply the intuitionistic fuzzy set to each window.
9. Enhanced image will be displayed the screen.

Figure 7. a) Fingerprint original image b) edge detected image using Robert method c) edge detected image using canny method d) edge detected image using proposed method

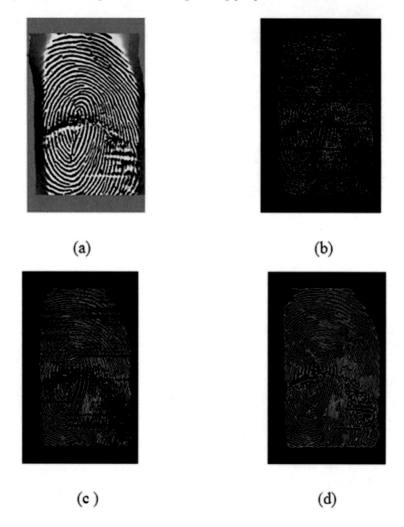

(a)   (b)

(c)   (d)

Figure 8. a) Fingerprint original image b) Edge detected image using Prewitt method c) edge detected image using Sobel method d) edge detected image using proposed method

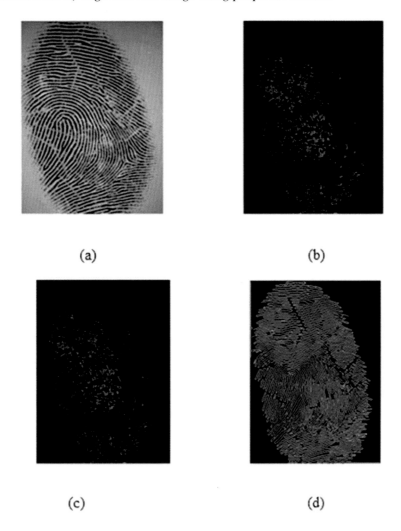

(a)   (b)

(c)   (d)

Intuitionistic Type -2 Fuzzy Divergence for Edge Detection

Pseudo code:

Input: Fingerprint Image.
Output: Fingerprint Image Binary Edge Detection.

1. Specify the input image with dimension.
2. The template pixel values of x and y.
3. Set of 16 type-2 fuzzy edge template, likewise $m_1, m_2, \ldots, m_{16}$.
4. Calculate

$$IT2FD(\widetilde{A}, \widetilde{B}) = \sum_i \sum_j 2 - (1 - \mu_{\widetilde{A}}(x_{ij}, u_{ij}) + \mu_{\widetilde{B}}(y_{ij}, u_{ij}) \exp\{\mu_{\widetilde{A}}(x_{ij}, u_{ij}) - \mu_{\widetilde{B}}(y_{ij}, u_{ij})\}$$
$$- (1 - \mu_{\widetilde{B}}(y_{ij}, u_{ij}) + \mu_{\widetilde{A}}(x_{ij}, u_{ij}) \exp\{\mu_{\widetilde{B}}(y_{ij}, u_{ij}) - \mu_{\widetilde{A}}(x_{ij}, u_{ij})\}$$

5. Calculating the max–min divergence for all pixel positions:

$$IT2FD(i, j) = \max_{N} \left[\min_{r} (IT2FD(\widetilde{A}, \widetilde{B}) \right].$$

6. Threshold the divergence matrix to obtain an edge-detection image:

```
for  i1 = 1 : dim
for  j1 = 1 : dim
if maxim  (i1, j1) >  Threshold value   w2(i1, j1) = 1
else  w2(i1, j1) = 0
end
end
end
```

7. Thinned the image.
8. Final binary edge detected image will be display on the screen.

CONCLUSION

This chapter discussed different enhancement and edge detection techniques using fuzzy, intuitionistic fuzzy, type-2 fuzzy and intuitionistic type-2 fuzzy set theoretic techniques on fingerprint images. Enhancement is the preprocessing of images to enhance or highlight the image structures and suppress unwanted information in the image. Fuzzy enhancement does provide better results, but in some cases, Intuitionistic fuzzy, type-2 fuzzy and Intuitionistic type- 2 fuzzy enhancement methods provide better results. Similarly, fuzzy methods do not show better edge images, and in that case, some advanced fuzzy edge detection techniques are used. This may be due to the fact that these advanced fuzzy sets consider either more number of uncertainties or different types of uncertainty. Also, MATLAB codes are discussed for better understanding to the readers.

REFERENCES

Aborisade, D. O. (2011). Novel fuzzy logic based edge detection technique. *International Journal of Advanced Science and Technology, 29*, 75–82.

Acharya, T., & Ray, A. K. (2005). *Image processing: principles and applications*. John Wiley & Sons. doi:10.1002/0471745790

Atanassov, K. T. (1986). Intuitionistic fuzzy sets. *Fuzzy Sets and Systems, 20*(1), 87–96. doi:10.1016/S0165-0114(86)80034-3

Babler, W. J. (1991). *Embryologic development of epidermal ridges and their configurations. In Dermatoglyphics: Science in Transition* (pp. 95–112). New York: Wiley-Liss.

Ballard, D. H., & Brown, C. M. (1982). *Computer vision, 1982*. Englewood Cliffs, NJ: Prenice-Hall.

Bansal, R., Arora, P., Gaur, M., Sehgal, P., & Bedi, P. (2009). Fingerprint image enhancement using type-2 fuzzy sets. In *Fuzzy Systems and Knowledge Discovery, 2009. FSKD'09. Sixth International Conference on* (Vol. 3, pp. 412–417). doi:10.1109/FSKD.2009.396

Bennet, D., & Perumal, D. S. A. (2011). *Fingerprint: DWT, SVD based enhancement and significant contrast for ridges and valleys using fuzzy measures.* arXiv Preprint arXiv:1106.5737

Biswas, R., & Sil, J. (2012). An improved canny edge detection algorithm based on type-2 fuzzy sets. *Procedia Technology, 4*, 820–824. doi:10.1016/j.protcy.2012.05.134

Bustince, H., Kacprzyk, J., & Mohedano, V. (2000). Intuitionistic fuzzy generators application to intuitionistic fuzzy complementation. *Fuzzy Sets and Systems, 114*(3), 485–504. doi:10.1016/S0165-0114(98)00279-6

Cao, K., Liu, E., & Jain, A. K. (n.d.). *Segmentation and Enhancement of Latent Fingerprints : A Coarse to Fine Ridge Structure Dictionary.* Academic Press.

Chaira, T. (2004). *Image segmentation and color retrieval: a fuzzy and intuitionistic fuzzy set theoretic approach* (PhD Thesis). Indian Institute of Technology, Kharagpur, India.

Chaira, T. (2013). Contrast enhancement of medical images using Type II fuzzy set. In *Communications (NCC), 2013 National Conference on* (pp. 1–5). doi:10.1109/NCC.2013.6488016

Chaira, T., & Ray, A. K. (2003). Segmentation using fuzzy divergence. *Pattern Recognition Letters, 24*(12), 1837–1844. doi:10.1016/S0167-8655(03)00007-2

Chaira, T., & Ray, A. K. (2014). Construction of fuzzy edge image using interval type II fuzzy set. *International Journal of Computational Intelligence Systems, 7*(4), 686–695. doi:10.1080/18756891.2013.862356

Chakraborty, A. (1996). *Feature and module integration for image segmentation.* Academic Press.

Choi, Y., & Krishnapuram, R. (1997). A robust approach to image enhancement based on fuzzy logic. *Image Processing. IEEE Transactions on, 6*(6), 808–825.

El-Khamy, S. E., Ghaleb, I., & El-Yamany, N. A. (2002). Fuzzy edge detection with minimum fuzzy entropy criterion. In *Electrotechnical Conference, 2002. MELECON 2002. 11th Mediterranean* (pp. 498–503). doi:10.1109/MELECON.2002.1014643

El-Khamy, S. E., Lotfy, M., & El-Yamany, N. (2000). A modified fuzzy Sobel edge detector. In *Radio Science Conference, 2000. 17th NRSC'2000. Seventeenth National* (pp. C32–1).

Ensafi, P., & Tizhoosh, H. R. (2005). Type-2 fuzzy image enhancement. In Image Analysis and Recognition (pp. 159–166). Springer. doi:10.1007/11559573_20

Feng, J., Zhou, J., Member, S., & Jain, A. K. (n.d.). *Orientation Field Estimation for Latent Fingerprint Enhancement.* Academic Press.

Gomez Lopera, J. F., Ilhami, N., Escamilla, P. L. L., Aroza, J. M., & Roldán, R. R. (1999). Improved entropic edge-detection. In *Image Analysis and Processing, 1999. Proceedings. International Conference on* (pp. 180–184). doi:10.1109/ICIAP.1999.797591

Gonzalez, R. C., & Wintz, P. (1977). *Digital image processing*. Academic Press.

Greenberg, S., Aladjem, M., Kogan, D., & Dimitrov, I. (2000). Fingerprint image enhancement using filtering techniques. In *Pattern Recognition, 2000. Proceedings. 15th International Conference on* (Vol. 3, pp. 322–325). doi:10.1109/ICPR.2000.903550

Hanmandlu, M., Jha, D., & Sharma, R. (2003). Color image enhancement by fuzzy intensification. *Pattern Recognition Letters*, *24*(1), 81–87. doi:10.1016/S0167-8655(02)00191-5

Hassanien, A. E., & Badr, A. (2003). A comparative study on digital mamography enhancement algorithms based on fuzzy theory. *Studies in Informatics and Control*, *12*(1), 21–32.

Ho, K. H. L., & Ohnishi, N. (1995). FEDGE—fuzzy edge detection by fuzzy categorization and classification of edges. In *Fuzzy Logic in Artificial Intelligence Towards Intelligent Systems* (pp. 182–196). Springer.

Jain, A., Flynn, P., & Ross, A. A. (2007). *Handbook of biometrics*. Springer Science & Business Media.

Jayaram, B., Narayana, K., & Vetrivel, V. (2011). Fuzzy Inference System based Contrast Enhancement. In *EUSFLAT Conf.* (pp. 311–318).

Karimi-Ashtiani, S., & Kuo, C.-C. J. (2008). A robust technique for latent fingerprint image segmentation and enhancement. In *Image Processing, 2008. ICIP 2008. 15th IEEE International Conference on* (pp. 1492–1495). doi:10.1109/ICIP.2008.4712049

Kass, M., Witkin, A., & Terzopoulos, D. (1988). Snakes: Active contour models. *International Journal of Computer Vision*, *1*(4), 321–331. doi:10.1007/BF00133570

Kim, B.-G., Kim, H.-J., & Park, D.-J. (2002). New enhancement algorithm for fingerprint images. In *Pattern Recognition, 2002. Proceedings. 16th International Conference on* (Vol. 3, pp. 879–882).

Lee, K. H. (2006). *First course on fuzzy theory and applications* (Vol. 27). Springer.

Maltoni, D., Maio, D., Jain, A. K., & Prabhakar, S. (2009). Handbook of fingerprint recognition. Springer. doi:10.1007/978-1-84882-254-2

Mao, K., Zhu, Z., & Jiang, H. (2010). A fast fingerprint image enhancement method. In *Computational Science and Optimization (CSO), 2010 Third International Joint Conference on* (Vol. 1, pp. 222–226). doi:10.1109/CSO.2010.76

Melin, P., Gonzalez, C. I., Castro, J. R., Mendoza, O., & Castillo, O. (2014). Edge-detection method for image processing based on generalized type-2 fuzzy logic. *Fuzzy Systems. IEEE Transactions on*, *22*(6), 1515–1525.

Russo, F. (1999). FIRE operators for image processing. *Fuzzy Sets and Systems*, *103*(2), 265–275. doi:10.1016/S0165-0114(98)00226-7

Russo, F., & Ramponi, G. (1994). Combined FIRE filters for image enhancement. In *Fuzzy Systems, 1994. IEEE World Congress on Computational Intelligence., Proceedings of the Third IEEE Conference on* (pp. 260–264).

Selvi, M., & George, A. (2013). FBFET: Fuzzy based fingerprint enhancement technique based on adaptive thresholding. In *Computing, Communications and Networking Technologies (ICCCNT), 2013 Fourth International Conference on* (pp. 1–5).

Sherlock, B. G., Monro, D. M., & Millard, K. (1994). Fingerprint enhancement by directional Fourier filtering. In *Vision, Image and Signal Processing, IEE Proceedings-* (Vol. 141, pp. 87–94). doi:10.1049/ip-vis:19949924

Sivanandam, S. N., Sumathi, S., & Deepa, S. N. et al. (2007). *Introduction to fuzzy logic using MATLAB* (Vol. 1). Springer. doi:10.1007/978-3-540-35781-0

Sonka, M. et al. (2001). *Image processing analysis and computing vision*. Brooks/Cole.

Szmidt, E., & Kacprzyk, J. (2001). Entropy for intuitionistic fuzzy sets. *Fuzzy Sets and Systems, 118*(3), 467–477. doi:10.1016/S0165-0114(98)00402-3

Tao, C.-W., Thompson, W. E., & Taur, J. S. (1993). A fuzzy if-then approach to edge detection. In *Fuzzy Systems, 1993., Second IEEE International Conference on* (pp. 1356–1360). doi:10.1109/FUZZY.1993.327590

Tizhoosh, H. R., & Fochem, M. (1995). Fuzzy histogram hyperbolization for image enhancement. *Proceedings EUFIT*, 95.

Vlachos, I. K., & Sergiadis, G. D. (2007). The role of entropy in intuitionistic fuzzy contrast enhancement. In *Foundations of Fuzzy Logic and Soft Computing* (pp. 104–113). Springer. doi:10.1007/978-3-540-72950-1_11

Wu, C., Shi, Z., & Govindaraju, V. (2004). Fingerprint image enhancement method using directional median filter. In Defense and Security (pp. 66–75). doi:10.1117/12.542200

Yang, J., Liu, L., & Jiang, T. (2002). Improved method for extraction of fingerprint features. In *Second International Conference on Image and Graphics* (pp. 552–558). doi:10.1117/12.477196

Yoon, S., Cao, K., Liu, E., & Jain, A. K. (2013). LFIQ: Latent fingerprint image quality. In *Biometrics: Theory, Applications and Systems (BTAS), 2013 IEEE Sixth International Conference on* (pp. 1–8).

Yoon, S., Feng, J., & Jain, A. K. (2011). Latent fingerprint enhancement via robust orientation field estimation. In *Biometrics (IJCB), 2011 International Joint Conference on* (pp. 1–8). doi:10.1109/IJCB.2011.6117482

Yoon, S., Liu, E., & Jain, A. K. (2015). On latent fingerprint image quality. In *Computational Forensics* (pp. 67–82). Springer. doi:10.1007/978-3-319-20125-2_7

Zadeh, L. A. (1965). Fuzzy sets. *Information and Control, 8*(3), 338–353. doi:10.1016/S0019-9958(65)90241-X

Zadeh, L. A. (1972). *A fuzzy-set-theoretic interpretation of linguistic hedges*. Academic Press.

Chapter 2
An Overview of Text Information Extraction from Images

Prabhakar C. J.
Kuvempu University, India

ABSTRACT

In this chapter, we present an overview of text information extraction from images/video. This chapter starts with an introduction to computer vision and its applications, which is followed by an introduction to text information extraction from images/video. We describe various forms of text, challenges and steps involved in text information extraction process. The literature review of techniques for text information extraction from images/video is presented. Finally, our approach for extraction of scene text information from images is presented.

INTRODUCTION

Digital images and videos form a larger part of archived multimedia data files, and they are rich in text information. Text present in images and videos provide valuable and important semantic information that may be of a particular interest as they are useful for describing the contents of an image. Text is therefore, becomes a Region of Interest (RoI), where, the points of interest must be clustered and extracted from the given image. Text Information Extraction (TIE) is concerned with the task of extracting relevant text information from digital images and videos. TIE system generally receives image or sequence of video frames as an input which can be either gray-scale or colored, compressed or un-compressed with still or moving text.

The TIE is a challenging problem because of variations occurring in images such as low contrast/resolutions, shaded or textured background, complex background, and variations in font size, style, artistic fonts, color, arbitrary text layouts, multi-script, effect of uncontrolled illumination, reflections, shadows, and distortion due to perspective projection (Crandall et al., 2003). These variations make the problem of automatic TIE extremely difficult. Figure 1 shows images containing variations in different aspects.

DOI: 10.4018/978-1-5225-2053-5.ch002

Figure 1. Natural scene text images: images with variations in size, alignment, color, blur, illumination and distortion
Courtesy: Lee & Kim, 2013.

Applications of Text Information Extraction

- **License/Container Plate Extraction:** Text information extraction techniques have been applied to automatically extract and recognize vehicle license plate and container plate, which helps for traffic surveillance and cargo container verification system (see Figure 2).
- **Address Block Extraction:** Letter cover has a high degree of global structure among a limited number of entities. Mails usually have a printed label containing a block of address and are always pasted arbitrarily in any position. TIE can be used to extract the address block from mails.
- **Search for Web-Pages:** Search engines have evolved over time due to growth of the web. Advanced search problems such as entity search and structured search on the web are facilitated by text information extraction.
- **Search for News Articles:** Standard information extractions such as entity recognition help users to find specific pieces of information from news articles.
- **Page Segmentation:** Document image analysis depends on the output of page segmentation technique which determines the format of a document page.
- **Retrieval of Intelligence Information:** Vital information about suspicious criminal elements can be identified and retrieved from documents using TIE extraction techniques.
- **Biomedical:** Discoveries related to biomedical field are searched and extracted from large scientific publications based on the identification of mentions on biomedical entities of interest from text and are linked to their corresponding entries in existing knowledge bases.
- **Navigation for Robots and Visually Impaired People:** Navigation of autonomous mobile robots and navigation aid to visually impaired persons are facilitated by extraction and recognition of text information.
- **Automobile and Tourist Aid:** Text information extraction and recognition are helpful for driving of automobiles and tourist systems.

Figure 2. Sample images containing text information for various applications: (a),(b) license plate extraction/recognition, (c) container plate recognition and (d) address block localization
Courtesy of Matas & Zimmermann, 2005; ALPR-INFOSEC Institute; Adaptive Recognition-Hungary; Gaceb, Eglin, Lebourgeois & Emptoz,2009, respectively.

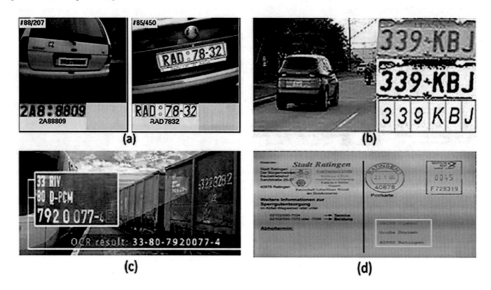

FORMS OF TEXT IN IMAGES

There exist a variety of sources where text can be found, which include images of historical manuscripts, books, journals, handwritten or printed documents, book covers, postal stamps, TV programs, advertisements, billboards, web pages and road signs. In this chapter, three forms of text are considered, such as scene text, caption text, and document text (printed or hand written). Each form is described in the below subsections:

Scene Text

Scene text exists naturally in both captured images and videos where text is written on trucks, t-shirts, buildings, billboards, etc. Sample images containing scene text are shown in the Figure 3. Generally, scene text is often affected by camera parameters such as illumination, focus and motion, perspective distortion and image blurring. In addition to these, other challenging factors are arbitrary text layouts, multi-scripts, artistic fonts, colors, complex and variable background, etc. Hence, scene text in images or videos is much more complex and challenging.

Scene text can be classified further based on text base-lines as: a) linear text and b) non-linear text. Linear text includes both horizontal and non-horizontal text with a linearly oriented baseline, while non-linear text includes curved text or irregularly oriented characters of the same word or sentence. Scene text extraction is very important and helpful in the applications such as, autonomous mobile robot navigation, tourist assistant systems, and navigational aids for automobiles, driving assistance for visually impaired people, identification and recognition of vehicle license plate.

Figure 3. Examples of images containing scene text

Caption Text

Caption text refers to text that is overlaid on existing image or video at a later stage, typically during image or video-editing process. The main sources of caption text are TV broadcastings, movies, etc. They usually annotate information about where, when, and name of the reported events, as well as represent the highlights in documentaries, depict titles, names of producers, actors, and credits, etc. Figure 4 shows some sample images containing caption text. Caption text plays a very important role in video skimming, browsing, and retrievals in large video databases. Since caption text is edited, it requires sophisticated techniques to be able to track and extract text from images and videos due to a number of challenges associated with it, which include, low resolutions, color bleeding, low contrast, variation in font size and orientations.

Document Text

Document text refers to text contained in digitized document materials. Document digitization is a crucial step in the process of building an archive to support preservation and access. The production of digital materials should represent the original contents as faithfully as possible. The sources of document text come from the following items: artworks, maps, photographs, handwritten/printed documents and historical records. Document text can be classified based on two major criteria: a) mode of data acquisition which include on-line or off-line and b) nature of text type comprising of either machine-printed or handwritten.

Figure 4. Examples of images containing caption text
Source: ABC News.

Figure 5. Examples of images with handwritten document text

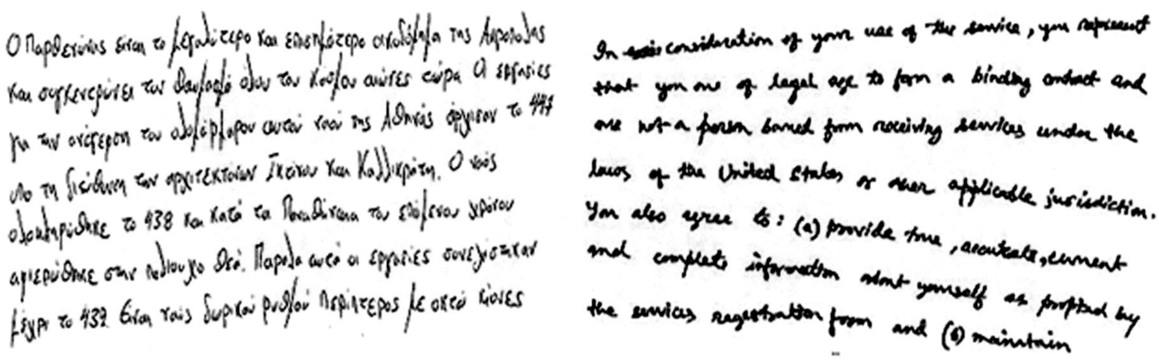

Document images are categorically faced by many challenges emanating from acquisition, processing and storage. The challenges faced in documents range from geometrical distortions, non-uniform illumination, degraded document page caused by aging, faded ink, seep-through, multi-oriented text-lines, high degrees of curl/curved, touching and overlapping components, noisy components, complex historical writing style and scripts.

Document text extraction technique finds its applications in areas such as, document database retrieval, automated processing/reading of documents and electronic/digital database archiving. Figure 5 shows some sample handwritten document images.

STEPS INVOLVED IN TIE

Typically, text information extraction approaches follow sequential sub-stages in the extraction of textual features from images, namely: detection, localization, extraction/enhancement, and recognition. Each of the sub-stages is very important as each performs a specific task in order to achieve the goal of TIE. Figure 6 provides a general flow diagram of text information extraction process.

Text Detection

Text detection is concerned with the process of determining if a given image contains text or not. Therefore, with no prior knowledge of existence or non-existence of text in the image, the detection algorithm should be capable of determine and give a favorable decision on whether text exists or not, based on the analysis of image contents.

In most of the TIE techniques, text detection has not been given enough attention, mainly because most applications of TIE are related to scanned images, such as book covers, compact disk cases, postal letter heads, and other forms of videos, etc., which are supposed to include text. With this assumption in mind, the authors purposely collected majority of our datasets from the sources where text is occurred. Text detection stage is indispensable to the overall system, alternatively, text localization module can also be used for detecting the presence of text in real-time (Zhong et al., 2000; Antani et al., 1999).

Figure 6. Flow diagram of text information extraction techniques

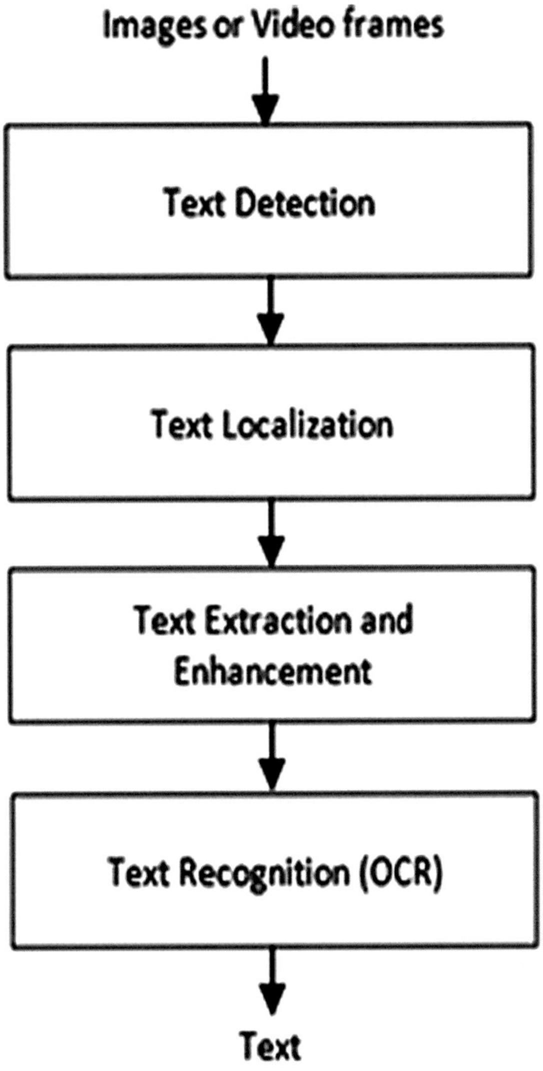

Images or Video frames

Text Detection

Text Localization

Text Extraction and Enhancement

Text Recognition (OCR)

Text

Text Localization

Text localization module is concerned with the task of detecting the regions where text is contained. The output of text localization is the generation/creation of bounding boxes around the text regions. Figure 7 show outputs of text localization method. Text localization uses important features of images in order to be able to perform its task efficiently, and these feature include the following: the size and color of the characters belonging to the same segment, text orientations and the contrast of the text against its boundaries. Another important text feature is that they appear in clusters (arranged compactly). Text localization should comply with the two requirements such as: 1) text localization must be robust with respect to font sizes, styles, orientations, alignment, and effects of lighting, reflections, shadows and perspective distortion and 2) the computation time must be small enough to be used in real-time.

Figure 7. Examples of candidate text region localization from images

Text localization techniques can be classified into two main groups: 1) threshold-based, and they include, histogram-based, adaptive/local and entropy-based techniques, 2) grouping-based, which include, region-based, clustering-based (density-based, k-means, Gaussian mixture modeling and graph theory) and learning-based techniques. The above-mentioned extraction techniques work with the assumption that text is brighter than the background and or vice versa.

Text Extraction and Enhancement

Text extraction is concerned with the separation of identified text pixels from background pixels in a binarized image map. Extraction module takes its input from the localization field and feeds its prepared output to the OCR. Text extraction mainly deals with uneven lighting and complex backgrounds. Most of the localized text in images and videos have a simple background and high contrast, which provide an easy task to extract text from background, others with low-resolution are prone to noise and becomes difficult to extract text accurately. Therefore, the later calls for development of enhancement technique to improve image quality. Figure 8 shows examples of text extraction from images.

Text Recognition

Text recognition is the last stage in TIE. Its results are critical to text indexing in images and videos. Recognition module's robustness depends solely on its predecessor, i.e. the extraction module. It is

Figure 8. Examples of text extraction from images

abc NEWS

CYBERSHAKE

podcast✳

ఏకీకృత అధ్యయన ఐఎస్ప కేంద్రం
एकीकृत अध्ययन विशेष केन्द्र
SPECIAL CENTRE FOR INTEGRATED
STUDIES
←

अक्रहम
అక్రహాఁ

noted that correctly extracted text increases the recognition rate and vice versa. Therefore, recognition module can work better when text is accurately separated from the background. The output of recognition technique is the identification of characters contained in the image or video in ASCII form in order to understand text and use it for particular applications. Many recognition techniques have been developed for specific languages and publicly available online. Therefore, this step is considered outside the problems addressed in this chapter. Figure 9 shows some sample results of text recognition on the ICDAR-2003 dataset, where the top rows show the original images, whereas, and bottom rows display accurately recognized text.

REVIEW OF RELATED WORK

The text exhibits its unique characteristics. These text characteristics motivated the researchers to develop techniques based on some assumptions and observations made on the text (Lee et al., 2013). First assumption is that, shapes of text regions are distinctive from the background region and the second one is that, characters are homogeneous in color and stroke width (or intensity). The existing methods can be classified into three groups based on the above assumptions. The former assumption leads to texture-based and edge-based techniques, whereas the latter leads to Connected Component (CC) based techniques.

In this section, a focus is made on the review of techniques for scene text, caption text and document text extraction from images and videos. Although, some of the existing methods have achieved good performance, it is noted that there is still room for improvement. The comprehensive survey on TIE techniques can be found in (Jung et al., 2004; Liang et al., 2005; Zhang et al., 2013). In the following sub-sections, related methods for extraction of each of the forms such as scene, caption and document text are provided.

Connected Component-Based Techniques

Connected Component (CC) based approaches are inspired by the observation that pixels constituting a particular region with the same color or stroke thickness often belong to the same object. CC-based methods use edge detection or color clustering to get the CCs. A geometrical analysis is performed in order to identify text components. The heuristic rules or classifiers are used to remove non-text CCs,

Figure 9. Sample results of text recognition on the ICDAR 2003 dataset
Courtesy of Neumann andMatas, 2010.

 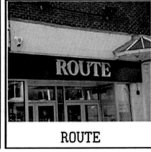 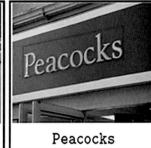

Figure 10. Sample results of connected component-based techniques: first row-simple connected components on various images and second row corresponding text localized regions

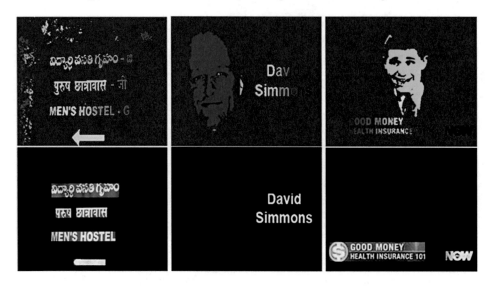

and finally the candidate CCs are grouped into lines. Connected Component-based methods perform a task through a bottom-up approach. Small initial components are grouped into successively larger components, and the process only stops when all regions have been identified in the image. Figure 10 shows some sample results of CC-based method.

CC-based methods work with various types of images such as binary document, web images, scanned color images, and videos, irrespective of font size, color and orientation. The main requirement of CC-based method is that text characters must be of uniform color, gray-level, low noise level and constant illumination, etc. In order to merge text components together, geometrical analysis of text is performed. Since text components are spatially arranged, the boundaries of text regions can be easily marked and remaining non-text components filtered out.

The CC-based techniques have several restrictions related to text alignment, such as upright and not connected, as well as the color of the text (monochrome). Several CCs approaches use the local thresholds (Lee & Kankanhalli, 1995), color reduction (Zhong et al., 1995), color clustering (Kim, 1996; Jain et al., 1998) and homogeneous intensity values (Shim et al., 1998). The existing methods were motivated by the fact that text strokes generally have homogeneous color. For instance, Zhong et al. (1995) use the connected component analysis to locate text in complex color images. Jain et al. (1998) propose a method based on connected component analysis. The method detects text in web images, video frames and document images such as newspapers. The original image is decomposed into a multi-valued map and connected components of color are selected. Text is identified if true to the following strategies: 1) inter-component features (geometry and connection property) and 2) projection profile features in both horizontal and vertical orientations. The probability of missing text is minimized at the cost of increasing false alarms.

Hase et al. (2001) segment the text regions with similar color based on CCA technique. Epshtein et al.(2010) use the CCs in a stroke width transformed image to from text-line. This method measured the stroke width for each pixel and merged neighboring pixels having approximately similar stroke thickness into a region. Although these methods are effective for most of the text detection tasks and fail when there are characters of different colors in a text-line.

Gllavata et al. (2004) utilize a slightly modified k-means algorithm to extract text pixels from the background. Shivakumara et al. (2011) used a k-means clustering performed in Fourier-Laplacian domain to extract CCs. They used straightness of text and edge density to remove false positives. Yi et al. (2012, 2013) presented a method to perform text localization through three steps: clustering of the boundary, segmenting the strokes and classifying the fragmented string. In the other method, they proposed a structure correlation model to extract discriminative appearance features of characters by local descriptors. Wang et al. (2013) proposed a method that uses Markov Random Field (MRF) with local contrasts, colors and gradients in each of the three channels of RGB image. The output of each channel is merged and grouped into words. Though the authors claim good results, but it fails to extract text in low contrast and poor illuminated images.

Chen et al. (2011) extracted edge-enhanced Maximally Stable Extremal Regions (MSER) and considered as text candidates and geometric filtering is done to remove non-text objects. Neumann et al. (2011) used MSER algorithm to detect stable regions in an image. These regions are then classified as foreground or background by further analyzing using heuristic methods or random field models. Pan et al. (2011) identified initial CCs using region based classifier and non-text components are pruned using the Conditional Random Field (CRF) method. In the work presented by H. Zhang et al. (2011), CRF has been used to give connected components either text or non-text labels. Text-like background regions are recognized as text characters with a low confidence. Ahmadi et al. (2015) proposed a statistical framework for binarizing degraded document images based on the concept of CRFs. The CRFs are discriminative graphical models which model conditional distribution and were used in structural classifications. The distribution of binarized images given the degraded ones is modeled with respect to a set of informative features extracted for all sites of the document image.

Li et al.(2014) proposed an approach that mirrors the move from saliency detection methods to measures of objectness. In order to measure the characterness, they developed three novel cues that are tailored for character detection and a Bayesian method for their integration. Because text is made up of sets of characters, they then design a Markov random field model to exploit the inherent dependencies between characters. Zhu et al.(2015) presented a robust system to detect natural scene text according to text region appearances. The framework they developed consists of three parts: auto image partition, two-stage grouping and two-layer classification. The first part partitions the image into unconstrained sub-images through statistical distribution of sampling points. Their designed two-stage grouping method performs grouping in each sub-image in first stage and connects different partitioned image regions in second stage to group connected components into text regions. A two-layer classification mechanism is designed for classifying candidate text regions. The first layer computes the similarity score of region blocks, and the second SVM classifier layer uses HOG features.

The CC-based methods yield a small number of segmented candidate components, hence, CC-based methods have lower computation cost. However, CC-based methods cannot segment text components accurately without prior knowledge of text position and scale. Another drawback is the existence of non-text components, which are easily confused with text when analyzed individually because of complex backgrounds.

Edge-Based Techniques

The edges are mostly preferred and widely used as a representative features in computer vision based techniques. Since the characters are composed of line segments, text regions contain rich edge information (Shivakumara et al., 2010). Edges are among the several textual properties available in an image, edge-based methods focus on the 'high contrast between the text and the background'. The edges of the text boundary are identified and merged, and then several heuristics are used to filter out the non-text regions. In order to detect text information and discriminate it from the background, edges are generated first, followed by a morphological operation to cluster text components and eliminate non-text regions. Usually, an edge filter is used for the detection of edges, and a smoothing operation or a morphological operator is used for the merging stage. Figure 11 display sample results of edge-based methods.

Some text regions that are prominent in the color images are difficult to detect in the gray-level image. After the color conversion, the edges are identified using a morphological gradient operator. The resulting edge map is then thresholded to obtain a binary edge map. Adaptive threshold is performed for each candidate region within the intensity image, which is less sensitive to illumination conditions and reflections. Edges that are spatially close are grouped by dilation to form candidate regions, while small components are removed by erosion. Non-text components are filtered out using size, thickness, aspect ratio, and gray-level homogeneity. This method seems to be robust to noise, as shown by experiments with noisy images. The method is insensitive to skew and text orientation, and curved text strings can also be extracted.

Smith et al.(1995) detected text by finding horizontal rectangle structure of clustered sharp edges. Their algorithm is scale-dependent that is, only text with certain font-size can be detected. Sato et al.(1998) also use edge features and structural constraint to detect captions in video frames. Wu et al.(1999) use nine second-order Gaussian derivatives to extract vertical strokes in horizontal aligned text regions. Strokes are connected into chip if they are connectable and there exists a path between them whose length is less than three times the height of the stroke. The chip will be further checked by structural properties like values of height, width and width/height. Xi et al.(2001) proposed an edge-based method using Sobel operator, followed by applying the smoothing filters, morphological operations and geometrical constraints on the edge map. Jain and Yu (1998) and Ezaki et al. (2004) presented edge-based methods based on pyramid decomposition followed by color-based edge detection and binarization. Mathematical morphology operations were employed for extraction of the text.

Lienhart et al. (2002) locate text in images and video frames using the image gradient feature and a neural network classifier. Ye et al.(2003) developed a text detection technique using edge features contained in the image. The empirical rules are employed on located edge dense image blocks in order to get the candidate text blocks. The texture property of text is represented using wavelet features. The SVM classifier is used to identify text from the candidate blocks Liu et al.(2005) used edge features for detection of text in video frames. They computed four edge maps in horizontal, vertical, up-right and up-left direction. The texture features are extracted from the four edge maps, and then a k-means algorithm applied to detect the initial text candidates. The text areas are identified by an empirical rule analysis and refined through projection profile analysis. Liu et al.(2006) proposed a multi-scale edge-based text extraction algorithm using edge strength, density and the orientation variance characteristics of the text.

Video temporal information has been used to detect video captions, considering that appearance of caption will bring a difference in successive frames, based on this, Tang et al.(2002) employed four edge filters to get the difference from successive frames, and their output were divided into a number of blocks. Furthermore, means and variances are computed from filtered blocks and a fuzzy clustering neural network (FCNN) classifier used to identify text. Lyu et al.(2005) proposed a method based on an adaptive local threshold algorithm by studying edge strength histogram.

Chen et al. (2001, 2004) used the Canny operator to detect edges in an image. Only one edge point in a small window is used in the estimation of scale and orientation to reduce the computational complexity. The edges of the text were then enhanced using this scale information. Morphological dilation is performed to connect the edges into clusters. Some heuristic knowledge, such as the horizontal-vertical aspect ratio and height, was used to filter out non-text clusters. Ye et al. (2005) use the Canny edge feature and morphological operation to detect candidate text blocks. The former uses the dist-map feature to verify the candidate text to reduce the false alarms. The above methods often have a high recall rate but produce many false alarms since background blocks may also have strong edges just as text does.

The edge-based methods presented by (Liu et al., 2004; Dubey, 2006; Cai et al., 2002; Shivakumara et al., 2009) locates potential text regions by finding dense edges. These methods are always simple but efficient. However, the performance of these methods can fail or degraded when the background contains features that give rise to dense edges.

Zhang et al.(2015) proposed an approach that employs the result of stroke width transform (SWT) as basic stroke candidates. These candidates are then merged using adaptive structuring elements to generate compactly constructed characters. Individual characters are chained using k-nearest neighbors algorithm to identify arbitrary oriented text strings, which are subsequently separated into words if necessary. Shivakumara et al.(2014) presented a method that integrates the Gradient-Spatial-Features (GSpF) and the Gradient-Structural-Features (GStF) at block level based on an error factor and the weights of the features to identify six video scripts, namely, Arabic, Chinese, English, Japanese, Korean and Tamil. Horizontal and vertical gradient values are first computed for each text block to increase the contrast of text pixels. Then the method divides the horizontal and the vertical gradient blocks into two equal parts at the centroid in the horizontal direction. Histogram operation on each part is performed to select dominant text pixels from respective subparts of the horizontal and the vertical gradient blocks, which results in text components. After extracting GSpF and GStF from the text components, the authors integrated spatial and structural features based on end points, intersection points, junction points and straightness of the skeleton of text components to identify the scripts.

Apart from the huge success rate of the edge based methods, the authors identified that these methods perform well on high contrast graphic text images, while they exhibit high false rate on low contrast in scene text and document text-lines. Pure structural property is not competent for eliminating false alarms.

Texture Based Techniques

The main motivation for texture-based techniques come from the fact that text contained in images has unique textural properties, which can be clearly distinguished from those belong to the background. These methods linearly transform textured images in order to locate text regions. The energy is measured and either linear or non-linear operator is used to separate text components from the background. Normally, classifiers are used to do classification of text and non-text components. The widely used texture analysis approaches are Gaussian filtering, Wavelet decomposition, Fourier transform, Discrete Cosine Transform (DCT), and Local Binary Pattern (LBP). The main advantage of texture-based techniques is their robustness to extract text information with high accuracy even when images suffer from noise. Sample results using a texture-based technique are shown in Figure 12.

Figure 11. Sample results of edge-based techniques: first row-initial edge map and second row-localized text region on various images

Zhong et al.(1995) proposed a method using features of color continuity and spatial variance in gray-level values. Then, the two features are combined sequentially. The results of their approach on various scanned images were good, but the limitation of this method rests on its inability to robustly detect ascending and descending components in characters. Li et al. (2000) proposed technique based on the intuition that texture for text differs from texture of the surrounding background and employed a wavelet transform to extract text features from selected key video frames. Jain et al.(2000) extracted graphic text in various images, which include binary, web, color and video frames. The authors use gray-level values and color continuity of the images as features. The method performed well on binary, web, and video frames, but it had poor results on color images. Zhong et al.(2000) presented a method that automatically performs localization of caption text directly in the DCT compressed domains using the intensity variation information. Caption regions are segmented from background using distinguishable texture characteristics. They first detect blocks of high horizontal spatial intensity variation as text candidates, and then refine these candidates into regions by spatial constraints. The potential caption text regions are verified by the vertical spectrum energy. But its robustness in complex background may not be satisfying for the limitation of spatial domain features.

Kim et al.(2003) propose a texture-based method using support vector machine (SVM). Classification models trained by an SVM on original gray values of a pixel's neighborhood are used to identify a pixel as text or non-text pixel. Text pixels will be post-processed by an adaptive mean shift (CAMSHIFT) algorithm and connected into text chips. Although the SVM-based learning approach makes the algorithm fully automatic, it is still difficult to discriminate text with non-text using pure texture features in complex background since the feature is insufficient to discriminate text with general textures. The classification on each of the pixels (image block) will be a time-consuming task. Lee et al.(2003) developed a technique using neighboring gray values as features for each individual pixel, they used SVM classifier to classify text and non-text components. Chen et al.(2004) presented a technique that detects text by extracting features from the text region, where they employed an adaptive binarization method to classify text and non-text pixels. Textual segmentations works very well with high resolution scene or document images, though their efficiency and effectiveness can be reduced when the images or videos are noisy or have low resolution. Other feature-based techniques such as Gabor filters, spatial variance and feature learning have been proposed, and they work well in extracting texture features from images.

Ye et al.(2005) proposed technique based on extraction of features from wavelet decomposition coefficients at different scales, and adaptive threshold is used to classify the text and non text regions. Ji et al.(2008) developed text detection approach based on local Haar Binary Pattern (LHBP), which is robust against variant illumination and text-background contrasts. Local binary pattern is extracted from high-frequency coefficients of the pyramid Haar wavelet. Directional correlation analysis (DCA) is used to locate candidate text regions. Three different types of features (Mean Difference Feature (MDF), Standard Deviation (SD) and Histogram of oriented Gradient (HoG) are extracted from a text segment on block level and weak classifier is used to develop text detection method by Hanif et al.(2009).

The partitioning based methods using gradient and color information of pixels are developed by Yi et al.(2011). Further, character level features are used in order to study the regularity of text so as to locate text in the images. Zhou et al. (2011) proposed a multilingual text detection method, which uses three different texture features to represent multilingual text such as histogram of oriented gradient, mean of gradients and local binary patterns. The cascade AdaBoost classifier is adopted to decide the text regions.

Yin et al.(2014) proposed an accurate and robust method for detecting text in natural scene images. A fast and effective pruning algorithm is designed to extract MSERs as character candidates using the strategy of minimizing regularized variations. Character candidates are grouped into text candidates by the single-link clustering algorithm, where distance weights and clustering threshold are learned automatically by a novel self-training distance metric learning algorithm. The posterior probabilities of text candidates corresponding to non-text are estimated with a character classifier, text candidates with high non-text probabilities are eliminated, and text is identified with a classifier. Wang et al.(2015) proposed an approach based on the confidence map and context information to robustly detect text in natural scenes. The authors build a confidence map model by integrating the seed candidate appearance and their relationships to highlight text from the background. The candidates with low confidence value are removed. In order to improve the recall rate, the text context information is adopted by the authors to regain them using text regions. Text-lines are formed and verified, whereas, words are obtained by calculating the threshold to separate the intra-word letters from the inter-word letters.

The main problems of texture based methods lie in the large number of features that heavily depend on the classifier in use and the number of training samples. The use of classifier with training samples restricts generalization capability such as multilingual text detection. In addition, determining the number of training samples for both text and non-text is non-trivial because of the unpredictable background in natural scene images. These methods only consider local information on text, so they cannot gather high-level information such as character relationships. As a result, many complex background regions such as human-made objects or leaves similar in shape to characters are misclassified as character regions. Speed is relatively slow, and the performance is sensitive to text alignment orientation. However, the whole process of extracting text features from images and videos using the traditional texture-based techniques become computationally expensive. The texture filters require an exhaustive scan of the input image for it to be able to extract features and classify them. The classification stage consumes much of the processing time, thus making the convolution operation costly.

Figure 12. Sample results of texture-based techniques: first row-simple texture map and second row-localized text region on various images

Other TIE Techniques

Other approaches falling within this category consist of a combination of two or more techniques described in the preceding sections, due to a large number of possible variations, which cannot be handled by a single approach. A Morphological-based methods have also been efficiently and effectively been applied to character recognition and document image analysis. They extract important text contrast features from the processed images which are invariant against various geometrical image changes like translation, rotation, and scaling. Even if lighting condition or text color is changed, the feature still can be maintained. These methods work better even if under different image alterations.

Chen et al.(2000) proposed a Binarization method for text extraction. Zhong et al.(1995) presented a hybrid method that combines both CC-based and texture-based methods. In their approach, the limitations of CC-based method such as low contrast characteristics, which cannot give a clear separation between characters and background can be handled by texture-based method. While, the drawbacks arising from texture-based methods, which include long character strokes extending beyond a generated bounding box are addressed through CC-based method. This is done by analyzing connected components. The drawback from this system is the lack of quantitative analysis in regard of enhanced performance. Gandhi et al.(2000) presented a gradient-based method to estimate motion model parameters. Their approach is based on assumption that scene text contained in planar surface (2D). An interactive split and merge technique is used to perform Multiple-motion segmentation.

Wu et al.(2008) presented a morphology-based text-line extraction algorithm to extract text regions from cluttered images. Initially, they defined a set of morphological operations to extract regions with strong contrast. The authors then used a moment based method to estimate text-line orientations in order to detect various text geometries for extraction. Saabni et al.(2014) presented a language independent global method for automatic text-line extraction. This approach computes an energy map from an image under investigation. The location of each seam is then determined. The authors developed two algorithms, the first one, works on binary document images with the possibility to extract the components along text-lines. The seam cuts through the text-line components. The text-line components, which the seam does not cut through are assigned to the closest text-line. The second algorithm works directly on gray-scale document images. It computes the distance transform directly from the gray-scale images and generate medial and separating seams. The medial seams determine the text-lines, whereas, the separating seams define the upper and lower boundaries.

Zhao et al. (2015) proposed a method consisted of both top-down and bottom-up processing, which are loosely coupled. They first use learning-based on partial differential equations to produce a text confidence map. Text region candidates are then detected from the map by local binarization and connected component clustering. In each text region candidate, character candidates are detected based on color similarity and then grouped into text candidates by simple rules. Finally, they adopt a two-level classification scheme to remove the non-text candidates. The structure of the method is flexible; the latter part can be replaced with CC-based methods to improve the detection accuracy.

OUR APPROACH FOR EXTRACTION OF SCENE TEXT

Text in scene images has been generally defined as text existing naturally in the image. Outdoor images containing sign or advertisement boards, walls, sidewalks, roads, roofs and other objects like vehicles can appear planar when viewed from a distance. Normally, the text information is written on the planar surfaces in order to read and interpret information easily. This motivated us to propose a scene text extraction technique based on detection and extraction of planar surface, which is followed by extraction of scene text within the extracted planar surface.

Many researchers, including Bobick et al. (1999), Corso et al. (2003) and Konolige et al. (2008) have used stereo disparity, which is estimated from stereo images in order to navigate the mobile robot based on detection of planar objects. As we mentioned, it is assumed that text is contained in planar surface, this drives our interest to identify a region within the video frames which represent a planar surface on the 3D world. We adopted technique proposed by Jeffrey et al. (2010) in order to detect and extract the planar surface from natural scene video frames. The approach comprises three major steps: a) estimation of disparity map using stereo frames, b) detection of candidate planar surface from the disparity space using gradient derivatives and c) fitting planar model d) segmentation of planar surface and e) extraction of scene text.

After extraction of planar surface from complex background, further processing can be done by considering the extracted planar surface (called as text block) instead of whole image area. The extraction of planar surface from the complex background reduces the complexity involved while extracting the text from complex background by considering the whole image as processing area. To increase the segmentation accuracy, plane fitting technique is introduced by constructing planar model based on a local surface normal computed through PCA and RANSAC. The image labeling is done by employing Markov Random Field (MRF) with Graph cuts algorithm where planar surface is segmented from other regions based on the labels assigned to it. The process is further extended to extract scene text by filtering the extracted text block (planar surface) with Fourier-Laplacian algorithm to generate points, which are classified using k-means as either belongs to text region or non-text region. Figure 13 shows the flow diagram of the proposed approach. For more explanation about our approach, refer the research paper (Boaz & Prabhakar, 2016).

Figure 13. Flow diagram of our approach

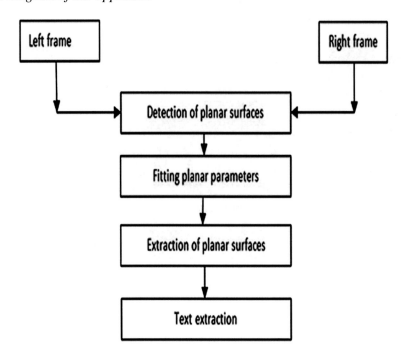

EXPERIMENTAL RESULTS

The author of this work believe that, this is the first work done directed to building a TIE technique based on stereo frames. Since there are no benchmark datasets with stereo frames of the natural scene containing text information. The stereo camera setup consists of two similarly calibrated video cameras positioned horizontally 3-4 inches apart with a frame rate of 29.99 frames per second. The video sequences were captured only focusing on the outdoor scene, where majorally planar objects contain text information. The video cameras are positioned just orthogonal to the objects of interest. The captured pair of video sequences of the same scene are between the length of 5 to 10 seconds. The authors created our own dataset from the pair of video sequences, which consists of high-quality stereo frames.

The stereo frames selected from video sequence must be of the same scene which contains text information. Our dataset contains one pair or more than one pair of frames per scene object and evaluation of our approach is carried out by giving input as one pair of frames per execution. The stereo frames are high quality and are between 320 x 270 and 450 x 350 resolutions. Measuring the performance of text extraction is extremely difficult and until now, there has been no comparison of the different extraction methods (Jung et al., 2004). Since, our work is focusing on text extraction rather than text recognition, the performance of text localization process is evaluated, which is one of the important steps in text extraction. Two metrics were adopted for evaluation, including: 1) recall-the fraction of positives which are detected rather than missed, 2) precision-the fraction of detections, which are positives.

Experiments are carried out using dataset, which contains stereo frames with horizontal text and experimental results were compared with other popular text extraction methods. The dataset contains 179 pairs of video frames, which were captured in the outdoor scene with horizontal English and regional Kannada script. In the pair of video frames, only left frame is used for employing other popular methods

Figure 14. Illustration of the overlap of a ground truth box and detected bounding box
Source: Ye et al., 2005.

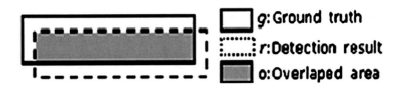

such as edge-based method (Liu et al., 2005), CCA method (Zhong et al., 1995), and gradient-based (Shivakumara et al., 2011). Ground truth is marked by hand on frames of dataset. Given the marked ground truth and detected result by the algorithm, the recall and precision are automatically calculated. The recall and precision rates have been computed based on the area ratio r of the bounding box between ground truth and result of our technique as shown in Figure 14.

$$ratio(r) = \frac{Area(DetectedBox \cap GroundTruthBox)}{Area(DetectedBox \cup GroundTruthBox)}. \qquad (1)$$

The following definitions were used for results evaluation process:

- **Truly Detected Box (TDB):** A detected box truly detects the texts if the area ratio r, defined is at least 50%.
- **False Detected Box (FDB):** The false detected box detects the texts if the area ratio r, defined is less than 50%.
- **Ground Truth Box (GTB):** Manually marked the text box by hand on test samples.

$$recall = \frac{(\#TDB)}{(\#GTB)} \qquad (2)$$

$$precision = \frac{(\#TDB)}{(\#TDB + \#FTB)} \qquad (3)$$

$$f - measure = \frac{(2 \times recall \times precision)}{recall \times precision} \qquad (4)$$

Figure 15 shows the result of our approach for extraction of planar surface from video frames of natural scene. The natural scene is synonymous with complex background. The experimental result shows that the proposed method detects and extracts the planar surface accurately.

Table 1 shows the recall, precision and f-measure obtained for stereo frames of our dataset using existing methods and proposed method. The results shown in Table 1 are the average value of recall, precision and f-measure computed for all the stereo frames of dataset. The proposed method has the highest recall, precision and f-measure when compared with the existing methods. The experimental

Figure 15. The results of planar surface extraction obtained by our method on video frames of our dataset: first row-original left frames and second row-extracted planar surface

Table 1. Comparison of text localization results using recall, precision and f-measure

Method	Precision	Recall	F-Measure
Edge-based method	0.64	0.67	0.65
CCA method	0.73	0.69	0.71
Gradient –based	0.59	0.82	0.69
Our approach	0.93	0.96	0.94

results show that the proposed method achieves high accuracy for scene text extraction for the video frames with complex background includes trees, building and other objects.

Figure 16 shows the visual comparison of text localization results of our approach with other popular existing methods for the stereo frames of our dataset. The connected component method locates the text area partially. This method locates the whole text area for the first frame, but includes background partially. The gradient based method locates the text area and part of background with many false positives. Edge based method failed to locate text area precisely, because scene images are rich in text like features such as tree-leaves, which produces many edges and are classified as text. The second row of Figure 16(c), which is an edge based result, is just visually same as the original image, due to the overlapping of the bounding boxes used to enclose text area.

Figure 16. The comparison of text localization result on our dataset: columns (a) original left frames, (b) results of connected component method, (c) results of edge-based method, (d) results of gradient-based method and (e) results of proposed method

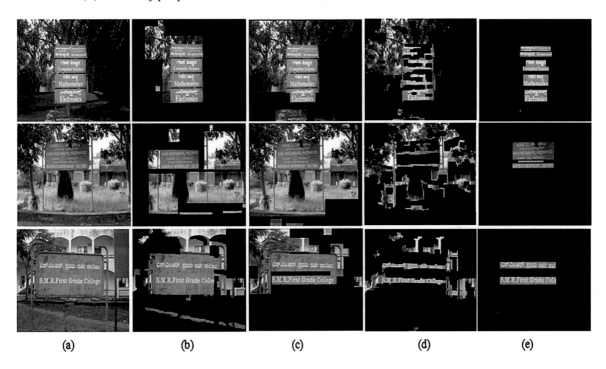

    (a)   (b)   (c)   (d)   (e)

Figure 17 shows intermediate results of edge-based method shown in the second row of Figure 16(c).

The proposed method initially extracts the planar surface as the first part of text localization (Figure 15) and thereafter proceeds to process these regions by employing Fourier-Laplacian technique to locate the text area accurately and precisely. The Figure 16(e) shows the text localization result of proposed method for video frames of the natural scene captured in a complex background. The proposed method locates all the text area correctly for third frame, but it shows the one false positive and two true negatives for the first and second frame respectively. The true negative for the second frame is due to occlusion of tree-leaves. The proposed method successfully locates the text area of the third frame, even though text is slightly oriented. The limitation of the proposed method is that it locates the supporting poles of the sign board, this due to fact that while extracting the planar surface it considers the supporting poles as part of planar surface.

Figure 18 displays sample results of text extraction by our approach for slightly oriented text information contained in video frames. The text extraction results for slightly oriented text demonstrate that our approach can be employed for both horizontal and slightly oriented text.

Figure 19 illustrates more extracted text results. It can be seen from the results that, most of the text is well detected and localized despite variations in character font, size, color, texture, script and orientation. Goodresults for the video frames with complex background consisting mainly trees and some other non-planar objects, which were easily labeled as non-text planar properties.

Figure 17. The text localization results from edge based method: (a) original left frame, (b) vertical edge results, (c) morphological operation results, (d) text area localization based on bounding box and (e) text

Figure 20 illustrates some failure examples. In the first frame, the text is not localized accurately, the reason that it contains multi colored text, during color clustering it consider and cluster the text with high contrast color and text having low contrast color is treated as background at binarization stage. The false alarm in second frame is due to low contrast and text does not appear properly because the frame was captured too far away from camera.

CONCLUSION

In this chapter, we addressed text information extraction problem, which involves two major processes, text localization and text extraction in three different environments and they include scene text, caption text and document text. The computer vision techniques developed for TIE were reviewed in this chapter which provides solutions to challenges associated with them. TIE technique for extraction of scene text from stereo frames acquired in the natural scene was presented. We presented a novel approach for the extraction of scene text where the novelty of our approach lies in the extraction of planar surface, as it is assumed that scene text are always written on planar objects for the purpose of readability. The extraction of planar surface provides an accurate candidate text block segmentation in complex environments such as tree-leaves which have text-like features are removed completely leaving only text features contained in planar surface. Further, text block segmentation reduces our working area for employing other low level

Figure 18. Sample results of text extraction for slightly oriented text by our approach: first column -original left frames and second column- corresponding extracted text information

processes to extract text within text block. The experimental results show that our approach is capable of handling multi-script text. Another important aspect is that, our technique is invariant to font sizes, noise contrast and or text-line orientation and can be used to extract all manner of text script. Though our approach proved to be computationally costly in terms of the time taken to complete the whole process, it is note worthy that the same approach produces an output which is most accurate for text information extraction in a highly complex environments which is still a pipe dream for the existing techniques.

Figure 19. Examples of text extraction results of our approach: columns (a) original frames, (b) disparity maps, (c) fitted planar models, (d) MRF segmentation and (e) text extraction results

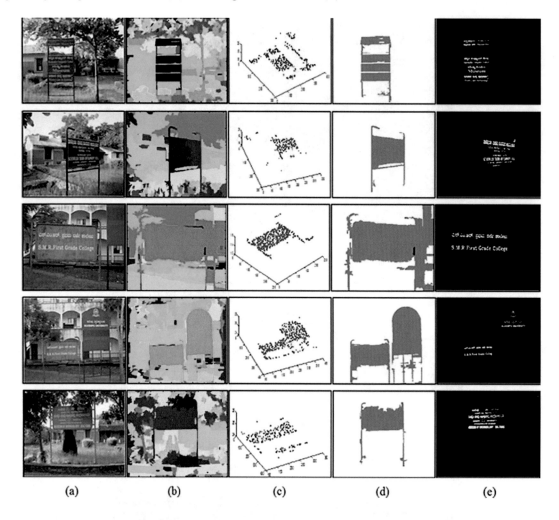

Figure 20. Frames with failures and false alarms of our approach: columns (a) original images, (b) disparity map, (c) fitted planar models, (d) MRF segmentation and (e) text extraction results

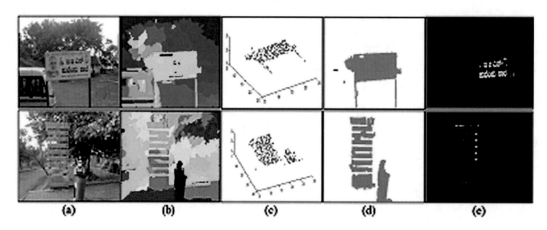

REFERENCES

Ahmadi, E., Azimifar, Z., Shams, M., Famouri, M., & Shafiee, M. J. (2015). Document image binarization using a dis criminative structural classifier. *Pattern Recognition Letters, Elsevier, 63*, 36–42. doi:10.1016/j.patrec.2015.06.008

Antani, S., Gargi, U., Crandall, D., Gandhi, T., & Kasturi, R. (1999). Extraction of Text in Video. Technical Report of Department of Computer Science and Engineering, Penn State University, CSE-99-016.

Boaz & Prabhakar. (2016). Extraction of Scene Text Information from Video, *International Journal of Image Graphics and Signal Processing, 1*, 15–26.

Bobick, A. F., & Stephen, I. S. (1999). Large occlusion stereo. *International Journal of Computer Vision, 33*(3), 181–200. doi:10.1023/A:1008150329890

Cai, M., Son, J., & Lyu, M. R. (2002). A new approach for video text detection. *Proceedings of International Conference on Image Processing*, 117-120.

Chen, D., Luettin, J., & Shearer, K. (2000). *A Survey of Text Detection and Recognition in Images and Videos.* InstitutDalleMolledIntelligenceArtificielle Perceptive (IDIAP) Research Report, 00-38.

Chen, D., Odobez, J. M., & Bourlard, H. (2004). Text detection and recognition in images and video frames. *Pattern Recognition, Elsevier, 37*(3), 595–608. doi:10.1016/j.patcog.2003.06.001

Chen, D., Shearer, K., & Bourlard, H. (2001). Text enhancement with asymmetric filter for video OCR. *Proceedings of International Conference on Image Analysisand Processing*, 192-197.

Chen, H., Tsai, S., Schroth, G., Chen, D., Grzeszczuk, R., & Girod, B. (2011). Robust text detection in natural images with edge-enhanced maximally stable extremal regions. *Proceedings of International Conference on Image Processing (ICIP)*, 2609-2612. doi:10.1109/ICIP.2011.6116200

Chen, X., Yang, J., Zhang, J., & Waibel, A. (2004). Automatic detection and recognition of signs from natural scenes. *IEEE Transactions on Image Processing, 13*(1), 87–99. doi:10.1109/TIP.2003.819223 PMID:15376960

Chen, X., & Yuille, A. (2004). Detecting and reading text in natural scenes. *Proceedings of IEEE Computer Society Conference on Computer Vision and Pattern Recognition (CVPR), 1*, 366-373.

Corso, J., Darius, B., & Gregory, H. (2003). Direct plane tracking in stereo images for mobile navigation. *Proceedings of International Conference on Robotics and Automation, 1*, 875-880. doi:10.1109/ROBOT.2003.1241703

Crandall, D., Antani, S., & Kasturi, R. (2003). Extraction of special effects caption text events from digital video. *International Journal on Document Analysis and Recognition, 5*(2-3), 138-157.

Dubey, P. (2006). Edge based text detection for multi-purpose application. *Proceedings of International Conference on Signal Processing*, 16-20. doi:10.1109/ICOSP.2006.346106

Epshtein, B., Eyal, O., & Yonatan, W. (2010). Detecting text in natural scenes with stroke width transform. *Proceedings of the IEEE Conference on Computer Vision and Pattern Recognition (CVPR)*, 2963-2970. doi:10.1109/CVPR.2010.5540041

Ezaki, N., Bulacu, M., & Schomaker, L. (2004). Text Detection from Natural Scene Images: Towards a System for Visually Impaired Persons. *Proceedings of International Conference on Pattern Recognition, 2*, 683-686. doi:10.1109/ICPR.2004.1334351

Gandhi, T., Kasuturi, R., & Antani, S. (2000). Application of Planar Motion Segmentation for Scene Text Extraction. *Proceedings of International Conference on Pattern Recognition, 1*, 445-449. doi:10.1109/ICPR.2000.905372

Gllavata, J., Ewerth, R., Stefi, T., & Freisleben, B. (2004). Unsupervised text segmentation using color and wavelet features. *Proceedings of International Conference on Image and Video Retrieval*, 216-224. doi:10.1007/978-3-540-27814-6_28

Hanif, S. M., & Prevost, L. (2009). Text detection and localization in complex scene images using constrained adaboost algorithm. *Proceedings of the 10th International Conference on Document Analysis and Recognition, ICDAR, IEEE*, 1-5. doi:10.1109/ICDAR.2009.172

Hase, H., Shinokawa, T., Yoneda, M., & Suen, C. Y. (2001). Character string extraction from color documents. *Pattern Recognition, Elsevier, 34*(7), 1349–1365. doi:10.1016/S0031-3203(00)00081-9

Huang, W., Lin, Z., Jianchao, Y., & Wang, J. (2013). Text localization in natural images using stroke feature transform and text covariance descriptors. *Proceedings of International Conference on Computer Vision ICCV)*,1241-1248. doi:10.1109/ICCV.2013.157

Iqbal, K., Xu-Cheng, Y., Hong-Wei, H., Sohail, A., & Hazrat, A. (2014). Bayesian network scores based text localization in scene images. *Proceedings of International Joint Conference on Neural Networks (IJCNN)*, 2218-2225. doi:10.1109/IJCNN.2014.6889731

Jain, A. K., Duin, R. P. W., & Mao, J. (2000). Statistical Pattern Recognition: A Review. *IEEE Transactions on Pattern Analysis and Machine Intelligence, 22*(1), 4–37. doi:10.1109/34.824819

Jain, A. K., & Yu, B. (1998). Automatic Text Location in Images and Video Frames. *Pattern Recognition, Elsevier, 31*(12), 2055–2076. doi:10.1016/S0031-3203(98)00067-3

Jeffrey, A. D., Corso, J. J., & Philip, D. (2010). Boosting with stereo features for building facade detection on mobile platforms. *Image Processing Workshop (WNYIPW)*,46-49.

Jung, K., Kim, K.I., & Jain, A.K. (2004). Text information extraction in images and video: A survey. *Pattern Recognition, 37*(5), 977-997.

Kim, H. (1996). Efficient automatic text location method and content-based indexing and structuring of video database. *Journal of Visual Communication and Image Representation, 7*(4), 336–344. doi:10.1006/jvci.1996.0029

Kim, K., Keechul, J., & Kim, H. J. (2003). Texture-based approach for text detection in images using support vector machines and continuously adaptive mean shift algorithm. *IEEE Transactions on Pattern Analysis and Machine Intelligence, 25*(12), 1631–1639. doi:10.1109/TPAMI.2003.1251157

Konolige, K., Agrawal, M., Bolles, R. C., Cowan, C., Fischler, M., & Gerkey, B. (2008). *Outdoor mapping and navigation using stereo vision. In Experimental Robotics* (pp. 179–190). Berlin: Springer.

Lee, C. M., & Kankanhalli, A. (1995). Automatic Extraction of Characters in Complex Images. *International Journal of Pattern Recognition and Artificial Intelligence, 9*(1), 67–82. doi:10.1142/S0218001495000043

Lee, C. W., Jung, K., & Kim, H. (2003). Automatic text detection and removal in video sequences. *Pattern Recognition Letters, Elsevier, 24*(15), 2607–2623. doi:10.1016/S0167-8655(03)00105-3

Lee, S., & Kim, J. H. (2013). Integrating multiple character proposals for robust scene text extraction. *Image and Vision Computing, Elsevier, 31*(11), 823–840. doi:10.1016/j.imavis.2013.08.007

Li, H., & Doermann, D. (2000). A Video Text Detection System Based on Automated Training. *Proceedings of International Conference on Pattern Recognition, 2*, 223-226. doi:10.1109/ICPR.2000.906053

Li, H., Doermann, D., & Kia, O. (2000). Automatic text detection and tracking in digital video. *IEEE Transactions on Image Processing, 9*(1), 147–156. doi:10.1109/83.817607 PMID:18255381

Li, Y., Po, L. M., Xu, X., Feng, L., Yuan, F., Cheung, C. H., & Cheung, K. W. (2014). No-reference image quality assessment with shearlet transform and deep neural networks. *Neurocomputing, Elsevier, 154*, 94–109. doi:10.1016/j.neucom.2014.12.015

Liang, J., Doermann, D., & Li, H. (2005). Camera-based analysis of text and documents: A survey. *International Journal of Document Analysis and Recognition, 7*(2-3), 84–104. doi:10.1007/s10032-004-0138-z

Lienhart, R., & Wernicke, A. (2002). Localizing and segmenting text in images and videos. *IEEE Transactions on Circuits and Systems for Video Technology, 12*(4), 256–268. doi:10.1109/76.999203

Liu, X., & Samarabandu, J. (2005). An edge-based text region extraction algorithm for indoor mobile robot navigation. *Proceedings of International Conference on Mechatronics and Automation, 2*, 701-706.

Liu, X., & Samarabandu, J. (2006) Multiscale edge-based text extraction from complex images, *Proceedings of International Conference on Multimedia and Expo*, 1721-1724. doi:10.1109/ICME.2006.262882

Liu, Y., Lu, H., Xue, X. Y., & Tan, Y. P. (2004). Effective video text detection using line features, *Proceedings of International Conference on Control, Automation, Robotics and Vision*, 1528-1532.

Lu, S., Chen, T., Shangxuan, T., Joo-Hwee, L., & Chew-Lim, T. (2015). Scene text extraction based on edges and support vector regression. *International Journal on Document Analysis and Recognition*, 1-11.

Lyu, M. R., Song, J., & Cai, M. (2005). A comprehensive method for multilingual video text detection localization, and extraction. *IEEE Transactions on Circuits and Systems for Video Technology, 15*(2), 243–255. doi:10.1109/TCSVT.2004.841653

Neumann, L., & Matas, J. (2010). A method for text localization and recognition in real-world images. *Proceedings of the 10th Asian Conference on Computer Vision*, 770-783.

Neumann, L., & Matas, J. (2011). Text localization in real-world images using efficiently pruned exhaustive search. *Proceedings of International Conference on Document Analysis and Recognition (ICDAR)*, 687-691. doi:10.1109/ICDAR.2011.144

Pan, Y., Hou, X., & Liu, C. (2011). A hybrid approach to detect and localize texts in natural scene images. *IEEE Transactions on Image Processing*, *20*(3), 800–813. doi:10.1109/TIP.2010.2070803 PMID:20813645

Saabni, R., Asi, A., & El-Sana, J. (2014). Text line extraction for historical document images. *Pattern Recognition Letters, Elsevier*, *35*, 23–33. doi:10.1016/j.patrec.2013.07.007

Sato, T., Kanade, T., Hughes, E. K., & Smith, M. A. (1998). Video ocr for digital news archives. *Proceedings of Workshop on Content Based Access of Image and Video Databases*, 52-60.

Shahab, A., Shafait, F., & Dengel, A. (2011). ICDAR-2011 robust reading competition challenge 2: Reading text in scene images. *Proceedings of International Conference on Document Analysis and Recognition (ICDAR)*, 1491-1496. doi:10.1109/ICDAR.2011.296

Shim, J. C., Dorai, C., & Bolle, R. (1998). Automatic Text Extraction from Video for Content-based Annotation and Retrieval. *Proceedings of International Conference on Pattern Recognition*, 1, 618-620.

Shivakumara, P., Huang, W., Phan, T. Q., & Tan, C. L. (2010). Accurate video text detection through classification of low and high contrast images. Pattern Recognition, 2165-2185.

Shivakumara, P., Kumar, N., Guru, D., & Tan, C. (2014). Separation of graphics (superimposed) and scene text in video frames. *Proceedings of the 11th IAPR International Workshop on Document Analysis Systems (DAS)*, 344-348. doi:10.1109/DAS.2014.20

Shivakumara, P., Phan, T. Q., & Tan, C. L. (2009). Video text detection based on filters and edge features. *Proceedings of International Conference on Multimedia and Expo*, 514-517. doi:10.1109/ICME.2009.5202546

Shivakumara, P., Phan, T. Q., & Tan, C. L. (2010). New wavelet and color features for text detection in video. *Proceedings of the 20th International Conference on Pattern Recognition (ICPR)*, 3996-3999. doi:10.1109/ICPR.2010.972

Shivakumara, P., Phan, T. Q., & Tan, C. L. (2011). A laplacian approach to multioriented text detection in video. *IEEE Transactions on Pattern Analysis and Machine Intelligence*, *33*(2), 412–419. doi:10.1109/TPAMI.2010.166 PMID:20733217

Smith, M. A., & Kanade, T. (1995). Video skimming for quick browsing based on audio and image characterization. Carnegie Mellon University.

Tang, X., Gao, X., Liu, J., & Zhang, H. (2002). A spatial-temporal approach for video caption detection and recognition. *IEEE Transactions on Neural Networks*, *13*(4), 961–971. doi:10.1109/TNN.2002.1021896 PMID:18244491

Wang, R., Sang, N., & Gao, C. (2015). Text detection approach based on confidence map and context information. *Neurocomputing, Elsevier*, *157*, 153–165. doi:10.1016/j.neucom.2015.01.023

Wang, X., Song, Y., & Zhang, Y. (2013). Natural scene text detection with multi-channel connected component segmentation. *Proceedings of the 12th International Conference on Document Analysis and Recognition (ICDAR)*, 1375-1379. doi:10.1109/ICDAR.2013.278

Wu, J. C., Hsieh, J. W., & Chen, Y. S. (2008). Morphology-based text line extraction. *Journal of Machine Vision and Applications, Springer, 19*(3), 195–207. doi:10.1007/s00138-007-0092-0

Wu, V., Manmatha, R., & Riseman, E. M. (1999). Text finder: An automatic system to detect and recognize text in images. *IEEE Transactions on Pattern Analysis and Machine Intelligence, 20*(11), 1224–1229. doi:10.1109/34.809116

Xi, S. X., Hua, X. R., Chen, L. W., & Zhang, H. (2001):.A video text detection and recognition system. *Proceedings of International Conference on multimedia and expo,* 873-876.

Ye, Q., Huang, Q., Gao, W., & Zhao, D. (2005). Fast and robust text detection in images and video frames. *Image and Vision Computing, Elsevier, 23*(6), 565–576. doi:10.1016/j.imavis.2005.01.004

Ye, W., & Gao, W., Wang, & Zeng, W. (2003). A robust text detection algorithm in images and video frames. *Proceedings of the Joint Conference of the 4th International Conference on Information, Communications and Signal Processing and 4th Pacific Rim Conference on Multimedia,* 802-806.

Yi, C., & Tian, Y. (2011). Text string detection from natural scenes by structure based partition and grouping. *IEEE Transactions on Image Processing,* 2594–2605. PMID:21411405

Yi, C., & Tian, Y. (2012). Localizing text in scene images by boundary clustering, stroke segmentation, and string fragment classification. *IEEE Transactions on Image Processing, 21*(9), 4256–4268. doi:10.1109/TIP.2012.2199327 PMID:22614647

Yi, C., & Tian, Y. (2013). Text extraction from scene images by character appearance and structure modeling. *Computer Vision and Image Understanding, Elsevier, 117*(2), 182–194. doi:10.1016/j.cviu.2012.11.002 PMID:23316111

Yi, F. P., Hou, X., & Liu, C. L. (2009). Text localization in natural scene images based on conditional random field. *Proceedings of the 10th International Conference on Document Analysis and Recognition,* 6-10.

Yin, X., Xuwang, Y., Huang, K., & Hong-Wei, H. (2014). Robust text detection in natural scene images. *IEEE Transactions on Pattern Analysis and Machine Intelligence, 36*(5), 970–983. doi:10.1109/TPAMI.2013.182 PMID:26353230

Zhang, H., Liu, C., Yang, C., Ding, X., & Wang, K. Q. (2011). An improved scene text extraction method using conditional random field and optical character recognition. *Proceedings of International Conference on Document Analysis and Recognition (ICDAR),* 708-712. doi:10.1109/ICDAR.2011.148

Zhang, H., Zhao, K., Song, Y., & Jun, G. (2013). Text extraction from natural scene image: A survey. Neurocomputing, 310-323.

Zhang, S., Zhang, J., & Liu, Y. (2011). A Window-Based Adaptive Correspondence Search Algorithm Using Mean Shift and Disparity Estimation. *Proceedings of International Conference on Virtual Reality and Visualization (ICVRV),* 319-322. doi:10.1109/ICVRV.2011.47

Zhang, Y., Lai, J., & Yuen, P. C. (2015). Text string detection for loosely-constructed characters with arbitrary orientations. *Neurocomputing, Elsevier, 168,* 970–978. doi:10.1016/j.neucom.2015.05.028

Zhao, Z., Fang, C., Lin, Z., & Wu, Y. (2015). A robust hybrid method for text detection in natural scenes by learning-based partial differential equations. *Neurocomputing, Elsevier*, *168*, 23–34. doi:10.1016/j.neucom.2015.06.019

Zhong, Y., Kalle, K., & Jain, A. K. (1995). Locating Text In Complex Color Images. *Pattern Recognition, Elsevier*, *28*(10), 1523–1535. doi:10.1016/0031-3203(95)00030-4

Zhong, Y., Zhang, H., & Jain, A. K. (2000). Automatic Caption Localization in Compressed Video. *IEEE Transactions on Pattern Analysis and Machine Intelligence*, *22*(4), 385–392. doi:10.1109/34.845381

Zhou, G., Liu, Y., Meng, Q., & Zhang, Y. (2011). Detecting multilingual text in natural scene. *Proceedings of the 1st International Symposium on Access Spaces (ISAS)*, 116-120. doi:10.1109/ISAS.2011.5960931

Zhu, A., Wang, G., & Dong, Y. (2015). *Detecting natural scenes text via auto image partition, two-stage grouping and two-layer classification. In Pattern Recognition Letters*. Elsevier.

Chapter 3
Exploring Image and Video Steganography Based on DCT and Wavelet Transform

Chantana Chantrapornchai
Kasetsart University, Thailand

Jitdumrong Preechasuk
Silpakorn University, Thailand

ABSTRACT

Steganography is one of the techniques used to communicate secret data through the cover media such as images, videos, audio, texts etc. In this work, we consider the algorithms of steganography based on DCT and wavelet transform. The aspects of media quality after hiding the information in the digital media are considered. Particularly, we compare the performance of the prototype algorithms, representing the DCT and wavelet-based image steganography algorithms respectively, using the PSNR, capacity, robustness and accuracy aspects. For video steganography, with various wavelet transforms, we compare the quality of the derived information, when frames are dropped and the effects of payload is studied. The application of using such steganography algorithm which can embed multiple messages, each of which requires a separate key is proposed. The application can estimate the capacity used and capacity remains for the given cover image and texts.

INTRODUCTION

Information hiding is important to applications such as military area (Rocha & Goldenstein, 2008) or the medical image such as a radiological image or Mammogram where a doctor will embed the patient information on the film or image (Li, Li & Wei, 2009). Steganography is a science hiding communicating secret data inside a cover media which can be any format such as text files, images, videos. On the contrary, cryptography attempts to encode the message with keys. The techniques used are such as RSA, DES, AES (Cheddad, Condell, Curram & McKevitt, 2010). Normally, the message is encrypted first and then hidden in the cover media.

DOI: 10.4018/978-1-5225-2053-5.ch003

Figure 1. Discipline of information hiding
Cheddad, Condell, Curram, & McKevitt, 2010.

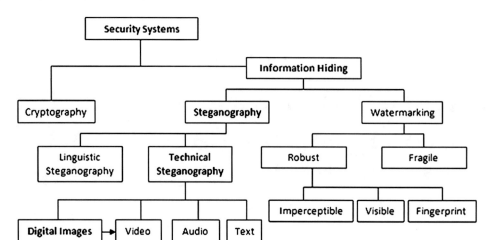

There are a number of aspects which are challenges of steganography, for example, the selected media type, and an encryption method, the algorithm of combining the message to the media. Criteria are considered for selecting embedded algorithms such as the noises of the resulting stego media, the size of the stego media, the robustness of the algorithm through the compression of the stego media etc. Some criteria may be a special case of the type of media such as video where the frame rate needed to be maintained during the transmission etc.

In this chapter, we first intend to make a comparative study of the steganography algorithms based on two types of transformations: DCT and wavelet. Both algorithms are compared in many related aspects: the quality of the stego images in terms of PSNR. Other aspects of comparison are considered such as capacity, accuracy and robustness. We next present the extension to the video steganography with the wavelet transform. Two wavelet transform approaches are considered for video steganography. The experiments compare the PSNR, robustness, and capacity of the stego video for these wavelet-based approaches. At last, we present an application of the approach combining with the hierarchical access control.

BACKGROUND

Steganography is a science that involves communicating secret data in a media. Figure 1 summarizes the fields in information hiding (Cheddad, Condell, Curram & McKevitt, 2010). It shows the relations between steganography, watermarking and cryptography. While watermarking focuses on copyrighting the media, the steganography emphasizes on the hiding message on the media (Stanescu, Borca, Groza & Stratulat, 2008). These techniques may be closed to each other while the metrics considered for both are different.

The media for hiding message can be many kinds as shown in Figure 2 (Morkel, Eloff, & Oliveir, 2005). Also the hidden message may be of many kinds such as a text, an image, an audio file etc.

Figure 2. Categories of media
Cheddad, Condell, Curram, & McKevitt, 2010.

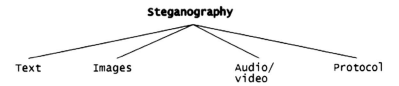

Figure 3. Types of steganography
Morkel, Eloff, & Oliveir, 2005.

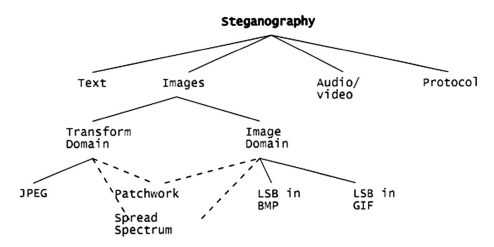

Consider images as a stego media. Many kinds of the transformation algorithms exist such as based on frequency domain or image domain as shown in Figure 3. There are many aspects that need to be considered in designing of the steganography algorithm. First, the secret message needs to be hidden completely in the cover media. However, when hiding the secret message to the cover media, the media property is affected. Once the media is brought to use such as playing video or displaying images, for example, the video may not display smoothly like before or the image may contain many noises etc. In addition, the size of media may change which affects the time for downloading or displaying the media in real-time.

The issues for designing steganography algorithms are summarized as follows (Cheddad, Condell, Curram, & McKevitt, 2010; Morkel, Eloffm & Oliveir, 2005).

1. **Realisticity:** The algorithm will alter the media property the least in terms of presentation of the media to the users. The users do not feel the changes on the media at all.
2. **Capacity:** All messages should be covered in the media. Thus, the algorithm should make use of the space of media carefully.
3. **Robustness:** There are two kinds of robustness. First, it is the robustness against the unintentional image manipulation such as rotating, cropping, etc. Besides, some media needs compression. The compression through the media format should not alter the correctness of the hidden message. Also, it should be robust against the attack especially by using the statistically attacks.

4. **File Format:** The algorithm should be applied to many file formats. Otherwise, it may be noticed that the communication occurs using the specific file format.
5. **Sizes:** The stego media should have the same size as the original image. This will not be noticed by a warden.
6. **Time to Process:** The last point concerns with the computation time of algorithm. The processing should be done within an acceptable amount of time.

Related Works

Many works have been done on image steganography in the past ten years. Some of them are related to the spatial domain while some of them are related to the frequency domain.

In the spatial domain, the information is hidden in the bits of image pixels. Usually LSB bit is used with different selection criteria. For example, Bailey and Curran presented the evaluation of the steganography methods. They consider the visual inspection such as considering colors of the methods using LSB approaches (Bailey & Curran, 2006; Curran & Bailey, 2003). Sur, Shyam, Goel, and Mukherjee used the statistical analysis for spatial desynchronization in the algorithm. The performance is measured based on the attack analysis (2012).

The transformation approach is said to be more robust than the spatial technique (Hamid, Yahya, Ahmad, & Qershi, 2012). It is tolerate to cropping, shrinking, image manipulation etc. and it also does not depend on the image format since it deals with the frequency domain although it has been affected by the lossy or lossless compression. The following discusses example techniques of wavelet or discrete cosine transform (DCT).

Reddy and Raja applied the discrete wavelet transform (HCSSD) (Reddy & Raja, 2010). The wavelet coefficients of both the cover and payload are fused into a single image using embedding strength parameters, alpha and beta. The cover media and payload are preprocessed to reduce the pixel range to ensure the payload is recovered accurately at the destination. Ali and Fawzi (2010) used the 2D wavelet transformation on the image and encrypted the message using RC4. With the payload of 73%, the approach yields PSNR at 22.84dB. Safy, Zayed and Dessouki (2009) proposed the adaptive approach where the message is hidden in wavelet coefficients with the optimum pixel adjustment selection. The approach selects the random coefficients for further security.

On the DCT side, Lin and Shiu used DCT to hide image data in coefficients (Lin & Shiu, 2010). Abed and Mustafa used steganography and cryptography, hiding a text in an image. They develop the application which embeds the text to the color image. Their approach is based on DCT transformation and gives the PSNR values about 28-30 dB on the test images (Abed & Mustafa, 2010). Hashad, Madani, Moneim, and Wahdan used LSB inserting bits to hide data and combined with the DCT transform (Hashad, Madani, Moneim & Wahdan, 2005).

Kavitha and Muruga (2007) sent maximum hidden information while preserving security against detection by an unauthorized person. A steganographic system is secured and effective when the statistics of the cover message and stego data are identical. The system proposes to increase the strength of the key by using UTF-32 encoding in the swapping algorithm and lossless stegano technique in the AVI file. Liu, Liu and Ni (2006) proposed a novel, low complexity chaotic steganography method applicable to MPEG-2 videos. Idbeaa et al. (2016) presented a video steganography using embedding-based byte differencing (EBBD). They considered to hide data within the same frame and between frames. Quantized

AC coefficients (AC-QTCs) were considered to manipulate hidden information. They measured the effectiveness of the approach using perceptibility, payload, and PSNR. Ramalingam M., Mat Isa N.A. (2015) considered spatial domain for hiding text message over the an image. Their approach was based on a randomized algorithm to select pixels for hiding data.

A number of papers has compared the two approaches: DCT and wavelet transformation. Most of them compare only the compression aspect. Radu and Iulian (n.d.) compared the DCT and wavelet transforms in the aspect of image compression. Elamaran and Praveen also compared in the aspect of compression. The energy performance is compared. Both transformations give comparable performance in the energy aspect (Elamaran & Praveen, 2012). Xiong, Ramchandran, Orchard, and Zhang compared both transformations for image coding and video coding. For image coding, DCT-based algorithm has lower complexity but the loss in the performance is about 0.7dB. For the video coding, the average PSNR of all frames for both are about the same. The difference is less than 0.5dB (Xiong, Ramchandran, Orchard, & Zhang, 1999). Katharotiya, Patel, and Goyani also compared both the compression of both approaches. DWT technique gives a better quality with slower speed than the DCT one (Katharotiya, Patel, & Goyani, 2009).

Goel, Rana, and Kaur presented a comparison of the basic steganography methods on hiding the image into the cover image using the algorithms such as DCT, DWT and LSB algorithms. They directly hid the image pixels in the LSB bits, and DCT and DWT coefficients correspondingly. The three techniques are evaluated on the basis of the parameters MSE, PSNR, NC, processing time, capacity and robustness. The results show that the DWT approach gives better invisibility, while yielding low PSNR values while the DCT approach gives medium performance in all tested aspects (Goel, Rana, & Kaur, 2013).

There are not a lot of video steganography tools in the literature (Sloan & Hernandez-Castro, 2015). Sloan, Hernandez-Castro evaluated nine approaches/tools for video steganography which covered most of current state-of-the art video steganography. Among these, the limitation of DCT has been observed in MSU Stego Video. Three of the studied tools used EOF data injection algorithm. Chandel and Jain (2016) surveyed approaches for video steganography. They based on the following criteria: Imperceptibility, payload, statistical attack, security, cost, and perceptual quality.

Several works studies the access control approach in applications. They concern the issues of privacy and security. Kawauchi, Maeta, Noda and Nozaki proposed a model of accessing digital content using the steganography via image data. Only the proper key is distributed to gain access to the digital content in the Internet (Kawaguchi, Maeta, Noda and Nozaki, 2007). With the access control application, the interesting study involved the security while allowing the hierarchical access right. Like the work by Hengartner and Steenkiste, they introduced a proof-based access control architecture which allows the hierarchical identity-based encryption while the client is required the proof to gain an access (Hengartner & Steenkiste, 2004). Akl and Taylor (1983) presented a method to solve the access control hierarchy. With the mathematical proof, the method generates the new key which can be used in the tree or graph structure. Ray et al. implemented the access control in the organization where several security classes are considered. The user at higher level can access the information owned by the user at lower level. The proper key generation was presented to this case. Several case studies of such scenarios were given (Ray, Ray & Narasimhammurthi, 2002).

IMAGE STEGANOGRAPHY BASED ON DCT AND WAVELET

In this work, we are interested in working with images in a frequency domain. First, an image must be transformed using transformations such as Discrete Cosine Transform and wavelet transform. The input text message may be encrypted using e.g. RC4 (Mousa & Hamad, 2006) algorithm and must be transformed into bits. Each pixel of the transformed image is considered as bit values. Algorithm 1 presents the framework for either DCT-based approach or wavelet-based approach for hiding text data into a cover image.

In the following, we select the prototype the DCT-Based algorithm and we briefly describe it. The selected DCT-Based algorithm is obtained (Abed & Mustafa, 2010).

Algorithm 1: Transformation-based Steganography.
Input: An input text message, and a cover image.
Output: A stego image.

1. Given the input text, the key for the message encryption is randomly generated. We use the key to encrypt the message based on the existing technique such as RC4.
2. The encrypted text is embedded in the cover image using the algorithms that are based on either DCT transform or wavelet transform algorithms.
3. The stego image is sent to the receiver. Assume that the receiver holds the key for decryption.

In Algorithm 1, Step 1, the message is converted into the binary format and encrypted using RC4 algorithm. The image is converted from RGB to YCbCr. The plane Y is only in used to hide the message. The image is divided into many 8x8 blocks. The DCT algorithm transformed each 8x8 block. The cipher text is hidden bit by bit. One 8x8 block is used to hide 1 bit of message. Or for wavelet-based, the message value is hidden in the coefficient of wavelets.

The algorithm steps are summarized as in Figure 4 where the inputs are a text message and a cover image (in RGB format). The output is a stego image (RGB).

From Figure 4, the color format is assumed. RGB image is transformed in to the YUV image using a subsampling. Then, the only Y plane is used for storing the message. Since the Y plane represents the brightness, it is assumed that the human eye should not be too sensitive with the small changes of brightness (Jantavong, 2009).

In the wavelet-based algorithm (Ali & Fawzi, 2010), the wavelet transform changes the image into low and high frequency regions. The inputs are a message, and a cover image (RGB). The output is the stego image. The flowchart is summarized in Figure 5.

For the message side, we encrypt the message using the RC4 algorithm and change the cipher text into the frequency domain using the wavelet transform. Then we normalize the obtained text values into the proper range. For the image side, it is applied with the wavelet transform to the image and the mean value of the transformed image (coefficients), *mean,* is computed. Then, we find the threshold of the image. In the experiments, we assume *alpha* = 0.9. The hiding positions are checked where the wavelet coefficients are less than T at every position. The text is stored at those positions.

To reduce the computation, little modification for the ease of storing the text positions is added. Rather than considering each position that has the coefficient less than the threshold, the contiguous submatrices that have the average coefficient values less than the threshold T is considered. In doing so,

Figure 4. DCT-based approach

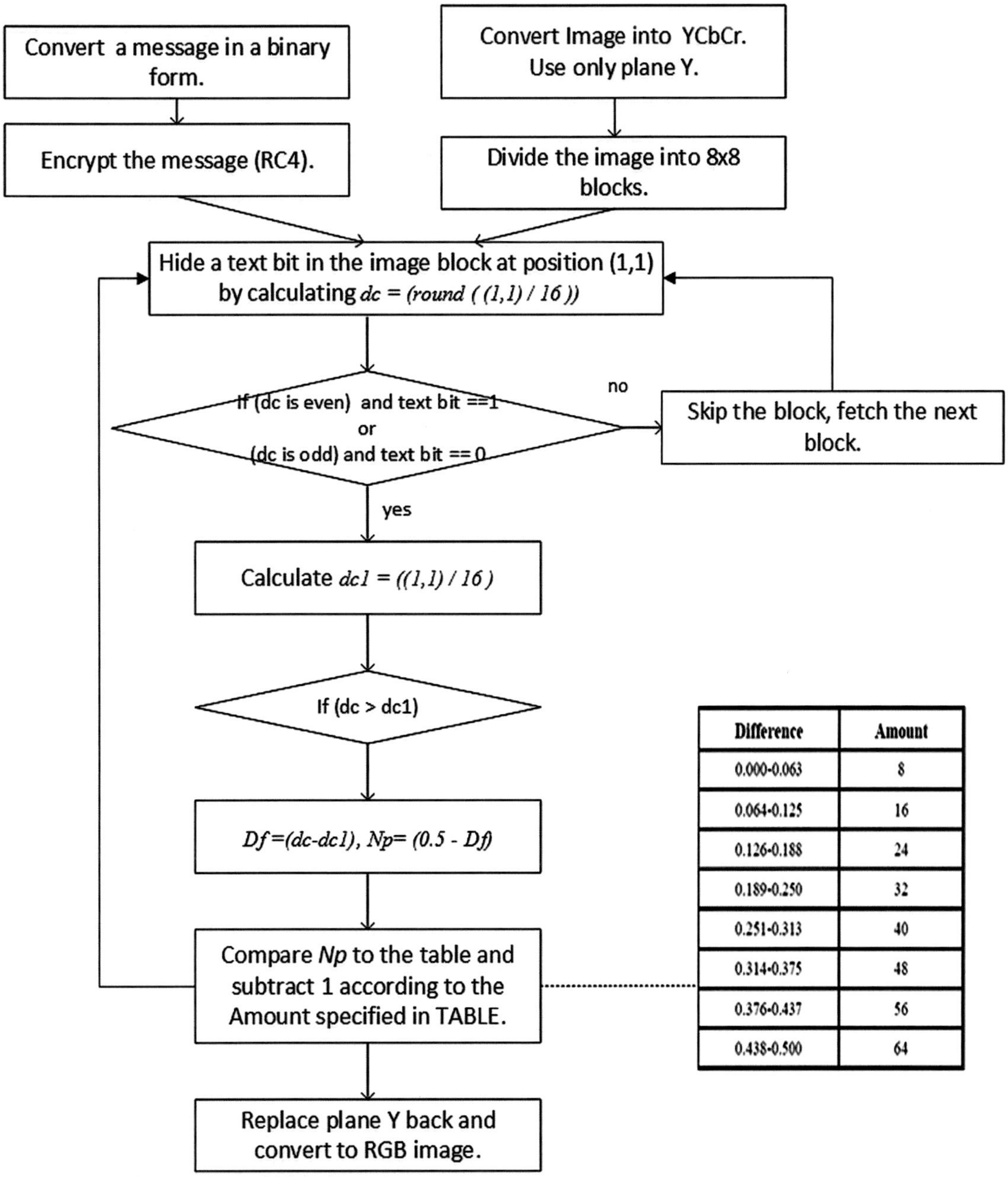

Difference	Amount
0.000-0.063	8
0.064-0.125	16
0.126-0.188	24
0.189-0.250	32
0.251-0.313	40
0.314-0.375	48
0.376-0.437	56
0.438-0.500	64

only the first positions where each message starts for each plane are stored. Note that this is just one of the heuristics to find the position to hide the text coefficient effectively and efficiently.

The previous literature did not mention about calculating the capacity explicitly. We further analyze the capacity as follows. First, we calculate the capacity for hiding texts, since each text contains characters which are represented as 8 bits. Each bit is hidden in the image according to the approach. For DCT-based approach, each 8x8 block can hide only 1 bit at position (0,0). Thus, the number of possible

Figure 5. Wavelet-based approach

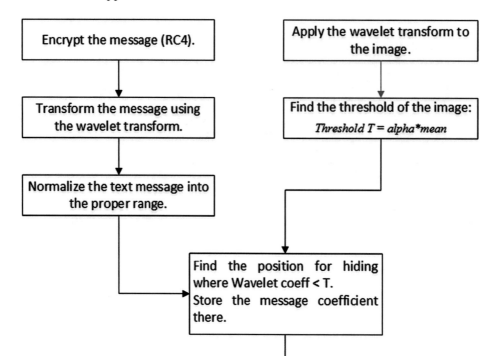

bits to hide is the total of 8x8 blocks. For the wavelet-based approach, after the transformation, there are 4 matrices, A,H,V, and D. Each of them has the half size of the original. The matrices A and H are used to hide texts. After the transformation, these two matrices contain values while matrices V and D contain zero values. Thus, texts are hidden in the two matrices. Then, the total capacity is calculated from the sizes of all A and H matrices. In reality, the capacity will be the number of positions that has the values less than the threshold (T) for each plane. When considering the two planes, the minimum number of positions is used. However, in the application, we estimate the capacity from the row and column size of matrix A.

VIDEO STEGANOGRAPHY BASED ON WAVELET

The above algorithm can be easily extended to hide data in a video. Algorithm 1 can be applied to each video frame. Hiding in the video has an advantage since it has more capacity due to several image frames. We pick a wavelet transform as a case study. For a video media, a video consists of many frames where each frame is considered as an image. At a higher level, video frame(s) must be picked to hide data. Some previous work considered to hide information at a specific frame (Ramalingam

& Mat Isa, 2015). In this work, we consider to hide in selected video frames where each frame is transformed using a wavelet-based approach.

It is also possible to explore various kinds of wavelet transformation, such as Discrete Wavelet Transform (DWT), Haar-DWT, Continuous Wavelet Transform, DjVu, Meyer, Fast wavelet transform, Lifting-based multi-level wavelet transform and etc. For most of the wavelet kinds, the hiding occurs in wavelet coefficients. The next question is how to pick wavelet coefficients to hide data. By intuition, the stego frame must look very close to the original framework. The Peak Signal to Noise Ratio (PSNR) is used to compare quality of stego frame to the original one. Also, since the hidden information may be spread out in many frames. If some frame is dropped during the video transmission, it is advantageous that the receiver can still figure out the hidden message. These are challenges due for video steganography beyond the image one.

In the experiment, we give an example in the application of hiding an image in the video media. The secret data is an RGB image. The Haar DWT and lifting-based wavelet transforms are selected as case studies. Two heuristics to consider the coefficients for hiding are used: random and similar values. The video frame is considered to hide data one by one in sequence. The proposed embedding model is as shown in Figure 6. The proposed doffing model is as shown in Figure 7.

From Figure 6, there are following steps. Step 1): Bring secret image and video file to transform using lifting based multi-level wavelet transform; then find and keep the positions with the same coefficient of color between the secret image and the frame of the video. Since we are interested in hiding in the frames containing pixels with the same coefficient as those of the secret image, this step searches for these pixels. Also, we are using the color image which is divided into RGB plane for each plane, we do this search. Step 2): Embed the pixels of the secret image with the same coefficient into those frames. In this work, we attempt to find the positions with the same coefficient values for each wavelet plane. If the number of coefficients that are same for the cover video frames is greater than that of the hidden image, the algorithm works fine. Also, if there are many positions with the same value, we randomly choose one. However, the values of the coefficients are not exactly matched, we find the coefficients with the "closest" values from the cover video frames. The "closest" means the values with the least absolute difference first. When there are two values with the save absolute values, we prefer the darker positions (the smaller value). Among these, we have to check whether the coefficient positions are already used. If not, we can use them. Otherwise, we do not consider them. At last, we cannot find any coefficient positions, e.g. the picture is dark background or white backgrounds. We randomly pick positions.

After embedding, the indices are kept in a file separately from the stego video. We keep the frame number, the row and column positions etc. They are also encrypted. For example, (1,5,5) means we keep the position at frame1, row5 and column5. Then we perform the inverse transform back for all the stego video frames.

On the decryption side, Figure 7 presents the steps which are described as follows: Doff pixel of the each frame of video file using the lifting discrete wavelet transforms. Then, the index files are decrypted. The indices are used to locate frames and positions to hide. The values from the coefficients are extracted as image coefficients. At last, the inverse lifting wavelet transform was applied to obtain the secret image.

Figure 6. A block diagram of finding the wavelet coefficients

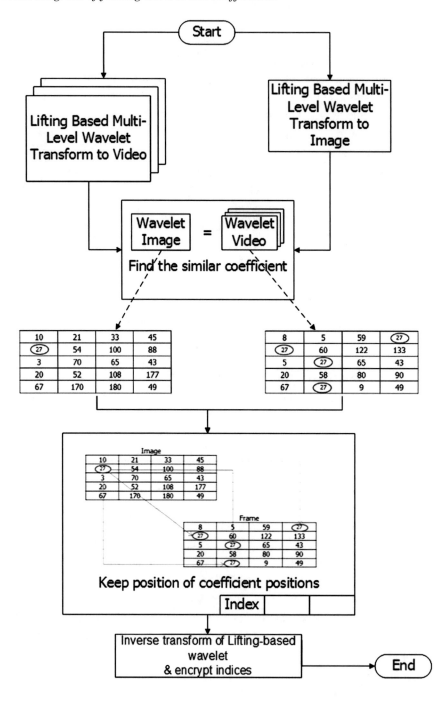

NUMERICAL RESULTS

Several metrics are considered and various images with different sizes are used for experiments. The algorithms' performance are compared using PSNR, capacity, accuracy, and robustness. For the PSNR value, it is computed by the following Equation (1).

Figure 7. A block diagram of the proposed doffing model

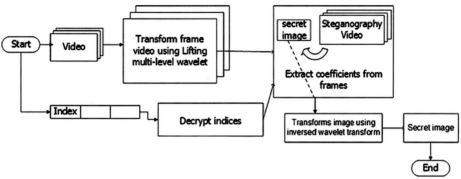

$$PSNR = 20 \log_{10} \left(\frac{b}{RMSE} \right) \tag{1}$$

where $RMSE = \sqrt{MSE}$ and

$$MSE = \frac{1}{N} \left(SUM_{ij} \left| Org_{ij} - Wmk_{ij} \right|^2 \right).$$

where Org_{ij} is the original image pixels and Wmk_{ij} is the stego image pixel, N is the total number of pixels. It is trivial to show that the good approach should result in a high PSNR value.

PSNR Comparison

Figures 8-10 compare the PSNR of both approaches for small, medium, and large images. The small size is between 100x100 and 500x500 pixels. The medium size is between 600x600 and 1,000x1,000 pixels and the large size is between 1,024x1,024 and 1,600 x1,600 pixels. The texts are ordered from small to long ones. The PSNR values of the DCT approach are consistent around 50dB while that of wavelet approach has a wide range from 40-70dB. For DCT approach, the ranges of the PSNR for the small size, medium, and large size image are 68-73dB, 67-81dB and 73-85dB. Also, compared all figures, PSNR is less when the message length is long. If using the same image to hide the short text, we should get the better PSNR comparing to use the image to hide the long text.

In Figure 11 and Figure 12, the longer messages are, the worse PSNR values are. The PSNR values remains about the same for all test cases. In this case, text1, text2 and text3 are "Where you go", "I know. It was a really good deal.", and "I think it came out of my pocket when I was in the taxi."

Table 1 compares the PSNR values when considering different quality lossy JPEG. Column "M" denotes the method where "D" is the DCT approach and "W" is the wavelet approach. The tests are done by setting various lossy levels. It is seen that we obtain higher values of PSNR for the short message (the first one) while in the second message and third message which are longer, the PSNR is reduced.

Figure 8. PSNR comparison for small images with 30 texts

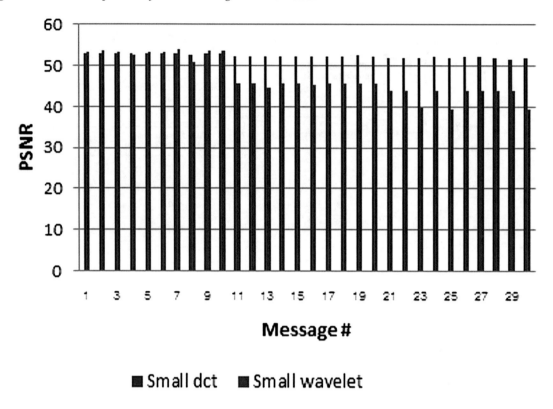

Figure 9. PSNR comparison for medium images with 30 texts

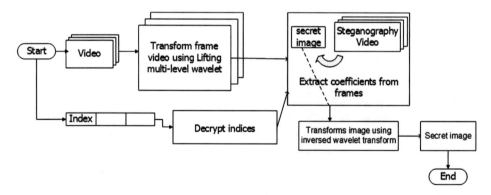

Accuracy Comparison

Table 2 presents detailed experiments on the correctness of the DCT-based approach. Column "Decrypted text from stego rgb" is the text obtained from decryption after extracting the cipher text from the RGB stego image. Column "Decrypted text from stego ycbcr" is the text obtained from extracting the cipher text from the YCbCr stego image. We need to convert the image into the YCbCr format before saving the bits. Column "Percent Correctness of stego rgb" is the correctness of characters obtained from decrypt-

Figure 10. PSNR comparison for large images with 30 texts

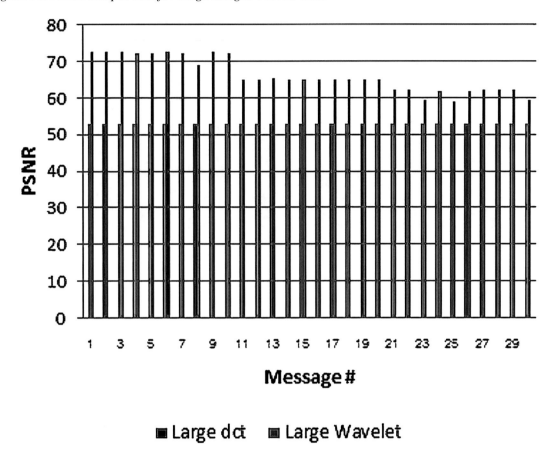

Table 1. PSNR values of both approaches when considering different quality lossy JPEGs

Image	Text	M	PSNR at Different Quality (dB)										
			1	10	20	30	40	50	60	70	80	90	100
200 x 200	Where you go	D	51.9045	51.8833	51.8790	51.8751	51.8919	51.8435	51.8647	51.8284	51.8826	51.8076	51.8239
		W	41.5264	40.1274	40.7774	40.3998	39.8979	40.4182	40.9277	40.9028	39.8902	39.8732	40.8816
	I know. It was a really good deal.	D	51.331	51.3858	51.3916	51.3574	51.3136	51.3256	51.3403	51.345	51.4451	51.4247	51.3894
		W	34.8696	34.7903	34.6735	34.5354	34.889	34.6575	35.1612	34.722	34.4676	34.6517	34.7488
	I think it came out of my pocket when I was in the taxi.	D	50.7254	50.8944	50.9468	50.8482	50.8579	50.8425	50.7948	50.7358	50.8696	50.8602	50.9334
		W	34.9306	34.8463	34.6875	34.7673	34.6302	34.9374	34.7094	34.9384	34.9811	35.0007	34.3118

ing the extracted text compared to the original hidden text. If we directly take the texts from the YCbCr cover image, we certainly get 100% correctness. However, when converting to RBG cover image from the YCbCr cover image, there is an error during the conversion due to some reasons. The error is due to many sources such as the colors of the cover image and the text values. The test shows that the error ranges between 0%-40%.

Figure 11. PSNR values considering various lossy levels and different size messages for DCT approach

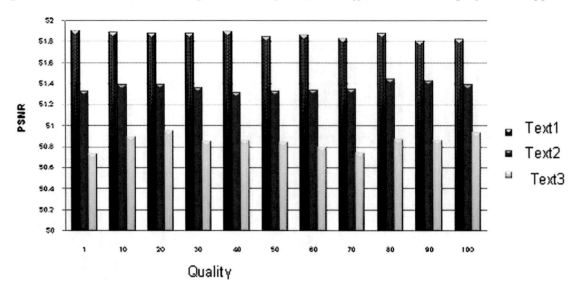

Figure 12. PSNR values considering various lossy levels and different size messages for wavelet approach

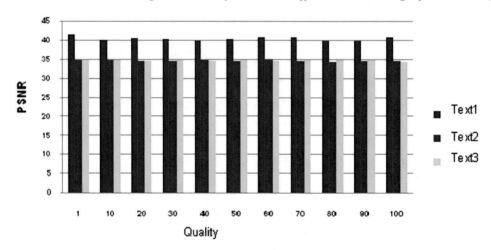

For the wavelet approach, the accuracy is 100% when deciphering directly from the raw image. However, after saving to the image file (RGB), there are rounding or truncation (from double to integer (0-255). Thus, when we open the file again for the decryption, the image which is in the RGB format is converted back to the double value again. The values are not the same as the ones before saving. This alter the results from decryption process. Hence, we cannot extract the store message right. This is one of the robustness problems of the approach. Note that in (Ali & Fawzi, 2010), this issue was not discussed.

For the DCT approach, also there are lots of error prone steps. The first problem is during the conversion from RBG to YCbCr images and the backward conversion vice versa ("Color Space,"n.d.). Secondly, it suffers from the saving process from the raw file to the other format such as JPEG, TIFF etc.

To convert to Y,Cr,B values, the following equations are used ("Quality of YUV-RGB conversion", n.d.)

Table 2. Accuracy of various images

Image	Text	Decrypted Text from Stego RGB	Decrypted Text from Stego YCBCR	Percent Correctness of Stego RGB
680 x 680	What to eat	Uiat to eat	What to eat	81.8%
	Where you go	WMere you go	Where you go	91.6%
	I'm going	I‡m going	I'm going	88.8%
	I like football	K%like footjaLl	I like football	73.3%
	I'd like to invite you to visit us at our new house	I₩d like to iNvite yo} to visit %s at oub FeW house	I'd like to invite you to visit us at our new house	88.2%
	We can lift weights or play basketball	UA can lift wuights oz plAy bask5vball.	We can lift weights or play basketball	82%
	I think it came out of my pocket when I was in the taxi.	Kthink it Kame out on my pocket vhEn I ga_%in the ɑapi.	I think it came out of my pocket when I was in the taxi.	78.5%
	There are six people in my family; my dad my mom, my older brother, my younger sister, my twin and I.	VMere are sax people an mY famil)8 my dataɪ,hY0mom, 'y(older "rother, my younger sister, my twin and)	There are six people in my family; my dad my mom, my older brother, my younger sister, my twin and I.	86.1%
	then stop at the next intersection. I'm gonna get out there and take the subway.	vLen stop al dhe next intersecti?m. I'm wofka get oₐt(there an`take the subway"	then stop at the next intersection. I'm gonna get out there andtake the subway.	86%
	I've been here many times. I come here for work all the time.Do you know how long it'll take?	Iₙve been herE many tames. I come hEre for,work all the timenDo you know how long it'll take?	I've been here many times. I come here for work all the time.Do you know how long it'll take?	94.6%
800 x 800	What to eat	What to eat	What to eat	100%
	Where you go	Where you go	Where you go	100%
	I'm going	I'm going	I'm going	100%
	I like football	I like football	I like football	100%
	I'd like to invite you to visit us at our new house	I'd like to invite you to visit us at our new house	I'd like to invite you to visit us at our new house	100%
	We can lift weights or play basketball	We can lift weights or play basketball	We can lift weights or play basketball	100%
	I think it came out of my pocket when I was in the taxi.	I think it came out of my pocket when I was in the taxi.	I think it came out of my pocket when I was in the taxi.	100%
	There are six people in my family; my dad my mom, my older brother, my younger sister, my twin and I.	There are six people in my family; my dad, my mom, my older brother, my younger sister, my twin a~d I	There are six people in my family; my dad my mom, my older brother, my younger sister, my twin and I.	99%
	then stop at the next intersection. I'm gonna get out there andtake the subway.	then stop at the next intersection. I'm gonna get out there andtake the subway.	then stop at the next intersection. I'm gonna get out there andtake the subway.	100%
	I've been here many times. I come here for work all the time.Do you know how long it'll take?	I've been here many times. I come here for work all the time. Do you know how long it'll take?	I've been here many times. I come here for work all the time.Do you know how long it'll take?	100%

continued on following page

Table 2. Continued

Image	Text	Decrypted Text from Stego RGB	Decrypted Text from Stego YCBCR	Percent Correctness of Stego RGB
1400 x 1400	What to eat	What to eat	What to eat	100%
	Where you go	Where you go	Where you go	100%
	I'm going	I'm going	I'm going	100%
	I like football	I like football	I like football	100%
	I'd like to invite you to visit us at our new house	I'd like to invte {ou to visit us at our new house	I'd like to invite you to visit us at our new house	96%
	We can lift weights or play basketball	We can lift weiGhts"or play basketball.	We can lift weights or play basketball	94.8%
	I think it came out of my pocket when I was in the taxi.	I think it came out of my pocket when I was in the taxi.	I think it came out of my pocket when I was in the taxi.	100%
	There are six people in my family; my dad my mom, my older brother, my younger sister, my twin and I.	There are six pEoplg in my family; my dad, my mom, my older brother, my younger sister, my pwin and I	There are six people in my family; my dad my mom, my older brother, my younger sister, my twin and I.	97%
	then stop at the next intersection. I'm gonna get out there and take the subway.	then stop at thɐ nezt intersection. I'm gonna get out there andtake the subway.	then stop at the next intersection. I'm gonna get out there and take the subway.	97.4%
	I've been here many times. I come here for work all the time.Do you know how long it'll take?	I've been here Many"times. I come here for work all the time. Do you know how long it'll tcka?	I've been here many times. I come here for work all the time.Do you know how long it'll take?	95.5%
1200 x 1200	What to eat	What to aaw	What to eat	81.8%
	Where you go	Wjure yoq d‹	Where you go	75%
	I'm going	I%m goinc	I'm going	77.7%
	I like football	I like fkoⱴal´	I like football	80%
	I'd like to invite you to visit us at our new house	I'd like$tm m{vi4e eou to vs̈ubuv at(w5r newl!ou2₁	I'd like to invite you to visit us at our new house	62.7%
	We can lift weights or play basketball	We0can lift?̃spg̃(ts0or play zaⱳ+gqbalt.	We can lift weights or play basketball	69.2%
	I think it came out of my pocket when I was in the taxi.	I''dhink it eye /ut(of my tos{dt when A was k/ɑtx% Taxi/	I think it came out of my pocket when I was in the taxi.	67.8%
	There are six people in my family; my dad my mom, my older brother, my younger sister, my twin and I.	Thure ara qix4ₒeOpli in my faẏ.y? my8dad, myk(/-- my odfer brőᴎerᵗy'ynunger sₒstᵤy(m}(twin and I	There are six people in my family; my dad my mom, my older brother, my younger sister, my twin and I.	73.2%
	then stop at the next intersection. I'm gonna get out there andtake the subway.	then stop aP$ae ̇@ neXt intersectkmn. I7m`gonncˇeᴎ!o]4 tdlre anltᵤk% 5he spĩway.	then stop at the next intersection. I'm gonna get out there andtake the subway.	68%
	I've been here many times. I come here for work all the time.Do you know how long it'll take?	I%ve beej hva mnytimes.$ⱬ8ⱳₒ/e herm ɳor wo~n ₒll4he)}ime.Do₵ou`jnot low lonO8itⱴ~h taca�口	I've been here many times. I come here for work all the time.Do you know how long it'll take?	69.8%

Y = (0.257 * R) + (0.504 * G) + (0.098 * B) + 16

Cr = (0.439 * R) - (0.368 * G) - (0.071 * B) + 128

B = 1.164 * (Y- 16) + 2.018 * (Cb –   128)

To convert from the YCbCr values back to RGB values, the following equations are used ("Everything about the data compression", n.d.).

R = 1.164 * (Y - 16) +1.596 * (Cr -128)

G = 1.164 * (Y - 16) - 0.813 * (Cr -128) - 0.391 * (Cb -128)

B = 1.164 * (Y -1 6) + 2.018 * (Cb -   128)

It is noted that the values for Y is [16,235] (220 steps), for Cr, and Cb is [16,239] (235 steps) while the values for RGB is (0-255). Thus, the conversion back to YCbCr and back to the RGB image will lose some accuracy since the scale steps are different and the rounding error due to integer values in RGB. All this will degrade the correctness of the DCT approach when decrypting back from the stego image. Note that, the purpose of using YCbCr is to hide in the Y plane which is a luma signal. Hopefully, hiding here will make less noticeable.

During the saving process from the raw data to the image file format, some information is lost which is unavoidable. It is interesting that the wavelet-based approach is less tolerate to the saving issue while the DCT-based approach is more robustness to the saving process although there are many steps which can cause the loss of information.

Capacity Comparison

We measure the capacity used to hide in terms of ratio to the overall capacity for different messages (1-30). The length of the messages is from short to long. Figure 13 and Figure 14 presents the capacity used for the DCT and wavelet approaches respectively. For example, the small size and medium size image the capacity is about 0.05-0.47, 0.01-0.14 and 0.0007-0.012, 0.000058-0.000913 for DCT and wavelet algorithms respectively.

Two figures implies the same conclusion: the larger the message the more capacity used. When the image is large, the more available capacity will be. Thus, small texts occupy small space in a large image size.

In details, the wavelet-based approach uses much less capacity. This is due to each bit is hidden in the pixel directly if the threshold agrees. For the DCT approach, each bit is hidden in an 8x8 pixel block. Thus, the DCT algorithm takes more space obviously.

Complexity Comparison

If we do not consider the issue of image saving, the DCT-based is a little less robust compared to the Wavelet-based one due to the YCbCr the conversion process. However, the DCT approach gives a stego

Figure 13. Capacity used from DCT approach for various image sizes

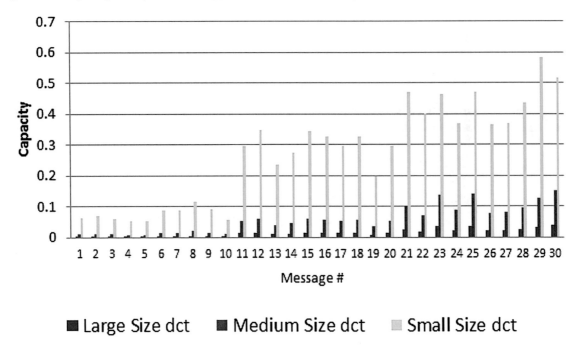

Figure 14. Capacity used from wavelet approach for various image sizes

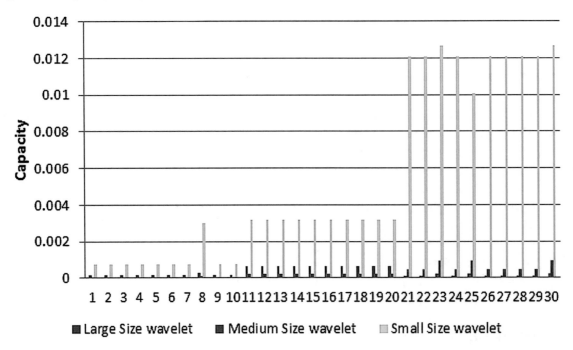

image with quite stable PSNR values where the wavelet approach is really depends in the color in the image and the text values. Nevertheless, the wavelet transformation usually consumes time to process less than that of the DCT transformation. The DCT transformation suffers from the block artifacts. The wavelet algorithm is better on the aspect of compression and coding (Elamaran & Praveen, 2012; Katharotiya, Patel & Goyani, 2011). It is noticed that though the wavelet transform usually outperforms, when putting with the algorithm to hide the message, the overall PSNR may not be as good as that of the DCT in some cases.

Table 3 summarizes the differences of the two algorithms. Assume that the size of image is $M \times N$. The wavelet-based algorithm performs the transformation once while the DCT-based algorithm performs the transformation to the 8×8 block. It iteratively performs the DCT to each block until the condition to hide the bit message is met. This is assumed to be p iterations. Each block may use different number of iterations. The hiding position for each block is always at (1,1). The wavelet-based algorithm computes the mean value of the image and selects the position to hide that use the value less than the means values. Thus, the algorithm has much less complexity compared to the DCT-based algorithm which attempts to distribute the difference in dc values through the quantization table.

Table 4 summarizes the results from all test aspects. It is shown that wavelet approach is better in most issues but less tolerate to the saving issue while the PSNR values are really sensitive to cover image color and text values.

Table 3. Complexity and method comparison

Aspects	Wavelet-Based Algorithm	DCT-Based Algorithm
Transformation	Wavelet	DCT
Size of block to transform	$M \times N$	$(M \times N)/64$
Number of times to transform	1	p
Iterations used to search to space to hide	At most $O(M \times N)$	$O(p \times ((M \times N)/64))$
Method to search for hiding position	Position has less than the threshold value	Always at (1,1) position of (8×8) block
How to message value is kept.	The value is replaced in the position.	The dc value is even and text bit is 0 or the dc value is odd and text bit is 1

Table 4. Performance comparison

Aspects	PSNR	Robustness to Saving	Robustness to Compression	Accuracy	Capacity
DCT-based algorithm	Less but stable values (51-53dB)	better	PSNR varying 50-52dB for varying quality.	Less due to YUV conversion (60%-100%)	Less due to blocking effect
Wavelet-based algorithm	Usually better but very sensitive to image colors and text values (39-73dB)	worse	PSNR varying 35-42dB for varying quality.	100%	more

Video PSNR and Capacity

For the video, the average PSNR values of all the video frames are calculated. Since the video is usually large, there should be lots of capacity to hide information. The secret image pixels are embedded in each frame of the video in wavelet coefficients. The experiments consider the effects due to frame dropping and payload. For the frame dropping, the goal is to test how well the method can reconstruct the stego image if there are some frame drops during the transmission. The frame dropping rates are varied and we calculate the PSNR of the reconstructed image. For payload, it presents the ratio of free capacity for storing the stego image. For example, when the payload is 10%, we consider the case where the size of the secret image size is 10% of the total size of all the frames. Obviously, the larger payload, the worse PSNR. The results are shown in Figure 15. In Figure 16, we compare PSNR when the frame drop percentage are varied by 10%, 20% 30% 40% and 50% of all frames of the video file. We test against various wavelet transform approaches, each of which hides the pixels in some different coefficient: lifting based multi-level wavelet transform with the similar coefficients (LMWT-Sim), using multi-level wavelet transform with the random coefficients (LMWT-Random), discrete wavelet transform with the similar coefficients (DWT-Sim) and discrete wavelet transform with random coefficients (DWT-Random).

Figure 15. Comparison of different payload size with different video files

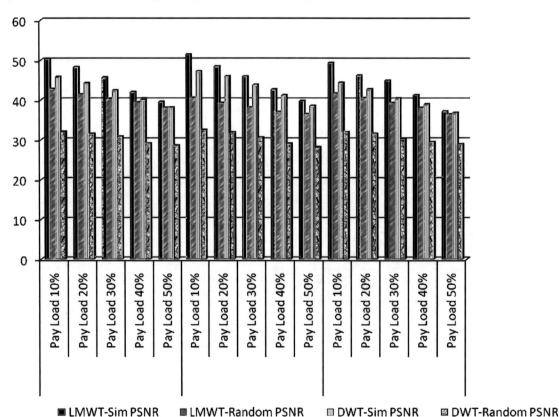

Figure 16. Comparison of different drop frame rates with different video files with the lena image 512*512

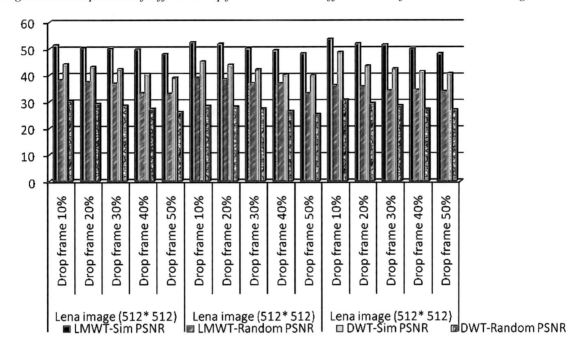

APPLICATIONS WITH ROLE-BASED ACCESS CONTROL FOR IMAGE STEGANOGRAPHY

The prototype applications for hiding messages in the cover image are developed. The application takes the image and text as inputs. The several texts can be hidden in the same image with the different access control. In the application, we can hide up to three messages with three levels of inclusion visibility as follows.

As in Table 5, user 3 with key level 3 has the most privileged. The user can see all messages that are hidden. User 2 with the key level 2 can only see the message owned by user 1 and himself. Finally, user 1 with the key level 1 can only see his message.

The key level 1 is the lowest-value key where level 3 is the highest-value key which can view all the three messages hidden. The key level 1 can be used to view the message level 1 only and the key level 2. To simplify the key construction complexity, we create three keys with tags. The user with the high privilege will hold the key file containing three keys while the user with the lowest privilege holds the key file containing one key which can be used to view his message only.

Table 5. Access options with different keys

	Key Level 1	Key Level 2	Key Level 3
Key level 1	√		
Key level 2	√	√	
Key level 3	√	√	√

To implement this prototype, we generate 3 keys for each user level, e.g. keys A, B, C respectively. The user level 3 can have three keys A,B,C while user level 1 owns only 1 key. The approach can be generalized to any level of users with this structure.

To be more secure, the key file may also be encrypted or the more complex key generation can be used to create a new single key to decrypt all three messages (Akl & Taylor, 1983).

- The key file contains each line containing the following items in one line separated by ":".
- Level (A = level 1, B = level 2, C = level 3)
- Key (32-characters long) which is randomly generated.
- The length of the hiding text.
- Block position or starting pixel for hiding (for DCT or Wavelet approach respectively). For the DCT approach, the 8x8 blocks are used to hide. This is the starting block used to hide. For the wavelet approach, the starting pixel for hiding is recorded. As in Section 3, we find the first consecutive pixels which have the average coefficients less than the threshold *T*. We record only the first pixel position (x,y).

For example, in the case of DCT, we obtain

```
A: wru3WoOb8hiSuQgIhpJaDsqGFeEYOm77:10:1:1
```

This line is the key level A, where the key == J6o0CdeWg9ETveZpddRAR0xHUyVC2rSi and the text length is 4, the starting pixels are (36,2) and (73,4). The wavelet approach hides the text in two planes: A,H; thus, the two pixel positions are used.

For the case that the file contains two keys, there are two lines in the file.

```
A: J6o0CdeWg9ETveZpddRAR0xHUyVC2rSi:4:36:2:73:4
B: OpBpVGgQP4ECP6ubVfHXHXtyDqWEMF0X:8:146:8:146:8
```

For the case that the file contains three keys, there are three lines.

```
A: J6o0CdeWg9ETveZpddRAR0xHUyVC2rSi:4:36:2:73:4
B: OpBpVGgQP4ECP6ubVfHXHXtyDqWEMF0X:8:146:8:146:8
C: CjxzIXqwhGX4iotFnxxTYUmd8aFjH3Ck:4:220:4:220:4
```

The application contains the interface as in Figures 17-18. The message can be entered increasingly from the lowest level. First, the user loads the cover image with Browse button (1). The "Max capacity" is shown in (2). The user enters the text (3) and he will see "Free capacity". The new key is generated after Encrypt button is clicked (4). The key is then saved in a file and the stego image (5) as in Figure 17. On the decryption side in Figure 18, the user needs to load both the stego image along with the appropriate key file (1). Then he will see the message(s) according to the key(s) he holds (2). As the text is typed, the capacity remained is shown in (3).

Figure 17. Application user interface (encryption)

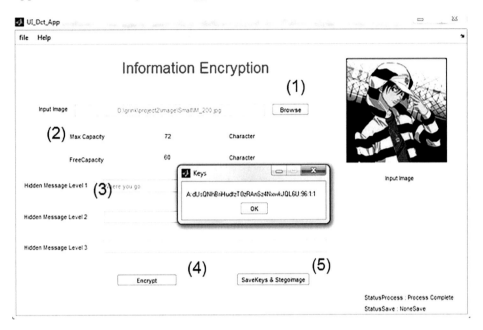

Figure 18. Application user interface (decryption)

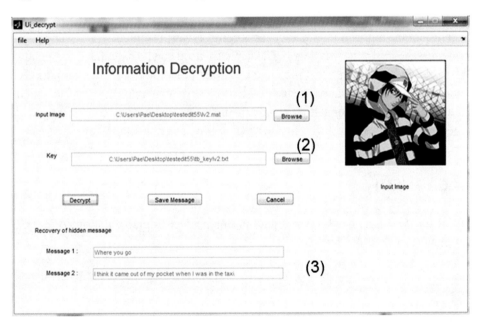

CONCLUSION

This paper studies the comparison of two steganography approaches: the DCT-based and wavelet-based algorithm. The DCT-based algorithm style usually divides an image into 8x8 blocks and hides data in each 8x8 block with the help of quantization. However, the wavelet-based algorithm usually hides the data in the coefficient matrices. The threshold value is used to determine whether the coefficient should be used to hide the message value. The experiments compare both approaches in the aspect of PSNR, accuracy, and capacity as well as robustness.

Comparing the quality of the stego images, PSNR values of the DCT approach has a smaller range while that of wavelet approach has a wide range. The short text with a large cover image gives the higher PSNR since there is much space in an image for hiding. For accuracy and robustness, the accuracy of the wavelet-based approach in decoded messages is very good while the accuracy of the DCT-based approach is 0-40% due to many factors such as JPEG compression or integer rounding or YCbCr conversion. Consider the capacity in hiding data, the wavelet-based approach has an advantage since it uses coefficients for hiding while the DCT-based method uses an 8x8 pixel block per bit. At last, the wavelet-based method has lower computation complexity in the hiding processes. From the video steganography experiment, selecting the coefficients that have values closed to the stego image pixels, to hide yields the best results. Selecting the similar coefficients can make the hidden data closed to the cover image, making the cover image unnoticeable. When measuring the average PSNR values of the stego videos and in different scenario such as frame dropping rates and payload sizes, lifting based multi-level wavelet transform with the similar coefficients gives the best average PSNR (40%-50%) compared to discrete wavelet transform.

The application of the algorithm with the access control was presented. The cover image can be used to hide several messages with the privileges. The capacity used can be calculated to see how much more information can be hidden. When a text message is entered, the key is generated randomly and used as an access to view the hidden message. The user with more privilege holds the key file which can decrypt all messages while the normal user can view only the message that his key can unlock. With the help of encryption theory, the multiple keys can further be combined to one single key.

ACKNOWLEDGMENT

We are thankful for the students who participate in this project implementation: Anongnart Boondee, Sirirat Saejung and Kornkanok Churin.

REFERENCES

Abed, F. S., & Mustafa, N. A. A. (2010). A proposed technique for information hiding based on DCT. *International Journal of Advancements in Computing Technology*, 2(5), 140–152. doi:10.4156/ijact. vol2.issue5.16

Akl, S. G., & Taylor, P. D. (1983). Cryptographic solution to a problem of access Control in a hierarchy. *ACM Transactions on Computer Systems*, 1(3), 239–248. doi:10.1145/357369.357372

Ali, A. A., & Fawzi, A. N. (2010). A modified high capacity image steganography technique based on wavelet transform. *The International Arab Journal of Information Technology.*, *7*(4), 358–364.

Bailey, K., & Curran, K. (2006). An evaluation of image based steganography methods using visual inspection and automated detection techniques. *Multimedia Tools and Applications*, *31*(8), 55–88. doi:10.1007/s11042-006-0008-4

Chandel, B., & Jain, S. (2016). Video steganography: A survey. *IOSR Journal of Computer Engineering.*, *18*(1), 11–17.

Cheddad, A., Condell, J., Curran, K., & McKevitt, P. (2010). Digital image steganography: Survey and analysis of current methods. *Signal Processing*, *90*(3), 727–752. doi:10.1016/j.sigpro.2009.08.010

Color Space. (n.d.) Retrieved from http://www.compression.ru/download/articles/color_space/ch03.pdf

Curran, K., & Bailey, K. (2003). An evaluation of image based steganography methods. *International Journal of Digital Evidence*, *2*(2). Retrieved from http://www.ijde.org

Elamaran, V., & Praveen, A. (2012). Comparison of DCT and wavelets in image coding.*Proceedings of International Conference on Computer Communication and Informatics (ICCCI).* doi:10.1109/ICCCI.2012.6158923

Everything about the data compression. (n.d.) Retrieved from http://www.compression.ru/index_en.htm

Goel, S., Rana, A., & Kaur, M. (2013). Comparison of image steganography techniques. *International Journal of Computers and Distributed Systems*, *3*(1), 20–30. Retrieved from http://www.ijcdsonline.com

Hamid, N., Yahya, A., Ahmad, R. B., & Qershi, O. A. M. (2012). Image steganography techniques: An overview. *International Journal of Computer Science and Security*, *6*(3).

Hashad, A. I., Madani, A. S., Moneim, A. E., & Wahdan, A. (2005). A robust steganography technique using discrete cosine transform insertion. *Proceedings of Enabling Technologies for the New Knowledge Society: ITI 3rd International Conference on Information and Communications Technology* (pp.255-264). doi:10.1109/ITICT.2005.1609628

Hengartner, U., & Steenkiste, P. (n.d.). *Exploiting hierarchical identity-based encryption for access control to pervasive computing information, October, CMU-CS-04-172.* Retrieved from https://cs.uwaterloo.ca/~uhengart/publications/securecomm05.pdf

Idbeaa T., Abdul Samad S., Husain H. (2016). A Secure and robust compressed domain video steganography for intra- and inter-frames using embedding-based byte differencing (EBBD) scheme. *PLoS One, 11*(3), 2. doi: 10.1371/journal.pone.0150732

Jantavong, J. (n.d.). *Chrominance and Luminance.* Retrieved from http://ladballbow.blogspot.com/2009_02_05_archive.html

Katharotiya, A., Patel, S., & Goyani, M. (2011). Comparative aalysis between DCT & DWT techniques of image compression. *Journal of Information Engineering and Applications*, *1*(2), 9–16. http://www.iiste.org

Kavitha, R., & Murugan, A. (2007). Lossless steganography on AVI file using swapping algorithm. *Conference on Computational Intelligence and Multimedia Applications*, 4, 83-88. doi:10.1109/IC-CIMA.2007.380

Kawaguchi, E., Maeta, M., Noda, H., & Nozaki, K. (2007). A model of digital contents access control system using steganographic information hiding scheme.*Proceedings of conference on Information Modelling and Knowledge Bases XVIII* (pp. 50-61).

Li, C. T., Li, Y., & Wei, C. H. (2009). Protection of digital mammograms on PACSs using data hiding techniques. *International Journal of Digital Crime and Forensics*, 1(1), 75–88. doi:10.4018/jdcf.2009010105

Lin, C. C., & Shiu, P. F. (2012). High capacity data hiding scheme for DCT-based images. *Journal of Information Hiding and Multimedia Signal Processing*, 1(3), 220–240.

Morkel, T., Eloff, J. H. P., & Olivier, M. S. (2005). An overview of image steganography.*Proceedings of the Fifth Annual Information Security South Africa Conference (ISSA)*.

Mousa, A., & Hamad, A. (2006). Evaluation of the RC4 algorithm for data encryption. *International Journal on Computer Science and Applications*, 3(2), 44–56. Retrieved from http:// www.tmrfindia. org/ijcsa/V3I24.pdf

Quality of YUV-RGB conversion. (n.d.) Retrieved from http://discoverybiz.net/enu0/faq/faq_YUVby-Breeze_test_00.html

Radu, C., & Iulian, U. (n.d.). *DCT transform and wavelet transform in image compression: Applications.* Retrieved from http://www.etc.tuiasi.ro/sibm/old/DCT_Wavelet_Transform_engl_v6.PDF?

Ramalingam, M., & Mat Isa, N. A. (2015). A Steganography Approach over Video Images to Improve Security. *Indian Journal of Science and Technology*, 8(1), 79–86. doi:10.17485/ijst/2015/v8i1/53100

Ray, I., Ray, I., & Narasimhamurthi, N. (2002). A cryptographic solution to implement access control in a hierarchy and more.*Proceedings of SACMAT'02*. doi:10.1145/507711.507723

Reddy, M. H. S., & Raja, K. B. (2010). High capacity and security steganograph using wavelet transform. *International Journal of Computer Science and Security*, 3(6), 462–472.

Rocha, A., & Goldenstein, S. (2008). Steganography and steganalysis in digital multimedia: Hype or hallelujah? *Research Initiative, Treatment Action*, 15(1), 83–110.

Safy, R. O. E., Zayed, H. H., & Dessouki, A. E. (2009). An adaptive steganographic technique based on integer wavelet transform.*Proceedings of International Conference on Networking and Media Convergence (ICNM 2009)* (pp.111-117). doi:10.1109/ICNM.2009.4907200

Sloan, T., & Hernandez-Castro, J. (2015). Forensic analysis of video steganography tools. *PeerJ Computer Science, 1*(e7). Retrieved from https://doi.org/10.7717/peerj-cs.7

Stanescu, D., Borca, D., Groza, V., & Stratulat, M. (2008). A hybrid watermarking technique using singular value decomposition. In *ProceedingsIEEE International Workshop on Haptic Audio visual Environments and Games (HAVE 2008)* (pp. 166 – 170). doi:10.1109/HAVE.2008.4685318

Sur, A., Shyam, D., Goel, D., & Mukherjee, J. (2012). An image steganographic algorithm based on spatial desynchronization. *Multimedia Tools and Applications*, *2012*(November). doi:10.1007/s11042-012-1261-3

Xiong, Z., Ramchandran, K., Orchard, M. T., & Zhang, Y. Q. (1999). A comparative study of DCT- and Wavelet-Based image coding. *IEEE Transactions on Circuits and Systems for Video Technology*, *9*(5), 692–695. doi:10.1109/76.780358

ADDITIONAL READING

Hashad, A. I., Madani, A. S., & Wahdan, A. E. M. A. (2005). A robust steganography technique using discrete cosine transform insertion.*Proceedings of International Conference on Information and Communication Technology*, Cairo, 255-264. doi:10.1109/ITICT.2005.1609628

Katzenbeisser, S., Fabien, Petitcolas A.P. (2000). Information hiding techniques for steganography and digital watermarking, Arctech House.

Kaur, B., Kaur, A., & Singh, J. (2011). Steganographic approach for hiding image in DCT domain. *International Journal of Advances in Engineering & Technology*, *1*(3), 72–78.

Kipper, G. (2003). *Investigator's guide to steganography*. CRC Press. doi:10.1201/9780203504765

Lo, H. Y., Topiwala, S., & Wang, J. (1998). Wavelet Based Steganography and Watermarking. Retrieved from http://www.cs.cornell.edu/topiwala/wavelets/report.html

KEY TERMS AND DEFINITIONS

Discrete Cosine Transform (DCT): A kind of transformation that changes from time domain to frequency domain, in terms of sum of cosine functions oscillating at different frequencies.

Discrete Wavelet Transform (Haar-DWT): A kind of DWT we used in the experiments. A 2-dimensional Haar-DWT consists of two operations, one is the horizontal operation and the other is the vertical one. Both are separate the image into a lower resolution approximation image or band (LL) as well as horizontal (HL), vertical (LH) and diagonal (HH). The Haar wavelet transform has the benefits of its ease. It is fast and uses small memory space.

Least Significant Bit (LSB): In spatial domain, it is very common to hide information in this LSB bit since it causes less error, making the cover media unnoticeable.

Lifting Based Multi-Level Wavelet Transform: Constituted of steps of split, predict, and update.

Lossless and Lossy Compression: Lossless compression is the method that every single bit of information remains like in the original format after the data is uncompressed. With lossy compression, it may remove redundant information in the original data file and when uncompressed, some original data are lost.

Peak Signal to Noise Ratio (PSNR): It is the metric to compare two images by calculating the sum of the squared errors.

Predict Step: The even samples are multiplied by the predicted factor. The results are summed to the odd samples to generate the new coefficients.

Split Step: The signal is split into even and odd points. The maximum correlation between adjacent pixels can be used for the next step.

Steganography: A science of communicating secret data through the cover media.

Update Step: The new coefficients computed by the predict step are multiplied by the update factors. The results are summed with the even samples to get the coarse coefficients.

Wavelet Transformation: A kind of transformation that changes from time domain to frequency domain by a wavelet function.

APPENDIX

The following are sample texts and images.

1. What to eat.
2. Where you go.
3. I love you.
4. I am busy.
5. I'm going.
6. I like football.
7. How old are you.
8. Would you like to do.
9. What's your name.
10. Why not go.
11. I'd like to invite you to visit us at our new house.
12. Would you please turn on the heat?
13. We can lift weights or play basketball.
14. I called you yesterday. Did you get my message?
15. It says your passport is ready. You can pick it up anytime.
16. I think it came out of my pocket when I was in the taxi.
17. We didn't go there. I'd like to go there next time.
18. I like it a lot. It's very pretty. Where did you buy it?
19. I know. It was a really good deal.
20. Lets play card? Do you know how to play Blackjack?
21. There are six people in my family; my dad my mom, my older brother, my younger sister, my twin and I.
22. I didn't know your sister lives in the city, when did she move there?
23. I think it depends on the situation. If it's urgent I'll take a plane. If it's not so urgent I'll choose the cheaper means of transport.
24. It's not big deal. He and I were supposed to talk to some new customer today.
25. Things are slow right now. Would you mind if I borrow your phone, mine's out of batteries and I have to call my boss to tell him about this.
26. She went to the store to buy some groceries. Would you like to leave a message?
27. Then stop at the next intersection. I'm got to get out there and take the subway.
28. I've been here many times. I come here for work all the time. Do you know how long it'll take?
29. I was going to cook dinner first, but I don't think I have enough time now. I'll just warm up some leftovers in the microwave.
30. She was feeling a bit strange because she had just had her hair cut. Her mom and the hairdresser had both agreed that her new haircut looked fantastic.

Short messages are number 1-10, medium messages are 11-20 and long messages are 21-30.

Chapter 4
Zernike–Moments–Based Shape Descriptors for Pattern Recognition and Classification Applications

Alex Noel Joseph Raj
VIT University, India

Vijayalakshmi G. V. Mahesh
VIT University, India

ABSTRACT

This chapter presents an analysis on Zernike Moments from the class of orthogonal moments which are invariant to rotation, translation and scaling. The chapter initially focuses on the review of Zernike moments as 1D, 2D and 3D based on their dimension and later investigates on the construction, characteristics of Zernike Moments and their invariants, which can be used as a shape descriptor to capture global and detailed information from the data based on their order to provide outstanding performance in various applications of image processing. Further the chapter also presents an application of 2D Zernike Moments features for plant species recognition and classification using supervised learning techniques. The performance of the learned models was evaluated with True Positive Rate, True Rejection ratio, False Acceptance Rate, False Rejection Ratio and Receiver Operating Characteristics. The simulation results indicate that the Zernike moments with its invariants was successful in recognising and classifying the images with least FAR and significant TRR.

INTRODUCTION

The area of pattern recognition and classification has grown due to its emerging applications towards machine vision, biometrics, medical imaging, optical character recognition, speech recognition, remote sensing and bioinformatics. Pattern recognition and classification is a process that involves acquisition of the raw data and taking certain necessary action based on the class or category of the pattern. This

DOI: 10.4018/978-1-5225-2053-5.ch004

process involves data sensing, preprocessing, feature extraction, recognition and classification, of which image representation and description by definite features is very important for pattern recognition and analysis problems. These set of features are the deciding factors in various classification problems. The utilization of good set of features decide the success of these methods. Shape (Loncaric,1998; Zhang & Lu, 2001) is an important visual feature that best describes and represents an image. It is extremely effective in capturing both holistic and structural information from an image. There are various shape descriptors been proposed and exist in the literature. These are broadly categorized into boundary based descriptors and region based descriptors (Zhang and Lu, 2002; Zhang and Lu, 2004) as shown in Figure 1. Boundary based descriptors exploit the boundary information. These include shape signatures (Davies, 2004), global descriptors (Niblack et al.,1993) and spectral descriptors (Folkers and Samet, 2002; Yang, Lee, and Lee, 1998). Global descriptors such as perimeter, eccentricity, circularity discriminate shape with large dissimilarities; hence they are usually suitable for filtering. With spectral descriptors (Zhang and Lu,2001), low frequency components capture global features while higher frequency components capture the enhanced features. Boundary based descriptors cannot capture the interior content of the image and they drop back when the boundaries are disjoint as the information is not completely available.

Region based descriptors (Zhang and Lu, 2004) consider all the pixels within the shape region which are considered to obtain the shape description. Region based methods make effective use of all the pixel information to represent the shape. These include area, euler number, convex hull,shape matrix and moment descriptors(Yang, Lee, and Lee, 1998; Teh and Chin, 1988; Flusser, 2006).The moment based descriptors are based on extracting statistical distribution from the image pixels. These moments have the property of being invariant to image rotation, scaling and translation which is significant for image recognition and classification methods (Teh and Chin, 1988).

The chapter is organized as follows. Section 2 provides a comprehensive review on Moment invariants. Section 3 outlines Zernike Moments (ZM) based on the dimensions as 1D, 2D and 3D; the computation of Zernike moments and their invariants and the applications of ZM in various image processing areas. Section 4 furnishes details about performance evaluation of the classifiers. Section 5 presents an application of 2D ZM in plant species recognition and classification. Finally Section 6 concludes the chapter.

Figure 1. Classification of shape descriptors

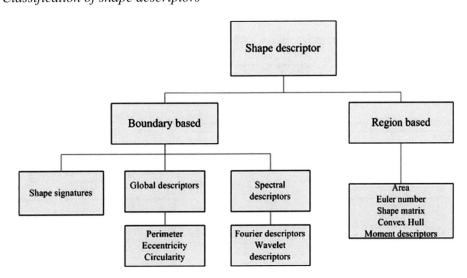

Review on Moment Invariants

Moments (Teh and Chin, 1988; Flusser, 2006) are projections of the image function onto polynomial basis functions. These moments and function of moments are best utilized as region based shape descriptors for various applications (Hosny, 2007; Rani and Devaraj, 2012; Khotanzad and Hong, 1990). Moments capture the global information from an image and further they do not require any boundary information. In literature various types of moments have been defined and described as shown in Figure 2.

Geometric Moments

Hu (1962) introduced geometric moments which are invariant to translation, rotation and scaling. For a digital image $f(x, y)$, they are defined as

$$m_{pq} = \sum_{x} \sum_{y} x^p y^q f(x, y) \tag{1}$$

where m_{pq} is the $(p + q)^{th}$ order moment of the image function

Geometric moments have attracted wide variety of applications. Dudani, Breeding and McGhee (1977) addressed the problem of aircraft type recognition from optical images using moment invariants. The work was conducted on 132 images with six aircraft types. Experimental results exhibited significantly lower error rate as compared to human observers. Prokop and Reeves (1992)reviewed geometric moments and its applications for unoccluded object representation and recognition. Noh and Rhee (2005) proposed palmprint recognition system based on Hu invariant method for a palmprint image of resolution 135 x 135. The results showed an improvement in False Acceptance Rate (FAR) and Genuine Acceptance Rate (GAR) by 0.002% and 0.1% respectively. From the geometric moments few invariants can be derived from the lower order moments, whereas computing higher order moments are computationally expensive. Also these lower order moments are insufficient to describe the shape accurately (Zhang and Lu,2004). Moreover the basis set $x^p y^q$ is not orthogonal indicating a definite amount of redundancy in the information content derived from the moments (Khotanzad and Hong, 1990).

Figure 2. Classification of moment descriptors

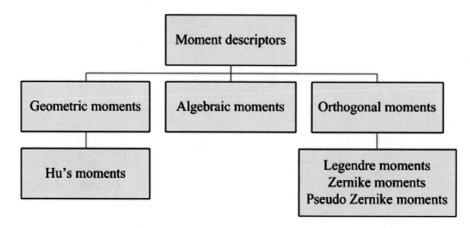

Algebraic Moments

Algebraic moment invariants have been initiated by Taubin and Cooper (1991a, 1991b), which are invariant to affine transformations and can be constructed up to an arbitrary order.They are derived from the first m central moments which and are given as the eigen values of the predefined matrices $M_{[j, k]}$, whose elements are scaled factors of the central moments. The central moments are given by

$$\mu_{pq} = \sum_x \sum_y (x - \overline{x})^p (y - \overline{y})^q f(x, y) \tag{2}$$

where $\overline{x}$ and $\overline{y}$ are the centroid co-ordinates of the image *f(x,y)*.

Scassellati, Alexopoulos and Flickner (1994) evaluated several similarity measures on planar, connected and non- occluded binary shapes using algebraic moments, spline curve distances, sign of curvature and Hausdroff distance. These similarity measures were compared to human similarity judgements on twenty test shapes from a large database of images. Niblack et al.(1993) proposed methods to query large online image databases using color, texture and shape contents of the images. The results from these works show that algebraic moment based method performed either very well or very poor on each of the query objects.

Orthogonal Moments

Orthogonal moments are obtained by projecting the image *f(x,y)* on to the set of orthogonal basis function. They are derived similar to geometric moments by replacing the basis $x^p y^q$ set by orthogonal polynomials set. Orthogonal moments were first proposed by Teague[23] which overcome the drawbacks of other moment descriptors.These include Legendre moments(LM), Zernike moments(ZM) and Pseudo Zernike moments(PZM).Zernike moments(ZM)outperforms other orthogonal moments(Tahmasbi, Saki and Shokouhi, 2011)as they possess important characteristics.

1.   They are rotationally invariant as the magnitudes of the ZM do not change when the image is rotated. These features can be constructed to an arbitrary higher order.
2.   With the orthogonality property the information contents obtained with different order moments does not overlap which indicate lowest possible redundancy.

Furthermore, to reconstruct an image, individual contribution from each order moment has to be added. With maximum order the reconstructed image is close to the original one. Additionally, the invariant features selected using ZM are only rotational invariant. To obtain the scale and translational invariant features (Khotanzad and Hong, 1990; Tahmasbi, Saki and Shokouhi, 2011), the image has to be normalized using the general moments before extracting the features.

ZERNIKE MOMENTS

ZM are characterized by the type of the base polynomials and are further classified based on their dimension or number of variables as 1D, 2D and 3D moment functions which are applied on 1D data, images and volumes respectively.

1D Zernike Moment

ZM is defined using a set of orthogonal polynomials defined on the unit circle $x^2 + y^2 \leq 1$. ZM features can only be extracted from 2D data, so it is difficult to apply ZM to derive features from the 1D data. Thus 1D data has to be mapped to 2D to accomplish the task. There are several methods that exist in the literature that achieve the mapping.

(W. Li, Xiao and Y. Liu, 2013) proposed low order auditory ZM for identifying music in the compressed domain. The problem of dimension mismatch was overcome by adapting Modified Discrete Cosine Transform (MDCT) -granule auditory image reconstruction which is done in time – frequency plan. The experiment was conducted on MP3 encoded data. The results indicate promising retrieval rate for 10-seconds long query excerpts from large data base of MP3 songs and distorted copies obtained due to pitch shifting and time scale modification. Senevirathna and Tayaratne (2015) presented audio music monitoring for analysing various techniques to recognize and identify music. The analysis include auditory ZM which can be applied to various application such as copyright infringement detection, effective search of audio objects, analysis of audio objects for video indexing and speech recognition.

2D Zernike Moment

Zernike (1934) introduced ZM which are orthogonal and invariant to rotation. ZM are projections of the image function *f(x, y)* on to set of complex Zernike polynomials defined on the unit circle. The Zernike polynomials are given by,

$$v_{nm}(x,y) = v_{nm}(\rho,\theta) = R_{nm}(\rho)\exp(jm\theta) \tag{3}$$

where

$n =$ The order of the polynomial.

$m =$ The repetition factor such that $|m| \leq n$ and $n-|m|$ is even.

$\rho =$ The length of the vector from the origin to the pixel located at spatial location (x, y) and is given by

$$\rho = \sqrt{x^2 + y^2}$$

$\theta =$ Angle of the vector from origin to the pixel located at spatial location (x, y) from the *x*-axis in counter clockwise direction and

$R_{nm}(\rho) =$ The radial polynomial defined as

$$R_{nm}(\rho) = \sum_{s=0}^{n-|m|} (-1)^s \frac{(2n+1-s)!}{s!(n-|m|-s)!(n+|m|+1-s)!} \rho^{n-s} \tag{4}$$

It can be noted that $R_{n-m}(\rho) = R_{nm}(\rho)$. These Zernike polynomials as defined in equation (3) are orthogonal and satisfy

$$\iint x^2 + y^2 \le 1 [v_{nm}(x,y)] * v_{pq}(x,y)dxdy = \frac{\pi}{n+1} \delta_{np} \delta_{mq} \tag{5}$$

such that

$$\delta_{ab} = \begin{cases} 1 & a = b \\ 0 & otherwise \end{cases}$$

Figure 3 shows some of the Zernike polynomials with variable orders and repetition factors. The ZM of a continuous image $f(x, y)$ with order n and repetition factor m is defined as

$$A_{nm} = \frac{m+1}{\pi} \int_x \int_y f(x,y) V_{nm}^*(\rho,\theta), x^2 + y^2 \le 1 \tag{6}$$

If the integrals in the above equation are replaced by summation, then the ZM of the digital image is obtained as below

$$A_{nm} = \frac{m+1}{\pi} \sum_x \sum_y f(x,y) V_{nm}^*(\rho,\theta), x^2 + y^2 = 1 \tag{7}$$

Also, $A_{n,-m} = A_{nm}$.

ZM Computation

To compute the ZM of an image with resolution N x N as given by equation (7), first it has to be mapped from cartesian co-ordinate system to polar co-ordinate system (unit circle) as shown in Figure 4, so that the pixels falling outside the unit circle are not considered to compute the ZM, where

$$d = \sqrt{\frac{(x-x')^2}{2} + \frac{(y-y')^2}{2}} \tag{8}$$

$$\rho = \sqrt{\frac{(x-x')^2 + (y-y')^2}{d}} \tag{9}$$

Figure 3. The plots of the magnitudes of the Zernike polynomials $V_{40}(x,y)$ (a), $V_{60}(x,y)(b)$, $V_{80}(x,y)(c)$, $V_{12,0}(x,y)$ (d), $V_{71}(x,y)(e)$ and $V_{11,1}(x,y)$ (f), respectively

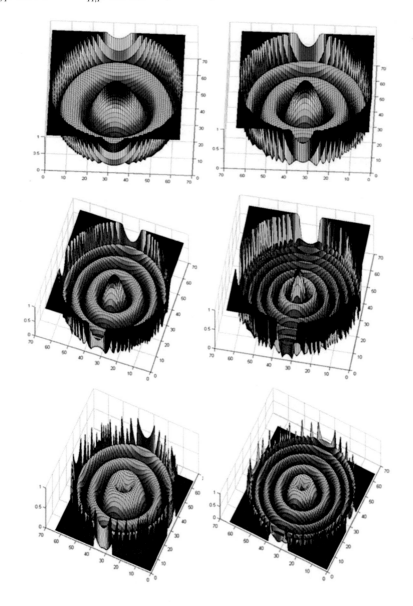

(x', y') is the centre of the unit disc

$$\theta = \tan^{-1} \frac{(x - x')}{(y - y')} \tag{10}$$

Figure 4. Mapping of rectangular image from cartesian co-ordinate system into polar co-ordinate system

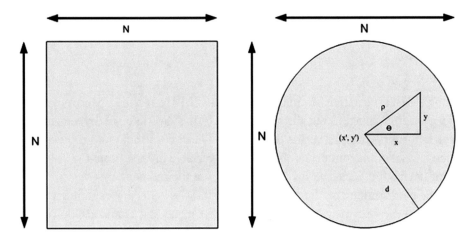

Feature Extraction

The magnitude of the ZM as given by $\left| A_{nm} \right|$ is rotation invariant. Rotation of an image has its influence on the phase of the ZM, whereas the magnitude of the ZM remains unaltered. If the image is rotated through an angle α, the rotated image obtained is as shown,

$$f^{r}\left(\rho,\theta\right) = f\left(\rho,\theta - \alpha\right)$$

The ZM of the rotated image is

$$A_{nm}^{r} = \frac{m+1}{\pi} \sum_{x}\sum_{y} f^{r}(\rho,\theta)V_{nm}^{*}(\rho,\theta) \qquad (11)$$

substituting for the Zernike polynomial $V_{nm}^{*}\left(\rho,\theta\right)$ in the above equation,

$$A_{nm}^{r} = \frac{m+1}{\pi} \sum_{x}\sum_{y} f^{r}(\rho,\theta)V_{nm}^{*}(\rho,\theta) \qquad (12)$$

$$A_{nm}^{r} = \frac{m+1}{\pi} \sum_{x}\sum_{y} f(\rho,\theta - \alpha)R_{nm}(\rho)\exp(-jm\theta)$$

replacing the variable $\theta - \alpha$ by θ_{1}

$$A_{nm}^{r} = \frac{m+1}{\pi} \sum_{x}\sum_{y} f(\rho,\theta_{1})R_{nm}(\rho)\exp(-jm(\theta_{1} + \alpha))$$

$$A^r_{nm} = \frac{m+1}{\pi} \sum_x \sum_y f(\rho, \theta_1) R_{nm}(\rho) \exp(-jm\theta_1) \exp(-jm\alpha)$$

$$A^r_{nm} = A_{nm} \exp(-jm\alpha) \qquad (13)$$

From equation (13) it is clear that, the magnitude of the ZM of a rotated image remains undistinguishable to that of the original image. Thus the magnitudes of the ZM obtained by varying the order n and repetition factor m form the feature vector that is effective in describing and representing the images. Table 1 provides few set of magnitudes of the ZM with variable orders. From the Table 1, it is apparent that the length of the feature vector varies with the order of the moment.

With the lower order moments, the global shape characteristics are captured whereas the higher order moments reveal the finer details of the image (Khotanzad and Hong, 1990; Tahmasbi, Saki and Shokouhi, 2011; Haddadnia, Faez and Moallem, 2001). Figure 5 displays the shape characteristics of an image when projected on to different Zernike polynomials with varying orders and repetition factor. It can be noted that, higher the order the more better are the features extracted.

Translation and Scale Normalization

ZM are invariant to rotation as explained and shown in equation (13), but are vulnerable to translation and scaling of images i.e. the ZM of the scaled and translated image is not identical to that of the original image. This problem can be resolved by normalizing the image by the use of regular moments (geometric moments) before its projection onto the Zernike polynomial for computing ZM. The steps employed to solve the dependency problems are,

The original image $f(x,y)$ has to be transformed into another image $f\left(x + \overline{x}, y + \overline{y}\right)$ where $(\overline{x}, \overline{y})$ is the centroid of the original image which is computed using

$$\overline{x} = \frac{m_{10}}{m_{00}}, \overline{y} = \frac{m_{01}}{m_{00}}$$

such that, the centroid of the image coincides with its centre to achieve translation invariance.

Table 1. Magnitude of ZM with variable orders

Order of the ZM	Magnitude of ZM $|A_{nm}|$ of Order n with Repetition Factor m	Length of the Feature Vector
0	$|A_{00}|$	1
0 - 1	$|A_{00}| |A_{01}|$	2
0 - 2	$|A_{00}| |A_{01}| |A_{20}| |A_{22}|$	4
0 - 3	$|A_{00}| |A_{01}| |A_{20}| |A_{22}| |A_{31}| |A_{33}|$	6
0 - 4	$|A_{00}| |A_{01}| |A_{20}| |A_{22}| |A_{31}| |A_{33}| |A_{40}| |A_{42}| |A_{44}|$	9
0 - 5	$|A_{00}| |A_{01}| |A_{20}| |A_{22}| |A_{31}| |A_{33}| |A_{40}| |A_{42}| |A_{44}| |A_{51}| |A_{53}| |A_{55}|$	12

Figure 5. Contour plots of the shape characteristics of an image selected from the ORL database projected on to the Zernike polynomials $V_{20}(x, y)$ (a), $V_{80}(x, y)(b)$, $V_{10,0}(x, y)(c)$ and $V_{20,0}(x, y)(d)$, respectively

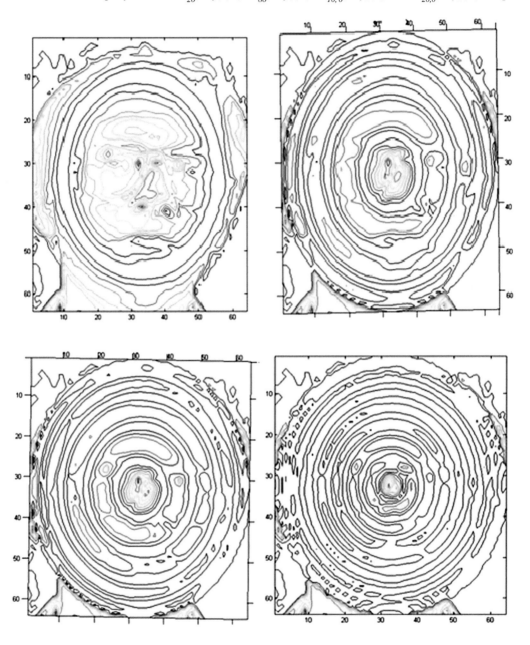

Transform the original image $f(x,y)$ into $f\left(\dfrac{x}{a}, \dfrac{y}{b}\right)$ to achieve invariance in scaling of the image with $a = \sqrt{\dfrac{\beta}{m_{00}}}$, where β is a predetermined value.

Consequently, with the combination of the prementioned steps, the image $f(x, y)$ can be normalized with respect to scaling and translation by transforming it into $f\left(\dfrac{x}{a} + \bar{x}, \dfrac{y}{a} + \bar{y}\right)$. Thus the invariance in rotation, scale and translation is achieved with the deployment of ZM as image descriptor.

Reconstruction of the Image

The image can be reconstructed from the ZM as given in equation (14) provided, all the moments A_{nm} of the image function $f(x, y)$ up to a given order n_{max} is known

$$f(x,y) = \sum_{n=0}^{n_{max}} \sum_{m} A_{nm} V_{nm}(\rho,\theta) \tag{14}$$

Applications of 2DZM

The evolution of ZM with its invariants has motivated its incorporation into significant areas of applications, where the ZM have provided essential solutions as compared to that of the state of the art methodologies.

- **Image Analysis:** The 2D ZM has the capability of capturing the global and local information from the images in a more compact way with less redundancy. With this the ZM were successful in image segmentation(Ghosal and Mehrotra, 1993), shape analysis(Wang, Mottershead, Patki and Patterson,2010; Bin and Jia-Xiong, 2002; Amayeh, Kasaei,Bebis, Tavakkoli and Veropoulos, 2007), sub pixel edge detection(Zhang, Bai and Zeng, 2010; Ghosal and Mehrotra,1994; Ghosal ; Lei and Jiafa,2008), image registration (Sarvaiya, Patnaik and Goklani,2010), image matching(H.K.Kim, J.D.Kim,Sim and Oh,2000) and medical image analysis(Iscan, Dokur, and Ölmez,2010; Liao and Pawlak, 1998).
- **Pattern Recognition:** Pattern recognition system relies on selection of appropriate features to achieve remarkable recognition performance. The features to be extracted from an object should be invariant to translation, scaling and rotation. ZM with its unique shape representing characteristics are utilized for pattern recognition applications such as face recognition(Haddadnia,Faez, and Moallem,2001; Wiliem, Madasu, Boles and Yarlagadda,2007), object recognition(Lemaitre, Smach, Miteran, Gauthier and Mohamed,2007), gesture recognition(Al-Rajab, Hogg and Ng, 2008), medical image classification(Tahmasbi, Saki and Shokouhi, S. B. (2011), character recognition (Trier, Jain andTaxt,1996; Liao and Pawlak,1996),leafrecognition(Wang, Huang, Du, Xu and Heutte,2008; Kulkarni, Rai, Jahagirdar and Upparamani,2013),fingerprint recognition(Qader,Ramli and Al-Haddad, 2007)and action recognition(Sun, Chen and Hauptmann, 2009).
- **Shape Based Image Retrieval:** Recent years have witnessed a rapid growth of images and videos in several areas. This has paved way for the efficient content based image retrieval systems (CBIR). Image retrieval retrieves images from a large database based on visual content. To achieve high retrieving performance and to generate the retrieved image ranking list, the content of the image

has to be described with proper and efficient features.2DZM with its invariants have been successfully used in shape based CBIR(Bakar, Hitam, Yussof and Jawahir,2013; Jadhav, Patil, Patil and Phalak,2013; Li, Lee and Pun,2009; Toharia, Robles, Rodríguez and Pastor, 2007)in particular trademark image retrieval(Shao and Jin,2012), medical image retrieval(Jyothi, Latha,Mohan and Reddy,2013), content based emblem retrieval(Cura, Tepper and Mejail, 2010).

In addition, the 2DZM are explored in areas such as image water marking(Kim and Lee, 2003), image authentication(Liu,Rui and Huang,2007) and 3D face recognition(Mahesh and Raj,2015)considering depth images. Also 2DZM are combined with other image descriptors to achieve a betterperformance. 2DZM are combined with wavelet transform(Foon, Pang,Jin and Ling,2004)for face recognition to attain an improved verification rate of 94.26%.A new edge detection approaches were proposed combining Zernike moment operator with Gaussianoperator(Li and Song,2010) and Roberts operator(Qin and Li) which provided a good precision in recognition. A neural network classifier based subcellular structure recognition system for fluorescence microscopic images of HeLa cells(Boland and Murphy,2001) was proposed using ZM with Haralick features.The system was able to achieve a recognition accuracy of 83%.

3D Zernike Moment

3D Zernike moments(3DZM) introduced by Canterakis (1999)are extensions of spherical harmonics based descriptors, which are orthonormal and compact. 3D ZM are the projections of 3D shape function $f(x)$: $x \in R^3$ on to the orthogonal basis functions. The orthogonal basis function for an order n, can be expressed as a linear combination of scaled geometric moments to fit a unit sphere as,

$$Z_{nl}^{m}(x) = R_{nl}(r)Y_{l}^{m}(\theta, \phi) \tag{15}$$

where,

{r, θ, φ} = Spherical co ordinates.
(l, m, n) = Integers representing the degree, order and repetition of the polynomial.
Y_{l}^{m} = The complex valued spherical harmonics expressed in terms of the spherical coordinates as

$$Y_{l}^{m}(\theta, \phi) = \sum_{j=0}^{\frac{l-m}{2}} Y_{lj}^{m}(\cos\theta)^{l-m-2j}(\sin\theta)^{m}e^{im\theta} \tag{16}$$

$$Y_{lj}^{m} = (-1)\frac{\sqrt{2l+1}}{2^l}\frac{\left(m|j|l-m-2j\right)\binom{2(l-j)}{l-j}}{\sqrt{m|m|l-m}} \tag{17}$$

such that $|m| \leq n, l \leq n$ and $n - |m|, (n - l)$ are even.

$R_{nl}\left(r\right)$ is the orthogonal radial polynomial given by

$$R_{nl}(r) = \sum_{v=o}^{K} Q_{klv} r^{2v+l} \tag{18}$$

The orthogonality of the basis functions is defined as

$$\frac{3}{4\pi} \int_{|x|\leq 1} Z_{nl}^{m}(x)\overline{Z_{n'l'}^{m'}}(x)dx = \delta_{nn'}\delta_{ll'}\delta_{mm'} \tag{19}$$

Though the Zernike polynomials are defined in spherical coordinates, but are actually functions on Cartesian coordinates.

The 3D Zernike moment of the 3D shape is defined as

$$F_{nl}^{m} = \frac{3}{4\pi} \int f(x)\overline{Z_{n'l'}^{m'}}(x)dx \tag{20}$$

also $F_{nl}^{-m}\left(x\right) = \left(-1\right)^{m} \overline{F_{nl}^{m}}$.

3DZM Computation and Feature Extraction

To compute the 3DZM, the 3D object has to be mapped into the unit sphere as depicted in Figure 6. These moments are able to represent the 3D object considerably and form the features that can be extensively used in image processing applications. These features are not normally rotation invariant. Hence to obtain the invariance to rotation, only the magnitude of the moments expressed in terms of the norms $\left\|F_{n}l^{m}\right\|$ are to be selected.

The number of 3DZM descriptors $\left(N_{3DZM}\right)$ obtained for a maximum moment order n_{max} is given by

$$N_{3DZM} = \left(\frac{n_{max}+2}{2}\right)^{2} \quad n_{max} \ is \ even$$

$$N_{3DZM} = \left(\frac{(n_{max}+1)(n_{max}+3)}{4}\right) n_{max} \ is \ odd \tag{21}$$

Table 2 provides the number of 3DZM developed with variable order, degree and repetition factor.

Figure 6. Mapping of rectangular 3D image to a unit sphere

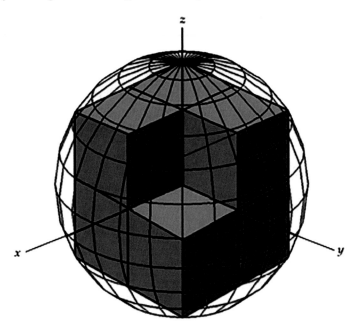

Table 2. Number of 3DZM descriptors with variable maximum order, degree and repetition factor

n_{max}	F_{nl}^m	N_{3DZM}
0	F_{00}^0	1
1	$F_{11}^{-1} F_{11}^1$	2
2	$F_{20}^0 F_{22}^{-2} F_{22}^0 F_{22}^2$	4
3	$F_{31}^{-1} F_{31}^1 F_{33}^{-3} F_{33}^{-1} F_{33}^1 F_{33}^3$	6

Translation and Scale Normalization

The 3DZM are invariant to rotation as explained above, but are variant to translation and scaling. Hence to obtain the invariance, the object has to be normalized before the computation of 3DZM. The normalizing procedure involves the following steps,

1. Compute the centroid of the object using the geometrical moments defined by

$$M_{rst} = \sum_x \sum_y \sum_z x^r y^s z^t f(x, y, z) \tag{22}$$

2.   Transform the centroid to the origin of the object.

3.   Scale the object so as to map it into the unit sphere.

Reconstruction of the Image

Since the functions Z_{nl}^{m} form a complete orthogonal system, it is possible to construct back the original function *f(x)* by a finite number of 3DZM F_{nl}^{m} as,

$$\bar{f}(x) = \sum_{n=0}^{N} \sum_{l=0}^{n} \sum_{m=-l}^{l} F_{nl}^{m} Z_{nl}^{m}(x) \tag{23}$$

such that (*n-l*) be an even number.

Applications of 3DZM

3DZM is able to capture the information content with no redundancy because of the orthogonality. Correspondingly, the moments have the benefit of extracting the global information from the 3D shape without the need of closed boundaries.

Due to its dominant and attractive properties, 3DZM has found applications in 3D facial expression recognition(Vretos, Nikolaidis and Pitas,2011) on depth images, content based shape retrieval(Novotni and Klein,2003), 3D image analysis and recognition (Canterakis,1999), shape based image similarity searching(Venkatraman, Chakravarthy and Kihara,2009), video action recognition(Lassoued,Zagrouba and Chahir,2011), protein surface shape analysis(Venkatraman, Sael and Kihara,2009), human behaviour recognition(Bouziane,Chahir, Molina and Jouen,2013), morphological characterization of intracranial aneurysms(Millán,Dempere-Marco, Pozo,Cebral and Frangi,2007), image matching.Also, the 3DZM are based on spherical harmonics, so are favourable for applications in biomolecular structure analysis(Venkatraman, Sael and Kihara,2009; Sael, La, Li, Rustamov and Kihara,2008; Sael et al., 2008).

PERFORMANCE MEASURES (PM)

PM follows the process of feature extraction and classification to evaluate the performance of the classifiers. The evaluation is based on the number of correct or incorrect predictions made by the classifier on the test samples.

Confusion Matrix

Confusion matrix or contingency table(Larose,2014) is most widely used method for evaluating the performance of the classifiers. The rows of the matrix represents the actual defined classifications and columns indicate the predicted classifications. The matrix constitute four entries as shown in the Table 3.

1.   **True Positive(TP):** Correctly classified test set samples, given positive samples.

2.   **False Positive (FP):** Accepted test set samples that should have been rejected.

Table 3. Confusion matrix

		Predicted Class	
		Class 1	Class 0
Actual Class	**Class 1**	True Positive (True accept)	False Negative (False reject)
	Class 0	False Positive (False accept)	True Negative (True reject)

3. **False Negative (FN):** Rejected test set samples that should have been accepted.
4. **True Negative (TN):** Correctly classified test set samples, given negative samples.

From the above entries, the following performance measures are calculated to evaluate the performance of a classifier

1. **True Positive Rate(TPR)/Hit Rate/Sensitivity:** Is the proportion of the positive samples that are correctly classified, which is given by

$$TPR = TP / \left(TP + FN\right) \tag{24}$$

2. **False Positive Rate/False Acceptance Rate (FAR):** Is the fraction of the invalid samples classified as valid and is found using

$$FAR = FP / \left(FP + TN\right) \tag{25}$$

3. **False Negative Rate/False Rejection Rate (FRR):** Is the proportion of the classifications, in which the valid samples are misclassified or rejected. This is calculated as

$$FRR = FN / (TP + FN) \tag{26}$$

4. **True Negative Rate/True Rejection Rate (TRR):** Is the fraction of the invalid samples exactly classified as invalid. It id found using the following equation

$$TRR = TN / \left(FP + TN\right) \tag{27}$$

Receiver Operating Characteristics (ROC) Curve

ROC curve (Fawcett, 2003) is a proficient technique for visualizing the performance of the classifiers. It is a 2 dimensional plot in which TPR is plotted on the Y axis and FPR on the X axis that depicts the trade off between hit rates and false alarm rate. A discrete classifier produces an (FPR, TPR) pair that corresponds to a single point in ROC space (Refer Figure 7).

Figure 7. ROC space

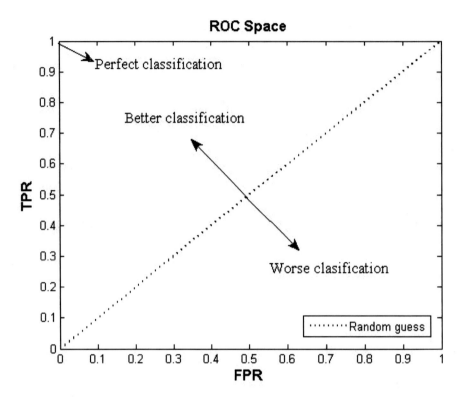

ROC Space Analysis

The performance evaluation criteria by means of ROC space include

1. The diagonal line in the ROC space indicates the random guess in identifying a class.
2. The lower left point in the ROC space (0,0) indicates an approach that never issues positive classifications. Such a classifier does not achieve true positives.
3. The upper right point (1,1) unconditionally furnishes positive classifications.
4. The upper left point (0,1) indicates perfect classification.
5. Classifiers observable in the left hand side of the space near X-axis makes positive classifications with a best training data set, thus leads to less false positive errors.
6. Classifiers noticeable on the upper right hand side makes positive classifications with a weak training data set. Such a classifier often leads to high false positive rates.
7. Classifiers appearing on the diagonal line does not have any information about the class.
8. Classifiers appearing below the diagonal line (lower triangle) performs worse classifications whereas appearing above the diagonal line (upper triangle) are better classifiers.

PLANT SPECIES RECOGNITION AND CLASSIFICATION USING 2D ZERNIKE MOMENT BASED SHAPE CHARACTERISTICS OF THE LEAVES

Plants species recognition has an important role to play in various areas such as medicinal science, food, natural dye making and cosmetics. The method of plant species recognition is based on the similarity of few physiological characteristics. As compared to various parts of the plants that include flower, fruit stem and bark, leaf provides more steady and universal features (Du, Wang and Zhang, 2007). The literature review reveals about the various works that have been carried out on plant species recognition and classification. (Du, Wang and Zhang,2007) presented a geometrical features based Move Median Centers (MMC) classifier, the results depicted excellent classification accuracy with reduced classification time. Wang, Huang, Du, Xu and Heutte (2008) proposed Hu geometric moments and Zernike moments(ZM) based Moving Center Hypershere (MCH) classifier. The results showed a classification accuracy of 92.6%. Wu,Zhou and Wang (2006) recommended a plant recognition system using neural networks, the effectiveness of the method was demonstrated efficiently with the experiments conducted. Li, Chi and Feng (2006) developed a method for identifying living plants through extraction of leaf veins and edges using Independent component analysis(ICA). The resulted obtained validated the performance of the ICA. Ehsanirad and Sharath Kumar (2010) classified 13 species of plants using Gray level co-occurrence matrix(GLCM) and principal component analysis(PCA). The results signified the performance of PCA with 98% accuracy whereas GLCM produced 78% of accuracy. Zulkifli, Saad and Mohtar (2011) performed a comparative analysis on the efficiency of Zernike moments(ZM), Legendre moments(LM) and Tchebichef moments(TM) for plant leaf identification using General Regression Neural Network. The analysis displayed a correct classification rate of 100% with TM. The chapter presents a plant species recognition and classification system using 2D ZM and machine learning techniques to exhibit noteworthy performance.

Methodology

The schematic representation of the proposed system is as shown in Figure 8.

The leaf images are binarized and processed to obtain translation and scale normalization. From the normalized leaf images features are extracted. Features are image descriptors that efficiently describe and represent the image and aids in image recognition and classification. The features are further used to train *k*-Nearest Neighbour (*k*NN), Linear Discriminant Analysis(LDA), Multilayer Perceptron Neural Network(MLPNN) and Radial Basis Function Neural Network(RBFNN)classifiers that learns the model

Figure 8. Plant species recognition and classification system

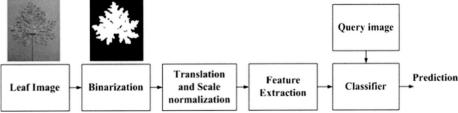

Figure 9. Ten sample images of a leaf species from leaf data set

and are able to predict the class label of the unseen leaf image samples. Also the performance of the classifiers is evaluated using confusion matrix and ROC curves.

The proposed method of plant species recognition and classification is carried out using 2D ZM as shape descriptors derived from the leaf images. The work was carried out on 340 leaf images obtained from the leaf dataset (Silva, Marçal and da Silva,2013). These 340 images include samples from 30 plant species with variations in scale. The sample images of a leaf species are as shown in Figure 9. The experiment was based on supervised learning, hence it incorporated two phases; the training phase and testing phase. The training phase involves the construction of labelled training data set and classifier training, while the trained classifier is tested with the test set in testing phase. Thus 77% of the dataset with 261 images were considered for training and the remaining 23% with 79 images as the test set. The flowchart for plant species recognition and classification is as displayed in Figure 10.

Results and Discussion

Case 1

Initially all the images from the training set were binarized and further normalized to achieve scale and translation invariance as explained in section 3.2.3. From the normalized images magnitudes of the ZM are computed using equation (7) by varying the order which forms the feature vector. At first 25 magnitudes of ZM $\left(\left| A_{nm} \right| \right)$ are computed using the orders 0-8 to form a feature vector. Consequently the length of the feature vector was varied to 36, 42 and 49. These feature vectors were labelled to form training data set and is provided as input to kNN(Taniar and Rahayu, 2013; Muja and Lowe, 2014)classifier for training. The classifier is trained by varying k(k=1, k=2, k=3 and k=4).

Following the method of constructing the training data set, the test data set is framed by considering all the images from the test set. Thus for all the images of the test set, feature vectors with lengths 25, 36, 42 and 49 are computed which forms the test data set. The trained models obtained with different values of k are tested with the test data set. During testing phase, the class labels of the unseen samples are predicted. Once the classifier is tested, its performance has to be evaluated, for which 30 confusion matrices with entries TP, FP, TN and FN are framed. From these confusion matrices, the performance measures TPR, TRR, FAR and FRR are computed and ROC curves are plotted. The results obtained with varying values of $k$and different lengths of feature vector is as described in Table 4 and Figure 11. From the results it is evident that the kNN classifier has delivered its best performance with 42 ZM which is noticeable from the ROC plots. Also it can be seen that for $k=1$, $k=2$ and $k=3$ the ROC curve with 42 ZM is closer to the left hand and top border of the ROC space, thus providing accurate results.

Figure 10. Flowchart for plant species recognition and classification

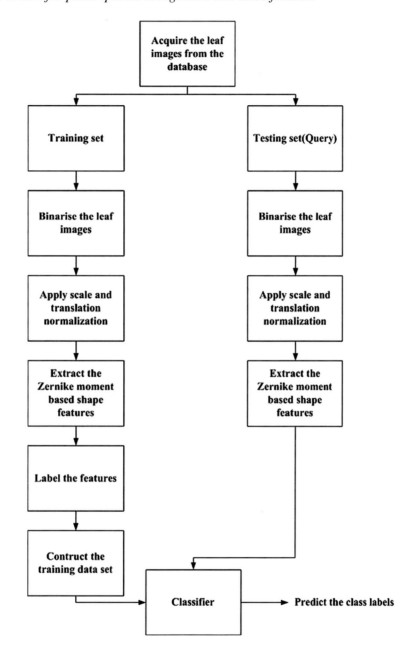

Case 2

Subsequently, the classification experiment was continued with LDA (Fisher,1936; Liu,2013) classifier. The labelled training date set is provided as input to the classifier. The classifier during training maximizes the inter class variance and minimizes the intra class variance to reduce the number of misclassification errors. After training, the model is tested using the test data set and its performance is evaluated. The results are as shown in Table 5 and the ROC plots of the classifier is illustrated in Figure 12. The results clearly indicate that the LDA classifier achieves better classification with 49 ZM.

Table 4. Results of kNN classifier with different values of k and variable lengths of feature vector

NZM	25				36				42				49			
PM (%)	kNN				kNN				kNN				*kNN*			
	k				*k*				*k*				*k*			
	1	**2**	**3**	**4**	**1**	**2**	**3**	**4**	**1**	**2**	**3**	**4**	**1**	**2**	**3**	**4**
FAR	1.92	1.92	2.05	2.22	1.74	1.74	2.05	2.05	1.61	1.61	1.87	1.87	1.74	1.74	1.96	1.96
FRR	54.55	54.55	58.44	63.64	49.35	49.35	58.44	58.44	45.45	45.45	53.25	53.25	49.35	49.35	55.84	55.84
TPR	45.45	45.45	41.56	36.36	50.65	50.65	41.56	41.56	54.55	54.55	46.75	46.75	50.65	50.65	44.16	44.16
TRR	98.08	98.08	97.95	97.78	98.26	98.26	97.95	97.95	98.39	98.39	98.13	98.13	98.26	98.26	98.04	98.04

NZM = Number of Zernike Moments (Feature vector)

PM = Performance Measures

Figure 11. ROC curves for k=1(a), k=2(b), k=3 (c) and k=4 (d) attained from kNN classifiers with feature vector(ZM) lengths of 25, 36, 42 and 49

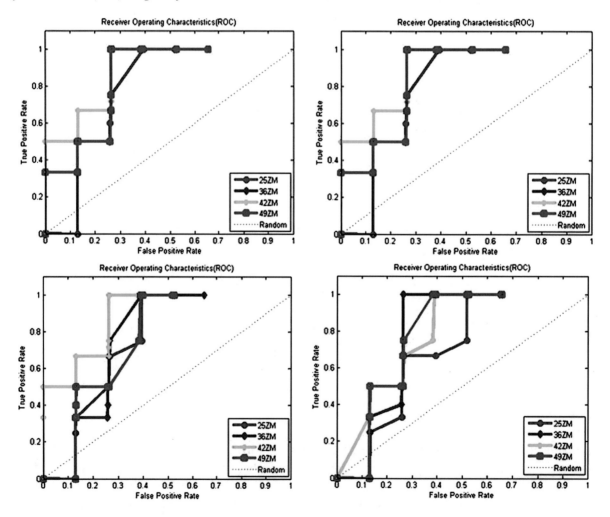

Figure 12. ROC curves for LDA classifier with feature vector (ZM) lengths of 25, 36, 42 and 49

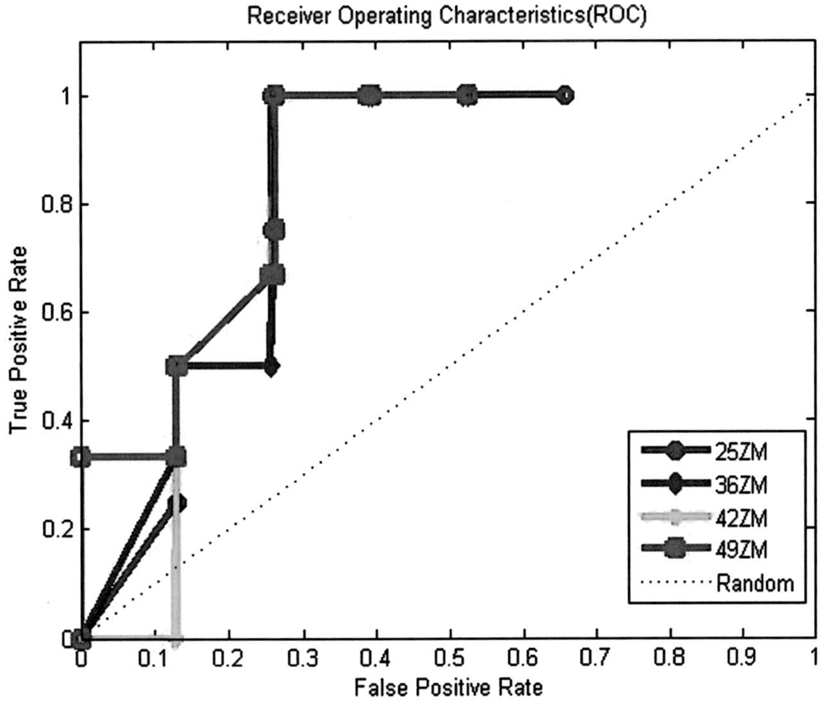

Case 3

Next, the experiment is repeated with MLPNN (Dougherty,2013; Fausett,1994) classifier. The classifier is trained with the training data set. During the process of training, the weights and biases of the network are modified to achieve the error goal of 0.01. The trained model under supervised learning is later tested and the performance is evaluated and analysed. The results attained with the MLPNN classifier is displayed in Table 5 and Figure 13. From the ROC curve, it is seen that the classifier touches the (1,1) point with 42 ZM which indicates unconditional positive classifications, whereas the classifier provides healthier classification with 49 ZM.

Table 5. Results of LDA, MLPNN and RBFNN classifiers obtained with variable lengths of feature vector

NZM	25			36			42			49		
PM (%)	LDA	MLPNN	RBFNN	LDA	MLPNN	RBFNN	LDA	MLPNN	RBFNN	LDA	MLPNN	RBFNN
FAR	1.79	1.70	1.70	1.70	1.83	1.79	1.70	1.74	1.53	1.70	1.66	1.57
FRR	50.65	48.05	48.05	48.05	51.95	50.65	48.05	49.35	42.86	48.05	46.75	44.16
TPR	50.00	57.95	51.95	51.95	48.05	49.35	51.95	50.65	57.14	51.95	53.25	55.84
TRR	98.21	98.30	98.30	98.30	98.17	98.21	98.30	98.26	98.47	98.30	98.34	98.43

NZM = Number of Zernike Moments(Feature vector)

PM = Performance Measures

Figure 13. ROC curve for MLPNN classifier with feature vector (ZM) lengths of 25, 36, 42 and 49

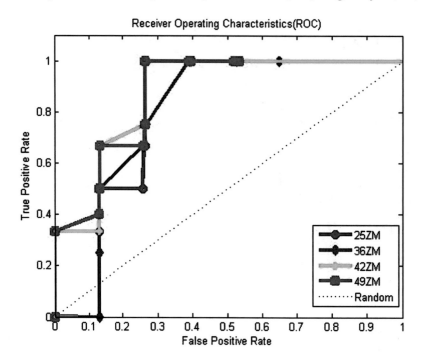

Figure 14. ROC curve for RBFNN classifier with feature vector (ZM) lengths of 25, 36, 42 and 49

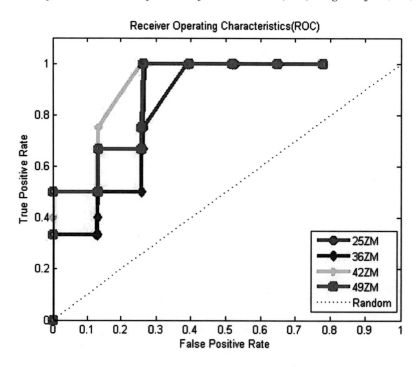

Case 4

Finally, the classification experiment is carried out with RBFNN(Ehsanirad and Sharath Kumar, 2010; Zulkifli, Saad and Mohtar, 2011) classifier. The classifier is trained providing the training data set and by varying the spread constant to achieve performance goal of 0.01. Soon after training, the trained model is tested, performance evaluated and analysed. The results are illustrated in Table 5 and Figure 14. The results indicate better classification with RBFNN using 42 ZM. The ROC curves displayed in Figure 10, Figure 11, Figure 12, and Figure 13 indicate the appearance of *k*NN, LDA and MLPNN classifiers in the lower triangle of the ROC space that indicate unacceptable classification with few feature vectors. On the other side, the RBFNN classifier with 25, 36, 42 and 49 ZM appear in the upper triangle of the ROC space that demonstrates acceptable classification. Also the RBFNN classifier with 49 ZM achieves better performance as the classifier is closer to upper left region of the ROC space where the number of misclassifications are less.

The comparison of the performance metrics TRR and FAR obtained with classifiers kNN, LDA, MLPNN and RBFNN for 25, 36, 42 and 49 ZM is presented in Figure 15a and Figure 15b.

From the Figures 14a and Figure 14b it is apparent that the RBFNN has shown noteworthy performance with 42 ZM. It can be noted that the RBFNN achieved highest TRR of 98.47% and lowest FAR of 1.53%. Lowest FAR indicates the reduction in frequency of invalid samples getting classified as valid samples. With maximum TRR the classifier is efficient in correctly rejecting a false claim of identity.

CONCLUSION

The chapter presented an analysis of Zernike moments based on their dimension. Zernike moments belong to orthogonal moments which capture the information content from the data with zero redundancy and have superior discrimination ability. Performance of a pattern recognition and classification systems depends upon the selection of the features. Zernike moments with its dominant and invariant characteristics have established a significant area in the fields of image analysis, object recognition, image registration, medical analysis and content based image retrieval.

Figure 15. TRR(a) and FAR(b) achieved from kNN, LDA, MLPNN and RBFNN classifiers with 25, 36, 42 and 49 ZM

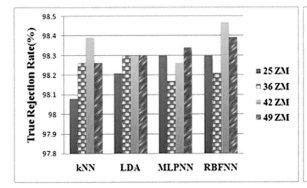
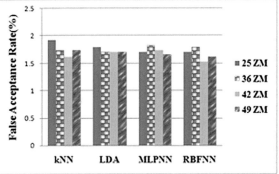

Exercises

1. Discuss about the rotation, translation and rotation invariance of the 2D Zernike moments.
2. List the magnitudes of the Zernike moments $|A_{nm}|$ by varying the order from $n=6$ to $n=12$.
3. Find the number of 3D Zernike moment descriptors (N_{3DZM}) for a maximum moment Order $n_{max} = 10$.
4. The row matrix 'C' indicates the classification result from a trained classifier. The number of classes/categories = 6. Number of samples per class=4.Using confusion matrix calculate the following performance metrics for all the classes
   a. True positive rate,
   b. False positive rate,
   c. True negative rate.
   d. False negative rate: $C = \begin{bmatrix} 1\,1\,3\,1\,2\,2\,2\,2\,3\,2\,3\,3\,4\,6\,4\,4\,5\,5\,5\,2\,6\,6\,6\,4 \end{bmatrix}$.

   The entries of 'C' indicate the class labels.
5. Consider a 3x3 matrix given as $A = \begin{bmatrix} 4 & 1 & 2 \\ 3 & 5 & 3 \\ 6 & 1 & 2 \end{bmatrix}$, find the Zernike moment of A for $n=2$ and $m=0$.

   Now rotate A by 45 degrees in counter clock wise direction to find the Zernike moment of the rotated matrix. Prove that the magnitude of the Zernike moment is invariant to rotation.
6. Write a MATLAB program to find the radial polynomial.

REFERENCES

Al-Rajab, M., Hogg, D., & Ng, K. (2008). A comparative study on using Zernike velocity moments and hidden Markov models for hand gesture recognition. In *Articulated Motion and Deformable Objects* (pp. 319–327). Springer Berlin Heidelberg. doi:10.1007/978-3-540-70517-8_31

Amayeh, G., Kasaei, S., Bebis, G., Tavakkoli, A., & Veropoulos, K. (2007, February). Improvement of Zernike moment descriptors on affine transformed shapes. In *Signal Processing and Its Applications, 2007.ISSPA 2007. 9th International Symposium on* (pp. 1-4). IEEE. doi:10.1109/ISSPA.2007.4555333

Bakar, S. A., Hitam, M. S., Yussof, H. W., & Jawahir, W. N. (2013, January). Investigating the properties of Zernike moments for robust content based image retrieval. In *Computer Applications Technology (ICCAT), 2013 International Conference on* (pp. 1-6). IEEE. doi:10.1109/ICCAT.2013.6522011

Bin, Y., &Jia-Xiong, P. (2002, October). Improvement and invariance analysis of Zernike moments using as a region-based shape descriptor. *Innull* (p. 120).IEEE.

Boland, M. V., & Murphy, R. F. (2001). A neural network classifier capable of recognizing the patterns of all major subcellular structures in fluorescence microscope images of HeLa cells. *Bioinformatics (Oxford, England)*, *17*(12), 1213–1223. doi:10.1093/bioinformatics/17.12.1213 PMID:11751230

Bouziane, A., Chahir, Y., Molina, M., & Jouen, F. (2013). Unified framework for human behaviour recognition: An approach using 3D Zernike moments. *Neurocomputing*, *100*, 107–116. doi:10.1016/j.neucom.2011.12.042

Cai, J. R., Yuan, L. M., Liu, B., & Sun, L. (2014). Nondestructive gender identification of silkworm cocoons using X-ray imaging with multivariate data analysis. *Analytical Methods, 6*(18), 7224–7233. doi:10.1039/C4AY00940A

Canterakis, N. (1999). 3D Zernike moments and Zernike affine invariants for 3D image analysis and recognition.*11th Scandinavian Conf. on Image Analysis.*

Cura, E., Tepper, M., &Mejail, M. (2010). Content-based emblem retrieval using Zernike moments. In *Progress in Pattern Recognition, Image Analysis, Computer Vision, and Applications* (pp. 79-86). Springer Berlin Heidelberg.

Davies, E. R. (2004). *Machine vision: theory, algorithms, practicalities*. Elsevier.

Dougherty, G. (2013). Pattern Recognition and Classification. Springer.

Du, J. X., Wang, X. F., & Zhang, G. J. (2007). Leaf shape based plant species recognition. *Applied Mathematics and Computation, 185*(2), 883–893. doi:10.1016/j.amc.2006.07.072

Dudani, S. A., Breeding, K. J., & McGhee, R. B. (1977). Aircraft identification by moment invariants. Computers. *IEEE Transactions on, 100*(1), 39–46.

Ehsanirad, A., & Sharath Kumar, Y. H. (2010). Leaf recognition for plant classification using GLCM and PCA methods. *Oriental Journal of Computer Science and Technology, 3*(1), 31–36.

Fausett, L. (1994). Fundamentals of Neural Networks. Prentice-Hall, Inc.

Fawcett, T. (2003). *ROC Graphs: Notes and Practical Considerations for Researchers*. Academic Press.

Fisher, R. A. (1936). The use of multiple meaures in taxonomic problems. *Annals of Eugenics, 7*(2), 179–188. doi:10.1111/j.1469-1809.1936.tb02137.x

Flusser, J. (2006, February). Moment invariants in image analysis. In *Proceedings of world academy of science, engineering and technology* (Vol. 11, No. 2, pp. 196-201).

Folkers, A., & Samet, H. (2002). Content-based image retrieval using Fourier descriptors on a logo database. In *Pattern Recognition, 2002.Proceedings.16th International Conference on* (Vol. 3, pp. 521-524). IEEE. doi:10.1109/ICPR.2002.1047991

Foon, N. H., Pang, Y. H., Jin, A. T. B., & Ling, D. N. C. (2004, July). An efficient method for human face recognition using wavelet transform and Zernike moments. In *Computer Graphics, Imaging and Visualization, 2004.CGIV 2004.Proceedings. International Conference on* (pp. 65-69). IEEE.

Ghosal, S. (n.d.). *Zernike Moment-Based Subpixel Edge Detection*. Centre for Robotics &Mfgsys., University of Kentucky.

Ghosal, S., & Mehrotra, R. (1993). Segmentation of range images: An orthogonal moment-based integrated approach. *Robotics and Automation. IEEE Transactions on, 9*(4), 385–399.

Ghosal, S., & Mehrotra, R. (1994). Detection of composite edges. Image Processing. *IEEE Transactions on, 3*(1), 14–25.

Haddadnia, J., Faez, K., & Moallem, P. (2001). Neural network based face recognition with moment invariants. In *Image Processing, 2001.Proceedings.2001 International Conference on* (Vol. 1, pp. 1018-1021). IEEE. doi:10.1109/ICIP.2001.959221

Hosny, K. M. (2007). Exact Legendre moment computation for gray level images. *Pattern Recognition*, *40*(12), 3597–3605. doi:10.1016/j.patcog.2007.04.014

Hosny, K. M., & Hafez, M. A. (2012). An algorithm for fast computation of 3D Zernike moments for volumetric images. *Mathematical Problems in Engineering*.

Hu, M. K. (1962). Visual pattern recognition by moment invariants. *Information Theory. IRE Transactions on*, *8*(2), 179–187.

Iscan, Z., Dokur, Z., & Ölmez, T. (2010). Tumor detection by using Zernike moments on segmented magnetic resonance brain images. *Expert Systems with Applications*, *37*(3), 2540–2549. doi:10.1016/j.eswa.2009.08.003

Jadhav, D., Patil, M., Patil, A., & Phalak, L. (2013). A Novel Three Stage CBIR using Varying Higher-Order Zernike Moments and its Performance Analysis. *International Journal of Computers and Applications*, *75*(3), 33–38. doi:10.5120/13093-0374

Jyothi, B., Latha, Y. M., Mohan, P. K., & Reddy, V. S. K. (2013). Medical Image Retrieval Using Moments. *International Journal of Application or Innovation in Engineering & Management*, *2*(1), 195–200.

Khotanzad, A., & Hong, Y. H. (1990). Invariant image recognition by Zernike moments. *Pattern Analysis and Machine Intelligence. IEEE Transactions on*, *12*(5), 489–497.

Kim, H. K., Kim, J. D., Sim, D. G., & Oh, D. I. (2000). A modified Zernike moment shape descriptor invariant to translation, rotation and scale for similarity-based image retrieval. In *Multimedia and Expo, 2000.ICME 2000.2000 IEEE International Conference on* (Vol. 1, pp. 307-310). IEEE.

Kim, H. S., & Lee, H. K. (2003). Invariant image watermark using Zernike moments. *Circuits and Systems for Video Technology. IEEE Transactions on*, *13*(8), 766–775.

Kulkarni, A. H., Rai, H. M., Jahagirdar, K. A., & Upparamani, P. S. (2013). A leaf recognition technique for plant classification using RBPNN and Zernike moments. *International Journal of Advanced Research in Computer and Communication Engineering*, *2*(1), 984–988.

Larose, D. T. (2014). *Discovering knowledge in data: an introduction to data mining*. John Wiley & Sons. doi:10.1002/9781118874059

Lassoued, I., Zagrouba, E., & Chahir, Y. (2011). An efficient approach for video action classification based on 3d Zernike moments. In *Future Information Technology* (pp. 196–205). Springer Berlin Heidelberg. doi:10.1007/978-3-642-22309-9_24

Lei, Y., & Jiafa, N. (2008). Subpixel Edge Detection Based on Morphological Theory. In *Proceedings of the world Congress on Engineering and Computer Science* (pp. 22-24).

Lemaitre, C., Smach, F., Miteran, J., Gauthier, J. P., & Mohamed, A. T. R. I. (2007). *A comparative study of Motion Descriptors and Zernike moments in color object recognition. In proceeding of International Multi-Conference on Systems, Signal and Devices*. Hammamet, Tunisia: IEEE.

Li, S., Lee, M. C., & Pun, C. M. (2009). Complex Zernike moments features for shape-based image retrieval. *Systems, Man and Cybernetics, Part A: Systems and Humans. IEEE Transactions on, 39*(1), 227–237.

Li, W., Xiao, C., & Liu, Y. (2013). Low-order auditory Zernike moment: A novel approach for robust music identification in the compressed domain. *EURASIP Journal on Advances in Signal Processing*, (1): 1–15.

Li, X., & Song, A. (2010, March). A new edge detection method using Gaussian-Zernike moment operator. In *Informatics in Control, Automation and Robotics (CAR), 2010 2nd International Asia Conference on* (Vol. 1, pp. 276-279). IEEE.

Li, Y., Chi, Z., & Feng, D. D. (2006, October). Leaf vein extraction using independent component analysis. In *Systems, Man and Cybernetics, 2006.SMC'06.IEEE International Conference on* (Vol. 5, pp. 3890-3894). IEEE. doi:10.1109/ICSMC.2006.384738

Liao, S. X., & Pawlak, M. (1996). On image analysis by moments. *Pattern analysis and machine intelligence. IEEE Transactions on, 18*(3), 254–266.

Liao, S. X., & Pawlak, M. (1998). On the accuracy of Zernike moments for image analysis. *Pattern Analysis and Machine Intelligence. IEEE Transactions on, 20*(12), 1358–1364.

Liu, H., Rui, W., & Huang, J. (2007, September). Binary image authentication using Zernike moments. In *Image Processing, 2007.ICIP 2007.IEEE International Conference on* (Vol. 1, pp. I-385). IEEE. doi:10.1109/ICIP.2007.4378972

Liu, Z. P. (2013). Linear discriminant analysis. In *Encyclopedia of Systems Biology* (pp. 1132–1133). Springer New York. doi:10.1007/978-1-4419-9863-7_395

Loncaric, S. (1998). A survey of shape analysis techniques. *Pattern Recognition, 31*(8), 983–1001. doi:10.1016/S0031-2023(97)00122-2

Mahesh, V. G., & Raj, A. N. J. (2015). Invariant face recognition using Zernike moments combined with feed forward neural network. *International Journal of Biometrics, 7*(3), 286–307. doi:10.1504/IJBM.2015.071950

Millán, R. D., Dempere-Marco, L., Pozo, J. M., Cebral, J. R., & Frangi, A. F. (2007). Morphological characterization of intracranial aneurysms using 3-D moment invariants. Medical Imaging. *IEEE Transactions on, 26*(9), 1270–1282.

Muja, M., & Lowe, D. G. (2014). Scalable nearest neighbor algorithms for high dimensional data. *Pattern Analysis and Machine Intelligence. IEEE Transactions on, 36*(11), 2227–2240.

Niblack, C. W., Barber, R., Equitz, W., Flickner, M. D., Glasman, E. H., Petkovic, D.,... Taubin, G. (1993, April). QBIC project: querying images by content, using color, texture, and shape. In *IS&T/SPIE's Symposium on Electronic Imaging: Science and Technology* (pp. 173-187). International Society for Optics and Photonics. doi:10.1117/12.143648

Noh, J. S., & Rhee, K. H. (2005). Palmprint identification algorithm using Hu invariant moments and Otsu binarization. In *Computer and Information Science, 2005. Fourth Annual ACIS International Conference on* (pp. 94-99). IEEE.

Novotni, M., & Klein, R. (2003, June). 3D Zernike descriptors for content based shape retrieval. In *Proceedings of the eighth ACM symposium on Solid modeling and applications* (pp. 216-225).ACM. doi:10.1145/781606.781639

Papakostas, G. A. (2014). *Over 50 Years of Image Moments and Moment Invariants.* Gate to Computer Sciece and Research. doi:10.15579/gcsr.vol1.ch1

Prokop, R. J., & Reeves, A. P. (1992). A survey of moment-based techniques for unoccluded object representation and recognition. *CVGIP: Graphical Models and Image Processing, 54*(5), 438–460.

Qader, H. A., Ramli, A. R., & Al-Haddad, S. (2007). Fingerprint Recognition Using Zernike Moments. *Int. Arab J. Inf. Technol., 4*(4), 372–376.

Qin, S., & Li, R. (n.d.). *An efficient algorithm for edge detection using Robert-Zernike moments operator.* Academic Press.

Qiuting, W., & Bing, Y. (2008, December). 3D terrain matching algorithm and performance analysis based on 3D Zernike moments. In *Computer Science and Software Engineering, 2008 International Conference on* (Vol. 6, pp. 73-76). IEEE.

Rani, J. S., & Devaraj, D. (2012). Face recognition using Krawtchouk moment. *Sadhana, 37*(4), 441–460. doi:10.1007/s12046-012-0090-4

Sael, L., La, D., Li, B., Rustamov, R., & Kihara, D. (2008). Rapid comparison of properties on protein surface. Proteins. *Structure, Function, and Bioinformatics, 73*(1), 1–10. doi:10.1002/prot.22141

Sael, L., Li, B., La, D., Fang, Y., Ramani, K., Rustamov, R., & Kihara, D. (2008). Fast protein tertiary structure retrieval based on global surface shape similarity. Proteins. *Structure, Function, and Bioinformatics, 72*(4), 1259–1273. doi:10.1002/prot.22030 PMID:18361455

Sarvaiya, J., Patnaik, S., & Goklani, H. (2010). Image registration using NSCT and invariant moment. [IJIP]. *International Journal of Image Processing, 4*(2), 119.

Scassellati, B. M., Alexopoulos, S., & Flickner, M. D. (1994, April). Retrieving images by 2D shape: a comparison of computation methods with human perceptual judgments. In *IS&T/SPIE 1994 International Symposium on Electronic Imaging: Science and Technology* (pp. 2-14). International Society for Optics and Photonics.

Senevirathna, E. N. W., &Jayaratne, L. (2015). Audio Music Monitoring: Analyzing Current Techniques for Song Recognition and Identification. *GSTF Journal on Computing (JoC), 4*(3).

Shao, Y., & Jin, Z. (2012). Trademark Image Retrieval Based on Improved Distance Measure of Moments. In Multimedia and Signal Processing (pp. 154-162). Springer Berlin Heidelberg. doi:10.1007/978-3-642-35286-7_20

Silva, P. F., Marçal, A. R., & da Silva, R. M. A. (2013). Evaluation of features for leaf discrimination. In *Image Analysis and Recognition* (pp. 197–204). Springer Berlin Heidelberg. doi:10.1007/978-3-642-39094-4_23

Sun, X., Chen, M., & Hauptmann, A. (2009, June). Action recognition via local descriptors and holistic features. In *Computer Vision and Pattern Recognition Workshops, 2009.CVPR Workshops 2009. IEEE Computer Society Conference on* (pp. 58-65). IEEE.

Tahmasbi, A., Saki, F., & Shokouhi, S. B. (2011). Classification of benign and malignant masses based on Zernike moments. *Computers in Biology and Medicine*, *41*(8), 726–735. doi:10.1016/j.compbiomed.2011.06.009 PMID:21722886

Taniar, D., & Rahayu, W. (2013). A taxonomy for nearest neighbour queries in spatial databases. *Journal of Computer and System Sciences*, *79*(7), 1017–1039. doi:10.1016/j.jcss.2013.01.017

Taubin, G., & Cooper, D. B. (1991, September). Recognition and positioning of rigid objects using algebraic moment invariants. In *San Diego,'91* (pp. 175–186). San Diego, CA: International Society for Optics and Photonics. doi:10.1117/12.48423

Taubin, G., & Cooper, D. B. (1991). *Object recognition based on moment (or algebraic) invariants.* IBM TJ Watson Research Center.

Teague, M. R. (1980). Image analysis via the general theory of moments. *JOSA*, *70*(8), 920–930. doi:10.1364/JOSA.70.000920

Teh, C. H., & Chin, R. T. (1988). On image analysis by the methods of moments. *Pattern Analysis and Machine Intelligence. IEEE Transactions on*, *10*(4), 496–513.

Toharia, P., Robles, O. D., Rodríguez, Á., & Pastor, L. (2007). *A study of Zernike invariants for content-based image retrieval. In Advances in Image and Video Technology* (pp. 944–957). Springer Berlin Heidelberg.

Trier, Ø. D., Jain, A. K., & Taxt, T. (1996). Feature extraction methods for character recognition-a survey. *Pattern Recognition*, *29*(4), 641–662. doi:10.1016/0031-3203(95)00118-2

Venkatraman, V., Chakravarthy, P., & Kihara, D. (2009). Application of 3D Zernike descriptors to shape-based ligand similarity searching. *J. Cheminformatics*, *1*(1), 19. doi:10.1186/1758-2946-1-19 PMID:20150998

Venkatraman, V., Sael, L., & Kihara, D. (2009). Potential for protein surface shape analysis using spherical harmonics and 3D Zernike descriptors. *Cell Biochemistry and Biophysics*, *54*(1-3), 23–32. doi:10.1007/s12013-009-9051-x PMID:19521674

Vretos, N., Nikolaidis, N., & Pitas, I. (2011, September). 3D facial expression recognition using Zernike moments on depth images. In *Image Processing (ICIP), 2011 18th IEEE International Conference on* (pp. 773-776).IEEE.

Wang, W. Z., Mottershead, J. E., Patki, A., & Patterson, E. A. (2010, August). Construction of shape features for the representation of full-field displacement/strain data. In Applied. *Mechanics of Materials*, *24*, 365–370.

Wang, X. F., Huang, D. S., Du, J. X., Xu, H., & Heutte, L. (2008). Classification of plant leaf images with complicated background. *Applied Mathematics and Computation, 205*(2), 916–926. doi:10.1016/j. amc.2008.05.108

Wiliem, A., Madasu, V. K., Boles, W., & Yarlagadda, P. (2007). A face recognition approach using Zernike Moments for video surveillance. *Recent Advances in Security Technology, 341.*

Wu, Q., Zhou, C., & Wang, C. (2006). Feature extraction and automatic recognition of plant leaf using artificial neural network. *Advances in Artificial Intelligence,* 3.

Yang, H. S., Lee, S. U., & Lee, K. M. (1998). Recognition of 2D object contours using starting-point-independent wavelet coefficient matching. *Journal of Visual Communication and Image Representation, 9*(2), 171–181. doi:10.1006/jvci.1998.0384

Zernike, F. (1934). Beugungstheorie des schneidenver-fahrens und seiner verbesserten form, der phasen-kontrastmethode. *Physica, 1*(7-12), 689–704. doi:10.1016/S0031-8914(34)80259-5

Zhang, B., Bai, L., & Zeng, X. (2010). A novel subpixel edge detection based on the Zernike moment. *Information Technology Journal, 9*(1), 41–47. doi:10.3923/itj.2010.41.47

Zhang, D., & Lu, G. (2001, June). A comparative study on shape retrieval using Fourier descriptors with different shape signatures. In *Proc. International Conference on Intelligent Multimedia and Distance Education (ICIMADE01).*

Zhang, D., & Lu, G. (2002). Shape-based image retrieval using generic Fourier descriptor. *Signal Processing Image Communication, 17*(10), 825–848. doi:10.1016/S0923-5965(02)00084-X

Zhang, D., & Lu, G. (2004). Review of shape representation and description techniques. *Pattern Recognition, 37*(1), 1–19. doi:10.1016/j.patcog.2003.07.008

Zulkifli, Z., Saad, P., & Mohtar, I. A. (2011, December). Plant leaf identification using moment invariants & general regression neural network. In *Hybrid Intelligent Systems (HIS), 2011 11th International Conference on* (pp. 430-435). IEEE. doi:10.1109/HIS.2011.6122144

Chapter 5

An Image De–Noising Method Based on Intensity Histogram Equalization Technique for Image Enhancement

Shantharajah S. P.
VIT University, India

Ramkumar T
VIT University, India

Balakrishnan N
Sona College of Technology, India

ABSTRACT

Image enhancement is a quantifying criterion for sharpening and enhancing image quality, where many techniques are empirical with interactive procedures to obtain précised results. The proposed Intensity Histogram Equalization (IHE) approach conquers the noise defects that has a preprocessor to remove noise and enhances image contrast, providing ways to improve the intensity of the image. The preprocessor has the mask production, enlightenment equalization and color normalization for efficient processing of the images which generates a binary image by labeling pixels, overcomes the non-uniform illumination of image and classifies color capacity, respectively. The distinct and discrete mapping function calculates the histogram values and improves the contrast of the image. The performance of IHE is based on noise removal ratio, reliability rate, false positive error measure, Max-Flow Computational Complexity Measure with NDRA and Variation HOD. As the outcome, the different levels of contrast have been significantly improved when evaluated against with the existing systems.

DOI: 10.4018/978-1-5225-2053-5.ch005

INTRODUCTION

In image processing applications, contrast enhancement technique plays a vital role in obtaining image quality. In today's world, applications of image processing dominates in various fields such as digital photography, remote sensing, LED and LCD display based images. The poor quality image fails to provide the best result while image operations are performed on it. The same result is obtained in the imaging devices also. In many image and video applications, these devices functions as human eyes which create the final result of visual quality. They usually correlate high image contrast with good image quality. Certainly, growth in image display and generation of knowledge are the focus for further enhancement in various image development methods.

The raw image has lesser contrast than the ideal one since the effects of the image have poor illumination conditions, low quality inexpensive imaging sensors, user operation errors, and media deterioration. For enhanced human analysis of image semantics and higher perceptual quality, contrast improvement is always focused. Broadly, the contrast development methods have been re-categorized into two folds namely, context-sensitive (point-wise operators) and context-free (point operators). In context-sensitive approach, the contrast is defined using the rate of change in intensity between adjacent pixels. The contrast is raised honestly by changing the local waveform on pixel by pixel forms.

Context-free contrast developmental method fails to change the local waveform on a pixel by pixel basis. As an option, the class of context-free contrast development methods changes with a statistical technique. They control the histogram of the input image to divide the gray levels of higher probability from the adjacent gray levels. Context-free techniques enhance the average difference between any two changed input gray levels. In relation to its context-sensitive counterpart, the context-free method fails to experience from the ringing artifact and it maintains the relative ordering of varied gray levels.

The technique, Minimization of Total Variation (TV) has been emerged as an approach for image de-noising. The correlation between the TV minimization issues and binary MRF models are discovered. A combinatorial optimization algorithm is planned for the TV minimization problem in the discrete setting using graph cuts. Image de-noising is the issue of improving a true image from an examined noisy image. The variation approach is a significant method for explaining the image de-noising issues when the image is described on the uninterrupted domain. Egil Bae et al. (2011) describes the Euler's elastica model which is the higher order model of essential meaning that reduces the curve of all level lines in the image. Traditional numerical technique for reducing the energy in higher order models is difficult. An effective minimization algorithm depending on the graph cuts for reducing the energy in the Euler's elastic model, by reducing the issues of explaining a series of simple graph representing issues. The sequence contains the links to the gradient flow of the energy function and joins to a minimum point.

The method for enhancing the contrast of the images is Histogram Equalization (HE). HE is an ease of using and yields better result comparing to other methods. Histogram Equalization procedures works on digital images by remapping the gray levels of the image which is by likelihood allocation of the input gray levels.

Histogram Equalization is a method that increases the contrast of an image by increasing the dynamic range of intensity given to pixels with the most probable intensity values. One transformation function that accomplishes this is a cumulative distribution function. The transformation of the histogram equalization function is scaled such that the least intense value in the original image is mapped to a zero intensity value in the equalized image. As well, the most intense value in the original image is mapped to an intensity value that is equal to the maximum intensity value determined by the bit depth of the image.

This produces results that have a dynamic range that is slightly larger than produced by the histogram equalization algorithm described by Gonzalez and Woods (2009). The HE methods can be grouped into two standard forms such as global and local histogram equalization method. Global Histogram Equalization (GHE) works on the histogram information of the entire input image for its function.

In GHE remaps the gray levels in the form that the contrast stretching becomes imperfect in several dominating gray levels. The grey level has larger image histogram components and source important disparity loss for other minute ones. Local Histogram Equalization (LHE) uses a minute slide window through each pixel of the photo image. The every pixel in the photo image consecutively falls in the window which is taken into account of HE method. The gray level mapping for improvement is completed only for the center pixel of that window. Conversely, LHE requires high computational cost and sometimes cause over-enhancement in some portion of the image. Another complexity is that LHE improve the noise level in the input photo image all the length of image features.

Multi Histogram Equalization (MHE) decomposes the image into several sub-images which is based on the histogram information of the image Vijay.A et.al (2013). This information consists of classes, threshold levels, where each histogram class represents a sub- image. The decompose process can be done as like image segmentation by using the threshold value. The number of sub-images depends on the decomposition process. MHE has three steps as: Multi histogram decomposition, Finding the optimal thresholds, and Automatic thresholding criterion.

Image enhancement via optimal contrast-tone mapping Xiaolin Wu (2011) has the primary departure of histogram equalization. Optimal contrast-tone mapping maximizes predictable difference and gain subject to an upper limit on tone distortion and optionally to other constraints. The minimization of the useful is explicitly acquired Olivier Bernard et al. (2009) with the B-spline coefficients. Each step of minimization is expressed during a convolution procedure. The color feature is one of the most broadly used image objects in image retrieval. It is relatively robust to backdrop complexity and self-governing of image size and direction.

An object illustration by sparse coding and multi-scale max pooling Qing Wang et al. (2012) symbolize a linear classifier to differentiate the objective from the background. The background image description for target and backdrop are measured on variations over time. The non-orthogonal, over-complete lexicon learned from local patches build visual prior more capable for object description. Max-margin learning algorithm Jianping Fan et al. (2011) attains more effectual training of a huge number of inter-related classifiers for multi-label picture annotation application. Max-margin learning algorithm fails to enlarge cluster-based parallel computing stage for inter-related classifier. It is also not very attractive to consider higher order nearest neighbors in inter-related classifier process.

The existing variation models based upon Higher Order Derivatives (Variation-HOD) Egil Bae et al. (2011) minimizes the curvature of all level lines in the image. An efficient minimization algorithm based upon graph cuts fails to have the exact relationship on gradient flow. Euler's Elastica model shortens the problem by solving a series of graph representable problems. Euler's Elastica model has relations to the gradient flow of the energy function, and joins to a least point. The curvature based models do not fit directly to exploit the max flow computation into the framework.

The Nonlinear Dynamic Range Adjustment (NDRA) Josef Strom Bartunek (2013) has four updated processing blocks: preprocessing, global analysis, local analysis and matched filtering. In the preprocessing and local analysis blocks, a nonlinear dynamic range adjustment method is used. In the global analysis and matched filtering blocks, different forms of order statistical filters are applied. These processing blocks yield an improved and new adaptive image processing method. But this efficient minimization algorithm based upon graph fails to have the exact relationship on gradient flow. This method combines and updates existing processing blocks but a comprehensive and efficient analysis of the different chosen design parameters are not performed. The effective optimization technique does not implement the preprocessing steps to reduce the number of instructions, noise and improve the quality.

The Intensity Histogram Equalization (IHE) method improves image contrast by removing the noise level on the preprocessing step. The IHE is a method that improves the contrast in an image, in order to stretch out the intensity range. That is, this method usually increases the global contrast of images, especially when the usable data of the image is represented by close contrast values. Histogram equalization accomplishes this by effectively spreading out the most frequent intensity values. By this way, the intensities can be better distributed on the histogram and allows for areas of lower local contrast to gain a higher contrast.

The IHE is incorporated here and the preprocessing step comprises of three steps: the mask production, enlightenment equalization, and color normalization. The intensity factor is used to improve the brightness on the photo image in IHE method. Further, the photo image uses the histogram threshold rate for exact association with gradient flow. IHE method improves the level of contrast enhancement and noise robustness.

The structure of paper is as follows. The Section-1 describes about the image contrast enhancement and drawbacks in the Histogram Equalization. The Intensity Histogram Equalization method is demonstrated in Section-2 to improve the brightness and to particularly remove the noise level. Then follows experimental performance in which the result analysis of image contrast enhancement on Corel Image Features Data Set is highlighted in section-3. Finally Section-4 concluded the notes offered from our outcomes.

IMAGE CONTRAST ENHANCEMENT USING INTENSITY HISTOGRAM EQUALIZATION METHOD

Intensity Histogram Equalization method is an easy and successful image contrast enhancement method. IHE has the following processes. Mask production, enlightenment equalization, and color normalization. IHE first removes the noise level using these processes. Mask production labels the pixels, and Region-of-interest (ROI) in the entire image eliminates the background completely from image and produces the binary image for each band. Further these bands are combined together using the logical operators which identifies the associated masks. The mean intensity value is calculated by using enlightenment equalization, by which it is possible to know the intensity values of each pixel.

The process of classifying the image and computing the color capacity in the images is termed as color normalization. In order to constantly point out colored objects and lesions, color must transmit directly to the inherent properties of the imaged objects and be self-determining of imaging conditions to enhance the quality. Intensity Histogram Equalization method is proposed for disparity enhancement and in that way introduces intensity to improve the brightness particularly to eradicate the noise level. IHE offer maximal brightness preservation using the intensity rate factor. After removing the noise level, the histogram threshold rate was mechanically calculated using pixel value statistics for each color band.

The IHE method looks into some level of contrast with neighbors by the max-flow computations. IHE method possible to relate practical approach with optimization based solutions for a successful contrast

Figure 1. Architecture diagram of intensity histogram equalization method

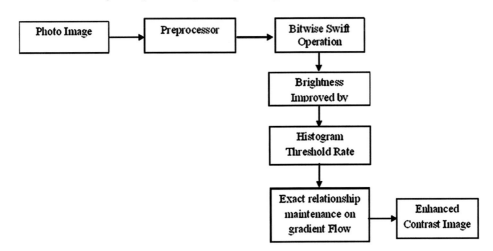

enhancement, brightness and for maintaining the histogram threshold rate. The architecture diagram of Intensity Histogram Equalization method is shown in Figure 1.

In Figure 1 IHE considers the photo image for enhancing the contrast. The photo image undergoes bitwise swift operation after the preprocessing phase. The brightness is improved by selecting associated intensity value of the image. IHE presents a histogram threshold rate which aims to enhance and preserve the image quality with exact relationship maintenance on gradient flow. In summing up, IHE method goal is to obtain a visually agreeable image enhancement method that has low computational intricacy and works well with picture images.

Preprocessing on IHE Method

The initial process for IHE is the preprocessing phase. The preprocessing phase has three levels of noise removal. They are mask production, enlightenment equalization and color normalization. The pictorial representation of the preprocessing step is shown in Figure 2.

As shown in Figure 2, the first step of the preprocessing is the mask generation which labels the pixels of the photo image. The background of the entire image is subtracted by Region-of-Interest (ROI). IHE produces the masks by the threshold value of the three color channel (i.e.,) R, G, B color bands. Each band has the output as a binary image. The threshold value was considered using pixel value statistics outside the ROI for each color band. The binary outcome of all bands is combined by using the logical operators, which identifies the major associated mask for max flow computation.

The second step is the enlightenment equalization, which is non-uniform due to the variation of the photo image. To overcome the non-uniform illumination, each pixel is equalized using the following equation

$$E_{mean}(rp,cp) = E(rp,cp) + i - \bar{E}(rp,cp) \qquad (1)$$

Figure 2. Preprocessor of IHE

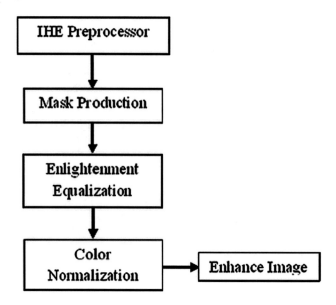

Enlightenment equalization 'E_{mean}' measures the mean intensity value using the row pixel 'rp' and column pixel 'cp'. 'i' is the average intensity and $\bar{E}(rp, cp)$ is the mean intensity value of pixels within a photo image 'p' of size N×N. IHE enlightenment equalization is used to calculate the mean intensity value, even though the resulting photo images look very similar.

The final step color normalization is useful in the classifying the given photo images showed with significant differences. In order to consistently point out colored objects and lesions, color must relate directly to the inherent properties of the photo imaged objects and be autonomous of imaging conditions. Usually, imaging conditions such as lighting geometry and the imaging device scales pixel values in a photo image.

IHE Function

The preprocessor of the IHE yields a binary image in which the mean intensity values are calculated. After this process, the Intensity Histogram equalization method utilizes the histogram of the photo image to obtain a distinct mapping D[n] which is used to modify the pixel values. IHE finds a mapping to obtain an image with a histogram that is as close as possible to a uniform distribution to fully exploit the dynamic range and to have a max-flow computation. D[n] is regarded as an intensity discrete probability mass function of the pixel intensities. The discrete mapping function in the IHE discrete form is given as

$$D[n] = (2^f - 1)\sum_{j=0}^{n} i(j) \tag{2}$$

In (2), f is the number of bits used to represent the pixel values, and n $\in$ [0, 2^f - 1]. IHE of the processed photo image is uniform with the discrete nature pixel intensities. IHE is possible to enhance the contrast by stretching the color of the photo image to make the pixels brighter. IHE produces more natural looking which enhances the contrast of the image by discrete mapping.

The approximated probability density function (PDF) and cumulative distribution function [CDF] c[n], can be obtained from the intensity histogram i[n] of a photo image. The discrete mapping function is a leveled version of IHE which uses the image histogram to obtain the higher contrast.

The probability density function (PDF) is defined as

$$PDF(l_n) = \frac{V_n}{N} \tag{3}$$

From (3), l_n = 0,1,.......R-1. V_n is the number of times level 'l' appears in an photo image. The probability density function $PDF(l_n)$ is used to attain exact relationship on gradient flow. P{i,j) is the given photo image with 'i' pixels and a contrast level of [0,R-1].

The cumulative density function (CDF) in IHE is obtained by

$$CDF(l_n) = \sum_{i=0}^{k} PDF(i) \tag{4}$$

The cumulative density function (CDF) in (4) is used to attain exact relationship on gradient flow and for efficient analysis of the different chosen design parameters. Using the execution sum of histogram values, histogram equalization plots an input level l_n into an output level $\overline{l_n}$.

$$\overline{l_n} = (R-1) * CDF(l_n) \tag{5}$$

The above equation indicates the relationship between l_n and $l_n + 1$ which has direct relation with PDF of the input photo image. In the IHE, the pixel values are uniformly distributed with values across their range. IHE method enhances the background of the photo image and often produces the probable effects in the photo image. The original photo image and the equalized IHE photo image are clearly seen with the enhanced photo image by removing the noise.

The IHE algorithm illustrates the processing step one by one and it is shown below,

Figure 3 illustrates the algorithmic step of IHE method is adjusted depending upon the photo input image's contrast. Low contrast photo images have narrow histograms in which de-noising are performed by intensity histogram equalization. The stretching IHE with histogram threshold rate improve the image quality with bitwise shift operation. Observation of these entire photo images show that the IHE method perform well. However, it is usually desired to have some quantitative measures in addition to subjective assessment.

Figure 3. IHE algorithm

Input: Corel Image Features Data Set photo Images taken for process

Output: De-noising and contrast Photo Images

Begin

Step 1: Read input image, perform preprocessing steps

    Step 1.1: Mask production which generate binary image

    Step 1.2: Enlightenment equalization forms mean intensity value

    Step 1.3: Color Normalization enhance image quality

Step 2: Perform the image contrast using a bitwise shift operation

Step 3: Calculate the histogram using pixels that has a magnitude larger than a given threshold which improves the brightness.

Step 4: Count the number of pixels included in the histogram threshold rate

Step 5: **Calculate** in the discrete mapping function, resulting in increased utilization of active range.

Step 6: Obtain enhanced contrast image with intensity value factor.

End

EXPERIMENTAL PERFORMANCE AND RESULT ANALYSIS

The Intensity Histogram Equalization method is implemented using MATLAB. The Corel Image Features Data Set is used for processing the IHE steps, which contain image features extracted from a Corel image collection. Corel Image Features Data Set holds 68,040 photo images from a mixture of categories. Four sets of features are accessible in Corel Image Features Data Set based on the color histogram, color histogram layout, color moments, and co-occurrences.

Each set of features in Corel Image Features Data Set is stored in a separate file and each line corresponds to a single image. These images are used in the evaluation of IHE method, Variation-HOD technique and Nonlinear Dynamic Range Adjustment (NDRA) method. The initial value in a line corresponds to the image ID and feature vector (e.g. color histogram) of the image. The similar image has the equivalent ID in all files but the image ID is not the same as the image filename in Corel Image Features Data Set.

Color Histogram and color histogram layout in Corel Image Features Data Set used for IHE method evaluation with 32 dimensions and each dimension value is the density of each color in the entire image. Histogram intersection between Color Histograms of two images is used to determine the correspondence surrounded by two images. Color Moments contain 9 magnitudes and each one contains H, S, and V in HSV color space with mean, standard deviation, and skew value. Euclidean distance between Color Moments of two images is used to represent the dissimilarity (distance) between two images.

Co-occurrence Texture contains 16 dimensions (4 x 4) which are transformed into 16 gray-scale images. The co-occurrence in 4 directions is worked out horizontal, vertical, and two diagonal directions. The 16 values are Second Angular Moment, Contrast, Inverse Difference Moment, and Entropy. Euclidean distance between Color Moments in Corel Image Features Data Set of two images is used to calculate the divergence (distance) among two images. Experiments evaluation is conducted with the set of images with varying parametric metrics namely reliability, noise removal ratio, intensity percentage value, brightness quality efficiency, max-flow computational complexity, and false positive error.

Intensity Histogram Equalization is compared against the existing variation models based upon Higher Order Derivatives, and Nonlinear Dynamic Range Adjustment method. The reliability in IHE method is the ability of the photo image to improve the image contrast under the stated conditions for a specified period of time. The noise level in the background of the photo image is measured and removes the noise from that image using the IHE method. The IHE method is measured in terms of Decibel (dB).

The brightness quality defines the contrast quality enhancement on the photo image and measured in terms of the pixel rate. Max-Flow Computational complexity in image contrast enhancement focuses on inherent difficulty, and relating those spatial frequency classes to each other. False Positive Error (FPE) denotes the incorrectly identified paths on the photo image.

The Figure 4 (a) and (b) denotes the FPE on the existing and proposed system, whereas the pixel count with errors is reduced in IHE method. Intensity of the photo image denotes the measurement of overall preprocessing, brightness and contrast histogram threshold rate.

The Image contrast reliability rate of the intensity histogram equalization is compared with Nonlinear Dynamic Range Adjustment Method and Variation HOD is shown in Table 1. Similarly, Figure 5 shows graph of the image contrast reliability of each technique and evaluates the system. The intensity histogram i[n] of a photo image give the approximate probability density function (PDF) of its pixel intensities to improve the reliability rate. The reliability rate is 11% improved when compared with the Variation-HOD [1]. The approximate cumulative distribution function [CDF] c[n], is obtained from i[n]. The discrete mapping function is a leveled version of IHE which uses the image histogram to obtain the higher contrast reliability by 5% when compared with the NDRA method [2].

Figure 4. (a) FPE on existing system; (b) FPE on IHE method

 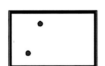

Table 1. Image contrast reliability tabulation

Technique	Image Contrast Reliability (%)
Variation-HOD	82
NDRA method	88
IHE method	93

Figure 5. Image contrast reliability measure

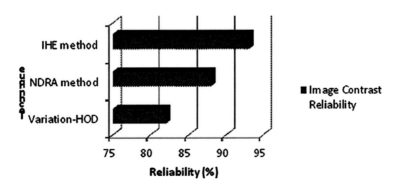

Table 2. Tabulation for noise removal rate

Photo Image Count	Noise Removal Rate (dB)		
	Variation-HOD	NDRA Method	IHE Method
5	8.54	9.24	10.00
10	7.18	7.88	8.45
15	7.15	8.22	9.33
20	6.82	7.52	8.53
25	7.43	8.19	9.12
30	7.92	8.45	9.89
35	7.47	8.12	9.54

Figure 6. Noise removal rate measure

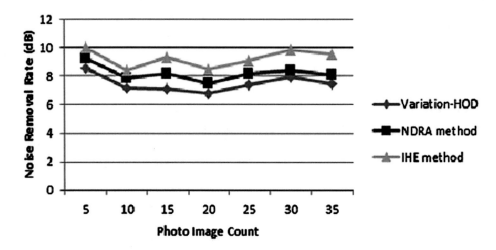

The noise removal rate is improved in IHE method when compared with the Variation-HOD [1] and NDRA method [2]. The cumulative density function (CDF) is used to attain exact relationship on gradient flow and for efficient analysis of the different chosen design parameters. Using the execution sum of histogram values, histogram equalization plots an input level l_n into an output level $\overline{l_n}$ and reduces the noise rate. The removal rate (Table 2, Figure 6) is 7 – 17% improved in IHE method when compared with Variation-HOD and 17 – 30% improved when compared with NDRA method [2].

Intensity Histogram Equalization (IHE) method for disparity enhancement introduces the intensity to improve the brightness particularly to eradicate the noise level. The brightness on the photo image is improved using the intensity factor in IHE method. The photo image uses the histogram threshold rate for exact association with gradient flow. IHE method improves the level of contrast enhancement and improves the noise removal rate.

CONCLUSION

Intensity Histogram Equalization method is developed for removing the noise defects. IHE method has the preprocessor with the process like mask production, enlightenment equalization, and color normalization for efficient analysis of different chosen parameters. Mask production labels the pixels and Region-of-Interest (ROI) in the complete photo image which eliminates the backdrop of the image to produce a binary image. To obtain a real-time implementable algorithm, IHE avoids complex calculations and improve the max-flow computational operations. IHE finds a mapping to get hold of a photo image with an intensity histogram, which is as close as credible to the equal distribution for making use of the dynamic range. The result analysis shows the effectiveness in IHE algorithm when compared to conventional NDRA method and Higher Order Derivatives algorithms. The noise removal ratio is averagely 11.798% improved in IHE method when evaluated on existing system. IHE offers a level of controllability and different levels of contrast enhancement with 5% improved result in reliability, noise removal ratio, and brightness quality efficiency.

REFERENCES

Bae, Shi, & Tai. (2011). Graph Cuts for Curvature Based Image Denoising. *IEEE Transactions on Image Processing, 20*(5).

Bartunek, Nilsson, Sallberg, & Claesson. (2013). Adaptive Fingerprint Image Enhancement with Emphasis on Pre-processing of Data. *IEEE Transactions on Image Processing, 22*(2).

Bernard, Friboulet, Thévenaz, & Unser. (2009). Variational B-Spline Level-Set: A Linear Filtering Approach for Fast Deformable Model Evolution. *IEEE Transactions on Image Processing, 18*(6).

Ciancio, A. (2011). *No-Reference Blur Assessment of Digital Pictures Based on Multifeature Classifiers. IEEE Transactions on Image Processing, 20(1)*.

Cui & Li. (2011). Adaptive Multi wavelet-Based Watermarking Through JPW Masking. IEEE Transactions on Image Processing, 20(4).

Fan, J. (2011). *Structured Max-Margin Learning for Inter-Related Classifier Training and Multilabel Image Annotation. IEEE Transactions on Image Processing, 20(3)*.

Gonzalez & Woods. (2009). *Digital Image Processing*. Pearson Education.

He, R., & Hu, B.-G. (2011). *Robust Principal Component Analysis Based on Maximum Correntropy Criterion. IEEE Transactions on Image Processing, 20(6)*.

Kayabol, & Zerubia. (2013). Unsupervised amplitude and texture classification of SAR images with multinomial latent model. *IEEE Transaction on Image Processing*.

Kotkar & Gharde. (2013). Review of Various Image Contrast Enhancement Techniques. *International Journal of Innovative Research in Science, Engineering and Technology, 2*(7).

Lin, H.-H. (2011). *Regularized Background Adaptation: A Novel Learning Rate Control Scheme for Gaussian Mixture Modeling. IEEE Transactions on Image Processing, 20(3)*.

Liu, Y.-F. (2011). *Inverse Halftoning Based on the Bayesian Theorem. IEEE Transactions on Image Processing, 20(4).*

McEwen, Puy, Thiran, Vandergheynst, Van De Ville, & Wiaux. (2013). Sparse image reconstruction on the sphere: Implications of a new sampling theorem. *IEEE Transactions on Image Processing, 22(6).*

Natarajan & Shantharajah. (2016). An Effective Segmentation Pattern Using Multi-Class Independent Component Analysis on High Quality Color Texture Images. *Research Journal of Applied Sciences, Engineering and Technology, 12*(9), 926-932.

Natarajan, & Shantharajah. (2014). Image Denoising and Contrast Via Intensity Equalization Method. *International Review on Computers and Software, 9*(6).

Nguyen, Patel, Nasrabadi, & Chellappa. (2013). Design of Non-Linear Kernel Dictionaries for Object Recognition. *IEEE Transactions on Image Processing, 22*(12).

Oikonomopoulos, A. (2011). *Spatiotemporal Localization and Categorization of Human Actions in Unsegmented Image Sequences. IEEE Transactions on Image Processing, 20(4).*

Pang, Huang, Yan, Jiang, & Qin. (2011). Transferring Boosted Detectors Towards Viewpoint and Scene Adaptiveness. *IEEE Transactions on Image Processing, 20*(5).

Tang & Zhang. (2011). Secure Image Encryption without Size Limitation Using Arnold Transform and Random Strategies. *Journal of Multimedia, 6*(2).

Wang, Q. (2012). Transferring Visual Prior for Online Object Tracking. *IEEE Transactions on Image Processing.*

Woolfe, F. (2011). *Autofluorescence Removal by Non-Negative Matrix Factorization. IEEE Transactions on Image Processing, 20(4).*

Wu. (2011). A Linear Programming Approach for Optimal Contrast-Tone Mapping. *IEEE Transactions on Image Processing, 20*(5).

Zhou, Bao, & Chen. (2013). Image Encryption Using a New Parametric Switching Chaotic System. *Signal Processing, 93*(11), 3039-3052.

Zhuang, H. (2012). *Multichannel Pulse-Coupled-Neural-Network-Based Color Image Segmentation for Object Detection. IEEE Transactions on Industrial Electronics, 59(8).*

Chapter 6

A New Image Encryption Method Based on Improved Cipher Block Chaining with Optimization Technique

Kuppusamy Krishnamoorthy
Alagappa University, India

Mahalakshmi Jeyabalu
Alagappa University, India

ABSTRACT

Security of images in transmission medium is most prime issue found in literature. Encryption of images is a way to secure it from unauthorized access. The authors in this chapter insist on the encryption of images via block ciphers. Block ciphers works simultaneously as well as on chunks. In this chapter, an encryption method using improved cipher block chaining is proposed to encrypt RGB color images. For every encryption methodology, key generation process is the most important phase. The authors proposed sub-optimal key generation algorithm and this nature inspired optimization technique reveals complex keys, remains very useful for decision making in dynamic environment. Key generation is crafted as complex with this mathematical model that overcomes the predicament key problem exists in existing methods and upgrades quality of encryption. Results of the proposed algorithm show the efficiency and its resistance against various cryptanalytic attacks.

INTRODUCTION

Security of the data, when transmitted through communication medium is most prime issue found in literature. In recent decades, images are used as a medium to transfer the messages between the consigner and consignee since it is considered to be more secure than the text data. It is used at various fields such as in defense services, Health care services, E- Learning etc. Fundamental issue is that the images need utmost protection while pass through networks, to resist it from various authentications and authoriza-

DOI: 10.4018/978-1-5225-2053-5.ch006

tion vulnerabilities. Intruders may hack the information completely or partially modify some content. Various security mechanisms like authentication, digital signatures, and cryptographic algorithms are used to protect images from unauthorized attacks (Mahalakshmi & Kuppusamy, 2016).

Cryptography is the science of designing mathematical models to secure the images from interloper attacks. Encryption and Decryption are the two phases to be handled in any cryptographic process. Encryption is the phase of converting the original user defined plain data into unintelligible format called cipher, where as decryption remains as the reverse to convert the cipher back to original. The encryption may be categorized either as full encryption or partial (Ramkrishna Das& Saurabh Dutta, 2013). Symmetric key Encryption and Asymmetric Key Encryption are the two categories of cryptography for which the Symmetric key uses single secret key shared between the consigner and consignee. In Asymmetric key encryption two keys are involved, one for the encryption and another for the decryption. The authors in this chapter focus on novel symmetric key encryption method to secure the images.

Various encryption algorithms are developed with ultimate goal to reduce the computational cost and increasing its performance (Yas & Alsultanny, 2008). Secret key algorithms are devised to work either as streams or as blocks. In stream cipher encryption finite numbers of characters are encrypted, and in block ciphers blocks or chunks of data is encrypted simultaneously (Panduranga, &Naveen Kumar, 2012). The main objective of this chapter is to develop an algorithm to elevate security to the images that are passed through the open networks between the sender and receiver. A plenty of approaches are employed to encrypt the images by various authors in the literature. This chapter brings out a new hybrid algorithm, to encrypt the RGB (Red, Green, Blue) image. This approach is expressed by a mathematical model formulated with improved cipher block chaining, the mode used for encrypting data at chunks. Every block of data differs and also it is the self synchronizing mode where the error propagation is less. It overcomes various security threats to the images when transferred between communicating entities.

Authentication and integrity maintenance of the images when transferred through open networks is considered in this chapter. Security policies must be examined by both sender and receiver so as to maintain the authenticity of the image. The image encryption method proposed in this chapter, is based on block cipher combined with logical substitution operations to strengthen the encryption code. In the scheme of key generation, the optimization technique is operated so as to minimize the cost of algorithm by means of time and speed. The genetic algorithm is one among the optimization technique, is the direct approach that uses a specific objective function to minimize the total cost of the taken for the execution. Genetic Algorithm is mainly consumed for specific selection of features in the images to extract or to cipher. Multi-objective function is generated for the proposed algorithm, one is to minimize the execution cost and the other is to reduce the execution speed. Genetic Algorithm is iterative optimization procedure used to solve complex optimization problems either it is maximize or to minimize (Kalyanmoy Deb, 2005). GA's are characterized by its robustness against attacks as well as ability to work with non-convex problems (Fossati et al., 2015).

Organization of the Chapter

In Section 2, the authors explained the various related symmetric key algorithms and their outcomes. After a fast overview, in section 3, the proposed encryption algorithm for the RGB color images is presented in more detail, particularly key scheming. In section 4, experimental results are placed to demonstrate the algorithm's performance on RGB images. Then, in section 5, the algorithm used in this chapter for image encryption and decryption using the proposed approach is in-depth compared with existing accepted algorithms of various authors by means of security analyses and verify the robustness of the algorithm. In Section 6, the conclusion of this approach is drawn.

BACKGROUND

Ali et al.(2015),proposed a method that, overcomes the fixed s-box limitations and improves the performance of AES for encrypting images, particularly when the image resolution is large. Replacement is done in the mix-column stage, with that of chaotic mapping and the exclusive disjunction operation is done to Reduce computational complexity. Heba Elhoseny et al. *(2015)*, explains the usage of various modes of operations, and presented a technique for chaotic map encryption. The authors of this article concentrated on fractional fourier transform domain for image encryption. According to the results evaluated the cipher feedback mode operation is suited for encryption, rather than in the block Cipher mode. The algorithm presented by the authors with its simplicity and high speed, provides security.

Manish Kumar, Mishra, and Sharma (2014), took over the credits on the first approach on the RGB color images. The authors have formulated a formula for all the possible range to choose keys for encrypting and decrypting an RGB image. The approach of the authors is suitable for larger size images that depend upon the possible keys parameterized. Color image encryption based on the affine transform in gyrator domain is given by Chen, Du, Liu, and Yang. *(2013)*. Ibrahim F. Elashry (2012), discussed on the method for encrypting images with few details using Rijndael and RC6 Block Ciphers in the Electronic Code Book Mode. According to the author's approach the preprocessing method gives the encryption algorithms the ability to encrypt images using parallel processing method. Repeated patterns are removed in the preprocessing phase leads to consistency in the image to be encrypted.

Liu Hongjun & Wang Xingyuan (2010), reported on the color image encryption using the Chaotic maps and one-time key generation. According to the authors report, the ciphered image is robust against noise, and makes known attack unfeasible. One-time key cryptosystem based on two robust chaotic maps generated by the authors encrypt the images for which the key space is large enough. Adbul Hamid Ragab, Osama S. Farag Alla, Amin Y. Noaman (2015), designed the robust chaotic block cipher (RCBC) encryption algorithm for image encryption. The authors of the paper have compared the performance of their algorithm against the RC6 and RC5 algorithms. The results of the algorithm show,it would stand better in the parameters of avalanche effect of the encrypted image, the correlation coefficient, maximum and irregular deviation and entropy factors.

Salim Wadi & Nasharuddin Zainal (2013), described a rapid encryption algorithm for Gray Scale High quality digital image encryption, based on the AES Algorithm. Some modifications are proposed by the authors that have increased the performance of AES algorithm in terms of time ciphering and pattern appearance. Number of rounds taken place initially is decreased, subsequently followed by replacement of the Substitution box, along with reducing the hardware requirements. The modified form reduces the time taken for an image to get encrypted and thus increases the execution speed. The method is compatible with High Definition images while fulfills the security requirements.

Osama Ahmed Khashan & Abdullah Mohd Zin (2013), explained on the Efficient Adaptive of Transparent Spatial Digital Image Encryption scheme. A model for transparent encryption and decryption on the fly for digital image files stored on hard disk is done by the authors providing sufficient level of security with reasonable computational complexity. Filter driver technology is used by the authors to encrypt the images with the transformation methods. Ch.-H. Lin T.-H. Chen & Ch.-S. Wu (2013), discussed on the chaining random grids for the batch image encryption scheme. The author's algorithm remains suitable to deal with batch binary, grey-scale and RGB color images. This method requires neither extra pixel expansion or any encoding basis matrix, which are basis and inevitable for adapted visual cryptography. The author's schemes are particularly suitable for a scenario in which clients with lightweight computation capability shoulder the role of decrypting the cipher-grids.

Noorul Hussain Ubaidur Rahman Chithralekha Balamurugan & Rajapandian Mariappan. (2015), focused on encryption of images using the DNA based computing. An unique nature inspired simulation based technique, applicable for DNA encryption and decryption is developed. It fulfills all of the functional and non-functional attributes for the encryption algorithm that reduces the cost of computation and increases the performance analysis.

Wang Xing-Yuan, Chen Feng, Wang Tian (2010), take the credit of designing the compound mode of confusion with diffusion for encrypting the images. The chaotic mapping technique is involved for the encryption process. The authors reveal the statistical analysis with higher order, key sensitivity and space analysis that show the effectiveness of the author's image encryption procedure. A block cipher encrypts plaintext in fixed-size n-bit blocks. Various modes of operation are there in literature to encrypt the data in blocks. One of the standard and efficient mode is the cipher block chaining, that is identical ciphertext blocks result when the same plaintext is enciphered under the same key and Initialization Vector.

Narendra K. Pareek & Vinod Patidar (2014), explained about protecting medical images using the genetic operations. An encryption method for gray scale medical images based on the features of genetic algorithms is brought out by the authors that have resulted in high order of security and thus can be used for real-time transmission of digital gray scale medical images. Various security analyses such as correlation coefficient, entropy, NPCR, key sensitivity and MSE are performed to reveal the work progress of the author's algorithm.

The literature review describes the use of various encryption modes that yields better results. Various security based services offered by the cloud paradigm along with the limitations is explained by the state of art. This chapter focuses on a novel encryption scheme for image encryption to enhance the encryption quality as well as to minimize the complexities in terms of cost and time with better results than traditional one.

PROPOSED ENCRYPTION ALGORITHM FOR RGB COLOR IMAGES

Image Encryption

Images are considered as a medium for transfer the messages between the consigner and consignee in confidential manner from the past decades. Maintaining the authentication of the images being transferred with raw information is major issue found in the state-of-art. Almost, a lot of algorithms have been there in the literature to secure the images from intruder attacks, each with their own merits and demerits. The goal of the researcher in this chapter focuses on delivering a compound algorithm, for RGB (Red, Green, Blue) color images that protects the images from illicit molest.

Images may be varied types such as in the form of Binary, Gray-Scale, CMYK, HSV, YIQ, RGB etc. In this chapter, the RGB color image encryption is taken into account. RGB is basic yet powerful color model almost engaged for a lot of encryption mechanisms. Encryption of color images rather than binary of gray-scale is little complicated. Color Spaces basically, mathematical model which contains color components as their elements. RGB color images are categorized between the ranges as follows in equation 1, each color channel as represented in above equation 2, in which "i" represents 0-255 pixel values to get encrypted. The authors in this research work, encrypt each color channel individually by dividing the channels, and finally have detached the separated color channel to produce the cipher image. Authors' contribution in this part is to separate the color components dynamically and encrypt them in such a manner to make the intrusion process complex to achieve.

$$
\begin{bmatrix}
R \to 0 - 255 \\
G \to 0 - 255 \\
B \to 0 - 255
\end{bmatrix}
\tag{1}
$$

$$
R_n = \int_1^n R_{n \to 1 to i} \, G_n = \int_1^n G_{n \to 1 to i} \, B_n = \int_1^n B_{n \to 1 to i}
\tag{2}
$$

INFORMATION ON THE PRELIMINARY STRUCTURE OF IMAGES

Color channels are one among various modes to transfer the messages in the communication medium with more security. The state of art makes it easy to define any color models in ease of mathematical structure. The basic model for RGB color image is as presented in Equation 1. This section consists of the information on separation and detachment of color components for the encryption of images.

Matrix Model is considered as the way to place the color components in this proposed research work. It takes around 8 x 8 sizes each with 64 pixels matrices. This structure is common way so as to alleviate ease of access and to maintain uniformity in the way of encryption. The image consists of the uncompressed image format such as in the JPEG is converted to individual color channels as red channel, green channel and blue channel respectively. This is then followed by bits conversion of every pixel between the positions 0-255, for depicted equation 3 to equation 4,

$$
\left(
\begin{array}{l}
R_0^{255} \to 138 R_0^{255} \to 153 R_0^{255} \to 28 R_0^{255} \to 46 \\
G_0^{255} \to 212 G_0^{255} \to 89 G_0^{255} \to 189 G_0^{255} \to 88 \\
B_0^{255} \to 76 B_0^{255} \to 131 B_0^{255} \to 98 B_0^{255} \to 190 \\
\\
R_0^{255} \to 78 R_0^{255} \to 210 R_0^{255} \to 89 R_0^{255} \to 8 \\
G_0^{255} \to 126 G_0^{255} \to 194 G_0^{255} \to 234 G_0^{255} \to 143 \\
B_0^{255} \to 167 B_0^{255} \to 90 B_0^{255} \to 174 B_0^{255} \to 95
\end{array}
\right)
\tag{3}
$$

$$\begin{aligned}
R \to 138 &\to \begin{bmatrix} 10001010 \end{bmatrix} \\
R \to 153 &\to \begin{bmatrix} 10011001 \end{bmatrix} \\
R \to 28 &\to \begin{bmatrix} 00011100 \end{bmatrix} \\
R \to 46 &\to \begin{bmatrix} 00101110 \end{bmatrix} \\
R \to 78 &\to \begin{bmatrix} 01001110 \end{bmatrix} \\
R \to 210 &\to \begin{bmatrix} 11010010 \end{bmatrix} \\
R \to 89 &\to \begin{bmatrix} 01011001 \end{bmatrix} \\
R \to 8 &\to \begin{bmatrix} 00001000 \end{bmatrix}
\end{aligned} \tag{4}$$

As depicted in equation4, consecutively for Green and Blue pixels also bits conversion is performed and transformed as block each consists of 8 x 8 color components. Let us assume, that if M_{ij} is a matrix of order n, then i,j represents the row and column elements respectively of order n. This conversion is done almost the last pixel is converted individually. The separation of color channel makes the process easier to encrypt whereas the bits conversion makes the process to perform faster.

KEY SCHEMING

Improved Cipher Block Chaining Key Generation for RGB Image Encryption

The proposed encryption method for RGB Image encryption is implemented with multiple key generations. The total number of keys involved for the encryption process is about three key generations. This section consists of the procedure for the first key generation from the cipher block chaining encryption operation mode. This encryption algorithm falls under symmetric key encryption method, which uses similar key for both encryption and decryption. The following is the procedure to generate the key from Cipher block chaining mode. [Figure 1depicts the basic construction of the CBC operation.

Step 1: Initialize the matrix M_{ij} with key elements of size 8x8, in which is the elements of the row and j is the elements of the column.

Step 2: Initialize the original image with the size M_{size}, with its size i*j, where i=row, j=column.

Step 3: Extract Pixel Values of original Image, for every color channels individually as per the equations 3 & 4.

Step 4: Individual color channels are separated and matrix is constructed till end of the file is reached, as R1 = (R_a, R_b,R_c, ...R_n.) and G1 = (G_a, G_b,G_c, ...G_n.), B1 = (B_a, B_b,B_c, ...B_n.), n ≤ Ri, Gi, Bi where i=1,2,3…n as in Equation 5,

Figure 1. Block Diagram of ICBC Process

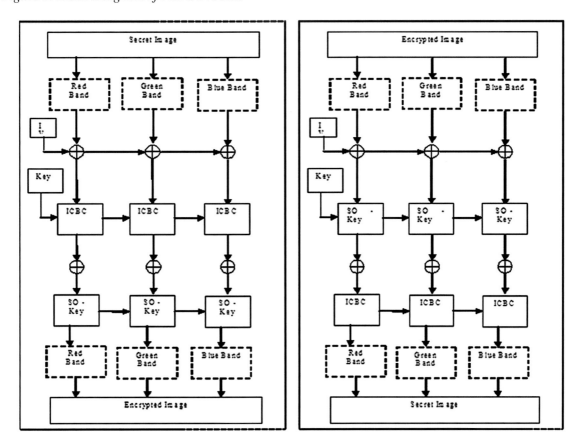

$$M_{ij} = \begin{bmatrix} 10101101 \\ 10010101 \\ 01011101 \\ 10010010 \\ 10101011 \\ 01010101 \\ 11001011 \\ 10011010 \end{bmatrix} \tag{5}$$

Step 5: Initialization Vector is provided with 8 elements, which is in binary positions as in equation 6.

$$M_{ij} = \begin{bmatrix} 11001010 \end{bmatrix} \tag{6}$$

Step 6: First row of the matrix is XORed with initialization vector elements.
Step 7: The output of the first row is then XORed with the second row element of the matrix.

Step 8: The process is repeated until all the pixel values of each color channel is converted.

Step 9: The modified sequence, thus obtained contains the binary message bits according to the appropriate type.

Step 10: The output matrices thus generated is considered as the first Key matrix to be substituted with the original matrix.

Key Generation for RGB Image Encryption from Psudeorandom Number Generators

The second key for the proposed encryption algorithm is generated from the pseudorandom number generators. The procedure for the process is given below,

Step 1: The output matrices obtained after the first substitution process is intended for the process.

Step 2: Key matrix of size 8 x 8 is generated from the pseudorandom number generators.

Step 3: Substitution operation is performed between the key matrix and the input matrix.

Step 4: Results obtain from the process is partially ciphered matrix.

Sub-Optimal Key Generation for RGB Image Encryption from Optimization Technique

The proposed image encryption algorithm comprises of sub-optimal key generation process and this nature inspired optimization technique reveals complex keys, remains very useful for decision-making. Optimization algorithms are employed so as to minimize the execution speed of the algorithm. Genetic Algorithm is one among the novel-searching technique filled with superior features designed specifically to work on hybrid algorithm. It is very hard to compute the code of genetic algorithm, also require relatively additional time to compute the optimization problem. Genetic Algorithms are characterized by their robustness as well as their ability to deal with non-convex problems in dynamic environment. The sub-optimal key is evolved as a result of four steps. The genetic algorithm optimization technique is one among the direct approach that uses a specific objective function to locate the minimum.The objective function is framed with the objective of minimizing the execution time of the algorithm with fastens key generation. The basic step to generate the key is comprised below,

Step 1: Population - The matrix space from which the key is to be generated.

Step 2: Selection - From the encrypted bits, some bits are randomly chosen to construct nearby optimal key. Evaluate the fitness function and select main constituent matrix to perform cross over.

Step 3: Crossover - The constructed matrix models of size 8 x 8 are crossover and two new offsprings are generated.

Step 4: Mutation - Between the pair of generated offspring's, mutation operation is performed. The fitness function is again calculated for this new offspring's.

Constraints are placed according to the need of the algorithm. The proposed encryption falls under linear type that computes the process within given time constraint. Genetic Algorithm is considered for the process, since it generated best solution from subset of solutions already available. Upon the exact arrival of the fitness function, from multiple iterations, the process stops and the new sub-optimal key is produced. The following is the steps for the full encryption of the images after the sub-optimal key generation.

Step 1: The output matrices obtained after the t substitution process is intended for the process.
Step 2: Key matrix of size 8 x 8 is generated from the sub-optimal key generation step.
Step 3: Substitution operation is performed between the key matrix and the partially ciphered matrix.
Step 4: Results obtained for the individual color channels from the process is completely ciphered.
Step 5: The detached color channels thus obtained is combined again for the generation of the ciphered image.
Step 6: The image thus evolved is the completely encrypted image.

Encryption and Decryption Process for RGB Image Encryption

The proposed RGB color image encryption algorithm consists of the encryption and decryption algorithm with multiple key generations. The proposed method ciphers the input secret image. The following are the stages of proposed method. Figure 2 shows the block diagram for the encryption and decryption method. The method is the combined architecture of improved cipher block chaining encryption mode with Exclusive Disjunction operator. The algorithmic description of the method is as follows. Consider the given input image as the format with the pixel resolution of 256x 256. Each color channel of the input image will get separately encrypted. This method well encrypts the image given by the user into inarticulate format. In any cryptographic process key generation is most significant part. In this technique multiple key generations takes place to strengthen encryption quality. The key generation process as explained in above sections follows then. Totally 32 matrices are created for every color bands is 8 x 8 matrix. The process is repeated recursively until all the pixels of the secret image are computed. Finally, the three bands are combined to generate the completely ciphered image.

Figure 2. Basic construction of cipher block chaining

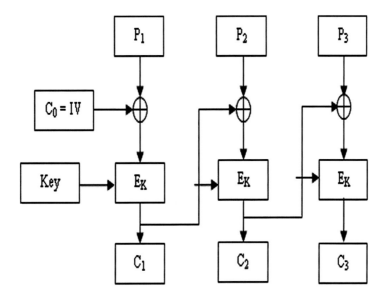

Decryption of the proposed algorithm is reverse process in which the key remains similar for both encryption and decryption. The encrypted image matrix is XORed with the key matrices. The resultant matrix is then fed to the improved cipher block chaining operation mode. Finally, the conversion to the pixel value is done. The detach bands are again combined to produce the original secret RGB image. Three levels of key generations are taken place to perform encryption as well as the decryption operation. XOR is the only self-invertible logical operator used for the encryption.

RESULTS AND DISCUSSIONS

The proposed method is implemented with Visual Studio 2010, C# language under the configuration of windows 7 operating system with Core-i3 and 3 GB RAM. The performance evaluation factors such as PSNR, MSE, NPCR and UACI are computed which show the differential attacks status to reveal the efficiency of the algorithm. Entropy value is computed to show the efficiency of the proposed encryption algorithm. The experimental result is done for various standard test images and their outputs are analyzed. Source of the standard images in obtained from (Fabien Petitcolas, 2015).

Experimental Analysis

This section contains the experimental results and their performance by using proposed encryption method. The standard test images such as the Lena, Baboon, Barbara, Bandon, Brandy Rose, Pueblo bonito, Waterfall, Wildflowers, Watch and Water are tested against the proposed algorithm. The results are depicted in Figure 3(a-j). There exists uniformity in pixel resolution of 256x256. Hence, the images are preprocessed and converted according to the standard pixel resolution form. From the experimental results it is confirmed that the proposed encryption algorithm effectively and completely convert the original input image into cipher image. The decryption without any loss deciphers the original image.

Performance Analysis

Various performance parameters are there in the literature to show the effectiveness of any cryptographic algorithm. In this research work to illustrate the efficiency of the encryption algorithm various parameters such as the Peak-Signal-to-Noise-Ratio (PSNR), Mean Square Error (MSE) are considered into account.

1. **Entropy:** Quality of the Encryption is analyzed to prove the strength of the algorithm. The entropy is one of the most outstanding features for measuring the randomness. The entropy values of original images are rarely generate uniformly distributed random messages and far from the ideal original images. The entropy values of the encrypted images are very close to the ideal value of 8, which means that the proposed encryption algorithm is highly robust against entropy attacks. In the equation given below $P(m_i)$ denotes the probability and the total states of the information source. For a purely random source emitting, the entropy should be M. Entropy is measured in the units of Shannon (Sh) as in equation 7. Table 1 shows the entropy value gained from the proposed image encryption method.

Figure 3. Experimental results of the proposed encryption algorithm

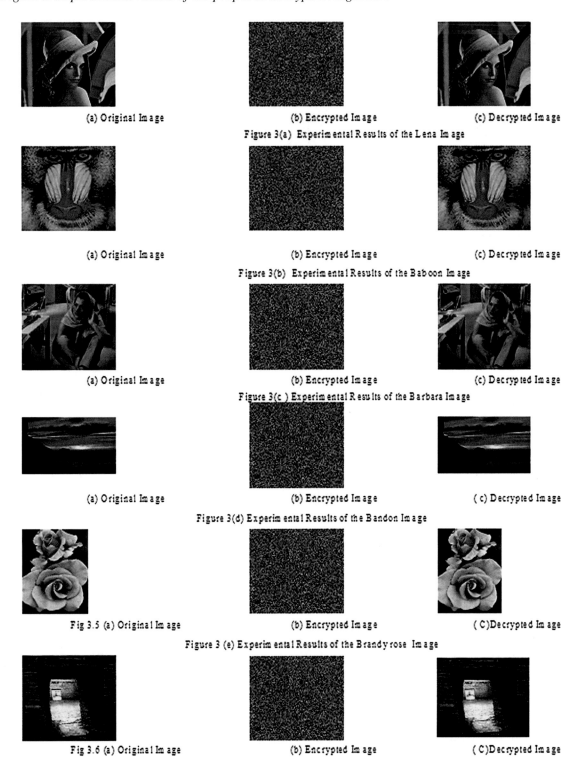

(a) Original Image   (b) Encrypted Image   (c) Decrypted Image

Figure 3(a) Experimental Results of the Lena Image

(a) Original Image   (b) Encrypted Image   (c) Decrypted Image

Figure 3(b) Experimental Results of the Baboon Image

(a) Original Image   (b) Encrypted Image   (c) Decrypted Image

Figure 3(c) Experimental Results of the Barbara Image

(a) Original Image   (b) Encrypted Image   (c) Decrypted Image

Figure 3(d) Experimental Results of the Bandon Image

Fig 3.5 (a) Original Image   (b) Encrypted Image   (C)Decrypted Image

Figure 3 (e) Experimental Results of the Brandy rose Image

Fig 3.6 (a) Original Image   (b) Encrypted Image   (C)Decrypted Image

Table 1. Entropy values for standard test images

Sl. No.	Image Name	Entropy Value (Sh)
1	Lena	7.999
2	Baboon	7.999
3	Barbara	7.998
4	Bandon	7.998
5	Brandy Rose	7.998
6	pueblo bonito	7.999
7	Waterfall	7.998
8	Wildflowers	7.998
9	Watch	7.998
10	Water	7.999

Table 2. Encryption and decryption time in seconds

Sl. No.	Image Name	Encryption Time in (Sec)	Decryption Time in (Sec)
1	Lena	3.8	3.8
2	Baboon	4.0	4.0
3	Barbara	3.0	3.0
4	Bandon	3.9	3.9
5	Brandy Rose	1.7	1.7
6	pueblo bonito	3.5	3.5
7	Waterfall	3.2	3.2
8	Wildflowers	3.0	3.0
9	Watch	2.9	2.9
10	Water	3.4	3.4

$$E = \sum \left[P\left(m_i\right) \times \log_2 \left(\frac{1}{p(m_i)} \right) \right] \tag{7}$$

2. **Encryption and Decryption Time:** Table 2 reveals the time taken for the encryption and decryption of the test images. The average execution time for both the encryption and decryption is around minimum time seconds.

Statistical Analysis

In this section the histogram analysis, one of the statistical measures is computed. It is performed to show the frequency distribution of continuous pixels between the original and encrypted image and also the density of the given image is determined. The cipher image with uniform histogram is found to be free from cryptanalytic attack. Figure 4(a-e) shows the histogram evaluated for the original image to that of encrypted images. The axis x and y represents the number of pixels of the original and encrypted images respectively.

Analysis of Differential Attacks

The differential attack analysis is one of the measure in which the attackers try to determine a rapport between the plain and the cipher images, through evaluating the differences in an input pixel. It can affect the resultant difference at the output image to obtain the key. NPCR (Number of Pixels Change Rate) and UACI (Unified Average Changing Intensity) are the two important measures used to test the influence of single-pixel change on the original and encrypted image as given in the equations 8 and 9. In the equations 8, 9 M, N denotes the dimension of the image and (i,j) stands for the image co-ordinates.

Figure 4. Histogram results of the proposed algorithm

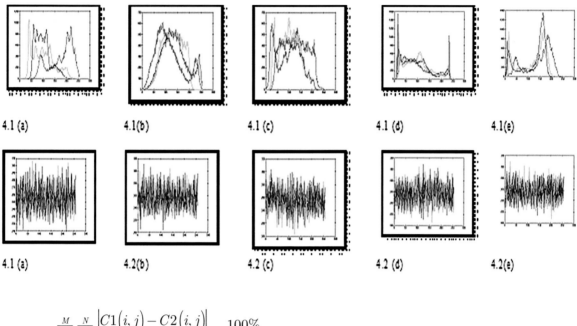

$$UACI = \sum_{i=1}^{M}\sum_{j=1}^{N} \frac{\left|C1\left(i,j\right) - C2\left(i,j\right)\right|}{255} \times \frac{100\%}{M \times N} \tag{8}$$

$$NPCR = \frac{1}{M \times N}\sum_{i=1}^{M}\sum_{j=1}^{N} D\left(i,j\right) \times 100\% \tag{9}$$

The results from the NPCR and UACI computations in Table 3 indicates that the method provided for image encryption is highly sensitive with respect to small changes in the original images. Hence, the given method is strongly capable of resisting the differential attack.

Table 3. NPCR and UACI values for encryped images

Sl. No.	Image Name	Size	NPCR(%)	UACI(%)
1	Lena	256 x 256	99.59	33.39
2	Baboon	256 x 256	99.62	33.46
3	Barbara	256 x 256	99.59	30.79
4	Bandon	256 x 256	99.68	30.09
5	Brandy Rose	256 x 256	99.62	32.20
6	pueblo bonito	256 x 256	99.67	33.40
7	Waterfall	256 x 256	99.62	29.51
8	Wildflowers	256 x 256	99.52	31.71
9	Watch	256 x 256	99.60	30.58
10	Water	256 x 256	99.61	30.34

Comparison of Proposed Approach with Existing Methods

A comparative study is conducted between the proposed encryption with the existing method. The following Table 4 shows a comparison between the proposed encryption method with existing method [Ref-10, 1]. The parameters considered are entropy, NPCR and UACI to illustrate the efficiency of the proposed algorithm. The existing method works on the exclusive logical operator and chaotic mapping is formulated for the color image encryption. A single standard test image results are presented to show the efficiency of the proposed method. The size of the image is converted to 256 x 256 for the proposed algorithm standard.

From the experimental analysis it is observed that the entropy value is very close enough to the ideal value 8 by using the proposed encryption method. This shows the proposed algorithm is defensive against attacks. Figure 5, plotted the variation in percentage of NPCR and UACI and Entropy between the existing and proposed method. The NPCR and UACI value computed are 99.59% and 33.39% says that a single pixel conversion in the image leads to major difference in encryption results. Thus it withstands the differential attacks effectually and is compared with the existing method.

Table 4. Comparision between the existing and proposed method

Parameters	Image Name	Existing Method-RCBC [Ref - 1]	ICBC Method [Ref-10]	Proposed Method
NPCR (%)	Lena (256 x 256)	78.4	99.60	99.59
UACI (%)	Lena (256 x 256)	31.2	32.17	33.39
Entropy (Sh)	Lena (256 x 256)	7.926	7.999	7.999

Figure 5. Variations between existing and proposed algorithms

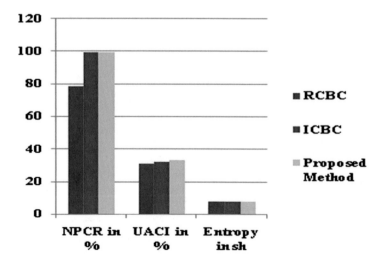

CONCLUSION

The existing algorithms prevail such as the AES-CBC and CBC- HMAC provides better results for encryption without any form of conversion of the image in general. The proposed RGB color image encryption works better by converting it into blocks of data, which can be computed simultaneously. This leads to less execution time and reduce computational complexity. The conversion into bits form helps in saving the space for processing as well as fastens the execution time. The key generation technique involved for this method remains complex to compute, since it is generated from the input itself and it is less prone to timing attacks as the time required to encipher or decipher a data block is same.

Multiple key generations involved in the process that increases the encryption quality and efficiency of the technique. The optimization technique involved in the key generation computes and generates sub-optimal key from subset of matrices. This will prevent the data from intruders since generation of the sub-optimal key from large set of matrices remains difficult. The association between input image and encrypted images is made more intricate by involving the logical operation applied on input image. The mathematical model, matrix access structure increases the speed of processing the elements in specific manner. Experimental analysis illustrates the effectiveness of the proposed method against various attacks, like differential attack, entropy analyzes etc. The encryption and decryption time calculation reveals the speed of the execution time of the algorithm. Histogram Analysis reveals the uniform distribution of pixels in the encrypted image. The performance metrics shows that the proposed image encryption method yields better security.

ACKNOWLEDGMENT

This research is supported by the AURF (Alagappa University Research Fellowship – Grant No. Ph.D/0833/ AURF Fellowship/2015), Alagappa University, Karaikudi, India.

REFERENCES

Abdulgader, , Iismail, Zainal, & Idbeaa. (2015). Enhancement of AES Algorithm based on Chaotic Maps and Shift Operation for Image Encryption. *Journal of Theoretical and Applied Information Technology*, *71*(1), 1–12.

Chen, H., Du, X., Liu, Z., & Yang, C. (2013). Color image encryption based on the affine transform and gyrator transform. *Optics and Lasers in Engineering*, *51*(6), 768–775. doi:10.1016/j.optlaseng.2013.01.016

Das & Dutta. (2013). An approach of bitwise Private-key Encryption, technique based on Multiple Operators and numbers of 0 and 1 counted from binary representation of Plain Text's single character. *International Journal of Innovative Technology and Exploring Engineering*, 1-6.

Deb, K. (2005). Practical Optimization Using Evolutionary Methods. KanGAL Report Number 2005008, Kanpur Genetic Algorithms Laboratory (KanGAL), Department of Mechanical Engineering, Indian Institute of Technology Kanpur.

Elashry, Faragallah, Abbas, El-Rabaie, & El-Samie. (2012). A New Method for Encrypting Images with Few DetailsUsing Rijndael and RC6 Block Ciphers in the Electronic Code Book Mode. *Information Security Journal: A Global Perspective, 21*(4), 193-205.

Elhoseny, Ahmed, Abbas, Kazemian, Faragallah, El-Rabaie, & El-Samie. (2015). Chaotic encryption of Images in the Fractional Fourier Transform domain using different modes of operation. Springer Verlag.

Fossati, J. P., Galarza, A., Martín-Villate, A., Echeverría, J. M., & Fontán, L. (2015). Optimal scheduling of a microgrid with a fuzzy logic controlled storage system. *Electrical Power and Energy Systems., 68,* 61–70. doi:10.1016/j.ijepes.2014.12.032

Hongjun, L., & Xingyuan, W. (2010). Color image encryption based on one-time keys and robust chaotic maps. *Computers & Mathematics with Applications (Oxford, England), 59*(10), 3320–3327. doi:10.1016/j.camwa.2010.03.017

Image Processing / Videocodecs/ Programming. (n.d.). Retrieved from http://www.hlevkin.com/TestImages/Boats.bmp

Khashan, O. A., & Zin, A. M. (2013). An Efficient Adaptive of Transparent Spatial Digital Image Encryption. *Procedia Technology, 11,* 288-297.

Lin, Ch.-H., Chen, T.-H., & Wu, Ch.-S. (2013). A batch image encryption scheme based on chaining random grids. *Scientia Iranica D, 20*(3), 670–681.

Mahalakshmi, J., & Kuppusamy, K. (2016). An efficient Image Encryption Method based on Improved-Cipher Block Chaining in Cloud Computing as a Security Service. *Aust. J. Basic & Appl. Sci., 10*(2), 297–306.

Manish Kumar, N., Mishra, D. C., & Sharma, R. K. (2014). Afirst approach on an RGB image encryption. *Optics and Lasers in Engineering, 52,* 27–34. doi:10.1016/j.optlaseng.2013.07.015

Panduranga, H. T., & Naveen Kumar, S. K. (2012). A Novel Image Encryption Technique using Multiwave based carrier Image.*Procedia Engineering, 38,* 2998-3004. doi:10.1016/j.proeng.2012.06.350

Pareek & Patidar. (2014). Medical image protection using genetic algorithm operations. *Soft Computing,* 1-10.

Petitcolas, F. (2015). *The Information Hiding Home page: Digital Watermarking & Steganography.* Retrieved from http://www.petitcolas.net/steganography/index.html

Ragab, Alla, & Noaman. (2015). Encryption Quality Analysis of the RCBC Block Cipher Compared with RC6 and RC5 Algorithms. In *International Bio-Metrics and Smart Government Summit, FTI Conference.*

Rahman, Balamurugan, & Mariappan. (2015). A Novel DNA Computing based Encryption and Decryption Algorithm. *Procedia Computer Science, 46,* 463 – 475.

Wadi & Zainal. (2013). Rapid Encryption Method Based on AES Algorithm for Grey Scale HD Image Encryption. *Procedia Technology, 11*(5), 1–5. doi:10.1016/j.protcy.2013.12.154

Xing-yuan, W., Feng, C., & Tian, W. (2010). A new compound mode of confusion and diffusion for block encryption of image based on chaos. *Communications in Nonlinear Science and Numerical Simulation*, *15*(9), 2479–2485. doi:10.1016/j.cnsns.2009.10.001

Yas, A. (2008). Testing Image Encryptionby Output Feedback (OFB). *Journal of Computer Science*, *4*(2), 125–128. doi:10.3844/jcssp.2008.125.128

Chapter 7

A Technique to Approximate Digital Planar Curve with Polygon

Mangayarkarasi Ramaiah
VIT University, India

Bimal Kumar Ray
VIT University, India

ABSTRACT

This chapter presents a technique which uses the sum of height square as a measure to define the deflection associated with a pseudo high curvature points on the digital planar curve. The proposed technique iteratively removes the pseudo high curvature points whose deflection is minimal, and recalculates the deflection associated with its neighbouring pseudo high curvature points. The experimental results of the proposed technique are compared with recent state of the art iterative point elimination methods. The comparative results show that the proposed technique produces the output polygon in a better way than others for most of the input digital curve.

INTRODUCTION

There had been significant interest in polygonal approximation of digital planar curve in the last two decades and it resulted in a large number of published papers. Another reason for its popularity is its application to a large number of problems viz. identifying registration number on cars (2002), for portrayal of geographical information (1998), recognizing handwritten forms (2016), in handling biological signal (electroocluography) (1990), in exploration of image (2002) and in matching similar images (1994, 1987, 1993).The technique polygonal approximation is classified as sequential, split and merge and heuristic search. The sequential algorithms use a linear probe to calculate error condition and if the condition is found to be false then the search for a new segment is started. Skalansky and Gonzalez (1980) and Ray and Ray (1994) presented sequential technique that performs a single pass along the digital curve and finds the vertices (pseudo high curvature vertices) of the closed curve. Skalansky and Gonzalez (1980)

DOI: 10.4018/978-1-5225-2053-5.ch007

use perpendicular distance as a measure to determine the vertices whereas Ray and Ray (1994), in an attempt to determine the longest promising line segment along a digital planar curve with minimum possible error optimize an objective function involving sum of squares of error and length of line segment. The output curve produced by Skalansky and Gonzalez (1980) depends upon the starting vertex of the input curve. Sequential techniques may not be able to retain features such as sharp corners and spikes. In contrast to sequential techniques, recursive splitting technique is based on divide-and-conquer method.

Pavlidis and Horowitz (1974) use split and merge technique which fits a line to an initial segmentation of the boundary vertices and computes the least squares error. It iteratively splits a curve if the error is too large and merges two segments if the error is too small. Dunham (1986) suggests an optimal algorithm (using dynamic programming), which instead of specifying the number of line segments specify the error and determine the minimum number of line segments. The recurrence relation used to determine the minimum number of line segments is simple. Sato (1992) also used dynamic programming to find the optimal approximating closed curve.

Yin (1998) presents a method for polygonal approximation that uses genetic algorithm. Yin (2003) presents Tabu search technique to reduce time and space complexity in polygonal approximation, but it is found to be computationally expensive.

The technique proposed in this chapter doesn't fall into anyone of the categories described above. The main objective of this chapter is to introduce a new measure to define the deflection associated with pseudo high curvature vertex more precisely than the other recent iterative vertex elimination techniques. The technique proposed in this chapter obtains the pseudo high curvature vertex using chain code and deletes the duplicate vertices on the digital curve iteratively and produce output polygon retaining with real vertices.

BACKGROUND

Most of the iterative vertex elimination methods begin with a set of pseudo high curvature vertices. The technique used to remove the duplicate vertices on the input curve iteratively based on different measure. In Iterative vertex elimination, the following are the challenges in front of the researchers. How to find a starting set of vertices? Since the technique iteratively deleting the vertices the methods have to take decision on how many number of vertices can possibly deleted in iteration. There are cases there may more than vertex delivers similar contribution towards in retains the shape of the curve, in such case how to choose the real vertices. Most of the techniques go with the decision by selecting the vertex with a small curve key. Masood (2008) says by choosing any vertex randomly also will not show any wrong impact on the performance of the technique. Most of the polygonal approximation techniques will make a search to detect the real vertices through various measures, whereas the type of algorithms discussed in this chapter is making a search to detect duplicate vertices and because of this reason this category of techniques has been referred to as 'reverse polygonization'.

Pikaz and Dinstein (1995) invented the concept of deleting duplicate vertices from the input curve iteratively. Authors choose three consecutive vertices of a curve and measure the of the middle vertex of these three vertices using two measures such as area of triangle and height of a triangle. Based on the data provided by these measures the method takes decision on the process of detecting duplicate vertices. Afterwards the technique removes the vertices whose contribution is less. Then the neighboring vertices deflection is calculated again. The algorithm may be stopped either with number of sides of the polygon or with some pre-specified value on the approximation error.

Zhu and Chirlian (1995) proposed some new criteria to evaluate the efficacy of critical vertex detection algorithms. To compute the deflection of each pseudo critical vertex p_i authors prefer the area of triangle formed by the pseudo critical vertex p_i and the preceding (p_{i-1}) and the succeeding (p_{i+1}) pseudo critical vertex and the vertices delivering small value for the deflection metric are detected. There may be more than one pseudo critical vertices may have the similar value of the deflection metric. The pseudo critical vertex will be deleted if its deflection measure is less than a threshold. Afterwards the technique recalculates the deflection for its preceding as well as succeeding pseudo critical vertices. The algorithm is stopped when no more pseudo critical vertices have the value for the deflection measure which is less than the threshold.

Latecki and Lakaemper (1999) present an algorithm for polygon evolution specially to fit discrete nature of a curve. The discrete curve evolution helps find vertices in the output polygon from the original boundary vertices in such a way that the output vertices preserve the original shape of the boundary. The method retains the real vertices by using the measure mentioned in equation 1.

$$K\left(v\right) = \frac{\beta l_1 l_2}{l_1 + l_2} \tag{1}$$

Note: β is the turn angle at the vertex v, l_1 is the distance between the vertex v and the preceding vertex u and l_2 is the distance between the vertex v and the next vertex w.

The method deletes the vertex whose measure for the criterion metric mentioned in equation 1 is smaller than other vertices. Then the technique recalculates the measure for the criterion metric for its immediate preceding and succeeding vertices on the curve.

Masood and Haq (2007) proposed an algorithm for polygonal approximation using iterative vertex elimination. Authors obtain initial segmentation vertices by Freeman chain code (1961). Authors use perpendicular squared distance as a metric to calculate the deflection associated with all break vertices. Then the technique iteratively deletes the duplicate vertices which have minimum deflection which Authors call associated error value. Most of the time in a single iteration more than one that may produce the same deflection as their neighboring vertices and in that scenario the technique chooses to eliminate the vertex that has lower curve index. Their analysis finds that if pseudo high curvature vertices with the same deflection differ in their curve index by unity then the order of removal of pseudo high curvature vertices may not produce an impact on increase in total deflection. But if the difference of the curve index is greater than unity then the sequence of removal may increase the total deflection. Authors state that the pseudo high curvature vertex with less deflection deleted may not find a place in the output polygon and the same pseudo high curvature vertex may be useful in later iteration. Whenever a pseudo high curvature vertex is removed, it creates an impact on its neighboring vertices. The procedure introduces a new pseudo high curvature vertex between two pseudo high curvature vertices when a pseudo high curvature vertex is deleted.

Masood and Haq (2007) introduce a stabilization process which in turn collects all unstable pseudo high curvature vertices and Authors are all moved to a new position in such a way that the overall distortion is diminished. This scenario may be clear if we look at the Figure 1 which shows a snapshot of the

Figure 1. a) Snapshot of chromosome curve when k=13; b) after stabilization process the chromosome curve at 13 numbers of pseudo high curvature vertices

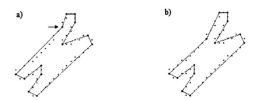

chromosome curve with thirteen pseudo high curvature vertices and the vertices indicated with arrow are the pseudo high curvature vertices with low deflection, the stabilization process introduces new pseudo high curvature vertex between its adjacent pseudo high curvature vertices. The fact how the technique will treat high curvature vertices i.e. sharp turnings is unknown. And the issues that are required to be addressed are noise tolerance and geometric invariance.

Masood (2008a) finds an initial segmentation of the curve through Freeman chain code (1961). The author computes the deflection for the pseudo high curvature vertices using the measure given in equation 2. The output polygon and the approximation error show that the deflection measure delivered via equation 2 is greater than unity. The shape of contour has been distorted which in turn returns high approximation error.

The perpendicular squared distance of any vertex. $p_k \equiv (x_k, y_k)$ from the straight line connecting vertex $p_i \equiv (x_i, y_i)$ and $p_j \equiv (x_j, y_j)$ is defined by equation 2

$$e_k = \frac{\left((x_k - x_i)(y_j - y_i) - (y_k - y_i)(x_j - x_i)\right)^2}{(x_j - x_i)^2 + (y_j - y_i)^2} \tag{2}$$

The vertices with low perpendicular squared distance will be deleted until the maximum deflection is less than 0.9. This threshold has been introduced based on trial and error and it doesn't suit for all curves. The fact how the technique will treat high curvature vertices i.e. sharp turnings is unknown. And also the following issues required to be addressed such as noise tolerance and geometrical-invariance.

Masood (2008b), presents an optimized algorithm which is similar to the one proposed by Masood and Haq (2007). Here it is unknown how the technique will treat high curvature vertices i.e. sharp turnings. And also the following issues required to be addressed such as noise tolerance and geometrical invariance.

Carmona et al. (2010) presents iterative vertex elimination where Authors use absolute perpendicular distance as a criterion measure. This technique also finds initial pseudo high curvature vertices through Freeman chain code (1961). This technique first detects the vertex with the highest deflection using perpendicular distance measure. Then it begins to delete the duplicate vertices whose deflection is less than a threshold. Afterwards the deflection of neighboring vertices is recalculated. When Authors are attempting to display the output curve at fewer vertices Authors observed that their method is able to retain vertex with the highest deflection. The polygonal approximation techniques applied to the four curves such as chromosome, leaf, infinity and semicircle are shown in Figure 2. The vertex with the highest deflection is marked with a solid circle. The algorithm is terminated based on the measure given by the equation 4.

Figure 2. Snapshot of the four bench mark curves highlighted with high deflection vertex: a) chromosome b) leaf c) infinity d) semicircle

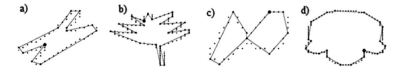

To prevent the heavy deformation threshold is imposed on the measure in equation 3.

$$r_i = \frac{\Delta l_{ij}}{E_{\infty j}} \qquad (3)$$

Ramaiah and Ray (2015) present a method for closed curve approximation which obtains the initial segmentation vertices using Freeman chain code (1960). Authors use the sum of square of deflection as a measure to calculate deflection associated with a pseudo high curvature vertex j_k from the line segment joining two immediate neighbors. This method iteratively removes the pseudo high curvature vertices from the curve until a polygonal approximation up to a desired level of detail is obtained. The technique has been tested with various digital curves to determine its ability in preserve the curvature portion in a better way than others. The experimental results reveal that the technique produce polygon by preserving high as well as low curvature region all most with equal precision. It is required to test whether the method is geometrically invariant and the noise tolerance issue too needs to be addressed.

PSEUDO HIGH CURVATURE VERTEX DETECTION AND POLYGONAL APPROXIMATION

The technique described in this chapter obtains pseudo high curvature vertices through Freeman chain code (1960) (Figure 3). A digital curve can be defined as

$$C_d = \left\{ p_i \left(x_i, y_i \right), where\ p_{i+1}\ is\ a\ neighbor\ of\ p_i\ modulon \right\} \qquad (4)$$

A vertex on a curve is called a pseudo high curvature vertex of the curve if the chain code at the vertex differs as one move from left of the vertex to its right. The Figure 4 shows the polygon with pseudo high curvature vertices for the human head shaped curve obtained by chain code assignment. To compute the deflection associated with each pseudo high curvature vertex (j_k) the metric used in this chapter is mentioned in equation 5.

The technique begins to deletes the pseudo high curvature vertex from the set of input vertices until the required output polygon is attained. In every iteration pseudo high curvature vertex having the lowest deflection is deleted. There are scenarios with more than one pseudo high curvature vertex with the lowest deflection and in this case the one with the lowest curve key is deleted. Once deleting the pseudo high curvature vertex (j_k), value of deflection of the two neighboring pseudo high curvature vertices $(j_{k-1}$

Figure 3. Freeman's chain code

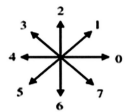

Figure 4. Pseudo high curvature vertices (in bold) for human shaped curve

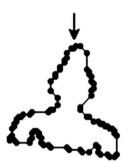

and j_{k+1}) are recalculated. The steps to delete the pseudo high curvature vertices are well established in Table 1 and 2.

$$\sum_{i=j_{k-1+1}}^{j_{k+1-1}} \frac{\frac{1}{4}\left\{ x_{j_k}\left(y_{j_{k+1}} - y_{j_k}\right) + x_{j_{k+1}}\left(y_i - y_{j_k}\right) + x_i\left(y_{j_k} - y_{k_{k+1}}\right)\right\}^2}{\left(x_{j_{k+1}} - x_{j_{k-1}}\right)^2 + \left(y_{j_{k+1}} - y_{j_{k-1}}\right)^2} \tag{5}$$

A sample pseudo high curvature vertex of the human head shaped curve with their deflection is listed in Table 1 where the vertex with the lowest deflection is highlighted in bold. After deleting the pseudo high curvature vertex, the deflections of the neighboring pseudo high curvature vertices are recalculated. (Neighboring pseudo high curvature vertices are highlighted in Table 2.)

The step for the proposed method is described below in the form of an algorithm. (Algorithm 1) This technique is capable of producing polygon with a dissimilar amount of pseudo high curvature vertices.

RESULTS AND DISCUSSIONS

The experimental results delivered by the proposed iterative vertex elimination are compared and analyzed with the results from other algorithms that use iterative vertex elimination methods. The performance of a polygonal approximation technique can be defined quantitatively by the approximation error and compression ratio. The approximation error is computed through maximum and total deflection of the curve from the approximating curve. The deflection of a vertex of a digital curve from its immediate side of the closed curve is measured by equation 2.

The maximum deflection (*Max_Dfl*) is confined as the highest of e_k and the total deflection (*Total_Dfl*) is confined as the summation of square of perpendicular distance of the all boundary vertices of the curve from the sides of the approximating polygon. The compression ratio (*CR*) is confined as the ratio of the number of vertices (*k*) of the output polygon to the total number of vertices in the input curve. Sarkar (1993) presents a metric where the ratio of the result from equation 6 (defining compression ratio) with the result from the equation 7 (defining total deflection) is called as figure of merit (*FOM*). The mathematical expression for the evaluation measures are given below.

Table 1. Sample j_k values for the inverted tomb shaped curve along with index of pseudo high curvature vertices and their deflection

j_k	Index of Pseudo High Curvature Vertex on the Curve	Deflection
1	35	1.83
2	43	2.71
3	46	1.89
4	54	39.04
5	61	9.44
6	65	7.66
7	68	12.38
8	**85**	**1.65**
9	89	2.02
10	94	27.5
11	100	18.7
12	109	81.86
13	118	18.03

Table 2. After deleting the pseudo high curvature vertex with curve key 85, recalculate the deflection of its neighboring vertices have been highlighted in bold

j_k	Index of Pseudo High Curvature Vertex on the Curve	Deflection
1	35	1.83
2	43	2.71
3	46	1.89
4	54	39.04
5	61	9.44
6	65	7.66
7	**68**	**26.43**
8	**89**	**44.89**
9	94	27.5
10	100	18.7
11	109	81.86
12	118	18.03

Algorithm 1

```
Input: The coordinates of the vertices of the closed digital curve.
Output: Coordinates of the vertices of the output closed curve.
Begin
1. Detect the pseudo high curvature vertices through chain code
2. Compute deflection of all j_k's using equation 5
3. While (termination condition)
a. Remove j_k with minimum dfl_{jk}
b. Recalculate the deflection of neighboring j_k
c. Compute maximum and total deflection
End.
```

$$CR = \frac{n}{k} \tag{6}$$

$$Total\_Dfl = \sum_{k=0}^{n} e_k \tag{7}$$

$$Max\_Dfl = \max_{k=1}^{n} \{e_k\} \tag{8}$$

$$FOM = \frac{CR}{Total\_Dfl} \tag{9}$$

When the input is the vertices of chromosome curve the method mentioned here, produces data for various evaluation measures are populated in Table 3 which conveys that for the following dissimilar amount of pseudo high curvature vertices 18, 17 and 16 the result of proposed method delivers a small value for total deflection which is lower than that of Ramaiah and Ray (2015). The proposed technique delivers smaller value for total deflection than others when k is ten. With nine pseudo high curvature vertices, the result of the proposed technique is smaller than that of Pikaz and Dinstein (1995), Masood (2008a) and Carmona et al. (2010) but greater than that of Ramaiah and Ray (2015). The output images of chromosome curve for various techniques with 10 pseudo high curvature vertices are displayed in Figure 5. With six pseudo high curvature vertices the proposed method produces smaller value for total deflection than others except Ramaiah and Ray (2015) and Carmona et al. (2010). The snapshot of chromosome curve for various techniques at 6 amounts of pseudo high curvature vertices is displayed in Figure 6.

For the vertices of semicircle curve the authors find that at 42 amounts of pseudo high curvature vertices all the methods produce the same value for maximum deflection but with respect to total deflection the result of the proposed method is a little higher than that of others. With 35 pseudo high curvature vertices the result of the proposed method is comparable to Ramaiah and Ray (2015) but is a little higher than that of others. With 15, 10 and 9 pseudo high curvature vertices the proposed method produces small value for total deflection which is less than all other methods, but the same is comparable to Ramaiah and Ray (2015). The comparative results are tabulated in Table 4. The snapshot of semicircle shaped curve using various techniques with 10 pseudo high curvature vertices is displayed in Figure 7. The experimental result of leaf shaped curve is displayed in Table 5 When the authors make an attempt to display the leaf shaped curve at 32, 20 amounts of pseudo high curvature vertices the results of the proposed techniques and others are comparable with each other except Carmona et al. (2010). With 16 pseudo high curvature vertices the proposed method and Ramaiah and Ray (2015) produce less value for approximation error than others, the snapshot for the same is shown in Figure 8.

For the infinity shaped curve (a curve which intersect itself), the comparative result is shown in Table 6. When k is 18, the proposed method yields smaller value for maximum deflection as well as

Figure 5. Polygonal approximation results of chromosome shaped curve at 10 numbers of pseudo high curvature vertices: a) digital curve; b) Pikaz and Dinstein (1995); c) Masood (2008a); d) Carmona et al. (2010); e) Ramaiah and Ray (2015); f) proposed method

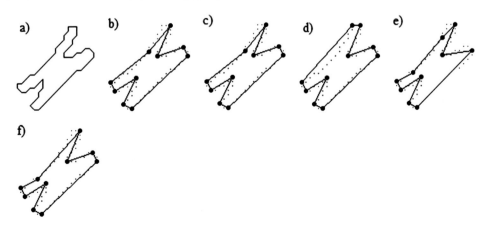

total deflection than others. With 17 and 15 pseudo high curvature vertices the proposed method delivers less value of total deflection than others. In terms of maximum deflection the results of the proposed technique are comparable to those of Ramaiah and Ray (2015) but with respect to maximum deflection the technique presented in this chapter produces a little higher value than those of Pikaz and Dinstein (1995), Masood (2008a) and Carmona et al. (2010). The output polygons are shown in Figure 9. When *k* is eight, the proposed technique produces smaller value for maximum deflection and total deflection than others (see the Figure 10). Then for the input vertices of infinity shaped curve the proposed method is able to produces a polygon with fewer amounts of pseudo high curvature vertices for the shape of the infinity curve and also with less total deflection than others see Figure 11.

The comparative results for the inverted tomb shaped curve are summarized in Table 7. The result at the following numbers of pseudo high curvature vertices 35, 32, 12, 10 and 7 the proposed method produces a polygon with less approximation error than others. The output curve of the various techniques for inverted tomb shaped curve at 21 and 10 pseudo high curvature vertices are displayed in Figure 12 and Figure 13.

The comparative result for the input of rabbit shaped curve is shown in Table 8. When the authors attempt to display the curve at 72, 36 amount pseudo high curvature vertices the proposed method delivers value for total deflection which is smaller than others. But at 20 pseudo high curvature vertices the result of the proposed method is comparable (in terms of total, maximum deflection and Figure of merit) to Pikaz and Dinstein (1995), Masood (2008a) but is higher than Carmona et al. (2010) and Ramaiah and Ray (2015). At sixteen amounts of pseudo high curvature vertices the proposed technique produces value for total deflection which is smaller than others. The snapshot at nineteen amount pseudo high curvature vertices is displayed in Figure 14 reveals that the proposed technique and Ramaiah and Ray (2015) produce a curve which did not intersect itself. Even at 16 amounts of pseudo high curvature vertices the proposed method is capable of producing an approximating polygon without intersection (please see Figure 14(g)). The experimental results for the human head shaped curve are displayed in Table 9. With 83 pseudo high curvature vertices, the proposed method approximation error in terms of total deflection is higher than the others. At 62, 30, 27, 23 numbers of pseudo high curvature vertices the proposed method result (total deflection) is smaller than others. The snapshot at 30 pseudo high curvature vertices are shown in figure 15 and the snapshot with 27 pseudo high curvature vertex are in figure 16. With 10 pseudo high curvature vertices the proposed method and Ramaiah and Ray (2015) produce visibly recognizable curve whereas the other techniques heavily deform the original shape of the curve.

Figure 6. Polygonal approximation results of chromosome shaped curve at 6 numbers of pseudo high curvature vertices: a) Pikaz and Dinstein (1995); b) Masood (2008a); c) Carmona et al. (2010); d) Ramaiah and Ray (2015); e) proposed method
Note: The digital planar curve shown from Figure 13 to Figure 16 are generated from the chain code appeared in Marji and Siy (2004).

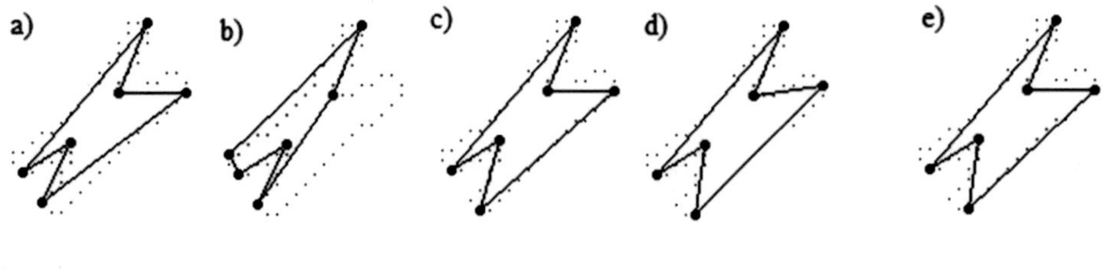

Table 3. Comparative results of chromosome curve

Methods	k	CR	Max_Dfl	Total_Dfl	FOM
Pikaz and Dinstein (1995)	18	3.33	0.51	2.88	1.15
Masood (2008a)			0.51	2.88	1.15
Carmona et al. (2010)			0.51	3.01	1.10
Ramaiah and Ray (2015)			0.6	3.32	1.00
Proposed			0.51	3.01	1.10
Pikaz and Dinstein (1995)	17	3.53	0.6	3.44	1.02
Masood (2008a)			0.6	3.44	1.02
Ramaiah and Ray (2015)			0.68	4.00	0.88
Proposed			0.60	3.57	0.98
Pikaz and Dinstein (1995)	16	3.75	0.51	3.84	0.97
Masood (2008a)			0.51	3.84	0.97
Ramaiah and Ray (2015)			0.74	4.88	0.76
Proposed			0.63	3.87	0.96
Pikaz and Dinstein (1995)	13	4.61	0.78	5.83	0.79
Masood (2008a)			0.78	5.82	0.79
Carmona et al. (2010)			1.21	12.47	0.36
Ramaiah and Ray (2015)			0.78	7.33	0.62
Proposed			0.78	5.95	0.77
Pikaz and Dinstein (1995)	10	6	1.53	14.73	0.40
Masood (2008a)			1.53	14.73	0.40
Carmona et al. (2010)			1.86	32.05	0.18
Ramaiah and Ray (2015)			1.41	14.86	0.40
Proposed			1.47	11.81	0.50
Pikaz and Dinstein (1995)	9	6.66	1.36	18.80	0.35
Carmona et al. (2010)			1.36	18.79	0.35
Masood (2008a)			1.36	18.79	0.35
Ramaiah and Ray (2015)			1.48	15.48	0.43
Proposed			2.12	17.11	0.38
Pikaz and Dinstein (1995)	8	7.5	1.98	34.49	0.22
Carmona et al. (2010)			1.98	34.49	0.22
Masood (2008a)			1.98	34.49	0.22
Ramaiah and Ray (2015)			2.12	20.76	0.36
Proposed			2.12	25.55	0.29
Pikaz and Dinstein (1995)	6	10	2.06	48.29	0.21
Carmona et al. (2010)			2.06	32.88	0.30
Masood (2008a)			5.66	300.0	0.03
Ramaiah and Ray (2015)			2.12	31.44	0.32
Proposed			2.12	37.90	0.26

Table 4. Comparative results of semicircle curve

Methods	k	CR	Max_Dfl	Total_Dfl	FOM
Pikaz and Dinstein (1995)	42	2.42	0.44	1.26	1.92
Masood (2008a)			0.44	1.26	1.92
Carmona et al. (2010)			0.44	1.43	1.69
Ramaiah and Ray (2015)			0.44	1.26	1.92
Proposed			0.44	1.50	1.61
Pikaz and Dinstein (1995)	35	2.91	0.44	2.09	1.39
Masood (2008a)			0.44	2.09	1.39
Carmona et al. (2010)			0.48	2.29	1.27
Ramaiah and Ray (2015)			0.44	2.25	1.29
Proposed			0.44	2.25	1.29
Pikaz and Dinstein (1995)	15	6.8	1.55	50.57	0.14
Masood (2008a)			1.55	50.57	0.14
Carmona et al. (2010)			1.55	50.57	0.14
Ramaiah and Ray (2015)			1.40	25.27	0.26
Proposed			1.40	25.27	0.26
Pikaz and Dinstein (1995)	10	10.2	2.04	65.29	0.15
Masood (2008a)			2.03	65.29	0.14
Carmona et al. (2010)			2.03	76.24	0.13
Ramaiah and Ray (2015)			2.04	61.02	0.16
Proposed			2.04	61.02	0.16
Pikaz and Dinstein (1995)	9	11.33	3.53	141.87	0.08
Masood (2008a)			3.53	141.87	0.08
Carmona et al. (2010)			3.53	141.87	0.08
Ramaiah and Ray (2015)			3.26	130.28	0.08
Proposed			3.26	130.28	0.08

COMPLEXITY

The proposed procedure eliminates only one pseudo high curvature vertices in a single iteration. Among n boundary vertices the proposed method calculates deflection associated with k pseudo high curvature vertices. Hence the time complexity of the proposed method is $O(kn)$.

CONCLUSION

A technique for polygonal approximation using iterative vertex elimination is presented in this chapter. This technique obtains initial set of pseudo high curvature vertices using chain code. The sum of square of height is used a measure to retain the real vertices on a curve. The proposed method is compared with

Table 5. Comparative results of leaf curve

Methods	k	CR	Max_Dfl	Total_Dfl	FOM
Pikaz and Dinstein (1995)	32	3.75	0.58	4.97	0.75
Masood (2008a)			0.58	4.97	0.75
Carmona et al. (2010)			0.74	6.38	0.58
Ramaiah and Ray (2015)			0.63	4.98	0.75
Proposed			0.63	4.98	
Pikaz and Dinstein (1995)	20	6	0.89	15.41	0.39
Masood (2008a)			0.89	15.41	0.39
Carmona et al. (2010)			0.98	14.16	0.42
Ramaiah and Ray (2015)			0.89	13.32	0.45
Proposed			0.89	13.32	0.45
Pikaz and Dinstein (1995)	15	8	3.0	101.12	0.08
Masood (2008a)			10.30	1161.49	0.01
Carmona et al. (2010)			5.14	215.77	0.04
Ramaiah and Ray (2015)			4.02	86.55	0.09
Proposed			4.02	86.55	0.09

Figure 7. A Semicircle shaped curve along with its polygonal approximation at k = 10: a) Digital curve; b) Pikaz and Dinstein (1995); b) Masood (2008a); d) Carmona et al. (2010); e) Ramaiah and Ray (2015); f) proposed method

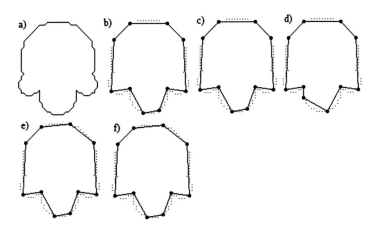

the recently proposed approaches that use iterative vertex elimination and it is found that the proposed technique produces better approximation than that produced by other existing iterative algorithms for most of the input curves.

Since the techniques proposed in this chapter finds initial segmentation vertices using Freeman chain code which yields more amount of initial set of vertices which may in turn increase the number of iterations. There is a demand for initial segmentation procedure for iterative vertex elimination to reduce the

Table 6. Comparative results of infinity curve

Methods	k	CR	Max_Dfl	Total_Dfl	FOM
Pikaz and Dinstein (1995)	18	2.5	0.51	1.67	1.50
Masood (2008a)			0.51	1.67	1.50
Carmona et al. (2010)			0.71	2.09	1.20
Ramaiah and Ray (2015)			0.55	1.85	1.35
Proposed			0.44	1.34	1.87
Pikaz and Dinstein (1995)	17	2.64	0.46	1.70	1.55
Masood (2008a)			0.46	1.71	1.54
Carmona et al. (2010)			1.14	4.59	0.58
Ramaiah and Ray (2015)			0.55	2.24	1.18
Proposed			0.55	1.72	1.53
Pikaz and Dinstein (1995)	15	3.0	0.46	1.92	1.56
Masood (2008a)			0.46	1.93	1.55
Carmona et al. (2010)			1.14	5.45	0.55
Ramaiah and Ray (2015)			0.55	2.90	1.03
Proposed			0.55	1.95	1.54
Pikaz and Dinstein (1995)	8	5.62	1.14	8.58	0.66
Masood (2008a)			1.14	8.58	0.66
Carmona et al. (2010)			1.14	8.85	0.64
Ramaiah and Ray (2015)			1.47	8.49	0.66
Proposed			1.10	7.49	0.75
Pikaz and Dinstein (1995)	4	11.25	2.60	56.50	0.20
Masood (2008a)			2.60	56.50	0.20
Carmona et al. (2010)			2.34	57.74	0.19
Ramaiah and Ray (2015)			3.75	148.54	0.08
Proposed			2.90	111.13	0.10

Figure 8. A leaf shaped curve along with its polygonal approximation at k = 16: a) Digital curve; b) Masood (2008a); c) Carmona et al. (2010); d) Pikaz and Dinstein (1995); e)Ramaiah and Ray(2015); f) proposed method

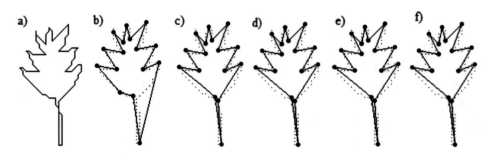

number of iterations. The iterative vertex elimination eliminates the point whose deflection is minimal. There are cases where may be more than one pseudo high curvature vertex produces same deflection then how to select the vertex. For that scenario the proposed techniques remove the vertex according to their curve index. So there is also demand for the steps which should optimally choose the vertex to delete.

Figure 9. Polygonal approximation results of infinity shaped curve when k is at 18: a) Digital curve; b) Pikaz and Dinstein (1995); c)Masood (2008a); d) Carmona et al. (2010); e) Ramaiah and Ray (2015); f) proposed method

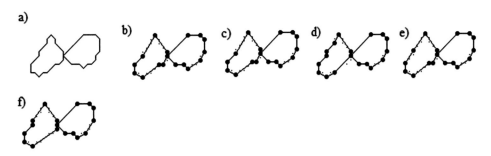

Figure 10. Polygonal approximation results of infinity shaped curve when k is at 18: a) Digital curve; b) Pikaz and Dinstein (1995); c)Masood (2008a); d) Carmona et al. (2010); e) Ramaiah and Ray (2015); f)Proposed method

Figure 11. Polygonal approximation results of various techniques at 4 numbers of pseudo high curvature vertices for the infinity curve: a) Pikaz and Dinstein (1995); b) Masood (2008a); c) Carmona et al. (2010); d) Ramaiah and Ray (2015); e) Proposed method

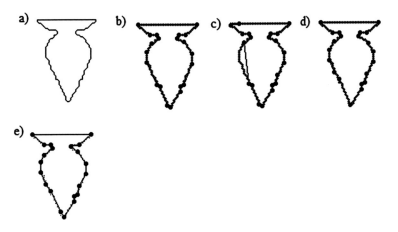

Figure 12. Polygonal approximation of inverted tomb shaped curve at k=21: a) digital-curve; b) Pikaz and Dinstein (1995); c) Masood (2008a); d) Ramaiah and Ray (2015); e) proposed method

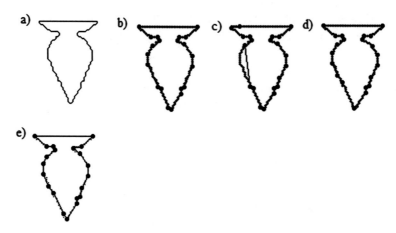

Table 7. Comparative results of inverted tomb shaped curve

Methods	k	CR	Max_Dfl	Total_Dfl	FOM
Pikaz and Dinstein (1995)	35	5.25	0.55	5.81	0.29
Masood (2008a)			0.55	5.81	0.29
Carmona et al. (2010)			6.28	345.26	0.02
Ramaiah and Ray (2015)			0,70	6.45	0.81
Proposed			0.70	6.40	0.82
Pikaz and Dinstein (1995)	32	5.83	0.71	7.00	0.83
Masood (2008a)			1.76	20.07	0.29
Carmona et al. (2010)			6.28	351.57	0.02
Ramaiah and Ray (2015)			0.63	6.64	0.88
Proposed			0.55	6.29	0.93
Pikaz and Dinstein (1995)	12	7	1.49	35.79	0.20
Masood (2008a)			8.87	681.90	0.01
Ramaiah and Ray (2015)			1.48	37.73	0.19
Proposed			1.48	30.81	0.23
Pikaz and Dinstein (1995)	10	10.5	1.49	44.15	0.24
Masood (2008a)			8.87	685.59	0.02
Ramaiah and Ray (2015)			1.41	44.86	0.23
Proposed			1.38	36.76	0.29
Pikaz and Dinstein (1995)	7	15	2.46	186.25	0.08
Masood (2008a)			8.87	701.58	0.02
Ramaiah and Ray (2015)			2.85	199.45	0.08
Proposed			3.05	162.45	0.09

Figure 13. Polygonal approximation of inverted tomb shaped curve at k=10: a) Pikaz and Dinstein (1995); b) Masood (2008a); c) Ramaiah and Ray (2015); d) proposed method

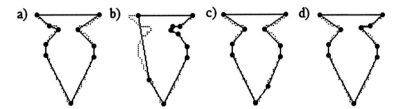

Table 8. Comparative results of rabbit curve

Methods	k	CR	Max_Dfl	Total_Dfl	FOM
Pikaz and Dinstein (1995)	72	2.91	0.44	2.26	1.29
Masood (2008a)			0.44	2.28	1.28
Carmona et al. (2010)			0.48	2.48	1.17
Ramaiah and Ray (2015)			0.44	2.86	1.02
Proposed			0.44	2.41	1.21
Pikaz and Dinstein,(1995)	36	5.83	0.69	9.72	0.60
Masood (2008a)			0.69	9.72	0.60
Carmona et al. (2010)			0.89	14.44	0.40
Ramaiah and Ray (2015)			0.74	10.51	0.55
Proposed			0.72	9.66	0.60
Pikaz and Dinstein (1995)	20	7	2.18	117.00	0.06
Masood (2008a)			2.18	117.00	0.06
Carmona et al. (2010)			2.09	105.95	0.07
Ramaiah and Ray (2015)			2.18	106.11	0.07
Proposed			2.84	117.74	0.06
Pikaz and Dinstein (1995)	19	10.5	2.18	141.51	0.07
Masood (2008a)			2.18	141.51	0.07
Carmona et al. (2010)			2.18	130.62	0.08
Ramaiah and Ray (2015)			2.18	130.62	0.08
Proposed			2.84	142.25	0.07
Pikaz and Dinstein (1995)	16	15	3.35	170.92	0.09
Masood (2008a)			3.35	170.93	0.09
Ramaiah and Ray (2015)			4	188.47	0.08
Proposed			3.35	140.92	0.11

Figure 14. A rabbit shaped curve along with its polygonal approximation at k=19: a) digital curve; b) Masood (2008a); c)Pikaz and Dinstein (1995); d) Carmona et al. (2010); e) Ramaiah and Ray (2015); f) proposed method; g) proposed method at 16

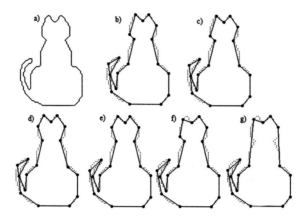

Table 9. Comparative results of human head shaped curve

Methods	k	CR	Max_Dfl	Total_Dfl	FOM
Pikaz and Dinstein (1995)	83	5.25	0.27	0.15	35.00
Masood (2008a)			0.27	0.15	35.00
Carmona et al. (2010)			0.27	0.14	37.50
Ramaiah and Ray (2015)			0.44	0.15	35.00
Proposed			0.44	0.40	13.13
Pikaz and Dinstein (1995)	62	5.83	0.44	2.51	2.32
Masood (2008a)			0.44	2.51	2.32
Carmona et al. (2010)			0.48	2.62	2.23
Ramaiah and Ray (2015)			0.44	2.66	2.19
Proposed			0.44	2.48	2.35
Pikaz and Dinstein (1995)	30	7	0.81	18.07	0.39
Masood (2008a)			0.82	18.07	0.39
Carmona et al. (2010)			1.21	23.11	0.30
Ramaiah and Ray (2015)			1.02	16.31	0.43
Proposed			1.02	15.35	0.46
Pikaz and Dinstein (1995)	27	10.5	0.92	21.78	0.48
Carmona et al. (2010)			1.21	24.40	0.43
Ramaiah and Ray (2015)			1.20	21.18	0.50
Proposed			1.20	20.06	0.52
Pikaz and Dinstein (1995)	23	15	1.24	30.57	0.49
Carmona et al. (2010)			1.54	39.91	0.38
Ramaiah and Ray (2015)			1.24	30.57	0.49
Proposed			1.24	29.44	0.51
Ramaiah and Ray (2015)	10	43.6	4.84	228.72	0.19
Proposed			4.84	231.34	0.19

Figure 15. Polygonal approximation results for human head shaped curve at k=30: a) digital curve; b) Pikaz and Dinstein (1995); c)Masood (2008a); d) Carmona et al. (2010); e)Ramaiah and Ray (2015); f) proposed method

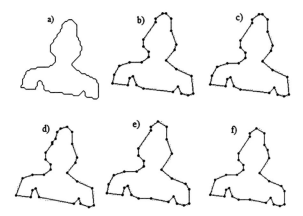

Figure 16. Polygonal approximation results at k =27: a) Pikaz and Dinstein (1995); b) Masood (2008a); c) Carmona et al. (2010); d) Ramaiah and Ray (2015); e) proposed method

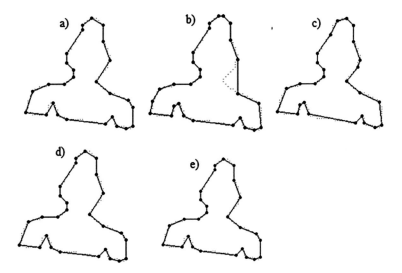

REFERENCES

Carmona-Poyato, A., Madrid-Cuevas, F. J., Medina-Carnicer, R., & Muñoz-Salinas, R. (2010). Polygonal approximation of digital planar curves through break point suppression. *Pattern Recognition*, *43*(1), 14–25. doi:10.1016/j.patcog.2009.06.010

Fardousse, K., & Qjidaa, H. (2016). Handwritten motives image recognition using polygonal approximation and chain-code. *WSEAS Transactions on Systems and Control*, *11*, 217–223.

Freeman, H. (1961). On the encoding of arbitrary geometric configurations. *IRE Transactions on Electronic Computers*, *EC-10*(2), 260–268. doi:10.1109/TEC.1961.5219197

Grumbach, S., Rigaux, P., & Segoufin, L. (1998, June). The DEDALE system for complex spatial queries. *SIGMOD Record, 27*(2), 213–224. doi:10.1145/276305.276324

Hu, X., & Ahuja, N. (1994). Matching point features with ordered geometric, rigidity, and disparity constraints. *IEEE Transactions on Pattern Analysis and Machine Intelligence, 16*(10), 1041–1049. doi:10.1109/34.329004

Kumar, M. P., Goyal, S., Jawahar, C. V., & Narayanan, P. J. (2002). *Polygonal Approximation of Closed Curves across Multiple Views.* ICVGIP.

Latecki, L. J., & Lakämper, R. (1999). Convexity rule for shape decomposition based on discrete contour evolution. *Computer Vision and Image Understanding, 73*(3), 441–454. doi:10.1006/cviu.1998.0738

Marji, M., & Siy, P. (2004). Polygonal representation of digital planar curves through dominant point detection—a nonparametric algorithm. *Pattern Recognition, 37*(11), 2113–2130. doi:10.1016/j.patcog.2004.03.004

Masood, A. (2008a). Dominant point detection by reverse polygonization of digital curves. *Image and Vision Computing, 26*(5), 702–715. doi:10.1016/j.imavis.2007.08.006

Masood, A. (2008b). Optimized polygonal approximation by dominant point deletion. *Pattern Recognition, 41*(1), 227–239. doi:10.1016/j.patcog.2007.05.021

Masood, A., & Haq, S. A. (2007). A novel approach to polygonal approximation of digital curves. *Journal of Visual Communication and Image Representation, 18*(3), 264–274. doi:10.1016/j.jvcir.2006.12.002

Neumann, R., & Teisseron, G. (2002). Extraction of dominant points by estimation of the contour fluctuations. *Pattern Recognition, 35*(7), 1447–1462. doi:10.1016/S0031-3203(01)00145-5

Pavlidis, T., & Horowitz, S. L. (1974). Segmentation of plane curves. *IEEE Transactions on Computers, 23*(8), 860–870. doi:10.1109/T-C.1974.224041

Ramaiah, M., & Ray, B. K. (2015). Polygonal approximation of digital planar curve using local integral deviation. *International Journal of Computational Vision and Robotics, 5*(3), 302–319. doi:10.1504/IJCVR.2015.071333

Sarkar, D. (1993). A simple algorithm for detection of significant vertices for polygonal approximation of chain-coded curves. *Pattern Recognition Letters, 14*(12), 959–964. doi:10.1016/0167-8655(93)90004-W

Sato, Y. (1992). Piecewise linear approximation of plane curves by perimeter optimization. *Pattern Recognition, 25*(12), 1535–1543. doi:10.1016/0031-3203(92)90126-4

Sethi, I. K., & Jain, R. (1987). Finding trajectories of feature points in a monocular image sequence. *IEEE Transactions on Pattern Analysis and Machine Intelligence, PAMI-9*(1), 56–73. doi:10.1109/TPAMI.1987.4767872 PMID:21869377

Sklansky, J., & Gonzalez, V. (1980). Fast polygonal approximation of digitized curves. *Pattern Recognition, 12*(5), 327–331. doi:10.1016/0031-3203(80)90031-X

Yin, P. Y. (2003). Ant colony search algorithms for optimal polygonal approximation of plane curves. *Pattern Recognition, 36*(8), 1783–1797. doi:10.1016/S0031-3203(02)00321-7

Yuen, P. C. (1993). Dominant point matching algorithm. *Electronics Letters, 29*(23), 2023–2024. doi:10.1049/el:19931350

Zhu, P., & Chirlian, P. M. (1995). On critical point detection of digital shapes. *IEEE Transactions on Pattern Analysis and Machine Intelligence, 17*(8), 737–748. doi:10.1109/34.400564

Chapter 8
Shape Determination of Aspired Foreign Body on Pediatric Radiography Images Using Rule-Based Approach

Vasumathy M
VIT University, India

Mythili Thirugnanam
VIT University, India

ABSTRACT

Foreign body aspiration (FBA) is a common problem among pediatric population that requires early diagnosis and prompt successful management. Conventionally the radiography image inspection processes are carried out manually by the experts of medical field. Recently automated systems are developed to improve the quality of the radiography images but none of the work carried out especially to determine the characteristics of the foreign bodies in pediatric foreign body aspired radiography images. The proposed approach focuses on characterizing the foreign body shape using sixteen various geometric and edge features. The shapes are determined by using fuzzy logical connectives formed by logically connecting two or more extracted information and a binary decision tree. More than 100 X-Ray radiography images are used to obtained the experimental research. The method proved that the results are more accurate in determining the foreign body shapes as circle, polygon, sharp and irregular automatically with less time.

INTRODUCTION

Worldwide, the foreign body aspiration is considered as most common cause of accidental death of children. First popular diagnostic tool for identifying foreign body is X-ray that can show the presence of abnormal region. This diagnosing tool has complemented the radiologists and medical practitioners to take right decision in right time in the pediatric foreign body aspiration treatment management process. The treatment management of foreign bodies are always depends on their size, shape and location.

DOI: 10.4018/978-1-5225-2053-5.ch008

Hence, it is important to develop an approach to identify the evidence such as size, shape and location for the early recognition and timely treatment of foreign body aspiration. The proposed work utilizes the knowledge of predefined foreign body characteristics and the knowledge of the various image processing operations used in the existing works for image enhancement and segmentation of foreign body aspired pediatric X-ray images. Some of the existing work has been surveyed for assessing the significance of aspired foreign body characteristics of the foreign body in pediatric foreign aspired radiographic images. The experimental test results are presented with classification accuracy to strengthen the proposed work significance in the process of aspired foreign body treatment management.

Related Works

Sajid Ullah Khan et al., (2016) proposed a novel and efficient enhancement algorithm based on image fusion using a discrete wavelet transform on pediatric X-ray image. The proposed algorithm has significant proficiency in the enhancement of degraded X-ray images. Raihan Firoz et al., (2016) proposed morphological transform for medical image enhancement. Contrast of various medical images can be enhanced using proposed approach. The results indicate that this morphological transform method improves the contrast of medical images and can help with better diagnosis. Thacker et al., (2016) discussed about most recent advances in Multi detector CT Diagnosis of Pediatric Pulmonary with imaging information. Reviews of most recent updates on MDCT diagnosis of pediatric pulmonary thromboembolism are presented. Xiao-ying Xing et al. (2015) summarize imaging features of pediatric spinal tuberculosis. The spinal X-ray, CT and MR presentations of 21 patients aged lesser than 18 years old patient's typical imaging findings are discussed with Pediatric spinal tuberculosis. Kramer et al., (2015), suggested that determining treatment management of FBA requires assessment of foreign body size, type of object ingested, location, clinical symptoms and time since ingestion and concludes, it is important to provide strong evidence base to develop guidelines for the treatment management of FBA. Jasani et al., (2015) discussed about various algorithms for shape detection and texture feature extraction of fruits and conclude that the Circular Hough Transform (CHT) and Edge Detection and Boundary Tracing algorithm are provided the best results. Kaviani et al., (2014), mentioned that the detection of foreign bodies is dependent on the imaging and the characteristics of the foreign body such as the material, size, and its location. Foreign bodies such as metal, stone, glass, and graphite are visible in radiographic images with size greater than or equal to 0.5 mm. Talati et al. (2014) proposed shape context descriptor for image feature extraction. The descriptor improves feature extraction efficiency by using shape parameter and shape representation method by using properties such as translation, rotation and scale invariant and gives good retrieval accuracy in gray scale dataset. Tirpude et al., (2013) conclude that introducing concept of image segmentation techniques in medical images will reduce the process of manual intervention. Park et al., (2013) presented a study to identify the risk factors of complication after foreign body removal. The most common foreign bodies in the pharynx, esophagus, and stomach were coins, fish bones, and springs. The mean size of the foreign body in failed cases is 3.6 cm and the successful cases mean size is 2.7 cm. Z.M. Raahat et al., (2013) Chances of coin impaction are directly proportional to its size and inversely with the age of child. The larger FB (20 to 23mm) tends to impact in the esophagus. Smaller pass into the stomach and intestine. Tian et al.(2013) presented a review on the recent development in feature extraction and provides survey on image feature representation techniques. The global, block-based and region-based features are compared for performance analysis and conclude the combination of all works better for images feature extraction. Erbil et al, (2013) described that plain radiography is useful in the localization of radiopaque foreign bodies and concludes, it is important to evaluate the type and location of the foreign body and to identify complications. Hemalatha et al.(2013) proposed an approach for image retrieval based on content based image retrieval techniques. The texture shape and color features are considered as descriptors for image retrieval process. The work further improved with global descriptor. Karthikeyan et al., (2012) proposed a segmentation algorithm for lung radiographic images. Fuzzy C-Means clustering was used to segment the lungs and the morphological operations were used for quality enhancement of the irregular boundary. Goshal et al., (2012) presented a water shed transformation technique for MRI image enhancement and concludes that the by using proposed segmentation technique, manual intervention and processing time for segmentation process is reduced. Chadha et al., (2012) made a comparative study on feature extraction techniques and their drawbacks for content based image retrieval. The obtained results are considerable and further need improvement in image with text queries. Kekre et al., (2010) discusses novel image retrieval methods based on shape features extracted using gradient operators and slope magnitude technique with Block Truncation Coding. The best performances are listed as Robert, Prewitt, Sobel and lastly the Canny based on block truncation coding. Saki et al., (2009) discussed about their 20 years experience of FBA in infancy. The detailed observation of common anatomic location is presented. Out of 1063 pediatric patients the foreign body were found in 560 (55.1%) patients followed by left main bronchus in 191 (18.8%), trachea in 173 (17.1%), vocal cord in 75(7.4%) and both bronchus in 16 (1.6%). Foreign body was not found during bronchoscope in 48 cases (8.7%). Monte C. Uyemura et al., (2005) had clearly explained about the clinical features, symptoms of esophageal foreign bodies, identification of ingested foreign bodies, and management of ingested foreign bodies, management of patients with suspected ingestion of radiopaque and radiolucent foreign bodies. The treatment management procedures are mainly depends on size, shape and location of the foreign body object. Withey et al., (2007) presented a survey of three generation segmentation techniques and concludes that each generation adds an additional level of algorithmic complexity. Park et al., (2004) reviewed 209 upper gastrointestinal tract foreign body aspiration cases. The review concludes that the size greater than 3 mm, sharp and long diameter foreign bodies are the risk factors for predicting complications related to removal of foreign bodies. Ying Liu et al., (2004) proposed a texture feature extraction algorithm based on POCS theory for arbitrary-shaped regions and

Table 1. List of foreign body objects based on radiolucent and radiopaque feature

Foreign Body	Radiolucent	Radiopaque
Plastic object	Yes	No
Meat	Yes	No
Peanut	Yes	No
Plastic toys	Yes	No
Fish bone	Yes	No
Chicken bone	Yes	No
Coin	No	Yes
Metal pin	No	Yes
Small nut	No	Yes
Small battery	No	Yes

concludes that the proposed algorithm is effective in retrieving arbitrary shaped regions. Van as et al., (2003) presented a study related to the impact of aspired foreign body location and size on children. From the existing work observation the commonly aspired foreign bodies are summarized in Table 1 based on radiolucent and radiopaque feature.

As per the literature survey the foreign body can be divided in two categories such as radiopaque foreign body and radiolucent foreign body. Plastic object, Meat, Peanut, Nail pieces, Plastic toys, Latex balloon, Marble ball normally are the type of the radiolucent foreign body and Coin, Fish Bone, Chicken bone, Metal pin, Metallic material like small nut, Small battery and Needles are the radiopaque foreign body. The significance of assessing the aspired foreign body descriptors such as size, shape, and anatomic location is more essential for the early recognition and timely treatment management of aspirated foreign bodies in pediatric X-ray images. At present many of the researches are focusing on enhancing the quality of the image to provide better visualization for medical experts but none of the research work carried for automatically determine the features of aspired foreign body. From the existing work it is understood that the significance of identifying features such as size shape and location of the aspired foreign body. Hence the proposed work aims to develop a knowledge or evidence base with automatic determination of shape of foreign bodies in X-ray images of pediatric patients.

Proposed Work

An approach for automatic shape determination of foreign body objects in X-ray images in introduced. Schematic view of determining the shapes of foreign body in pediatric radiography images is shown in Figure 1.

Figure 1. Schematic view of determining the shapes of foreign body in pediatric radiography images

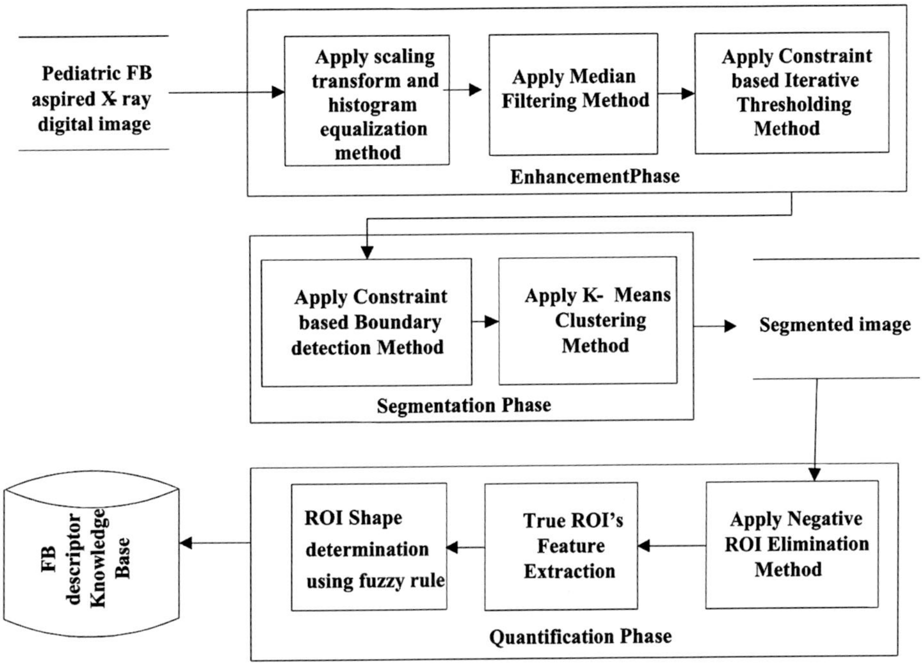

Figure 2. Sample segmentation process results of pediatric radiography images

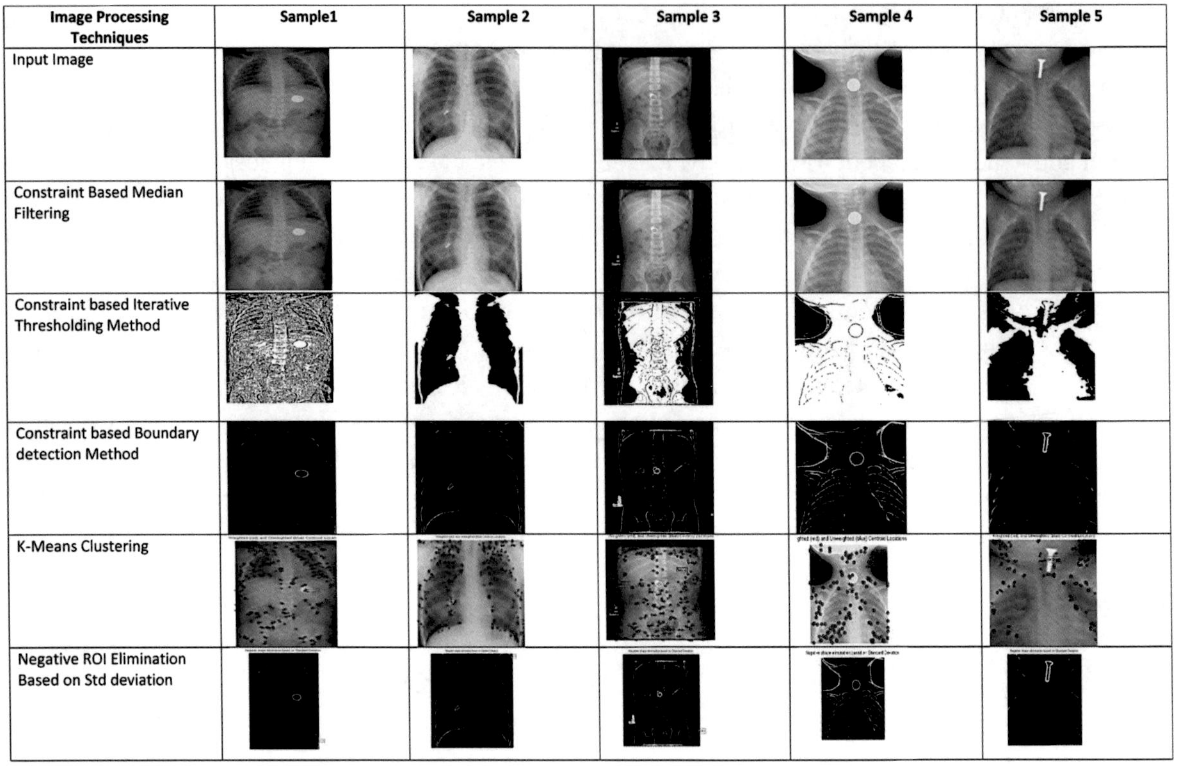

Image Processing Techniques	Sample1	Sample 2	Sample 3	Sample 4	Sample 5
Input Image					
Constraint Based Median Filtering					
Constraint based Iterative Thresholding Method					
Constraint based Boundary detection Method					
K-Means Clustering					
Negative ROI Elimination Based on Std deviation					

Enhancement methods such as scaling transformation and histogram equalization allows the observer to focus on specific intensity band of interest, constraint based median filtering, constraint based iterative thresholding methods are used to reduce noise and increase the contrast of structure of interest. Segmentation methods are operate based on pixel intensity and texture variations of the images which include Sobel boundary detection and pattern recognition method such as K-Means clustering. The K-means clustering method is used to group the normal and abnormal pixel in the image and thus determines the size of the interested region in the preprocessed image. Decision based negative ROI elimination method is used to rapidly rule out infeasible segmentations. The result of segmentation process is shown in Figure 2. Quantification methods are applied to segmented structure to extract the essential diagnostic information such as shape, size, circularity and etc., The shapes are determined by using fuzzy logical connectives formed by logically connecting two or more extracted information. A knowledge or evidence base with the identified influenced descriptors such as size, shape is created to assist the treatment management process of pediatric foreign body aspiration. Finally a knowledge or evidence base with the identified influenced descriptors such as size, standard deviation, circularity, shape and etc., is created to assist the medical practitioner in treatment management process of pediatric foreign body aspiration.

True ROI's Feature Extraction

The negative ROI elimination method highlights the true ROI. For feature extraction, the true ROI boundaries are detected, and from the boundary, the features such as Area, Perimeter, Standard Deviation of edges, Eular Number, Maximum Intensity, Minimum Intensity, thinness ratio, etc., are calculated. By using boundary descriptors, shape descriptors such as Convex Area, Circularity, Compactness, Rectangularity, Eccentricity, and Solidity are calculated for further classification. Table 3 shows the various descriptors with description.

Steps involved in feature extraction

Step 1: Loop over the region values to determine the labeled true ROI.
Step 2: Obtain (X, Y) boundary coordinates corresponding to label 'k' region.
Step 3: Find minimum and maximum values of x and y coordinate
Step 4: The size of the region (Area) is calculated using the boundary coordinates.

$$Area = \sum_{i=0}^{n} r(x_i, y_j)$$

Step 5: Find radius of each labeled region using following formula

$$Radius = \sqrt{(x_2 - x_1)^2 + (y_2 - y_1)^2}$$

Step 6: Calculate various boundaries and shapes metrics using the formula described in Table 2.

ROI Shape Determination Using Fuzzy Rules and Binary Decision Tree

For each region, the features are extracted and constructed as feature vector and is given below:

FV (Shape) = {FV (descriptors)}

where FV (descriptors) is a shape and boundary features extracted from of the regions presented in the input Pediatric X-ray image. Various shapes of the foreign bodies used in this work are shown in Table 4. The shapes are determined by using fuzzy logical connectives formed by logically connecting two or more extracted information called descriptors. Table 5 shows the Fuzzy Logical connective rules involved in ROI shape determination method. Figure 2 shows the decision tree which is used for determining shape of ROI in FB radiography images.

Steps Involved in ROI Shape Determination Method

Step 1: The features of the true ROI are calculated and stored in a database.
Step 2: Using the shape parameters, the rules have been constructed to determine the shape of the True ROI region.
Step 3: The metric ranges 0 as lowest and 1 as the highest value
Step 4: The circularity metric determines the shape of circle and polygon
Step 5: The Eccentricity metric determines the shape of Elongated

Table 2. Various descriptors with description

S. No.	Descriptor	Expression	Description
1	Area	$Area = \sum_{i=0}^{n} r(x_i, y_j)$	Total pixels in the region
2	Perimeter	$Perimeter = \sum_{i=0}^{n} B_r(x_i, y_j)$	The number of pixels of boundary of the region
3	Standard Deviation	$Sd_r = \sqrt{\dfrac{1}{n}\sum_{i=1}^{n}\left(x_i - \bar{x}\right)^2}$	A measure of average contrast of the region boundary
4	Eular Number	Number of connected components – number of holes	Euler number is relation between the number of contiguous parts and the number of holes on a region
5	Maximum Intensity	Pixel with the greatest intensity	Specifying the value of the pixel with the greatest intensity in the region
6	Minimum Intensity	Pixel with the lowest intensity	Specifying the value of the pixel with the lowest intensity in the region.
7	Thinness Ratio	$Tr = \left(\dfrac{4 * \pi * Area}{Perimeter}\right)$	Used to distinguish circle and line from other region
8	Circularity	$Cir = \left(\dfrac{4 * \pi * Area}{(Perimeter)^2}\right)$	Measure of circularity of the region
9	Convex Area	$ConAr = \sum_{i=0}^{n} r(x_i, y_j)$	Total pixels in the region
10	Compactness	$Compact = \left(\dfrac{2 * \sqrt{Area * x}}{Perimeter}\right)$	Degree of deviation of the region from a perfect circle
11	Elongation	$Elong = \left(\dfrac{Area}{(2 * RMax)^2}\right)$	Ratio of minimum dimension to maximum dimension of the rectangle
12	Rectangularity	$Rect = \left(\dfrac{Area}{perimeter}\right)$	Represents how a region is similar as rectangle
13	Eccentricity	$Ecc = \sqrt{1 - \left(\dfrac{R\min}{R\max}\right)^2}$	The eccentricity is the ratio of the distance between the ellipse and its major axis length.
14	Solidity	$Solidity = \left(\dfrac{Area}{ConvexArea}\right)$	Specifying the proportion of the pixels in the convex area that are also in the region.
15	Dispersion	$Disp = \left(\dfrac{RMax}{Area}\right)$	Measure of irregularity of region
16	Centroid	The x and y coordinate of the center of region	The x and y coordinate of the center of region

Figure 3. Various shapes of the foreign bodies

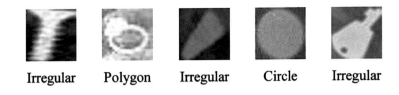

Irregular   Polygon   Irregular   Circle   Irregular

Table 3. Fuzzy logical connective rules for shape determination

Class	Logically Connected Descriptors (P)	Logical Connective Rule (Implication P→Q) where P Is Descriptor and Q Is Input Value	Output ([2] B. Surendiran et al., (2012))
Class A	Circularity	$if\left(Circularity \geq 0.90\right)$	Circle
Class B	Circularity	$if\left(Circularity \geq 0.70 \,\&\,\&Circularity \leq 0.89\right)$	Polygon
Class C	Eccentricity	$if\left(Eccentricity \geq 0.80\right)$	Elongation
Class D	Rectangularity	$if\left(Rectangularity \geq 0.80\right)$	Rectangle
Class E	Dispersion	$if\left(Dispersion \leq 0.20\right)$	Irregular

Figure 4. Procedure used to determine the shape of ROI

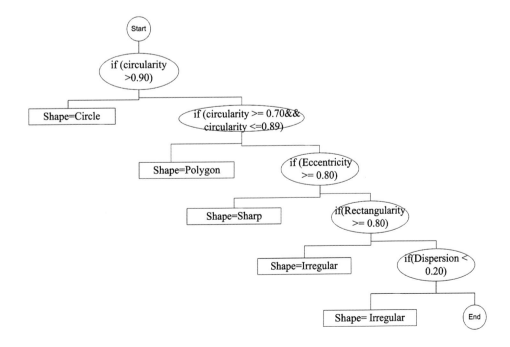

Table 4. Computed values for geometric and edge based features

Sample	F1	F2	F3	F4	F5	F6	F7	F8	F9	F10	F11	F12	F13	F14	F15	F16
Sample 1	5.9	2336	223.92	50.03	39	17	1	1	3.05	0.01	10.43	0.99	0.45	10	0.59	Irregular
Sample2	8.4	741	105.4	12.99	0	77	1	2	1.86	0.02	7.03	0.29	0.6	4.54	0.84	Polygon
Sample3	23.13	683	107.4	0.71	2	1	2	0	0.01	0.5	0.87	1	0.59	50	0.74	Polygon
Sample4	9.1	1024	119.05	53.67	101	25	1	5	3.94	0.02	8.6	0.9	0.26	22.02	0.91	Polygon
Sample5	0.63	114	47.8	0.91	4	1	18	0.01	0.01	0.5	0.91	0.83	3.51	38.07	0.63	Circular
Sample6	49.82	1471	538.84	20.12	107	1	21	0	0	0.5	0.83	0.55	0.27	20.46	0.06	Polygon
Sample7	32.82	969	119.4	1.88	7	1	54	0.01	0.02	0.5	0.86	0.8	0.41	3.91	0.85	Polygon
Sample8	15.85	468	89.11	27.86	146	1	46	0.03	0.01	0.5	0.54	0.55	0.85	57.77	0.74	Polygon
Sample9	92.07	1934	246.59	1.77	6	1	8	0	0.01	0.5	0.87	1	0.13	20.5	0.62	Polygon
Sample10	6.81	201	82.77	35.78	141	1	82	0.02	0.01	0.5	0.66	0.68	1.99	31.71	0.37	Sharp
Sample11	3.4	321	74.26	29.32	152	2	60	0.02	0.01	0.4	0.57	0.77	1.66	28.14	0.28	Sharp
Sample12	5.8	156	67.07	32.65	149	1	73	0.05	0	0.5	0.99	0.57	1.89	29.77	0.38	Sharp
Sample13	6.06	179	77.46	1.41	5	1	8	0.01	0.01	0.5	0.91	1	2.23	34.5	0.37	Sharp
Sample14	4.61	136	66.28	1.95	10	1	47	0.01	0.01	0.5	0.99	0.67	2.94	2.74	0.39	Sharp
Sample15	0.39	103	57.8	3.71	11	1	8	0.01	0.01	0.5	0.93	0.75	3.88	37.67	0.39	Sharp
Sample16	3.62	107	55.11	1.35	7	1	89	0.01	0.01	0.5	1	0.67	3.74	3.84	0.44	Irregular
Sample17	13.31	393	106.85	3.71	14	2	9	0.01	0.01	0.5	0	1	1.02	29	0.43	Irregular
Sample18	6.5	2154	204.07	0	1	8	8	1	0	0.01	10.56	0	1	10.33	0.73	Irregular
Sample19	97.82	3479	263.18	45.72	182	1	682	0.01	0.01	0.5	0.93	0.56	0.11	17.26	0.63	Irregular
Sample20	30.31	895	659.55	81.76	255	1	124	0	0	0.5	0.78	0.42	0.45	99.04	0.03	Irregular

F1 = Size, F2 = Area, F3 = Perimeter, F4 = Standard Deviation, F5 = Minimum Intensity, F6 = Maximum Intensity, F7 = ConvexArea, F8 =Compactness, F9 = Elongation, F10 = Rectangularity, F11 = Eccentricity, F12 = Solidity, F13 = Dispersion, F14 = Centroid, F15 = ThinnessRatio, F16= Shape.

Step 6: The Rectangularity metric determines the shape of rectangle

Step 7: The Smaller value of the dispersion metric determines the shape of Irregular

The procedure used for determine the shape of ROI using binary decision tree is shown in Figure 4.

Experimental Results

Experimental testing shows efficient results in shape determination. The proposed approach focuses on characterizing the foreign body shape using sixteen various geometric and edge features. The computed value for geometric and edge based features have been shown in Table 4.

The geometric features such as size denotes the identified foreign body size in centimeter, area denotes the total number of pixels in the foreign body, perimeter, standard deviation, minimum intensity, maximum intensity, solidity, centriod, Thinness ratio are calculated based on the standard deviation. These calculated edge based features are the base for calculating shape based features such as convex area, compactness, elongation, rectangularity, eccentricity and dispersion. The 60% misclassification in circle determination shows under polygon in most of the samples. This is because of the experiment is developed to identify the perfect circle by considering the variation in thinness ratio of the interested

Figure 5. Classification rate of shape determination

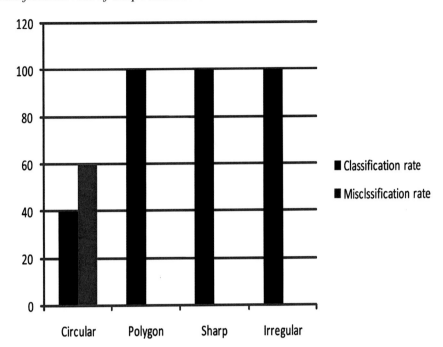

Table 5. Performance analysis of shape determination

Shape	Correct Classification (in %)	Misclassification (in %)
Circular	40%	60%
Polygon	100%	0%
Sharp	100%	0%
Irregular	100%	0%

region. For experimental test 60 radiographic images from various public medical databases like gopix were used and the results achieved 85% of correct classification accuracy in determining the shape as circle, polygon, sharp and irregular. The performance analysis of shape determination such as circle, polygon, sharp and irregular is shown in Table 5. The percentage of correctly determined shape and the misclassification percentage of shape determination are showed in Figure 5.

CONCLUSION

The developed system is efficient for analyzing the pediatric foreign body aspired X-Ray images for doctors and medical practitioners. Figure 3 shows the experimental results with 100% accuracy in shape determination for polygon sharp and irregular, 40% prediction accuracy in circle detection. Overall the proposed shape determination approach achieves 85% of correct classification accuracy in determining the aspired foreign body shape as circle, polygon, sharp and irregular on pediatric radiographic images.

The doctors can able to decide the further treatment procedure based on the shape of the foreign body. The future work aims to propose an approach that helps to standardize the clinical practice and to provide efficient evidence-base for the treatment management process of foreign body removal.

REFERENCE

Chadha, A., Mallik, S., & Johar, R. (2012). Comparative Study and Optimization of Feature-Extraction Techniques for Content based Image Retrieval. *International Journal of Computers and Applications*, *52*(20), 35–42. doi:10.5120/8320-1959

Erbil, B., & Karaca, M. A. (2013). Emergency admissions due to swallowed foreign bodies in Adults. *World Journal of Gastroenterology*, *19*(38), 6447–6452. doi:10.3748/wjg.v19.i38.6447 PMID:24151363

Firoz, R., Ali, M. S., Khan, M. N. U., Hossain, M. K., Islam, M. K., & Shahinuzzaman, M. (2016). Medical Image Enhancement Using Morphological Transformation. *Journal of Data Analysis and Information Processing*, *4*(12), 1–12. doi:10.4236/jdaip.2016.41001

Hemalatha P. A. (2013). Image Retrieval by Content Using Descriptors. *International Journal of Engineering Sciences & Research Technology, 2*(10), 1-7.

Jasani, D., Patel, P., Patel, S., Ahir, B., Patel, K., & Dixit, M. (2015). Review of Shape and Texture Feature Extraction Techniques for Fruits. *International Journal of Computer Science and Information Technologies*, *6*(6), 4851–4854.

Karthikeyan, C., Ramadoss, B., & Baskar, S. (2012). Segmentation Algorithm for CT Images using Morphological Operation and Artificial Neural Network. *International Journal of Signal Processing. Image Processing and Pattern Recognition*, *5*(2), 115–122.

Kaviani, F., Rashid, R. J., Shahmoradi, Z., & Gholamian, M. (2014). Detection of Foreign Bodies by Spiral Computed Tomography and Cone Beam Computed Tomography in Maxillofacial Regions. *Journal Dental Research and Dental Clinical Prospects*, *8*(3), 166–171. PMID:25346836

Kekre, H. B., Thepade, S., Mukherjee, P., Kakaiya, M., Wadhwa, S., & Singh, S. (2010). Image Retrieval with Shape Features Extracted using Gradient Operators and Slope Magnitude Technique with BTC. *International Journal of Computers and Applications*, *6*(8), 28–33. doi:10.5120/1094-1430

Khan, S. U., Chai, W. Y., See, C. S., & Khan, A. (2016). X-Ray Image Enhancement Using a Boundary Division Wiener Filter and Wavelet-Based Image Fusion Approach. *Journal of Information Process System*, *12*(1), 35–45.

Liu, Y., Zhou, X., & Ma, W.-Y. (2004). Extracting Texture Features from Arbitrary-shaped Regions for Image Retrieval. *Multimedia and Expo 2004 IEEE International Conference*, *3*(3), 1891-1894.

Park, J. H., Park, C. H., Park, J. H., Lee, S. J., Lee, W. S., & Joo, Y. E. (2004). Review of 209 cases of foreign bodies in the upper gastrointestinal tract and clinical factors of successful endoscopic removal. *The Korean Journal of Gastroenterology*, *4*(3), 226–233. PMID:15100486

Park, Y.-K., Kim, K.-O., Yang, J.-H., Lee, S.-H., & Jang, B.-I. (2013). Factors Associated with Development of Complications After Endoscopic Foreign Body Removal. *Saudi Journal of Gastroenterology*, *19*(5), 230–234. doi:10.4103/1319-3767.118136 PMID:24045597

Raahat, , Raza, Umar, Hussain, Rasheed, & Rao. (2013). Coin Impaction at Upper end of Esophagus; Wait or Intervene. *Pakistan Journal of Otolaryngology*, *29*(3), 77–79.

Robert, E. (2015). Management of Ingested Foreign Bodies in Children: A Clinical Report of the NASP-GHAN Endoscopy Committee. *Journal of Pediatric Gastroenterology and Nutrition*, *60*(4), 562–574. doi:10.1097/MPG.0000000000000729 PMID:25611037

Saki, N., Nikakhlagh, S., Rahim, F., & Abshirini, H. (2009). Foreign body aspirations in Infancy: A 20-year experience. *International Journal of Medical Sciences*, *6*(6), 322–328. doi:10.7150/ijms.6.322 PMID:19851473

Surendiran, B., & Vadivel, A. (2012). Mammogram mass classification using various geometric shape and margin features for early detection of breast cancer. *International Journal of Medical Engineering and Informatics*, *4*(1), 36–54. doi:10.1504/IJMEI.2012.045302

Talati & Shah. (2014). Feature Extraction Technique using Shape Context Descriptor for Image Retrieval. *Indian Journal of Applied Research*, *4*(8), 1-2.

Thacker, P. G., & Lee, E. Y. (2016). Advances in Multidetector CT Diagnosis of Pediatric Pulmonary Thromboembolism. *Korean Journal of Radiology*, *17*(2), 198–208. doi:10.3348/kjr.2016.17.2.198 PMID:26957904

Tian. (2013). A Review on Image Feature Extraction and Representation Technique. *International Journal of Multimedia and Ubiquitous Engineering*, *8*(4), 385-396.

Tirpude, & Welekar. (2013). A Study of Brain Magnetic Resonance Image Segmentation Techniques. *International Journal of Advanced Research in Computer and Communication Engineering*, *4*(3), 279–284.

Uyemura, M. C. (2005). Foreign Body Ingestion in Children. *American Academy of Family Physicians*, *72*(2), 287–291. PMID:16050452

Van As,, A.B., duToit, N., Wallis, L., Stool, D., Chen, X., & Rode, H. (2003). Pediatric coin ingestion: A prospective study of coin location and symptoms- The South African experience with ingestion injury in children. *International Journal of Pediatric Otorhinolaryngology*, *67*(1), 1–8. PMID:12560141

Withey, D. J., & Koles, Z. J. (2007). Three Generations of Medical Image Segmentation, Methods and Available Software. *International Journal of Bioelectromagnetism*, *9*(2), 67–68.

Xiao-ying, X., & Hui-shu, Y. (2015). Imaging and differential diagnosis of pediatric spinal tuberculosis. *Radiology of Infectious Diseases*, *1*(20), 78–82. doi:10.1016/j.jrid.2015.02.005

Chapter 9
Evaluation of Image Detection and Description Algorithms for Application in Monocular SLAM

Claudio Urrea
Universidad de Santiago de Chile, Chile

Gabriel Solar
Universidad de Santiago de Chile, Chile

ABSTRACT

The results of new experiments on the detection and description of images for an EKF-SLAM monocular application are employed in order to obtain a dispersed set of features without related data association problems. By means of different detectors/descriptors, the number of features observed and the ability to observe the same feature in various captures is evaluated. To this end, a monocular vision system independent of the EKF-SLAM system is designed and implemented using the MatLab software. This new system allows for—in addition to image capture—the detection and description of features as well as the association of data between images, thus serving as a priori information to avoid incorrect associations between the obtained features and the map of an EKF-SLAM system. Additionally, it enables the evaluation and comparison of the precision, consistency and convergence of various algorithms.

INTRODUCTION

In the field of mobile robots, autonomy is one of the most important features that need further development to improve decision-making before unknown conditions of a medium. Therefore, describing the environment in which the robot is located and the relation of the robot with it becomes fundamental. Simultaneous Localization and Mapping (SLAM) techniques address this problem by gradually constructing a metric map and simultaneously localizing the robot in that map. Through obtaining both entities, it is possible for a robot to navigate in unknown and remote environments, being able to perform risky tasks sometimes impossible for a human being. Notwithstanding, research conducted is not pertinent to all types of applications; for instance, land mobile hexapod robots, that is, with three pairs of legs, have

DOI: 10.4018/978-1-5225-2053-5.ch009

not been studied in depth. These robots are suitable for navigation in non-structured environments, i.e. without regular properties; thus, the study of SLAM applied to them would allow for exploring environments deemed unreachable for other robots.

Nowadays, different authors have proposed a large variety of SLAM algorithms, several of which are available in open code (Chen & Cheng, 2010) and accessible via MatLab software. Among the proposed systems, a predominant research field is SLAM based on artificial vision, specifically SLAM systems based on EKF applied to monocular vision or monocular EKF-SLAM. In this context, the implementation of Civera et al. (2010), which comprises the study of RANdom SAmple Consensus (RANSAC) to establish correspondence between distinctive features of an image, stands out.

In a monocular EKF-SLAM system, the information for detection of a feature is used to define in pixels the coordinates at which a point of interest, i.e. a point of the landmark 3D space, is projected on the image plane. Meanwhile, the information for the description of one feature is employed in the association of data between points of interest. Classically, detection is achieved by means of corner detectors such as Harris, Shi-Tomasi, and FAST[1]'s. Then, an 11x11-pixel image patch is saved from the first observation and projected on the image plane to search for and establish correspondence with features obtained in the captures of Davison (2003), and Davison et al. (2007). Although the classical combination between corner detectors and image patch descriptors is computationally one of the fastest, it lacks in precision (Gauglitz et al., 2011).

Considering the above, in this chapter we present results of new experiments in the detection and description of images with the purpose of improving the precision when obtaining visual features for an application of monocular EKF-SLAM, using MatLab as computational support. Firstly, new detection and description algorithms used in this platform are introduced. Secondly, the design and implementation of a program for the study and analysis of detectors and descriptors is detailed. Finally, the results of the tests conducted, along with the conclusions and projections of this work are presented.

RELATED WORK

At present, there is a wide range of algorithms for the detection and description of image features, therefore a comparative study of those algorithms becomes necessary to evaluate their behavior in a SLAM system. Although the comparative work of these technologies focuses on artificial vision applications, three important studies in the field of visual localization and SLAM should be noted. Firstly, the work of Gauglitz et al. (2011) presents an extensive analysis of the various combinations between detection and description algorithms for a visual localization application. Secondly, Gil et al. (2010) conduct a comparative study on detectors and descriptors for visual SLAM, which is based on the measurement of the repetition in which features appear in successive images (recall) and on the precision of the features obtained by the compared algorithms. However, despite the comparison being useful to improve the system's precision, this study does not consider the uncertainty inherent to SLAM. Finally, Klippenstein and Zhang's (2009) work proposes a new methodology that employs various detectors in order to evaluate the performance of a SLAM system by means of a test of accumulated consistency and uncertainty.

We now present an evaluation of various image detectors and descriptors using MatLab R2014a Computer Vision System Toolbox. A monocular vision system that allows generating a disperse map of visual features is introduced, thereby simplifying data association. Thus, the evaluation of the detectors and descriptors is performed based on the quality of the generated map. The detectors and descriptors studied are defined in sections 3 and 4, respectively. Section 5 addresses the correspondence and selection algorithms, while section 6 deals with the implementation of those algorithms. The program developed to obtain the visual features map is presented in section 7 and the results obtained with each algorithm are shown in section 8. To conclude, conclusions and further developments are analyzed in section 9.

FEATURE DETECTORS

Harris

The Harris detector is one of the first and most widely used algorithms for the detection of points of interest (Harris & Stephens, 1988) in robotic navigation. It is classified as a corner detector that captures intensity variations of an image from a small position change. Mathematically, each pixel is described by a matrix in which the eigenvalues define the intensity gradient with respect to each coordinate axis of the image. A corner is a pixel whose two eigenvalues are high. Figure 1 illustrates detection of corners by means of an intensity gradient. In Figure 1a, it can be clearly seen a flat region, which represents the absence of intensity variation in both directions. On the other hand, Figure 1b shows an intensity variation in only one direction, which is denominated an edge, while the important variation in both directions presented in Figure 1c is denominated a corner.

The Harris detector describes the high eigenvalues by means of a law of response to a corner, based on an autocorrelation function applied to the matrix of each pixel, where the corner is defined by the pixels with a correlation value greater than a given threshold (Klippenstein & Zhang, 2009).

Shi-Tomasi

The Shi-Tomasi detector, which is a variation of the Harris detector, applies the same principle of the intensity gradient to identify a corner, but changing its response law definition (Shi & Tomasi, 1994). In this algorithm, the response law is calculated directly using the minimum of the eigenvalues, and a corner is defined by the pixels with a response law greater than a certain threshold.

Compared to the Harris detector, the Shi-Tomasi detector reduces the region in which a point is detected as a corner. The studies presented by Shi-Tomasi propose that corners obtained by this method are more stable for follow-up (Shi & Tomasi, 1994).

Figure 1. Detection of corners by means of an intensity gradient: a) flat region; b) edge; c) corner

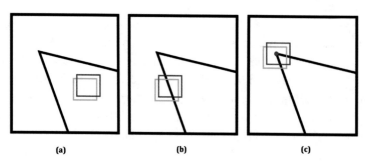

(a)   (b)   (c)

FAST

In contrast with the corner detectors abovementioned, the FAST algorithm does not identify a point of interest by intensity gradients in the image. In this case, the law of response to a corner is based on the identification of the intensity difference in a corner candidate with respect to the circular neighborhood of pixels around that point, which is called test segment (see Figure 2a). The main feature of this algorithm is its execution speed, achieved thanks to the training of a decision tree in the context of machine learning systems (Rosten & Drummond, 2005; Rosten & Drummond, 2006).

BRISK

The Binary Robust Invariant Scalable Keypoints (BRISK) algorithm is a detector as well as a descriptor of image features (Leutenegger et al., 2011). As a detector, it employs the FAST algorithm in different scale-spaces, interpolating the detections to find the localization of a point of interest. This property allows detection to be invariant to image scale changes.

SURF

The Speeded-Up Robust Features (SURF) algorithm is a detector and a descriptor of image features; as a detector, it is denominated Fast Hessian (Bay et al., 2008). Compared to the corner detectors presented above, it is a detector of invariant regions (blob detector) based on the efficient calculation of an approximation of the Hessian matrix determinant obtained at different image scales.

MSER

In contrast with the algorithms presented thus far, Maximally Stable Extremal Regions (MSER) is a blob detector that generates a region of pixels that is typically used for the correlation between stereo images and the recognition of objects (Matas et al., 2004). In this type of detection, a point of interest is defined as the center of gravity of the detected region (see Figure 2b).

Figure 2. Detection of points and regions of interest: a) FAST; b) MSER

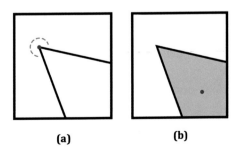

(a)   (b)

FEATURES DESCRIPTORS

Image Section

This is a descriptor of the neighborhood of a point of interest based on a square section of a, generally, 11x11 pixel image in gray scale. It has been studied together with corner detectors such as Harris and Shi-Tomasi's by Davison (2003), and Davison et al. (2007). Additionally, Schmidt and Kasinski (2010) have conducted image section research including FAST-type detectors.

SURF

The SURF algorithm is a descriptor of the circular sampling region neighboring a detected point of interest (Bay et al., 2008). It represents a distribution to the response of a filter based on the convolution of the sampling region with Haar Wavelets. This distribution, which depends on the scale at which a point of interest has been detected, provides orientation information on each point of interest, reproducible under image rotations (Bay et al., 2008). The SURF descriptor is in itself complementary to the Fast Hessian detector, which allows for obtaining the scale information required by the descriptor.

BRISK

Similarly as performed by SURF, the BRISK algorithm describes a point of interest by means of a circular sampling region. However, with the BRISK algorithm, this description is carried out through a binary vector that contains information of image intensity on the sampling pattern, akin to the Binary Robust Independent Elementary Features (BRIEF) descriptor (Calonder et al., 2010). The sampling pattern produced by the BRISK algorithm is characterized by obtaining N equidistant points concentric to the detected point of interest (symbolized by small blue circles in Figure 3a), with a smaller standard deviation toward the center of the circular pattern (symbolized by dashed- line red circles in Figure 3a). This information is used, in turn, to find the orientation of a point of interest, as is conducted with SURF.

FREAK

The Fast Retina Keypoint (FREAK) algorithm is a descriptor inspired on the human visual system's retina (Alahi et al., 2012). Similar to the BRISK algorithm, FREAK is characterized by obtaining a circular sampling pattern of binary information on image intensity around a point of interest. However, it differs in its distribution, which has a greater density of points towards the center, as shown in Figure 3b, as it is based on the distribution of the retinal ganglion cells and their corresponding receptors. The algorithm calculates a cascade of binary chains by the efficient comparison of image intensity to the sampling pattern. The FREAK descriptor has been studied based on the Adaptive and Generic Accelerated Segment Test (AGAST) corner detector, akin to the FAST algorithm for corner detection (Alahi et al., 2012).

Figure 3. Sampling pattern of binary descriptors: a) BRISK; b) FREAK

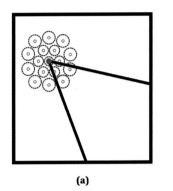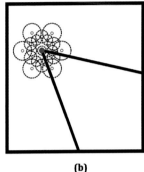

(a)   (b)

DATA ASSOCIATION

Data association allows the recognition of the same feature in various images, by identifying the feature with a label. Thereby, a monocular EKF-SLAM system can recognize the correspondence between an observed feature and a landmark of the map identified with the same label. To recognize the points of interest, detected and described by any of the previously mentioned algorithms, the system matches the points of the previous image with each point of the current image and selects the correct correspondences one-to-one.

The matching stage is carried out with the description information, employing the Nearest Neighbor (NN) algorithm, which rejects ambiguous correspondences through a ratio of the distance between two similar correspondences, as described by Lowe (2004). This also allows obtaining a metric between corresponded features by means of Sum of Squared Differences (SSD).

The selection stage is conducted by the detection information from the corresponded features in the matching stage. By means of the M-estimator Sample Consensus (MSAC) algorithm, which is a generalization of the RANSAC algorithm (Torr & Zisserman, 2000), correspondences that present a behavior similar to that of an estimated model of projective geometric transformation are accepted as valid. Furthermore, to ensure the one-to-one association between the current points of interest and those of a previous instant, the correspondence that has a greater metric is accepted. Thus, points of interest accepted by the selection (inliers) are identified with the same label, whereas those that are not (outliers) are rejected.

DESCRIPTION OF THE IMPLEMENTED FUNCTIONS

The system for obtaining points of interest is based on the feature detection algorithms presented in the previous sections, i.e.: Harris, Shi-Tomasi, FAST, BRISK, SURF and MSER, description Patch, SURF, BRISK and FREAK, NN-Ratio correspondence, and MSAC selection. Table 1 presents the functions implemented in the MatLab R2014a Computer Vision System Toolbox, which allows for the evaluation of those algorithms.

The point of interest detection functions (Category: Detector, in Table 1), corresponding to the previously presented detectors, give as a result a data structure that defines the detected type of point or region

Table 1. Functions implemented in the MatLab 2014a Computer Vision System toolbox

Name	Category
detectHarrisFeatures	Detector
detectMinEigenFeatures	Detector
detectFASTFeatures	Detector
detectBRISKFeatures	Detector
detectSURFFeatures	Detector
detectMSERRegions	Detector
cornerPoints	Class
BRISKPoints	Class
SURFPoints	Class
MSERRegions	Class
extractFeatures	Descriptor
matchFeatures	Correspondence
estimateGeometricTransform	Selection

(Category: Class, in Table 1), which are cornerPoints class with Harris, Shi-Tomasi and FAST, and other classes denominated after their detector's name. The description function (Category: Descriptor, in Table 1), is executed by default according to the type of point of interest used. Specifically, FREAK is used as a descriptor for cornerPoints and BRISKPoints, while SURF is for SURFPoints, and MSERRegion. With the purpose of comparing the performance of all the presented detectors/descriptors, each set is evaluated by modifying the default method. The correspondence function (Category: Correspondence, in Table 1) is configured with an SSD metric and under the NN-Ratio method. Finally, the selection function (Category: Selection, in Table 1), which uses the MSAC method, is configured under a projective transformation according to what was expressed above.

DESCRIPTION OF THE MONOCULAR VISION SYSTEM

The monocular vision system allows for obtaining a set of features repeatedly observed in different captures, which is called visual features map. In other words, the system registers a history of the features that have been corresponded by means of data association, with at least one image. When one feature is corresponded for the first time, it is added to the visual features map, and then identified with a label. On the other hand, if the correspondence of one feature is repeated, the information of the visual features map is updated and the new observation is identified with the previously designed label. In this way, the monocular vision system allows the evaluation of detectors and descriptors according to the behavior of the visual features map.

The features map obtained is independent of the SLAM system, allowing this system to be implemented in an embedded form in a CMUcam3[2] type monocular camera or by means of FPGA, as in the work developed by Krajník et al. (2014) on the detection and description of SURF features. In the context of scene 3D reconstruction, this approach is similar to camera trackers or match movers systems, such as the noncommercial Voodoo Camera Tracker[3] software.

In the proposed system, the camera's localization information is not estimated as it is obtained naturally from a monocular EKF-SLAM system. Consequently, it is not possible to identify whether a feature of the visual map is visible or not due to rotation and translation effects on the monocular camera. As a result, correspondence between features is effective only when they are observed repeatedly within the camera's field of view. However, this is not sufficient for a SLAM system in which data association is carried out by means of the estimated probability region (search region) of an observation in the image plane[4]. In fact, the information obtained with the proposed system may be used to define a priori the correspondences between the map of the SLAM system and the observations made, allowing this map to be corrected and, in turn, reducing the estimated probability region, and simplifying the data association problem. The work of Shi et al. (2013) shows that, by feature selection, the reliability of data association is improved, therefore the consistency of the monocular EKF-SLAM system is ensured.

Additionally, the system possess a graphic interface, administered by the main interface (Figure 4a), and composed of a capture system (Figure 4b) and an image processing system (Figure 4c) in which the detection and description algorithm used for each test is configured.

Finally, the algorithm developed to obtain the visual features map is described. The system functions through the consecutive association of the points of interest of current and previous captures, as well as with the features map obtained thus far, which is composed of the formerly validated associations between pairs of captures. Therefore, the system is governed by the structure shown in Figure 5 flow chart.

Initializing and updating the points of interest are two noteworthy stages in the association system. The former is meant to add new points of interest to the map, while the latter intends to update the information of the points on the map with the new associations made.

Two important functions are performed in the initialization stage: establishing new and disperse features to initialize the process, and defining the feature with an identification label. The points of interest that have no correspondence with the matching algorithm are considered as new features. To obtain dispersed points based on the set of new points associated between captures, a certain minimum radius of the distance between the points on the image in the image plane is defined, accepting as valid points those with the largest metric provided by the matching algorithm.

In the updating stage, in addition to renewing the description and detection information on the points of interest, the number of times that a point has been reconsidered is updated. With this purpose, given a minimum number of captures, a certain threshold is established that allows defining whether the number of updates made is sufficient to retain the point of interest on the map; otherwise that point is deleted.

RESULTS

Using various detectors/descriptors, the quality of the obtained features map is evaluated. To define that quality, the number of features observed, based on the number of initiated labels, as well as the capacity for observing the same feature in different captures, which is determined by the ratio of the number of labels deleted in the process to the total number of initiated labels, are measured.

In this analysis, the tests were conducted using static scenes, with a natural movement of the monocular camera, to exclude from the evaluation the labels deleted due to lack of visibility of the feature caused by rotation and translation effects. In particular, tests were carried out considering three different environments: the first two were outdoors under natural light, an unstructured environment of a tree and a dirt street (Figure 6a) and a structured environment of a street and buildings (Figure 6b),respectively; and the third was an indoor structured environment under artificial light (Figure 6c).

Experiments consisted in capturing the same scene using various detectors/descriptors during 10 seconds. This allowed to run a performance evaluation of the system, in which the number of possible captures was different for each set of algorithms evaluated.

Figure 4. Interface developed on MatLab R2014a: a) main interface; b) capture system; c) image processing system

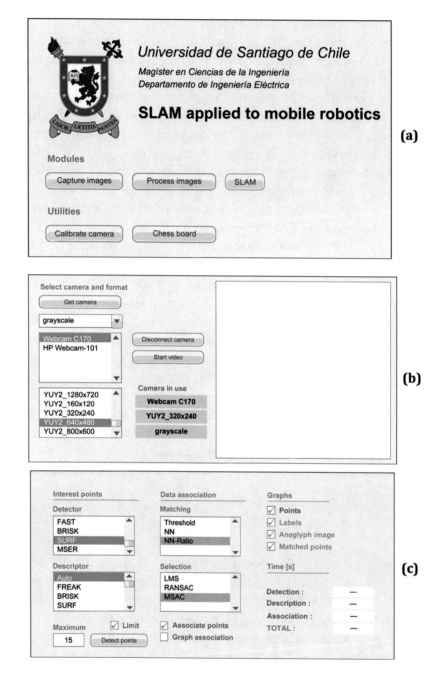

The results obtained for each of the three experiments are provided below. Figures 7, 11 and 15 show the numbers of labels obtained per capture using the detectors/descriptors, and Figures 8, 12 and 16 present the ratio of labels deleted in each capture. Considering the results delivered by the previously described graphs, Figures 9, 13 and 17 show the mean (symbolized by bars) and the variance (symbol-

Figure 5. Flowchart of the data association system structure

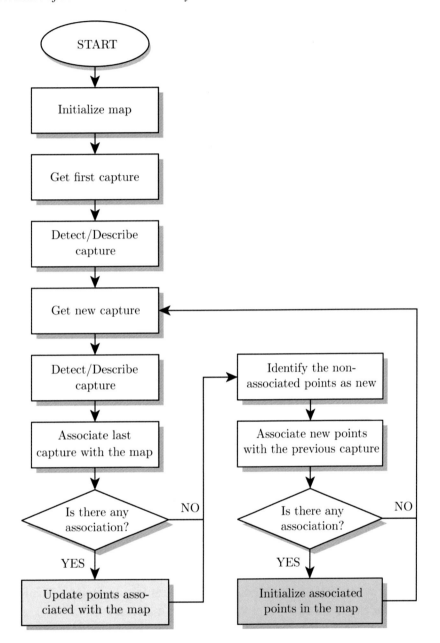

ized by error bars) of the evaluation of descriptors vs. detectors, and Figures 10, 14 and 18 present the mean and the variance of the evaluation of detectors vs. descriptors.

For the experiment conducted in the environment composed of the tree and the street (Figure 6a), results are shown in Figures 7, 8, 9, and 10.

In Figure 7 it can be seen that, in general, the FAST, BRISK and SURF detectors are the ones that process more captures. However, this does not represent a generalized advantage. An example of this feature is the BRISK/FREAK set, which, in particular, presents a very limited number of labels (Figure 7b).

Figure 6. Detection/description tests in three different environments: a) tree and dirt street; b) street and buildings; c) house corridor

(a)   **(b)**

(c)

Figure 8 shows that the SURF detector, besides processing a large number of captures, has a low deleted/total ratio. Specifically, the SURF/SURF combination shows a remarkable performance.

With respect to Figure 9, it is seen that the detector that provides the largest number of labels is the Shi- Tomasi, albeit having a high deleted/total mean ratio for all types of descriptors. In addition, the Harris/BRISK, SURF/BRISK, SURF/SURF, SURF/Block and MSER/BRISK sets are the ones that deliver the lowest mean and variance of the deleted/total ratio. Nevertheless, the Harris/BRISK and SURF/ SURF sets are the ones with the highest mean for the number of labels obtained. The BRISK detector is particularly variable for each kind of descriptor. Despite the mean and the variance of the deleted/total ratio being small, the number of labels obtained with this detector has a low mean or a very high variance.

Figure 10 shows that the Block descriptor has the largest mean in the number of captures, in spite of having a high deleted/ total mean in general, with the exception of the SURF/Block pair. It must be noted that the BRISK and SURF descriptors deliver the best results.

The results of the experiment in the environment composed of buildings and street (Figure 6b) are shown in Figures 11, 12, 13, and 14.

Figure 11 and Figure 12 show that the performance observed in the previous experiment is enhanced; label detections with BRISK are much fewer than those of the others, and Shi-Tomasi presents the largest number of detected labels in spite of processing a smaller number of images compared to the other detectors. On the other hand, SURF presents a curve of the deleted/total ratio lower than the one

Figure 7. Number of features identified for each capture in the Tree+Street experiment: a) Block; b) Freak; c) BRISK; d) SURF

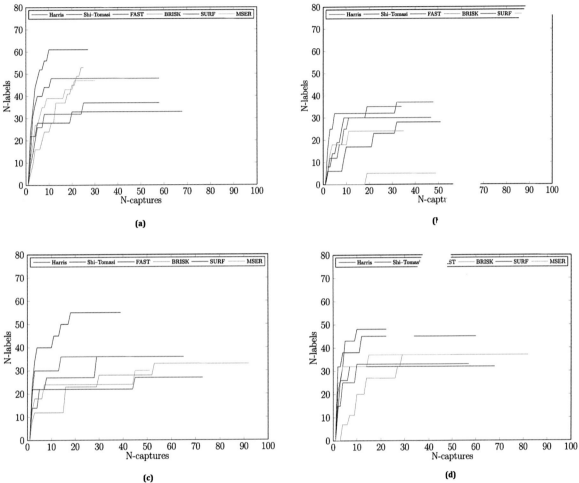

delivered by the other detectors. The Harris/BRISK and Shi-Tomasi/BRISK combinations, which also have good performance, stand out.

Figure 13 reveals a performance similar to that of the previous experiment; in particular, the SURF/SURF combination is of note due to its high mean, minimum variance in the number of captures, and lower mean and variance of the deleted/total ratio.

Figure 14 exhibits, in increasing order, a clear trend of the FREAK, BRISK, SURF and Block detectors towards greater numbers of captures. However, the BRISK and SURF detectors present a lower mean and variance of the deleted/total ratio.

The results of the third and last experiment, carried out in an environment composed of an indoor corridor (Figure 6c), are shown in Figures 15, 16, 17, and 18.

This experiment is very interesting since the number of possible detections can be, in general, low, because of the scarce distinctive regions that constitute the scene.

Figure 8. Ratio of deleted features for each capture in the Tree+Street experiment: a) Block; b) Freak; c) BRISK; d) SURF

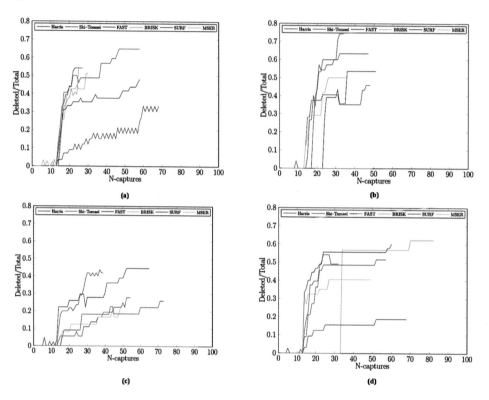

Figure 9. Mean and variance for each type of detector in the Tree+Street experiment: a) Number of labels; b) Deleted/Total

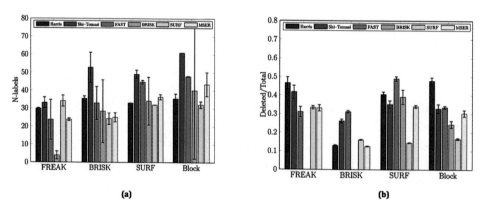

Furthermore, although the texture of the scene capture allows for an easier detection of the wall corners, it renders the association of data by means of descriptors more difficult.

Figure 15 shows that the largest number of label detections correspond, as well as in the previous experiments, to Shi-Tomasi. For the other detectors, the number of detected points is much less.

Figure 16 reveals that the deleted/total ratio is highly variable, especially for the Block descriptor (Figure 16a).

Figure 10. Mean and variance for each kind of descriptor in the Tree+Street experiment: a) Number of labels; b) Deleted/Total

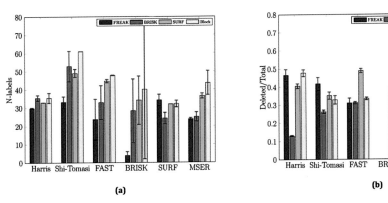

Figure 11. Number of features identified for each capture in the Street+ Buildings experiment: a) Block; b) Freak; c) BRISK; d) SURF

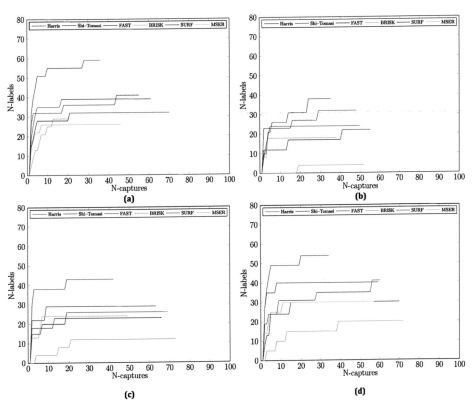

As for the FREAK descriptor, the deleted/total ratio for all detectors is small, which may be attributed to small number of detected labels (Figure 15b).

Figure 17 shows that the greatest number of detections is achieved by Shi-Tomasi. Nevertheless, this detector presents a high variance as well as a high mean and variance with respect to the deleted/

Figure 12. Ratio of features deleted per each capture in the Street+Buildings experiment: a) Block; b) Freak; c) BRISK; d) SURF

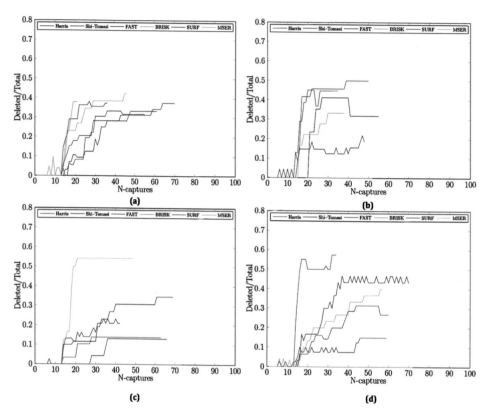

Figure 13. Mean and variance for each kind of detector in the Buildings+Street experiment: a) number of labels; b) deleted/total

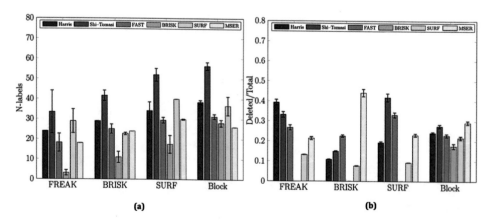

total ratio. The Harris/SURF and SURF/SURF pairs performed best, albeit delivering a low mean for the detected number of labels.

In Figure 18, it can be seen that the worst component is achieved using the Block descriptor, due to the limited visual information in the pixels around a point of interest.

Figure 14. Mean and variance for each kind of descriptor in the Buildings+Street experiment: a) number of labels; b) deleted/total

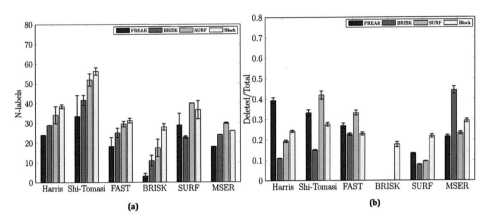

Figure 15. Number of identified features for each capture in the house corridor experiment: a) Block; b) Freak; c) BRISK; d) SURF

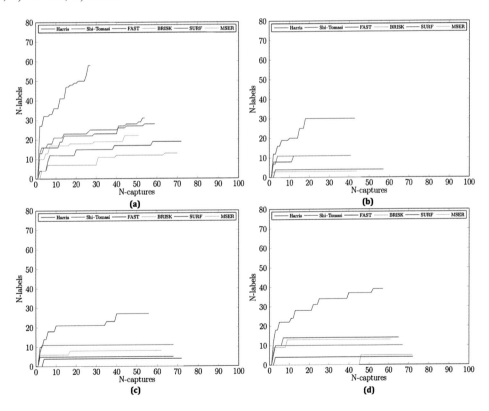

LIMITATIONS OF THE PROPOSED WORK

Regarding processing time and under the hardware conditions formerly described, the modified system spends around 1 second per capture for tests with few landmark detections (Figure 19a and 19b). This

Figure 16. Ratio of deleted features for each capture in the house corridor experiment: a) Block; b) Freak; c) BRISK; d) SURF

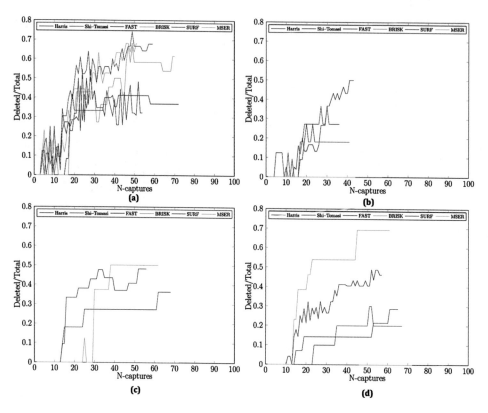

Figure 17. Mean and variance for each kind of detector in the house corridor experiment: a) number of labels; b) deleted/total

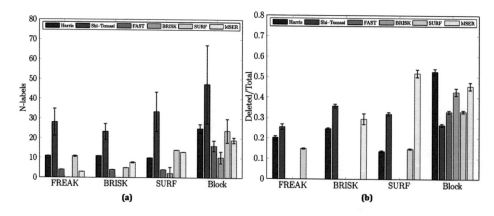

is a considerable decrease, taking into account that it takes the original system from 4 to 10 seconds approximately to capture images with a greater number of landmarks. This decline in processing time is due to the use of the FAST detector available in MatLab 2014a artificial vision toolbox, which enhances the update of graphic objects by the set and get methods aforementioned and by limiting the maximum quantity of searches for a feature.

Figure 18. Mean and variance for each kind of descriptor in the house corridor experiment: a) number of labels; b) deleted/total

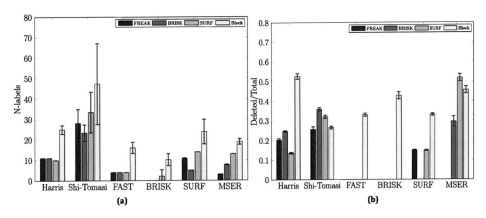

It has been demonstrated that the system, when tested in a simple environment, is able to correctly follow a reduced number of landmarks, as presented in the right window of figures 19a and 19b, where a triangle symbolizes the position of the camera and red ellipses point up the uncertainty region of the landmarks detected in the image (left window). Nevertheless, the system operates more slowly when confronted with a greater number of points, and especially with those that require more complex search (in Figures 19a and 19b, detected points are clearly identifiable corners). Consequently, observations are made between camera positions from longer distances, thus reducing localization and mapping corrections and delivering landmarks with greater uncertainty, as shown in the test performed in figure 19c.

Likewise, tests in non-structure open environments have been conducted. Figure 19d illustrates one of them, in which a greater number of blue points can be observed. These correspond to points previously identified and that could not be matched along the process. This phenomenon is principally due to the

Figure 19. Tests of Civera et al.'s system modified for running SLAM online with a Logitech c170 webcam

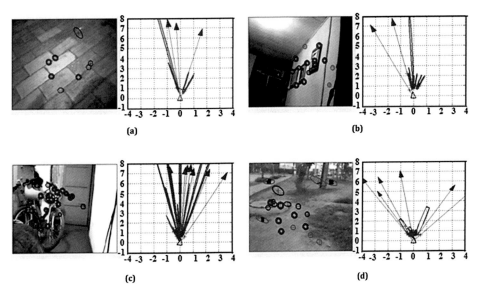

flat texture of the environment. Therefore, implementation of the system in non-structured environments with high relief is proposed.

One of the effects present in all tests is a clear divergence in the system state when the camera suddenly changes its speed and direction, due to the model of motion proposed and to the slowness of the algorithm for greater quantity of landmarks.

CONCLUSION

This chapter presents the evaluation of various detectors/descriptors of image features by measuring the number of features observed and the ability of observing the same feature in different captures, according to the results from the monocular vision system designed and implemented in order to obtain the dispersion of points of interest. In this context, out of the three experiments carried out considering image detection and description, the SURF algorithm is the one that delivers the best results. Results generated by Harris/BRISK and Shi-Tomasi/BRISK are also acceptable, but at the expense of a greater variability of the detected labels.

From the results, it is concluded that the proposed system allows for the creation of an independent monocular vision system based on the SURF detector/descriptor, which permits the observation of points of interest and the association of data between captures, forming an a priori association between the map of a SLAM system and the observations made, and thereby reducing incorrect associations that may affect the consistency of a monocular EKF-SLAM system.

Algorithm Design

The proposed system is a sequential algorithm supported in the EKF structure, in which the localization of a hexapod robot equipped with a monocular sensor is estimated, and a spatial representation of the environment, called map, is constructed by means of the detection and description of visual features from the images captured with the camera.

This algorithm design is based on mobility and environmental conditions recorded in an autonomous navigation application with a hexapod robot, as well as on the studied IT solutions for SLAM. Therefore, in order to develop a VSLAM program in MatLab 2014a that allows the comparison of solutions and can also be implemented under the defined software conditions, the structure of a problem is defined, current solutions based on artificial vision are studied, and the nomenclature used is standardized. The program is then validated through simulation and implemented in the robot being studied. The characteristics of the systems that constitute the program, which were defined in the study, are the following:

1. **Structure of the SLAM System:** Predicts the robot localization and, by constructing a map, corrects through observation of the environment. A data association algorithm is defined with the purpose of obtaining a relation between the map and the observations, which would allow for correcting, increasing and managing this map. Furthermore, an SPD approximation function is implemented and applied to the covariance matrix of estimates, for these not to cause conflict with calculations.
2. **Mobile System:** Types of translation and rotation the robot is able to execute, which are described in the control signal and are implemented by motion strategies. The system mobility is studied,

implementing two models of motion mentioned in the literature review and proposing a new model that describes the sudden speed variations of the hexapod robot.

3. **Observation System:** A type of spatial representation suitable for non-structured environments is defined by means of points. Then, detection and image description algorithms that enable point detection are evaluated, and the model of motion is implemented according to this representation. System observability is assessed based on the camera intrinsic parameters. Additionally, a new method for obtaining extrinsic parameters that relate the camera coordinate systems to the robot is proposed.

4. **Data Association:** An algorithm for the association of images acquired from the monocular camera is implemented in order to relate consecutive observations. Additionally, data association algorithms that match observations with the map are studied.

Implementation Problems Detected

During the development of the proposed program, a number of problems that impaired the implementation or that affected estimates were detected. Some have already been tackled, while other were partially solved and, thus, require a definitive solution in future. These problems are detailed below:

1. Covariance matrices symmetry:
   a. Inversion errors,
   b. Cholesky decomposition errors.
2. Stability and mobility of the robot.
3. Communication with embedded computer.
4. Sudden speed variations.
5. Discrete movement. Low frequency sampling.
6. System speed.
7. Reduced FOV.
8. Uncertainty of the camera's extrinsic parameters.

Proposed Solutions

The proposals for solving the problems detected are considered a principal contribution of this work, since they advance the characterization of SLAM applied to a hexapod robot. The solutions established for each aforementioned item are discussed below:

1. A SPD approximation is carried out.
2. Crab-like lateral motion is no longer employed.
   a. To execute lateral motion, the camera must be rotated in a certain angle, ideally 90°. As this is not mechanically possible, the camera is rotated in a smaller angle. The lateral motion corresponds to the perpendicular component of the camera translation.
   b. In further studies, mechanical problems must be corrected so the robot is able to perform the movement.
3. Direct communication with the SCC-32 card is implemented. This should be corrected in a future approach for the robot to be capable of executing a program in embedded form.

4. A new model of motion based on control pulse is designed.
5. Sampling must be increased:
    a. In frontal translation, the motion strategy with the highest sampling frequency is used.
    b. In order to conduct a movement parallel to capture sampling and that allows obtaining images at high frequency, the state of the robot must be estimated by determining its speed instead of its position.
6. Despite not affecting the results, since the robot moves sequentially during capture and system execution (i.e., it is motionless while these operations are conducted), this problem must be corrected if the motion occurs concurrently with the sampling of image captures.
7. A Genius WideCam F100 camera that possess a wide FOV is used. For this reason, the observation model takes into account radial distortion.
8. Parameters are estimated by the natural correction of EKF-SLAM. This methodology has been proven by simulation and verified through frontal, lateral, and rotational translation tests. Nevertheless, to obtain parameters that are more precise, improving the proposed system in such a way that it becomes more robust before uncertainties is necessary. The correction of the side motion problem will also assist in the execution of tests.

FUTURE PROSPECTS

Based on the theoretical background, it must be acknowledged that a number of fields could not been included, due to its breadth and scope, which were different from the specific objectives of this work. However, it is noteworthy that the contemporaneity of this study renders it the onset of new research lines. Therefore, several proposals that may be implemented in the presented system are herein detailed. The future prospects of this work are as follows:

1. To increase the program's performance by its translation into a low-level language, such as C or C++, which would allow for an embedded implementation in Raspberry Pi computers. Additionally, techniques of efficient processing as well as other SLAM schemes, such as particle filter and key frames, should be taken into account.
2. To parallelize independent stages of the system using parallel and distributed processing. Specifically, the motion instruction to be executed by the robot and image processing can be parallelized.
3. To train the robot with multiple sensors that provide, through data fusion, more information on the dynamics of the system, thereby improving SLAM correction. In particular, combining an IMU sensor and collaborative cameras may enrich the robot dynamic information and the medium structure. In this sense, the design of a device composed of an IMU sensor, a camera and embedded processing is proposed for use in SLAM. This device would allow for obtaining observations by association between captures, at high frequency and using localization information from SLAM when this has finished.
4. To use the state estimated by SLAM for controlling robot position and for assessing the precision of estimates.
5. To study different environment models, such as rigid bodies or thick clouds of points and objects to enhance spatial representation.

ACKNOWLEDGMENT

This work has been supported by Proyectos Basales and the Vicerrectoría de Investigación, Desarrollo e Innovación (VRIDEI), Universidad de Santiago de Chile, Chile.

REFERENCES

Alahi, A., Ortiz, R., & Vandergheynst, P. (2012). *FREAK: Fast retina keypoint*. Paper presented at IEEE Conference on Computer Vision and Pattern Recognition (CVPR), Providence, RI. doi:10.1109/CVPR.2012.6247715

Bay, H., Ess, A., Tuytelaars, T., & Gool, L. V. (2008). Speeded-up robust features (SURF). *Computer Vision and Image Understanding, 110*(3), 346–359. doi:10.1016/j.cviu.2007.09.014

Calonder, M., Lepetit, V., Strecha, C., & Fua, P. (2010). BRIEF: binary robust independent elementary features. In K. Daniilidis, P. Maragos, & N. Paragios (Eds.), *Computer Vision – ECCV 2010* (pp. 778–792). Berlin: Springer-Verlag; doi:10.1007/978-3-642-15561-1_56

Chen, C., & Cheng, Y. (2010). *MatLab-based simulators for mobile robot simultaneous localization and mapping*. Paper presented at 3rd International Conference on Advanced Computer Theory and Engineering (ICACTE), Chengdu, China. doi:10.1109/ICACTE.2010.5579471

Civera, J., Grasa, O. G., Davison, A. J., & Montiel, J. M. M. (2010). 1-Point RANSAC for extended Kalman filtering: Application to real-time structure from motion and visual odometry. *Journal of Field Robotics, 27*(5), 609–631. doi:10.1002/rob.20345

Davison, A. J. (2003). Real-time simultaneous localisation and mapping with a single camera.*Proceedings of the Ninth IEEE International Conference on Computer Vision (ICCV'03)*. doi:10.1109/ICCV.2003.1238654

Davison, A. J., Reid, I. D., Molton, N. D., & Stasse, O. (2007). MonoSLAM: Real-time single camera SLAM. *IEEE Transactions on Pattern Analysis and Machine Intelligence, 29*(6), 1052–1067. doi:10.1109/TPAMI.2007.1049 PMID:17431302

Gauglitz, S., Höllerer, T., & Turk, M. (2011). Evaluation of interest point detectors and feature descriptors for visual tracking. *International Journal of Computer Vision, 94*(3), 335–360. doi:10.1007/s11263-011-0431-5

Gil, A., Martínez, O., Ballesta, M., & Reinoso, O. (2010). A comparative evaluation of interest point detectors and local descriptors for visual slam. *Machine Vision and Applications, 21*(6), 905–920. doi:10.1007/s00138-009-0195-x

Harris, C., & Stephens, M. (1988). A combined corner and edge detector. In *Proceedings of the Fourth Alvey Vision Conference*. Manchester, UK: Alvety Vision Club. doi:10.5244/C.2.23

Klippenstein, J., & Zhang, H. (2009). *Performance evaluation of visual SLAM using several feature extractors*. Paper presented at IEEE/RSJ International Conference on Intelligent Robots and Systems (IROS), St. Louis, MO. doi:10.1109/IROS.2009.5354001

Krajník, T., Sváb, J., Pedre, S., Cizek, P., & Preucil, L. (2014). FPGA-based module for SURF extraction. *Machine Vision and Applications, 25*(3), 787–800. doi:10.1007/s00138-014-0599-0

Leutenegger, S., Chli, M., & Siegwart, R. Y. (2011). *BRISK: Binary robust invariant scalable keypoints.* Paper presented at IEEE International Conference on Computer Vision (ICCV), Barcelona, Spain. doi:10.1109/ICCV.2011.6126542

Lowe, D. G. (2004). Distinctive image features from scale-invariant keypoints. *International Journal of Computer Vision, 60*(2), 91–110. doi:10.1023/B:VISI.0000029664.99615.94

Matas, J., Chum, O., Urban, M., & Pajdla, T. (2004). Robust wide-baseline stereo from maximally stable extremal regions. *Image and Vision Computing, 22*(10), 761–767. doi:10.1016/j.imavis.2004.02.006

Rosten, E., & Drummond, T. (2005). Fusing points and lines for high performance tracking. In *Proceedings of the Tenth IEEE International Conference on Computer Vision (ICCV'05)*. Beijing, China: IEEE. doi:10.1109/ICCV.2005.104

Rosten, E., & Drummond, T. (2006). Machine learning for high-speed corner detection. In A. Leonardis, H. Bischof & A. Pinz (Eds.), Computer Vision – ECCV 2006 (pp. 430–443). Berlin: Springer-Verlag. doi: 34 doi:10.1007/11744023_34

Schmidt, A., & Kasinski, A. (2010). The visual SLAM system for a hexapod robot. In L. Bolc, R. Tadeusiewics, L. J. Chmielewski & K. Wojciechowski (Eds.), Computer Vision and Graphics (pp. 260-267). Berlin: Springer-Verlag. doi: 32 doi:10.1007/978-3-642-15907-7_32

Shi, J., & Tomasi, C. (1994). Good features to track. In *Proceedings of IEEE Computer Society Conference on Computer Vision and Pattern Recognition (CVPR'94)*. Seattle, WA: IEEE. doi:10.1109/CVPR.1994.323794

Shi, Z., Liu, Z., Wu, X., & Xu, W. (2013). Feature selection for reliable data association in visual SLAM. *Machine Vision and Applications, 24*(4), 667–682. doi:10.1007/s00138-012-0440-6

Torr, P., & Zisserman, A. (2000). MLESAC: A new robust estimator with application to estimating image geometry. *Computer Vision and Image Understanding, 78*(1), 138–156. doi:10.1006/cviu.1999.0832

ENDNOTES

[1]   Features From Accelerated Segment Test.

[2]   CMUcam, Open Source Programmable Embedded Color.

[3]   Voodoo Camera Tracker Copyright © 2002-2012.

[4]   Also called active vision or active search, by Davison (2003), and Davison et al. (2007).

Chapter 10
Diophantine Equations for Enhanced Security in Watermarking Scheme for Image Authentication

Padma T
Sona College of Technology, India

Jayashree Nair
AIMS Institutes, India

ABSTRACT

Hard mathematical problems having no polynomial time algorithms to determine a solution are seemly in design of secure cryptosystems. The proposed watermarking system used number theoretic concepts of the hard higher order Diophantine equations for image content authentication scheme with three major phases such as 1) Formation of Diophantine equation; 2) Generation and embedding of dual Watermarks; and 3) Image content authentication and verification of integrity. Quality of the water-marked images, robustness to compression and security are bench-marked with two peer schemes which used dual watermarks.

INTRODUCTION

The past two decades have witnessed revolutionary advancements in the areas of technology and communication. The availability of cheap technological solutions has initiated and nurtured newer avenues in business, entertainment and collaboration, where digital multimedia represents a primary source of communication due to its huge expressive capability. The advancements have also facilitated the efficient storage and proliferation of digital multimedia and along with it issues like data vulnerability and fraud. The rampant availability of digital media processing tools has made copying and manipulation of multimedia an easy task.

DOI: 10.4018/978-1-5225-2053-5.ch010

This vulnerability has necessitated the need for inherent mechanisms in multimedia applications to ensure 1) trust worthiness of the media - to prove ownership, protect copyright and to certify the integrity of the media for assurance that the received media is from an authorized source and is identical to the original one and 2) security during the storage and transmission. Any act or attempt of modification on the digital medium is called an attack and security mechanisms are the methods intended to prevent, detect or recover from a security attack.

Authentication is the act of ensuring trust worthiness of digital media and watermarking is a preferred technique used to implement it. Security of a watermark based authentication scheme lies in the complexity and randomness involved in the watermark generation and embedding process. This is to prevent or make it complex for an adversary to detect, read, remove or tamper with the watermark or watermarked image. Mathematical problems that are hard to solve like RSA, Diffie-Hellman key exchange scheme, El-Gamal and Elliptic curve cryptosystems (ECC) have always been favorites in the design of secure cryptosystems where a polynomial time algorithm does not exist as on date to determine whether there is a solution to the problem or not. Number theory based approaches have been used in literature to generate secret keys and pseudorandom sequences but they involve the use of very large seeds with hundreds of digits. Managing and sharing large keys between the communicating parties is complex and leads to its compromise. They are seldom adopted due to the nature of complex computations and time involved.

Diophantine equation is an algebraic equation relating integer quantities. They are expressed usually in two or more unknowns such that only integer solutions are sought or allowed. Solvability of higher order Diophantine equations is a hard problem and is considered a prospective candidate in the design of secure cryptosystems.

The objective is this study is to design a secure, hierarchical, blind and content based image authentication scheme in the Discrete Wavelet Transform (DWT) domain. Diophantine equations that are hard to solve or those with large number of unknown variables are used as the building block in ensuring security of the scheme. Compression, exposure to channel noise and security being important concerns during the regular storage and transmission of images, the proposed scheme is designed to be robust to common incidental noise and fragile to malicious manipulations especially common attacks like collusion, counterfeiting, cut/copy paste and brute force attacks.

IMAGE AUTHENTICATION

According to Cox and Miller (2002), digital image authentication is the act of verifying the integrity and authenticity (or credibility) of digital images, i.e. to check if the image has undergone any tampering since its creation. Judging the authenticity of an image is hard, if not impossible, and a judgement cannot be made unless it passes certain tests of integrity and authentication confirmation. An image authentication system is expected to detect manipulations, localize it and to some extent recover the manipulated or altered regions. Measures are needed to ensure that the image is protected against illegal tampering and manipulations. Authentication mechanisms do not protect the image from being stolen or copied.

Image authentication techniques, in general, consist of a stamping stage and a verification stage. During the stamping stage, an authentication code like an external logo or a watermark generated from the image is incorporated with the image. During the verification stage, the authentication code extracted from the query image and the authentication code generated from the query image or original watermarked image are correlated to judge the authenticity of the image. Watermarking techniques have been proposed in the spatial domains by Mintzer and Yeung (1999), Holliman and Memon (2000) and Tanaka, Nakamura and Matsui (1991), in the transform domains like Discrete Transform (DCT) by Ahmed, Natarajan and Rao (1974) and Koch and Zhao (1995) in the Discrete Wavelet domain (DWT) domains by Chun-Lin (2010) and Qi, Xin and Chang (2009) and in the Discrete Fourier domain (DFT) domains by Gonzalez, Woods and Eddins (2004).

Based on the requirement of the application and level of robustness expected of the watermark required and the distortions that may be affect the image during storage and transmission of the image, authentication schemes can be categorized as strict or selective. Strict or complete authentication techniques are applied to the entire image and do not accept any type of distortion or manipulation of the watermarked image. The watermarks are usually generated from hash functions on the image and any attempt to distort the watermarked image or exposure to incidental noise will alter the embedded watermark. The scheme rejects an image as inauthentic for the slightest alteration since its creation - if there is even a single bit change in representation of the image (Walton, 1995; Wong, 1998).

Selective or content authentication techniques verify an image for the integrity of the contents and not its representation. Changes in the perceptual quality of the image and distortions that alter the content within pre-defined levels are considered acceptable as the perceptual quality and semantics of the image is preserved; rest of the distortions is rejected as malicious manipulations. Selective authentication is commonly achieved using semi-fragile watermarking techniques using image content based watermarks. They provide robustness against specific types of image processing operations. According to Haouzia and Noumeir (2008), accurately defining image content is a challenge. Image content can be expressed in terms of its pixel or transform representation, color, edges, histogram, relationship with neighboring pixels, moments and so on. For image authentication, it may be defined in terms of the image semantic content, its visual representation or its interpretation. A variety of generating functions have been proposed in literature for use in content authentication. Moment is used as the feature by Kim and Lee (2003), edge by Chang and Chuang (2002), DCT coefficients by Barni, Bartolini, Cappellini and Piva (1998), Chang, Chuang and Chen (2002), Mursi, Assassa, Aboalsamh and Alghathbar (2009) and Lin and Chang(2001), wavelet coefficients by Fei, Kundur and Kwong (2006) and Kundur, Zhao and Campisi, (2004) and Frobenius norm by Parameswaran and Anbumani (2008) and Radharani and Valarmathi (2012).

Common image processing operations like quantization, transmission noise, filtering and compression change the pixel values without altering the content or semantics. Selective authentication applications are expected to differentiate content altering image processing operations from those that do not alter the content and design the authentication scheme accordingly. The performance of an authentication system can be evaluated based on the parameters as defined by Cox and Miller (2002) with variable significances in different applications like imperceptibility, robustness, capability of tamper detection and localization, security, blind or informed detection, capacity, complexity and portability

Security of Authentication Systems

An attack can be defined as data manipulation either with the purpose of impairing, removing or destroying the embedded watermark or that which occurs during the storage and transmission of the watermarked data. In image authentication, the attacks may be classified as acceptable or malicious based on the requirements of the application. Acceptable manipulations are the attacks which do not change the semantic meaning of content and are acceptable by an authentication system if desired by the application. Common acceptable manipulations include format conversions, lossless and high-quality lossy compression, re-sampling, etc. Malicious manipulations are the attacks that change the semantic meaning and should be rejected. Common malicious manipulations include cropping, inserting, replacing, reordering perceptual objects in images, collusion, brute force key search, etc.

Improving the security aspect of an authentication system, without any cost of imperceptibility and robustness, is a key challenge of today's research in watermarking. Any authentication scheme is as robust as the mechanisms used to generate the secret keys, share the keys, randomness mechanisms involved and the hardness involved in deriving parameters or solutions. Any watermarking system for authentication is incomplete without a secret key or random sequence that is used to generate sufficient random noise to scramble or mask the watermark, sensitive information or the embedding pattern. Even if the presence of the watermark is detected, it would not be possible to see or read the watermark in the absence of the secret key. Secrecy of the key ensures security of the system and wherever necessary, they have to be shared using an appropriate private or public key system with the authenticator. The security of an authentication scheme also lies in the complexity and randomness involved in watermark generation and embedding process.

Authentication is a cryptographic service that is very mathematical and draws solutions from Mathematics and Computer Science. Diophantine equations have prominent application in factoring, public key signature schemes and are based on the efficient non-solubility of such equations. In spite of many efforts to design a general algorithm, finding solutions to Diophantine equations is usually a hard task and individual equations present a kind of puzzle that require specialized techniques to solve. Diophantine Equations are introduced in the next section.

DIOPHANTINE EQUATIONS

According to Menezes, Van Oorschot and Vanstone (1996), a Diophantine equation is an algebraic equation, usually in two or more unknowns, such that only integer solutions are sought or allowed. The word Diophantine refers to the Hellenistic mathematician of the 3rd century, Diophantus of Alexandria, who made a study of such equations and was one of the first mathematicians to introduce symbolism into algebra. Diophantine equations have prominent application in factoring, public key signature schemes and are based on the efficient non-solubility of such equations.

Diophantine equations are polynomial equations of the form

$$f\left(a_1, a_2, a_3, \ldots a_n, x_1, x_2, x_3, \ldots \ldots x_n\right) = C$$

where a_1 and c are integers.

The simplest of the equations are the linear equations of the form

$$ax_1 + bx_2 = c$$

where a, b and c are integers and a, b are both not zero. A solution to this equation is a pair of integers, x_1 and x_2, which when substituted into the equation, satisfy it.

Determining the solutions of Diophantine equation is difficult in general when the order of the Diophantine equation is higher than one. General formulae for solving equations exist only for equations with degrees up to 3, and the general equation of degree 4 and higher are still considered un-solvable. This is because of the fact that the Diophantine equation may have zero non trivial solution, finite number or infinite number of solutions. Moreover, determining the solution of each type of Diophantine equation has to be dealt with independently as there doeas not exist a algorithm to determine if there exists a common method to solve it. The main difficulty in finding efficient solutions to Diophantine problems is the fact that most of the proofs known to show existence of solutions usually are brute force search. The condition for solvability for a Linear Diophantine Equation (LDE) is elaborated by Shlapentokh (2007).

Lin, Chang and Lee (1995) proposed a public key cipher scheme based on Diophantine equations to solve the key management problem in which the keys can be easily generated. The equation selected is practically non-soluble and the scheme involves simple encryption and decryption procedures where to encrypt a message, the sender needs to conduct a vector product of the message being sent and the enciphering key and the receiver can easily decrypt it by conducting several multiplication operations and modulus operations. Yosh (2011) proposed a key exchange cryptosystem where two higher order Diophantine equations are considered for encrypting shared secret between sender and recipient. The senders and recipients exchange Diophantine equations as their public key. Although this key exchange cryptosystem has the intrinsic security, it requires a complicated implementation compared with other key exchange cryptosystems. This complexity is due to generating Diophantine equations in an unpredictable manner so as to avoid cases of generating equations that have unique solutions. Hirata-Kohno and Hirata-Kohno and Petho (2013) analyzed and eliminated several weaknesses of the protocol proposed by Yosh (2011). They suggested a choice of the parameters, which is secure against cipher text-only attack. Bérczes, Hajdu, Hirata-Kohno, Kovács and Pethő (2014) proposed a key exchange protocol that depends on the hardness of solving Diophantine equations and combined it with the complexity of S-integers, where the public key size is much less but provides same level of security. Anuradha and Praveen (2014) proposed a method for recovering the key in a key exchange protocol using Diophantine equations. The ambiguity regarding the solutions of a Diophantine equation is considered as a potential source for trapdoor functions to recover the key by the sender and receiver in the key exchange protocol. Okumura (2015) proposed a new public key cryptosystem based on Diophantine equations and analyzed its security. Diophantine equations of increasing type over integers were considered for the cryptosystem where the security is based on the hardness of finding a solution to them. They have proposed a field analogue by incorporating a key idea, to avoid some attacks, of "twisting" the plaintext by using some modular arithmetic and Euler's theorem as in the RSA cryptosystem. They use a polynomial as the public key of degree increasing type to recover the plaintext.

PROPOSED AUTHENTICATION SCHEME

A semi-fragile watermarking system that exploits the difficulty in solving certain Diophantine equations to enhance security of the image authentication scheme is proposed. Watermark embedding locations are identified based on selected solutions of Diophantine equations and keeping certain parameters a secret. Majorly two watermarks with varied intended purposes are used. The first watermark comprises multiple unique watermarks generated for every pair of sub blocks of the image to make it resistant to replacement attacks. The second watermark is a quantized down sampled representation of the original image and is used for visual verification. Both the watermarks are embedded in the DWT domain of the image.

The authentication scheme is explained in three major phases 1) Formation of Diophantine equation 2) Generation and embedding of the dual Watermarks and 3) Image content authentication and verification of integrity.

Formation of Diophantine Equation

The watermarking scheme has to consider the following pre-requisites to ensure adequate security of the authentication process:

- Consider or construct linear Diophantine equation in more than 3 variables or non-linear Diophantine equations that have infinite solutions, i.e. avoid constructions for which the equation will have unique solutions that will enable an intruder to guess the values of the variables or
- Select an appropriate form of Diophantine equation that is hard to solve.
- Design an automated system to construct Diophantine equations that will have infinite solutions as it may be very expensive in terms of time to construct such equations manually
- Mechanism to change the form of the Diophantine equations dynamically and periodically so as to prevent an adversary from analyzing the output patterns to break the system.

A linear Diophantine equation with number of variables, n, where $n \geq 3$ is used in the design of the authentication system. At the owner's end, a linear Diophantine equation of the form

$$a_1 x_1 + a_2 x_2 + a_3 x_3 + \ldots a_n x_n = C$$

for $n \geq 3$ and $a_i, x_i, C \in \mathbb{Z}$ that will have infinite solutions is selected or constructed by repeated application of Euclid's extended algorithm [15]. The coefficients are selected such that the equation will have infinite solutions. The constructed Diophantine Equation will be the public key with the coefficients a_i being the private keys.

A specific solution of the equation is determined using which all the unknowns, x_i's can be determined. One of the solutions is selected as the particular solution and the corresponding *t-value* is chosen as the secret key, K_1, which is securely exchanged with the authenticator. The Diophantine equation is shared publicly and the coefficients $a_1, a_2, ..a_n$ are the secret keys that may be shared using a public or private key system by the owner with the authenticator. The authenticator will use the secret *t-value* to determine the particular solution and to calculate the values of the unknowns, $x_1, x_2, x_3, ..., x_n$, which are used to identify watermarking locations as explained in Embedding Authentication Watermark section.

Result 1 (Shlapentokh, 2007): A linear Diophantine equation $a_1, b_1, C \in \mathbb{Z}$ represented by

$$a_1 x + a_2 y = C$$

has an integer solution in $x, y \in \mathbb{Z} \Leftrightarrow \gcd\left(a_1, a_2\right) \mid C$

Result 2 (Shlapentokh, 2007): The linear Diophantine equation $a_1 x + a_2 y = C$ admits a solution if and only if $d \mid C$, where $d = gcd\left(a_1, a_2\right)$. If x_0 and y_0 is any particular solution of this equation, then all other solutions are given by

$$x = x_0 - \left(\frac{a_1}{d}\right)t \text{ and } y = y_0 - \left(\frac{a_1}{d}\right)t$$

where t is an arbitrary integer.

Generation and Embedding of Dual Watermarks

Two watermarks are generated and embedded in the image – the Authentication watermark W_A and Visual Authentication watermark W_{VA}. The Authentication watermark W_A is a collage of multiple watermarks generated for each sub block of the image that is used to detect incidental or malicious tampering. W_{VA} is the quantized approximation of the original image and is used for visual authentication. Multiple copies of W_{VA} are embedded in the selected coefficients of 2D DWT of LH_1 sub band using a quantization based technique.

Generation of Authentication Watermark W_A

The 1st level 2D DWT transform of the host image *I* of size $M \times N$ decomposes it into four sub bands – LL_1, LH_1, HL_1 and HH_1 as shown in Figure 1. The low frequency LL_1 sub band contains the low frequency approximation coefficients of the original image. LL_1, LH_1, HL_1 and HH_1 sub bands represent the high frequency components that contain the edge information in the vertical, horizontal and diagonal frequencies. The LL_1 sub band is used to generate the content based Authentication watermark W_A as follows:

- The LL_1 sub band is divided into non-overlapping $m \times m$ sized blocks and the DCT is computed for each block. The blocks are placed into two disjoint groups A and B based on a pre-defined secret mapping function and pairs of blocks $\left(P, Q\right)$ are formed where $P \in A, Q \in B$ and $A \cap B = \varnothing$. For each pair of block $\left(P, Q\right)$, low frequency DCT coefficients comprising the DC coefficient and $n - 1$ low frequency AC coefficients are selected.

The feature vector FV_{pq} for a pair of blocks $\left(P, Q\right)$ is computed as:

$$FV_{pq}\left(v\right) = \begin{cases} 1 & if \ DCT_p\left(v\right) \geq DCT_q\left(v\right) \\ 0 & if \ DCT_p\left(v\right) < DCT_q\left(v\right) \end{cases}$$

where v is the number of low frequency coefficients considered for generating the feature vector in each block pair and $DCT_p(v)$ and $DCT_q(v)$ are the DCT coefficients of the block pair (P, Q) at the corresponding position v.

- One of the solutions of the Diophantine equation, x_i, is used to extract the Key Vector KV from a pseudorandom sequence generated using a secret key. The Feature Vector $FV_{pq}(v)$ is scrambled by exclusive OR-ing with the KV to generate the scrambled Feature Vector $SFV_{pq}(v)$. The Majority bit M_b from $SFV_{pq}(v)$ is extracted and the string of majority bits is the content based Authentication watermark W_A.

Selection of Coefficients and Determination of Side Information

Authentication watermark W_A is embedded in the HHL_2 and HLH_2 sub bands obtained after 2D DWT of HL_1 sub band by altering the ratio of the selected coefficients of the corresponding block pairs as they are robust to JPEG 2000 compression and mild image processing operations. For this, the HHL_2 and HLH_2 sub bands are further divided into sub blocks of size $p \times p$ each as shown in Figure 1.

Block pairs (T_i, V_i) are mapped such that $T_i \in HHL_2$ and $V_i \in HLH_2$ for all the sub blocks i. The pairs are chosen randomly or by a pre-defined mapping function such that each block is considered only once to be a part of a block pair. The coefficients for embedding the watermark are identified based on the select solution, x_i, of the Diophantine equations. Another solution of the Diophantine equations is used as the selection index to extract the Map Vector MPV_2 from the pseudorandom sequence. For each block pair, (T_i, V_i), w corresponding coefficients are selected from each of the block pairs where $MPV_2 = 1$ (or $MPV_2 = 0$).

Prior to embedding the watermark, the relationship between each pair of blocks R_i is established by determining the absolute sum of the selected coefficients for each block pair is determined as

$$S1_i = \sum_{k=1}^{w} \left| T_i(k) \right|$$

$$S2_i = \sum_{k=1}^{w} \left| V_i(k) \right|$$

where $S1_i$ is the sum of selected coefficients of block T_i of HHL_2 sub band and $S2_i$ is the sum of selected coefficients of block V_i of HHL_2 sub band. Side information ratio, R_i, for the block pair (T_i, V_i) is determined as

$$R_i = S1_i / S2_i$$

Figure 1. Locations identified for watermark embedding

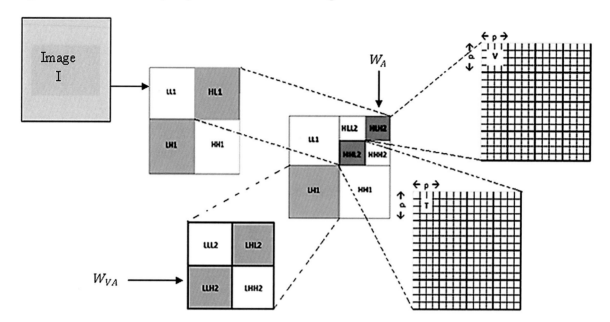

Side information, *R*, for all the block pairs is computed and transmitted securely along with the image or separately using a private or public key system to the authenticator to be used during the authentication and verification of the query watermarked image.

Embedding the Authentication Watermark W_A

Each bit of the Authentication Watermark W_A is embedded in the block pairs HHL_2 and HLH_2 sub bands by modifying the amplitude of the coefficients of the block pair $\left(T_i, V_i\right)$ that were selected by procedure described in the previous section as follows:

$$\text{if } M_b = 1, \begin{cases} T_i\left(k\right) = T_i\left(k\right) * \alpha \\ \quad and \\ V_i\left(k\right) = V_i\left(k\right) / \alpha \end{cases}$$

$$\text{if } M_b = 0, \begin{cases} T_i\left(k\right) = T_i\left(k\right) / \alpha \\ \quad and \\ V_i\left(k\right) = V_i\left(k\right) * \alpha \end{cases}$$

where $k=1..w$ and α is the watermark strength factor that is experimentally determined so as to ensure adequate robustness and imperceptibility of the watermark.

If $S1_w$ and $S2_w$ are the sum of the modified coefficients after embedding M_b, then for the ratio $R_w = S1_w / S2_w$ and the ratio R_i before embedding, then

$$R_w > R_i \text{ if } M_b = 1 \text{ and}$$

$$R_w < R_i \text{ if } M_b = 0$$

This result is used by the authenticator to verify the authenticity of the watermarked image.

Generation and Embedding of Visual Authentication Watermark

In order to add a second level authentication to the watermarking scheme, a coarse approximation of the original image is embedded as the second watermark to enable visual authentication.

The Visual Authentication watermark, W_{VA}, generated from 2D DWT of the LL_1 sub bandto obtain LL_2, a coarser representation of the original image. The LL_2 coefficients are then quantized using Quantized Index Modulation (QIM) (Chen & Wornell, 1998) to generate a quantized approximation of the image so as to reduce the cost involved in representing it. Quantization allows flexibility to work on the quality of the watermark to be embedded and retrieved. The watermark is embedded in the sub bands obtained after 2D DWT of the LH_1 sub band. The computational cost is reduced as a downscaled version of the image is processed here.

Determination of Watermark Embedding Locations for W_{VA}

W_{VA} is embedded in the sub bands obtained after 2D DWT of the LH_1 sub band to obtain the LLH_2 and LHL_2 sub bands. The embedding sub bands are highlighted in Figure 1. Multiple copies of W_{VA} are embedded in the two selected sub bands for redundancy.

The Diophantine equations selected in earlier section such that it has infinite solutions is solved for its basic solution. The secret *t-value* is used to select the desired set of solutions which are used to identify embedding locations for the watermark W_{VA}. Multiple copies of Visual Authentication watermark W_{VA} is embedded in the locations given by

$$EL_1 = x_1 \bmod u$$

$$EL_2 = x_2 \bmod u$$

$$EL_n = x_n \bmod u$$

where u is the number of coefficients in the sub band and $x_1, x_2, \ldots, x_n$ are the solutions of the Diophantine equation and EL_i. *Modulo(u)* ensures locations within the designated range for the coefficients available for watermark embedding. Two instances of the watermark W_{VA} are embedded in the selected sub bands in positions indicated by EL_i and EL_j, where $i \neq j$ and $i, j < n$

Embedding Authentication Watermark W_{VA}

W_{VA} is embedded in the LLH_2 and LHL_2 sub bands by modifying the LSB of the selected coefficients. Vectors V_1 and V_2 are formed of the coefficients of LLH_2 and LHL_2 sub bands starting with positions EL_1 for the LLH_2 sub band and EL_2 for the LHL_2 sub band. The binary of each coefficient (r bits) of the quantized Visual Authentication watermark, W_{VA} is embedded in the selected coefficient of the sub band by replacing its r LSBs. A second copy of the approximation of the image is embedded in vector V_2. The vectors are restored as sub bands and inverse DWT of the image generates the watermarked image W_m.

Image Content Authentication and Verification of Integrity

All the secret keys –the selected coefficients of the Diophantine equation, *t-value*, seed to generate pseudorandom sequence, the side information R, secret mapping function to pair the blocks are to be made available at the authentication end in a secure manner using a private key or public key system or kept in the repository secured by means of Public Key Infrastructure (PKI).

The authentication scheme enables authentication at multiple levels. Visual authentication can be used for preliminary verification. Visually examining and comparing the two copies of the extracted Visual Authentication watermarks is done at the first level. At the second level, the visual authentication watermark is compared with the query watermarked image to get a first hand impression of the authenticity of the image. The third level of authentication can be achieved by extracting the Authentication Watermark $\widetilde{W}_A$ to identify or confirm tampering of the image. The Diophantine equations shared publicly and the coefficients, $a_i's$, shared secretly with the authenticator are used to reconstruct the Diophantine equation which is solved for the basic solution. Using the secret *t-value*, corresponding solutions for $x_i's$, are computed. The solutions are also used to identify the coefficients of the DWT sub bands to extract the Visual Authentication watermarks, $\widetilde{W}_{VA1}$ and $\widetilde{W}_{VA2}$ by applying the reverse procedure used to embed the Authentication watermark W_{VA}.

At the first level of authentication, the extracted copies of the Visual Authentication watermarks are visually correlated to determine the extent of similarity between the two, i.e. $\widetilde{W}_{VA1}$ and $\widetilde{W}_{VA2}$.

At the second level, the extracted Visual Authentication watermarks are visually correlated with the query watermarked image to determine the visual authenticity of the query image i.e. $\widetilde{W}_{VA1}$ and W_m.

For authentication at a more objective level, at the third level, the generated and extracted Authentication Watermarks, $\widetilde{W}_A$ and $\widehat{W}_A$ are correlated to determine the authenticity or nature of $\widetilde{W}_A$ if the first or second levels fail.

The Authentication watermark $\widehat{W}_A$ is generated from the query watermarked image W_m by applying the procedure in generation of authentication watermark section. The Authentication watermark $\widehat{W}_A$ embedded at the source is extracted from the query watermarked image by using the reverse of procedure used to embed the watermark. 2D DWT is applied to the HL_1 sub band to get the HHL_2 and HLH_2 sub bands. These sub bands are further divided into sub blocks of size $p \times p$ and block pairs are mapped using the secret mapping function. For each block pair, w coefficients are selected based on the Map Vector and absolute sum of selected coefficients of each sub block, $\widehat{S1}$ and $\widehat{S2}$, is determined. The side information ratio, $\widehat{R}$ is determined as

$$\widehat{R} = \widehat{S1} \Big/ \widehat{S2}$$

The Majority bit $\widehat{M}_b$ is extracted using the side information ratio, R_w generated at the time of watermark embedding and secretly shared with the authenticator:

$$\widehat{M}_b = \begin{cases} 1, & if \ \widehat{R} \Big/ R_w > 0 \\ 0, & otherwise \end{cases}$$

The extracted majority bit $\widehat{M}_b$ is correlated with the Majority bit $\widetilde{M}_b$ to verify the authenticity of a block pair for an objective evaluation. The degree of correlation determines the authenticity of the image.

If a possible modification is detected during correlation of the majority bits then the inference as to whether the modification is incidental or malicious is based on the strength of manipulation, φ. This is determined as the percent difference between $\widehat{R}$ and R_w, the extracted and received side information for the block under consideration and is given by:

$$\varphi = \frac{\left| \widehat{R} - R_w \right|}{\max\left(\widehat{R}, R_w\right)} * 100$$

The strength of manipulation is correlated with experimentally decided threshold values of ∂, μ and σ to decide on the authenticity of the image. The results of authentication based on the value of φ will be:

$$Outcome \ of \ authentication = \begin{cases} authentic, & if \ \varphi < \partial \\ incidentally \ tampered, & if \ \partial \leq \varphi < \mu \\ maliciously \ tampered, & if \ \varphi \geq \mu \end{cases}$$

Figure 2 gives an illustration of the generated Visual Authentication watermark W_{VA}. The quantized watermark is represented in Figure 2 (b). The sub bands selected to embed the watermark are shown in Figure 2 (c) and the sub bands after embedding the quantized Visual Authentication watermark W_{VA} is

Figure 2. a) Coarse approximation of Visual Authentication watermark of Lena image; b) quantized approximation of the Visual Authentication watermark, W_{VA}; c) identified DWT sub band of Lena image to embed W_{VA}; d) sub band after embedding W_{VA}; e) extracted Visual Authentication watermark

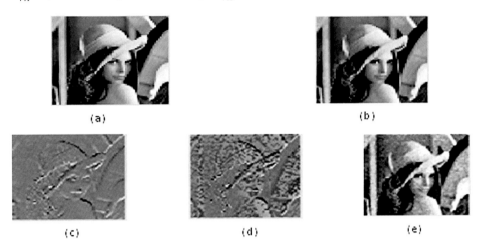

shown in Figures 2 (d). At the time of authentication the Visual Authentication watermark W_{VA} is extracted from the selected sub bands to visually authenticate the query image and is depicted in Figure2 (e).

Experimental Results

The authentication schemes described in this chapter are implemented using MATLAB version 7.12.0.635 (R2011a) environment where grey scale images of type tiff, bmp, jpeg and png formats were chosen for the experiments.

Perceptual Quality Analysis

The quality of the watermarked images after embedding only the Authentication watermark, W_A, only the Visual Authentication watermark W_{VA} and both W_A and W_{VA} for $\alpha = 0.9$ is summarized in Table 1. The Peak Signal to Noise Ratio (PSNR) of the images watermarked with only W_A are in the range 64 – 67 dB, after embedding only W_{VA}, the PSNR is in the range of 50 - 54 dB and after embedding both W_A and W_{VA}, the ratio are in the range 50 – 54 dB. A PSNR of 38 dB and above indicates good quality of the watermarked image. The PSNR values vary according to the embedding strength, α. The experimental results show that embedding strength $\alpha = 0.9$ gives the highest value of PSNR. Structural Similarity (SSIM), Pearson Correlation Coefficient (PCC) and Bit Error Rate (BER) are the other measures used to determine imperceptibility of the watermark.

The SSIM and PCC values are very close to 1 indicating good quality. From the results it is evident that embedding the Visual Authentication watermark W_{VA} causes a fair degradation in the quality of the image and is comparable to the quality after embedding both the watermarks W_A and W_{VA}. Depending

Table 1. Quality metrics of watermarked image after embedding: only W_A, only W_{VA} and after embedding both W_A and W_{VA} for embedding strength, $\alpha = 0.9$

Image	Only W_A			Only W_{VA}			Both W_A and W_{VA}		
	PSNR	SSIM	PCC	PSNR	SSIM	PCC	PSNR	SSIM	PCC
Lena	67.48	1	1	52.1	0.94	0.998	53.39	0.94	0.998
Einstein	67.97	1	1	53.8	0.96	0.997	53.82	0.96	0.997
MRI	66.51	1	1	52.4	0.98	0.998	51.38	0.98	0.996
Rice	64.73	1	1	51.4	0.98	0.998	51.37	0.99	0.998
Pirate	66.86	1	1	50.1	0.96	0.998	50.07	0.96	0.998

Figure 3. Watermarked images after watermark embedding: a) only W_A; b) only W_{VA}; and c) after embedding both W_A and W_{VA} for embedding strength, $\alpha = 0.9$

(a)   (b)   (c)

the nature of the application, if the emphasis on quality is non-negotiable, then the watermarking scheme need embed only W_A. Figure 3 gives an illustration of the quality of the watermarked image after embedding only W_A, only W_{VA} and after embedding both.

Authentication of the Watermarked Image

The generated and extracted watermarks are correlated on a block by block basis. In case of a mismatch between the re-generated and extracted watermark bits and before categorizing the concerned pair of blocks are non-authentic, the strength of manipulation, φ between $\widehat{R}$ and R_w, the extracted and received side information ratios is determined as given by Equation (12).

Threshold values ∂ and μ are experimentally determined as 0.8% and 12% based on a battery of experiments with incidental and malicious manipulations carried out on a variety of images. A watermarked image that has not been exposed to any kind of incidental or malicious operation will have φ values in the range of 0% to δ. If $\delta \leq \varphi < \mu$, it implies that the block pair may be incidentally modified - operations like compression, filtering, etc and can be considered as authentic. If $\varphi \geq \mu$ then the block pair may be implied as maliciously tampered - operations like heavy compression, cut and paste attack

Table 2. PSNR and BER of extracted Visual Authentication watermark W_{VA} after JPEG 2000 compression with respect to the Visual Authentication watermark extracted from watermarked image after JPEG 2000 compression

Quality Factor	Watermarked Image		QF=95		QF=90		QF=85		QF=80	
	PSNR (dB)	BER %	PSNR (dB)	BER %	PSNR (dB)	BER %	PSNR (dB)	BER %	PSNR (dB)	BER %
pentagon	48.2	0.03	45.4	0.11	43.27	0.31	41.7	0.37	39.2	0.40
bridge	47	0.02	46.52	0.15	43.54	0.22	41.23	0.26	39.13	0.32
Einstein	53.82	0.14	49.2	0.33	47.6	0.36	45.83	0.39	43.2	0.41
Lena	49.27	0.07	46	0.15	44.3	0.23	42.67	0.25	39.56	0.43
Living room	48.17	0.03	45.1	0.21	42.32	0.22	41.54	0.31	39.7	0.36
Lena	51.39	0.08	49.02	0.19	46.4	0.29	45.3	0.32	42.01	1.3

Figure 4. Watermarked image with: a) dual watermarks W_A and W_{VA} and after JPEG2000 compression; with b) QF = 90%; c) QF = 85%; and d) QF = 80%

(a)   (b)   (c)   (d)

or any geometric attack. Figure 5 illustrates the Visual Authentication watermark $\widetilde{W}_{VA}$ recovered from the watermarked Lena and Cameraman images which are used to endorse the results of verification with the Authentication Watermark $\widetilde{W}_A$.

Robustness to Compression

The watermarked images were subject to various levels of JPEG and JPEG 2000 compression and the results are summarized. JPEG 2000 is the current compression standard used for images and is carried out in the DWT domain of the image. By choosing the watermark generation and embedding in the same domain as used by the compression scheme, properties of the DWT transform of the image can be suitably used to ensure robustness to loss of information that will occur during compression.

The quality of the extracted Visual Authentication watermarks in comparison to the watermark extracted from images that are not compressed is shown in Table 2. The PSNR of the extracted Authentication watermark $\widetilde{W}_{VA}$ varies from 45 dB to 50 dB for QF=95 and between 39 dB and 44 dB for QF = 80. The BER is also quite low which indicates good quality of the extracted watermark. The performance of the authentication scheme under JPEG compression is visually illustrated in Figures 4 and 5.

Figure 5. Visual Authentication watermark extracted from: a) dual watermarked image after JPEG 2000 compression; with b) QF = 90%; c) QF = 85%; and d) QF = 80%

As JPEG 2000 standard is still in the various stages of adoption and the progress is slow, it will take some time before it is universally implemented. Till such time, JPEG compression will be prevalent. The watermarked test images were subject to various levels of JPEG compression and the authentication results are illustrated in Figure 6 and Figure 7. The results indicate that the scheme is robust to JPEG compression of the watermarked images for $QF > 95\%$ The watermark is slightly degraded at $QF=95\%$ and the degradation increases considerably for compression beyond $QF > 95\%$ and the strength of manipulation, φ, between the computed ratios of the generated and extracted watermarks is beyond the set limits for the scheme.

Table 3 shows the PSNR values of the Visual Authentication watermark recovered from the watermarked images that have been JPEG compressed with respect to the watermark extracted from the watermarked image that has not been compressed.

Figure 6. Watermarked boat image with dual watermarks W_A and W_{VA} and after JPEG compression for: a) QF = 98%; b) QF = 95%; c) QF = 90%; d) QF = 85%

Figure 7. Visual Authentication watermark extracted from dual watermarked Boat image after JPEG compression for: a) QF = 98; b) QF = 95; c) QF = 90; d) QF = 85

Table 3. Quality of extracted Visual Authentication watermark W_{VA} before and after JPEG compression

Quality Factor	Watermarked Image		JPEG with QF= 98%		JPEG with QF= 95%		JPEG with QF= 90%		JPEG with QF=85%	
	PSNR	BER	PSNR	BER	PSNR	BER	PSNR	BER	PSNR	BER
pentagon	48.2	0.3	38.32	1.3	32	12.4	28.2	32.1	23.3	37.2
bridge	47	0.2	38	1.45	30	11.6	25.3	28.1	24	32.1
Einstein	53.82	0.34	40.16	2.06	33.74	8.67	29.02	30.0	25.4	32.8
Lena	49.27	0.27	38.76	1.98	32.4	12.3	29.2	27.6	25.2	30.7
living room	48.17	0.3	36.4	2.0	32.02	11.8	29.01	31.1	24.83	34.4

Robustness to Incidental Noise

Noise distorts and degrades the image which in turn distorts the content based watermark. The watermarked images were subject to various types of incidental noise and the robustness of the scheme evaluated. Table 4 summarizes the performance of the authentication scheme to various incidental noise and quality of the extracted Visual Authentication watermark. Figure 8 illustrates the watermarked images after being subject to various types of noise and Figure 9 illustrates the Visual Authentication watermarks extracted from the watermarked images that were subject to the noise attacks. The authentication scheme is robust to Gaussian noise with zero mean and variance of 0.001 and salt and pepper noise up to density = 0.01 beyond which the noise is considered malicious. The scheme is also fragile to median filtering. When a non-watermarked image is subject to image authentication, it gives negative value for the correlation and the recovered Visual Authentication watermark is of very poor quality as illustrated in Figure 9 (d).

Table 4. Authentication results for watermarked image of Lena under various attacks

Attacks	Authentication Results	Recovery Results		
	Strength of Manipulation	Correlation Value	PSNR of Watermarked Image (dB)	PSNR of Recovered Watermark W_{VA}
Original watermarked image	Nil	1	51.39	47
Wrong key	94%	-	-	8
Median Filter [3 3]	40%	0.3	13	23
Median Filter [4 4]	36%	0.4	17	24.7
Gaussian noise M=0; V=0.001	8%	0.87	31	35.2
Salt and pepper Noise density =0.02	23%	0.53	21	29
Salt and pepper Noise density =0.01	12%	0.82	30	31
Non watermarked image	70%	-0.03	9	13

Figure 8. Watermarked images subject to noise attacks: a) salt and pepper, d=0.02; b) Gaussian noise with M=0, variance=0.01; c) median filter (3 3); d) non-watermarked image

Figure 9. Visual Authentication watermarks recovered from the watermarked images that were subject to noise attacks: a) salt and pepper, d=0.02; b) Gaussian noise with M=0, variance=0.01; c) median filter (3 3); d) non-watermarked image

Robustness against Malicious Attacks

Cropping is usually carried out in the spatial domain which results in a substantial distortion in the frequency domain of the image. The proposed scheme being implemented in the frequency domain, cropping attacks are considered malicious and the image is subsequently designated as maliciously tampered. The DWT transform is also shift and rotation invariant and thereby cannot tolerate geometric attacks.

Figure 10 depicts the extracted Visual Authentication watermark from the tampered images that gives a very close approximation to the original watermarked image in spite of the manipulation. In Figure 10 (a), the frame on the wall is removed from the watermarked image. The authentication result of the same indicates a dense alteration in one region and multiple patches in the other regions. This is attributed to the watermark generation and embedding scheme which involved random pairing of blocks of size $p \times p$ and generating the watermark for every pair of blocks. At the time of verification, the Authentication

Figure 10. a) Watermarked image of living room that is altered; b) detection of possible tampered locations; c) localization of the tampered locations; d) approximation of Visual Authentication watermark extracted from the tampered image

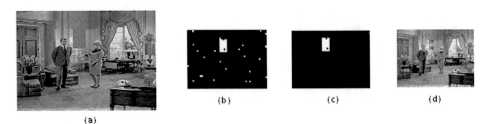

watermark bits are re-generated for each pair of blocks that were paired using the secret mapping function and compared with the watermark bits extracted from the query watermarked image. Any mismatch in the watermarks for a pair of blocks will raise suspect on both the pairs as indicated in Figure 10 (b).

The manipulation may be exactly localized by incorporating additional side information like the mean of significant coefficients of each sub block - DC and one or two low frequency AC coefficients of each sub block can be used. This side information is used to compare the mean of each of the sub blocks as determined by the authenticator and the variation is used to pin point the exact block that is tampered as reflected in Figure 10 (c). The side information generated at the embedding end has to be secretly shared with the authenticator, involving additional cost in terms of time and space.

Security Analysis

The proposed image authentication system is as secure as the randomness of the pseudorandom sequences used to scramble the watermark or its embedding sequence and the difficulty in estimating the secret parameters used in the scheme.

Randomness in Selection of Embedding Locations

In order to enhance the security of the proposed scheme and ensure complexity for the adversary to break it, integer solutions of selected Diophantine equations are used to identify the embedding locations. By choosing randomizing procedure to select the start location for embedding the watermark using solutions of hard to solve Diophantine equations, the scheme ensures high resistance to brute force attack by an adversary thus increasing the cost of attack in extracting the Visual Authentication watermark, W_{VA}. Given a 1024 x 1024 image, W_{VA} will have 65,536 coefficients. Each of the HHL_2 and HLH_2 sub bands are 256 x 256 by dimension which implies that each of sub bands have 65,536 coefficients each, totally 1,31,072 coefficients. The adversary has to either try all possible locations as starting location for presence of the watermark or has to try to solve the Diophantine equation by trying all possible values of the coefficients to get integer solutions. The legitimate authenticator can solve the equation using the coefficients values exchanged secretly by the sender and derive the selected solution of the

Figure 11. a) Watermarked bridge image; b) Visual Authentication watermark recovered using wrong starting location

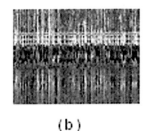

(b)

(a)

equation using the secret *t-value*. This makes the computational complexity quite high for an adversary to determine the embedding locations thus increasing security of the scheme. When wrong locations were used to indicate the embedding locations, the extracted Visual Authentication watermark is shown in Figures 11 (b).

Key Sensitivity Analysis

Diophantine equations selected in the scheme are such that they are hard to solve and each Diophantine equation requires a specific approach to solve it. A general method does not exist for all Diophantine equations. The coefficients of the equation are kept a secret and exchanged securely with the authenticator. An adversary who has the Diophantine equation but not its coefficients or the *t-value* that determines the selected solution, has to execute a brute force attack to break the system – identify watermarking locations and break the watermark scrambled using the pseudorandom sequence making it an expensive process. Thus the use of right keys is very crucial to the authentication process as the scheme is extremely sensitive to it.

Cut/Copy Paste Attack

In this attack an attempt is made to replace some parts of the image with an equivalent set of pixels or delete objects. For every block being replaced / modified, the adversary has also to find its pair and make suitable changes to it to avoid being detected. Moreover, an equivalent image block to replace the watermarked one also has to be determined. At the time of verification, the test will fail as the other pair of the block will also be identified as manipulated. This makes it difficult for an adversary to execute a cut / copy paste attack on the watermarked image.

Collusion Attack

The scheme is by nature resistant to collusion attack in which an adversary obtains multiple images watermarked with the same watermark and executes an averaging exercise to eliminate it. In the proposed scheme, each pair of sub blocks of the image is watermarked separately using the content based watermark generated from them. Thus the image has a collage of watermarks embedded in it. The watermark varies from image to image and within it block by block. It is computationally complex for an adversary to attempt to detect the watermark, remove or manipulate it without setting off alarms of manipulation. Thus the scheme is not prone to collusion attack by design.

Performance Analysis of the Proposed Scheme

In this section, the results of the DWT based semi-fragile authentication scheme are analyzed and compared with the related DWT based image authentication techniques. The use of Diophantine equation in image watermarking and authentication schemes have not been attempted before according to literature and hence the comparative analysis presented here is subjective. The features and performance of the proposed scheme is compared with dual watermarked based schemes implemented by Woo, Du and Pham (2006) and Chamlawi, Khan and Usman, (2010) and results summarized in Table 5.

The scheme proposed by Woo et al., (2006) uses a down scaled version of the host image as the content based watermark. Quantization is used to map the DWT coefficient to its binary value from which four MSB's are embedded in horizontal sub band of the 2nd level 2D DWT of the LL_1 sub band and the remaining four LSB's in the vertical sub band. A secret key is used to pick random pixel positions to embed the bits of the watermark. For authentication, the embedded watermark is extracted and compared with a down sampled version of the original host image. Correlation based thresholding is used to determine the tampered locations. For recovery of the original image, the extracted watermark is up-scaled to the original size of the host image. The scheme claims to be blind but insists on the use of a down sampled version of the test image for accurate authentication. The scheme is fragile to JPEG compression and mild incidental noise.

The scheme proposed by Chamlawi et al. (2010) for image authentication and recovery is non-blind and multiple watermarks based. Two watermarks are used – one for authentication and the other to recover tampered regions. The authentication watermark is a signature or its binary equivalent and the recovery watermark is multiple instances of quantized and JPEG compressed version of DCT of the image. The watermarks are embedded in DWT sub bands. During authentication the embedded authentication watermark is extracted and compared with the original authentication watermark to identify manipulations. Visual authentication is done by comparing the query image with the recovery watermark extracted from the sub bands. The nature of tampering is determined by observing the density of error pixels – dense

Table 5. Performance analysis of proposed Diophantine equations based image authentication scheme with peer schemes

Feature	Woo, Du and Pham's (2006) scheme	Chamlawi, Khan and Usman's (2010) scheme	Pillai and Padma's (2015, 2017) scheme
Watermarking Domain	DWT	DWT	DWT - DCT
PSNR (Lena)	≈ 41 dB	≈ 39 dB	≈ 53 - 67 db
Tamper Detection	Non Blind - By difference with test image	Non Blind - By difference with test image	Blind – By Correlation
Localization	Yes	Pixel level	4x4 Block level
Tolerance to JPEG 2000 Compression	Nil	High	High
Tolerance to JPEG Compression	Up to QF = 90%	Up to QF = 70%	Up to QF = 95%
Watermark Type for Authentication	Down scaled version of original image	Binary image	Relationship between DCT coefficients
Watermark Type for Recovery	Down scaled version of original image	Quantized DCT of image that is JPEG compressed	Quantized down scaled version of original image
Watermark Security	Nil	Pseudorandom sequence	N private keys based on Diophantine Equations and block mapping function
Randomizing Watermark Embedding Locations	Using secret key	Using secret key	Secret Key and Diophantine equations
Tolerance to Signal Processing	Very low	Not specified	Average
Computational Cost	low	low	high

pixels indicate malicious manipulations and sparse pixels indicate incidental operations. The scheme is non-blind and uses the difference of the original and query images to detect the tampered regions.

The scheme uses a content based watermark derived from the features of the image and ensures a unique watermark for every pair of blocks ensuring that the scheme is robust to collusion attack. In the peer schemes, in both the cases, an external logo is used as the watermark.

Security of the proposed scheme is enhanced by the use of solutions of hard to solve Diophantine equations to identify locations to embed the quantized down sampled approximation of the original image in the selected DWT sub bands. Secret keys and a mapping function are used at various stages of the watermarking to add to security of the scheme. Security of the scheme is much higher compared to the peer schemes but at the cost of time.

CONCLUSION

A watermarking scheme using number theoretic concepts that tries to balance the requirements of an effective watermark authentication scheme including imperceptibility, tamper detection, localization of tampered areas, security and ability to differentiate between incidental distortions and malicious manipulations is proposed.

The number theory based watermarking scheme for image content authentication uses dual watermarks, the Authentication watermark and Visual Authentication watermark, one to authenticate the watermarked images and the other to reinforce the authentication. Both the watermarks are sensitive to malicious manipulations but robust to high level JPEG 2000, mild JPEG compression and other incidental noise. The choice of whether to embed one or both the watermarks is open and can be decided based on the requirements of the application. The scheme can recover an approximate version of the original image with reasonable quality after compression and some incidental noise. Quality of the watermarked images is good even with multiple watermarks embedded in it.

Diophantine equations enhance the security of the authentication scheme. Multiple keys are used at the various stages of the watermarking to add to the security of the scheme. The authentication is also carried out at multiple levels based on the nature of authentication required, visual or factual.

Limitations

Despite the good performance of the watermarking scheme, determining the secret embedding locations using Diophantine equations involves higher computational costs. This is contributed by the additional time and iterations required to form the desired Diophantine equation that generates integer solutions. The equation must be constructed carefully so as to avoid equations that have no solution or only one unique solution as it may be easily inferred by the adversary. Each Diophantine equation will have a unique approach to determine its solution as there is no polynomial time algorithm to determine the general solution. The constraints used to select the Diophantine equations require skill that are difficult for common man to implement, hence automated solutions are required to generate the equations and determine the solutions.

REFERENCES

Ahmed, N., Natarajan, T., & Rao, K. R. (1974). Discrete Cosine Transform. *IEEE Transactions on Computers, 100*(1), 90–93. doi:10.1109/T-C.1974.223784

Anuradha Kameswari, P., & Praveen Kumar, L. (2014). A Method for Recovering a Key in the Key Exchange Cryptosystem by Diophantine Equations. *International Journal of Computers and Applications, 100*(14), 11–13. doi:10.5120/17592-8302

Barni, M., Bartolini, F., Cappellini, V., & Piva, A. (1998). A DCT-domain system for robust image watermarking. *Signal Processing, 66*(3), 357–372. doi:10.1016/S0165-1684(98)00015-2

Barreto, P. S., Kim, H. Y., & Rijmen, V. (2002). Toward secure public-key block wise fragile authentication watermarking. *IEE Proceedings. Vision Image and Signal Processing, 149*(2), 57–62. doi:10.1049/ip-vis:20020168

Bérczes, A., Hajdu, L., Hirata-Kohno, N., Kovács, T., & Pethő, A. (2014). A key exchange protocol based on Diophantine equations and S-integers. *JSIAM Letters, 6*(0), 85–88. doi:10.14495/jsiaml.6.85

Chamlawi, R., Khan, A., & Usman, I. (2010). Authentication and recovery of images using multiple watermarks. *Computers & Electrical Engineering, 36*(3), 578–584. doi:10.1016/j.compeleceng.2009.12.003

Chang, C. C., & Chuang, J. C. (2002). An image intellectual property protection scheme for gray-level images using visual secret sharing strategy. *Pattern Recognition Letters, 23*(8), 931–941. doi:10.1016/S0167-8655(02)00023-5

Chang, C. C., Chuang, J. C., & Chen, T. S. (2002). Recognition of image authenticity using significant DCT coefficients quantization. *INFORMATICA-LJUBLJANA, 26*(4), 359–366.

Chen, B., & Wornell, G. W. (1998). Digital watermarking and information embedding using dither modulation. In *Multimedia Signal Processing, 1998 IEEE Second Workshop on* (pp. 273-278). IEEE. doi:10.1109/MMSP.1998.738946

Chun-Lin, H. (2010). *A Tutorial of Wavelet Transform*. Academic Press.

Cox, I. J., & Miller, M. L. (2002). The first 50 years of electronic watermarking. *EURASIP Journal on Advances in Signal Processing*, (2): 1–7.

Fei, C., Kundur, D., & Kwong, R. H. (2006). Analysis and design of secure watermark-based authentication systems. *IEEE Transactions on Information Forensics and Security, 1*(1), 43-55.

Gonzalez, R. C., Woods, R. E., & Eddins, S. L. (2004). *Book*. Digital Image Processing Using Matlab.

Haouzia, A., & Noumeir, R. (2008). Methods for image authentication: A survey. *Multimedia Tools and Applications, 39*(1), 1–46. doi:10.1007/s11042-007-0154-3

Hardy, G. H., & Wright, E. M. (1979). *An introduction to the theory of numbers*. Oxford University Press.

Hirata-Kohno, N., & Petho, A. (2013). On a key exchange protocol based on Diophantine equations. *Infocommunications Journal, 5*(3), 17–21.

Holliman, M., & Memon, N. (2000). Counterfeiting attacks on oblivious block-wise independent invisible watermarking schemes. *IEEE Transactions on Image Processing, 9*(3), 432–441. doi:10.1109/83.826780 PMID:18255414

Kim, H. S., & Lee, H. K. (2003). Invariant image watermark using Zernike moments. *IEEE Transactions on Circuits and Systems for Video Technology, 13*(8), 766–775. doi:10.1109/TCSVT.2003.815955

Koch, E., & Zhao, J. (1995). Towards robust and hidden image copyright labeling. In *IEEE Workshop on Nonlinear Signal and Image Processing* (pp. 452-455). NeosMarmaras, Greece: IEEE.

Kundur, D., Zhao, Y., & Campisi, P. (2004). A stenographic framework for dual authentication and compression of high resolution imagery. In *Circuits and Systems, 2004. ISCAS'04.Proceedings of the 2004 International Symposium on* (Vol. 2, pp. II-1). IEEE. doi:10.1109/ISCAS.2004.1329193

Lin, C. H., Chang, C. C., & Lee, R. C. T. (1995). A new public-key cipher system based upon the Diophantine equations. *IEEE Transactions on Computers, 44*(1), 13–19. doi:10.1109/12.368013

Lin, C. Y., & Chang, S. F. (2001). SARI: self-authentication-and-recovery image watermarking system. In *Proceedings of the ninth ACM international conference on Multimedia* (pp. 628-629). ACM. doi:10.1145/500141.500266

Menezes, A. J., Van Oorschot, P. C., & Vanstone, S. A. (1996). *Handbook of applied cryptography*. CRC Press. doi:10.1201/9781439821916

Mintzer, F. C., & Yeung, M. M. Y. (1999). *U.S. Patent No. 5,875,249*. Washington, DC: U.S. Patent and Trademark Office.

Mursi, M. F., Assassa, G. M., Aboalsamh, H. A., & Alghathbar, K. (2009). A DCT-based secure JPEG image authentication scheme. *World Academy of Science. Engineering and Technology, 53*, 682–687.

Okumura, S. (2015). A public key cryptosystem based on Diophantine equations of degree increasing type. *Pacific Journal of Mathematics for Industry, 7*(1), 1. doi:10.1186/s40736-015-0014-4

Parameswaran, L., & Anbumani, K. (2008). Content-based watermarking for image authentication using independent component analysis. *Informatica, 32*(3).

Pillai, J. S., & Padma, T. (2015). Secure Watermarking using Diophantine Equations for Authentication and Recovery. *Journal of Network and Information Security, 3*(2), 2–9.

Pillai, J. S., & Padma, T. (2017). Semi Fragile Watermarking for Content based Image Authentication and Recovery in the DWT domain. *International Arab Journal of Internet Technologies*. (in press)

Qi, X., Xin, X., & Chang, R. (2009). Image authentication and tamper detection using two complementary watermarks. In *2009 16th IEEE International Conference on Image Processing (ICIP)* (pp. 4257-4260). IEEE.

Radharani, S., & Valarmathi, M. L. (2012). content based hybrid DWT-DCT watermarking for image authentication in color images. *International Journal of Engineering Inventions, 1*(4), 32–38.

Shlapentokh, A. (2007). *Hilbert's tenth problem: Diophantine classes and extensions to global fields* (Vol. 7). Cambridge University Press.

Tanaka, K., Nakamura, Y., & Matsui, K. (1991). Secret transmission method of character data in motion picture communication. In *Visual Communications,'91* (pp. 646–649). Boston, MA: International Society for Optics and Photonics. doi:10.1117/12.50295

Walton, S. (1995). Image authentication for a slippery new age. *Dr. Dobb's Journal of Software Tools for the Professional Programmer*, 20(4), 18–27.

Wong, P. W. (1998). A public key watermark for image verification and authentication. In *Image Processing, 1998. ICIP 98. Proceedings. 1998 International Conference on* (Vol. 1, pp. 455-459). IEEE.

Woo, C. S., Du, J., & Pham, B. (2006). Geometric invariant domain for image watermarking. In *International Workshop on Digital Watermarking* (pp. 294-307). Springer Berlin Heidelberg. doi:10.1007/11922841_24

Yosh, H. (2011). *The key exchange cryptosystem used with higher order Diophantine equations.* arXiv preprint arXiv:1103.3742

Chapter 11

Design, Construction, and Programming of a Mobile Robot Controlled by Artificial Vision

Claudio Urrea
Universidad de Santiago de Chile, Chile

Alex Yau
Universidad de Santiago de Chile, Chile

ABSTRACT

The design, construction and programming of a mobile robot controlled by means of artificial vision, capable of recognizing, grabbing and moving specific objects in a completely autonomous way is presented, together with the conceptual and theoretical-practical grounds for the work. A mechanically robust robot is built and a system is designed, allowing the mobility of two sensors jointly, i.e., artificial vision camera and distance sensor. This makes it possible to improve the range of artificial vision, over approximately 180°, achieving precise positioning of the mobile robot. The artificial vision camera, CMUCam 2, provides the mobile robot with great autonomy thanks to its excellent interaction with its surrounding world. Having a mobile robot like this will allow interesting developments to be made in various areas of mobile robotics.

INTRODUCTION

In recent years, there has been increasing interest in research on mobile robots due to the endless number of remote applications that can be developed with them, particularly in areas of high risk to human beings. Currently, thanks to the degree of development that has been reached in the field of mechanisms and sensors, the implementation of systems with a high degree of interaction with the environment has been achieved. This has allowed robots to get a more accurate description of their environment, such as sampling, analysis of the surrounding, detection of gases, leakage, or even sending video signals so that the observer is not exposed. Since mobile robots can now carry out their tasks with greater accuracy,

DOI: 10.4018/978-1-5225-2053-5.ch011

precision and autonomy, the developments of control methods, as well as the implementation of new prototypes, are of high importance in the field of robotics.

Mobile robots exhibit the advantage of integrating the functionality of a device or system with the mobility of an autonomous vehicle, offering a number of advantages, but also a number of yet unsolved technological barriers such as:

- Increased duration of battery charge to achieve greater autonomy.
- Increased potentialities of the navigation systems to allow automatic mobility in the most efficient, flexible, fault-tolerant and safe possible manner.
- Improved efficiency of the control of fleets consisting of various mobile robots to solve problems such as optimized scaling, routing or traffic management, etc.

RELATED WORK

Location is one of the key technologies in autonomous mobile robot navigation, as it is the foundation of the route plan and obstacle avoidance of mobile robots. The work of Wang and Zhao (2010) is concerned with the problem of determining the position of mobile robots by vision. A type of infrared landmark was designed; a system software based on Visual C++6.0 and OpenCV was build; and a location system for vision-based mobile robot and artificial landmark was developed. The infrared landmark image was acquired by a vision sensor and its mass center in the image was recognized by image processing. By the triangulation method, the robot's position in the world coordinate system was obtained. Experimental results show that the method could be applied in the field of self-localization of mobile robots.

On the other hand, this study focuses not only on controlling a mobile robot through artificial vision, but also on controlling the vision of one camera by the joint work of algorithms and the robot's motion. Shaikh et al. (2011) introduces a vision tracking system for mobile robots using Unscented Kalman Filter (UKF). The proposed system accurately estimates the position and orientation of the mobile robot by integrating information received from encoders, inertial sensors, and active beacons. These position and orientation estimates are used to rotate the camera towards the target during robot motion. The UKF, employed as an efficient sensor fusion algorithm, is an advanced filtering technique that reduces the position and orientation errors of the sensors.

Recent research by Pilar et al. (2014) present and emulate a wheeled robot for object transportation in a distribution center. The robot follows a free trajectory, which is controlled by artificial vision and fuzzy logic modules. The artificial vision system includes a webcam located in the upper part of the distribution center, which was used to calculate the location of the robot. Specifically, image segmentation technique of red color was implemented in the artificial vision system to determine the robot's position and orientation. The information obtained from the webcam is also employed by the fuzzy controller to estimate the robot's velocity, which is then send to the mobile robot wirelessly. The control of the motors and the wireless communication of the robot are performed by an Arduino platform, which supports an Xbee module for communications. The image processing and fuzzy control are implemented on a PC using Matlab. The light source selected generated a uniform diffuse lighting with not much glare in the environment, which enabled the artificial vision system to retrieve traits of interest from the physical surroundings.

The work of Figueiredo et al. (2016) presents the last developments in vision-based target tracking by an Autonomous Underwater Vehicle (AUV). The main concepts behind the visual relative localization are provided and the results from a statistical analysis for the relative localization algorithm are presented. The purpose of this analysis is to ensure properness of data used to feed controllers that are responsible for governing the AUV motion. A new set of controllers enabling the AUV to track a visual target is given. Experimental data obtained from tests in tank are presented, validating both the visual relative localization and control of the AUV.

GENERAL ASPECTS OF ROBOTICS

Background of Mobile Robots

The use of mobile robots is justified in applications in which tasks that are unpleasant or risky to humans are carried out, such as transporting hazardous materials, mining excavations, industrial cleaning, or inspection of nuclear power plants. In these situations, a mobile robot can perform the task and avoid uncalled-for risks to the workers' health. Another group of applications in which these kinds of robots complement the operator's activities are supervision, inspection, or assisting disabled people. Also, in surgical teleoperation applications, where there is considerable backwardness in communications, the use of vehicles with some degree of autonomy is interesting.

An autonomous mobile robot is characterized by having an intelligent connection between the operations of perception and action, which defines its behavior and allows it to fulfill the programmed objectives in surroundings with some uncertainty. The degree of autonomy depends largely on the ability of a robot to disregard the surroundings and convert the obtained information into orders, so that when orders are applied to the locomotion system's actuators, the efficient performance of the task is guaranteed. From this, it can be concluded that the main characteristics of a mobile robot, in contrast with any other kind of vehicle, are the following:

- Perception, which determines the relation of the robot with its work environment, by means of its onboard sensors.
- Reasoning, which determines the actions that must be carried out at all times according to the state of the robot and its surroundings to reach the assigned goals.

In this way, the reasoning ability of an autonomous mobile robot is translated into the planning of safe trajectories that will allow it to fulfill the assigned objectives. The execution of a task in particular must be carried out in a closed loop for the robot to adapt to navigating through unstructured surroundings. A traditional control loop is not used because the action is not generated by simple output feedback.

It is therefore necessary to use a planner skilled in geometric analysis that knows the conditions of the surroundings and of the mobile robot, together with its kinematic and dynamic characteristics. Starting from this point, the mobile robot can transform data supplied by the perception into adequate control references that do not go beyond any of its physical limitations, and that define trajectories free from obstacles that guarantee the achievement of the goals established for the specific task. Thus, the planner becomes responsible, to a large extent, of the mobile robot's navigation efficiency; therefore its design requires special care. To carry out these tasks it is necessary to have fine control of the movements of the mobile robot. The following techniques stand out for this purpose:

- Pure Pursue.
- PI-PD-PID control techniques.
- Ziegler-Nichols controllers.
- Cohen and Coon methods.
- Fuzzy control.

In addition to the above control techniques, there are methods for the execution of its specific tasks, e.g., the geometric method for following routes explicitly, the methods based on control theory applied to following trajectories and routes, as well as predictive and reactive control following, based on the direct reaction to environmental perception sensors (Caracciolo et al., 1999; Ollero, 2001).

Morphology of Mobile Robots

The design of the mobile robot that will be constructed is based on a configuration that consists of four wheels. Various configurations that comply with these characteristics are presented below (Silva et al., 2007; Holz et al., 2014; Wang et al., 2014; Shang et al., 2016).

Ackermann

The arrangement and mobility of its axles is similar to that of a conventional vehicle. The inner front wheel turns at a slightly larger angle than the outer wheel to prevent sliding. The extensions of the front axles intersect at some point on the extension of the axle of the rear wheels. The locus of the points drawn on the ground by the centers of the wheels are concentric circumferences centered on axle P1, as shown in Figure 1.

Figure 1. Ackermann configuration

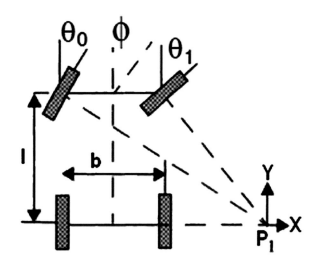

Skid-Steer

They are composed of several wheels on both sides of the vehicle that act simultaneously. The motion consists of the combination of the movements of the left and right sides, which result in advance, reverse, turning motions, etc. It is important to point out that, in contrast with the Ackermann, there is no axle movement.

Other kinds of four-wheel robots exist with hybrid configurations of wheels with differential traction and omnidirectional, as well as others with four omnidirectional wheels. For the design of the mobile robot presented in this chapter, this four-wheel configuration without axle movement was chosen, thanks to its great maneuverability.

Kinematics of Mobile Robots

Kinematics is the simplest study of the behavior of a mechanical system. In mobile robots, it is necessary to understand the mechanical behavior of both the approximate design for the task to be performed and the process of creation of the control software for the robot's hardware.

Mobile robots are not the first complex mechanical systems to require such analysis. Manipulator robots have been subjected to intensive research for over 40 years (from the 70s), because to a certain extent they are more complex than other mobile robots, thus the robotics community has reached a deep understanding of the kinematics and even of the dynamics of manipulator robots.

Representation of the Robot's Position

In the kinematic analysis, the mobile robot is considered as a rigid body on four wheels operating on a horizontal plane. To specify the position and orientation of this mobile robot, a two-dimensional movement is established between a global reference framework of the (X_g, Y_g, Z_g) plane that is chosen arbitrarily, and a local reference framework of the robot (x_1, y_1, z_1), associated with a point on the frame that corresponds to the robot's Center of Mass (COM). According to Figure 2, this COM can be described in the global reference system as COM=(X, Y), and the angular difference between the global and local system of reference is θ. Therefore, its position and orientation are determined by equation (1):

$$\xi_G = \begin{bmatrix} X \\ Y \\ \theta \end{bmatrix} \tag{1}$$

The velocity vector is defined on a two-dimensional coordinate system of the COM and expressed as a function of the local reference system by means of V_x and V_y, which determine the vehicle's longitudinal and lateral velocities (Figure 3). To obtain the robot's movement in global terms, its local movement is mapped along the global reference axes, leading to equation (2):

Figure 2. Reference system

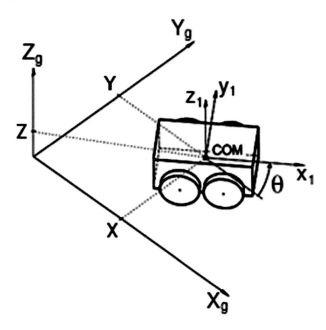

Figure 3. Velocities of the robot and global reference

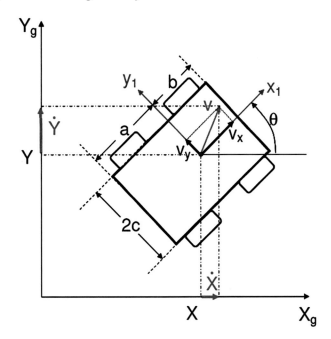

$$\dot{q} = \begin{bmatrix} \dot{X} \\ \dot{Y} \\ \dot{\theta} \end{bmatrix} = \begin{bmatrix} \cos\theta & -sen\theta & 0 \\ sen\theta & \cos\theta & 0 \\ 0 & 0 & 1 \end{bmatrix} \begin{bmatrix} V_x \\ V_y \\ \omega \end{bmatrix} \tag{2}$$

Velocity Ratio

The representation of the mobile robot in space does not impose any restriction on its motion in the plane, therefore only its free body kinematics is described. However, it is necessary to include the ratio between the velocities of the wheels and the local velocities. Then we have that the cinematic model for this mobile robot is constituted by the system of equations (3), (4), (5):

$$\dot{X} = r\left(\frac{\omega_L + \omega_R}{2}\right)\cos\theta + x_{ICR}r\left(\frac{-\omega_L + \omega_R}{2c}\right)sen\theta \tag{3}$$

$$\dot{Y} = r\left(\frac{\omega_L + \omega_R}{2}\right)sen\theta + x_{ICR}r\left(\frac{-\omega_L + \omega_R}{2c}\right)\cos\theta \tag{4}$$

$$\dot{\theta} = r\left(\frac{-\omega_L + \omega_R}{2c}\right) \tag{5}$$

where x_{ICR} is a coordinate of the center of instantaneous rotation, and ω_L and ω_R denote the angular velocities of the left and right wheels, respectively. At the kinematic level, they can be considered as control entries and can be used to control the longitudinal and angular velocity according to equation (6):

$$\omega = r\frac{-\omega_L + \omega_R}{2c} \tag{6}$$

where r is the presumed effective radius of the wheels and 2c is the spacing between the wheels. In this way, kinematic control of the mobile robot is achieved, as shown schematically in Figure 4.

Figure 4. Kinematic control of the robot

GUIDANCE OF MOBILE ROBOTS

The navigation problem of a mobile robot can be summarized in three questions: Where am I? Where am I going? And how should I get there? therefore a navigation system consists in the set of sensors, systems, methods and technologies that try to situate a mobile robot in its surroundings. Now, for a mobile robot to be completely autonomous and be able to go over its workspace without the occurrence of any inconveniences, it is necessary to answer the above questions by means of the following stages in the process of mobile robot guidance: localization, mapping and planning of trajectories.

The localization process consists in finding the location of the mobile robot within its work setting. The mapping process consists in creating a representation of the setting in which the mobile robot is performing, which must be comprehensible by it. The trajectory planning consists in determining the route that the mobile robot must follow, from an initial to a final configuration. This trajectory must be planned in such a way that the mobile robot does not collide with objects that it finds along its way.

Localization

The concept of localization arises as a need to estimate the position of the mobile robot within the work setting (map). There are different localization techniques that can be grouped into two kinds:

- Local Localization, which consists in determining the position of the mobile robot from a known initial position; *i.e.*, follow-up the movements made by the mobile robot, estimate its degree of advance and orientation, and make calculations to estimate the current position from the starting point of the movement, for example, odometry and landmarks may be mentioned.
- Global Localization, which consists in finding the position of the mobile robot without knowing its location at a previous instant, or having uncertain information. Kalman filtering, Markov filtering, and particle filtering may be mentioned.

Map Generation

It is important for the mobile robot to get in some way a map of the surroundings in which it must move. This must be done so that in a later stage it can use that map to trace the trajectory that it must follow. In general, maps are not adapted to the requirements of the robot and elaborating them manually is a time-consuming and costly process. If a robot builds its own map, the map will be suitable for the robot sensory capacities, and thus for use in navigation or localization.

- **Sensory Maps:** They are based on invariant characteristics or on grid maps of spatial occupation (probabilistic). In the grid maps the space is represented as a set of 2D or 3D cells, associating an occupation (1) or free (0) state. The number of cells is (n^d), where n is the number of cells per dimension and d is the number of dimensions.
- **Geometric Maps:** It is considered that the space can be represented by a series of geometric primitives (such as straight lines or polygons). The exploration is based on algorithms inspired in computational geometry. For instance, there are some techniques based on reaching a goal by moving in a straight line.

- **Topological Maps:** A map of the different situations that the robot will face is constructed. Then this map is represented by means of a graph, so when the map indicates a change of situation, i.e., differences with the expected, a new node and an arc are included. The resultant graph represents a map of the free space of the surroundings.

Trajectory Planning

The trajectory-planning problem consists in determining a trajectory between an initial and a final configuration, so that the mobile robot does not collide with the obstacles and complies with its kinematic restrictions. To do this it is necessary to consider the following specifications: minimum distance trajectory, semi-unknown environments, dynamic environments, additional restrictions, and efficiency.

To tackle the trajectory planning problem there are various methods that are grouped into graph search, dynamic programming, Voronoi diagrams, and visibility graphs.

CHOICE OF ELECTRIC COMPONENTS

Each of these elements must be chosen according to the task for which the robot was constructed, since they play a fundamental role for the configuration of the robot to perform specific tasks. It is necessary to know in advance what these specific tasks are in order to determine the electrical elements to be used.

The electric components chosen for the designed and implemented mobile robot are presented below:

- **Servomotors:** The total number of servomotors of the mobile robot is 17.
- **Microcontroller:** The microcontroller used is a Basic Stamp by Parallax.
- **Servo controller:** Because of the large number of servomotors used in the configuration of the mobile robot and for a better compatibility performance, the Parallax Servo Controller (PSC) board is used.
- **Sensors:** Due to the various tasks that this mobile robot will carry out, two types of sensors are chosen: an ultrasonic distance sensor, and a shape and color sensor (Acroname CMUCam 2+).
- **Batteries:** Two 6-V rechargeable batteries are used.
- **Computer:** To improve the processing capacity with respect to the artificial vision task, a netbook was incorporated.

CONSTRUCTION OF THE MOBILE ROBOT

The construction process of this mobile robot was divided into three main mechanical stages: the frame of the mobile robot, a manipulator with clamp as terminal effector, and a manipulator of the artificial vision camera.

Frame of the Mobile Robot

The frame of the mobile robot is the structure that integrates all its components, *i.e.*, the camera with its manipulator, the manipulator, batteries, circuits, and sensors, among other components, forming the robot's main structure. The design criteria were selected considering that the mobile robot has the following characteristics:

- Great mobility,
- Acceptable autonomy time,
- Light and easily transportable,
- Expansion and connectivity capacity,
- Acceptable construction cost.

A rail capable of displacing the artificial vision camera linearly to increase its range of vision is designed. This configuration was performed imitating the motion of the head of a turtle, in this way increasing its vision range by almost 180°.

Therefore, in its final design, the mobile robot consists of the following elements:

- **Base0:** Inside there are two supports for each wall for the servomotors in charge of the traction.
- **Base1:** This base contains all the robot's wiring and the battery supports, as well as the converters that allow communication between the camera and the netbook
- **PC Casing:** It is mounted on top of Base1, and its main function is to protect the netbook from possible impacts.
- **Manipulator Support:** It is fixed on Base1 and rests on the PC casing to provide more stability and strength to the manipulator.
- **Microcontroller Casing:** Its function is only to protect the microcontroller and its servo controlling board from dust as well as from possible impacts, in addition to avoiding possible accidental disconnections of elements like the sensors, servomotors, artificial vision camera, and batteries.

Figure 5 shows the above-mentioned elements, assembled to form the frame.

Figure 5. Frame of the mobile robot

Manipulator

This manipulator has four all rotational DOF on the same axle, and a terminal effector composed of a clamp. Out of these DOF, the first one allows a 180° turning motion that enables the handling and deposit of grasped objects. The second one allows the reaching motion and practically has a function akin to that of the shoulder joint. The third allows bringing close, fulfilling the function of the elbow, also with a 180° motion; and the fourth allows a fine and precise motion, serving a function similar to the motion of the human wrist, with a movement over 180°. The terminal effector allows grasping objects, and in general performs the function of the human fingers.

Figure 6 illustrates the manipulator, which is composed of the following mechanical elements: base manipulator, arm, forearm, wrist, and terminal effector.

Camera Manipulator

The camera manipulator consists of the following elements:

- **Camera-Sensor Support:** It supports the camera as well as the ultrasonic sensor, and it also performs the PAN motion by means of the servomotor.
- **TILT Support:** The part supports the servomotor in charge of performing the PAN movement.
- **Cart:** It has the function of sliding the artificial vision camera into or out of the frame of the mobile robot, to expand its vision range.
- **Adjustment Support:** It consists of two parts that are fixed on base0, whose function is to provide mechanical adjustment to the cart.

These three mechanical parts, assembled, constitute the mobile robot shown in Figure 7.

Figure 6. Manipulator arm

Figure 7. Designed and implemented mobile robot

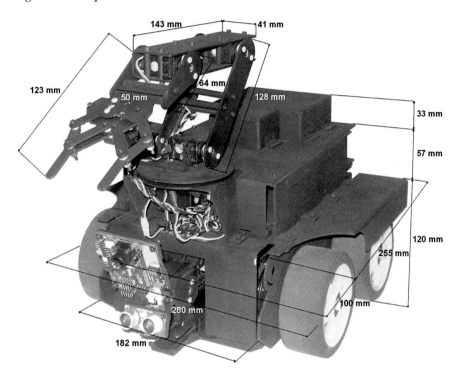

PROGRAMMING AND RESULTS

The microcontroller used for programming the mobile robot is a Basic Stamp, whose programming language is Basic. On the other hand, the commands of the artificial vision camera are very important for the development of object recognition, because if one of these commands is poorly configured, the recognition cannot take place. In addition to these commands, the artificial vision camera has others with different work characteristics and properties. The advantage of using this artificial vision camera is that, by means of its own commands, it allows the use of a technique for recognizing objects by means of their color. The mobile robot also has a netbook with the purpose of making it carry out specific tasks and work in general, as complex as its programming and its sensors allow.

Camera Programming

The robot starts functioning by searching for an object based on its color. Thus, the first program to execute is that of the configuration of the camera, which is presented below:

```
'-----------------------------------
'CONFIGURACION DE CAMARA
'-----------------------------------
CONFIGURACION_CMU:
        SEROUT  6, 84, ["RS",13]
        PAUSE   200
```

```
        SEROUT  6, 84,  ["PM 1",13]
        SERIN   7, 84,  [WAIT (":")]
        PAUSE   200
        SEROUT  6, 84,  ["RM 2",13]
        SEROUT  6, 84,  ["OM 0 63",13]
        SEROUT  6, 84,  ["NF 10",13]
        SEROUT  6, 84,  ["CR 19 32 18 40",13]
        SERIN   7, 84,  [WAIT (":")]
        GOSUB   PARPADEO_LED
RETURN
`----------------------------------
'OBTENCION DE COLORES DE IMAGEN
`----------------------------------
obtencion_color:
        SEROUT  6, 84,  ["RM 3",13]
        PAUSE   200
        SEROUT  6, 84,  ["TC 60 240 16 17 16 16",13]
        SERIN   7, 84,  [STR datorecibido\8]
RETURN
```

The first subroutine configures the camera by means of the values 6 and 84, which correspond to the output pin of the controller and to the constant defining speed of serial transmission, respectively. Through these values, communication between the camera and microcontroller is established.

Obtaining colors becomes very simple when applying this configuration, which, as may be seen, is mainly made up of a single command line, namely TC, which defines the maximum and minimum value of each RGB. However, in this case we are only interested in red.

Below it may be seen part of the principal program, by which subroutines are directed, that has direct relation with the detection of objects in front of the camera.

```
UBICACION:
  GOSUB obtencion_color
  IF (datorecibido(6) >= 72) THEN
    'DEBUG "Detecto Color Rojo",CR
    IF (datorecibido(3) < 44) AND (datorecibido(5) < 44) THEN
            'DEBUG "Objeto rojo a IZQ",CR
            GOSUB posicion
            pos  = 1
            GOSUB centrar_izq
            ELSEIF (datorecibido(3) > 44)AND(datorecibido(5) > 44) THEN
                    'DEBUG "Objeto rojo a DER",CR
                    GOSUB posicion
                    pos  = 2
                    GOSUB centrar_der
    ELSEIF ((datorecibido(3) < 44)AND(datorecibido(5) > 44))THEN
```

```
            IF ((88-datorecibido(5)) > datorecibido(3))THEN
                    'DEBUG "OBJETO ROJO DELANTE HACIA LA IZQ",CR
                    GOSUB posicion
                    pos   =  3
                    GOSUB centrar_izq
            ELSEIF ((88-datorecibido(5)) < datorecibido(3))THEN
                    'DEBUG "OBJETO ROJO DELANTE HACIA LA DER",CR
                    GOSUB posicion
                    pos   =  4
                    GOSUB centrar_der
              ELSEIF ((88-datorecibido(5)) = datorecibido(3))THEN
                    'DEBUG "OBJETO ROJO FRENTE A ROBOT",CR
                    GOSUB detectado
            ENDIF
      ENDIF
   ELSE
      GOSUB mover_camara
   ENDIF
```

This program runs a series of conditional statements to define whether the camera has found the red object or not, as well as in which position the object is by comparing values obtained from the camera, specifically, the coordinates of the square that encloses the object, thereby determining if the object is left, right or at the center.

The program has two types of motion, to the left and to the right, each one destined to determine more accurately the object's position. The first motion, whether to the left or to the right, has the aim of approaching the camera to the object, while the second motion conducts a fine control to place the camera in front of the object.

When the camera is in front of the object due to the fine movement of the manipulator robot, motion stops and is directed to the subroutine 'detected', this allows the robot to continue with its configuration to grab the identified object.

It must be noted that when none of the statements is true, the camera motion subroutine starts and remains in this loop until the red object is localized. Once the camera has covered its view range, close to 180°, the robot turns clockwise and starts the search again.

Distance Sensor Programming

The program used for programming the distance sensor is shown below:

```
'------------------------------
'MEDICIÓN DE DISTANCIA
'------------------------------
distancia_adelante:
        PULSOUT         10, Trigger
        PULSIN          10, 1, rawDist
```

```
rawDist  =  rawDist */ Scale
rawDist  =  rawDist / 2
cm  =  rawDist ** RawToCm
PAUSE  1000
'DEBUG  "cm=", DEC cm,CR
PAUSE 1000
 IF (cm > 10)                    THEN AVANZAR
 IF ((cm >= 8) AND (cm <=10))    THEN mover_manipulador
 IF (cm <= 7)                    THEN RETROCEDER
```

With this program, it is known at what distance from the sensor an object is; by means of the PUL-SOUT command a signal is sent through the pin to which the sensor is connected, while the information is received by the same pin using the PULSIN command, storing information in a variable previously created for such end.

PSC Control Card Programming

In order to control all the servomotors, a PSC control card must be programmed. The following program is used for this purpose:

```
'{$STAMP BS2px}
'{$PBASIC 2.5}
Sdat          PIN 15          ' Pin para configuración serial
Baud CON 1646          ' Constante para velocidad de 2400 baud
buff          VAR Byte(3)     ' Variable temporal
FindPSC:               ' Encuentra y obtiene la versión
DEBUG    "Encontrando PSC", CR          'Número de la PSC.
SEROUT   Sdat, Baud, ["!SCVER?",CR]
SERIN    Sdat, Baud, 500, FindPSC, [STR buff\3]
DEBUG    "PSC ver: ", buff(0), buff(1), buff(2), CR
STOP
```

This program in independent from the general programming of the robot. However, it is crucial to carry it out; otherwise, it will be impossible for the PSC card to communicate with the microcontroller, impeding control of each servomotor.

Servomotor Programming

In addition to Hitec servomotors, there are two different servomotors, namely a Futaba servomotor—in charge of performing the motion to push the cart of the camera—and a GWS servomotor—in charge of opening and closing the clamp. Both respond to the same pulse train to be in central position. Below is presented a table (Table 1) with the values that must be sent to each servomotor for it to carry out motion.

Table 1. Pulse train values for servomotors

Servomotor	0°	90°	180°
Hitech 311HB	250	750	1250
Hitech 475HB	250	750	1250
Hitech 965MG	250	750	1250
Hitech 7955TG	380	750	1120
Futaba 3004	240	750	1240
GWS 2BBMG	250	750	1250

Servomotor Initial Movement

To initiate the complete configuration of the robot, each servomotor must be in initial position. This subroutine is as follows:

```
'-----------------------------------------------------------------------
'POSICIÓN INICIAL SERVOMOTORES
'-----------------------------------------------------------------------
mov_iniservos:
  pw = 950
    SEROUT 15, 1646,["!SC", 0, 10, pw.LOWBYTE, pw.HIGHBYTE, CR]
  pw = 800
    SEROUT 15, 1646,["!SC", 1, 10, pw.LOWBYTE, pw.HIGHBYTE, CR]
  pw = 750
    SEROUT 15, 1646,["!SC", 2, 10, pw.LOWBYTE, pw.HIGHBYTE, CR]
    SEROUT 15, 1646,["!SC", 3, 0, pw.LOWBYTE, pw.HIGHBYTE, CR]
    SEROUT 15, 1646,["!SC", 4, 0, pw.LOWBYTE, pw.HIGHBYTE, CR]
  pw = 1090
    SEROUT 15, 1646,["!SC", 5, 10, pw.LOWBYTE, pw.HIGHBYTE, CR]
  pw = 1130
    SEROUT 15, 1646,["!SC", 6, 10, pw.LOWBYTE, pw.HIGHBYTE, CR]
  pw = 1070
    SEROUT 15, 1646,["!SC", 7, 10, pw.LOWBYTE, pw.HIGHBYTE, CR]
  pw = 700
    SEROUT 15, 1646,["!SC", 8, 10, pw.LOWBYTE, pw.HIGHBYTE, CR]
  pw = 750
    SEROUT 15, 1646,["!SC", 9, 10, pw.LOWBYTE, pw.HIGHBYTE, CR]
RETURN
```

The motion of each servomotor is determined by a variable previously created for that end, namely the *Word*-type pw variable, which varies according to the direction towards which each servomotor carries out motion.

Camera Servomotors Motion

It comprises three servomotors: the one that pushes the cart and the other two that move the camera's manipulator. In addition, its programming includes the following subroutines:

```
'POSICION INICIAL DE CÁMARA
'--------------------------------------------------------------------------
posini_camara:
          pw = 240
          SEROUT 15, 1646,["!SC", 0, 10, pw.LOWBYTE, pw.HIGHBYTE, CR]
          PAUSE 100
          pw = 800
          SEROUT 15, 1646,["!SC", 1, 0, pw.LOWBYTE, pw.HIGHBYTE, CR]
          PAUSE 1000
          pw = 350
          SEROUT 15, 1646,["!SC", 2, 10, pw.LOWBYTE, pw.HIGHBYTE, CR]
          PAUSE 200
RETURN
'--------------------------------------------------------------------------
'MOVER CÁMARA
'--------------------------------------------------------------------------
mover_camara:
            pwa = pwa+50
            pwb = pwa
            pw  = pwa
            SEROUT 15, 1646,["!SC", 2, 10, pw.LOWBYTE, pw.HIGHBYTE, CR]
            PAUSE 1500
            IF (pwa = 1100) THEN nueva
            GOTO salir
nueva: pwa = 350
            SEROUT 15, 1646,["!SC", 2, 8, pwa.LOWBYTE, pwa.HIGHBYTE, CR]
            GOSUB GIRO
            RETURN
salir:  RETURN
```

The first subroutine aforementioned is directly related to the initial position of the manipulator robot before initiating the object search process. The second subroutine is responsible for performing the Pan motion of the camera's manipulator to localize the object.

These programs were insufficient to localize the object placed just in front of the camera. Therefore, it was necessary to configure a new subroutine called 'position' that was able to do it. The 'position' subroutine allows localizing the position of the Pan servomotor when it sweeps the surroundings searching for the object. With the values obtained from 'position' subroutine, 'centrar_izq' or 'centrar_der' subroutines are entered. These routines are in charge of moving the manipulator of the camera towards those directions and of positioning the camera in front of the object by means of the conditional statements associated.

Servomotors Traction Motion

The robot traction motion is made up of the following subroutines:

```
`------------------------------------------------------------------------
`UBICACIÓN DEL ROBOT FRENTE AL OBJETO
`------------------------------------------------------------------------
centrar_robot:
    IF (((buff(1)= 2) AND (buff(2) > 229 AND buff(2) <= 256)) OR ((buff(1)= 3)
AND
(buff(2) >= 0 AND buff(2) < 9)))THEN
                GOSUB DETENER
                GOSUB calc_dis
`Giro Izquierda
    ELSEIF ((buff(1)= 1) AND (buff(2)<=256)) OR ((buff(1)= 2) AND (buff(2) <
230)) THEN
                pwb = pwb+40
                SEROUT 15, 1646, ["!SC", 2, 0, pwb.LOWBYTE, pwb.HIGHBYTE, CR]
                PAUSE 100
                pw=780
                SEROUT 15, 1646, ["!SC", 3, 0, pw.LOWBYTE, pw.HIGHBYTE, CR]
                SEROUT 15, 1646, ["!SC", 4, 0, pw.LOWBYTE, pw.HIGHBYTE, CR]
                PAUSE 300
                GOSUB DETENER
                GOSUB UBICACION
`Giro Derecha
ELSEIF ((buff(1)=2) AND (buff(2)>247) OR ((buff(1)= 3) AND (buff(2) < 256)) OR
        ((buff(1)= 4) AND (buff(2) < 146))) THEN
                pwb = pwb-40
                SEROUT 15, 1646, ["!SC", 2, 0, pwb.LOWBYTE, pwb.HIGHBYTE, CR]
                PAUSE 100
                pw=720
                SEROUT 15, 1646, ["!SC", 3, 0, pw.LOWBYTE, pw.HIGHBYTE, CR]
                SEROUT 15, 1646, ["!SC", 4, 0, pw.LOWBYTE, pw.HIGHBYTE, CR]
                PAUSE 300
                GOSUB DETENER
                GOSUB UBICACIÓN
    ENDIF
```

The first part of this subroutine indicates that the robot is already in front of the object. Then the robot is directed to the 'stop' subroutine and when it returns heads to the distance calculation subroutine. The following conditional statement moves the camera to the right and turns the robot to the left, to subsequently go to the 'stop' subroutine and then to the 'location' subroutine to center the camera in front of the object one more time. Meanwhile, the other statement does the same but in the opposite direction.

Manipulator Servomotors Motion

The manipulator robot motion is defined by the following subroutine:

```
'----------------------------------------------------------------------
' MOVIMIENTO DEL MANIPULADOR
'----------------------------------------------------------------------
mover_manipulador:
        pw = 390
        SEROUT 15, 1646,["!SC", 6, 10, pw.LOWBYTE, pw.HIGHBYTE, CR]
        pw = 550
        SEROUT 15, 1646,["!SC", 7, 10, pw.LOWBYTE, pw.HIGHBYTE, CR]
        pw = 600
        SEROUT 15, 1646,["!SC", 8, 10, pw.LOWBYTE, pw.HIGHBYTE, CR]
        PAUSE 2500
        pw = 945
        SEROUT 15, 1646,["!SC", 9, 10, pw.LOWBYTE, pw.HIGHBYTE, CR]
        PAUSE 2000
        pw = 1130
        SEROUT 15, 1646,["!SC", 6, 10, pw.LOWBYTE, pw.HIGHBYTE, CR]
        pw = 1070
        SEROUT 15, 1646,["!SC", 7, 10, pw.LOWBYTE, pw.HIGHBYTE, CR]
        pw = 900
        SEROUT 15, 1646,["!SC", 8, 10, pw.LOWBYTE, pw.HIGHBYTE, CR]
        PAUSE 2000
        pw = 700
        SEROUT 15, 1646,["!SC", 8, 10, pw.LOWBYTE, pw.HIGHBYTE, CR]
GOSUB fin
```

For the manipulator robot to capable of grabbing the object, the only action executed is sending different values of the pw variable to each servomotor. These values are set according to the motion performed by the manipulator robot, which is a single movement. In addition, pauses in the programming allow the associated servomotor to perform its movement without making the next one, so it can grab the object adequately. When the object has been grabbed, the manipulator robot returns to its initial position, except for the clam that is holding the object.

All the subroutines aforementioned, together with other subroutines for analysis, are part of the complete program that allows the robot to identify the object, head to it and finally grab it. Each subroutine can be configured separately to observe its functioning, regardless of the general program.

Results from each subroutine can be seen by the DEBUG command and can be accessed within the program in the form of remarks, since they consume great part of the memory available in the microcontroller. Some of the results are the localization of the object, which indicate when, where and at what distance it is detected.

To conclude, results are satisfactory because the robot performs the tasks for which it was programmed.

CONCLUSION

The design, construction and programming of a mobile robot controlled by means of artificial vision, specifically by means of the recognition of different color objects, has been presented. This mobile robot also has a notebook that provides it with a large artificial intelligence capacity, which depends mostly on the programming given.

A mechanically robust robot has been built and a system has been designed that allows the mobility of two sensors jointly, *i.e.*, artificial vision camera and distance sensor. This makes it possible to improve the range of artificial vision to approximately 180°, achieving precise positioning of the mobile robot.

The Basic Stamp microcontroller provides efficiency in the algorithms, allowing good coordination between all the constitutive elements of the mobile robot.

Incorporating the PSC card allows a simpler and controlled programming of each servomotor in terms of speed and position, making the navigation system more reliable.

The artificial vision camera, CMUCam 2, provides the mobile robot with great autonomy thanks to its excellent interaction with its surrounding world.

Having this mobile robot facilitates to carry out interesting developments in various areas of mobile robotics.

DISCUSSION

Problems

The manual manufacturing of the majority of pieces constituting the robot, such as chassis, brackets, basis, axles, among others, is time-consuming.

Unfortunately, Basic Stamp is not the optimal microcontroller for the development of a wide range of algorithms, due to its limited memory, which does not allow the new robot to perform tasks that are more complex.

Challenges

Although the results obtained were satisfactory, some lines can be developed to improve and optimize the current design:

- Addition of arms capable of lifting the robot to overcome obstacles of certain height. Specifically, the gear case used in this motion needs to be improved.
- Substitution of the microcontroller for one of greater capacity in terms of memory and algorithm processing.
- Development of research on trajectory planning, mobile robots' kinematics, among others, and of algorithms for artificial vision, mainly for recognition of objects or shapes, incorporating a netbook.

ACKNOWLEDGMENT

This work has been supported by Proyectos Basales and the Vicerrectoría de Investigación, Desarrollo e Innovación (VRIDEI), Universidad de Santiago de Chile, Chile.

REFERENCES

Bin, M. R. (2008). *Vision based autonomous robot*. Malaysia: Universiti Teknologi Malaysia.

Caracciolo, L., De Luca, A., & Iannitti, S. (1999). Trajectory tracking control of a four-wheel differentially driven mobile robot. In *Proceedings of the 1999 IEEE Internatonal Conference on Robotics & Automation*. Detroit, MI: IEEE. doi:10.1109/ROBOT.1999.773994

Del Pilar, F., Guarnizo, J., & Benavides, G. (2014). Emulation system for a distribution center using mobile robot, controlled by artificial vision and fuzzy logic. *IEEE Latin America Transactions*, *12*(4), 557–563. doi:10.1109/TLA.2014.6868855

Figuereido, A. B., Ferreira, B. M., & Matos, A. C. (2016). *Visión-based localization and positioning of an AUV*. Paper presented at OCEANS 2016 Conference, Shanghai, China. doi:10.1109/OCEANSAP.2016.7485384

Holz, D., Nieuwenhuisen, M., Droeschel, D., Stückler, J., Berner, A., Li, J., Klein, R., & Behnke, S. (2014). Active recognition and manipulation for mobile robot bin picking. In F. Röhrbein, G. Veiga, & C. Natale (Eds.), Gearing up and accelerating cross-fertilization between academic and industrial robotics in Europe (pp. 133-153). Springer International Publishing.

Ollero, A. (2001). *Robótica: Manipuladores y robots móviles*. Barcelona: Marcombo S.A.

Shaikh, M. M., Bahn, W., Lee, C., Kim, T., Lee, T., Kim, K., & Cho, D. (2011). *Mobile robot vision tracking using unscented kalman filter*. Paper presented at 2011 IEEE/SICE International Symposium on System Integration (SII), Kyoto, Japan. doi:10.1109/SII.2011.6147622

Shang, W., Yang, C., Liu, Y. & Wang, J. (2016). Design on a Composite Mobile System for Exploration Robot. *Shock and Vibration*.10.1155/2016/6363071

Silva, R., García, J. R., Barrientos, V. R., Molina, M. A., Hernández, V. M., & Silva, G. (2007). State-of-the-art of the movable wheels robots. *Telématique: Revista Electrónica de Estudios Telemáticos*, *6*(3), 1–14.

Wang, L., & Zhao, G. (2010). A localization system for mobile robots based vision. In *Proceedings of the 8th World Congress on Intelligent Control and Automation*. Jinan, China: IEEE. doi:10.1109/WCICA.2010.5554159

Chapter 12
Review and Applications of Multimodal Biometrics for Secured Systems

Chitra Anil Dhawale
P. R. Pote College of Engineering and Management, India

ABSTRACT

Biometric Systems provide improved security over traditional electronic access control methods such as RFID tags, electronic keypads and some mechanical locks. The user's authorized card or password pin can be lost or stolen. In order for the biometrics to be ultra-secure and to provide more-than-average accuracy, more than one form of biometric identification is required. Hence the need arises for the use of multimodal biometrics. This uses a combination of different biometric recognition technologies. This chapter begins with the basic idea of Biometrics, Biometrics System with its components, Working and proceeds with the need of Multimodal Biometrics with the emphasis on review of various multimodal systems based on fusion ways and fusion level of various features. The last section of this chapter describes various multimodal Biometric Systems.

INTRODUCTION

In an identity management system like banking site log in, ATM login, Airport verification for a traveler, traditional token based user verification methods based on license, passport, PINS or passwords prove as weak authentication methods since they can be missed or stolen. Authentication measure is thus required to exist with user, not lost in any case and must be unique of course! Such a reliable measure is nothing but the person itself!, Here the term biometrics came into existence.

The term Biometrics contains two words – *Bio* (Greek word for Life) and *Metrics* (Measurements). Biometrics is a branch of information technology that aims towards finding one's identity based on personal traits. Biometric systems are developed based on the individual's physical characteristics or behavioral characteristics. The physical characteristics or features or attributes like finger prints, color

DOI: 10.4018/978-1-5225-2053-5.ch012

Figure 1. Components of biometric system

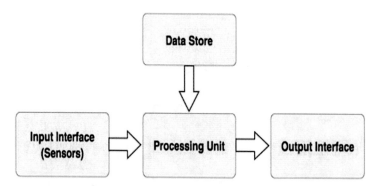

of iris, color of hair, hand geometry, and behavioral characteristics such as tone and accent of speech, signature, etc. make a person stand separate from the rest.

These are the unique characteristics which are selected. This means that we should have feel of uniqueness when we look at the object. Not only one part should be different but together the entire object must be found unique. Also it is necessary that it should be existing with everybody.

Biometric systems use these unique features for:

- Identification and verification of a person,
- Authentication of person,
- Security of system from unauthorised access.

A biometric system is a technology which takes input as person's physiological, behavioral, or both traits as input, analyzes it, and authenticate the person for accessing the system.

COMPONENTS OF A BIOMETRIC SYSTEM

In general, a biometric system can be divided into four basic components (Figure 1).

1. **Input Interface (Sensors):** It is the sensing component of a biometrics system that converts human biological data into digital form. For example,
   a. A Metal Oxide Semiconductor (CMOS) imager or a Charge Coupled Device (CCD) in the case of face recognition, handprint recognition, or iris/retinal recognition systems.
   b. An optical sensor in case of fingerprint systems.
   c. A microphone in case of voice recognition systems.
2. **Processing Unit:** The processing component is a microprocessor, Digital Signal Processor (DSP), or computer that processes the data captured from the sensors. The processing of the biometric sample involves:
   a. Sample image enhancement,
   b. Sample image normalization,
   c. Feature extraction,
   d. Comparison of the biometric sample with all stored samples in database.

Figure 2. Working of biometric system

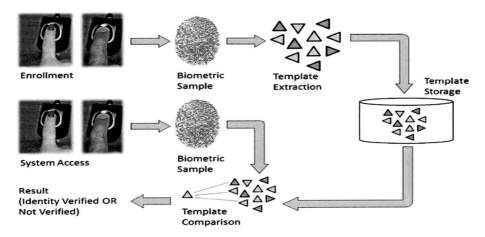

3. **Database Store:** The database stores the enrolled sample, which is recalled to perform a match at the time of authentication. For identification, there can be any memory from Random Access Memory (RAM), flash EPROM, or a data server. For verification, a removable storage element like a contact or contactless smart card is used.

4. **Output Interface:** The output interface communicates the decision of the biometric system to enable the access to the user. This can be a simple serial communication protocol RS232, or the higher bandwidth USB protocol. It could also be TCP/IP protocol, Radio Frequency Identification (RFID), Bluetooth, or one of the many cellular protocols.

General Working of a Biometric System

There are four general steps a biometric system takes to perform identification and verification (Figure 2):

*   Acquire live sample from candidate. (using sensors)
*   Extract prominent features from sample. (using processing unit)
*   Compare live sample with samples stored in database. (using algorithms)
*   Present the decision. (Accept or reject the candidate.)

The biometric sample is acquired from candidate user. The prominent features are extracted from the sample and it is then compared with all the samples stored in the database. When the input sample matches with one of the samples in the database, the biometric system allows the person to access the resources; otherwise prohibits.

Biometrics Terminology

*   **Biometric Template:** A digital reference of the distinct characteristics that are extracted from a biometric sample.
*   **Candidate/Subject:** A person who enters his biometric sample.
*   **Closed-Set Identification:** The person is known to be existing in the database.

- **Enrollment:** It is when a candidate uses a biometric system for the first time, it records the basic information such as name, address, etc. and then records the candidate's biometric trait.
- **False Acceptance Rate (FAR):** Number of False Acceptances / Number of Identification Attempts. A biometric system providing low FAR ensures high security. It is the measure of possibility that a biometric system will incorrectly identify an unauthorized user as a valid user.
- **False Reject Rate (FRR):** Number of False Rejections/ Number of Identification Attempts. It is the measure of possibility that the biometric system will incorrectly reject an authorized user as an invalid user.
- **Open-Set Identification:** The person is not guaranteed to be existing in the database.
- **Task:** It is when the biometric system searches the database for matching sample.

NEED OF MULTIMODAL BIOMETRICS

Single feature selection for biometric recognition can lead to wrong identification of the objects in rare cases where dirty data acquisition is done or the cases where people are trying to crack the system by proxy input. It has also the drawback of non-availability of universal biometric traits. Also in this case the issues of interclass-variations (variation in biometric traits due to age) and intra-class similarities (twins with similar physical characteristics) hold true. In this case multimodal biometric system is used, for example use of (Photograph+signature) for person identification. Multimodal biometrics does not always refer to the use of two or more separate biometric trait samples but the multiple inputs can come from variety of sources (Andreas Humm, 2009). These sources are summarized in Figure 3. The need of multiple attributes vary with applications. For example, employee attendance system require person's unique thumb print, while detecting a criminal running among the crowd at a public place requires walking style and body silhouettes to be traced and matched. In a vehicle license management system face and signature of the driver may work whereas in online course tutorial conduction student's keystroke dynamics can play a good part to find him unique.

Figure 3. Sources of input: multimodal biometric systems

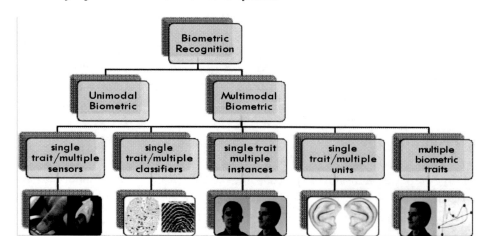

REVIEW OF MULTIMODAL BIOMETRICS

In multibiometric systems the biometric traits are fused at different level like feature level, match score level, decision level, etc. with the help of various fusion methodologies; some of which can be listed as concatenation, weighted summation, product, min, max, borda count, majority voting etc. following section summarizes work by different authors on Multibiometric systems with respect to modalities, fusion ways, fusion levels, database, dataset size, algorithms, performance, etc.

Multibiometric Fusion Ways

Different modalities in Multibiometrics are fused in different ways at various levels right from input acquisition to decision making. Those are summarized below-

1. **Single Biometric Multiple Sensors:** In these systems, a single biometric trait is imaged using multiple sensors in order to extract diverse information from the images. For example, the system may record the 2-D texture content of a person's face using a CCD camera and the 3-D surface shape of the face using a range sensor in order to perform authentication. The availability of multi-sensor data pertaining to a single trait can assist the segmentation and registration procedures also besides improving matching accuracy (Ross, 2006). In the literature pioneer work on multiple-sensors is given about multisensory fingerprint verification (Marcialis & Roli, 2004) where the system is based on the fusion of optical and capacitive sensors.

2. **Multiple Biometrics:** Under these systems combination of different physical\behavioral biometrics can be used to identify\verify accurate users. For ex. Some of the earliest work has used face and speech (Souheil Ben-Yacoub, 1999). Physically uncorrelated traits handwriting and speech (Andreas Humm S. M., 2009) are found to give superior results than that of correlated traits palm print and fingerprint (Yong Jian Chin, 2009).

3. **Single Biometric Multiple Units/Instance:** The input samples are multiple instances of same trait. For ex. use of left and right index fingers. In this case an individual's own biometric data can be used to verify its own identity. For ex. If a person's single unit is found badly captured due to some inherent problems like skin decease, then the combination of facts across multiple will become a good identifying feature. For big number of subjects in database, multiple instance systems are more useful (Ross, 2006). For example Ajay Kumar (Ajay Kumar, 2011) has proposed fusion of multiple representations of Palmprint.

4. **Multiple Algorithms/Classifier/Matcher:** These systems are cost-effective and user-convenient, since they do not incorporate usage of different sensors; instead makes use of various matcher algorithms for different features. For example for the same fingerprint image different algorithms for minutiae extraction and ridges separation. For example in the work on verification for the feature of finger knucle (AlMahafzah, Imran & Sheshadri, 2012) the authors have used multiple algorithms like Log-Gabor Filters (LG), Local Phase Quantization (LPQ), Principal Component Analysis (PCA) and Locality Preserving Projections (LPP).

5. **Hybrid Systems:** These are the biometric systems where combined approaches using any of the types stated above. For ex. Ramli et al. (Ramli, Rani, & Ishak, 2011) provide solution to identify a person by making use of multiple instances of speaker output combined with face modality by employing weighted sum rule fusion and Min-max technique for normalization. Thus the system is multi-instance and multimodal in its design.

Fusion Levels

The goal of fusion is to determine the best set of experts in a given problem domain and devise an appropriate function that can optimally combine the decisions rendered by the individual experts (Ross, 2006). The information can be consolidated at various levels. These levels are primarily categorized based on right from capturing an image to taking final decision via feature extraction and matching modules. The different fusion levels thus defined are either before matching or after matching. These are summarized as follows-

Fusion before Matching

1. **Fusion at the Sensor Level:** Different sensors have different quality and capacity of image acquisition; this fact leads to capturing of different levels of details of the underlying structure of biometric trait. Integration of these details creates a composite image with more information. For example mosaicing of different Palmprint images taken from various cameras to form a single good quality Palmprint image (Ross, 2006). Marcialis et al. (Marcialis & Roli, 2004) described a multi-sensor fingerprint matcher based on optical and capacitive sensors followed by feature enhancement to extract Minutae points by two algorithms viz. Fourier enhancement and rank order transformation. A String algorithm is used as a matcher to form respective scores which are fused further to claim the identity.

2. **Fusion at the Feature Extraction Level:** It is about concatenation of feature set vectors extracted from different biometric sources/algorithms followed by feature normalization to change the location and scale parameters of distributions of the individual features sets into a single feature set or vector (AlMahafzah, Imran, & Sheshadri, 2012). Harbi AlMahafzah et al. (2012) performs multi-algorithm feature level fusion for the feature of finger knuckle (7,920 images of FKP database) for various feature extraction algorithms like Log-Gabor Filters (LG), Local Phase Quantization (LPQ), Principal Component Analysis (PCA) and Locality Preserving Projections (LPP). Various feature normalization techniques like Min-Max, Median and absolute Median, Z-Score, Tanh are used for two or three algorithms combination. Yong Jian Chin (Yong Jian Chin, 2009) proposed to fuse palmprint and fingerprint using Gabor Filter after image pre-processing and enhancement by filtering, STFT and 2D-DWT algorithms.

Fusion after Matching

1. **Fusion at the Rank Level:** After matching the input trait, the matcher assigns a rank to inputs in descending order. Highest the rank highest is the matching rate. In multiple traits, the ranks of different modalities are combined to find a joint rank for best identity purpose. The ranks of individual classifiers are combined using the highest rank method, the Borda count method, and the logistic regression method (Ross, 2006). Rank level fusion is applied for Face, ear and signature to include matched identities that appear in top identities given by matcher of individual trait and only those identities are included that appear in all matcher results (Maruf Monwar, 2009). Rank-level fusion can be applied to multiple biometric representations by consolidating ranks given by four palm print matchers in non-linear fashion (Ajay Kumar, 2011).

2. **Fusion at the Matching Scores:** Fusion at the match score level is the foremost in multimodal biometrics fusionas it provides very higher information of input data than earlier levels and results into better categorization (Ajay Kumar, 2010). In the initial literature it was found that face and speech data was combined at score level to confirm that classification schemes like support vector machines and Bayesian classifier prove to be the best for person identity verification (Souheil Ben-Yacoub, 1999). The very first demonstration of multimodal fusion of fingerprint and face was done under match score level (Robert Snelick, 2005). The identification system can be made more robust and secure by embedding voice with the facial features by watermarking algorithms (Vatsa, 2007). A user can be asked by writing some text and reading the same while writing, thus recording speech and handwriting signals at the same time reducing extra time required for input access. The matching outcomes are fused later at match score level to give maximum of 1% equal error rate (Andreas Humm, 2009).Two fingerprints (Marcialis & Roli, 2004) are be examined to extract minute points after capturing the image by two sensor, optical sensor and capacitive sensor, followed by matching using String matcher algorithm The match score thus produced is fused to get final score to take decision about confirming claimed identity.

3. **Fusion at the Decision (Abstract Level) Level:** The fusion at decision level is made when the already existing commercially available biometric matchers give access to final decision. In the study of multi-biometric systems, researchers have proposed decision level fusion approaches making use of "AND" and "OR" rules, majority voting, weighted majority voting, Bayesian decision fusion, the Depster-Shafer theory of evidence and behavior knowledge space.

Performance of Biometric Systems

The biometric system may not always respond in intended manner at some rare cases; this may be due to certain external factors leading to undesired outputs. These factors are discussed below in terms of various types of errors they cause. By the incorporation of a biometric systems these errors can be minimized and the methods can be optimized to tolerate certain unavoidable errors to identify a legitimate user.

1. **False Rejection Rate (FRR):** For some reasons like malfunctioning of sensor or alteration in physical structure of a person due to health reason such as damage to some organs like finger or hand due to accidental cases may lead a biometric system to find a genuine user as an imposter which we call as false rejection. The identities with highintra-class variations are more prone to give high FRR.

2. **False Acceptance Rate (FAR) or False Match Rate (FMR):** Here an imposter is accepted as a legitimate user.The identities with less inter-class variations are more prone to give high FAR. Identities in the form of twin siblings or father-son duo, are the best cases for such failures.

3. **Failure to Capture Rate (FCR):** In some cases biometric samples are not properly located due to poor sensor intensity leading to bad quality images. The corresponding ratio is called FCR.

4. **Failure to Enroll Rate (FTE):** Unawareness about enrollment process may denote the rate of failure. User training may help in this situation.

The reliability of the multimodal biometric system is depends on the experimental results. As per the case study, the training database contains a face, iris, two fingerprint images and one or two signature image(s) for each individual. The face image has been taken from the operated environment with the

Table 1. The accuracy, FAR, and FRR of individual recognizers

Trait	Algorithm	FAR (%)	FRR (%)	Accuracy (%)
Face	EBGM	0.59	22	88.70
Fingerprint	Reference Point	11	6	91.05
Iris	Haar	3.42	8.45	92.50
Signature	Global and Local Features	10	8	91.00

help of high definition digital camera. The face images acquired using the frontal view with the help of various orientations and different lightning. The fingerprints collected with the help of optical sensor. The iris image is collected with the help of high definition Camera.

The performance parameter is tested and is depicted in Table 1.

CHALLENGES OF MULTIMODAL BIOMETRICS SYSTEM

1.   The challenging part of the multimodal biometric system is the automatic acknowledgement of the indoor, outdoor and lighting environment and compatible for the other outsider system to communicate and adjust it.
2.   The sensors are multi adjusted and high quality and faster to gain the different type of data along with the low cost.
3.   The system should be consistent to work with the different type of data such as images, videos, gestures, bio-impressions. Though, this data is a different input from various sources, the algorithm is efficient to gain the required the data to find the perfect match.
4.   This system must be work on any type of image and the multi type data in integration.
5.   The matching algorithms should be efficient enough to recognize the incoming contents. Either single algorithm or the integrated approach can be helpful.
6.   Should be 100% Accurate, Consistent, Independent and Durable.

CASE STUDIES OF APPLICATIONS FOR SECURED MULTI MODAL SYSTEMS

Various applications of biometrics fall into areas like forensics, government and commercial applications. Corpse identification, Criminal investigation, Parenthood determination and Missing children are some of the forensic applications of biometrics. Government sector can utilize this means of identification for National ID, Driver's license, voter registration, Welfare disbursement, Border crossing, etc. commercial applications include ATM, Access control and computer login, Mobile phone, e-commerce, Internet, banking, smart card, so on (Kong, 2009).

Some other applications where biometrics is used as a means for authenticating individuals is described in Figures 4, 5, 6, and 7.

Figure 4. P.R. Pote College of Engineering and Management, Amravati in India have hosted an employee attendance system where an employee has to mark his attendance every day by putting any of his hand fingers which is acquired and matched with already enrolled database for the corresponding employee across his employee id. Once the match is found message displays successful attendance for the found id.

Figure 5. Identity recognition technology has improved sufficiently in Japan as a result of which, Japan plans to deploy mobile biometric terminals at airports to take photos and fingerprints of foreign visitors, cutting down the processing time at the immigration desk. The terminals, called Biocart, will be installed at all airports with international operations, from April 2016. After capturing the visitors' images and fingerprints, the terminals will send the information to the immigration desk. The Justice Ministry expects Biocarts to reduce waiting time for travelers as well as ease the burden on the immigration staff.
Japan, 2015.

Figure 6. Air transport communications and information technology specialist SITA has partnered with AOptix Technologies to deploy automated biometric identity solutions at airports and borders to enhance passenger security by making use of iris recognition and face biometric technology to facilitate identity screening at airports. The AOptix InSight family of iris and face biometric systems provides enhanced accuracy, speed, and intuitive capability by working at a comfortable distance of 1.5m to 2.5m. It captures ISO-ICAO quality iris and face images to ensure reliable matching accuracy.
SITA, 2012.

Figure 7. A device FV 350 by ZKAccess is able to capture and process both finger vein and fingerprint biometric data simultaneously. Authorized users can enroll and authenticate themselves fast and seamlessly by simply pressing their finger on the device's combined fingerprint/vein sensor. The device will then illuminate the user's finger vein pattern and capture both their finger vein and fingerprint minutiae points. The device converts them into vein and fingerprint templates, and stores the data in the FV 350 database for future identification and verification. The FV 350 has a capability of storing up to 1000 vein and 1000 fingerprints and is able to identify users in less than two seconds.
Lee, 2015.

CONCLUSION

In this chapter, various issues have been presented that are related to multimodal biometric systems. The performance of the biometric system can be higher by integrating multiple sources of information. Independent and hybrid levels and scenarios of multimodal systems are discussed. Integration at the match score level is attractive. Performance gain is strongly marked when non varied attributes are used in a multimodal system. Though, the challenges faced by multimodal biometric system is presents, but the literature presented in this chapter helps to improve the multimodel biometric system.

This chapter summarize the different components of the biometric system such as input interface, processing unit, database store and output interface. The general working of the biometric system is presented in terms of identification and verification. The multimodel biometric system is reviewed by presenting the concepts of multibiometric fusion way, fusion levels. The performance analysis of the biometric systems are presented precisely. The challenges occur during implementing and using the multimodel biometric system is given. At the end of the chapter, a case sdudy of applications for secured multimodel biometric system is presented in the appendix (Table 2).

REFERENCES

Ajay Kumar, S. M. (2010). A New Framework for Adaptive Multimodal Biometrics Management. *IEEE Transactions On Information Forensics And Security, 5*(1), 92–102. doi:10.1109/TIFS.2009.2031892

Ajay Kumar, S. M. (2010). A New Framework for Adaptive Multimodal Biometrics Management. *IEEE Transactions On Information Forensics And Security, 5*(1), 92–102. doi:10.1109/TIFS.2009.2031892

Ajay Kumar, S. S. (2011). Personal Identification Using Multibiometrics Rank-Level Fusion. *IEEE Transactions on Systems, Man and Cybernetics. Part C, Applications and Reviews, 41*(5), 743–752. doi:10.1109/TSMCC.2010.2089516

AlMahafzah, H., Imran, M., & Sheshadri, H.S. (2012). *Multi-algorithm Feature Level*. Academic Press.

AlMahafzah, H., Imran, M., & Sheshadri, H. S. (2012). *Multi-algorithm Feature Level Fusion Using Finger Knuckle Print Biometric*. Springer-Verlag Berlin Heidelberg. doi:10.1007/978-3-642-35594-3_42

Andreas, U., & Wild, P. (2009). Single-sensor multi-instance fingerprint and. *International Journal of Biometrics, 1*(4), 442–462. doi:10.1504/IJBM.2009.027305

Andreas Humm, J. H. (2009). Authentication, Combined Handwriting and Speech Modalities for User. *IEEE Transactions on Systems, Man, and Cybernetics. Part A, Systems and Humans, 39*(1), 25–35. doi:10.1109/TSMCA.2008.2007978

Andreas Humm, S. M. (2009). Combined Handwriting and Speech Modalities for User Authentication. *IEEE Transactions on Systems, Man, and Cybernetics. Part A, Systems and Humans, 39*(1), 25–35. doi:10.1109/TSMCA.2008.2007978

D. A., N. H., & K. A. (2011). Performance of weighted sum- rule fusion scheme in multi-instance and multi-modal biometric systems. *World Applied Science journal, 12*(11), 2160-2167.

Deshpande, A.S. Patil S.M. & Lathi R. (2008). A Multimodal Biometric Recognition System based on Fusion of Palmprint, Fingerprint and Face. *International Journal of Electronics and Computer Science Engineering, 3*(1), 1315-1320.

Frischholz, R.W. (2000). BioID: A Multimodal Biometric Identification System. *IEEE Transaction,* 64-68.

Hyunsoek, C., & Hyeyoung, P. (2014). *Gestures, A Multimodal User Authentication System Using Faces*. Hindawi Publishing Corporation.

Jain, A. R., & Ross, A. (2004). Multibiometric systems. *Communications of the ACM, 47*(1), 34–40. doi:10.1145/962081.962102

Jain, K. (2004). Multimodal Biometrics: An Overview.*12th European Signal Processing Conference (EUSIPCO)*, 1221-1224.

Jain, K., & Ross, A. (2004). Multibiometric systems. *Communications of the ACM, 47*(1), 34–40. doi:10.1145/962081.962102

Japan airports to install mobile biometric terminals to screen foreign passengers. (2015, September 8). Retrieved from http://www.airport-technology.com/news/newsjapan-airports-to-install-mobile-biometric-terminals-to-screen-foreign-passengers-4665642

Kar-Ann Toh, S. M.-Y. (2004). Exploiting Global and Local Decisions for Multimodal Biometrics Verification. *IEEE Transactions on Signal Processing, 52*(10).

Kassem, M. A. (2014). An Enhanced ATM Security System Using Multimodal Biometric Strategy. *International Journal of Electrical & Computer Sciences IJECS-IJENS, 14*(04), 9–16.

Kong, A., Zhang, D., & Kamel, M. (2009). A survey of Palmprint recognition. *Elsevier. Pattern Recognition, 42*(7), 1408–1418. doi:10.1016/j.patcog.2009.01.018

Lee, J. (2015, August 26). *ZKAccess releases multi-biometric access control device.* Retrieved from http://www.biometricupdate.com/201508/zkaccess-releases-multi-biometric-access-control-device

Liang Wang, H. N. (2004). Fusion of Static and Dynamic Body Biometrics for Gait Recognition. *IEEE Transactions on Circuits and Systems for Video Technology, 14*(2).

Marcialis, G. L., & Roli, F. (2004). Fingerprint Verification by Fusion of Optical and Capacitive Sensors. *Pattern Recognition Letters, 25*(11), 1315–1322. doi:10.1016/j.patrec.2004.05.011

Marcialis, G. L., & Roli, F. (2004). Fingerprint Verification by Fusion of Optical and Capacitive Sensors. Pattern Recognition Letters, 11(25), 1315-1322.

Md. Maruf Monwar, S. M. (2009). Multimodal Biometric System Using Rank-Level Fusion Approach. *IEEE Transactions on Systems, Man, and Cybernetics. Part B, Cybernetics, 39*(4), 867–878. doi:10.1109/TSMCB.2008.2009071 PMID:19336340

Ramli, D. A., Rani, N. H. C., & Ishak, K. A. (2011). Performance of weighted sum- rule fusion scheme in multi-instance and multi-modal biometric systems. World Applied Science Journal, 11(12), 2160-2167.

Robert Snelick, U. U. (2005). Large-Scale Evaluation of Multimodal Biometric Authentication Using State-of-the-Art Systems. *IEEE Transactions on Pattern Analysis and Machine Intelligence, 27*(3), 450–455. doi:10.1109/TPAMI.2005.57 PMID:15747798

Ross, A. (2006). *Handbook of Multibiometrics*. New York: Springer.

SITA and AOptix partner to offer automated biometric systems. (2012, February 10). Retrieved from http://www.airport-technology.com/news/newssita-aoptix-partnership-to-offer-airport-automated-biometric-identity-solutions

Souheil Ben-Yacoub, Y. A. (1999). Fusion of Face and Speech Data for Person Identity Verification. *IEEE Transaction*, *10*(5), 1065–1074. PMID:18252609

Uhl, A., & Wild, P. (2009). Single-sensor multi-instance fingerprint. *International Journal of Biometrics*, *4*(1), 442-462.

Uhl, A., & Wild, P. (2009). Single-sensor multi-instance fingerprint and. International. *Journal of Bioethics*, *1*(4), 442–462.

Vatsa, R. S. (2007). Feature based RDWT watermarking for multimodal biometric system. Academic Press.

Vincenzo Conti, C. M. (2010). A Frequency-based Approach for Features Fusion in Fingerprint and Iris Multimodal Biometric Identification Systems. *IEEE Transactions on Systems, Man and Cybernetics. Part C, Applications and Reviews*, *40*(4), 384–395. doi:10.1109/TSMCC.2010.2045374

Yang, W. (2015). Mutual dependency of features in multimodal biometric systems. Electronics Letters, 3(51), 234–235.

Yong Jian Chin, T. S. (2009). Integrating Palmprint and Fingerprint for Identity Verification. Third International Conference on Network and System Security. *IEEE Transaction*, 437-442.

APPENDIX: COMPARISON OF VARIOUS MULTIMODAL BIOMETRIC SYSTEMS

Table 2. Comparison of various multimodal approaches

Authors	Biometric Modalities	Fusion Way	Fusion Level	Approaches	Database	Performance
(Souheil Ben-Yacoub, 1999)	face and speech	Multiple biometrics	Match score	Elastic graph matching algorithm for face recognition	XM2VTS database with 295 people	SVM-polynomial and the Bayesian classifiers give best results in terms of accuracy and performance of a multimodal system for identity verification
(Robert W. Frischholz, 2000)	face, voice and lip movement	Multiple biometrics	Sensor	• Model-based algorithm for face detection • Synergeticcomputer to classify • The optical features like face and lip • Vector quantifier to classifythe audio feature	150 persons for three months	Guarantees a high degree of security from falsification and unauthorized access keeping the privacy rights of system users protected.
(Gian Luca Marcialis & Fabio Roli, 2004)	Fingerprint Feature: Minutae points	Multiple biometrics	Multi-sensor, Match score	• A multi-sensor fingerprint matcher based on optical and capacitive sensors • Fourier enhancement and rank order transformation • String Algorithm as matcher • Score transformation for fusion	unavailable	FAA-1%, FRR-1%
(Liang Wang, 2004)	Gait (static and dynamic)	Single biometric multiple units	Decision	• Static information analysis by Procrustes shape analysis method • Model-based approach track the walker • Analysis of users video for static and dynamic body movements independently by exemplar classifier	Dataset of 20 persons	The results using dynamic information(87.5%) are somewhat better than those using static information (83.75%)
(Kar-Ann Toh, 2004)	Fingerprint, speech and hand geometry	Multiple biometrics	Decision	A reduced multivariate polynomial model	NA	• Local learning alone can improve verification equal error rates of about 50%. • Current investigation is for verification purpose, future work will be for identification applications.

continued on following page

Table 2. Continued

Authors	Biometric Modalities	Fusion Way	Fusion Level	Approaches	Database	Performance
(Robert Snelick, 2005)	fingerprint and face	Multiple biometrics	Match score	Quadric-Line-Quadric (QLQ) adaptive normalization method	FERET image database for face images and	● Min-max (MM) and user-weightage (UW) normalization methods give best results for EER ● Simple-score (SS), matcher weighting (MW) and User Weighting (UW) fusions methods give best results for EER.
(Mayank Vatsa, 2007)	face, voice	Multiple biometrics	Match score	3-level RDWT biometric watermarking algorithm		Accuracy 94%
(Andreas Humm S. M., 2009)	Handwriting and speech	Multiple biometrics	Match score	Expectation–Maximization algorithm for data acquisition	70 users from MyIdea biometric database	● EER for spoken signatures is 1.1% ● EER for spoken handwriting is 0.3% ● Best overall performance: spoken handwriting ● Spoken signature: much less data and shorter authentication time.
(Yong Jian Chin, 2009)	Palmrpint and fingerprint	Multiple biometrics	Feature	● 2D-DWT for Image decomposition ● Gabor filter for feature extraction	F1:100 subjects/8 images each F2: 103 subjects/10 Images each P1: 7750 Palmprint images from 386 subjects P2: 5160 cropped Palmprint images from 208 subjects	EER is 0.91% for the combination of fingerprints by optical sensors and Palmprint captured using a contact-less Palmprint acquisition device.
(Md. Maruf Monwar, 2009)	face, ear and signature	Multiple biometrics	Rank	● PCA and LDA for feature matching ● Highest rank, borda count and logistic regression for rank fusion	virtual multimodal database	Average training time is 2.6 mins and average response time is 0.5 mis.

continued on following page

Table 2. Continued

Authors	Biometric Modalities	Fusion Way	Fusion Level	Approaches	Database	Performance
(Ajay Kumar S. M., 2010)	Palmprint, iris, face, speech and fingerprint	Multiple biometrics	Comparison of Score-level and decision-level	Iterative evolutionary approach to determine optimal fusion level by adaptive nature of security requirement.	Public biometric database	Proposed Score-level approach generates more stable performance with lesser number of iterations as compared to that of decision-level fusion.
(Ajay Kumar S. S., 2011)	Palm print	Multiple biometric representations	Rank	Consolidations of rank given by Nonlinear independent matchers	NIST Biometric set Release-1	99.28% recognition rate
(Harbi AlMahafzah, Mohammad Imran, & H.S. Sheshadri, 2012)	Finger knuckle	Multi-algorithm	Feature	Feature extraction algorithms like, • Log-Gabor Filters (LG) • Local Phase Quantization (LPQ) • Principal Component Analysis (PCA) • Locality Preserving Projections (LPP)	FKP database, 7,920 images	Multi-algorithm fusion gives better performance than single-algorithms fusion
(Vincenzo Conti, 2010)	Iris and fingerprint	Multiple biometrics	Template	• Frequency based approach • Hamming distance based matching algorithm	FVC 2002 DB2B/BATH database (10-50 users)	FAR=0% FRR=5.71%

Chapter 13

Background Subtraction and Object Tracking via Key Frame–Based Rotational Symmetry Dynamic Texture

Jeyabharathi D
Anna University Regional Campus – Tirunelveli, India

Dejey D
Anna University Regional Campus – Tirunelveli, India

ABSTRACT

Developing universal methods for background subtraction and object tracking is one of the critical and hardest challenges in many video processing and computer-vision applications. To achieve superior foreground detection quality across unconstrained scenarios, a novel Two Layer Rotational Symmetry Dynamic Texture (RSDT) model is proposed, which avoids illumination variations by using two layers of spatio temporal patches. Spatio temporal patches describe both motion and appearance parameters in a video sequence. The concept of key frame is used to avoid redundant samples. Auto Regressive Integrated Moving Average model (ARIMA) (Hyndman & Rob, 2015) estimates the statistical parameters from the subspace. Uniform Local Derivative Pattern (LDP) (Zhang et al., 2010) acts as a feature for tracking objects in a video. Extensive experimental evaluations on a wide range of benchmark datasets validate the efficiency of RSDT compared to Center Symmetric Spatio Temporal Local Ternary Pattern (CS-STLTP) (Lin et al., 2015) for unconstrained video analytics.

INTRODUCTION

Object Detection and Tracking

Video analysis commonly has three key steps: moving region detection, tracking that region of object in the video sequences, analysing the behaviour of that object. One of the essential tasks in the field of image processing and computer vision is background subtraction.

DOI: 10.4018/978-1-5225-2053-5.ch013

Background subtraction is the process of moving target detection from background model. It is used for further processing in video sequences. The main purpose of background subtraction is segmenting out the image into foreground and background. It is a widely used approach to reduce the problem and process only the relevant information from the image. Background subtraction is still a research area because of the necessity of a fast and lighting independent method. In fact, foreground detection has long been an alternative path to image segmentation. Whichever way is inherently the better approach, foreground detection has the additional advantage in that it immediately reduces the problem by extracting the moving regions.

The proposed Key Frame Based Rotational Symmetry Dynamic Texture framework includes background learning and subtraction and vehicle-object identification and tracking. The proposed work is based on two layers of spatio temporal patches. A Spatio temporal patch is the grouping of spatio temporal blocks. It describes not only the appearance of spatial structural information but also describes the temporal motion between two spatio temporal blocks. Key frames concept has been used to drastically reduce the processing overhead between spatio temporal blocks. Auto Regressive Integrated Moving Average (ARIMA) is a time serial analysis model used for parameter estimation, and forecasting. Object tracking is also one of the challenging tasks in the field of computer vision. Tracking can be defined as the problem of estimating the trajectory of an object in the image plane as it moves around the scene. Feature identification is an important step in object tracking. Selected feature must be insensitive against the appearance variation caused by numerous factors such as illumination, pose angle, and background clutter and camera motion. Uniform Local Derivative Pattern for each object is taken as the feature for tracking the objects. The way for tracking multiple objects whose number is unknown and varies is also presented in this chapter. This chapter focuses on traffic surveillance and monitoring. The camera is mounted stationarily and the vehicles are in motion. Monitoring the vehicles helps to manage better the traffic flows.

Application of Object Detection and Tracking

The primary motivation behind background subtraction is that it can be used to reduce the problem set for further processing that is a just processed part of the picture that contains the relevant information. It segments the image into foreground and background.

Some of the applications are as follows (Huang, 2011; Kuralkar & Gaikwad, 2012):

- **Visual Surveillance:** A human action recognition framework processes image sequences captured by video cameras by observing delicate zones, for example, bank, departmental stores, parking areas and country border to figure out whether one or more humans engaged are suspicious or under criminal activity.
- **Content Based Video Coding:** This system generates the video content. Video has to be segmented into video objects and tracked as they traverse across the video frames.
- **Traffic Is Consistently Observed Using Cameras:** Any vehicle that breaks the traffic rules or is included in other illegal act can be tracked down easily if the surveillance system is supported by an object tracking system. This framework can be utilized to check the number of the vehicles, identify the vehicles and track them.
- **Animation:** Object tracking algorithm can also be extended for animation.

- Motion capture in sports and tracking of multiple human in crowded environments.
- **Content Based Video Retrieval:** This process needs to identify moving objects prior to the generation of video semantics and performance of high level video analysis such as similarity retrievals.
- Background subtraction is also used in applications such as optical motion capture, teleconferencing (Elgammal et al., 2004) and even 3D modelling (Cheung et al., 2000).

BACKGROUND

Brief History of Background Subtraction and Tracking

Background Subtraction

There are a lot of background subtraction techniques, many of which are reviewed in surveys like Cheung and Kamath, (2004), Brutzer (2011), and Bouwmans (2011). It can be broadly divided into 3 categories: pixel-based, region-based, and frame-based (Vosters et al., 2010).

Pixel-based algorithms are based on forming a statistical background model for each pixel separately. Such algorithms are based on simple statistics such as mean value to complex multimodal distributions. The most simple techniques in this category include use of previous frame as background model, median value of pixels from a fixed number of recent images, running average and modelling of each pixel as a Gaussian (Cheung & Kamath, 2004; Brutzer, 2011). Most of the techniques based on these simple statistics including the unimodal Gaussian methods are very fast and computationally inexpensive but produce poor segmentation results due to complex real world scenarios such as camera noise, moving background, camera jitter, sudden illumination changes, etc. The most popular techniques in pixel based category are pixel-wise Gaussian Mixture Model (GMM) (Stauffer & Grimson, 1999) and kernel densities (Elgammal et al., 2000).

The second class of techniques are region-based techniques, which unlike their pixel based counterpart exploit local spatial relationships among pixels. Sheikh and Shah (2005) have presented a non-parametric kernel density estimate to model probability of foreground and background pixels but they include pixel location in the model (Piccardi, 2004; Wren et al., 1997; Elgammal et al., 2000). Another region based method presented by Liu and Fu (1998), uses Statistical Circular Shift Moments (SCSM) in image regions for change detection. Apart from these, there are a number of region based techniques (Barnich et al., 2011; Seki et al., 2003; Power & Schoonees, 2002) that take into account spatial dependencies by considering blocks of different sizes instead of pixels individually.

Frame-based methods create statistical Background (BG) models for the entire frame. Many of the frame-based techniques are based on a shading model, which calculates the ratio of intensities between an input image and the reference frame or BG model (Skifstad & Jain, 1989; Vosters et al., 2010). Frame based techniques have not gained much popularity as pixel based approaches but are known to offer more robust solutions against gradual as well as sudden illumination changes (Bouwmans, 2011). Based on the shading model, Pilet et al. (2008), have proposed a method that makes use of the ratio of intensities between an input image and background image.

Frame based methods greatly reduce computation overhead and it is robust against gradual as well as sudden illumination changes. So the proposed system uses frame based background subtraction.

Object Tracking

In object tracking techniques, the most difficult task is the representation of objects in a frame. For object representation color histogram (Comaniciu et al., 2003; Birchfield, 1998) image features (Collins & Liu, 2000; Kanhere et al., 2005) feature vector (Zhao & Nevatia, 2004) have been used.

In kernel based tracking, kernel refers to object's shape or appearance. Comaniciu et al. (2003) have proposed a kernel based tracking where in the color histogram of the object is used for tracking. Similarity measurement is based on the Bhattacharyya coefficient. Comaniciu et al.(2000) have proposed mean shift based approach. For 3-D target objects and monochromatic object, this method is not suitable. In those cases, it often fails to track object, even if there is a small variation in illumination.

In point tracking, detected objects in consecutive frames are represented by a point. (Hue et al., 2002) describe an extension of the classical particle filter. These methods only take the largest posterior probability based on current and previous observations. They often fail with background clutter, occlusion and multi-object confusion. In MacCormick and Blake (2000); Perez et al.(2002); and Rasmussen and Hager (2001) object tracking is based on probabilistic model.

Feature based algorithm tracks objects based on similarity between features such as edge, color, histogram, size in successive frames (Kanhere et al., 2005; Collins & Liu, 2000). Li et al. (2008) have proposed a corner feature based object tracking method using Adaptive Kalman Filter. Each moving object is represented by its corner. Then, tracking is achieved through the corner point variation between successive frames. Xue et al. (2010) have used the voting strategy to choose discriminative features to represent the objects. Then object tracking is done using mean shift algorithm utilizing discriminative features. Fazli et al. (2009) have presented an improved tracking method based on SIFT features, which can track both single object and multiple objects in video sequences where the object movement may be fast or slow.

In region tracking, object regions are extracted using previous frame (Xue et al., 2008). Bascle and Deriche (1995) have described a new approach to tracking of complex shapes through image sequences, which combines deformable region models and deformable contours. Wei et al. (2008) have introduced a novel technique with the help of region derived descriptors for segmentation and tracking. The homogeneous regions of an image are obtained by partitioning the image into a series. Thus, the problem of object extraction changes from pixel based to database analysis.

Feature based tracking method for detecting vehicles can be used to track object effectively under challenging conditions such as more congestion, shadows and lighting transition. Instead of tracking entire vehicles, vehicle features are tracked to make the method robust to partial occlusion. Under varying lighting condition the system is fully functional because most significant features are used for tracking purpose. So the proposed system uses feature based tracking method.

Local Patterns

Ojala et al. (1996) have proposed Local Binary Pattern (LBP) in the field of texture classification. To reduce the complexity of feature vectors (Ojala et al., 2012; Pietikainen et al., 2000) they have proposed rotational invariant texture classification. Spatio temporal local binary pattern has been proposed by Zhao et al. LBP has been used for texture segmentation (Zhao et al., 2009), background modeling and detection (Heikkila et al., 2006), interest region description (Heikkila et al., 2009), image retrieval

(Unay et al., 2010), Local Derivative Pattern (LDP) templates extract high order local information by encoding various distinctive spatial relationships contained in a given local region (Zhang et al., 2010). This observation has been motivational in this work to use LDP feature to track the objects in a video.

Video Surveillance and Monitoring

Video surveillance can be a key technology to fight against terrorism, crime, public safety and for efficient management of traffic.

There are immediate needs for automated surveillance systems in commercial, law enforcement and military applications. Mounting video cameras is cheap, but finding available human resources to observe the output is expensive. Although surveillance cameras are already prevalent in banks, stores, and parking lots, video data is currently used only "after the fact" as a forensic tool, thus losing its primary benefit as an active, real-time medium. What is needed is a continuous 24-hour monitoring of surveillance video to alert security officers to a burglary in progress, or to a suspicious individual loitering in the parking lot, while there is still time to prevent the crime.

In addition to obvious security applications, video surveillance technology has been proposed to measure traffic flow, detect accidents on highways, monitor pedestrian congestion in public spaces, compile consumer demographics in shopping malls and amusement parks, log routine maintenance tasks at nuclear facilities, and count endangered species. Numerous military applications include patrolling national borders, measuring the flow of refugees in troubled areas, monitoring peace treaties, and providing secure perimeters around bases and embassies.

Video Surveillance cameras are to be installed to improve the traffic management in city and ensure road and traffic safety. Increased level of car ownership, worse conditions of roads, lack of respect for the traffic rules cause rising number of car accidents and collisions. Such a situation requires strong measures to eliminate the number of road accidents and collisions. Traffic surveillance systems installed in the busiest and most dangerous intersections in the city can play an essential role in incident detection, traffic management and can increase the respect for the traffic rules.

Even though several background subtraction algorithms have been proposed in the literature, the problem of classifying moving objects in a complex environment is still far from being totally solved. There are numerous problems that a good background subtraction algorithm must solve correctly. Consider a video sequence from a stationary camera overseeing a traffic intersection. As it is an outdoor environment, a background subtraction algorithm should familiarize too many levels of illumination at different times of the day and handle adverse weather conditions such as fog or snow that modifies the background. Changing shadow, cast by moving objects, should be detached so that consistent features can be extracted from the objects in subsequent processing. The complex traffic flow at the intersections also poses trials to a background subtraction algorithm. The vehicles move at an usual speed when the traffic signal light is green, but comes to a stop when it goes red. The vehicles then continue to remain stationary until the light turns green again. A good background subtraction algorithm must handle the moving objects that first merge into the background and then develop foreground at a later time. In addition, to accommodate the real-time requirements of numerous applications, a background subtraction algorithm must be computationally inexpensive and have low memory supplies, while still being able to correctly identify moving objects in the video. Even though many background subtraction techniques have been proposed, they are typically obtainable as parts of a larger computer vision application. In this chapter, these challenges are identified in those associated with the sudden, fast illumination changes in the high traffic environment and a regression model is built as a compensation to update the background model (Piccardi, 2004). The objective of this work is to develop an automated video understanding technology for use in urban and battlefield surveillance applications in future.

BACKGROUND SUBTRACTION

Basis of Background Subtraction

Background subtraction is widely used for detecting moving objects. The ultimate goal is to "subtract" the background pixels in a scene leaving only the foreground objects of interest. In real world scenes, the situation will be more challenging.

Background subtraction usually consists of three steps besides the basic structure of the background model:

- Background initialization (construction of the initial background model).
- Background maintenance (updating the background model to account for temporal changes in subsequent frames).
- Foreground/background pixel classification.

Background modeling is at the heart of any background subtraction calculation. Much research has been dedicated to build up a background model that is robust against environmental changes in the background, however sensitive enough to distinguish every single moving object of interest. Figure 1 gives the overall structure of background subtraction.

Figure 1. Basic structure of background subtraction

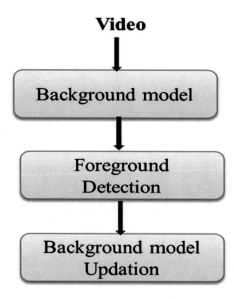

1. **First Frame as a Background:** The basic idea is that the first frame in the image is considered as the background. Then the current frame is subtracted from the background image. Based on a pixel by pixel threshold comparison, it determines whether the pixel is moving target or background pixel. This method is easy and fast in many applications, but some problems appear when tracking multiple objects or when an object stops in which the moving object is not accurately detected.
2. **Average Frame as a Background:** The background model is calculated, by averaging a series of preceeding frames. This averaging refers to averaging corresponding pixels in the given images.
3. **Frame Differencing:** Frame difference method is also known as the adjacent frame difference method or the image sequence difference method. This approach considers the current frame as the background model of the next frame (Power & Schoonees, 2002).

The experimental result of the three basic methods are shown in Figure 2. These approaches are not suitable for dynamic background, illumination changes and heavy traffic environments.

Challenges in Background Subtraction

There are many challenges in developing a good background subtraction algorithm. First and the most challenging problem in foreground segmentation is sudden illumination changes. Numerous state-of-the art systems can deal with gradual illumination changes, however, stay vulnerable to sudden changes.

Figure 2. (a) First frame as a background; (b) average frame as a background; (c) frame differencing

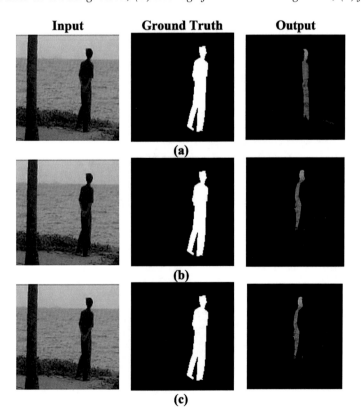

The sudden illumination change in "lobby" sequence is shown in Figure 3. Initially all the lights are turned on up to frame#126. At frame#127 suddenly one light is turned off and at frame#135 again two lights are turned off. These situations cause most of the subtraction methods to fail (false positive i.e. detecting background pixels as foreground pixels). In outdoor environment also, sudden illumination changes are caused by a vehicle's headlight. Figure 3(b) is the output of the Kalman filter (Li et al., 2008) under sudden illumination.

Second, the dynamic background, that is, the scene environment is not always static. Sometimes it is highly dynamic. A good background model ought to additionally respond rapidly to changes in background and adapt itself to accommodate changes occurring in the background, for example, moving of a chair from one place to another. In the "campus" sequence, the dynamic textures are present in the background that is a waving tree. Results of subtraction using Kalman filter is shown in Figure 4. The result has many false positives around the regions of dynamic texture.

In this proposed work, the above mentioned problems are solved by making a robust background model. The main aim of the work is to get an efficient real time system suitable for both the indoor and the outdoor environments.

Figure 3. Result of moving object detection for "lobby" sequence under sudden illumination changes

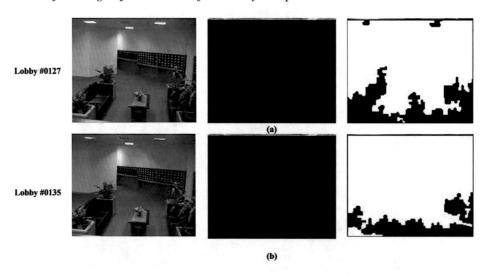

Figure 4. Result of moving object detection for "Campus" sequence under dynamic background: (a) original frame; (b) ground truth; (c) result of Kalman filter

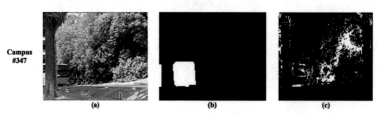

Figure 5. The complete sketch of the proposed background subtraction algorithm

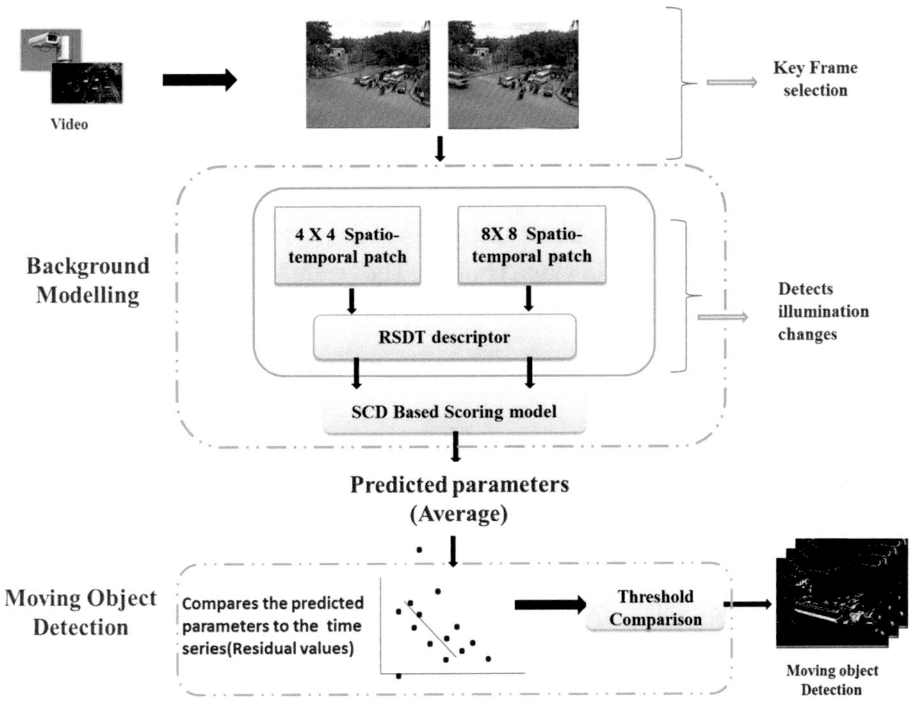

BACKGROUND SUBTRACTION: A NEW APPROACH

Introduction

The following are the steps in the proposed work. Figure 5 shows the complete map of the proposed work. The proposed work has three parts: (i). Dynamic key frame selection, (ii). A novel background model construction (iii). Moving object detection. Background modelling involves two layers for the construction of effective subspaces. Auto Regressive Integrated Moving Average model (ARIMA) has been used to estimate the statistical parameters from the subspaces. Moving object detection is based on thresholding. Finally, a new observation at time t is identified to be the foreground, based on the threshold value.

Contribution

The contributions in this paper are as follows:

- A dynamic algorithm for background subtraction is proposed. Background model is estimated using Auto Regressive Integrated Moving Average model. This is used to correctly estimate the appearance and temporal relationships between blocks.
- All the background subtraction methods discussed in the literature process the entire frames in the sequence. To reduce processing overhead, key frame selection is introduced.

- Line and rotational symmetry concepts are used to predict the similarity between each block of pixels. Directional codes of each spatio temporal patches give exact subspace.

Key Frame Selection

Methods of Key Frame Selection

Key frames are characterized as the representative frames of a video stream, that is, the frames that give the most exact and minimal outline of the video content. The "right" key frame detection procedure depends on the application as well as on the individual "definition" of the user/developer of what a video summary should include.

Some ideas of key frame selection process are:

- Most key frame extraction strategies begin with the decomposition of a video into temporal segments (shots or scenes) and then extract a fixed or a number of key frames per temporal segment. In few applications even the determination of the center frame of every shot may be a tolerable methodology for key frame estimation (the center, not the first or the last because at the beginning and at the end of shots or scenes there may be frames belonging to artistic passages from one shot to another, i.e. visual effects, such as fade in/fade out).
- Another class of approaches employ a sequential search to video stream. Such techniques start by a "root" key frame (usually randomly selected as one of the first frames of the video) and then compare one by one the next frames, until a frame with significantly different low-level visual content is found. Then, this becomes the "root" key frame and the process continues from the next video frame.

Advantages of Key Frame in Background Subtraction

- The Figure 6(a) denotes the redundant area in the successive frames. The static areas in the frames are hidden by white color. Traditional methods utilize each frame and construct background model for each frame. The observation from the above Figure 6(a) is that, the active moving area is very small. The remaining is the redundant one. It may also lead to redundant values in the spatio temporal blocks. To avoid this redundancy one representative or key frame is chosen among every 10 successive frames.
- The smallest amount of deviation occurs in between each 10 frames. So one representative frame is enough to generate the background model for the 10 frames. It can be used to reduce the computational complexity.
- In Figure 6(b), the man enters in frame#0586. From frame#0001 to frame#0585 there is no movement in the frames. So there is no need to generate the background model for every frame. Hence the concept of key frame is included in background subtraction.

Figure 6. (a) Moving area in the frames; (b) key frame selection

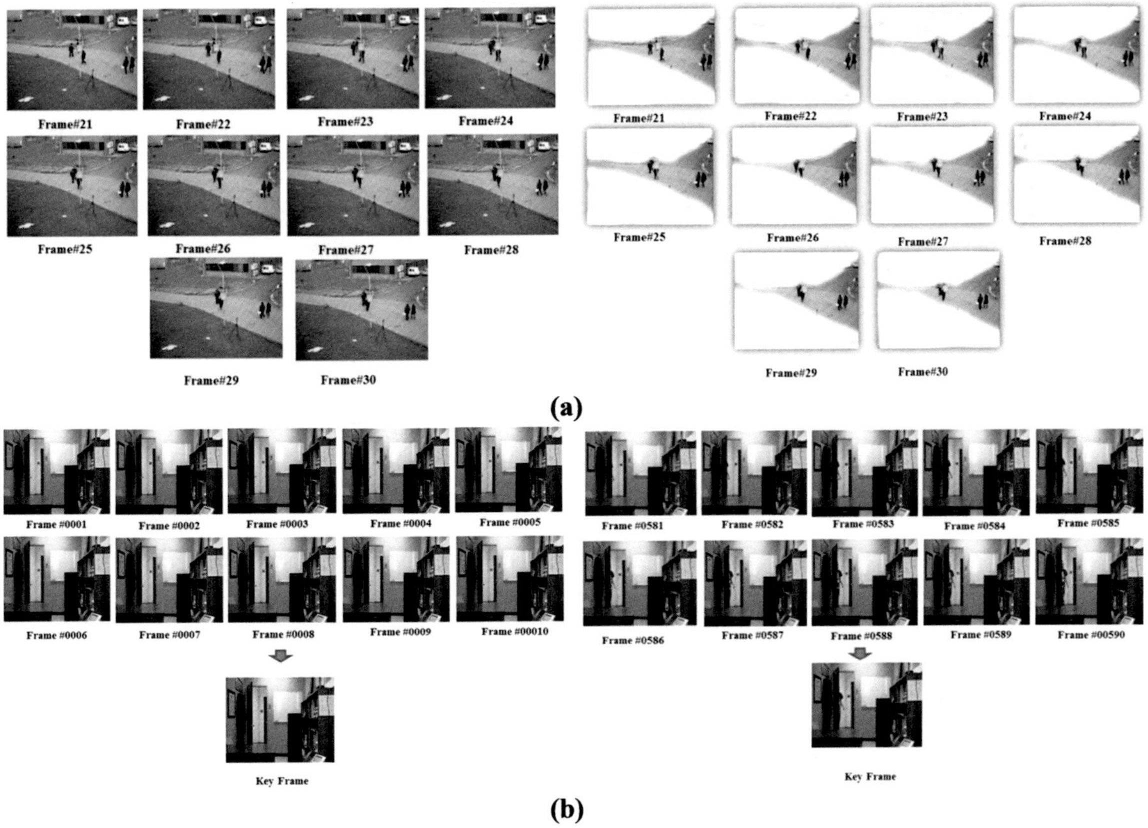

(a)

(b)

Key Frame Selection in RSDT

Key frame selection is based on the absolute difference between successive frames in the video. One key frame is selected for every 10 frames in the video. Key frame selection methodology is demonstrated in Algorithm 1.

Background Model

Spatio Temporal Patches

A spatio-temporal patch is grouping of simultaneously captured spatio-temporal information in surveillance video. Commonly spatio temporal patches can be used to reduce the uncertainty in detecting and tracking moving objects in a video. For every two key frames, two layers of spatio temporal patches are constructed on behalf of proceeding 20 consecutive frames.

The first layer spatio temporal patches include smaller spatio temporal blocks of size 4×4. These smaller size blocks are useful for detecting a slight deviation, but it leads to increase the false positive error rate. That is it falsely predicts some background pixel as foreground. To reduce this type of error a second layer is essential for moving object detection.

Figure 7. The sketch of the key frame selection algorithm

Input: Video

Output: Set of Key frames

N – Number of frames, F – Frame, Th – Threshold, KF – Key frame, N_1=1, N_2=10

do   //Read the frame until the end of the video

    Setting threshold (Th)

    • Calculate sum of the histogram difference between successive frames using imhist(), imabsdiff()

$$SumAbsDiff_{i=N_1.....N_2} = Sum\left(imabsdiff\left(imhist(F_i), imhist(F_{i+1})\right)\right)$$

    • Calculate overall mean value of SumAbsDiff

$$Th = mean2(SumAbsDiff)$$

    for frame F=$N_1 : N_2$ //Execute 10 frames

        Key Frame selection

        • Extract frame (F) one by one

        • Calculate sum of the histogram difference between successive frames using imhist(), imabsdiff()

        • If it is greater than threshold then set as key frame (KF)

        if two key frames (KF) are encountered

            o Detect moving object of the 10 frames corresponding to the first key frame

        end

    end

N_1=1+N_2

N_2=10+N_2

while N2 > N

The second layer of spatio temporal patches have 8×8 sizes of spatio temporal blocks. For sudden and gradual illumination changes two layers of spatio temporal patches are necessary. To reduce computational overhead the larger block of size 16×16 is not included.

Rotational Symmetry Dynamic Texture

One of the main challenges of background subtraction for video surveillance is dynamic background. Some parts of the scenery may contain movement, but should be regarded as background, according to their relevance. Such movement can be periodical or irregular (e.g., traffic lights, waving trees). In that situation, the invariant and effective representation of subspace is essential. So a symmetry pattern of each block is necessary to make the invariant subspace. Line symmetry of each block alone is not enough to generate the invariant subspace. Hence, rotational invariant directional codes of each block are also estimated. This invariant subspace can be used to maintain the accurate background model. This idea significantly reduces the memory requirements.

1. **Line Symmetry:** The line of symmetry is a line segment that is drawn on a diagram in order to divide the diagram equally divided into two. The line of symmetry divides a picture into two parts so that one forms a mirror image of the other. In other words, the images on the other side of the line of symmetry must be the reflection of each other. The shapes that have a line of symmetry are known as "symmetrical", while those which do not possess any kind of line of symmetry, are termed as "asymmetrical" (Diane et al., 1988).

2. **Rotational Symmetry:** Rotational symmetry is also known in biological context as radial symmetry. According to rotational symmetry objects may look the same even after a certain amount of rotation. The degree of rotational symmetry is how many degrees the shape has to be turned to look the same on a different side or vertex. It cannot be the same side or vertex (Diane et al., 1988).

3. **Generation of Directional Codes:** Spatio temporal patches are used to jointly model spatial and temporal information. Specifically, at every location of the consecutive two key frames, a sequence of spatio temporal patches are extracted as for observations, and then learnt to update the background models. Moreover, to compactly encode the spatio temporal patches against illumination variations, patch based descriptor, namely Rotational Symmetry Dynamic Texture (RSDT) is used.

Directional codes are calculated using the similarity of the blocks in the spatio temporal patches by checking whether the pixels within the blocks hold line symmetry or rotational symmetry. This is given in Equation(1).

$$
Dir\left(j,k\right) = \begin{cases} 0, & \begin{aligned} &STB_i\left(j,k\right) = STB_i\left(k,p-\left(j-1\right)\right) = STB_i\left(p-\left(k-1\right),j\right) \\ &= STB_i\left(p-\left(j-1\right),p-\left(k-1\right)\right) \end{aligned} \\ -1, & \begin{aligned} &STB_i\left(j,k\right) = STB_i\left(p-\left(j-1\right),p-\left(k-1\right)\right) \| STB_i\left(k,p-\left(j-1\right)\right) \\ &= STB_i\left(p-\left(k-1\right),j\right) \end{aligned} \\ 1 & Otherwise \end{cases}
\tag{1}
$$

Figure 8 illustrates an example of RSDT in 4×4 sized spatio temporal block. During one complete rotation how many times a shape will fit over itself is called the order of rotational symmetry. A square has 4 sides and the rotation measurement angle is 90 degrees. So the square objects have order 4 rotational symmetry. At the same time the line of symmetry of square objects have order 2 and its corresponding angle is 180 degrees.

The RSDT process in a 4×4 sized spatio temporal block yields 4 directional codes in the form of -1, 0, 1.

For a 16×16 spatio temporal block, RSDT process can create 16 directional codes. It is shown in Figure 9. At last, the length of the directional code for each spatio temporal patch is 4*2, 16 *2 because every two key frames are taken for the RSDT process.

The grouping of those directional codes forms the subspace of the corresponding layer in which each column contains the feature of each spatio temporal patch. Figure 10 demonstrates the conceptual illustration for subspace construction.

Figure 8. Rotational symmetry on 4 × 4 spatio temporal block

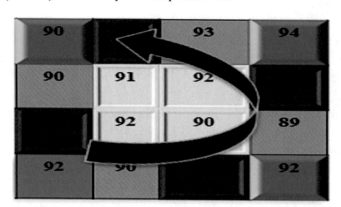

Figure 9. Rotational symmetry on 8 × 8 spatio temporal block

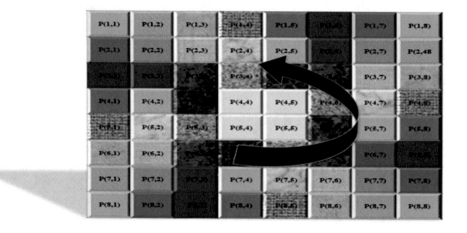

Auto Regressive Integrated Moving Average Model

1. **Auto Regressive Moving Average (ARMA) Model:** Auto regression model can be used to forecast the variable of interest using a linear combination of past values of the variable. The term auto regression indicates that it is a regression of the variable against itself. In time series analysis, the Moving-Average (MA) model is a common approach for modeling univariate time series. The notation MA(q) refers to the moving average model of order q.

A model which depends only on the previous outputs of the system is called an Auto Regressive model (AR), while a model which depends only on the inputs to the system is called a Moving Average model (MA), and of course a model based on both inputs and outputs is an Auto Regressive-Moving-Average model (ARMA) (Hyndman & Rob, 2015).

2. **Auto Regressive Integrated Moving Average (ARIMA) Model:** An ARMA model contains parts for an AR and MA model. So is ARMA(p,q). An ARIMA model is an extension as it includes the extra part for differencing. This simply takes each data point and calculates the change from the

previous data point. The ARIMA model is ARIMA (p,d,q) where p is the order of the AR part, d is the number of times differencing has been carried out and q is the order of the MA part. The extension allows the model to deal with long term variation better or improves the usefulness of this modelling technique (Hyndman & Rob, 2015).

3.   **ARIMA Model in Background Subtraction:** In time series analysis, an Auto Regressive Integrated Moving Average (ARIMA) model is a generalization of an Auto Regressive Moving Average (ARMA) model (Hyndman & Rob, 2015). These models are fitted to time series data either to understand the data better or to predict future points in the series (forecasting).There are many ways in which a time series fails to be stationary. ARIMA model is used to fit the series to be stationary by applying difference of the data points.

The surveillance videos have atleast small amount of movement and are not stationary. In such a situation ARIMA model can be used. Traffic on a stretch of road is said to be stationary if an observer does not detect movement in an arbitrary area of the time space diagram. Traffic is stationary if all the vehicle trajectories are parallel and equidistant. It is also stationary if it is a superposition of families of trajectories with these properties (e.g. fast and slow drivers). The above environment is not possible in traffic area i.e. Stationary traffic does not exist. That is why ARIMA model is also suitable for traffic time series data.

The observed subspace of each layer is expressed in the form of data matrix in which each column contains the RSDT directional codes of Spatio temporal patches. The state of each column in the subspace is defined as Equation(2).

$$Z_{i+1} = CZ_i + A \qquad (2)$$

where Z_i is the state of ith column, C is an appearance consistency parameter, A is temporal coherence between spatio temporal blocks.

Figure 10. Subspace construction

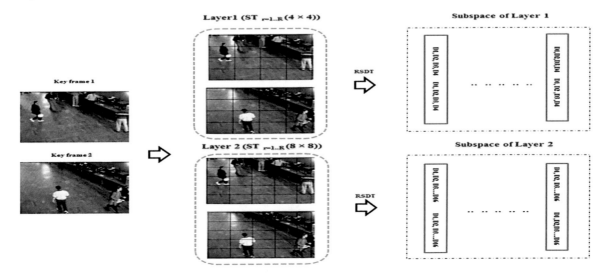

Figure 11. RSDT background model generation

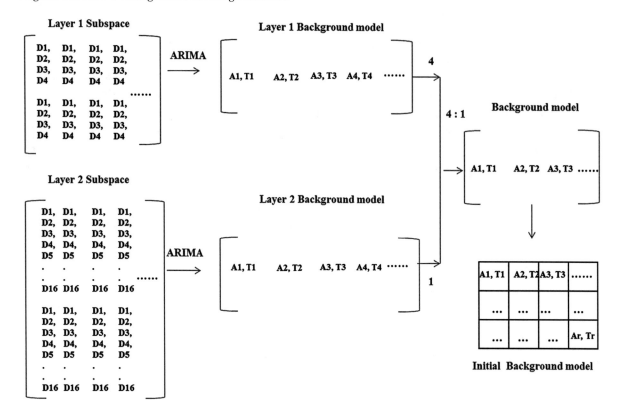

The linear dynamic system ARIMA can be used to characterize the spatio temporal statistics of the subspace and estimate the above two parameters for each column in the data matrix.

In the proposed method, background is modelled at block level by maintaining the parameters such as Appearance Consistency (C) and Temporal Coherence (A). This is shown in Figure 11. The mean values of the two layers of parameters are used in the segmentation of foreground from background.

Foreground Detection

Given a newly appearing spatio temporal block $STB_{i_{(8\times8)}}$, determining whether pixels in $STB_{i_{(8\times8)}}$ belong to the background or not is decided by thresholding its appearance residual and state residual. The background model is generated by taking the average of two layers in the ratio of 4:1 that's why the block of size 8×8 is chosen to detect moving regions. Appearance residual is the deviation of spatio temporal block from its state. State residual is the deviation from one state of spatio temporal block to another state of spatio temporal block. The state of $STB_{i_{(8\times8)}}$ with appearance consistency A_i (Lin et al., 2015) is denoted by Z_i and is given in Equation(3).

$$Z_i = A_i * STB_{i_{(8\times8)}} \qquad (3)$$

and further the appearance residual of $STB_{i_{(8\times8)}}$ is W_i and is given in Equation(4)

$$W_i = \left\| STB_{i_{(8\times8)}} - Z_i \right\| \tag{4}$$

With state Z_i and the Temporal Coherence T_i, state residual $\in_i$ is estimated as in (5)

$$\in_i = \left\| Z_{i+1} - T_i * Z_i \right\| \tag{5}$$

State residual value is used to find the variation between two states. Variation of state residual is used to determine whether the pixel is foreground or background.

Finally, the background subtraction is effected by making the decision on the pixel S_i as foreground or background as given in Equation (6).

$$S_i = \begin{cases} 1\left(Foreground\right), & if\left(W_i > T_w\right) \\ 0\left(Background\right), & if\left(\in_i < T_\in\right) \end{cases} \tag{6}$$

where W_i is appearance residual, $\in_i$ is state residual, T_w, $T_\in$ are threshold values obtained from the mean values of W_i and $\in_i$.

Updating Model Parameters

The model parameter is updated using learning rate α. There is no need to change the appearance consistency (A) of each spatio temporal block in the successive 10 frames. The key frame appearance constancy is taken as 10 consecutive frames appearance consistency. There is need to update the temporal relationship between successive spatio temporal blocks. It is given in Equation(7)

$$T_{i+1} = \left(1 - \alpha\right) * T_i + \alpha Z_i \tag{7}$$

where T_i is the temporal coherence of the ith block. Z_i is the corresponding state variable. $\alpha = 0.01$ is that learning rate.

FEATURE EXTRACTION

Unique identification of each object is necessary to track the objects in a video. Then only tracking can be performed faster using this reduced representation instead of using complete objects. Texture based feature descriptors are used to describe the appearance of objects. Compared to color, gradient features in the object, texture feature can be used to efficiently represent the feature. Local Derivative Patterns (LDP) (Zhang et al., 2010) is known as one of the efficient features. LDP gone through an analysis operator is defined as a grayscale invariant texture measure, derived from a general definition of texture in a local neighbourhood. The most important property of the LDP operator is its tolerance against illumination changes. LBP encodes all directions first order derivative binary result while LDP encodes the higher order derivative information which contains more detailed discriminative features that the first order Local Binary Pattern (LBP) cannot obtain from an image (Zhang et al., 2010)

For the local patterns with p=8 neighborhoods, 2^p combinations of feature vectors are possible. To reduce the length of the feature vector and the computation cost, uniform patterns (Pietikainen et al., 2000) are used. The pattern is called uniform if the binary pattern contains at most two 0-1 or 1-0 transition. It can be used to reduce the length of the feature vector and implement a simple rotation invariant descriptor. These rotational invariant descriptors can be used to extract the unique features from each background subtracted object in the frames. Uniform Local Derivative Pattern (LDP) has $p \times (p-1)$ possible feature vectors. It is illustrated in Figure 12.

Apply Local Derivative Pattern (LDP) (Zhang et al., 2010) on each 5×5 blocks of every object. Padding is done if necessary. The result of each block's four decimal pattern is grouped into an array. The length of the array is $4 * R$, where R is the total number of decimal value of the corresponding binary patterns in the object. Further it is reduced by using uniform patterns. Finally feature vector is constructed using Equation(8).

$$f\left(LDP^2_{Direction[i=1..(4*R)]}, l_s\right) = \begin{cases} 1, & if \ LDP^2_{Direction[i]} = l_s \\ 0, & Otherwise \end{cases} \tag{8}$$

$$Fv = \frac{1}{U \times V} \sum_{i=1}^{R} f\left(LDP^2_{Direction[i]}, l_s\right), 1 \leq s \leq 58 \tag{9}$$

where $U \times V$ is the size of each object in the background subtracted video. l_s is the uniform patterns have the index s. It varies from 1 to 58.

OBJECT TRACKING

Automatic tracking of objects can be the foundation for many interesting applications. An accurate and efficient tracking capability is essential for building higher level vision-based intelligence. The aim of an object tracker is to generate the trajectory of an object over time by locating its position in every frame of the video.

Each object in the first frame is considered as a target object. Target object's location is predicted and its corresponding features are extracted using Local Derivative Patterns (LDP). That is each object is represented by its LDP feature. In the subsequent frames, candidates are defined and are represented by its corresponding LDP features. Tracking procedure starts with the calculation of distance between feature vector of the target objects and candidate objects in the next frame. Based on minimum distance each object is tracked. This is shown in Figure 13.

Figure 12. Uniform pattern representation

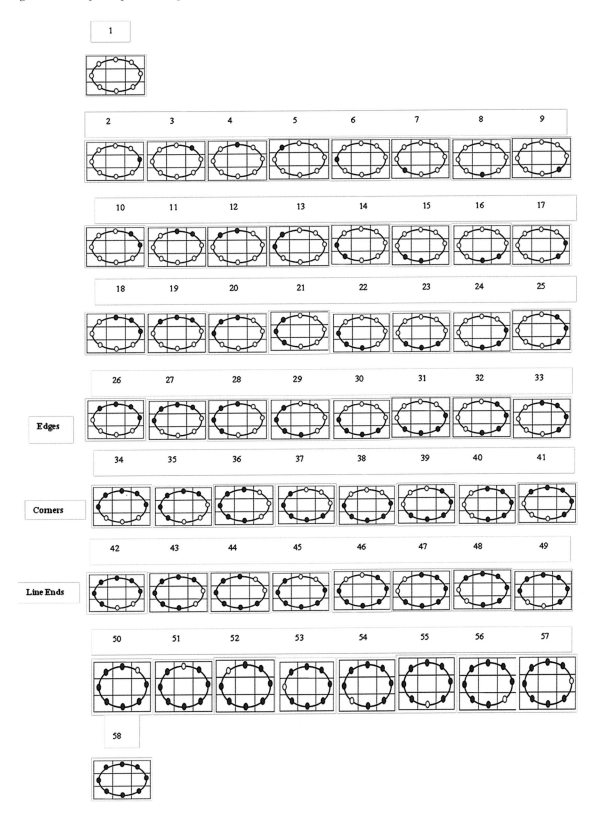

Figure 13. Object tracking using LDP feature

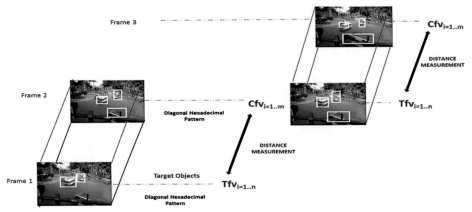

EXPERIMENTS

The performances of the proposed work are evaluated against six most widely used techniques MOG (Power & Schoonees, 2002) and GMM (Stauffer & Grimson, 1999), as well as XC-LBP (Xue et al., 2010), Sigma-Deltal Z (Manzanera, 2007), Bayesian Histogram (Li et al., 2003), CS-STLTP (lin et al., 2015). No post processing (e.g., noise filtering) is applied to evaluate the unaided strength of each technique. The two other variants attempted are listed below:

- CS-STLTP with ARIMA,
- RSDT with ARMA.

Center Symmetric Spatio Temporal Local Ternary Pattern (CS-STLTP) (Lin et al., 2015) is a brick based descriptor, which is inspired by the 2D scale invariant local pattern operator. For each sequence of video bricks, subspace is pursued by employing the Auto Regressive Moving Average model (ARMA) (Hyndman & Rob, 2015). ARIMA model is used instead of ARMA model.

The rest of this section is organized as follows. The experimental setup is presented in the next section, while different quantitative and qualitative evaluation results are presented in subsequent sections.

Experimental Setup

The different datasets, including PETS (Performance Evaluation of Tracking and Surveillance, 2006), BMC (Background Models Challenge, 2012), Institut fur Algorithmen und Kognitive Systemes (Kollnig & Nagel, 97) have been used to compare the performance of the proposed work with that of the benchmark methods. The test sequences are categorized in the following classes based on the characteristics of the operating environments: Indoor, Outdoor and Traffic sequences. Both classes-wise and overall performances of all techniques are analyzed to assess the strengths and weaknesses of the benchmark methods and the proposed method.

Metrics

Each background subtraction technique is a binary classifier as all pixels of a frame image are classified as either background or foreground. Most widely used metric in computer vision to evaluate the performance of a binary classifier is the F-score. This metric combines the following four measures: True Positive (TP) that counts correctly classified foreground pixels; True Negative (TN) that counts correctly classified background pixels; False Positive (FP) that counts background pixels incorrectly classified as foregrounds; and False Negative (FN) that counts foreground pixels incorrectly classified as background. F-score is thus measured as

$$FScore = \frac{2 * Precision * Recall}{Precision + Recall} \tag{10}$$

where

$$Precision = \frac{TP}{TP + FP} \tag{11}$$

and

$$Recall = \frac{TP}{TP + FN} \tag{12}$$

Implementation

The proposed work is implemented using Matlab version 8.3. The parameters used for the implementation are given below:

- The subspace model is newly constructed for every 10 consecutive frames. The parameters are updated in every frame.
- The threshold value for background subtraction is approximately set between 0.03 and 0.08.
- Learning parameter α=0.01.

Background Subtraction

Results of the background subtraction against the existing benchmark methods are tabulated in Table 1. It can be seen that the F-score of the proposed work is relatively higher than those of other methods. Experimental results for indoor, outdoor, traffic sequences are shown in Figure 14 and Figure 15.

In indoor, for example " waving curtain", sequence one man is walking around a room in front of a waving curtain. That is there is a dynamically varying background. In that situation the system needs to update its background model. The proposed work can cope with dynamically varying background effectively. Another challenging sequence in indoor environment is "lobby". The challenging criteria is gradual and sudden illumination changes. An invariant subspace is necessary to overcome this problem. The proposed method uses the concept of rotational symmetry and line symmetry in between and within spatio temporal blocks which can yield an invariant subspace. Compared to other methods RSDT shows better performance.

In outdoor, "Fountain" sequence the dynamic textures are present in the background, that is, the fountain is spouting in the middle of the lake. For this sequence also, the proposed work shows better performance than others.

In traffic sequences the main challenge is inconsistent lighting where the weather introduces unpredictable variations in both lighting and background movement. Such sequences are shown in Figure 16 where the proposed work gives a better result when compared to others.

In Table 2, reported F-score values achieved by the proposed approach on the PETS, BMC, Institut für Algorithmen und Kognitive Systeme datasets, are compared with those achieved by other three state-of-the-art methods. The comparison of F-score in Table 2 clearly demonstrates the superiority of RSDT among the other variants attempted.

Object Tracking

One of the most frequently used approaches for detecting and tracking human objects and vehicles is Kalman filter approach (Ning et al., 2008). This algorithm is compared with the proposed approach for performance evaluation. The tracking strategy of Kalman filter algorithm and the proposed technique

Table 1. Performance analysis of benchmark methods and the proposed method based on the metric F-score

Sequences	GMM	MOG	XCS-LBP	Sigma-Delta Z	Bayesian Histogram	CS-STLTP	Proposed RSDT-ARIMA
PETS Dataset							
Water surface	0.3212	0.3908	0.4578	0.5691	0.6201	0.8809	0.8817
Active fountain	0.3101	0.4673	0.4601	0.5200	0.6197	0.8471	0.8470
Waving curtain	0.3875	0.5009	0.5271	0.5826	0.6423	0.7502	0.8286
Shopping mall	0.3409	0.4998	0.5198	0.5421	0.5822	0.7623	0.7720
Airport	0.3423	0.5291	0.5291	0.5312	0.5621	0.7509	0.7609
Bootstrap	0.2892	0.4712	0.4712	0.4821	0.5012	0.5712	0.5923
Loppy	0.2513	0.4527	0.3527	0.4011	0.4402	0.5829	0.6301
BMC Dataset							
Video_001	0.5278	0.5124	0.6324	0.5901	0.6276	0.8102	0.8421
Video_002	0.5201	0.5301	0.6423	0.6302	0.6300	0.8012	0.8401
Video_003	0.5400	0.5487	0.6587	0.6490	0.6512	0.8154	0.8500
Video_004	0.5512	0.5623	0.6623	0.6499	0.6710	0.8423	0.8492
Video_005	0.5730	0.5219	0.6420	0.6511	0.6932	0.8322	0.8301
Institut für Algorithmen und Kognitive Systeme Traffic Sequence							
Durlacher-Tor	0.3890	0.4011	0.4200	0.6091	0.6299	0.6324	0.7524
Ettlinger-Tor	0.3912	0.4010	0.4512	0.5932	0.6300	0.6291	0.7811
Taxi	0.4210	0.4587	0.4635	0.5910	0.6012	0.6120	0.7402

Table 2. Performance analysis of variants attempted and the proposed work based on the metric F-score

Sequences	CS-STLTP-ARMA	CS-STLTP-ARIMA	RSDT- ARMA	Proposed RSDT-ARIMA
PETS Dataset				
Water surface	0.8809	0.8810	0.8817	0.8817
Active fountain	0.8471	0.8471	0.8471	0.8470
Waving curtain	0.7502	0.7601	0.7609	0.8286
Shopping mall	0.7623	0.7629	0.769	0.7720
Airport	0.7509	0.7600	0.7609	0.7609
Bootstrap	0.5712	0.5709	0.5816	0.5923
Loppy	0.5829	0.5900	0.5900	0.6301
BMC Dataset				
Video_001	0.8102	0.8102	0.8129	0.8421
Video_002	0.8012	0.8065	0.8296	0.8401
Video_003	0.8154	0.8190	0.8209	0.8500
Video_004	0.8423	0.8421	0.8421	0.8492
Video_005	0.8322	0.8300	0.8302	0.8301
Institut für Algorithmen und Kognitive Systeme Traffic Sequence				
Durlacher-Tor	0.6324	0.6392	0.7310	0.7524
Ettlinger-Tor	0.6291	0.6210	0.7518	0.7811
Taxi	0.6120	0.6282	0.7265	0.7402

Figure 14. Results of background subtraction on PETS dataset by the proposed approach RSDT-ARIMA and other three benchmark methods

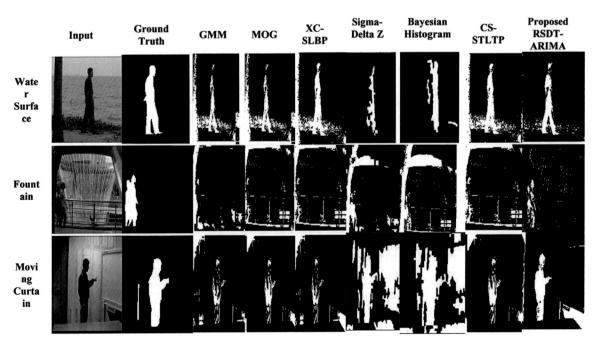

Figure 15. Results of background subtraction on BMC dataset by the proposed approach RSDT-ARIMA and other three benchmark methods

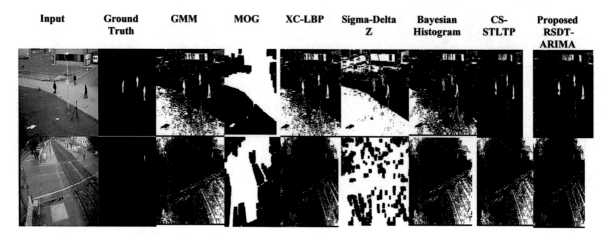

Figure 16. Results of background subtraction on Institut für Algorithmen und Kognitive Systeme dataset by the proposed approach RSDT-ARIMA and other three benchmark methods

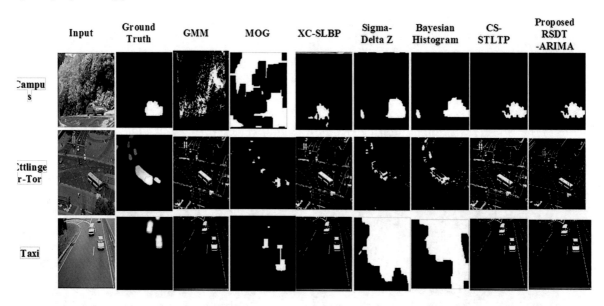

are shown in Figure 17. Compared to the Kalman filter, the proposed work with LDP feature tracks the objects without any failure. In Kalman filter approach, the moving human objects are not tracked due to the static behavior of objects in the consecutive frames. This issue is overcome by utilizing the unique LDP feature to track the objects in a video. This is shown in Figure 17. A rectangular colour bounding box is plotted around the foreground objects in the video.

1.   **Indoor Dynamic Variation:** Figure 17 (a) shows the tracking results for a video of moving human bodies in an indoor scene, in front of dynamic scene. It contains a set of strongly waving curtains due to the wind. Due to the correct background modelling strategy, tracking is performed correctly.

Figure 17. Example of object tracking experimental: (a) a frame of a video sequence with dynamic background (waving curtain); (b) tracking in the outdoor environment; (c) tracking vehicles in the traffic environment

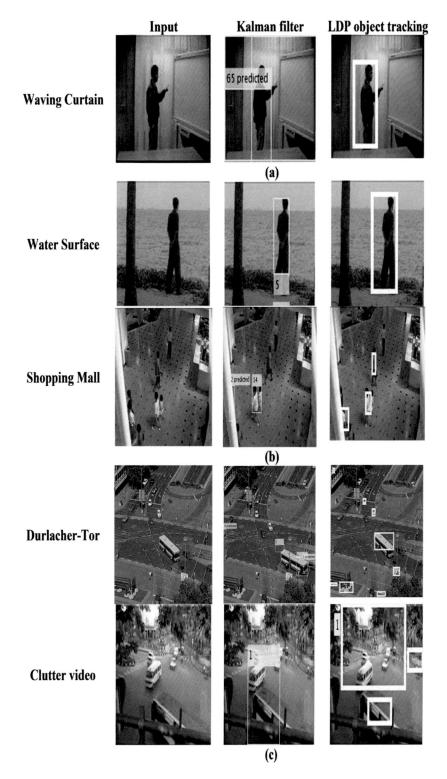

2. **Outdoor Moving Human Body Tracking:** Figure 17 (b) shows the tracking results for a video of moving human bodies in an outdoor scene. Among the moving objects two of them in the scene, walk with the same wave length. It is difficult to track moving human bodies because their shape change is difficult to track and their motion is difficult to learn and predict. However, the proposed work is able to track multiple persons correctly even if they merge and separate.

3. **Vehicle Tracking:** Traffic sequences are also taken to verify the tracking methods. The proposed method has a good tracking speed and it can track fast moving objects such as vehicles as well. When a car comes into the scene, it is seen as a new tracking object, and a tracking window for that car is assigned. The objects in the traffic sequence (Figure 17(c)) exhibit drastic change in scale. It is a challenging task because based on scaling, tracking algorithm must enlarge the size of the bounding box. The texture based feature can be used to overcome this challenge.

4. **Discussion:**

    a. **Time Complexity:** Key frame selection is the first phase in the Rotational Symmetry Dynamic Texture (RSDT) process. Key frame is the frame which best reflects the content among the consecutive frames in the video. It can represent the salient content of the frames. This step greatly reduces complexity and the processing overhead. Also it guarantees faster background subtraction.

The running time of existing methods is O(2N) where N is the number of frames in the video. The proposed work takes 1 frame for every 10 frames and hence the running time is O(1.1N). This step greatly reduces complexity and the processing overhead. Also it guarantees faster background subtraction.

Only one key frame is taken in the RSDT-SCD process. That key frame is a representative frame for 10 consecutive frames. In general, reading time is less than the processing time. Key frame selection step can automatically reduce the remaining 9 frames' processing time. It decreases the delay in processing.

    b. **Efficiency:** Two different sizes of spatio temporal patches are used to make the background model. So it creates the background model accurately. RSDT process is used to create the directional code based on line symmetry and rotational symmetry effectively. ARIMA model is based on first difference, so it can detect even the mild changes also. So the proposed work is more accurate in yielding results for background subtraction than the existing state-of-the-art methods.

CONCLUSION

A novel Rotational Symmetry Dynamic Texture (RSDT) for background subtraction is proposed which generates directional codes based on the concept rotational symmetry and line symmetry. This provides effective subspace. The result of the proposed method is compared with techniques like GMM, MOG, XC-LBP, Bayesian Histogram, Sigma-Delta Z, Center Symmetry - Spatio Temporal Local Ternary Pattern (CS-STLTP) by using the parameter such as F-Score. The proposed method outperforms the other background subtraction methods.

The time series model Auto Regressive Integrated Moving Average model (ARIMA) has been widely used to estimate the parameters appearance, consistency and temporal coherence. Compared to ARMA, ARIMA produces better performance. Also new combinations of CS-STLTP with ARIMA, RSDT with ARMA are compared. The results show the effectiveness of the proposed RSDT with ARIMA model.

At last the moving object is tracked by matching the LDP feature of each object frame by frame. Sufficient experiments as well as empirical analysis are presented to validate the advantages. In future, the proposed method is to be put in use for GPU based implementation so as to adapt the work for real time video surveillance system.

REFERENCES

Background Models Challenge (BMC). (2012, November). *Asian Conference on Computer Vision.* Retrieved from http://bmc.iut-auvergne.com

Barnich, O., & Van, M. (2011, June). Vibe: A universal background subtraction algorithm for video sequences. *IEEE Transactions on Image Processing, 20*(6), 1709–1724. doi:10.1109/TIP.2010.2101613 PMID:21189241

Bascle, B., & Deriche, R. (1995). Region Tracking through Image Sequences.*Proc.Fifth Int'l Conf. Computer Vision*, 302-307. doi:10.1109/ICCV.1995.466925

Birchfield, S. (1998). Elliptical Head Tracking Using Intensity Gradients and Color Histograms.*IEEE Conf. Computer Vision and Pattern Recognition*, 232-237. doi:10.1109/CVPR.1998.698614

Bouwmans, T. (2011, September). Recent Advanced Statistical Background Modeling forForeground Detection: A Systematic Survey. *Recent Patents on Computer Science, 4*(3), 147–176.

Brutzer, S., Hoferlin, B., & Heidemann, G. (2011). Evaluation of background subtraction techniques for video surveillance.*IEEE Conf. CVPR*, 1937–1944. doi:10.1109/CVPR.2011.5995508

Cheung, G. K. M., Kanade, T., Bouguet, J. Y., & Holler, M. (2000). *Real time system for robust 3 D voxel reconstruction of human motions.* CVPR. doi:10.1109/CVPR.2000.854944

Cheung, S. C., & Kamath, C. (2004). *Robust techniques for background subtraction in urban traffic video.* SPIE Video Comm. Image Process. doi:10.1117/12.526886

Collins, R., & Liu, Y. (2000). Online Selection of Discriminative Tracking Feature. *IEEE Transactions on Pattern Analysis and Machine Intelligence, 27*(10), 1631–1643. doi:10.1109/TPAMI.2005.205 PMID:16237997

Comaniciu, D., Ramesh, V., & Meer, P. (2000). Real time tracking of non-rigid objects using mean shift. *IEEE Conference on Computer Vision and Pattern Recognition (CVPR '00), 2*, 142-149. doi:10.1109/ CVPR.2000.854761

Comaniciu, D., Ramesh, V., Meer, P. (2003). Kernal Based Object Tracking. *IEEE Transaction on Pattern Analysis and Machine Intelligence, 25*(5), 564-577.

Elgammal, A., Harwood, D., & Davis, L. (2000). Non-parametric Model for Background Subtraction. *European Conf. Computer Vision, 2*, 751–767.

Elgammal, A., Harwood, D., & Davis, L. (2004). *Non-parametric model for background subtraction. IEEE Frame-Rate Workshop*, (Vol. 4). IEEE.

Fazli, S., Pour, H. M., & Bouzari, H. (2009). Particle Filter based Object Tracking with Sift and Color Feature. *Machine Vision, 2009. ICMV '09.Second International Conference*, 89 – 93.

Heikkila, M., & Pietikainen, M. (2006, April). A texture based method for modelling the background and detecting moving objects. *IEEE Transactions on Pattern Analysis and Machine Intelligence, 28*(4), 657–662. doi:10.1109/TPAMI.2006.68 PMID:16566514

Heikkila, M., Pietikainen, M., & Schmid, C. (2009, March). Description of interest regions with local binary patterns. *Pattern Recognition, 42*(3), 425–436. doi:10.1016/j.patcog.2008.08.014

Huang. S., (2011, Jan.). An Advanced Motion Detection Algorithm with Video Quality Analysis for Video Surveillance Systems. *IEEE Transaction on Circuit and Systems for Video Technology, 21*(1).

Hue, C., Le Cadre, J. P., & Perez, P. (2002, July). Tracking multiple objects with particle filtering. *IEEE Transactions on Aerospace and Electronic Systems, 38*(3), 791–812. doi:10.1109/TAES.2002.1039400

Hyndman, R. J., & Athanasopoulos. (2015, May). *8.9 Seasonal ARIMA models*. Academic Press.

Kanhere, N. K., Pundlik, S. J., & Birchfield, S. T. (2005). Vehicle segmentation and tracking from a low-angle off-axis camera.*IEEE Conference on Computer Vision and pattern Recognition*. doi:10.1109/CVPR.2005.365

Kollnig, N. (1997). *Institutfür Algorithmen und Kognitive Systeme*. Retrieved from http://i21www.ira.uka.de/image_sequences

Kuralkar, P. (2012). Human Object Tracking using Background Subtraction and Shadow Removal Techniques. *International Journal of Advanced Research in Computer Science and Software Engineering, 2*(3).

Li, L., Huang, W., Gu, I., & Tian, Q. (2003). Foreground object detection from videos containing complex background.*ACM International Conference on Multimedia*, 2-10. doi:10.1145/957013.957017

Li, N., Liu, L., & Xu, D. (2008). Corner feature based object tracking using Adaptive Kalman Filter, Signal Processing. *ICSP 2008.9th International Conference*, 1432 – 1435.

Lin, Xu, Y., Liang, X., & Lai. (2014, July). Complex Background Subtraction by pursuing Dynamic Spatio – Temporal Models. *IEEE Transaction on Image Processing, 23*(7), 3191-3201.

Liu, S., & Fu, C. (1998, September). Statistical change detection with moments under time varying illumination. *IEEE Transactions on Image Processing, 7*(9), 1258–1268. doi:10.1109/83.709658 PMID:18276338

MacCormick, J., & Blake, A. (2000). A Probabilistic Exclusion Principle for Tracking Multiple Objects. *International Journal of Computer Vision, 39*(1), 57–71. doi:10.1023/A:1008122218374

Manzanera, A. (2007). Σ-Δ Background Subtraction and the Zipf Law.*Pattern Recognition, Image. Analysis and Applications*, 42–51.

Ojala, T., Pietikainen, M., & Harwood, D. (1996, January). A Comparative study of texture measures with classification based on feature distribution. *Pattern Recognition, 29*(1), 51–59. doi:10.1016/0031-3203(95)00067-4

Ojala, T., Pietikainen, M., & Maenpaa, T. (2012, July). Multiresolution grayscale and rotation invariant texture classification with local binary patterns. *IEEE Transactions on Pattern Analysis and Machine Intelligence, 24*(7), 971–987. doi:10.1109/TPAMI.2002.1017623

Perez, P., Hue, C., Vermaak, J., & Gangnet, M. (2002). Color-Based Probabilistic Tracking.*European Conf. Computer Vision*, 661-675.

Performance Evaluation of Tracking and Surveillance (PETS). (2006, June). *Ninth IEEE International Workshop on Performance Evaluation of Tracking and Surveillance*. Retrieved from http://perception. i2r.a-star.edu.sg

Piccardi, M. (2004). Background subtraction techniques: a review.*IEEE Int. Conf. Systems, Man and Cybernetics*, 3099–3104.

Pietikainen, M., Ojala, T., Scruggs, T., Bowyer, K. W., Jin, C., & Hoffman, K. (2000, January). Rotational invariant texture classification using feature distribution. *Pattern Recognition, 33*(1), 43–52. doi:10.1016/S0031-3203(99)00032-1

Pilet, J., Strecha, C., & Fua, P. (2008). *Making background subtraction robust to sudden illumination changes*. ECCV. doi:10.1007/978-3-540-88693-8_42

Power, P., & Schoonees, J. (2002). Understand background mixture models for foreground segmentation. *Image and Vision Computing*, 267–271.

Rasmussen, C., & Hager, G. (2001, June). Probabilistic Data Association Methods for Tracking Complex Visual Objects. *IEEE Transactions on Pattern Analysis and Machine Intelligence, 23*(6), 560–576. doi:10.1109/34.927458

Seki, M., Wada, T., Fujiwara, H., & Sumi, K. (2003). Background subtraction based on cooccurrence of image variations.*IEEE Int. Conf. CVPR*, 65–72. doi:10.1109/CVPR.2003.1211453

Sheikh, Y., & Shah, M. (2005). Bayesian modeling of dynamic scenes for object detection. *IEEE Transactions on Pattern Analysis and Machine Intelligence, 27*(11), 1778–1792. doi:10.1109/TPAMI.2005.213 PMID:16285376

Skifstad, K., & Jain, R. (1989). Illumination independent change detection for real world image sequences. *Comp. Vision. Graphics, and Image Process., 46*(3), 387–399. doi:10.1016/0734-189X(89)90039-X

Stauffer, C., & Grimson, W. (1999). Adaptive background mixture models for real-time tracking.*IEEE Conf. CVPR*, 2246-2252. doi:10.1109/CVPR.1999.784637

Unay, D., Ekin, A., & Jasinschi, R. S. (2010, July). Local structured based region of interest retrieval in brain MR images. *IEEE Transactions on Information Technology in Biomedicine, 14*(4), 897–903. doi:10.1109/TITB.2009.2038152 PMID:20064763

Vosters, L. P. J., Shan, C., & Gritti, T. (2010). Background subtraction under sudden illumination changes. *IEEE Conf. AVSS*, 384–391.

Wei, F., Chou, S., & Lin, C. (2008). A region-based object tracking scheme using Adaboost-based feature selection. *IEEE International Symposium on Circuits and Systems*, 2753– 2756.

Wren, C., Azarbayejani, A., Darrel, T., & Pentland, A. (1997). Pfinder, Real time tracking of the human body. *IEEE Transactions on Pattern Analysis and Machine Intelligence, 19*(7), 780–785. doi:10.1109/34.598236

Xue, C., Chun, C., Zhu, M., & Chen, A. (2008). A Discriminative Feature-Based Mean-shift Algorithm for Object Tracking. *Knowledge Acquisition and Modeling Workshop, 2008. KAM Workshop 2008. IEEE International Symposium*, 217 – 220. doi:10.1109/KAMW.2008.4810464

Xue, G., Sun, J., & Song, L. (2010, July). Dynamic Background Subtraction Based On Spatial Extended Center-Symmetric Local Binary Pattern. *International Conference in Multimedia and Exposition*, 1050-1055. doi:10.1109/ICME.2010.5582601

Zhang, B., Gao, Y., Zhao, S., Liu, J. (2010, February). Local Derivative Pattern Versus Local Binary Pattern: Face Recognition With High-Order Local Pattern Descriptor. *IEEE Transaction on Image processing, 19*(2), 533-545.

Zhao, G., Barnard, M., & Pietikainen, M. (2009, November). Lipreading with local spatial temporal descriptor. *IEEE Transactions on Multimedia, 11*(7), 1254–1265. doi:10.1109/TMM.2009.2030637

Zhao, T., & Nevatia, R. (2004). Tracking Multiple Humans in Crowed Environment. *IEEE Computer Society Conference on Computer Vision and Pattern Recognition (CVPR'04)*, 2, 406.

Chapter 14
A Novel Approach of Human Tracking Mechanism in Wireless Camera Networks

Usha Devi Gandhi
VIT University, India

ABSTRACT

The sensing power of traditional camera networks for efficiently addressing the critical tasks in the process of cluster – based target tracking of human, such as measurement integration, inclusion/exclusion in the cluster and cluster head rotation. The Wireless Camera Networks efficiently uses distribution friendly representation and methods in which every node contributes to the computation in each mechanism without the requirement of any prior knowledge of the rest of the nodes. These mechanisms and methods are integrated in two different distributed schemas so that it can be implemented in the same mean time without taking into the consideration of cluster size. Thus, the experimental evaluation shows that the proposed schemes and mechanisms drastically reduce the energy consumption and computational burden with respect to the existing methodology.

INTRODUCTION

Limitations & tracking through GPS deprived of situations is an open exploration environment where a high range of sensors and procedures have been anticipated in the late periods. A decent number of following techniques for WCNs have been implemented. A large portion of them receive the clustering technique, in which the head moves about as the cluster scheduler. The Cluster based plans oblige strategies to incorporate the estimations of the objective accumulated by the bunch individuals. Moreover, there is a need of instruments for selecting the incorporation and prohibition of hubs in the group and for dealing with the revolution of the group head part. These systems will have a straight effect on implementation and the asset utilization. Case in point, consideration/prohibition is connected to initiation/deactivation: hubs are kept dynamic while they fit in with the group and deactivated at the point when prohibited with a specific end goal to spare vitality. Various strategies for these instruments have

DOI: 10.4018/978-1-5225-2053-5.ch014

been produced. Be that as it may, the majority of them is clear adjustments of instruments intended for conventional camera systems and regularly dismiss the qualities of WCNs. This particularly designed to get into consideration that the capabilities and demands of wireless sensor networks namely conservation of energy, minimal computational ability and potentially greater transmission defects. Mechanisms uses such as Extended Information filter for the unique measurement of data rates, an effectively based mechanism for the activation or deactivation of cameras which can balance the sensing expectation and resource consumption. Another methodology involved is that selects the chief role to the eligible node for the effective integration of more information regarding the target by making use of the previously active nodes in the cluster. These three methods apply calculated approach which are devised for disseminated implementation such as a) the utilization of proficient and distributed open representations and statistics measurements; b) every cluster nodes adds to the calculation in every structure; and c) nodes don't require any prior knowledge of the remaining nodes. Two differently conveyed schemes are proposed to amicably incorporate these components enormously abusing computation reuse.

LITERATURE REVIEW

The distributed wireless sensor micro sensor frameworks will allow the keen observation of a diverse kind of situations for both general and defense purposes. Goshorn et al.(2007) discussed communication protocols that have a massive effect on the general vitality dissemination of the respective systems. Taking into account our experiments and results that the conventional protocol of direct broadcast, multihop routing, minimum energy transfer, and static clustering may not be suitable for sensor systems, suggesting "LEACH (Low-Energy Adaptive Bunching Hierarchy)", which is an clustering based method that implements distinct rotation of cluster heads to equally distribute the energy level in the system for each sensors in it. "LEACH" deploys partial organization to have robustness of dynamic networks and scalability, and sums up all the collected information form the sensors into the routing protocol in order to limit the measurement of collected information which has to be transferred to the base station. Simulations results shows that "LEACH" can achieve as an element of 9 reductions in terms of dissipation in contrast with the conventional routing protocols.

Various mechanisms have been held to track the moving objects in any geographical environment which may include rotating the head cluster node among the other cluster nodes within the system. This cluster head node is responsible for managing the impact of the cluster nodes respectively. Various large numbers of distinct methods and systems such as "LEACH" and its variations intend to normalize the consumption of energy by selecting the node which has a high remaining energy level and memory level as the head node. However, these criteria will not be of any use to improve the sensing ability or to have reduced energy consumption. While in the other system environment the head role is allocated to the node that is very much near to the estimated target location (Medeiros et al., 2011). The node which collects the exact information about the assigns target need not be close to the target; hence it is free to be located anywhere in the system. Various methods have tried for implementation which deals with addition and elimination of nodes in the respective cluster techniques (Zhang et al., 2007). This keeps the node active whose distance is less than presumed values from the target.

Viola Jones Algorithm

The main characteristic of the face detection algorithm is it's i) robustness, ii) easy pimplementation in real time iiii) detecting the human face or frames. There are four steps or stages followed by this algorithm are Haar selection, Creation of an internal image, Adaboost training and applying Cascading filter technique. There are five type of features used by this algorithm (Figure 1)

- **Haar Features:** This step works based on similar human features that can be detected in every human face such as eyes which is darker than the upper cheek region (Figure 2). While the nose region will be brighter than the eye region.

The rectangular features are applied to the gray scale image ie integral image along with a time constant. As a result (Figure 3), we can obtain a sophisticated alternative features. This uses the rectangle features which have array values such as three in 8 rectangle and four in nine rectangle.

SIFT Algorithm

Human frames have to be composed with and without reference images by implementing the SIFT algorithm techniques. In the beginning of this process, initial frames has to be extracted from the preprocessed human frames and this is compared with all other remaining frames which are categorized

Figure 1. Sub window features

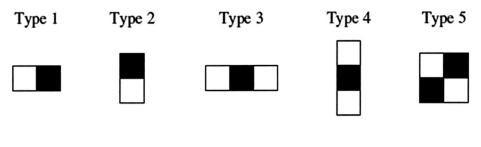

Figure 2. The Haar features

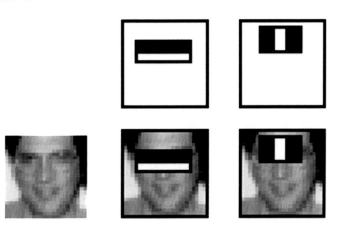

Figure 3. Array values of integral image

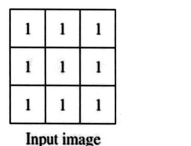

Table 1. Detailed comparisons of shift and its variants

	Keypoint Detection		Keypoint Description		
	Scale-space	Selection	Main direction	Feature Extraction	#Dimensions
SIFT	Different-scale images convoluted with a Gaussian function	Detect extrema in DoG space; do non-maxima suppression	Calculate a gradient amplitude of a square area; regard the direction with the maximum gradient strength as the main direction	Divide a 16×16 region into 4×4 sub-regions; create a gradient histogram for each sub-region	128
PCA-SIFT	Same as SIFT	Same as SIFT	Same as SIFT	Extract a 41×41 patch; form a 3042-dimension vector; use a project matrix to multiply with it	20 or less
GSIFT	Same as SIFT	Same as SIFT	Same as SIFT	For each keypoint, create a vector consisting of SIFT description and a global texture vector	188
CSIFT	Replace grayscale with color invariant; convolute with a Gaussian function	Same as SIFT	Same as SIFT	Same as SIFT	384
SURF	Different-scale box filter convoluting with an original image	Use a Hessian matrix to determine candidate keypoints; do non-maxima suppression	Calculate a Haar wavelet response in x and y directions of each sector in a circular area; regard the direction with maximum norm as the main direction	Divide a 20×20s region into 4×4s sub-regions; calculate a Haar wavelet response	64
ASIFT	After a preprocessing - viewpoint transformation, follow SIFT's steps (i.e., the same as SIFT)				

under non-human frames. Thus, compares the characteristic of the objects and its process. Once this process is triggered and completed, all the frames are been collected and stored in the new folder. These frames are composed into a single length video. The next frame is extracted and all the above mentioned processes are repeated. Thus this is done for all human frames. Suppose the reference image is not having any data or it is empty, the frames which are saved in each folder is composed to form videos of the non-human frames of each individual. But if the reference image is full or consist of data then the frames are separately categorized in separate unique folders. Thus divides and categorizes frames into video frames for separate individuals. Hence this SIFT algorithm is implemented by the following steps: Creating the Difference of Gaussian Pyramid, Noise Elimination, Orientation Assignment, Keypoints Matching.

An series of experiments have been carried out based on various characteristics such as blurring the image quality and extracting frames, changing the brightness of the image and rotating the angle view point of the image. The images (Mikolajczyk et al., 2005) used for this experimental analysis are all

Figure 4. Experimental result for Blur radius

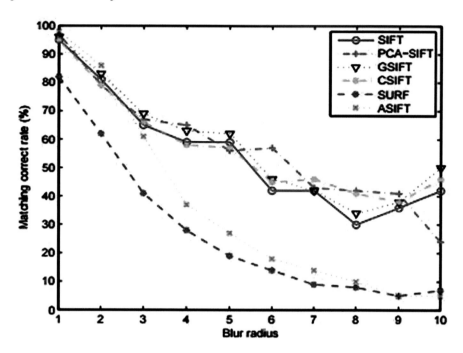

Figure 5. Experimental result for brightness changes

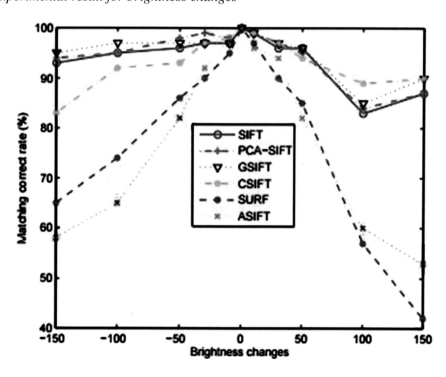

Figure 6. Experimental result for change in view point angle

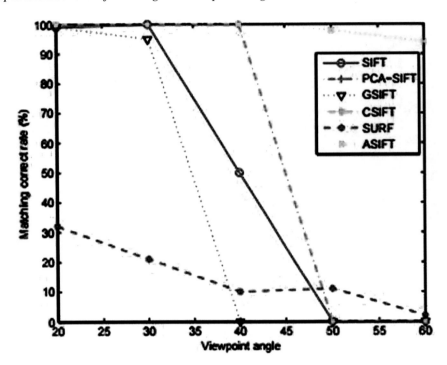

converted into gray scale images initially. Thus obtain the result as in Figure 4 about the performance range of the SIFT algorithm.

All most each and every image data does not have the same frame value if the brightness property of images are changed. Each pixel of the image gets a new value every time when there is a slightest change in the brightness value. The SIFT algorithm has shown better performance in this brightness changes experimental analysis (Figure 5) and the change in the view point angle as in Figure 6.

PROPOSED SYSTEM

It includes developing a distinct activation method that considers transmission errors for the enhanced version of cameras and can utilize all the data matrix uncertainty metric, which allows computation distribution and reutilize the data involving interesting advantages. The cluster selection mechanism is based on similar technology and tools in comparison with those implemented in the camera activation techniques. The performance of each methodology and the comparison of similar experiments, new robustness analysis and more practical performance analysis are measured. Unlike the previous techniques of a single hop cluster schema, here the preference is given to the multicast socket methodology where each and every neighboring nodes are detected for collection and transmission of data. The implementation of SIFT (Soto et al., 2009) algorithm for extraction of human and non-human frames helps to retrieve unique information of any particular object or an individual as per the demand. This has a high reduction of noise and can straight alignment of key point matching in each frame as shown in Figure 7.

Figure 7. Architecture diagram

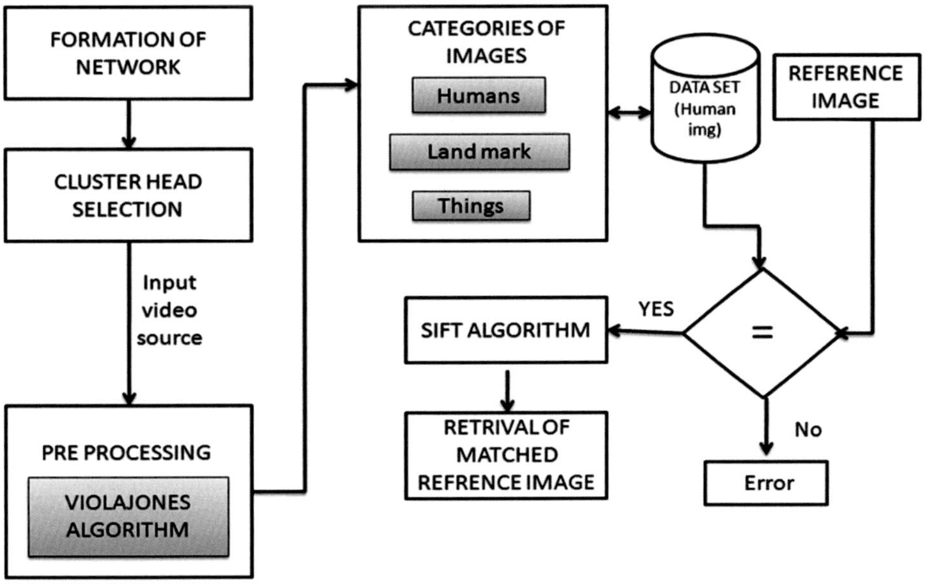

Modules Description

There are mainly four modules in this system.

- Network formation,
- Cluster head selection,
- Pre-processing,
- Retrieval of matched images using SIFT algorithm.

Network Formation

The first module deals with the mechanism of network formation. This network is formed by various camera sensors which acts as an individual nodes in a network. Each node sends a "hello" message to other nodes within the network in order to detect the neighboring nodes. Once the node detects the "hello" message from other nodes or separate node from the system, it maintains a contact record to store the data about the neighboring nodes. Once the neighbor nodes are found, a queue is maintained at each neighbor node called real queue.

Cluster Head Selection

The main diploma of performance tracking purely depends on the cluster head selection process. In order to select the cluster head, certain conditions are used as metrics for obtaining the higher performance. Hence the node that obtains estimation tentatively uses the measurement of the currently available active nodes. The selection of a bad cluster head node will increase the uncertainty level. The selected cluster node which will act as the cluster head must have an active communication with it's cluster members in the network. Let us consider node i as the cluster head is measured using EUi, the expected ambiguity regarding the target at time t+1 if the node is selected as the cluster head. Let us consider that at time t, St is the set of node that are active. St consists of the nodes that are both in tracking mode and the current mode. The cluster head is mainly selected by considering battery usage and the memory usage. Among all the nodes present in the cluster the node which is having the highest memory space and the higher battery power will be selected as the cluster head. By using the information matrix we can drastically reduce the burden as regarding to the previous entropy analysis (De San Bernabe et al., 2012).

Preprocessing

After the selection of the cluster head now the collected data which are in the image format has to be preprocessed. In preprocessing the collected input videos are bisected and converted into frame format. Now these preprocessed frames are categorized into information less frames and the frames which are having valid information. These are determined on the bases of the metrics for the frames which are having a mean input frame value of less than 15 in terms of Matlab measurements and metrics. In order to make this process less complicated and easy to evaluate the preprocessed frames are clubbed together to form a single video for its categorization. This clubbed video consists of only valid information frames. The video categorization involves the separation of human frames and non-human frames using the Viola-Jones algorithm. The frame which comes under the Region of Interest comes under human frame category whereas the other frames are evaluated and categorized as non-human frames.

Retrieval of Matched Images Using SIFT Algorithm

Videos are categorized by using transition clues like human, object. In this module Human frame has to Compose with and without Reference image by using BPN with the help of Trainee Database. Trainee Database has to be Created after Processing has been completed. It consists of list of human frames with different angles in a specific Group. Each human frame is stored in a uniform manner. Initially Each Human Frames are checked and evaluated with the Trainee Database Frames. Suppose the initial starting human frames is in match with First groups in Trainee Database, then a separate Folder will create and write the Frame on that. Repeating the process until all the Human Frames has to be completed in Human categorized. If the Reference image is empty, on that condition Frames in the Each Folder will be composed and formed videos for individual all humans. If the Reference image is not empty, Frames will be categorized depending on the Reference image for a specific human face.

Activity Diagram

This diagram represents the graphical flow of various activities in an ordered and stepwise manner. This is one of the important unified diagram that clearly shows (Figure 8) the operational steps in accordance to the algorithm and the methods used in the thesis. The concurrency of this diagram has to be accurate because this represents the actual methodological ways stepwise. It also represents the flow control of the proposed mechanism.

Figure 8. Activity diagram

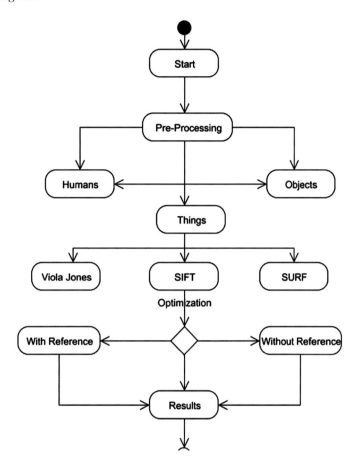

IMPLEMENTATION OF THE SYSTEM

Selection of Cluster Head

In the cluster head selection technique let us consider three nodes A, B, C. Assume that the nodes are linked in A-B and A-C manner. Thus these links is having high memory space and high primary reception rate. If A is selected as the cluster head in this scenario then there will be high contribution probability from the nodes B and C. now le us consider the node link B to C is having less primary reception time. If suppose B is selected as the cluster head, then the high contribution will be from the node A but not from the node C. therefore if node A is selected as the cluster node then the resulting estimation will be more accurate.

Step 1: First we have to calculate the information matrix.

$$EU_i = tr\left(\bar{\Omega}_{t+1}\right) + \sum_{j \in S_t} p_{j,i}^2 \, tr\left(\Omega_{j,t+1}\right)$$

Step 2: EUi should not be maximizes for cluster head selection.

$$CL = \arg\max_{i \in S_t}\left(EU_i\right)$$

Step 3: Removing the independent values we get the final metric.

$$CL = \arg\max_{i \in S_t}\left(\sum_{j \in S_t} p_{j,i}^2\, tr\left(\Omega_{j,t+1}\right)\right)$$

Thus by the above formulation prioritization is given to the node which is having the high primary reception rate as shown in Box 1.

Enhanced Voila Jones Implementation

The steps shown in Box 2 are implemented for identifying human frames.

The Matlab script is able to condition the database images into positive data. Various examples was constructed for the evaluation process. The script does the following:

1. It opens a facial image and it is transformed into a greyscale image.
2. The user places a boundary box around the face in the displayed image.
3. The faces are scaled to 24*24 pixels.
4. This process saves the rescaled face as an image and data file as an normalized information set

The normalization process for variance was suggested by Viola-Jones as a mean to reduce the effect of various lighting conditions as shown in Figure 9

A total number of 5000 positive examples has to be adequate to train the individual stages of the staged classifier, but these examples should be chosen wisely (Figure 10). The final detector will only detects the similar faces to those in the training set so the training set should signify the most familiar facial variation.

Box 1.

Algorithm : Proposed Cluster Head Selection Method

Require : $p_{j,i}, tr(\Omega_{j,t+1})\ \forall j, i \in S_t$
1: **for** $\forall i \in S_t$ **do**
2:    $EU_i = \sum_{j \in S_t} p_{j,i}^2 tr(\Omega_{j,t+1})$
3: **end for**
4: $CL = \arg\max_{i \in S_t}(EU_i)$
5: **if** $(EU_{CL} > 0)$ **then**
6:    Assign CL as the new cluster head
7: **end if**

Box 2.

- Given examples images $(x_1, y_1), \ldots, (x_n, y_n)$ where $y_1 = 0, 1$ for negative and positive examples.
- Initialize weights $w_{1,i} = \frac{1}{2m}, \frac{1}{2l}$ for $y_1 = 0, 1$, where m and l are the numbers of positive and negative examples.
- For $t = 1, \ldots, T$:

1) Normalize the weights, $w_{t,i} \leftarrow \dfrac{w_{t,i}}{\sum_{j=1}^{n} w_{t,j}}$

2) Select the best weak classifier with respect to the weighted error:

$$\varepsilon_t = \min_{f,p,\theta} \sum_i w_i \left| h(x_i, f, p, \theta) - y_i \right|$$

3) Define $h_t(x) = h(x, f_t, p_t, \theta_t)$ where f_t, p_t and θ_t are the minimizers of ε_t.

4) Update the weights:

$$w_{t+1,i} = w_{t,i} \beta_t^{1-e_i}$$

where $e_i = 0$ if example x_i is classified correctly and $e_i = 1$ otherwise, and $\beta_t = \frac{\varepsilon_t}{1 - \varepsilon_t}$

- The final strong classifier is:

$$C(x) = \begin{cases} 1 & \text{if } \sum_{t=1}^{T} \alpha_t h_t(x) \geq \frac{1}{2} \sum_{t=1}^{T} \alpha_t \\ 0 & \text{otherwise} \end{cases}$$

where $\alpha_t = \log \frac{1}{\beta_t}$

Figure 9. Positive image

Figure 10. Data graph

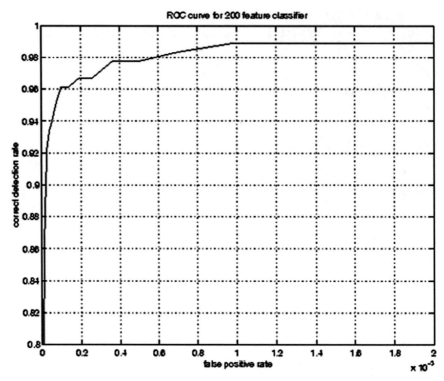

ROC curve for 200 feature classifier

Thus the human faces are detected and the output frame is received. Example of an output frame is shown in Figure 11.

CASSCADE CLASSIFIER

- It gives us 100% detection rate and the false rate is very low ie below 30%
- All the sub windows are given equal time for compilation
- This is a two feature simple classifier
- This acts (Figure 12) as the 1st filter layers to eliminate the negative windows

SIFT Algorithm Implementation

The construction of Gaussian Pyramid is the first step. So an Gaussian "Scale Space" function is constructed obtained form the input image. This function of Gaussian pyramid is formed by filtering the original image by using various Gaussian functions with different type of widths. There are two Gaussian functions: DoG, $D(x,y,6)$. The difference between these two functions is calculated between two filter images.

Figure 11. Successful detection of face

Figure 12. Casscade classifier

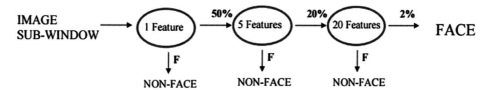

$$D(x, y, \sigma)e = L(x, y, k\sigma) - L\left(x, y, e\right)$$

$$L\left(x, y, \sigma\right)\left[PUB1\right]e = G\left(x, y, \sigma\right) * I\left(x, y\right)e$$

$$G\left(x, y\right)e = 1\exp\left\{-x^2y^2\right\}$$

$$G_i * G_0 * fe \; xGe_0^G F$$

The Fourier transform of a Gaussian function, e^{ax2} is given by

$$F_x\left[e^{ax2}\right]^e - \pi^2 t^2$$

$$t = e\Pi / a$$

Figure 13. Orientation subset window

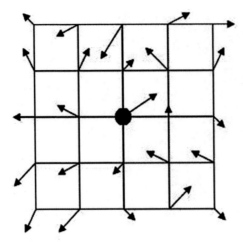

Substituting this and equating it to a covolution with a single Gaussian of width k_0 is shown in Figure 13.

These steps will assigned over the key points based on the properties of local image source. Thus a histogram for the respective orientation (Figure 13) is formed from the orientation gradient of sample points within a area in and around the keypoints. An 16*16 square is selected for this implementation. The orientation histogram consists of 36 bin enclosing 360 degree range orientations. The gradient magnitude is preprogrammed as well as the orientation {m(x,y) ø(x,y)} is also already computed using the pixel variations.

This calculates the location, orientation and scaling of SIFT features that are found in the images. These characteristics of the images respond firmly ro the edges and the intensity gradients. The SIFT characteristics generally appears in the eye region, nose, top of the nose, corner of lips for a human face image.

Figure 14 shows the keypoints in arrow mark. The length of these arrow marks indicates the contrast magnitudes in the input human face image. These arrows points from the darker region in the image towards the lighter region.

Therefore the computed SIFT features of the given image is evaluated and it has been experimented with some simple images with similar matching schemas. The most important and essential part of this

Figure 14. Detected human frame image

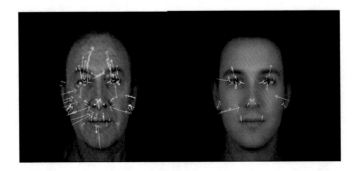

methodology is noise adjustment which results in false or in efficient matching. Thus the requested image of a particular human face has been detected and extracted successfully by using SIFT algorithm.

RESULTS AND DISCUSSION

For sample figures and screenshots, please see Figures 15-36.

CONCLUSION

The core objective of this project is to track a particular selected object from an video frame captured by group of camera networks. These are based on the static node approaches which as specially developed for the implementation distribution. Each node of the cluster in the system environment contributes to the evaluation of each single and every methodology so that the work done by each cluster node is shared in an consistent way despite the consequences of the size of the cluster. There are 2 schemas usede for the selection of cluster process. This first schema is a straight forward integration mechanism. While the second schema is an approximated execution technique. This work paves way for a wide opening in the study area of tracking methods using a wireless camera networks. This wisely ignores the usage of RSSI which further involves extra energy consumption. Thus the main advantage of energy consumption is achieved by neglecting the RSSI factor. The SIFT algorithm also gave extra advantage of the exact extraction of human frames and detecting the particular selected human frame from the input Trainee Dataset.

Figure 15. Main page

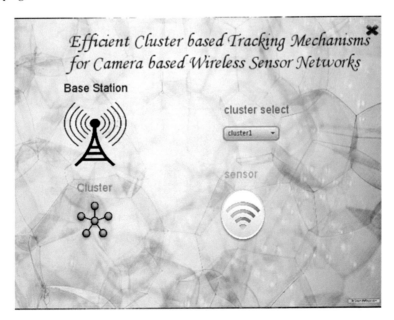

Figure 16. Base station page

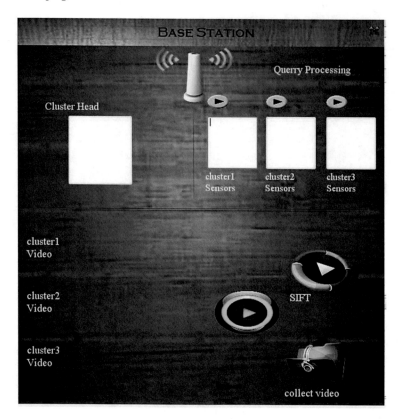

Figure 17. Input box for distance

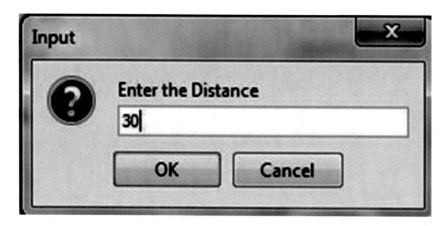

Figure 18. Input box for range

Figure 19. Input box for no. of sensors

Figure 20. Cluster head

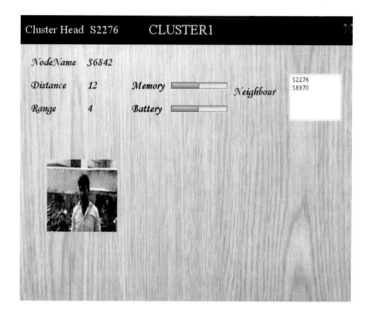

Figure 21. Neighbor node

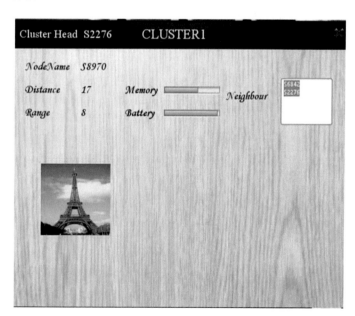

Figure 22. Input box for cluster 2

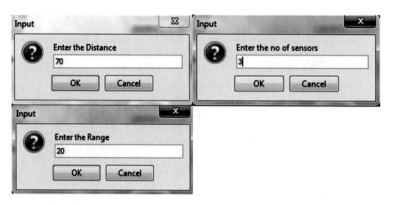

Figure 23. Cluster head

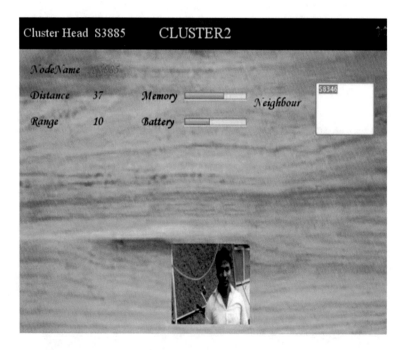

Figure 24. Neighbor nodes of Cluster 2

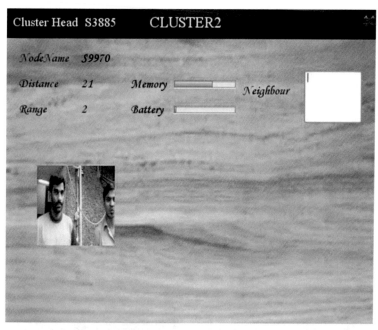

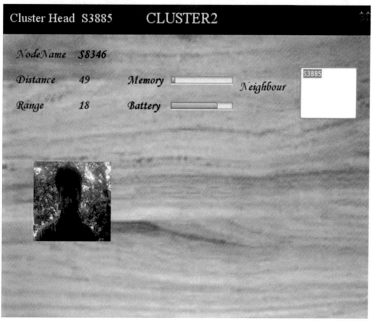

Figure 25. Input box for cluster 3

Figure 26. Cluster head

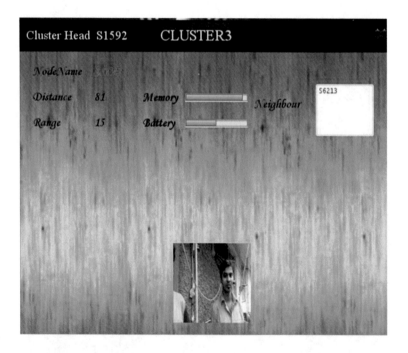

Figure 27. Neighbor nodes of Cluster 3

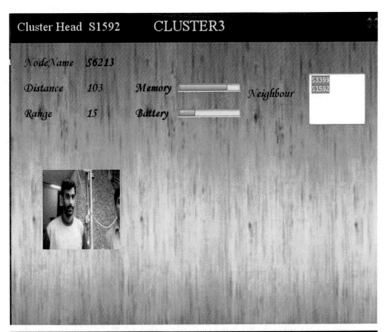

Figure 28. collection of data from each cluster

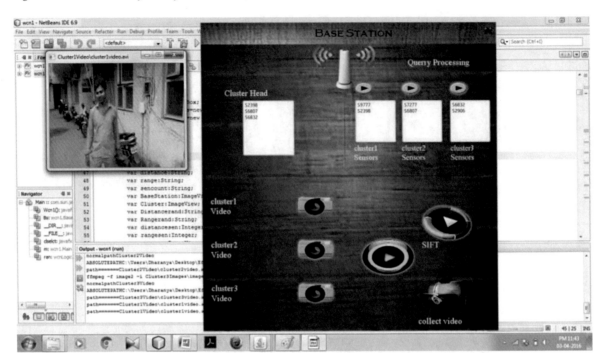

Figure 29. Collection of videos from each cluster

Figure 30. Calling of SIFT algorithm

Figure 31. Detection of human face

Figure 32. Human frames extraction

Figure 33. Separate video extraction

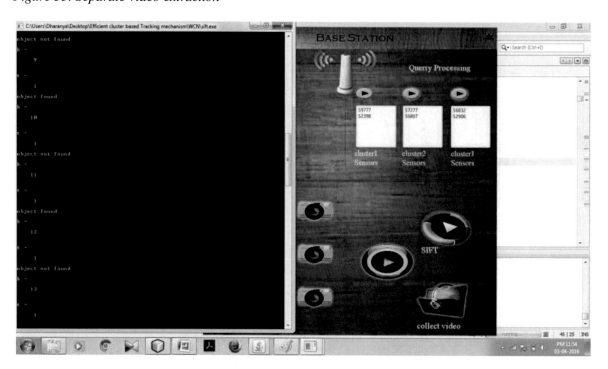

Figure 34. Detecting each frame values

Figure 35. Selection of input image

Figure 36. Output

REFERENCES

De San Bernabe, A., Martinez-de Dios, J.R., & Baturone, A.O. (2012). Entropy-aware cluster-based object tracking for camera wireless sensor networks. *IEEE/RSJ International Conference on Intelligent Robots and Systems, IROS'12*.

De San Bernabe, A., Martinez-de Dios, J. R., & Ollero, A. (2012). A WSN-based tool for urban and industrial fire-fighting. *Sensors (Basel, Switzerland), 12*(12), 15009–15035. doi:10.3390/s121115009 PMID:23202198

Desai P. and Rattan K.S. (2009). Indoor localization and surveillance using wireless sensor network and pantilt camera. *IEEE National Aerospace & Electronics Conference (NAECON),* 1–6.

Dore, A., Cattoni, A. F., & Regazzoni, C. S. (2007). A particle filter based fusion framework for video-radio tracking in smartspaces.*IEEE Conf. on Advanced Video and Signal Based Surveillance, AVSS'07,* 99–104.

Ercan, A. O., El Gamal, A., & Guibas, L. J. (2007). Object tracking inthe presence of occlusions via a camera network.*Int. Conf. on Information Processing in Sensor Networks, IPSN'07,* 509–518. doi:10.1145/1236360.1236425

Ercan, A. O., Yang, D. B., El Gamal, A., & Guibas, L. J. (2006). Optimal placement and selection of camera network nodes fortarget localization. In Distributed computing in sensor systems. Springer.

Goshorn, R., Goshorn, J., Goshorn, D., & Aghajan, H. (2007). Architecture for cluster-based automated surveillance network for detecting and tracking multiple persons.*ACM/IEEE Int. Conf. on Distributed Smart Cameras, ICDSC'07*, 219–226. doi:10.1109/ICDSC.2007.4357527

Gray, R. M. (2011). *Entropy and information theory*. Springer. doi:10.1007/978-1-4419-7970-4

Heinzelman, A. B. H., & Chandrakasan, W. (2000). Energy-efficient communication protocol for wireless microsensor networks.*Int. Conf. on System Sciences*. doi:10.1109/HICSS.2000.926982

Jimenez-Gonzalez, A., Martínez-de Dios, J. R., & Ollero, A. (2015). An integrated testbed for cooperative perception with heterogeneous mobile and static sensors. *Sensors (Basel, Switzerland)*, *11*(12), 11516–11543. doi:10.3390/s111211516 PMID:22247679

Jimenez-Gonzalez Martınez-de Dios, J., De San Bernabe, A., & Ollero, A. (2011). WSN-based visual object tracking using extended information filters. *Int. Workshop on Networks of Cooperating Objects*, 11.

Medeiros, H., Park, J., & Kak, A. (2007). A light-weight event-driven protocol for sensor clustering in wireless camera networks.*ACM/IEEE Int. Conf. on Distributed Smart Cameras, ICDSC'07*, 203–210. doi:10.1109/ICDSC.2007.4357525

Medeiros, H., Park, J., & Kak, A. (2011). Distributed object trackingusing a cluster-based kalman filter in wireless camera networks. *IEEE Journal of Selected Topics in Signal Processing*, *2*(4), 448–463. doi:10.1109/JSTSP.2008.2001310

Mikolajczyk, K., Tuytelaars, T., Schmid, C., Zisserman, A., Matas, J., Schaffalitzky, F., & Gool, L. V. et al. (2005). A comparison of affine region detectors. *International Journal of Computer Vision*, *65*(1-2), 43–72. doi:10.1007/s11263-005-3848-x

Miyaki, T., Yamasaki, T., & Aizawa, K. (2007). Multi-sensor fusion tracking using visual information and wi-fi location estimation.*ACM/IEEE Int. Conf. on Distributed Smart Cameras, ICDSC'07*, 275–282.

Onel, T., Ersoy, C., & Delic, H. (2009). Information content-based sensor selection and transmission power adjustment for collaborative target tracking. *IEEE Transactions on Mobile Computing*, *8*(8), 1103–1116. doi:10.1109/TMC.2009.12

Sanfeliu, A., Andrade-Cetto, J., Barbosa, M., Bowden, R., Capitian, R., & Corominas, A. (2010). Decentralized sensor fusion for ubiquitous networking robotics in urban areas. *Sensors (Basel, Switzerland)*, *10*(3), 2274–2314. doi:10.3390/s100302274 PMID:22294927

Song, B., & Roy-Chowdhury, A. K. (2007). Stochastic adaptive tracking in a camera network.*IEEE Int. Conf. on Compute Vision*, 1–8. doi:10.1109/ICCV.2007.4408937

Soto, C., Song, B., & Roy-Chowdhury, A. K. (2009). Distributed multi-target tracking in a self-configuring camera network. *IEEE Conf. on Computer Vision and Pattern Recognition, CVPR'09*, 1486–1493. doi:10.1109/CVPR.2009.5206773

Thrun S. Burgard W. Fox D. (2005). *Probabilistic robotics*. MIT Press.

Zhang, W., & Cao, G. (2004). DCTC: Dynamic Convoy Tree-based Collaboration for target tracking in sensor networks. *IEEE Transactions on Wireless Communications*, *3*(5), 1689–1701. doi:10.1109/TWC.2004.833443

Chapter 15
Digital Image Steganography:
Survey, Analysis, and Application

Chitra A. Dhawale
P. R. Pote College of Engineering and Management, India

Naveen D. Jambhekar
S. S. S. K. R. Innani Mahavidyalaya, India

ABSTRACT

Digital data transmitted over the insecure communication can be prone to attacks. Intruders try various attacks to unauthorized access of the confidential information. The Steganography is such as security system that provide the protection to the images, text and other type of data digitally transferred through the data communication network. This chapter elaborates the basics of Digital Image Steganographic techniques from ancient era to digital edge, types of images used for the steganography, payload used for the steganography, various attacks and different algorithms that can provide the information security. The performance analysis of the various Digital Image Steganographic algorithms are discussed. The current applications and their necessities are discussed in this chapter.

INTRODUCTION

Digital data in the form of text, images, audio and video are transmitted over the internet by means of communication links. The confidentiality of secret data should be preserved from intruders. Steganography contains a group of methods with which different algorithms are available to embed the secret data under the cover medium such as image, without any detectable indications on the cover image. Many algorithms are designed to provide the security for the communication of data over the Internet. The good steganographic algorithm is identified by the performance of the algorithm measured with the help of the parameters such as PSNR, MSE, robustness and capacity to hide the information in the cover image. This chapter explores the steganographic methods used from many years, the methods used currently and the capabilities of steganography in future. The crucial part of the steganographic algorithms are the carrier and its payload. There are various types of carriers available for the steganographic applications.

DOI: 10.4018/978-1-5225-2053-5.ch015

Steganography is the technique that covers the confidential data under the cover medium such as image, without reflecting any clue on the cover image (Chan & Cheng, 2004). Secrete Message transmission is possible by the technique steganography with the help of entities such as a secret message, message carrier and the embedding algorithm who embed the secret message in the cover message i.e. image. The Message is the secret data which is being hidden and carrier is the entity that covers the secret message (Valandar, Ayubi & Barani, 2015). Using the image steganographic method, the secret message is covered by an image in such way that the secret message can be easily extracted as well as the cover image does not lose its visibility (Bender, Morimoto & Lu, 2010). The variations are done slightly, that do not reflect the visual changes in the image.

The mathematical techniques, available in the cryptography have some limitations and can prone to crack mathematically. The image steganography is more secure, but the processing and extraction of the secret message from the cover image need some more processing time. The good steganographic algorithms are able to hide the sensitive data under the cover medium such as image, without remaining any noticeable clue to the intruders (Sun & Liu, 2010). The strength of the steganographic algorithms is to keep the confidential information under an image such a way that, no any steganalysis method, or tool extracts the original message from the cover image without the proper stego key (Mishra, Tiwari & Yadav, 2014).

In the spatial domain, the spatial based methods carried out by the image pixel base using the techniques such as Least Significant Bit (LSB) insertion, SVD and spread spectrum methods. In the frequency based methods, the Discrete Cosine Transformation (DCT), Discrete Wavelet Transformation (DWT), Discrete Fourier Transformation (DFT) and Integer Wavelet Transformation (IWT) steganographic transformation based methods hide secret image i.e. the payload to another cover image (Verma, 2011).

Figure 1. Digital image steganographic algorithms

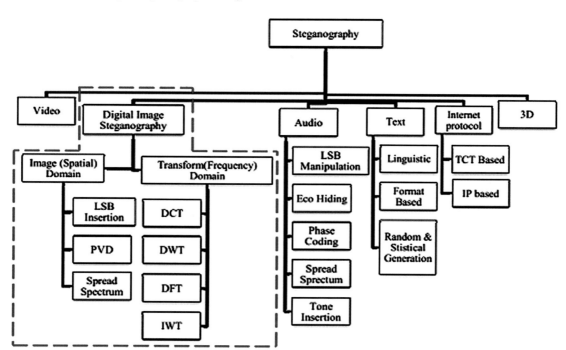

The efficiency of the above steganographic algorithms can be analyzed by comparing the cover image with the stego image. This comparison is carried out by calculating the parameters viz. Peak Signal to Noise Ratio (PSNR), Mean Squared Error (MSE) with the help of programming the code in MATLAB (Gonzalez, Woods & Eddins, 2010). Figure 1 shows the digital image steganographic algorithms.

The steganographic algorithms are classified using text, digital image, audio, video, internet protocols and 3d domain as shown in the Figure 1. This chapter explores the Digital Image Steganographic Algorithms by evaluating using image (spatial) domain and transform (frequency) domain. The spatial or image domain consists of the LSB insertion, PVD and spread spectrum methods while the transform or frequency domain consists of DWT, DCT, DFT and IWT methods which are discussed below (Barni, 2001).

Effective and efficient steganographic algorithms are those who hide the sensitive data under the cover medium such as image, without leaving any detectable clue to the intruders. The strength of the steganographic algorithms is to keep the confidential information under an image such a way that, no any steganalysis method, or tool extracts the original secret message from the cover image without finding right stegokey (Denemark, Boroumand, &Fridrich, 2016). Stegokey is used to merge the secret data under the cover image. The stegokey is unique and used for encryption and same for decryption. This stegokey must be preserved by both sender and receiver (Khan et al., 2014). Recently, many researchers have worked on steganography and written the benefits of the different steganographic algorithms.

Steganography is a group of methods used for securing the secret information under the cover medium such as an image using some translation rules. Here the translation rules merge the selected text into the image, that makes the simple text secure and no one can easily plunder the secret information.

Because of steganography, two communication sides transfer the confidential data secretly where attacker unknown the secret message covered in other medium such as cover images. Steganography is the technique in which the original message which is being transmitted over the unsecured communication channel will be masked into the cover medium such as image, audio or video such that any human being, the device or the specialized software cannot predict the original hidden data. In steganography, the secret message transmission is possible using two entities such as the original message to be transmitted and the message carrier used to cover the transmitting message (Chakrabarti & Samanta, 2015).

Using the digital image steganographic method, the secret message is covered by an image in such way that the original message cannot predict by the intruders. The variations are done slightly that do not reflect the visual changes on the cover image.

STEGANOGRAPHY ON THE EARLY AGE

The Steganography suggest itself as a Greek word made from steganos - covered or secret and graphy - writing or drawing. The first steganographic technique was coming in the history of ancient Greece around 440 B.C. The Greek swayer Histaeus use the steganography in a new way to hide secret messages by shaving messenger's head, waiting to grow hair again, then again shaving the head and waiting to grow hair, so that the it will hide the secret message under long hair. On the other side, recipient finding the secret message by trimming hairs of messenger. The recipient was also using the same method to reply.

During 480 B.C. the next steganographic technique was evolved. Demerstus use the technique of writing the secret message to the Spartans that warns high intrusions by Xerxes. The secret message was put on the surface of wooden wax tablet and again covered with fresh wax. This tablet was delivered to the destination place with its hidden secret message.

Johannes Trithemius (1 February 1462 – 13 December 1516) is a first person who was the German Renaissance humanist, advisor to Emperors in Germany, the founder of scientific bibliography and one of the founders of modern cryptography also wrote the "Steganographia". He is a first author of the first printed work on cryptography, the Polygraphia.

With the publication of Auguste Kerchoffs', cryptography militaire, although this work was mostly about cryptography, but describes the principal that was helpful in designing the new steganographic system, known as Kerchoff's principal regarding the steganography. During both world wars, steganography helped to hide the confidential message using invisible ink which would gleam by keeping on the flame.

DIGITAL STEGANOGRAPHY TODAY

Thereafter the ancient steganographic techniques, many researchers discovered the steganographic algorithms that provide the high security features to secure the digital document. Intruders also develop methods that evacuate the safe message known as the steganalysis. Moreover, the ultimate use of the internet for the communication of the digital document was coming into existence in the recent days. Due to intensive use of internet- an unsecured communication channel, the sensitive data is not safe today.

The mathematical techniques that available in the cryptography, have some limitations and can prone to crack mathematically by anyone with little efforts. The digital image steganography is more secure, but the processing and extraction of the secret message from the cover image required some processing time. However, in the present digital era, by using the advanced computer systems with massive processing speed, this task is under control. Today the secret sharing over the internet is possible by applying the steganography, by carrying the following process effectively.

- Confidential data to be transmitted firmly.
- Cover image selection to hold secret message.
- Selection and implementation of the method that merge the secret message in the cover medium.
- The key that is used for the conversion method and also to uncover the secret message.

To secure the text using the steganographic techniques, the original text message is scrambled, shuffled or mixed with other text data with the help of mathematical function. Only the legal receiver can reverse this process to extract the message. The digital image steganographic technique hides the secret information under the cover image. In audio steganography, the multimedia such as text, image or sound can be put in the other cover audio signals that do not give the impression of this mixing (Tayel, Gamal & Shawky, 2016). This is similar for the video steganography, where two videos intermix with each other, or any carrier date like text, image or audio signals are merged with the covert video.

The algorithms used today to secure the digital document, commonly follows the steganographic rules as the one shown in the following figures.

Figure 2 and Figure 3 show the steganographic system.

Figure 2. Sender side steganographic system

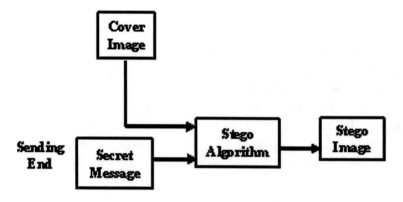

Figure 3. Receiving side steganographic system

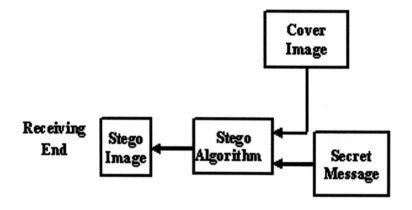

BASICS OF STEGANOGRAPHY

Terminology

1. **Digital Image:** A digital image is a series of pixels having different intensity can be represented by the hexadecimal value for every pixel. The image can be monochrome or colour image. The image can be 8, 16 or 32 bit image and can be represented by the pixel's intensity at different position where the image I is a represented by the function $I(x, y)$ where x and y are the address of pixel.
2. **Cover Image:** It is a carrier image which keep the secret image or message during transmission. The cover image can be large enough to keep the secret message or image.
3. **Secret Key:** The secret key can be optional. The work of secret key is to provide a special function even if the use of the specific steganographic algorithm.
4. **Payload:** The secret message or image to be hidden into the cover image.
5. **Stego Image:** The image that keep the secret image or message and used for the the actual transmission. The receiver end extract the confidential data from this stego image.
6. **Steganographic Algorithm:** The selected method that hide the payload in the cover image.

Figure 4. Steganographic Performance Evaluation Criterions

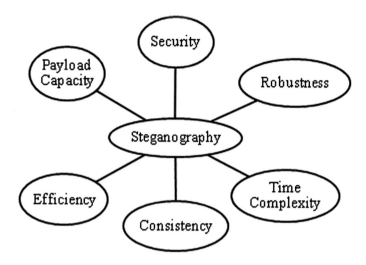

Steganographic Performance Evaluation Criterions

The use of steganographic functions for the secure data transmission depends on some criterions that define the efficiency of specific algorithm. These criterions are payload capacity, security, robustness, time complexity, consistency and efficiency (Cheddad, Condell, Curran & McKevitt, 2010). Figure 4 depicts the evaluation criterions.

Payload Capacity

The number of bits to be hidden inside the cover image. The capacity of payload i.e. the secret message or image is smaller than the cover image. Therefore, it can be easily hidden inside the cover image without disturbing the visual quality of the cover image.

Security

The secret image or message should not revealed in the cover image and preserve the security. Any digital image steganographic algorithm must accurate in its security assistance, otherwise it helps to the intruders to break the confidentiality. The security of the algorithms is measured through the algorithmic complexity.

Robustness

The secret message or image remain original and extracted accurately even if the stego image goes through worst transmission conditions, cropping, compression, rotation and filtering. The robustness of the steganographic algorithm must maintain even if the use of different size of payload with different types of cover images.

Time Complexity

The time complexity plays a crucial role during the stego message transmission. Large time complexity can generates the bigger message. The transmission can be affected by the bandwidth of the network. However, the large time required to embed the secret data inside the cover image can be due to the big size of the payload and the high security of the steganographic algorithm.

Consistency

The steganographic algorithm used at both the ends of the transmission must be consistent in it working. The data embedded at one end must be extracted accurately that proves the consistency of the steganographic algorithm.

Efficiency

How much size of payload embedded in the cover object is the efficiency of the steganographic algorithm. Also, the quality of cover image that keep the secret message or image is the efficiency of the steganographic algorithm.

Steganographic Data Hiding Capacity and Cover Selection

The primary goal of image steganography is to embed the secret image in another image known as a cover image. The selection of the cover is completely dependent on the size of the secret image. The cover image is large enough to hold the secret image (Fang, Liu, Gu & Tang, 2011). To select the cover image, the distortion measure along with a threshold value has been analyzed. Before embedding an image, the quality of the cover image is tested against the measures such as MSE, PSNR results into the efficient distortion less embedding which tends to the stego image undetectable by any steganalyzer. The steganalyzer verify the stego image for the micro changes and distortion in the image to guess and extract the secret message or image from the stego image (Provos & Honeyman, 2003). The cover image selection is the issue of sender and receiver who are engaged in the secret communication using the digital image steganographic algorithms. The secrecy of the secret communication is depends on the key image i.e. the cover image keep secretly. This secret cover image must be transferred from sender to receiver secretly without giving any indication to the intruders.

Steganographic data hiding capacity refers to the maximum amount of data that can be embedded into a cover-medium. It also essentially required to be reliably extracted from the stego-object in terms of perceptual perfection, undetectability and robustness. As compared to other data hiding system, the steganographic system must posses the feature of undetectability and perceptual quality that can be possible through the effective implementation statistical properties for the cover medium.

Before moving to the steganographic techniques, let us first understand about the digital image formats. For the steganographic applications, the BMP- Bitmap, GIF- Graphics Interchange Format, JPEG- Joint Photographic Experts Group image formats are widely used today. For the steganographic applications monochrome and color images can be used (Srinivasan, Arunkumar & Rajesh, 2015). The time complexity of the color image can be calculated as

$$C = \left(C_r + C_g + C_b\right) / 3 \tag{1}$$

where C is the complexity and r, g & b are the intensity of the pixels available for complexity analysis.

- **BMP: Bitmap** - Most operating systems support bitmap images with 1, 4, 8, 16, 24 and 32 bits per pixel. Here, the concentration is largely on the monochrome i.e. grayscale images and 24 bit color images because of the requirement of processing power, storage and transmission capacity of the network.
- **GIF: Graphics Interchange Format** - GIF is CompuServe's standard that defines the generalized color raster images. This Graphics Interchange Format permits high-quality, high-resolution graphics compatible for a variety of graphics hardware and is proposed as an exchange and display mechanism. It uses up to 256 colors from the 24-bit RGB color space, and stores both the palette and the pixel matrix.
- **JPEG: Joint Photographic Experts Group** - It is the most commonly used standard for lossy and lossless compression till today. It is very efficient photographic image technique and can make an excellent quality image even if it is a lossy compression technique. Because of the lossy compressed nature, some visual quality is lost in the compression process. With the lossless compression, the quality is great. The images used for the steganography are the 8-bit grayscale images as well as color images.

The steganographic methods used today are categories into image domain, transform domain, spread spectrum domain and statistical technique.

DIGITAL IMAGE STEGANOGRAPHIC ALGORITHMS

Secret data hiding through the digital image steganographic techniques can be preformed through the spatial and frequency domain as depicted using figure 3.

A steganographic security system can be represented as

$$Y = f\left(C, M, K\right) \tag{2}$$

where

Y is the stego object,
C is the cover medium,
M is the message embedded in the C,
K is the security key, and
f is the steganographic function.

Here, the security key K is optional and not required during some of the steganographic algorithms. The digital image steganographic algorithms are discussed below.

Image or Spatial Domain

The image or spatial domain is the field through which the embedding of secret message can be performed by using working with the pixel of the image, by embedding the secret image in the pixels intensity. The techniques covered under the spatial domain are

Least Significant Bit Insertion (LSB)

The LSB insertion technique implants secret information in a cover image by changing the intensity of Least Significant Bits (Ker, 2005). Image's every Least Significant Bits are somewhat randomly noisy and when replaced or modified, do not affect the visual quality of the image. The pixel value of the digital image can be represented as

$$P_i = \sum_{n=0}^{7} b_n X 2^n \tag{3}$$

where P represents the pixels at a specific position and b_n represents the number of bits in each pixels. The above equation represents the pixels value using 8-bits of binary data.

Using the LSB substitution technique, the secret message in binary format is first permuted and then substituted in the image in place of every bytes least significant bit place, bit by bit fashion (Chan & Cheng, 2004). The bit insertion depends on the bits available in the secret message. If the message is bigger, then the cover image should be enough bigger to hide it (Kong, 2009). The LSB substitution is suitable for BMP images where they are lossless. Digital images are commonly available in 8 bits, 16 bits and 24 bits. The embedding can be possible for one, two and three bits for each image pixel for the 8 bits, 16 bits and 24 bits images respectively. The embedding positions are the LSB for each byte. Some or every byte of cover image can hide one bit of secret image information (Singh & Singh 2015).

The following is the procedure to embed a secret message under a digital image.

LSB Substitution Algorithm

Step 1: Scan the secret message (text or image) along with the cover image.
Step 2: Convert secret message to binary data.
Step 3: Permute the binary bits of secret message
Step 4: Calculate LSB position of every byte of the cover image.
Step 5: Substitute every bit of cover image to the LSB of the cover image bit by bit.
Step 6: Save the image after LSB substitution and is the Stego image.

The following procedure is used to extract the secret message hidden under the digital image

LSB Algorithm to Read the Secret Message from Stego Image

Step 1: Scan the Stego image.
Step 2: Estimate LSB position of each byte of Stego image.

Step 3: Extract each LSB bit and convert each 8 bits into a character.

The hiding and extracting of the secret data in the least significant bit position of the cover image is carried out by converting the secret data to pixels data. The hiding and unhiding principal is depicted below.

The secret message embedding is carried with the help of following procedure.

The secret and cover image bit position is calculated by Secret(i,j) and Cover(i,j).

Three possibilities are calculated as

if LSB(Cover(i,j)) = MSB(Secret(i,j)) then no change and continue to next position

if LSB(Cover(i,j)) >MSB(Secret(i,j)) then LSB(Stego(i,j)) = LSB(Cover(i,j)) -   1

if LSB(Cover(i,j)) <MSB(Secret(i,j)) then LSB(Stego(i,j)) = LSB(Cover(i,j)) + 1

Here the new image after embedding is the stego image similar with the cover image. The similarity is because of the change in the LSB of the cover image, which cannot affect the visual perception of the cover image. Here Stego(i,j) is the stego image.

The process of extracting secret image bits from stegoimage is straightforward.

if LSB(Stego(i,j)) = 0 then MSB(Secret(i,j)) = 0

if LSB(C(i,j)) = 1 then MSB(S(i,j)) = 1

For this embedding process, the cover image large enough to hold the secret image's all bits.

Pixel-Value Differencing (PVD)

Secret data hiding in digital images with the help of the pixel-value differencing (PVD) method gives higher embedding capacity without reflecting any clue on the cover image. The pixel-value differencing (PVD) method was originally developed for hiding the secret messages into 8 bits grayscale images (Wu & Tsai, 2003). Even though the large amount of secret information is embedded, the PVD produces high definition stego image. PVD partitions the cover image into non overlapping blocks with two consecutive non overlapping pixels. The embedding of secret message get started using PVD with upper left corner of the cover image that reads the cover image in a zigzag fashion as shown in Figure 5. Each two-pixel blocks are used to maintain the smoothness properties of the cover image. There is a difference in the edge and the block pixels. If the difference is larger, more bits can be embedded in the cover image pixels pair. From each block the difference value d_i is calculated by subtracting P_i from P_i+1. The difference values are in between -255 to 255.

Following algorithm describes the PVD embedding process.

Figure 5. Blocks of images with zigzag scan

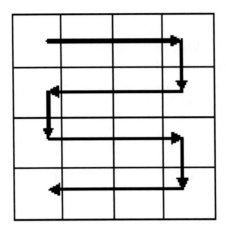

PVD Algorithm

Step 1: Difference between two consecutive pixels p_i and p_{i+1} is calculated as $di = |p_i - p_{i+1}|$

Step 2: Determine the number of bits to be embedded d_i in the quantization range table.

Step 3: Read secret bits s_1 from secret stream and convert into decimal value b

Step 4: Calculate the new difference $s_i = l_i + b$ where l_i is the lower bound of the range table and d_i and s_i must be in the range

Step 5: The new pixel value can be determined as

$$\left(s_i, s_{i+1}\right) = \left(p_i + \left\lceil\frac{\left||s_i - d_i|\right|}{2}\right\rceil, p_{i+1} + \left\lfloor\frac{\left||s_i - d_i|\right|}{2}\right\rfloor\right), \text{if } p_i \geq p_{i+1}, s_i \succ d_i \left(s_i, s_{i+1}\right),$$

$$\left(s_i, s_{i+1}\right) = \left(p_i + \left\lceil\frac{\left||s_i - d_i|\right|}{2}\right\rceil, p_{i+1} + \left\lfloor\frac{\left||s_i - d_i|\right|}{2}\right\rfloor\right), \text{if } p_i \prec p_{i+1}, s_i \succ d_i,$$

$$\left(s_i, s_{i+1}\right) = \left(p_i + \left\lceil\frac{\left||s_i - d_i|\right|}{2}\right\rceil, p_{i+1} + \left\lfloor\frac{\left||s_i - d_i|\right|}{2}\right\rfloor\right), \text{if } p_i \geq p_{i+1}, s_i \leq d_i$$

$$\left(s_i, s_{i+1}\right) = \left(p_i + \left\lceil\frac{\left||s_i - d_i|\right|}{2}\right\rceil, p_{i+1} + \left\lfloor\frac{\left||s_i - d_i|\right|}{2}\right\rfloor\right), \text{if } p_i \prec p_{i+1}, s_i \leq d_i$$

Step 6: Repeating steps 1 to 5 for complete embedding of secret bits.

Spread Spectrum

In spread spectrum techniques, data hidden inside the cover image is spread completely making undetectable. Using this technique, the message is planted in noise and then mixed with the cover image producing the stego image. The cover image has powerful signals than the embedded signals. Therefore, it is difficult to notice by the human eye or even by the computer system (Marvel, Boncelet Jr. & Retter, 1999).

Here the secret data are dispersed throughout the cover image, without modifying the statistical parameters of the cover image. Most steganographic applications now use the spread spectrum techniques because of its extreme mathematical and complex approach.

Using spread spectrum method, secret information is distributed around the cover image therefore it is difficult to locate the secrets. Using spread spectrum method, the data from secret image is planted in noise and then mixed with the cover image to generate the stego image. Here the secret image data are embedded having lower signal than the cover image, the secret image is not noticeable by human as well as steganalyzer. The Spread spectrum technique is statistically strong and proves the robustness practically, even if the secret data is scattered all over the cover image, without modifying the statistical properties.

Transform Domain Techniques

Transform domain provides the robust watermarking feature because of its data embedding technique and greater capacity. Transforms domain techniques include the discrete cosine transform (DCT), discrete Fourier transform (DFT) and discrete wavelet transform (DWT). When data inserted or embed using the transform techniques, the secret data can stay in the robust zones, scattered across the cover image and provides safety against any signal processing attack.

The transform or frequency domain methods hide a secret message in the significant parts of the cover image which makes the stego image more robust. In this, the image is transformed from pixel domain to frequency domain. The following methods are the frequency domain techniques used in the digital image steganography.

Discrete Cosine Transformation

Digital steganography for images can be done with the help of two techniques- spatial domain and transform domain. The DCT is an orthogonal transformation for the digital and signal processing (Hashad, Madani & Wahdan, 2005). During 2-dimensional DCT, the image is divided into 8 x 8 blocks and then each block is transformed to the DCT domain. The different equal size band of the image is selected such as low, middle and high frequency bands (Figure 6).

DCT coefficients are organized frequency wise by zigzag fashion so that the frequency positions 0 to 63 can be acquired.

Thereafter, it is easier to embed secret image to the selected frequency band(s). The visual part is kept under the low frequency. The low and high frequency bands are targeted for the compression and noise removal (Sakr, Ibrahem, Abdullkader & Amin, 2012). Therefore, the middle frequency bands are more suitable for embedding because the secret image resides in without any loss and it cannot affect the visibility of the image. JPEG compression is accomplished with the help of DCT coefficients. It divide the cover image into portions. It translates cover image from the image domain to the frequency domain.

The following equation shows the 2-dimensional DCT

Figure 6. Bands of an image

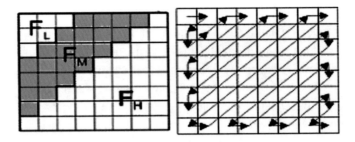

$$F\left(u,v\right) = \frac{c(u)c(v)}{4}\sum_{i=0}^{7}\sum_{i=0}^{7}\cos\left[\frac{\left(2i+1\right)\mu\pi}{16}\right]\cos\left[\frac{\left(2j+1\right)\mu\pi}{16}\right]f\left(i,j\right) \tag{4}$$

$$c\left(e\right) = \begin{cases} \dfrac{1}{\sqrt{2}} & \text{if} \quad e = 0 \\ 1 & \quad e \neq 0 \end{cases} \tag{5}$$

Here, $f(u,v)$ and $f(i,j)$ present a DCT coefficient at the (u,v) coordinate and a pixel value at the (i,j) coordinate, respectively. $f(0,0)$ is the DC component, which corresponds to an average intensity value of each block in the spatial domain. $f(u,v)$ is the AC component, in which u $\neq$0 and v $\neq$0.

Input: Cover and secret image
Output: Stego image embedded with secret image

```
while end of secret image file do
        read adjacent f(i,j) of cover image
        if f(i,j) = 0 and f(i,j)= 1 then
            get adjacent LSB of secret image
            replace DCT LSB with secret image bit
        end if
        insert f(i,j)  into stego image
end while
```

Discrete Wavelet Transformation

The Discrete Wavelet transform (DWT) widely used in the signal processing, watermarking and image compression. The DWT decompose an image mathematically into a set of functions, known as wavelets (Demirel & Jafari, 2011). Wavelets are produced by converting and expanding of an existing original wavelet. The data are represented using high pass and low pass coefficients. The DWT divides the signal into low and high frequency bands. The low frequency band contains coarse information of the signal while the edge components are represented by the high frequency band. The high frequency band is suitable for embedding because these regions are unnoticeable to the human eye on their edges. In two dimensional object, The DWT in vertical direction followed by horizontal direction is performed (Kumar & Kumar, 2010). At the end of the first level decomposition, the four sub-bands: LL1, LH1, HL1, and HH1 are generated. The previous level decomposed LL band is used as input for the next successive decomposition (Shejul & Kulkarni, 2010). To carry DWT for second level, The DWT on LL1 & for third Level decomposition is performed and the DWT on LL2 is applied & finally 4 sub band of third level that are LL3, LH3, HH3, HL3 is collected.

Discrete Fourier Transformation

The embedding of a secret message into cover image is done by converting the cover image from the spatial domain to frequency domain. Then divide the image into equal blocks 2x2 pixels. Then the secrete message data get hidden in the LSB part of the real image using the DFT method. Thereafter the conversion is done from frequency domain to spatial domain to generate the stego image. The frequency domain works in the analog nature of the image. The image is the collection of pixels, while the DFT converts image into the analog signals.

Integer Wavelet Transformation

Integer Wavelet Transformation (see Figure 7) is a frequency domain method efficiently produces the lossless compression. It represents the image coefficient into an integer number. The IWT uses a complete technique of DWT but maps integers to integers in the output (Ghasemi, Shanbehzadeh & ZahirAzami, 2011). In discrete wavelet transform, the wavelet filter has the floating point coefficients. When the secret

Figure 7. Three level discrete wavelet decomposition

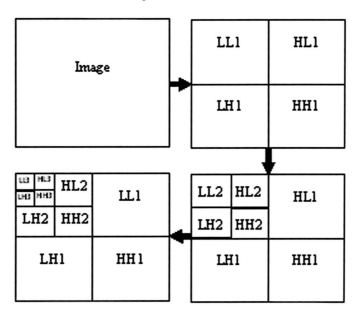

information is stored, then data loss occurs because of the truncation of integer value due to floating point coefficient (Hemalatha, Acharya, Renuka & Kamath, 2012). This loss cannot persist in the Integer Wavelet Transformation, because it maps integer to integer in the output.

Statistical Method

Encrypt valuable information by applying specific statistical functions on a cover image and performing the variable possible test to extract the hidden information.

Patchwork

This uses statistical method to create a redundant pattern of secret data scattered over the cover image. In this, two different sections of cover image selected, where the secret message will completed embedded on two different patches. The implementation is redundant because, if any patch get destroyed, then the secret message can be easily available from other patch. But if the message is bigger, then only the single patch is possible depending on the size of the cover image. All this procedure is done on the grayscale image, because of the time, speed and space complexity of the algorithms and processors. This patch work is done by increasing the pixel intensity of one patch and decreasing the pixel intensity of another patch, also known as masking approach. Here the change is not noticeable and do not affect the quality of the cover image.

Because of its robustness, it is advantageous over the malicious manipulation of images. Because of the secret data distributed over various parts of the cover image and if the data is lost due to cropping of modification in the image, then it can be accessed through other part because of the multiple copies embedded as patches. Patchwork is beneficial to transfer highly sensitive small amount data.

The steganographic system is efficient enough to secure the hidden messages, but many researchers are working on the Steganalysis that accept the challenge to break the security to extract the secrets.

PERFORMANCE PARAMETERS

The performance of the algorithms used for the embedding of secret image on the cover, is measured by analyzing the cover image with the stego image (Kumar & Kumar, 2010). The analysis can be effictively done by finding the parameters such as Peak Signal to Noise Ratio (PSNR), Mean Squared Error (MSE), Normalized Cross-Correlation (NCC), Average Difference (AD), Structural Content (SC), Maximum Difference (MD) and Normalized Absolute Error (NAE) (Joseph & Vishnukumar, 2015). The following parameters are helpful to analyze the cover image with stego image and the difference will be calculated mathematically.

Peak Signal to Noise Ratio (PSNR)

The Peak Signal-to-noise ratio (PSNR) is the ratio between the peak signal and alteration noise signals that affects the accuracy of its presentation of stego image. PSNR is described using logarithmic decibel scale. The lower the PSNR rate indicates the low quality and compression, where higher the PSNR, the better the quality of the compressed or reconstructed image (Yoo & Ahn, 2012). The PSNR is calculated by following formula

$$PSNR = \log_{10}\left(\frac{MAX_i^2}{MSE}\right) \qquad (6)$$

The PSNR is calculated via Mean Squared Error (MSE). Here, MAX_I is the highest existing pixel value. If pixels are defined by a 8 bit value, then it becomes 255.

Mean Squared Ratio (MSE)

The MSE is the successively incremented squared error between the stego and the cover image. The Mean Squared Error (MSE) is used to quantify the difference between values implied by an estimator and the true values of the quantity being estimated. It is calculated by following formula

$$MSE = \frac{1}{mn}\sum_{i=0}^{m-1}\sum_{j=0}^{n-1}\left[l(i,j) - k(i,j)\right]^2 \qquad (7)$$

where $I(i,j)$ am the original image and $K(i,j)$ is the stego image. The m & n are the dimensions of the images. If MSE is low, then errors are less having high quality.

Normalized Cross-Correlation (NCC)

Normalized cross correlation is used to match template, i.e. it is a process used to find the relevancy of the structure or object in an image. Correlation is widely used as an effective similarity measure in matching tasks. This function returns the normalized cross correlation between the calling data series and the argument, the input data series. It is calculated by following formula:

$$NCC = \frac{\sum_{j=1}^{m}\sum_{k=1}^{n}\left(l(x,y) - l'(x,y)\right)^2}{\sum_{j=1}^{m}\sum_{k=1}^{n}\left(l(x,y)\right)^2} \qquad (8)$$

Average Difference (AD)

It is an average difference between the two selected pixel values of cover and stego image. If it is lower, both images match the correctness and without noise. It is calculated by following formula

$$AD = \frac{1}{M*N}\sum_{i=1}^{m}\sum_{j=1}^{n}\left(S(i,j) - C(i,j)\right) \qquad (9)$$

Structural Content (SC)

The structural correlation or Content measures the similarity between the cover and stego image by analyzing the small areas having nearest low level structural information. The similarity is measured by counting the number of similar regions. If similar regions are large, then both images are more similar. The large value indicates the low quality and small value indicates the high quality. It is calculated by following formula:

$$SC = \frac{\sum_{j=1}^{M} X_i \sum_{k=1}^{N} l(x,y)^2}{\sum_{j=1}^{M} X_i \sum_{k=1}^{N} l'(x,y)^2} \tag{10}$$

Maximum Difference (MD)

It is used to measure the cover and stego images and the compressed quality of stego image. Large value indicates poor quality. It is calculated by following formula

$$MD = \max\left(\left|x_j,k - x_j,k\right|\right) \tag{11}$$

Normalized Absolute Error (NAE)

It is the statistical difference between the cover and stego image. The large value indicates the low quality and small value indicates the high quality. It is calculated by following formula

$$NAE = \frac{\sum_{j=1}^{M}\sum_{k=1}^{N}\left|X_j,k - X_j,k\right|}{\sum_{j=1}^{M}\sum_{k=1}^{N}\left|X_j,k\right|} \tag{12}$$

ATTACKS ON STEGANOGRAPHY: A STEGANALYSIS

Steganalysis is the technique with which, anyone can extract the secret message from the cover image. But the requirement is only the right algorithms or method to unhide the information from the cover image. Many researchers work on the steganalysis to break the hidden system of steganography and extract the secret message (Wang & Wang, 2004). The attacks on the steganography in the form of steganalysis are discussed below.

- **Stego-Only Attack:** Only the Stego image is analyzed and feasible methods are applied to discover the secret signals.

- **Known Cover Attack:** Both cover and stego object is compared and pattern differences are detected suck as the secret image and the image with the hidden information are selected for comparison.
- **Known Message Attack:** The sample stego image with known secret hidden message is analyzed. The similar technique will be applied to extract the hidden message from other stego images.
- **Chosen Stego Attack:** The hidden information is known with respect to the stego object and the steganographic method (tools) to extract it.
- **Chosen Message Attack:** The stego object is generated from the chosen message using the steganographic tools. This type of attack checks the matching patterns of the newly generated stego object and can determine the particular steganographic algorithm or tools used.
- **Known Stego Attack:** The verification of actual and stego object is done using known stegonography algorithms or tool.

APPLICATIONS OF STEGANOGRAPHY

Security plays a vital role for every individual who resides and communicate digitally over the insecure communication channels. Steganography plays a crucial role in securing the confidential information. Some of the applications needs high security while some needs moderate. Depending on the security need, capacity and type of data to be hidden, the type of steganographic algorithms are available. Some of the applications that require steganographic security are

- **Military:** Early years in the military data security suffers from the confidential data transmission. The transmission was possible through the paper courier medium. With the advanced technology, the transmission is done through the electronic medium. The hacking of confidential messages by the intruders are done frequently. The steganography gives the assurance to transmit images, text, audio and video security by keeping them in the competent cover medium without reflecting any clue to intruder. Military data can be hidden into the cover medium before transmission to the destination.
- **Business:** Business data such as online money transaction between authorized parties, stock market data and personnel information can be protected by the steganographic means. This is a secure medium where the legal party get the data without revealing to the intruder.
- **Government:** Government confidential information such as departmental files, pan cards, government resolutions and orders can be protected by the steganography.
- **Medical:** The medical records such as DNA reports, patients pathological reports can be protected by the steganography therefore intruder cannot tamper it.
- **Academic and Research:** Most of the research and valuable academic record are completely online can be prone to attack. The steganography protect the confidential research and their design interested to intruder.
- **Intellectual Property:** The patents, logos, copyrights and other intellectual properties valuable for any nation can be efficiently protected by various steganographic algorithms such as digital watermarking.

CONCLUSION

The steganography itself is a secret for many hundred years. The appearance and use it in secret writing or hiding is different. The secrets are something that baffles understanding and cannot be explained is in existence because of the steganography. In the current era, efficient algorithms are designed that helps to keep the intruders away from the secret information hidden in the cover image. Many steganalysis methods are developed to extract the hidden information. The effectiveness of the steganographic algorithms will be increased by Security Enhancement discuss in this paper such as efficient embedding, reducing distortion, suitable cover selection. Therefore, no any type of steganographic attack breaks the security mechanism implemented by the advanced steganographic algorithm.

This chapter elaborates different digital image steganographic technique along with the type of images required. The payload capacity and the cover image richness have been discussed. The performance parameters used for the analysis of images before and after the steganographic activity have been discussed. Various digital image steganographic applications have been discussed in terms of the security and confidentiality.

REFERENCES

Chan, C.-K., & Cheng, L. M. (2004). Hiding data in images by simple LSB substitution. *Pattern Recognition Society, 37*(3), 469–474. doi:10.1016/j.patcog.2003.08.007

Barni, M. (2001). Improved Wavelet-Based Watermarking Through Pixel-Wise Masking. *IEEE Transactions on Image Processing, 10*(5), 783-791.

Kong, F.-H. (2009). Image Retrieval using both Color and Texture Features. *Proceedings of the Eighth International Conference on Machine Learning and Cybernetics, 4,* 12-15. doi:10.1109/ICMLC.2009.5212186

Demirel, H., & Jafari, G. A. (2011). Image Resolution Enhancement by Using Discrete and Stationary Wavelet Decomposition. *IEEE Transactions on Image Processing, 20*(5), 1458–1460. doi:10.1109/TIP.2010.2087767 PMID:20959267

Fang, J., Liu, Gu, W., & Tang, Y. (2011). A method to improve the image enhancement result based on image fusion. *International Conference on Multimedia Technology (ICMT)*, 55-58.

Provos, N., & Honeyman, P. (2003). Hide and seek: An introduction to steganography. *Security & Privacy. IEEE Journals & Magazines, 1*(3), 32–44.

Bender, D. G., Morimoto, N., & Lu, A. (2010). Techniques for data hiding. *IBM Systems Journal, 35*(3 & 4), 313–336.

Ker, A. D. (2005). Steganalysis of LSB matching in grayscale images. *Signal Processing Letters, IEEE, 12*(6), 441–444. doi:10.1109/LSP.2005.847889

Cheddad, A., Condell, J., Curran, K., & McKevitt, P. (2010). Digital image steganography: Survey and analysis of current methods. *Signal Processing, 90*(3), 727–752. doi:10.1016/j.sigpro.2009.08.010

Yoo, J.-C., & Ahn, C. W. (2012). Image matching using peak signal-to-noise ratio-based occlusion detection. *IEEE. Image Processing, IET, 6*(5), 483–495. doi:10.1049/iet-ipr.2011.0025

Gonzalez, R. C., Woods, R. E., & Eddins, S. L. (2010). *Digital Image Processing Using Matlab* (2nd ed.). New Delhi: Tata McGraw Hill Education Private Limited.

Wu, D.-C., & Tsai, W.-H. (2003). *A steganographic method for images by pixel-value differencing. In Pattern Recognition Letters 24* (pp. 1613–1626). Elsevier.

Wang, H., & Wang, S. (2004). Cyber warfare: Steganography vs. Steganalysis. *Communications of the ACM, 47*(10).

Marvel, L. M., Boncelet, C. G. Jr, & Retter, C. (1999). Spread Spectrum Steganography. *IEEE Transactions on Image Processing, 8*(8).

Chan, C. K., & Cheng, L. (2004). Hiding data in images by simple LSB substitution. *Pattern Recognition Society, 37*(3), 469–474.

Hashad, A. I., Madani, A. S., & Wahdan, A. E. M. A. (2005). A robust steganography technique using discrete cosine transform insertion. *Enabling Technologies for the New Knowledge Society: ITI 3rd International Conference on Information and Communications Technology,* 255-264.

Sakr, A. S., Ibrahem, H. M., Abdullkader, H. M., & Amin, M. (2012). A steganographic method based on DCT and new quantization technique.*22nd International Conference on Computer Theory and Applications (ICCTA),* 187-191. doi:10.1109/ICCTA.2012.6523567

Kumar, V., & Kumar, D. (2010). Performance evaluation of DWT based image steganography. *IEEE 2nd International Advance Computing Conference (IACC),* 223-228.

Shejul, A. A., & Kulkarni, U. L. (2010). A DWT Based Approach for Steganography using Biometrics.*International Conference on Data Storage and Data Engineering (DSDE),* 39-43. doi:10.1109/DSDE.2010.10

Ghasemi, E., Shanbehzadeh, J., & ZahirAzami, B. (2011). A steganographic method based on Integer Wavelet Transform and Genetic Algorithm. *International Conference on Communications and Signal Processing (ICCSP),* 42-45. doi:10.1109/ICCSP.2011.5739395

Hemalatha, S., Acharya, U. D., Renuka, A., & Kamath, P. R. (2012). A secure image steganography technique using Integer Wavelet Transform.*World Congress on Information and Communication Technologies (WICT),* 755-758. doi:10.1109/WICT.2012.6409175

Sun, F., & Liu (2010). Selecting Cover for Image Steganography by Correlation Coefficient.*Second International Workshop on Education Technology and Computer Science (ETCS),* 2, 159-162. doi:10.1109/ETCS.2010.33

Mishra, M., Tiwari, G., & Yadav, A. K. (2014). Secret Communication using public key steganography. *IEEE International Conference on Recent Advances and Innovations in Engineering (ICRAIE-2014),* 1-5.

Verma, N. (2011). Review of Steganographic Techniques.*International Conference and Workshop on Emerging Trends in Technology (ICWET–TCET),* 990-993. doi:10.1145/1980022.1980237

Srinivasan, B., Arunkumar, S., & Rajesh, K. (2015). A Novel Approach for Color Image Steganography Using NUBASI and Randomized. *Secret Sharing Algorithm. Indian Journal of Science and Technology, 8*(S7), 228–235. doi:10.17485/ijst/2015/v8iS7/64275

Khan, A. S., Fisal, N., Bakar, Z. A., Salawu, N., Maqbool, W., Ullah, R., & Safdar, H. (2014). Secure Authentication and Key Management Protocols for Mobile Multihop WiMAX Networks. *Indian Journal of Science and Technology, 7*(3), 282–295.

Chakrabarti, S., & Samanta, D. (2015). A novel approach to Digital Image Steganography of key-based encrypted text.*IEEEInternational Conference on Electrical, Electronics, Signals, Communication and Optimization (EESCO)*, 1-6. doi:10.1109/EESCO.2015.7254009

Singh, A., & Singh, H. (2015). An improved LSB based image steganography technique for RGB images. *IEEE International Conference on Electrical, Computer and Communication Technologies (ICECCT)*, 1-4. doi:10.1109/ICECCT.2015.7226122

Valandar, M. Y., Ayubi, P., & Barani, M. J. (2015). High secure digital image steganography based on 3D chaotic map.*7th Conference on Information and Knowledge Technology (IKT)*, 1-6. doi:10.1109/IKT.2015.7288810

Denemark, T. D., Boroumand, M., & Fridrich, J. (2016). Steganalysis Features for Content-Adaptive JPEG Steganography. IEEE Transactions on Information Forensics and Security, 11(8), 1736-1746.

Tayel, M., Gamal, A., & Shawky, H. (2016). A proposed implementation method of an audio steganography technique.*18th International Conference on Advanced Communication Technology (ICACT)*.

Joseph, P., & Vishnukumar, S. (2015). A study on steganographic techniques.*Global Conference on Communication Technologies (GCCT), 206-210.* doi:10.1109/GCCT.2015.7342653

APPENDIX: QUESTIONS AND ANSWERS

Q1: What is Steganography?

Ans. Steganographic system contains a group of methods with which different algorithms are available to embed the secret data under the cover medium such as image, without any detectable indications on the cover image. The steganography is a way to hide any type of digital object such as image, audio, video, text to the digital cover object.

Q2: What is digital image steganography?

Ans. Digital image Steganography is the technique that covers the confidential data under the cover medium such as digital image, without reflecting any clue on the cover image. Secret data hiding through the digital image steganographic techniques can be preformed through the spatial and frequency domain techniques.

Q3: Does Steganography advantageous over Cryptography?

Ans. The mathematical techniques available in the cryptography have some limitations and can prone to crack mathematically. These cryptographic techniques are not suitable for the digital data such as images, audio and videos.

The steganographic techniques are basically meant for the digital data such as images, audio and video, where the methods are work on the spatial and frequency domains. The concept of security in steganography is possible by hiding the digital secret material under the other digital cover object, without reflecting any perception to the intruders.

Q4: What are the types of Steganographic methods?

Ans. Steganography is a group of methods used for securing the secret information under the cover medium such as an image using some translation rules. Secret data hiding through the digital image steganographic techniques can be preformed through the spatial and frequency domain techniques. The spatial domain techniques deal with the digital images. These techniques are Least Significant Bit insertion (LSB), Pixel Value Differencing (PVD), Spread Sprectrum (SS). Where, the transform or frequency domain techniques include the discrete cosine transform (DCT), discrete Fourier transform (DFT) and discrete wavelet transform (DWT).

Q5: What is Payload?

Ans. The payload is the number of bits to be hidden inside the cover image. The capacity of payload i.e. the secret message or image must smaller than the cover image. Therefore, it can be easily hidden inside the cover image without disturbing the visual quality of the cover image.

Q6: What are the criterion for evaluation of Steganographic system Performance?

Ans. The use of steganographic functions for the secure data transmission depends on some criterions that define the efficiency of specific algorithm. These criterions are payload capacity, security, robustness, time complexity, consistency and efficiency.

Q7: Which digital image steganographic algorithm is superior?

Ans. The Average Difference i.e. noise is higher in using spatial domain methods as compared to the frequency domain methods such as medium in DCT and lower in the DWT. The DWT has lower difference and ideal for steganography. The lower invisibility of the secret image is occured using the DWT method. DWT is robust due to the lower noise impression on the stego image. DWT method is distortion less with less noise and greater image quality because of the Average Difference and Structural Content. Though the spatial methods are simple and more suitable but the transform domain method such as DWT is more attractive as compared to all the steganographic methods.

Q8: Which digital image steganographic algorithm is suitable for data hiding in terms of low overhead processing?

Ans. The spatial algorithm such as LSB insertion is more suitable because of its simplicity and suitability. The extra overhead processing to compute the cover object structure and embedding process is less using the LSB insertion.

Q9: Which parameters are effective in comparing the performance of the digital image before and after steganographic operation?

Ans. The performance of the algorithms used for the embedding of secret image on the cover, is measured by analyzing the cover image with the stego image. The analysis can done by finding the parameters such as Peak Signal to Noise Ratio (PSNR), Mean Squared Error (MSE), Normalized Cross-Correlation (NCC), Average Difference (AD), Structural Content (SC), Maximum Difference (MD) and Normalized Absolute Error (NAE).

Q10: What is steganalysis?

Ans. Steganalysis is the technique with which, anyone can extract the secret message from the cover image. But the requirement is only the right algorithms or method to unhide the information from the cover image.

Chapter 16
Vegetation Index:
Ideas, Methods, Influences, and Trends

Suresh Kumar Nagarajan
VIT University, India

Arun Kumar Sangaiah
VIT University, India

ABSTRACT

This is the survey for finding vegetation, deforestation of earth images from various related papers from different authors. This survey deals with remote sensing and normalized difference vegetation index with various techniques. We survey almost 100 theoretical and empirical contributions in the current decade related to image processing, NDVI generation by using various new techniques. We also discuss significant challenges involved in the adaptation of existing image processing techniques to generation NDVI systems that can be useful in the real world. The resolution of remote sensing images increases every day, raising the level of detail and the heterogeneity of the scenes. Most of the existing geographic information systems classification tools have used the same methods for years. With these new high resolution images, basic classification methods do not provide satisfactory results.

SATELLITE IMAGE PROCESSING AND AIR POLLUTION DETECTION

Prochdxka and Kolinovd of their paper was devoted to the analysis of mathematical methods allowing for detection of concentration of aerosol particles observed at ground measuring stations and by satellites (Prochdxka & Kolinovd, 2004). Their whole paper is focused on satellite images and their processing. Owing to simultaneous observations at different frequencies.

This is devoted to the design and verification of algorithms of image denoising including wavelet use and their correlation. They use image segmentation, feature extraction, classification, and detection of the most important sources of pollution, prediction and control of pollution sources for this analysis. This paper discusses problems of image analysis and image processing applied to satellite images allowing to obtain information on air pollution due to solid particles. The extracted information of solid particles in the air obtained via surface measurements.

DOI: 10.4018/978-1-5225-2053-5.ch016

Correlation methods assumes in many cases proper signal preprocessing to remove specific signal components and to reduce substantial signal errors. For this research first they used data acquisition. In data acquisition many techniques they were used like ground observations, remote satellite sensing. Second thing is image processing. For image processing they handle some techniques like image denoising, image correlation. Then parts of the figure were evaluated to compare results of this correspondence for i) different time instants of ground observations, ii) different sizes of regions used for satellite channels correlation. For correlation they used two images stored in two matrices assumes evaluation of the correlation coefficient for the corresponding sub image regions which can be obtained using the relation

$$r = \frac{\sum_m \sum_n \left(A(m,n) - \bar{A} \right)\left(B(m,n) - \bar{B} \right)}{\sqrt{\sum_m \sum_n \left(A(m,n) - \bar{A} \right)^2 \sum_m \sum_n \left(B(m,n) - \bar{B} \right)^2}}$$

Then the best correspondence has been found.

Results presented in this paper is justify correspondence between satellite and ground observations in the case of appropriate weather conditions as correlation of the surface and satellite measurements gives very satisfactory results for some regions in which the (Figure 1) concentration of aerosol particle's in the air is measured. Then more detailed statements on how such information can be used for evaluation of air pollution will be made after greater volumes of data are processed.

Studies of their given data motivate subsequent research of general mathematical problems and they form a basis for further research in this area. Mathematical background used for these studies will include further methods of i) time series processing including two dimensional interpolation using non-linear methods and wavelet functions, ii) image preprocessing, filtering, image enhancement and channels correlation. It was assumed that general methods of image processing will contribute both to environmental sensing and to the area of signal analysis.

Figure 1. Correlation of aerosol particles evaluated in satellite images

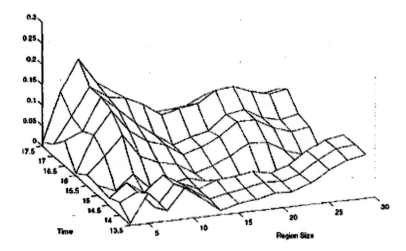

Interval and Fuzzy Methods in Remote Sensing and Satellite Image Processing

Mr. Starks analyzed about remote sensing problems, that was remote sensing is the enormous amount of data that is typically available for processing, in many cases, traditional data processing methods, that work well for data sets of smaller size, often require too much computational time and storage when applied to satellite images. In order to combat the data explosion problem encountered in remote sensing applications, interval and fuzzy methods may be employed. This paper presented several applications that have been addressed using some approaches. This paper tells a number of applications that involve remote sensing of earth based phenomena were presented that lead to solution based upon interval computations and fuzzy methods (Starks, 2004).

First that was, an application of interval computations in Hyperspectral Image Processing. Actually Landsat images consists of seven bands, Increasing the number of spectral bands by several orders of magnitude places additional demands on processing demands for remote sensing applications. They offered discrimination application that currently, that time it couldn't be effectively addressed using Landsat data; it was amenable to solution using hyperspectral information. This application involves the discrimination between two mineralsm kaolinate and dickite. Because of the inevitable imprecision in measurements among the seven spectral bands offered by Landsat, it was difficult to discriminate between kaolinate and its rare amorphous yet chemically similar form dickite. That time NASA launched a new series of satellites, named Lewis after the famous 19th century explorer. So from the hyper spectral imagery provided by satellites such as Lewism it wasm in principle possible to distinguish Kaolinate and dickite. So they used a fast (linear-time) algorithm for solving this problem has been proposed.

Next they subdivided geological areas using interval methods. Due to the evaluation of different evidence and different interpretation of experts, subdivision of a geological area into segments was often a controversial issue. Thus, they seek an objective method of performing the subdivision process in order to remove the subjectivity that enters into the geological interpretation of remotely sensed landscape imagery.

To make geological subdivision more reliable, they used, instead of limited geological samples, a more abundant source of topographical information that may be obtained through remote sensing. The volume of data associated with such a study can be overwhelming. This interval approach leads to reliable subdivision of geological areas is presented. Here the zone is divided into three segments. In the viewpoint of many scientists, this evidence is not yet sufficiently convincing. It was showed that if topographical information obtained from satellite remote sensing platforms is processed using interval methods.

Next they used Geological Decision-Making Based upon Fuzzy Clustering. To enhance the ability to make good decisions, it makes good sense to utilize the information that is made available through remote sensing. One of the most effective ways to combat the information explosion associated with the processing of satellite images is through clustering. Suppose that they were presented with a training set consisting of a large number of remotely sensed satellite images. Instead of analyzing each image individually, they instead classify the images into a few meaningful clusters.

For geologically based decision-making schemes, fuzzy clustering can be a valuable tool. Finally they found the typical representative for each cluster can be accomplished by means of the Fuzzy C-Means method. This method is premised on the natural idea that each characteristic of a typical representative should be equal to an average over all elements of the corresponding cluster. The problem of formulating the problem of choosing the optimal fuzzy clustering as a precise mathematical problem was solved; the empirically best fuzzy clustering methods were indeed optimal.

The advent of geographical information systems has increase the effectiveness of remote sensing in applications where data are spatially correlated. In many cases, information stored in GIS systems may be expressed in terms of collections of entities and phenomena that are structured aggregations of spatial entities. Thus features found in GIS systems tend to form natural class hierarchies. Because data found in GIS systems is often inexact and vague, it is natural to examine the interaction of fuzzy set theory and object oriented databases in an attempt to develop powerful tools for knowledge representation in GIS systems. This paper presents the results of work aimed at developing a fuzzy object data model that is currently being developed. Prototype implementations of this model using an integrative approach with commercial software packages are also described in this work.

Estimating Net Primary Productivity of Terrestrial Vegetation Based on Remote Sensing

Mr. Wenquan Zhu, his research was fully based on estimating net primary productivity of terrestrial vegetation. An estimation model of net primary productivity (NPP), based on geographic information system (GIS) and remote sensing (RS) technology, is presented. The model, driven with ground meteorological data and remote sensing data, moves beyond simple correlative models to a more mechanistic basis and avoids the need for a full suite of ecophysiological process algorithms that require explicit parameterization. Therefore, it is relatively easier to acquire data (Zhu, Pan, Hu, Li, & Gong, 2004).

Application and validation of this model in Inner Mongolia, China, was conducted. After the validation with observed data and the comparison with other NPP models, the results showed that the predicted NPP was in good agreement with field measurement, and the remote sensing method can more actually reflect the forest NPP than Chicago model. These results illustrated the utility of the model for terrestrial primary production over regional scales.

Accurate estimate of Net primary productivity (NPP) is critical to understand the carbon dynamics within the atmosphere-vegetation-soil continuum and the response of terrestrial ecosystem to future climate warming. Model simulation is commonly used to estimate regional and global NPP given the difficulties to directly measure NPP at such spatial scales. These models range in complexity from statistical climate-correlation models to mechanistic ecophysiological models. Typically, such models operate on point measurements that are extrapolated spatially. Spatial scaling of point measurements to the landscape or regional scale is problematic owing to great landscape heterogeneity relative to sampling density. With the increasing availability of remote sensing measurements that provide the complete global coverage with a high revisit frequency, light utilization efficiency models based on remote sensing data opened a new phase in the study of NPP, and they made the global and regional NPP estimation possible. In this paper, an estimation model of NPP, based on geographic information system (GIS) and remote sensing (RS) technology, was presented. Application and validation of this model in Inner Mongolia, China, was also conducted.

Their study site is Inner Mongolia. It is located in the northern part of china. The average elevation is about 100 m above sea level. The Inner Mongolia grassland is a typical kind of semi-aridity temperature grassland ecosystem in the middle latitude. It is located in the Northeast china transect of the terrestrial transect for global change study in the International Geosphere-Biosphere Programme. Model description is for a given area; the amount of photo synthetically active radiation absorbed annually by green vegetation (APAR) multiplied by the efficiency by which that radiation is converted to plant biomass increment (ε) equals the NPP.

$$NPP = APAR \times \varepsilon$$

- **APAR:** APAR is calculated at each monthly time step. It is the product of PAR surface irradiance and the fraction of photo synthetically active radiation (FPAR). PAR surface irradiance is calculated as 1/2 the total solar surface irradiance

(SSI). APAR is represented as:

$$APAR = SSI \times FPAR \times 0.5$$

Next thing is data acquisition and processing. The MODIS NDVI images were provided by the Global Land Cover Facility (GLCF), University of Maryland. The spatial resolution is 500 m × 500m. The 32-day composite data were taken from Dec. 2001 to Dec. 2002. These images were rectified to the reference topographic map. The verification result showed that the registration error was less than 1 pixel. The residual error of NDVI was corrected with the assumption that the NDVI in deserts was zero.

- **Meteorological Data:** Daily meteorological data, derived from 84 meteorological stations in the study area in the same period as MODIS images, included total daily precipitation, mean daily temperature, and total daily solar irradiance. All these data were validated with the missing and suspicious data eliminated. The data were then interpolated at the same scale with remote sensing data using Kringing method.
- **Vegetation Map:** The vegetation map of China with a scale of 1: 1 000 000 was provided by Institute of Botany, Chinese Academy of Sciences.

The NPP and its distribution in Inner Mongolia were estimated. The gradient distribution of NPP in Inner Mongolia was very distinct because of the different constraints from water and temperature. The higher NPP value was found in the northeastern Inner Mongolia, which was mainly covered by boreal needle-leaf forests. The vegetation coverage was very low. Global and regional validation of estimated NPP is very difficult due to the heterogeneity among different ecosystems. There are two common methods to validate the estimated NPP. One is to compare the measured value with the field observation data, and the other is to compare with other models. Field observation data from 30 stations were acquired from Institute of Botany, Chinese Academy of Sciences. They were the calculated mean value for a biome based on extensively measured plot data.

Conclusion of their paper is an NPP estimation model was presented. After the application and validation in Inner Mongolia, China, some results acquired. That was NPP can be estimated just using ground meteorological data and remote sensing data. The remote sensing method integrates some plant eco-physiological Process bases and makes some parameters simple to compute. It is relatively easier to acquire data and its application can be enhanced. After the validation with observed data and the comparison with other NPP models, the results showed that the predicted NPP was consistent with observed values, and the remote sensing method can more actually reflect the forest NPP than Chicago model. The spatio-temporal distribution of NPP in Inner Mongolia was analyzed. It was good agreement with other research results, which illustrated the utility of the model for terrestrial primary production over regional scales.

Analysing NDVI Using the Geostationary Meteosat Second Generation SEVIRI Sensor

Mr. Rasmus Fensholt, he presents first results on Normalized Difference Vegetation Index (NDVI), from the Spinning Enhanced Visible and Infrared Imager (SEVIRI) sensor onboard the geostationary satellite Meteosat Second Generation (MSG) covering the African continent. With a temporal resolution of 15 min MSG offers complementary information for NDVI monitoring compared to vegetation monitoring based on polar orbiting satellites. The improved temporal resolution has potential implications for accurate NDVI assessment of the African continent (Fensholt, Sandholt, & Stisen, 2006).

This analysis illustrated the diurnal NDVI dependency of illumination conditions, view angle and vegetation intensity and pinpoints the importance of proper BRDF modeling to produce daily values of MSG NDVI normalized for acquisition time.

With the launch of the geostationary Meteosat Second Generation, Meteosat-8 satellite with its Spinning Enhanced Visible and Infrared Imager (SEVIRI), unprecedented data for scientific exploration are now available to Earth System Scientists. The SEVIRI sensor detects radiation in 12 spectral bands among which two are specifically suited for vegetation studies. MSG data have the great advantage over data from the polar orbiting satellites that the frequency of observations is so much higher (15 min interval versus one time a day acquisitions), thus the chances to avoid cloud cover are much improved, which open up for a new vegetation monitoring scheme, in particular for the African continent over which MSG is located. Data from polar orbiting satellite sensors have been used extensively for vegetation monitoring during the last decades based on spectral vegetation indices, in particular the Normalized Difference Vegetation Index, NDVI.

- **Vegetation Index:** Vegetation is traditionally monitored using information from the red (high absorption) and near-infrared wavelengths (high reflectance) combined into the Normalized Difference Vegetation Index (NDVI). NDVI is defined as:

NDVI = NIR - RED / NIR + RED

where NIR is reflectance in the near-infrared wavelengths and RED is reflectance in the red wavelengths. The applicable satellite data for estimation of NDVI have so far been based on polar orbiting satellites carrying sensors detecting radiation in red and near-infrared wavelengths. Much effort has been put into development of improved measures of vegetation. Geostationary data have been used to assess information on surface anisotropy but this is the first paper introducing NDVI from a geostationary satellite including results analyzing diurnal variation in observed NDVI from a fixed view position with varying solar zenith angles.

The MSG satellite was launched on 29th of August 2002 and, after the commissioning phase, the satellite was put into its nominal operational position at 3.4° West longitude at an altitude of 36.000 km. Routine operations with MSG-1 started 28th of January 2004 and since then, data have been available to the scientific community. The SEVIRI sensor is equipped with 12 spectral channels, ranging from visible wavelengths to far infrared wavelengths. Several application areas have been foreseen, for terrestrial applications. In the near future, the possibility of further improvements to the accuracies is expected, due to the potential of getting information about atmospheric constituents giving input to atmospheric correction algorithms.

- **MSG Data Preprocessing:** At the Institute of Geography, University of Copenhagen, a prototype of an operational real time MSG SEVIRI processor has been build and tested in WinCHIPS, and an optimized version of the processor is currently being rewritten in IDL. Final result is, the reflectance and brightness temperature images are subsequently geo rectified to a relevant geographical map Projection with a pixel spacing of three kilometers and saved as 16 bit integer images.

- **Assessment of NDVI:** The Normalized Difference Vegetation Index is calculated from cloud masked surface reflectance in the red and near infrared channels for each image acquisition. They use the MSG cloud mask distributed with the HRIT data. Acknowledging the solar zenith angle influence on observed NDVI only data from 10 am to 2 pm local solar time are included in these analyses. The diurnal variation of observed NDVI and the selection of a 4-h time interval are subject for further discussion in the subsequent sections of this paper. Descriptive statistics are estimated, and a preliminary estimate of daily NDVI is made from a simple averaging of the images from 10 am to 2 pm local solar time. The full processing chain from Level 1.5 product received via EUMETCast to the final NDVI images.

Final result is improvements in image frequency and comparison to in situ measurements Time series of MSG SEVIRI NDVI (10 am–2 pm local solar time) are plotted together with MODIS Terra and Aqua NDVI. Only cloud free scenes are included as specified by the MODIS quality flags and the MSG cloud mask. Pixel size of MSG SEVIRI NDVI data is 3000 m and the MODIS MOD/ MYD09GQK daily 250 m red and near-infrared reflectances have been aggregated to match the MSG SEVIRI spatial pixel resolution before calculation of NDVI. From the combined use of the Terra (overpass time 10:30 am) and Aqua (overpass time 1:30 pm) data, 47 days of cloud free scenes (either Terra or Aqua) were available at the test site during the 2004-growing season. The full processing chain is given in Figure 2.

NDVI Based Vegetation Rendering

Mr. Stefan Roettger tells about Terrain Rendering, Vegetation Rendering, and Texture Splatting. Terrain rendering has a long tradition now. Ten years back the publication of the so called continuous level of detail (C-LOD) method (Gorgan et al, 2009; Petcu et al., 2008)enabled the display of very large landscapes. These approaches use a very fine grained triangulation that is driven by the screen space error of the coarsened mesh. This means that objects that are far away from the viewer are represented at a lower level of detail than objects that are nearby. In order to achieve a high degree of realism plain terrain rendering is not sufficient. Man-made objects and the various types of vegetation such as grass, bushes and trees have to be considered as well. A wide variety of methods exists that are able to model virtual landscapes and plant ecosystems in a very realistic way. Due to the huge amount of detail of an ecosystem it is very difficult to apply these techniques to the large scenes that are visible in a typical GIS scenario. Several approaches have been made to increase the rendering performance: point based, volume rendering based and billboard based (Roettger,2006).

Figure 2. Analyzing NDVI

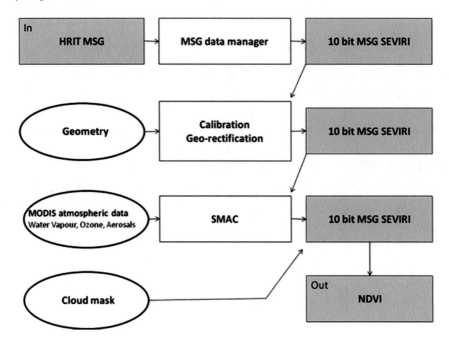

- **NDVI Measurement:** While the described approaches try to model vegetation in a procedural or stochastically way few approaches are known that can display the vegetation of a real GIS scene located somewhere on earth. Partly this was due to the restricted availability of data that describes the distribution of vegetation in a specific area. Vegetation usually has NDVI values in the range from 0.1 to 0.7. Higher index values are associated with higher levels of healthy vegetation cover, whereas clouds and snow will cause index values near zero.
- **Large Scale Forest Rendering:** The NDVI data is available from the GLCF as tiled grey scale images that cover a geo-referenced area. Together with the DEMs (digital elevation maps) from the SRTM (Space Shuttle Radar Mission) and the visible channels 1-3 of the Landsat data they effectively have a high resolution landscape and vegetation description of any particular area in the world. Since the data is overlapping each other, the first step to visualize the scene is to resample the data.

Also, the usage of a double buffered render cache enables us to store the geometry in a vertex buffer so that the graphics hardware is able to process the triangles very efficiently. Additionally, the render cache has the advantage (Figure 2). Prism stacked on a base triangle with one bush placed randomly inside the prism volume. That it can be easily extended for the purpose of large scale forest rendering as described in the following, The C-LOD algorithm uses a height field for the compact storage of terrain data. From this data the mesh is generated in a view-dependent way and stored tile by tile in the render cache. They introduce a second height field which represents the height of the associated vegetation. From this vegetation height field they generate a volumetric description of the space occupied by the vegetation in the following way: For each triangle that is output by the terrain renderer a prism is stacked on top of these base triangles. The height of the 3 vertical edges of each prism is taken from the vegetation height field, so that the set of prisms is a view-dependent volumetric description of the vegetation on the landscape. Since the base triangles are coupled with the stacked prisms, the screen space error which drives the triangulation must be modified to be the maximum of the screen space error for both the height field and the vegetation field.

Additionally, the placement density decreases with the viewing distance in order to keep the total number of generated plants within a manageable limit. All the generated plants are stored in a tree render cache which is also double buffered. Currently the plants are rendered as billboards in each frame. Due to the view dependency of the tree generating process the number of visible trees in a scene is reduced dramatically. At the same time the forest is still stretching out very far, since the render cache allows to render a large number of trees in real-time. Since the cache is updated permanently, the placement of the plants is also repeatedly updated. As a result, the height of the plants corresponds with the elevation of the terrain even though the elevation may change over time due to a changing view point. A practical example for this case is a tour on the highway through a forest, where basically only the highway and the trees on its side are visible.

- **Rendering the Grass Layer:** High to medium values of the NDVI usually corresponds to trees or bushes, respectively. These can be displayed efficiently using our described billboard approach. NDVI values correspond to either very sparse vegetation or grass. For the display of meadows with a large extent billboards are not suitable, so they use an approach which is commonly known as texture Splatting. In general, texture Splatting means that from a set of appearance parameters a selection of tilable patterns is blended together and then splat onto the surface.

The described C-LOD method reduces this to an amount of roughly 100.000 visible trees depending on the point of view. Another possible option is to accelerate the display of the cached geometry by using impostors and/or billboard clouds for distant trees. Additionally, a geometrical plant representation can be used to improve the appearance of nearby trees.

Sensitivity of the EVI and NDVI to Topographic Effects

Mr. Bunkei Matsushita described about NDVI and EVI vegetation indices. These Vegetation indices play an important role in monitoring variations in vegetation. The Enhanced Vegetation Index (EVI) proposed by the MODIS Land Discipline Group and the Normalized Difference Vegetation Index (NDVI) are both global-based vegetation indices aimed at providing consistent spatial and temporal information regarding global vegetation. However, many environmental factors such as atmospheric conditions and soil background may produce errors in these indices (Matsushita, Yang, Chen, Onda1 & Qiu,2007).

The topographic effect is another very important factor, especially when the indices are used in areas of rough terrain. In this paper, they theoretically analyzed differences in the topographic effect on the EVI and the NDVI based on a non-Lambertian model and two airborne-based images acquired from a mountainous area covered by high-density Japanese cypress plantation were used as a case study. The results indicate that the soil adjustment factor "L" in the EVI makes it more sensitive to topographic conditions than is the NDVI. Based on these results, they strongly recommend that the topographic effect should be removed in the reflectance data before the EVI was calculated—as well as from other vegetation indices that similarly include a term without a band ratio format (e.g., the PVI and SAVI)—when these indices are used in the area of rough terrain, where the topographic effect on the vegetation indices having only a band ratio format (e.g., the NDVI) can usually be ignored.

The vegetation index (VI), defined as the arithmetic combination of two or more bands related to the spectral characteristics of vegetation, has been widely used for the phonologic monitoring, vegetation classification, and biophysical derivation of radiometric and structural vegetation parameters. Among existing VIs, the Normalized Difference Vegetation Index (NDVI) is the most often used and is an operational, global-based vegetation index, partly due to its "ratio" properties, which enable the NDVI to cancel out a large proportion of the noise caused by changing sun angles, topography, clouds or shadow, and atmospheric conditions.

EVI reduces the adverse effects of environmental factors such as atmospheric conditions and soil background; it does not take into consideration the topographic effect, which is defined as the variation in radiance that accompanies a change in orientation from a horizontal to an inclined surface, in response to a change in light source and sensor position. In fact, the topographic effect is probably another important environmental factor contributing to the noise in calibration, especially in hilly areas. As is well known, the topographic effects in the visible and near infrared parts of a surface's solar spectrum are comparable. Therefore, the topographic effect could be eliminated or weakened when VIs are expressed as band ratios, such as in the NDVI, RVI, *etc.*

Unlike the NDVI, the EVI includes a constant term, the soil adjustment factor L, in its denominator. This constant allows the EVI to include a term without a band ratio format. Therefore, the topographic effect on the EVI cannot be ignored as simple as that on the NDVI.

Theoretical analysis of topographic effects on EVI and NDVI: To explain theoretically how topography affects the vegetation index, they assume that there exists a pixel Ω, whose slope and aspect are S and A, respectively. The reflectance's of the single channels, especially the blue and red channels, should be saturated and unchanged if in the case of a level surface. However, it can be clearly seen that the reflectance images of the single channels and the EVI image all show a greater variation than does the NDVI image in regard to spatial distribution. The reflectance's of the single channels and EVI values are all very different between the north and south aspect, and even within the same aspect area these values also vary among different slopes. In contrast, the NDVI image shows little spatial variation. The results show that the spatial variations of the reflectance in single channels and EVI are all due mainly to the topographic effects, while the NDVI can eliminate or weaken the topographic effects because of its band ratio format.

The Enhanced Vegetation Index (EVI) was proposed to reduce both atmospheric and soil background noise simultaneously. Although the EVI performs better than does the NDVI in many applications, they showed in the present paper that it is more sensitive to topographic conditions than is the NDVI. Based on a non-Lambertian model, they quasi-quantitatively interpreted the reason for the difference of the topographic effect between the EVI and NDVI, and two airborne-based images obtained from a high-density mountain area in Japan were used as a study case to evaluate the conclusion. Their study shows that the NDVI can be expressed as a function of the ratio vegetation index (RVI), which can reduce the direct effect of topography absolutely. However, the EVI cannot be written as a function of the RVI because of the soil adjustment factor "L". Thus, they may conclude that it is the soil adjustment factor in the EVI that makes it much more sensitive to the direct effect than is the NDVI. And both the EVI and NDVI may be influenced by the indirect effect of topography, which is determined by the BRDF of the surface. Furthermore, they need to be aware that the topographic effect is relative to spatial scale: as the size of the pixel increases, the effect of topography may decrease or even disappear. The quantitative relationship between spatial scale and topographic effect needs further study. Lastly, they strongly recommend that the topographic effect be removed from the EVI—as well as from other vegetation indices that similarly include a term without a band ratio format (e.g., the PVI and SAVI)—when these indices are used in conjunction with a high spatial resolution image of an area of rough terrain, where the topographic effect on the vegetarian indices having only a band ratio format (e.g., the NDVI) can usually be ignored.

Fusion of Vegetation Indices Using Continuous Belief Functions and Cautious-Adaptive

Research paper of Mr. Abdelaziz Kallel is to propose a methodology based on vegetation index fusion to provide an accurate estimation of the fraction of vegetation cover (fCover). Because of the partial and imprecise nature of remote-sensing data. The defined fCover belief functions are continuous with the interval [0, 1] as a discernment space. Since the vegetation indices are not independent (e.g., perpendicular vegetation index and weighted difference vegetation index are linearly linked), so they defined a new combination rule called "cautious adaptive" to handle the partial "nondistinctness" between the sources (vegetation indices). In this rule, the "nondistinctness" is modeled by a factor varying from zero (distinct sources) to one (totally correlated sources), and the fusion rule varies accordingly from the conjunctive rule to the cautious one. In terms of results, both in the cases of simulated data and actual data, they showed the interest of the combination of two or three vegetation indices to improve either the accuracy of fCover estimation or its robustness (Kallel, Hégarat-Mascle, Hubert-Moy, & Ottlé, 2008).

Estimation of vegetation features from space is a great challenge for agronomist, hydrologist, and meteorologist communities. For example, land cover during winter in agricultural regions strongly influences soil erosion processes and water quality. Therefore, the identification and monitoring of vegetation cover the physical parameter being the fraction of vegetation cover (fCover)] constitutes a prior approach for the monitoring of water resources. Now, the use of vegetation indices to estimate vegetation characteristics is very popular. They are empirical combinations between visible generally Red (R)] and near-infrared (NIR) reflectance's that show good correlation with plant growth, vegetation cover, and biomass amount.

- **Vegetation Index Mass Function:** Here, they presented the way the mass functions (or bbd in the continuous domain) associated to the different vegetation indices are derived. Using the Adding model, they obtained simulations of satellite measurements (and then vegetation indices computed from) conditionally to fCover value and assuming vegetation/soil/acquisition parameters. Then, they could derive some distributions of fCover values versus vegetation index ones. However, the obtained knowledge is only partial and imprecise since the vegetation/soil parameters are unknown in their application, and therefore, the distributions of fCover values are spread by the necessary variability of vegetation/soil parameters in our simulations. Therefore, assuming that knowledge corresponds rather to a potential betting behavior on the fCover value (in continuous domain), they model it by a pignistic probability density. Now, since the pignistic transform is a many-to-one transform, there is an infinite number of belief densities, which is said to be "isopignistic," that induce the same pignistic probability density.

- **New Combination Rule:** They said that the vegetation indices to be combined are not necessarily independent (some of them are even strongly correlated). Therefore, the orthogonal sum $\oplus$ or the conjunctive rule $\_\cap$ are not suitable.

- **Application to the Fusion of Vegetation Indices:** They analyze the performance of the proposed model through our application that is the combination of several vegetation indices in order to estimate the vegetation fraction cover. They first present the vegetation indices considered. Then, the performance of their fusion is evaluated in the case of simulated data: with or without noise. Finally, the case of actual data is considered. The first thing is Considered Vegetation Indices, during the last 20 years; works have been carried to follow continental surfaces from space. Numerous vegetation indices combining the reflectance measurements at two or several wavelengths have been proposed.

The more popular index is probably the NDVI that combines reflectance measurements in the Red and in the NIR domains without any other data. However, it suffers from some problems related to its dependence to acquisition geometry (sun position and looking angle) and spectral properties of the soil. Such dependences are at least partially taken into account by more recent indices. Indeed, more performing indices has been developed, particularly those that are taking into account the soil reflectance such as the soil-adjusted vegetation indices. All these indices are highly correlated to the leaf area index (LAI) of the vegetation cover, particularly during the growing stage of the vegetation until a saturation level. The interests of these indices, particularly relative to the factors to which the indices are assumed robust, such as the acquisition conditions, the soil and vegetation spectral properties, the geometry of the vegetation cover, and the row effects, has been evaluated from robustness experiences using radioactive transfer model simulations.

Table 1 lists the different vegetation indices, its abbreviations, and its formulations.

Table 1. Vegetation indices

Index	Abbreviation	Formulation
Perpendicular Vegetation Index	PVI	$\dfrac{rNIR - a0rR - b0}{\sqrt{a_0^2 + 1}}$
Weighted Infrared-Red Vegetation Index	WDVI	$rNIR - a0rR$
RATIO Vegetation Index	RVI	$\dfrac{rNIR}{rR}$
Normalized Difference Vegetation Index	NDVI	$\dfrac{rNIR - rR}{rNIR + rR}$
Soil-Adjusted Vegetation Index	SAVI	$\left(1 + L\right)\dfrac{rNIR - rR}{rNIR + rR + L}; L = 0.5$
Transformed Soil Adjusted Vegetation Index	TSAVI	$\dfrac{a0\left(rNIR - a0rR - b0\right)}{a0rNIR + rR - a0b0 + X\left(1 + A_0^2\right)}; X = 0.08$
Modified Soil Adjusted Vegetation Index	MSAVI	$\dfrac{1}{2}\left(2rR + 1 - \sqrt{\left(2rR + 1\right)2}\right) - 8\left(rR - rNIR\right)$

Results in the Case of Simulated Data are considered in order to evaluate the fusion independent of the accuracy of the ground truth. These simulations have been obtained from the coupled Adding/ PROSPECT. In the Visible domain, the albedo is mainly due to pigment concentration (chlorophyll *a* + *b*) *Ca+b*.

They proposed to derive semi empirical method allowing the inversion of the fCover. It was based on the inversion of a four parameter model combining the reflectances in the Red and NIR domains. This model is semi empirical since it is based on radioactive transfer modeling. To calibrate the model parameters, two optimization methods are used: the Simplex and the Shuffled Complex Evolution algorithm, which are deterministic and heuristic methods, respectively. SCE-UA is a priori more accurate, but it is also more complex and needs longer running time.

In this paper the simulated data considered in order to evaluate the fusion independent of the accuracy of the ground truth. These simulations have been obtained from the coupled Adding/Prospect. In the visible domain, the albedo is mainly due to pigment concentration (chlorophyll a + b) Ca+b. In the NIR domain, the absorption is lower, the albedo is higher. Adding inputs are the leaf reflectance and transmittance simulated by PROSPECT, the vegetation density (fCover), the leaf area distribution, and the sun and observation geometries: the sun Zenithal angles (θo, ϕo), the hot-spot parameters, and the soil reflectance's (Rsoil,R,Rsoil,NIR) that are entirely determined by Red soil reflectance variation [min$R$so,R, max$R$so,R] and the soil-line equation slope and intercept ($a0, b0$). These values are then used to simulate remote sensing measurements, from which the vegetation indices are computed.

Numerous simulations have been done. Here, they only presented the two following typical cases, respectively: without noise and with noise. Finally in this paper the correlation between vegetation indices was set as an a priori parameter that can be defined from general knowledge about the indices. They assumed the independence between vegetation indices except PVI and WDVI that are linearly linked, RVI and NDVI that are unlinearly linked, Sx and SCE-UA which only differ by the kind of optimization.

The performance of the method has been evaluated through two parameters: 1) the method accuracy represented by the mean L1 error that is the average of the absolute difference between the estimated fCover value and the actual one 2) the method robustness represented by the standard deviation of L1 error. They considered each vegetation index individually or the combination of two or three vegetation indices. When three indices are combined, they compared the result using the classical conjunctive rule and the proposed cautious-adaptive combination rule.

They mentioned the comparison of these two combination rules through the results called "PVI+WDVI+1IVEG" and "PVI, WDVI, 1IVEG" that correspond to the conjunctive rule applied to three indices. The result of a combination of two indices is generally better than the use of only one index and that the combination of three indices is generally better than the combination of three indices is generally better than the combination of two. They compared the fusion with the conjunctive rule to the one with the cautious-adaptive rule. The results are plotted with empty and full symbols, respectively. They noted that there is a quasi-systematic slight improvement using the cautious-adaptive rule. In order to evaluate precisely the performance of the fusion was relative to the individual vegetation indices.

Results in the Case of Actual Data: In order to test the fusion in the case of actual data, they consider both remote-sensed data and reference field data (ground truth) measurements acquired simultaneously over the Yar watershed. This watershed, which is located in a fairly intensive farming area (field size is about 1 ha) in northern Brittany, France, has been carried out for several years. In 2006, over 81 fields, ground-truth measurements off Cover values have been acquired with a 5% precision for low fCover values (fCover ≤ 25%) and a 10% accuracy for high fCover values (fCover > 25%). The distribution of the observed fCover values presents two modes: one mode around one since the majority of fields are covered in winter, and one mode around 0.1. Indeed, fields with mean vegetation are few since the leaseholders are either respecting the law (winter coverage) or not respecting it, but rarely respecting it only partially.

Conclusion of this paper is they consider the problem of fusion of different sources that are not necessarily independent and in a continuous discernment space. This problem was raised in the framework of the fCover estimation from remote-sensing data. However the defined solutions may be applied to similar problems, particularly data fusion of different sensor measurements to estimate other real parameters. Then, the contributions of this paper are of two kinds: theoretical, in the domain of fusion, and thematic, in the domain of vegetation monitoring.

The results were first, to handle the continuous case; second, they proposed a new combination rule called cautious adaptive that allows taking into account the particle redundancies between sources through a supervised parameter. They showed that, when this parameter varies from zero to one, the proposed rule varies from the classical conjunctive combination to the cautious rule defined by smets. The main advantage of the proposed rule is then to control the level of a priori redundancy between the sources since two sources may be apparently correlated but independent in a cognitive way.

Concerning the vegetation monitoring, they showed that combination several vegetation indices can improve either the accuracy of the fCover estimation or its robustness. In some optimal cases, it can even lead to improvement of both accuracy and robustness. These conclusions were drawn from the analysis of simulated data using the coupled Adding/PROSPECT radiative transfer model, either with or without noise simulating the natural variability of soil/vegetation parameters. In the case of actual data, results seem less clear which is mainly due to the specific distribution of the ground. In the case of classical vegetation indices, the combination of two or three of them may improve the estimation relatively to the best estimator among the indices involved. However, in the case of more sophisticated inversion methods (such as the Sx or the SCE-UA), there is no real improvement.

Future studies will deal with automatic learning of the "correlation" or "redundancy" between sources. This learning can only be based on the analysis of the conjoint statistics of the considered sources. Another problem that will occur is the modeling of the partial redundancy between three or more sources. Indeed, to preserve the associative of the combination, this notion of redundancy has to be carefully defined. The second perspective is related to our specific application. A more discerning model of the vegetation index "correlation" function could be defined by introducing the fCover dependence. It will allow modeling, for example, a higher "correlation" of the indices, taking into account the soil line at lower fCover values. More precise *a priori* information about the reliability of each vegetation index versus the fCover inversion domain can also be taken into account.

MedioGrid: A Grid-Based Platform for Satellite Image Processing

Mr. Dana Petcu and Daniela Zaharie tells about Grid based software's involvement in Remote sensing areas. Recently Grid-based software platform was developed to allow remote sensing image processing for preventing disasters like river floods and forest fires. While several innovative components were presented in research papers in the past few years, this paper presents a state-of-the-art of the whole platform and exposes the novelty elements that distinguish it from other similar approaches (Petcu, Zaharie, Gorgan, Pop, & Tudor,2009).

Satellite image processing is both data and computing intensive. It confronts several difficulties or even impossibilities when using one single computer. Moreover, space satellites ensure the download from space to ground of many images per day. The analysis and sharing of this huge amount of data is a big challenge for the remote sensing community. The Grid technologies are expected to make feasible the creation of a computational environment handling hundreds of distributed databases, heterogeneous computing resources, and simultaneous users.

There are at least three reasons for using Grid computing for satellite image processing: location – the required computing performance is not available locally, the solution being the remote computing; cooperation – the required computing performance is not available in one location, the solution being co-operative computing; specialization – the required computing services are only available at specialized centers, the solution being application specific computing.

Architecture and Main Components, the main objectives of the Mediogrid project are to develop a Grid structure to support the parallel and distributed processing of geographical and environment data; develop algorithms for Grid based processing of satellite images; develop the MedioGrid's Software Platform to support Grid services; develop and experiment environment supervising applications with data extracted from satellite images; model and visualize the virtual geographical space.

The kernel contains the basic software components and services which are used by most of the environment oriented Grid applications:

1. MediogridService provides services for creating, executing and scheduling jobs;
2. MediogridFactory is a stateful web service which creates entities that manage job information;
3. MedioGridResource contains information about the job state, the starting and the ending time of the job;
4. MediogridOGSADAI provides access to the image database;
5. MediogridUrlCopy supports file transfer using the GridFTP protocol – by using this service the worker node accesses the image files and processes the data;
6. MediogridRLS returns a list of physical images in order to allow the worker to decide, based on its location, which is the most appropriate GridFTP server for downloading the required data.
7. Condor is used to schedule, manage and monitor every job created by the MedioGridService.

In a second stage of the project the software platform kernel has been developed. It consists of software components implementing fundamental algorithms for image segmentation, as well as applying parallel and distributed data processing. Mediogrid components are performing basic image processing of MODIS and Landsat images, or more sophisticated operations like vegetation classification, water detection, cloud detection, or unsupervised image classification. Modeling and visualization of the virtual geographical space, GIS and LBS (Location Based Services) were also considered. Grid services were developed to publicly expose into Web interfaces the basic operations that can be performed on satellite images by executing general or specialized legacy codes. Parallel processing has been used as an effective solution in the case of time-consuming algorithms like the classification ones.

In Figure 3 they discuss some details about the platform functionality.

This project focused on the data model and execution environment represented in Figure 3. The main objective what concerns the data model was to define a proper data access interface and an efficient replication scheme. Data access patterns have been analyzed both statically and by using monitoring techniques and tools. An open source solution for the Grid environment, based on the Debian Linux

Figure 3. Grid based platform for satellite image

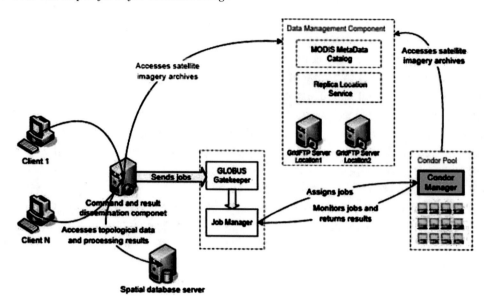

distribution and community provided tools, has been chosen. Data distribution and a generic data model based on OGSADAI interfaces have been proposed.

Next step was to address the data distribution problem together with data life cycle. The initial proposal was to make use of a static replication scheme. Such a scheme wastes storage, especially for seldom used data. A dynamic policy based replication scheme was proposed, giving the possibility to adapt replicated application data distribution based on usage patterns. The dynamic policy based replication framework architecture is depicted.

Research activities toward the execution environment are ongoing and they aim to address the problem of providing uniform and proper tools to ease the development and deployment of MedioGrid applications. They started to analyze both performance and usability of existing Grid programming tools and aim to provide alternative paradigms based on shared data models. A Service example, one distinct application of MedioGrid is Greenland. It studies the extent and structure of the vegetation cover for a certain geographic area.

Great attention was paid to the difference in reflectance between the visible and the near infrared domains. Each geographic area has a specific spectral signature, depending on the structure of vegetation that is expressed by the wavelengths emitted or reflected by that surface. The Greenland application classifies the vegetation areas based on vegetation indices. In the first phase the user specifies the time interval and the geographical area the satellite images address to, and the vegetation based classification operation. The system displays a list of images selected from the database according with the previous criteria. Next, the user can choose for classification a subset of them and the corresponding vegetation indices.

Another distinct application is Waterland. It performs the water detection by using short-wave infrared, red and near infrared spectral bands of Landsat images. It returns a GeoTIFF image that highlights the water boundaries. A preliminary test service for detecting changes in river beds, based on wrapping

Figure 4. Multispectral image segmentation integrated into the platform

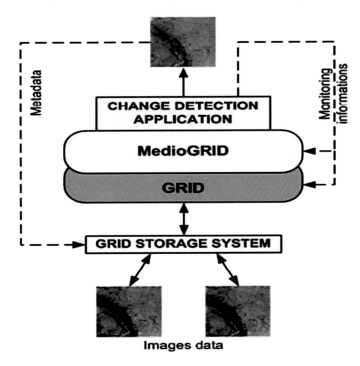

Images data

an open-source image processing tool, was reported. A distributed algorithm for multispectral satellite image segmentation was recently developed and presented. Multispectral image segmentation is used in remote sensing for land cover and land use classification and change detection. Regions of the image are clustered separately and then the results are combined.

The algorithm employs two types of clustering techniques; each specialized to its task and steered towards obtaining a final meaningful segmentation. The results show good spatial coherency in segments and coherent borders between regions that were segmented separately. Figure 4 says the algorithm seeks to find more spectrally and spatially coherent clusters by employing spatial information and spectral knowledge. It also seeks to distribute the computation to be able to overcome the temporal complexity of the algorithms used as well as the considerable memory requirements.

Another approach for unsupervised image segmentation is based on distributed versions of K-means and fuzzy C-means algorithms, While MedioGrid platform is built on the latest version of standard Grid middleware that is implementing Web service concepts (Service Grid), tests were performed also on a classical Grid infrastructure (Computational Grid), SEE-Grid (South-Eastern European Grid infrastructure II), to study the potential of using a joint infrastructure. In this scenario, the satellite images and the client's codes should be available at the client side as well as some minimal facilities to access the computational Grid infrastructure. The Grid middleware allows the execution of client codes on client's data at remote computing nodes. The case study refers to the implementation of a simple classification algorithm based on the binary decision tree. The classification process involves translating the pixel values in a satellite image into meaningful categories. The inputs are two MODIS bands (the red and the infrared ones).

The detected land-cover classes include: water, cloud, non-forest, forest, and scrub. Since the classification algorithm is applied on the pixel level, the splitting of the computational effort into similar tasks acting on parts of the image is straightforward: the bands are split into equal sub-images. The code prepared for the Computational Grid consists of three components: the splitter that takes the two bands and splits them into a number of sub-images; the classifier that receiving two images (pieces from the red and infrared bands) applies the binary decision tree and produces the sub-image storing for each pixel the color of the associated land cover class; and the composer that gathers the colored subim ages. Parameter studies were performed to detect the best choice of the number of tasks (sub-images) depending on the image's dimension.

The conclusion of this paper is current Grid technologies provide powerful tools for remote sensing data sharing and processing. Realizing this fact, a new platform based on open-source software was built to serve the requests coming from field specialists as well as beginners. The platform was already populated with several complex applications that were enumerated in this paper. Further developments of the platform are related to the issue of real-time processing and new service integration.

Monitoring of Vegetation Changes Using Multi-Temporal NDVI

Mr. Youhao, Mr. Wang Jihe of their research studies tells about Time series of Normalized Difference Vegetation Index (NDVI) derived from seven Landsat TM/ETM+ satellite images were used quantitatively to monitor the vegetation change in peripheral regions around the Minqin Oasis. Based on field observation and re-adjustment, the TM-based NDVI values from 0 to 0.21 were classified as natural and artificial vegetation such as herbage, desert shrub, and landscapes such as semi-fixed sand dunes, fixed sand dunes and sand dunes, while the NDVI values more than 0.22 as the crops and shelter belt beside the crops (Youhao, Jihe, Shangyu, Ping, & Zihui,2008).

The variations of NDVI values less than 0.21 indicating the natural and human planted vegetation were analyzed. Results show that the areas of NDVI values ranging from 0.09- 0.14 indicating semi-fixed sand dunes planted perennial herbage and desert shrub have decreased gradually. The human planted shrubs (NDVI 0.15-0.21) have reduced in short time occurring during 1987-1991. While the areas indicating shifting sand dunes and inter-dunes planted annual or perennial herbages and scrubs (NDVI less than 0.09) fluctuated. The correlation analysis between NDVI and annual precipitation shows that NDVI is statistically correlated with the variations in the annual precipitation, implying that the precipitation-controlled natural vegetation coverage in the margins of the Minqin oasis has overshadowed the made-planted vegetation in dominating the ecological landscape since late 1980's.

Minqin Oasis, encircled by the Badain Jaran Desert in north and Tengger Desert in east to south, lies in the lower reach of Shiyang River Watershed, Northwest China. The conflict between invading of sand dunes with anti-invading has long history in Minqin area. Therefore, the peripheral desert ecological system around the Minqin oasis is quite important and absolutely necessary to the oasis economic systems in terms of protecting the oasis from desertification and ensuring sustainable development, meaning that the oasis economic systems have to co-exist with the peripheral ecological systems in the Minqin oasis. In order to enhance the ability of combating sand dunes invasion and alleviate the damage of oasis from sandy desertification, a large number of artificial vegetation been planted within the peripheral regions from the end of 1950s to the middle of 1970s to recruit the lack of natural. Meanwhile, the groundwater within the oasis has been extracted since the middle 1960s due to the decrease in surface water resource from the upstream and the increase of irrigated acreage in the oasis.

However, the excessive human activities mainly including overexploitation of groundwater and afforestation have lowered rapidly the groundwater table, resulting in an overall decrease in soil water content. In response to the soil moisture decrease in the periphery, some plant species relying on groundwater resource have been dying out and other more mesic species have been replaced with more xerosere species (Yang, 1999). Consequently, the peripheral eco-system has been changed greatly. The safe existence and sustainable development of Minqin oasis have been threatened by the desertification, bringing the great attention to the environment deterioration problems. In order to develop the strategies of retrieving the vegetation and preserving the oasis, the deterioration process of vegetation must be documented clearly. In this study, three representative study areas growing mainly artificial plants, natural vegetation as well as natural halophytes respectively were selected, and, Time series of normalized difference vegetation index (NDVI) derived from seven Landsat TM/ETM+ satellite images were used quantitatively to monitor the vegetation changes in peripheral regions around the Minqin Oasis.

The data utilized in their research were: seven Landsat data sets (Row 33/ Path 131) of TM images (dated 18 September 1987, 13, September 1991; 5 September 1994; 31 August 1998; 20, August 2000; 8, September 2001 and ETM+ 17, July 2002) acquired under clear atmospheric condition during July to September, 1:100,000 topographic maps and DEM with 30- m resolution, field observation data including plant species, vegetation coverage, canopy and biomass of individual as well as rainfall station data for the period 1980-2006.

The utilized Landsat data sets have been geo-referenced on the Transverse Morcator coordinate system, zone 18 North by Landsat station. Before using them, calibrations need to be done. Based on 1:100,000 scale topographic maps, twenty ground control points (GCP) were positioned. Then, the 1987 image was used as a reference image and was calibrated using polynomial model using polynomial model with root mean square errors of 0.41. The Digital Number (DN) between 0-255 of 1, 2, 3, 4, 5 and 7 bands were transformed to the top atmospheric reflectance. Then, the local observed meteorological information was put into the Simulation of Satellite Signals in the Solar Spectrum (5S) radiation correction model to get the surface reflectance. After calibrating, the geo-referenced seven images were clipped by the polygons of A01, Ao2 and A03. The Normalized difference vegetation index (NDVI) were computed by taking difference between TM/ETM+ near infrared (NIR) and red (R) channel reflectance values and then normalizing by the sum of these two channel: NDVI = $\rho4$- $\rho3/\rho4+\rho3$ ($\rho4$ and $\rho3$ are the reflectance values of the channel 4 and channel 3 respectively).

Statistical analysis including average, variations, deviation as well as cumulative deviation of rainfall station data during 1980 to 2006, NDVI values and average NDVI less than 0.21 were performed. Specially, for analyzing variation of areas occupied by different NDVI series, the GRID NDVI data involving floating point values were converted into GRID data with integral values of NDVI. The entire tasks were carried out on ENVI 3.0, Arcview3.0 and Microsoft Excel 2000 running on Windows 2000.

Final conclusion of this paper is, the NDVI derived from TM/ETM + images provide useful information to monitor vegetation changes, especially the natural plants growing on sand dunes and semi-fixed sand dunes in arid Minqin region. The analysis of NDVI variations showed that the landscapes on which grow perennial herbage, and desert shrub, The correlation analysis between NDVI (less than 0.21) and annual precipitation shows that NDVI is statistically correlated with the variations in the annual precipitation, implying that the precipitation-controlled natural vegetation coverage in the margins of the Minqin oasis has overshadowed the made-planted vegetation in dominating the ecological landscape since late 1980's.

Forest-Cover Change Detection Using Multi-Temporal High-Resolution Remote Sensing Data

Mr. Jun Huang, Mr. Youchuan, of their research studies deals about Forest Cover change detection using Multi-Temporal high-resolution Remote Sensing Data. The forest-cover change detection system includes several key modules: image segmentation, difference images processing and binary change detection model using threshold. These modules are evaluated by multi-temporal QuickBird remotely sensed data set: 1) In the image segmentation module, multi-scale segmentation algorithm was used to form the image objects. 2) In the difference image module, spectral value and NDVI (normalized difference vegetation index) were taken as input data. Correlation coefficient and t-test algorithms based on objects are used to develop difference images. 3) In the binary change detection module, change maps obtained from spectral value and NDVI are compared. Finally, experimental results carried out on multi-temporal QuickBird remotely sensed data set confirm the effectiveness of the proposed system (Huang, Wan, & Shen, 2009).

The global concerns in terms of ecosystem monitoring require more attention on forest-cover changes. Recently, with the development of high spectral and spatial resolution remote sensing satellite, forest-cover change detection using satellite images is an efficient technique to overcome the high complexity of forest-cover changes. Automatic change detection in images of a given scene acquired at different time is one of the most interesting topics in the remote sensing field. The main difficulties affecting change detection in remote sensing images arise from following factors: (1) the lack of prior information of changed areas; (2) relative radioactive changes in obtained images of the same area at different time (light conditions, atmospheric conditions, sensor calibration, ground moisture and so on).

In this paper, an unsupervised technique for detecting forest-cover changes in high resolution satellite images has been proposed. From an operational point of view, it is obvious that using unsupervised techniques is feasible and efficient while ground truth information is not available. Forest-cover change detection in this paper is based on a direct comparison of original raw images, and NDVI acquired in the same area at two different times.

Figure 5 shows the Architecture of the proposed method: For object-based change detection tasks, radioactive calibration and image coregistration are very important process. Manual coregistration method was used. Automatic radioactive calibration and image registration are pre-processing step of this study. Multi-scale Segmentation Algorithm: Image segmentation is the important basis for object-based approach. Multi-scale segmentation algorithm has been developed and implemented in the commercial software eCognition. The idea of this algorithm is to minimize the average heterogeneity of image objects weighted by their size during the merging process. In the algorithm, the heterogeneity change caused by a possible merge is evaluated by calculating and mixing the spectral and shape differences between the situations before and after the merge. For any pair of adjacent objects, an overall heterogeneity change for a possible merger is broken.

Which are linearly combined to calculate a value as the following

$$\Delta hoverall = (1 - Wshape)\Delta hspectral + Wshape\Delta hshape$$

In this paper they discussed about many algorithms,

Figure 5. Flow chart of object-based forest-cover change detection

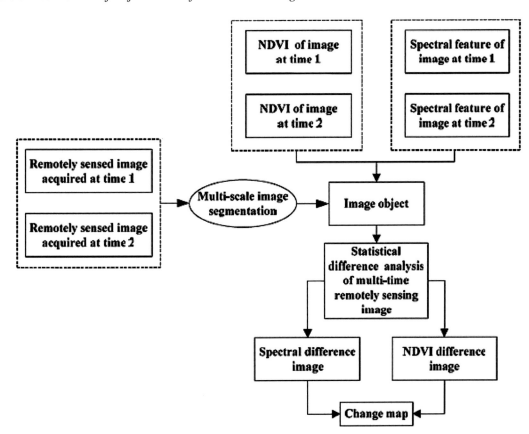

1. **Correlation Coefficient Method:** Correlation coefficient is widely used in probability and statistics theory to measure the similarity between two variables. Correlation coefficient can be used to measure the spectral similarity of the two pixels. Low correlation coefficient means that there are changes between two variables and high correlation coefficient means there are not any changes.

2. **t-Test Method:** Compared to correlation coefficient method, they used t-test method for multi-temporal remotely sensed image change detection purpose. The main idea of t-test method is by calculating the image means and variances within the given region to measure the similarity. The t value denotes the change degree of the objects, and lager t values mean changed area, otherwise, smaller t values mean unchanged area.

3. **Data Set Descriptions:** In order to carry out an experimental analysis aimed at assessing the performances of the proposed approach, they considered multi-temporal data set corresponding to geographical area of Hubei province, China. The data set consist of two QuickBird images acquired at the same area by a passive multispectral scanner equipped on a satellite. The spatial resolution is 2.4 m and spectral channels include three visible spectral channels and one near-infrared spectral channel. The test area shown in the two images was a section of a scene acquired in 2004 and 2005, and the size of the area is 1257 *1312 pixels.

4. **Multi-Temporal Image Segmentation:** The input data of Multi-scale segmentation is the band-combined image of multi-temporal remotely sensed images obtained at different times. The basic

task of segmentation algorithms is the merge of image elements based on spectral homogeneity to the neighboring regions. In this research, the image was multi-scale segmented by Fractal Net Evolution Approach.

5. **Difference Image:** NDVI and spectral values are taken as input information to develop difference images. NDVI (normalized difference vegetation index) is an important index to measure the forest volume and forest-cover. Comparing the results of correlation coefficient and t-test method, they found that the changed regions in difference image using t-test show higher contrast than which using correlation coefficient, so they use the two t-test difference images for the next process.

6. **Binariation and Change Map:** NDVI is a more feasible index to forest-cover change detection. In the spectral change map, some buildings and roads are taken as changed region because of the influence of relative radioactive conditions. Therefore, the change map forming by NDVI value is useful and effective in forest-cover change detection.

Final conclusion of this paper is a novel automatic approach to unsupervised change detection in multi-temporal remotely sensed images has been proposed. The approach presents some important advantages over the classical unsupervised change detection techniques that are used in remotely sensed application:

1. It provides a well-defined methodological framework for automatic analysis of the difference image, thus avoiding heuristic approaches generally used in operational remote sensing;

2. It does not require any prior assumption for the statistical distribution model of changed and unchanged pixels in the difference image.

3. It allows the spatial-contextual information to be exploited efficiently in the change-detection process. Experimental results carried out on multi-temporal QuickBird remote sensing data set confirm the effectiveness of the proposed system. It is worth noting that the object-based forest-cover change detection has limits. The results have been influenced by different radioactive condition at different times. How to decrease the influence of relative radioactive difference will be the next work.

Grid Services and Satellite Image Processing for Urban and River Bed Changes Assessment

Mr. Cristina Gherghina tells about Grid based architectures might be suitable platforms for their digital processing and analysis because the required computational power to process satellite data in real time. Here, they described several Grid Services which implement some of the satellite images processing and analysis techniques used to detect urban growth and river bed changes. Thus, they have implemented a supervised image classification algorithm which marks out the urban or river bed areas, and a comparison image algorithm, which compares two classified images, taken in 1970 and 2000, and highlights the urban or river bed changes (*Cristina Gherghina* from "Ovidius" University of Constantza, *Eliza Isbasoiu* from Spiru, 2009).

Satellite images can be very useful in providing valuable information, but the human eye is not very sensitive to subtle changes in brightness and color. To overcome this difficulty we can use digital image processing, the only practical technology for classification, feature extraction, pattern recognition, projection, and others. The size of a typical satellite image is about 15-40 MB per spectral band. An image may include up to 7 bands (or more for multi-temporal processing). It is thus desirable to distribute the processing of satellite images over a heterogeneous network of computers, where each of them contributes to a faster result according to its capabilities. In this context, Grid based architectures may be a solution. Grid computing hooks up geographically or departmentally separate machines to create a "virtual" supercomputer. This virtual machine appears as a single pool of computing resources and possesses the computational muscle to do jobs that individual machines cannot.

Grid computing provided a favorable and consolidated way to combine and exploit computational power, being the best technology that allows the efficient and coordinated use of heterogeneous resources geographically distributed. Grid approach to a problem guarantees to achieve the needed level of abstraction from aspects such as data sources and computational resources. The software applications developed so far support image processing of MODIS images, cloud Detection, vegetation classification, unsupervised image classification. One of the Grid services developed within this project is the one that uses freely distributed software – GIMP, to detect river bed changes.

The Grid services they developed met the requirements of a user who wants to apply some standard image processing techniques to extract particular information from specific large satellite images. If the available computing power and storing resources are not allowing the local processing of the satellite images, the user will have to use the resources of a Grid infrastructure. Spectral-Scanners and Landsat 7 TM. The supervised image classification method used is the parallelepiped algorithm or the "box decision rule classifier". The parallelepiped classifier uses intervals or bounded regions of pixels' values to determine whether a pixel belongs to a class or not. The intervals' bounding points are obtained from the values of the pixels of the classes' samples. The sample of a class represents an area of known identity delineated on the digital image, usually by specifying the corner points of a rectangular or polygonal area using the line and column numbers within the coordinate system of the digital image.

The analyst who makes the samples must, of course, know the correct class for each area. Since this classifier is supervised, there are two steps in its use: signature creation and classification. Signatures can be considered as descriptors for the classes, often containing statistical information about the pixels used as samples. The signature creation's steps use as input the original image pixels, class description and samples data files to calculate the minimum and maximum bounding coordinate for each class. The classification operation input consists of the original image pixels, class description and the signatures created. based on an image from the list, the user creates the class description and samples' files (text files) and copies them through GridFTP on the storage-and-computing node where the image resides.

Apply the classification and comparison algorithms on the original image of the previously selected one, and saw the resulted from the classification and comparison algorithms. And it helps the user to easily upload any data or to download and visualize any image from the distributed database, by hiding the specific commands of the GridFTP file transfer.

The testing environment consists in a cluster with PC nodes which is shown in Figure 6. They performed the following test: first, apply classification method simultaneously on two images; next, apply comparison algorithm simultaneously on two couples of images. Processing time depended on the images size and processing algorithm invoked. The tests proved that the applications are efficient and easy to use.

Grid Based Satellite Image Processing Platform for Earth Observation Application Development

Mr. Dorian Gorgan of his research studies about the grid based Satellite Image Processing platform. The satellite images supplying information of earth surface, vegetations, weather conditions, geographic areas, pollution, and natural phenomena. This satellite data has multispectral bands. The data exploration

Figure 6. Services and its relationships

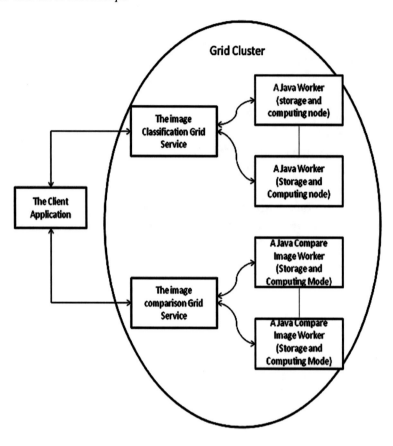

and interpretation should consider general and particular parameters. These specific conditions require flexible tools and friendly user interfaces to support the optimal search for appropriate solutions (Gorgan, Bacu, Stefanut, Rodila, & Mihon, 2009)

This paper describes the Environment oriented Satellite Data Processing Platform Architecture and the gProcess basic toolset. The ESIP platform has been developed through the SEE-GRID-SCI. ESIP supports the development and the execution of the Grid based applications concerning particularly with the processing of satellite images and generally with environmental related processing and studies.

The solutions for Grid processing description were based on workflow description by languages and graphs. Such projects were GridAnt, GWorkflowDL and BPEL4WS. Condor DagMAN handles direct acyclic graphs by dependencies between the jobs. It was based on condor job manager. Any failure in job execution triggers the resubmitting of that job. Another one is Pegasus, Which was used for two workflow models, abstract and concrete workflows. At execution time, Pegasus transforms the concrete workflow in Condor DagMAN specification.

Another Grid workflow management system GridFlow. This workflow management system focuses on service-level scheduling and workflow management rather than on workflow specification. This ESIP was based on the gProcess platform developed through the MedioGrid. The gProcess platform is an interactive toolset supported the flexible description, instantiation, scheduled and execution of the Grid processing. It was collection of Web and Grid services, and tools providing basic functionalities such as:

- Development of hypergraphs as complex composition of basic operators, Grid and Web services, and subgraphs;
- Pattern workflow instantiation for a particular satellite images;
- Satellite data access, management, and visualization;
- Workflow based Grid execution;
- Process execution control and visualization;
- Optimal execution for appropriate mapping of the processing over the Grid resources. The optimal processing is achieved in terms of code optimization, total execution time, and data communication costs over the Grid.

ESIP layers on gProcess a set of Web and Grid services, and image oriented basic operators such as Arithmetic - addition, division, multiplication, subtraction (applied to two input image files), exponent, complement, and negation (applied to a single input image file); Radiometric transformations - histogram equalization, mean, histogram scaling, linear scale and threshold based filtering of an image; Spatial domain transformations – blurring, convolution, sharpening, and median filters; Edge, line and spot detection - gradient transformation; Color conversion operators - transform image from a color model (such as RGB, CYMK, HSV) to another one, pseudo coloring multispectral image; Geometric transformations - rotation, scale, translation, and warp; Statistics – compute histogram, mean, and standard deviation pixel values of an image; and Nonspatial domain transforms - forward and inverse Fourier transformation, spectrum computation of a Fourier domain image. A few Multispectral Imagery Operators has been experimented as well, such as vegetation indices: DVI, NDVI, IPVI, RVI, OSAVI, GEMI; Water indices: NDWI, VWC, WI; Nonlinear interpolation; and Change detection. The compatibility with known image processing software packages such as GDAL, GRASS GIS, GIMP, and OpenGIS is the subject of current research and experiments as well.

The gProcess platform provided a flexible diagrammatical description solution for imagery processing workflows. Conceptually, a DAG describes the imagery processing algorithm. The nodes represent operators, services, subgraphs and input data, and the arcs represented the execution dependencies between nodes. The gProcess architecture is based on the client-server model. At the server side the Grid Infrastructure supported the access to computing resources and distributed databases through a set of services such as EditorWs, ManagerWS, ExecutorWS and Viewer WS.

EditorWS provides relevant information on available resources (e.g. lists of operations, subgraphs, satellite image types, data types). This information is then published by the EditorIC in some interaction components for designing and developing the graph editor's user interface. ManagerWS provides information on workflows (i.e. PDG, iPDG), and fetches and uploads related resources (i.e. workflows, operators, services, subgraphs, data). This service supports the main interaction with the gProcess operators, services, and resources available in the database. ExecutorWS executes the instantiated workflows (iPDG) over the Grid, and monitors this execution. The service maps the workflow into an internal data structure, and analyzes and schedules the operators for sequential and parallel execution over the Grid. ViewerWS gets and formats the input and output data (e.g. initial and processed satellite images).

It supports the access and visualization functionality of the satellite images. The client side encapsulates Client Java API, User Oriented Application Level, and Applications. The Web and desktop applications access the gProcess services by the Client Java API level. A set of user interaction supporting components, such as EditorIC, ManagerIC, and ViewerIC are exposed through the User Oriented Application Level.

The upper level, the Applications' one combines the editor, manager, and viewer related functionality into complex user interactive tools.

The Condor job manager is responsible with the scheduling and execution of processing graph nodes, and every atomic node is submitted as a request to the job manager. The gProcess database stores graph nodes related real time data such as execution status, output resource location, and starting and final execution time, supporting the visualization of the execution progression in the graphical user interface.

Several test cases were developed using various sets of data. The focus of this phase was on running complete and complex workflow in the gProcess that contained Service computational nodes in different relations with simple operators and sub graphs. This research was focused on integrating Web services into the gProcess application using BPEL business workflows. The future work includes developments such as complex workflow template files to allow a more flexible composition of several Web services, Accurate way of discovering and selecting web services, Failure aware, which implies adding a fault manager component to allow detection and recovery for faults that can appear at different levels.

Conclusion of this paper is, ESIP experiments the flexible components and tools provided by gProcess platform in the context of satellite imagery processing over the Grid. It explored the description and execution of workflows as complex hypergraphs combining satellite imagery processing atomic operators, simple and combined Web services, and subgraphs. ESIP is the basic platform for the development methodology used to build up and experiment the EO application over the Grid.

A Quantitative Evaluation of Image Segmentation Quality

Mr. Honglei Zhu tells about image segmentation qualities in satellite image processing. Segmentation is a procedure to group spatially adjacent image pixels into segments. Spatially adjacent pixels formed one image segment if they met some criteria. A segmentation results may vary, it's depending on generalization levels and other constraints. Their research gives a quantitative estimate of a segmentation result using indices such as: a) a summed standard deviation of the input images within each image segment; b) a summed absolute difference within each image segment; and c) a summed difference of a segment to its adjacent segments. A series of segmentation results were studied from two perspectives (Zhu & Chen, 2009).

The findings of their study can be used a) to guide an algorithm optimization for image segmentation, b) to assist the evaluation of different software programs to be used for a certain application and, c) to assist in identifying an optimal segmentation result for a given analysis. The advances of remote sensing sensor technology and improvements in image processing techniques, object oriented image analysis has been one of the most active research topics in satellite image processing. Image segmentation is often the first procedure employed in such an analysis and its result may then be utilized for further analysis. The quality of image segmentation is fundamental to a high quality object oriented image analysis. There are different segmentation algorithms for forming segments within an image.

Their research proposed three indices for a quantitative estimate: a) a sum of size-weighted standard deviation within each segment, derived from the input images, b) a sum of absolute differences within each image segment and, c) a sum of sized-weighted difference of a segment to its adjacent segments. A series of segmentation results were studied from two perspectives. One focused on a series of segmentation results with different generalization levels, and the other compared two series of segmentation results obtained using two different segmentation algorithms.

- **Segmentation Methods, Data Set, and Analysis:** Two commonly used segmentation approaches they were chosen to derive the series of segmentation. One is a watershed-based segmentation and the other, a region-grow approach. The detailed description about the region-grow approach can be found from Baatz and Schape (2000), and a watershed-based method is given as follows.
- **Watershed-Based Segmentation:** There were three steps involved in watershed-based image segmentation. 1) Derive surface image: a variance image is derived from each image layer. Centered at every pixel, a 3 by 3 moving window is used to derive its variance for that pixel. The surface image for watershed delineation is a weighted average of all variance images from all image layers. Equal weight is assumed in this study. 2) Delineate watersheds. From the surface image, pixels within a homogeneous region form a watershed. 3) Merge segments. Adjacent watershed may be merged to form a new segment with larger size according to their spectral similarity and a given generalization level.
- **Data Set:** QuickBird multispectral satellite imagery was used. The data set was collected on October 29, 2005. The area was around (42.4N, 83.8W), in the southeast of Michigan, U.S.A.. The image consisted of four bands, at the wavelengths of blue, green, red, and near infra-red. A subset with 1024 by 1024 rows and columns was utilized for this study. With a spatial resolution of 2.6 meters, the data set covers about 7.1 square km.
- **Statistical Analysis:** A series of segmentation for both watershed-based and region-grow approaches were derived. And each series contained 20 generalization levels, from as fine as 39595 segments, to as coarse as one segment for the whole imagery. They were at the intermediate generalization level. The breakdown of the 20 levels can be seen from the x-axis. Measured the quality of three indices. In order to describe the degree of compactness, a measured of sum of perimeters of segments was adopted.

Their Study given a quantitative estimate about the statistical characteristics of a segmentation result. Three indices, sum of size-weighted standard deviation, sum of absolute differences to mean, and sum of size-weighted differences to neighboring segments, were introduced for a quantitative estimate from two perspectives. The first perspective was the responses of the indices to the generalization levels.

Analysis of Time Series of Landsat Images

Mr. Thomas Bauer study was temporal changes of coca fields interpreted by SIMIC II interpreters on Landsat images of consecutive years. Next thing is analysis of spectral and shape features of coca fields. Influence of spraying and the relation between the image acquisition date and the date of the spraying was investigated. Their research input data is Landsat 7 ETM+ of October 2005, January 2006, December 2006, and January 2008. Survey of coca fields was taken. Final processed data is Orthophotograph of January 2008 (*Bauer & Schneider, 2009*).

Methodology of their paper was 1) Stability of coca fields, that means GIS analysis of the temporal change of coca fields: 2005, 2006, and 2007. 2) Investigations on the spectral characteristics, NDVI vegetation index. 3) Analysis of the influence of spraying lines. From Vegetation index they found sensitive indicator of the presence and condition of green vegetation, Vegetated areas – high values because of relatively high near infrared reflectance and low visible reflectance, Bare soil areas – similar reflectance in the two bands; vegetation indices near zero, NDVI.

Final conclusion of their paper is GIS analysis: Shape features(size, area), they found Normalized Difference Vegetation Index of different year. From that they analyzed influence of spraying in conjunction with NDVI. From NDVI they showed the seasonality investigations based on Normalized Difference Vegetation Index.

Analysis of Spatiotemporal Difference of NDVI

Mr. Lei and Bian of their study was to compare the spatiotemporal difference of the vegetation index extracted from TM and MODIS images by time series analysis and spatial statistics, and found the relationship among between the vegetation, climate factors, coal mining etc..The study area is located at an arid mine area, where the mining activities and ecology reconstruction is ongoing. It was found that the MODISNDVI (monthly or 16 days) products can provide results close to the NDVI derived from atmosphere corrected TM images. Time series analysis found that the monthly NDVI, rainfall and temperature are consistently subjected to annual periodical rhythm under the impacts of coal mining. And there was a significant correlation between NDVI and rainfall & temperature in the arid mine area. NDVI-TM (30 m) or NDVI-MODIS (250 m) are feasible for spatial statistics at their study area. Higher value of NDVI is accompanied by higher spatial variation of NDVI with a squared correlation coefficient (R2 =0.6983). It was probably because the natural arid landform was damaged by human activities (Lei & Bian, 2010).

The objective of their study was to find the spatial and temporal variation of vegetation under the influence of local arid climate, vegetation reconstruction and mining activities, at a mine area with arid and semi-arid climate and located in north of China. Their case study area was Shendong coal mine area located at the border of Shanxi province and Inner Monogolia. The total area size is about 3200 km2; and the elevation is between 1000 m to 1500 m. The average annual rainfall is about 436.7 mm, about 70% of which happens in July, August and September (Cui et al., 2001). And the groundwater is deep below the surface and intermittent. The surface was Aeolian landform with sparse vegetation which is typical sandy land vegetation.

- **Dataset:** Landsat TM/ETM+ satellite data, three Landsat TM images were acquired and processed. The NDVI calculated based on equation, then the mean NDVI of the study area can be obtained by statistics. MODIS-NDVI products, there are several types of MODIS-NDVI products with different spatial and temporal resolution produced by Earth Observation System. In their study67 MODIS-NDVI-Monthly-1km and several MODIS-NDVI-16 days-250m images from January 2000 to August 2005 were processed.
- **Spatiotemporal Statistics:** Temporal changes of mean NDVI were derived from monthly MODIS vegetation products to reflect the vegetation change varying with time. The correlations between the NDVI and the climates factors, e.g. monthly rainfall and air temperature were analyzed to determine the influences of climate factors on the vegetation in arid mining region. A semivariogram analysis was used to describe the spatial variance and spatial structure of the NDVI. The semi variance statistic was calculated as one half of the average squared.
- **Temporal Change of NDVI:** They showed the NDVI derived from Landsat TM and MODIS images at the same period. It was noticed that the NDVI with FLAASH correction provides a much closer and more reasonable fit with the MODIS-NDVI than the uncorrected NDVI. Therefore, they remove the atmosphere effect before calculation of NDVI. Moreover, the difference between

the corrected NDVI and MODIS-NDVI was due to the different methods of NDVI acquisition. The NDVI of Landsat was for one day; but MODIS-NDVI was the maximum NDVI over a period.

The spatial characteristics obtained from different spatial resolution (30 m, 250 m, and 1 km) of NDVI were analyzed and compared by semi variance analysis. It was found that the NDVI of 2002 and 2003 in July are of higher semi variance, because of the higher value of NDVI. Detailed analysis can be made by using an empirical semi variance model. The exponential model was determined as optimal empirical semi variance model, the key parameters of which were provided.

Conclusion of their paper was MODIS-NDVI and Landsat-TM images were processed to study the spatiotemporal variance of vegetation in an arid mining area. It was found that MODIS-NDVI products can provide results close to the NDVI derived from atmosphere corrected TM images. Time series analysis found that the monthly NDVI, rainfall and temperature are consistently subject to annual periodical rhythm. The arid climate variables are still the dominating factors, instead of underground coal mining.

Remote Sensing Monitoring for Vegetation Change in Mining Area Based on Spot-VGT NDVI

Mr. Baodonga and Mr. Lixinb of their research paper includes the composition of time series data, the vegetation variation analysis and gradation of desertification land. The variation of NDVI is divided into 7 levels according to the slope of the fitted line by using NDVI time series data. The desertification land is divided into 5 levels according to the vegetation coverage, which was transformed from NDVI. The method was validated in Ningdong coal mining area, Northwest China and their results showed that the method was valid and effective (Baodonga, Lixinb, & Shanjuna,2011).

The change in vegetation was the most direct indicator of land degradation. The Normalized Difference Vegetation Index was frequently used to assess the condition of vegetation. The environment and vegetation cover in mining area were influenced by the exploitation and utilization of mineral resources. SPOTVGT NDVI as information source and considered the characteristics of mining areas in China, their paper introduced how to monitor the vegetation change and desertification in mining area.

- **Data Set:** The investigations were performed by using NDVI data derived from the VEGETATION sensor on board the SPOT satellite platforms with 1 km spatial resolution. The data were subjected to atmospheric corrections performed by CNES on the basis of the simplified method for atmospheric corrections (SMAC). That allows for reducing the contamination effects due to residual clouds, atmospheric perturbations, variable illumination and viewing geometry that are generally present in daily NDVI maps.
- **Changing Trend Analysis to NDVI:** Based on the yearly SPOT-VGT NDVI data, the linear regression of one variable was used to simulate the changing trend of the vegetation in mining area. For each pixel, the slope of the fitted line shows the changing trend of the vegetation. For example, it means that good trend for vegetation if the slope is positive; on the other hand, it means bad trend for vegetation if the slope is negative. In detail, the degree of vegetation variation was divided into 7 levels according to the slope of the fitted line by using NDVI time series data. Second method Land desertification grading, the relationship between NDVI and vegetation coverage was known from other objects.

Next thing was for the variation analysis based on NDVI, the linear regression of one variable was used to simulate the changing trend of the vegetation in the coal mining area. The degree of vegetation variation was divided into 7 levels according to the slope of the fettle line. The results showed that improved vegetation are accounted and degraded vegetation area accounted.

Conclusion of the paper is the time series data of SPOT-VGT NDVI could be composed accordingly to reveal the vegetation information evidently. By the linear regression of one-variable, the changed trend of vegetation could be depicted during a period. By grading the land desertification according to vegetation coverage, multi-temporal desertification in mining area could be monitored. The vegetation variation and land desertification in mining area can be monitored dynamically and evaluated effectively.

MODIS-NDVI-Based Crop Growth Monitoring

Mr. Huang quing and Mr, Zhang Li of their paper tells about, a MODIS-NDVI based method for operational crop growth monitoring in China agriculture remote sensing monitoring system was presented. Some meteorological data such as temperature, precipitation and sunshine, as well as the field observation data were used to modify the models parameters. The crop growth conditions were categorized into three classes, better than usual, usual and worse than usual, and application of this method to bring wheat, winter wheat, spring maize, summer maize, cotton, soybean and paddy rice and its results were introduced (Quing, Li, Wenbin, & Dandan, 2010).

In large-scale for farmers, it was difficult to applications because of time, people and accuracy of information could not be assured. With an objective, timely feature, remote sensing can get a wide range of ground-based information in a short time and it has a unique advantage in monitoring the agricultural situation. Their project was divided into three phases; the first phase was to monitor the changes of wheat acreage, estimate the yield and total production to nine wheat production states of the U.S. Great Plains; The second phase was to monitor the crops growth condition and food production not only their own country, but also Canada and parts of the former Soviet Union; The third phase is to monitor the changes of wheat acreage, estimate the yield and total production to the world's major grain-producing countries, such as Canada, Mexico, Argentina, Brazil, the former Soviet Union, China, India, the Middle East, Australia and etc., which established an agricultural monitor system of global level.

- **Data Preparation:** Remote sensing data preparation and preprocessing, Vegetation indexes are important parameters which carry abundant information of earth surface vegetation properties. NDVI (Normalized Difference Vegetation Index) which can be generated from the red and near-infrared bands of the MODIS data enhance the identify capacity to soil background and weaken the impact of atmosphere and terrain shadow, and NDVI values increase with the growth of the crops, and gradually decrease after reaching the maximum at a certain growth stage of the crops. NDVI has more advantages in monitoring crop growth condition than other index. In order to effectively eliminate the cloud cover, atmospheric affects and other unfavorable factors, NDVI maximum values of monitoring period were composite.

The process of remote sensing data preparation and preprocessing is as follows: Firstly, everyday MODIS data covering the whole China are received by MODIS satellite receiving station, then these data are transferred to the processing unit where processing is performed using the remote sensing image processing system. After the preprocessing, including radiometric correction, geometric correction, projection changes, clouds marks etc, the red and near-infrared bands of the MODIS data were used to composite NDVI. Daily images are used to produce a sixteen-day, cloud free composite image for NDVI with maximum value composite method.

- **Other Data Preparation:** Some other data related to crop growth condition were collected to a have some basic information about the study area and crops. These data include: regional topographic map; regional administrative division map; land use and land cover maps; crop distribution maps; historical MODIS data of monitoring period; meteorological data of temperature, precipitation and sunshine, as well as the field investigation data.
- **Methodology:** In their study, an improved NDVI difference model in CHARMS was used to assess different crops growth situation. Based on crop growth condition of current monitoring period, the maximum average NDVI data of the last five years was subtracted by the maximum NDVI of study period by using the Equation, resulting in a NDVI difference data, which showed could indicate the spatial difference of crop growth condition at a certain period. Since NDVI value for individual pixel can be affected by atmospheric condition, a 3 by 3 filter approach was applied to each pixel, namely, the value of each pixel is generated from the average NDVI values of itself and its adjacent 8-pixels.

Based on the calculated R values, the crop growth condition were categorized into three classes, better than usual, usual and worse than usual, or well, general and bad. If there is cloud cover over the area, this area was processed as a non-monitored area, crop growth was not evaluated. Last, crop growth condition was assessment at four different scales. And the spatial distribution maps of crop growth condition were also created. That method was then used to monitor the growth condition of spring wheat, winter wheat, spring maize, summer maize, and cotton, soybean and paddy rice. The monitoring results can supply real time crop growth information for relevant department and relevant provinces or regions.

Conclusion of the paper was Crop growth dynamic monitoring was significance in guarantying national food security and promoting agriculture sustainable development. To understand the Agricultural production condition timely and accurately is related to government decision-making, agricultural production management and the general public concerns. Remote sensing could get a wide range of ground-based information in a short time and it has a unique advantage in monitoring the agricultural situation. The early crop growing condition monitoring in CHARMS were invaluable to decision makers and analysts within government agencies for better management of agriculture.

Colour Based Image Segmentation Using K-Means Clustering

Mr. Anil Chitade, Mr. Katiyar of their work presents a novel image segmentation based on colour features with K-means clustering unsupervised algorithm. In this we did not used any training data. The entire work is divided into two stages. First enhancement of color separation of satellite image using decorrelation stretching is carried out and then the regions are grouped into a set of five classes using K-means clustering algorithm. Using this two step process, it was possible to reduce the computational cost avoiding feature calculation for every pixel in the image. Although the colour is not frequently used for image segmentation, it gives a high discriminative power of regions present in the image (Chitade & Katiyar, 2010).

The most common features used in image segmentation include texture, shape, grey level intensity, and colour. The constitution of the right data space is a common problem in connection with segmentation/classification. In order to construct realistic classifiers, the features that are sufficiently representative of the physical process must be searched. It was observed that different transforms were used to extract desired information from remote-sensing images or biomedical images. Segmentation evaluation techniques can be generally divided into two categories (supervised and unsupervised). The first category was not applicable to remote sensing because an optimum segmentation (ground truth segmentation) was difficult to obtain. Moreover, available segmentation evaluation techniques have not been thoroughly tested for remotely sensed data. Therefore, for comparison purposes, it was possible to proceed with the classification process and then indirectly assess the segmentation process through the produced classification accuracies.

De-correlation stretching enhances the color separation of an image with significant band-to-band correlation. The exaggerated colors improve visual interpretation and make feature discrimination easier. They applied decorrelation stretching with the de-corrstretch function. The number of color bands, NBANDS, in the image is taken three. But they could applied de-correlation stretching regardless of the number of color bands. The original color values of the image are mapped to a new set of color values with a wider range. The color intensities of each pixel were transformed into the color eigenspace of the NBANDS-by-NBANDS covariance or correlation matrix, stretched to equalize the band variances, and then transformed back to the original color bands. To define the band wise statistics, they could use the entire original image, with the subset option, or any selected subset of it.

- **K-Means Clustering:** Clustering algorithms used for unsupervised classification of remote sensing data vary according to the efficiency with which clustering takes Place. K-means was the clustering algorithm used to determine the natural spectral groupings present in a data set. This accepts from analyst the number of clusters to be located in the data. The algorithm then arbitrarily seeds or locates, that number of cluster centers in multidimensional measurement space. Each pixel in the image was then assigned to the cluster whose arbitrary mean vector is closest. The procedure continues until there was no significant change in the location of class mean vectors between successive iterations of the algorithms. K-means approach was iterative; it was computationally intensive and hence applied only to image subareas rather than to full scenes and can be treated as unsupervised training areas.
- **Color-Based Segmentation Using K-Means Clustering:** For that the image was read from particular source. For colour separation of an image they applied the decorrelation stretching. Then they convert that image from RGB color space to L*a*b color space. After that they classified the color in a*b* space using K-Means clustering. Images were created by segment the image by color. Next that was segmented from Nuclei into a separate image.

Conclusion was color based image segmentation; it was possible to reduce the computation cost avoided feature calculation for every pixel in the image. Although the color was not frequently used for image segmentation may be used for mapping the changes in land use land cover taken over temporal period in general but not in particular.

Calculating NDVI for Landsat7-ETM Data after Atmospheric Correction Using 6S Model

Mr. Yaowen Xie, Mr. Xiaojiong of their study tells about, firstly atmospheric correction parameters identified for landsat7-ETM remote sensing image in Zhangye city. And then the Normalized Difference Vegetation Index (NDVI) of desert, grassland and forest from May 2001 to November 2002 was calculated before and after making the atmospheric correction. The spatio-temporal changes in the NDVI were analyzed, thus the effect of atmospheric correction was evaluated for different land covers spectral response characteristics of ETM satellite image. The result showed that firstly the intercept of the regression line, between the NDVI of before and after correction, was almost the same for each land cover type. In all of the desert, grassland and forest land, atmospheric correction made the NDVI larger by at least 0.05; In the desert, NDVI before correction less seasonal change than NDVI after correction; in the grassland, NDVI before correction and NDVI after correction showed the same seasonal trend; in the forest land, NDVI after correction increased more rapidly and decreased more gradually than the NDVI before correction before and after the peak. Next the aerosol optical thickness and elevation in each pixel were considered in this 6S model, so the results of atmospheric correction could be more reasonable and more truly reflect the surface vegetation conditions (Xie, Zhao, Li, & Wang, 2010).

Due to the absorption and scattering of atmospheric composition such as atmospheric molecules, aerosols and cloud particles impact on the remote sensing information, which lead to a certain amount of non-target features information were mixed in the remote sensing information required, so preprocessed accuracy of data less than requirements of quantitative analysis. The aim of atmospheric correction is to eliminate the effects of atmospheric interference on satellite data. Atmospheric correction is particularly important in calculating the vegetation index using reflectance in the red and near-infrared spectral bands, because aerosol increases, and precipitable water decreases, the reflectance in each spectral band, with the rate fixed for each spectral band. Consequently, these effects made the NDVI values smaller than their true value.

When 6S model was used to simulated the atmospheric scattering process, it was necessary to input a number of atmospheric correction parameters, in which aerosol optical thickness and elevation have a greater impact on the results of Atmospheric correction. Therefore, in their study, first, atmospheric correction parameters for the Landsat-ETM images were analyzed, in order to evaluate the atmospheric correction impact on spectral response characteristics of surface features for ETM images, the Normalized Difference Vegetation Index (NDVI) of desert, grassland, and forested areas were calculated after making the atmospheric correction. And also the spatio-temporal change in the NDVI was analyzed, aiming at obtained the true surface vegetation conditions, improved the accuracy of vegetation remote sensing studies, so that the research ideas will be provided for the choice of atmospheric correction in vegetation remote sensing.

Atmospheric correction were affected by various parameters, including geometric parameters, atmospheric model, aerosol model, spectrum conditions, ground reflectance and elevation parameters of the target and the sensor. When all of the time, longitude and latitude in center point required from image header file were inputted into the 6S model, which can calculate automatically solar zenith angle, observation zenith angle and azimuth to determine the geometric parameters. Standard atmospheric model, which was mid-latitude summer atmospheric model, was used in this 6S model. Although the results of atmospheric correction were more accuracy adopting measured atmospheric conditions, the acquisition process of measured data is difficult. Therefore, the selection of standard atmospheric model is a simple and practical method of the atmospheric correction.

The best method for aerosol optical thickness required was measurement using spectrophotometer in the study area, whereas many number of samples need to be measured for images with wide coverage area and complex underlying surface, and for the historical image data, aerosol optical thickness data could not be given. For the aerosol conditions of ETM image, the gray level of aerosol optical thickness with a resolution of 1 km can be got from MODIS aerosol products AOT, which is a good way of ETM aerosol status obtained. In their study, MODIS 550 nm aerosol products AOT with a resolution of 1 km and the SRTM data with a resolution of 90 m were resample into a resolution of 30m, which was registered with the corrected image. The surface reflectance in a pixel was calculated using this pixel of the aerosol optical thickness and elevation as the calibration parameters.

The different seasons and months, the concentration of the water vapor, aerosol was not same in the same point of image. So in order to evaluate the effect of correction for different time images, it was necessary to analyze the change of NDVI before and after correction. For the desert, grassland and forestland areas, atmospheric correction made the NDVI larger by at least 0.05. In the desert, seasonal change in the NDVI was small, NDVI-b was less seasonal change than NDVI-a, the range of NDVI-a have a distinct increase.

Their research paper presented a method of atmospheric correction for Landsat-ETM, taken into account existing research results, the input parameters, including aerosol optical thickness, elevation, which had the significant effect on the results of the correction, were detailedly analyzed. The changes in the relationship between NDVI before and after atmospheric correction were analyzed, indicating that it was valid that 6S atmospheric correction model was applied to this study area, the NDVI after correction had a clear upward trend. So the 6S model can effectively reduce the atmospheric influence in the transmission of electromagnetic waves.

Analysis of Spectral Vegetation Indices Related to Soil-Line for Mapping Mangrove Forests Using Satellite Imagery

Mr. Ibrahim and Mr. Usali of their study was for finding the variation of spectral vegetation indices related to soil-line typically found in Mangrove forest. That was done by using soil-line based vegetation indices such as Perpendicular Vegetation Index (PVI), Soil-adjusted Vegetation Index(SAVI), Optimized Soil-Adjusted Vegetation Index, Transformed Soil-Adjusted Vegetation Index (TSAVI) and Modified Soil-Adjusted Vegetation Index (MSAVI). The Landsat TM image was used to identify and classify mangrove areas within the study area. Intercept and parameter were introduced in mangrove mapping in order to remove the soil background. A total of five mangrove classes were mapped out. The accuracy of mapping using five indices was ranges 70% to 79% respectively. Results the SAVI were the best indices for mangrove mapping compared to other indices with accuracy of 79% and able to determine four mangrove classes (Kasawani, Norsaliza, & Hasmadi,2010).

Vegetation indices derived from satellite image data became one of the primary information sources for monitoring vegetation conditions and mapping land cover change. Many remote sensing studies utilized vegetation indices to study vegetation, with assuming that the properties of the background are constant or soil variations are normalized by the particular vegetation index used Mangroves have a wide geographical distribution. Mangrove vegetation has a vital function in maintaining the equilibrium and secondary productivity of coastal lagoons and estuaries and forms the base of most coastal trophic structures by means of a constant organic matter production throughout the year. Vegetation indices have typically been obtained from spectral reflectance's of red and near infrared bands to evaluate vegetation canopies.

Mangrove was an important component of global ecosystems and knowledge of the Earths mangrove is important to understand land-atmosphere interactions and their effects on climate. Thus, their study investigates the variation of spectral vegetation indices related to soil-line typically found in mangrove forest. Several soil line based vegetation indices were used such as Perpendicular Vegetation Index (PVI), Soil-adjusted Vegetation Index (SAVI), Optimized Soil-Adjusted Vegetation Index (OSAVI), Transformed Soil-adjusted Vegetation Index (TSAVI) and Modified Soil-adjusted Vegetation Index (MSAVI).

Application of Vegetation Index's and Soil-line based Vegetation Index's in mangrove forest: Study conducted and identified that the vegetation species in the East Coast mangrove of Peninsular Malaysia using Vegetation Index's. The spectral reflectance of a plant canopy was combination of the reflectance spectra of plant and soil component. The spectral was governed by the optical properties of the elements and photon exchange with the canopy. The severity of soil noise decreased in both sparser vegetation canopies and in more humid. The soil-line was a linear relationship between the NIR and R reflectance of bare soil originally discovered by Richardson and Wiegand, with NIR=aR+b, Where 'a' is the soil line slope and 'b' is the intercept.

A total of 60 trained areas were used using stratified random sampling to determine the accuracy for each output images of the unsupervised classification. The overall classification accuracy obtained for all indices were determined more than 70%. Soil reflectance's in mangroves areas of Kelantan Delta are low in all bands. It might due to four factors such as minerals composition, soil moisture content, organic matter contents and soil texture. PVI, SAVI, OSAVI and TSAVI all mangrove vegetation showed a bright reflectance but non-mangroves areas represent by darker reflectance. On the other than the vegetation index value of mangrove forests for SAVI is not altered by soil background. It might be due to SAVI values seem to be less affected by soil-brightness variation and thus VI values obtained for a given canopy cover are rather the same, independently of soil background.

The grey scale image of MSAVI it was differs than other indices. It might be possible because mangroves area reflected in dark while non-mangroves reflected in lighter color. The value of the mangrove forests was lower compared to non-mangroves. This was occurred although MSAVI considering reducing the soil effects. The SAVI, OSAVI, and TSAVI exhibits the similar index value for the mangrove forests based on the ratio between NIR and Red reflectance. The PVI expressed the distance between canopy R and NIR reflectance and the soil line. Although it was better than NDVI at low vegetation densities case but it was still affected by the soil. MSAVI was performed and results occurred better than other PVI, SAVI, OSAVI and TSAVI. MSAVI was designed to correct weakness of SAVI for vegetation responds as it moves away from the soil line. MSAVI was increased the dynamic range for vegetation signal, as well as further minimizing the soil background influences, and resulting in greater vegetation sensitivity as defined.

Conclusion of their paper was soil-based Vegetation Index approach was successful in discriminating mangrove species and therefore successful to map and identify mangrove forests in Kelantan Delta. The SAVI was found as the best indices with maximum accuracy, which distinguished mangrove in four classes, compared to normal unsupervised classification of same accuracy for five classes. It was also better compared to the others selected VI's in their study.

Table 2. Research issues

S. No.	Research Issues	Proposed Work
1	Studies of their data are to motivate subsequent research of general mathematical problems. They include further methods of time series processing of two dimensional interpolation using non-linear methods, image preprocessing, filtering, image enhancement and channels correlation. it contribute both to environmental sensing and to the area of signal analysis	They missed to generate graph representation of all processed data. They didn't continue this for more places, more time sequences. They forget to differentiate their results for multiple observed objects.
2	Fuzzy C-Means method was premised on the natural idea that each characteristic of a typical representative should be equal to an average over all elements of the corresponding cluster. Problem of choosing the optimal fuzzy clustering as a precise mathematical problem was solved. This paper presents the results of work aimed at developing a fuzzy object data model that was developed. Prototype implementation of this model using an integrative approach with commercial software packages are also described.	K-Means clustering method was not introduced. Geological decision making based upon fuzzy clustering is should make good sense to utilize the information that is made available through remote sensing.
3	NPP estimation model was presented by using ground meterological data and remote sensing data. After the validation with observed data and comparison with other NPP models. The spatio-temporal distribution was analyzed for particular place.	For NPP they did not use other techniques for validation. GPP was not estimated.
4	Time series of MSG SEVIRI NDVI are plotted together with MODIS terra and aqua NDVI. Cloud free scenes are included as specified by the MODIS quality flags and the MSG cloud mask. Red and near-infrared reflectances have been aggreated to match the MSG SEVIRI spatial pixel resolution before calculation of NDVI. every data were combined.	Identification of precipating cloud type, rainfall analysis was missed
5	Described C-LOD method reduces roughly 100.00 visible trees depending on the point of view. Another possible option is to accelerate the display of the cached geometry by using impostors and billboard clouds for distant trees. Additionally a geometrical plant representation can be used to improve the appearance of nearby trees.	GIS parameters didn't used to find average rainfall and soil classifications.
6	The Enhanced Vegetation Index was proposed to reduce both atmospheric and soil background noise simultaneously. Although the EVI performs better than does the NDVI in many applications. It shows that the NDVI can be expressed as a function of the ratio vegetation indiex, which can reduce the direct effect of topography absolutely.	There is no aware of that the topographic effect is relative to spatial scale: as the size of the pixel increases, the effect of topography may decrease or even disappear. The quantitative relationship between spatial scale and topographic effect was not defined.
7	Concerning the vegetation monitoring, they proved several vegetation indices can improve either the accuracy of the fCover estimation or its robustness. These conclusions were drawn from the analysis of simulated data using the coupled, with or without natural variability parameters.	In the case of more sophisticated inversion methods, there is no real improvement. They didn't show much concentration on correlation and redundancy between sources. Another problem is the modeling of the partial redundancy between three or more sources.
8	Grid technologies provide powerful tools for remote sensing data sharing and processing. Realizing this factm a new platform based on open-source software was built to serve the requests coming from field specialists as well as beginners.	Developments of the platform are related to the issue of real-time processing and new service integration didn't occur.
9	NDVI derived from TM/ETM + images provide useful information to monitor vegetation changes. The analysis of NDVI variations showed that the landscapes on which grow perennial herbage, and desert shrub. The correlation analysis between NDVI and annual precipitation-controlled natural vegetation coverage in the margins of the Minqin oasis has overshadowed the made-planted vegetation.	Vegetation might not be calculated at different time series and different seasons.
10	a novel automatic approach to unsupervised change detection in multi-temporal remotely sensed images has been proposed. The approach presents some important advantages over the classical unsupervised change detection techniques that are used in remotely sensed application.	They used only NDVI vegetation method. They didn't use other vegetation methodologies.

From Table 2, the proposed system for Vegetation Index will be introduced. This proposed system has many image processing techniques and solution for finding vegetation. It is new and better than previous research study. The derived proposed system is given below and its descriptive explanations are also mentioned. Figure 7 shows the proposed architecture.

Figure 7. Proposed architecture

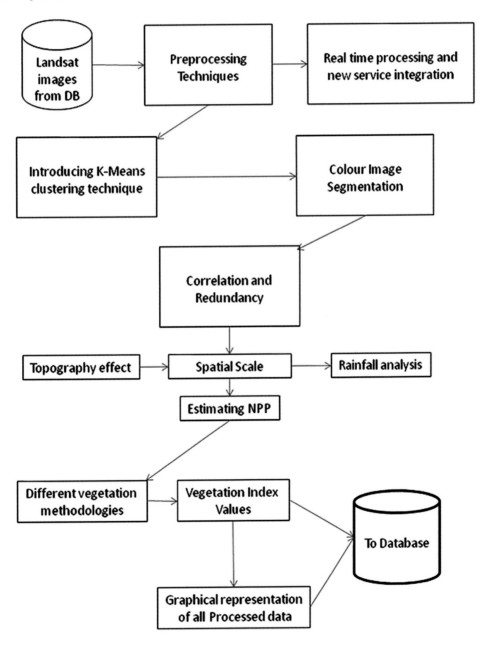

Proposed Work

- **Landsat Images from DB:** Here the required data is retrieved from US Glovis Landsat area. The USGS now offers all users the entire Landsat 1-5 and 7 archive data at no charge using a standard data product recipe. So that all the current up-to-date data can be stored to one particular database. Landsat image file type is.jpg. This data available from two different views, they are 1000 m and 250 m. We can use 250 m Landsat image for vegetation index.

- **Preprocessing Techniques:** Pre-processing techniques are used to attenuate geometric and radiometric variations in orbital images. In order to get a cartographic uniformity of the different scenes used, a geometric correction technique was applied based on control points from a pre-registered image. The correction were made using first order polynomial transformation model and nearest neighbor method for resampling. Some of the preprocessing techniques are contrast the image, resize the image, sharpen the image, etc.

- **Real Time Processing and New Service Integration:** After completion of preprocessing some real time processing should be introduce along with new service integration. Some examples are introducing segmentation methods, different correlation methods.

- **Introducing K-Means Clustering Technique:** Cluster analysis or clustering is the task of assigning a set of objects into groups (called clusters) so that the objects in the same cluster are more similar (in some sense or another) to each other than to those in other clusters. Clustering is a main task of explorative data mining, and a common technique for statistical data analysis used in many fields, including machine learning, pattern recognition, image analysis, information retrieval, and bioinformatics. The most common algorithm uses an iterative refinement technique. Due to its ubiquity it is often called the *k*-means algorithm; it is also referred to as Lloyd's algorithm, particularly in the computer science community

Fuzzy C-means clustering is a soft version of K-means, where each data point has a fuzzy degree of belonging to each cluster. Gaussian mixture models trained with expectation-maximization algorithm (EM algorithm) maintains probabilistic assignments to clusters, instead of deterministic assignments, and multivariate Gaussian distributions instead of means. Several methods have been proposed to choose better starting clusters. One recent proposal is k-means++. The filtering algorithm uses kd-trees to speed up each k-means step.

- **Colour Image Segmentation:** After introducing of Clustering techniques, the image should be segment to find NDVI of the particular area. So the Colour Image Segmentation is very important to find Vegetation index. By this way we can use multiple image segmentation methods over an image.

- **Spatial Scale, Rainfall Analysis:** After completing the colour image segmentation we can find out NDVI easily. From that we can scale about the spatial value of the processing image, with the help of NDVI we can easily conclude about the Rainfall of that particular area by variation in biospheric activities. Significant relationships are finding between seasonal rainfall and NDVI range (NDVI) with better correlations.

- **Estimating Net Primary Productivity:** Conversion of native forests to agriculture and urban land leads to fragmentation of forested landscapes with significant consequences for habitat conservation and forest productivity. The Normalized Difference Vegetation Index (NDVI) and its subsequent are use to predict biophysical parameters such as the fraction of photo synthetically active radiation intercepted by forest canopies (fPAR). This means that simulated aboveground net primary productivity (NPPA) using canopy radiation interception models such as 3-PG (Physiological Principles for Predicting Growth), coupled with remote sensing observations, can yield different results in fragmented landscapes depending on the spatial resolution of the remotely sensed data.

- **Different Vegetation Methodologies:** Other than NDVI, we can use other vegetation index finding methodologies and its formulations. They are Perpendicular Vegetation Index, Weighted Infrared Vegetation Index, Ratio Vegetation Index, Soil-adjusted Vegetation Index; Transformed Soil adjusted Vegetation Index, Modified Soil Adjusted Vegetation Index. Each can have different abbreviations with different formulations.

- **Vegetation Index Values with Graphical Representation:** After using the different vegetation methodologies we can get the perfect Vegetation Index values, from that value we can generate Histograms, Visible bands of the images, True color images, Scatter plots of images, Cluster images. These Vegetation index values with respective graphical images are stored to output database.

REFERENCES

Bauer & Schneider. (2009). *Analysis of time series of Landsat images*. Institute of Surveying, Remote Sensing and Land Information, University of Natural Resources and Applied Life Sciences (BOKU).

Chitade & Katiyar. (2010). *Colour Based Image Segmentation using K-Means Clustering*. Department of Civil Engineering, Manit, Bhopal, Madhyapradesh.

Fensholt, Sandholt, & Stisen. (2006). *Analysing NDVI for the African continent using the geostationary meteosat second generation SEVIRI sensor*. Compton Tucker at Institute of Geography, University of Copenhagen, University of Copenhagen.

Gherghina. (2009). *Grid Services and Satellite Image Processing for urban and river bed changes assessment*. "Ovidius" University of Constantza.

Gorgan, Bacu, Stefanut, Rodila, & Mihon. (2009). *Grid based Satellite Image Processing Platform for Earth Observation Application Development*. Technical University of Cluj-Napoca.

Huang, Wan, & Shen. (2009). *An Object-Based Approach for Forest-Cover Change Detection using Multi-Temporal High-Resolution Remote Sensing Data*. School of Remote Sensing and Information Engineering, Wuhan University.

Huang, Zhang, Wu, & Li. (2010). *MODIS-NDVI-Based crop growth monitoring in China Agriculture Remote Sensing Monitoring System*. Grassland Ecosystem Observation and Research Station Institute of Agricultural Resources and Regional Planning of Chinese Academy of Agricultural Sciences.

Kallel, Hégarat-Mascle, Hubert-Moy, & Ottlé. (2008). *Fusion of Vegetation Indices Using Continuous Belief Functions and Cautious-Adaptive*. Academic Press.

Kasawani, Norsaliza, & Hasmadi. (2010). *Analysis of Spectral Vegetation Indices Related to Soil-Line for Mapping Mangrove Forests Using Satellite Imagery*. University of Malaysia Terengganu.

Lei & , Bian. (2010). Analysis of Spatiotemporal Difference of NDVI in an Arid Coal Mining Region using. *Remote Sensing*.

Ma, Wu, & Liu. (2010). *Remote Sensing Monitoring For Vegetation Change In Mining Area Based On Spot-VGT NDVI*. Institute for Geoinformatics & Digital Mine Research, Northeastern University.

Matsushita, Yang, Chen, Onda1, & Qiu. (2007). *Sensitivity of the Enhanced Vegetation Index (EVI) and Normalized Difference Vegetation Index (NDVI) to Topographic Effects: A Case Study in High-Density Cypress Forest*. Graduate School of Life and Environmental Sciences, University of Tsukuba.

Prochdxka & Kolinovd. (2004). *Satellite Image Processing and Air Pollution Detection*. Prague Institute of Chemical Technology.

Roettger. (2006). *NDVI Based Vegetation Rendering*. Computer Graphics Group, University of Erlangen.

Starks. (2004). *Interval and Fuzzy Methods in Remote Sensing and Satellite Image Processing*. University of Texas at El Paso.

Xie, Zhao, Li, & Wang. (2010). *Calculating NDVI for Landsat7-ETM Data after atmospheric correction Using 6S Model*. Key Laboratory of West China's Environmental System.

Youhao, Jihe, Shangyu, Ping, & Zihui. (2008). *Monitoring of Vegetation Changes Using Multi-temporal NDVI in Peripheral Regions around Minqin Oasis, Northwest China*. College of Resources Science and Technology.

Petcu, Zaharie, Gorgan, Pop, & Tudor. (2008). *MedioGrid: A Grid-based Platform for Satellite Image Processing*. Western University of Timisoara.

Zhu & Chen. (2009). *A Quantitative Evaluation of Image Segmentation Quality*. Clark University.

Zhu, Pan, Hu, Li, & Gong. (2004). *Estimating Net Primary Productivity of Terrestrial Vegetation Based on Remote Sensing: A Case Study in Inner Mongolia, China*. College of Resources Science and Technology, Key Laboratory of Environmental Change and Natural Disaster of Ministry of Education, Beijing Normal University.

Chapter 17
Expert System through GIS-Based Cloud

Prabu Sevugan
VIT University, India

Swarnalatha Purushotham
VIT University, India

Ajay Chandran
VIT University, India

ABSTRACT

Enthusiasm for accuracy farming practices and advances is becoming quickly all through the agrarian world. The accuracy farming can make utilization of the current methods, for example, GPS (Global Positioning System) innovation, GIS (Geographical Information System) innovation, RS (Remote Sensing) innovation and ES (Expert System) innovation et cetera, with a specific end goal to separate the agribusiness specialized measures among plots to acquire the better peripheral advantage of economy and environment. The study demonstrates to those generally accepted methods to utilize GIS (Geography Information System), Data mining and Web innovations in the rural master choice framework. This security with mass storage is satisfied by using GIS cloud server. This chapter discuss with an Integrated Geographic Information System with ES using Cloud Computing.

INTRODUCTION

Precision farming means soil specific farming such as Tillage, Drilling, Fertilizing, Spraying, Irrigation and harvesting phases. The consecutive reforms in agricultural policy have created adequate environment for the above to facilitate the farmers. Besides, wireless sensor network (WSN) architecture for vegetable greenhouse (Sun et al.,2013) is suggested to fulfill the dreams of farmers by way of scientific cultivation and minimum management costs from the aspect of environmental monitoring.

DOI: 10.4018/978-1-5225-2053-5.ch017

As of late, the interest on agribusiness item has risen. Be that as it may, the information of science and innovation underway is deficient. The expansion of farming yield is limited by numerous issues, for example, absence of logical administration on development; diminish on the amount of individuals on exploration and promo, which additionally expand the expense of generation (Liping et al.,2002). Master framework can without much of a stretch and precisely direct agriculturists to experimentally treat, control bug and convey outfield administration as indicated by reality. Master framework for agrarian creation innovation, consolidated GIS with master framework, can do spatial investigation and administration and take care of the issue of learning reason met in geographic exploration. Master framework taking into account GIS can take care of the issue confronted with underway and expansion the yield and efficiency (Mao Kebiao, Tan et al., 2004; Wu Weiying, 2004).

The utilization of ES can give another plan to the rural generation. GIS can artificially deal with the different space-time information to give the choice and the interview administrations for the agribusiness creation. (Kebiao & Zhihao, 2004) Combination of ES and GIS can make the geology data to bring into the ES choice procedure. It can raise scientificity of the ES choice to utilize the logical aftereffect of GIS. In the meantime, discharging the ES choice result by GIS can fortify the visual presentation. (Miao et al.,2004) The system innovation can settle on the choice plan quicker and all the more advantageously this can be send to the rancher. It is not just a key mechanical step how to settle on logical choice and to get experimental solution to guide cultivating; additionally it is a key step regardless of whether to accomplish the point of accuracy. Step by step instructions to manufacture clever spatial choice emotionally supportive network by mix of GIS and ES innovation is not yet a completely investigated subject in Information Technology. Thusly, it is not just has essential hypothetical essentialness to examine and fabricated farming keen spatial choice emotionally supportive network, additionally it has vital down to earth meaning.

BACKGROUND

The use of Geographical Information System (GIS) methods in watering system water administration can be utilized as a capable device for the investigation of spatially disseminated databases and the assessment of situations under various neighborhood conditions. The fruitful mix of GIS systems can be connected to the examination of watering system water necessity and the estimation of future interest (Ray & Dadhwal, 2001). Also, the spatial examination and administration abilities of GIS have rendered it an effective instrument for extending the watering system estimation from a ranch scale to a local level. Moreover, such coordinated watering system frameworks are fit for expanding crop efficiency and encouraging determination of the most suitable editing design. Its applications in accuracy cultivating and groundwater appraisal are additionally talked about Recent years there was an inadequacy of water asset in numerous parts of the world because of expanding populace, uneven appropriation of water supply and other temperate or mechanical reasons. It is accounted for that more than 70% of the world water asset is utilized for watering system purposes. In spite of the fact that much proof has demonstrated an overemployment of water, the interest for watering system is as yet expanding. In this way, it is broadly recognized that key water arranging is crucial for maintainable water supply later on (Qing & Linvill, 2002). Much work has been done on the estimation of watering system water request, which requires an extensive comprehension of nearby natural elements, for example, soil, atmosphere and water dissemination. The majority of these information are spatially conveyed and the perplexing general impact has prompted the presentation of Geographical Information System (GIS) and different advancements to this field. GIS based models have been connected meaning to build up a database which gives a premise to further examination and understanding(Hashmi et al.,1995). The foundation of various watering system situations has encouraged the estimation of watering system necessities and the appropriation of water asset, which is crucial for selecting the correct editing design and figuring out where, when and the amount to flood.

Colossal measure of exertion has been made on the estimation of yield evapotranspiration (ET), for the most part centered around discovering water prerequisites for various harvests under different nearby conditions, i.e. soil, climate (Chowdary, Rao, & Sharma, 2003). Far less work has been done on a district wide scale. Like the homestead level situation, varieties in components, for example, soil assume an imperative part. The spatial examination and administration abilities of GIS have rendered it an effective apparatus for extending the past work from ranch scale to a local level. The fundamental information for watering system water request estimation are gathered with a spatial determination. These information (soil, atmosphere, crops and so forth.) in this way shape a spatial database.

Territorial watering system water request estimations are ordinarily in light of editing examples or area use. An illustration would be the estimation in an order region with a few waterway bowls where a vector based information model is connected. Contrasted with other important studies, this model maps watering system request, as well as catches spatial varieties and reflexes any adjustments in watering system water request once trimming example is modified. A Decision Support System (DSS) is likewise used to help choice making (Cottenier, Elrad, & Prunicki, 2005). Once all important information are caught, DSS would go about as a successful device as far as creating so as to enhance interest arranging distinctive situations and imagining the effects under these situations. Another appealing component is the way that GIS can without much of a stretch arrange the consequences of watering system water requests. For instance, information characterized by various trench frameworks can prompt an a great deal more compelling and precise estimation.

GIS web administration can successfully adapt to a few issues of conventional GIS applications, for example, difficult to upgrade old frameworks, lacking of good interoperability and difficult to incorporate with different frameworks, and so on. Accuracy treatment and exactness watering system were utilized to clarify key innovations of the SDSS development taking into account GIS web service (Lun, Jing, Dashi, & Zuo, 2001). The exploration result demonstrates that GIS web administration is suitable for creating spatial choice emotionally supportive network for exactness cultivating, and GIS web administration based applications has clear favorable circumstances in managing issues, for example, sharing spatial information, programming reuse and decreasing the expense of framework reconciliation.

As one of the vital parts of accuracy cultivating (PF) specialized design, spatial choice emotionally supportive network (SDSS) for PF is a sort of programming which can be utilized to address the issues of quantitative investigation and keen choice making support in exactness cultivating generation. Through farmland-related spatial data investigation, the SDSS for PF can give choice making administrations to rural generation, and backing shrewd ranch hardware practically speaking. The exploration of SDSS for PF is exceptionally important for advancing and applying innovations of exactness cultivating. A large portion of the current spatial choice emotionally supportive networks for PF are desktop based or site based software's, which would be hard to keep up and redesign in light of the fact that the information and framework capacities are firmly coupled. It is likewise difficult to share data and accomplish interoperability among these delicate products since they were built up into disconnected islands of data. The issues above have as of now lead the exceptional misuse of asset, and due to these issues, the current spatial choice emotionally supportive network for PF are not fit for reacting the progressions from the business sector based rural creation. To put it plainly, the current SDSS for PA have confined the improvement of PF in light of their inalienable deficiencies, it is earnestly important to create cutting edge SDSS for PF, which would be on interest, significantly more open, and simple to keep up and upgrade. The ascents of web administration innovation advance the improvement of programming engineering from customary mode (Host, Client/Server, Browser/Server style) to arrange intelligent mode. This web administration based programming engineering mode can adapt to the characteristic weaknesses of conventional frameworks, so it is conceivable to plan and set up an open, approximately coupled SDSS for PF by utilizing the design. Study had been directed for the suitable spatial examination and choice making techniques for accuracy preparation and watering system. On this premise, the outcomes had examined the likelihood of the framework development, and gave plan and usage arrangement of the SDSS for PF. The plan of web administration parts accumulation, which would be utilized to execute the examination and choice making elements of SDSS for PF were additionally been concentrated on,

GIS web administration can viably adapt to the conventional GIS applications' issues, for example, hard to keep up, lacking of good interoperability and difficult to incorporate with different frameworks, and so on (Xinling, 1993). Exactness preparation and accuracy watering system, as cases, were utilized to depict key advancements of GIS web administration based SDSS for PF. The exploration result demonstrates that GIS web administration is suitable for creating Spatial Decision-production Support System for PF, and GIS web administration based applications has evident focal points in managing issues, for example, sharing spatial information, programming reuse and lessening the expense of framework mix.

Late advancement and future point of view of Wireless Sensors in horticulture and nourishment industry is finished. The innovation points of interest other than financially savvy arrangements and how WSN have been utilized as a part of PA to help with spatial information accumulation, exactness watering system and supplying information to ranchers are all said (Liping, Chuanjiang, Xuexine, & Xiahong, 2002). Points of interest of airborne remote detecting for recognizing and mapping weeds in yields in PA have been extraordinarily acknowledged overall (Cottenier, Elrad, & Prunicki, 2005). Detecting and information securing alongside mapping is done inside of hours. Possibility surveys on GSM-SMS innovation application to handle information securing done (Chu et al., 2003). Utilization of Wireless Sensor Networks (WSNs) results in minimal effort and low-control utilization organizations, in this way turning into a prevailing alternative (Xiang, Baozhu, Tiancai, Chun jiang, & Ping, 2003). It is additionally surely understood that harvests are likewise adversely influenced by gatecrashers (human or creatures) and by inadequate control of the generation process. Video observation is an answer for recognize and distinguish interlopers and also to better deal with the creation process (Deren, 1997). WSN advancements empowered checking and control of nursery parameter in accuracy horticulture, particularly control of equivalent appropriation of water to all harvests in the entire homestead or according to the necessity of the product (Bo & Yingjie, 1996). Green house innovation might be the best arrangement. The fundamental targets of site-particular administration of agrarian inputs are to expand gainfulness of harvest creation, enhance item quality, and secure nature (Liangzhi & Zhiqing, 1992). Data about the variability of various soil characteristics inside of a field is vital for the choice making process. The failure to get soil qualities quickly and modestly stays one of the greatest impediments of exactness farming (Zhou et al.,2004).

The quick creating period of PC innovation has experienced the marvelous advances in registering stockpiling, preparing abilities and systems administration innovation, which have permitted the clients to produce, process, and impart enormous volume of data to high dependability and proficiency (Sun,

Yan, Shi, Zhang, & Zhang, 2006). The requirement for preparing and appropriation of tremendous information prompts the improvement of distributed computing, which empowers helpful, boundless, on interest system access to a common pool of registering assets set at better places. Various clients and examination associations are presently applying distributed computing ideas or simple and productive answers for their figuring and information sharing needs.

Despite the fact that few meanings of distributed computing exist in the writing, the definition authored by the US National Institute of Standards and Technology (NIST) Information Technology Laboratory in 2009 is normally considered as an all-around acknowledged standard one. As indicated by NIST (Hou, 2000) "Distributed computing is a model for empowering advantageous, on-interest system access to a mutual pool of configurable figuring assets (e.g., systems, servers, stockpiling, applications, and administrations) that can be quickly provisioned and discharged with negligible administration exertion or administration supplier communication. The rising cloud abstracts base complexities of servers, applications, information, and heterogeneous stages". Distributed computing emphasizes (Gosavi, Shinde, Dhakulkar, 2012) wide utilization of Wide Area Networks (WANs), i.e. the Internet, which permit association between cloud administration suppliers and shoppers.

Administration suppliers are extending their offerings running from introductory equipment and stages to programming administrations and the entire programming applications. It for the most part comprises of three segments viz; Infrastructure, Platform and Application and Users. In a word Cloud figuring is an "on interest administration" in which shared assets, data, programming and different gadgets are given by customer's necessity at a particular time. For the most part, it comprises of an application, a stage and an infrastructure (Paul & Ghose, 2012; Bento & Bento, 2011). The base is dispersed in nature. These conveyed bases are in charge of giving on-interest administrations. Administrations might be of programming assets (e.g. Programming as a Service, SaaS), physical assets (e.g. Stage as a Service, PaaS), equipment (e.g. Equipment as a Service, HaaS) or foundation (Infrastructure as a Service, IaaS). There are number of ways to deal with distributed computing are called attention to alongside its design model. It has been seen that after such a large number of years, distributed computing today is the start of "system based dispersed processing" and is viewed as the innovation of this decade (Chui, Loffler, & Roberts, 2010).

METHODOLOGY

The accuracy horticulture intends to finely acclimate to a wide range of soil and harvest administration measures, to streamline use amount for every single rural material, for example, manure, pesticide, water, seed etc, as indicated by the unique state of every cultivating unit, to acquire high return and most financial advantage, in the meantime to diminish the use of synthetic matter, and to secure rural situations and cultivating land asset GIS-based yield item innovation master framework is made out of human-PC interface, database, master learning base, model base and framework upkeep and administration (Figure 1).

- **Database:** The framework incorporates foundation, redesign, alter, reproduce and yield of database, which made out of spot, line and polygon (Hori, Kawashima, &Yamazaki, 2010).

Spatial databases speak to geographic information and use uniform Geographic Coordinates, furthermore give vector and raster position. The records incorporate harvest natural circulation, amass tempera-

Figure 1. System architecture

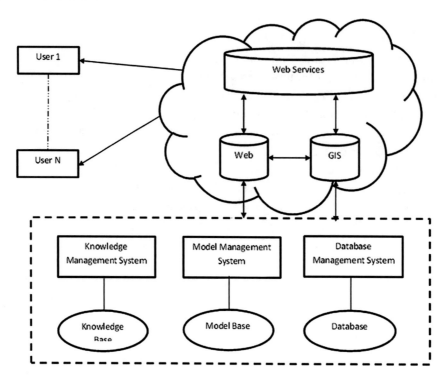

ture appropriation, soil sort dissemination, precipitation dispersion, farmland conveyance, authoritative guide, furthermore quality database, land assets, compost, watering system, manure value, seed, water assets, climatic asset thus on (Bo & Wang, 2011).

- **Information Base Administration:** Expertise, gave by master, is put away in learning base, including reality, rules.

The amount and nature of learning base is the key variable that decides the capacity to take care of the issue. The foundation of information base is the center mission of master framework. In Object-Oriented learning base, idea and substances, included in the critical thinking, are considered as items to frame object model as per order and structure. Substance of guidelines are conveyed in the characteristic and technique for reason and conclusion, which are shown by the inferred relationship between objects (Qirui, 2012). Each suggested relationship has two states, static enduring state and dynamic state, reflecting whether a standard has been received. The truth can be acquired from learning base, which is the accumulation of articles. Surmising is done by induction motor by transmission of article to choose whether a guideline is initiated and shape a grouping of exercises issued to the database

- **Model Base:** Model base, which gives figuring procedure, can give leader capacity of taking care of issue and data to take care of issue by coordinating, examine and analyze distinctive arrangement.

Estimation model and projects, which have been investigated and analyzed some time recently, are put away in model base (Mitsuyoshi, Kawashima, & Yamazaki, 2011). Amid projects run, reality, information and tenets are coordinated. Depend on and need exist between models in model base, which implies that whether a model is done or not is controlled by whether another model is done or not. Model base incorporates crop development model, development period model, manure ideal portion models thus on (Xu, Fei, Geng, Bai, & Zhang, 2011).

- **Framework Support and Administration:** The module is with a specific end goal to ensure framework to run well, including upkeep and overhaul of database, model base and learning base. Framework functions and its details are clarified in figure 2.
- **Information Inquiry:** Master experience and learning for different sorts of yield are put away in the framework, which can give clients much data. Keeping in mind the end goal to encourage clients to inquiry data, numerous photos related with malady and vermin control are inserted in the system (Wang, Song, Liu, Jiang, & Liu, 2013). Clients' needs can be met by various methods for looking data, by inventory question or by catchphrases.
- **Agronomic Decision-Making:** It is the center module in the framework, which is made out of sub-modules, including readiness before sowing, sowing choice making, preparation choice making, column crop administration, malady analysis and control of sickness and vermin.
- **Result Output:** The data chose and comes about originating from smart choice making can be yield and printed.
- **System Maintenance:** The principle capacity of this module is to look after database, model base and information base, for database, essentially the redesign of property database and spatial database, the change of model parameter in model base and learning change and upkeep in information base.

INTEGRATION OF GIS AND EXPERT SYSTEM INTEGRATED DEVELOPMENT

GIS part and question arranged visual programming dialect is coordinated to do auxiliary advancement. Capacity of administration and examination of spatial database was completed by GIS segment and protest arranged visual advancement apparatus was utilized to extend framework capacity. In view of current scripting language and new capacities in GIS, that is Object Linking and Embedding, innovation, capacity menu can be composed utilizing uniform human-machine interface and choice making module, likewise some basic choice and investigation module can be inserted into GIS. At that point entangled model can be changed into executable system by scripting language with Object Linking and Embedding, function (Mitsuyoshi, Kawashima, & Yamazaki, 2011). At long last, GIS and convoluted model can be connected together by programming and Object Linking and Embedding, innovation in GIS. The methodology exploits encoding capacity in visual programming advancement devices and does numerous entangled examinations. In the interim, it can make full utilization of complete capacity of spatial information visual investigation, which enhances advancement productivity and give a decent appearance, immaculate capacity, high unwavering quality, simple support and simple to utilize.

Figure 2. System functions

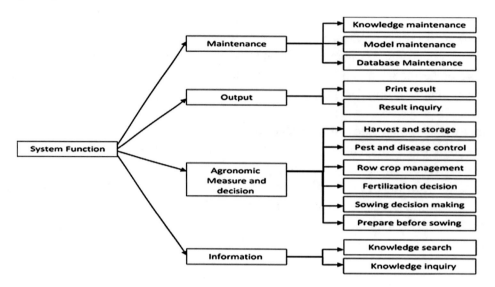

Knowledge Representation

There numerous courses for information representation in master framework. Many-sided quality and vagueness in horticulture make rationale structure of learning confused and arrangement space extensive. Information representation method for "standards frame+ rules body" can speak to rationale relationship between sub-issue and parent issue in horticulture, gives master a decent way to deal with break down muddled issues and make issue simple (Wang, Song, Liu, Jiang, & Liu, 2013). In the interim, it gives a technique, which makes a simple innovation of information procurement taking into account PC cooperation to be completed.

Application of Intelligent Reasoning Technology

Clever thinking innovation is the key innovation of GIS-based master framework for soybean creation, demonstrating intellectualization of the framework. One of the noteworthy elements of the framework is clever thinking capacity, whose primary assignments are: getting conclusion from truths, which are sent to thinking machine by principles or other learning structure (in information base); including suitable data; clarifying conclusion and data as per prerequisites. Reasoning so as to think driven methodology is dictated bearing. In GIS based master arrangement of soybean creation, the primary thinking innovation is half breed thinking, or mixture control, which implies that forward thinking to choose target, in reverse thinking to affirm thinking way or control methodology. Forward thinking is additionally called driven-by-database control, which are suitable for issues with expansive arrangement space, such outline, rules, forecast, supervision and control, administration etc. In reverse thinking is likewise called driven by-target control, which implies that selecting an objective first and afterward searching for substandard set which can reason the objective in entire principle set. On the off chance that one guarantees of a guideline is coordinated with the reality in database, then the tenet is executed. Generally, the framework will execute past project by the reason of this tenet until the general target is met or come up short.

FUTURE RESEARCH DIRECTIONS

The study can be built the fundamental casing of choice emotionally supportive network for treatment as per the supplement substance of soil on the distinctive soil testing focuses and the yield meteorological information and soil information into a database. The framework could insert soil properties map by the extensive assessment arrangement of soil ripeness. Taking into account the database framework and learning framework, the framework can create remedy confronting the laborer and produce solution map confronting the ranch by GIS with information model, for example, adjusted preparation objective of yield model et cetera. The clients will get the treatment medicine which can manage them to exactness preparation. It cannot just raise the objectivity and unwavering quality of preparation plan and spare compost additionally enhance financial and environment advantages. Another fascinating use of Geographical Information System (GIS) strategies is in watering system water administration where GIS can be utilized as an intense device for the investigation of spatially circulated databases and the assessment of situations under various nearby conditions. The effective coordination of GIS strategies can be connected to the examination of watering system water necessity and the estimation of future interest. In addition, the spatial examination and administration capacities of GIS have rendered it an effective instrument for extending the watering system estimation from a homestead scale to a local level. Also, such incorporated watering system frameworks are fit for expanding crop efficiency and encouraging determination of the most suitable editing design. Its applications in accuracy cultivating and groundwater appraisal are likewise plausible.

CONCLUSION

GIS-based agrarian creation innovation master framework, as a stage of innovation exchange, enhances the level of insight in horticultural generation, furthermore coordinates flow examination to furnish clients with mechanical administration. Issues of ranchers scattered and absence of master were additionally tackled by this master framework, which gives administration to laborer in a more noteworthy extent. Business-situated and handle arranged were done from data gathering, preparing and choice making in this framework. The helpfulness was enhanced through coordinating master framework and GIS. The exchange from halfway analysis to large scale direction and full scale choice making comes right, which is helpful to advance the change of thorough farming creation limit and gives a clever agrarian data innovation for accomplishing high return development.

The study could clear base on learning model of product administration for keen choice and coordinate GIS and information model in system stage. The framework conquers some shortcoming, for example, conventional yield development example and space-time appropriation second rate of experienced learning in the master framework. The framework which gives the quantitative device and standard model for product administration will do a ton to the hypothetical and down to earth improvement of shrewd agribusiness data innovation.

REFERENCES

Zhou & Zhou. (2004). Agricultural Expert System application in cultural growth. *Agriculture Network Information, 11*, 32–35.

Avancha, S., Korolev, V., Joshi, A., Finin, T., & Yesha, Y. (2002). On Experiments with a Transport Protocol for Pervasive Computing Environments. *Computer Networks, 40*(4), 515–535. doi:10.1016/S1389-1286(02)00294-3

Bento, A., & Bento, R. (2011). Computing: A new phase in information technology management. Journal of Information Technology Management, 22(1).

Bo, Y., & Wang, H. (2011). The Application of Cloud Computing and The Internet of Things in Agriculture and Forestry. *International Joint Conference on Service Sciences.* IEEE Computer Society.

Li, Cheng, Yan, & Gong. (2010). *Monitoring System for Vegetable Greenhouses based on a Wireless Sensor Network.* National Library of Medicine.

Chowdary, V., Rao, N., & Sharma, P. (2003). GIS based decision support system for groundwater assessment in large irrigation project areas. *Agricultural Water Management, 62*(3), 229–252. doi:10.1016/S0378-3774(03)00144-6

Chui, M., Loffler, M., & Roberts, R. (2010). *The Internet of Things. McKinsey Quarterly.*

Cottenier, T., Elrad, T., & Prunicki, A. (2005). Contextual Aspect-Sensitive Services. T*he 4th International Conference on Aspect-Oriented Software Development (AOSD'05)*, 84-92.

Chen, Zhao, Liu, & Du. (2002). Design and Implementation of Intelligent Decision Support System for Precision Agriculture. *Transactions of the Chinese Society. Agricultural Engineering, 18*(3), 145–148.

Gao & Jin. (1992). *Rice cultivation computer simulation and optimization decision system.* Beijing: China Agricultural Science Technology Publishing House.

Gosavi, N., Shinde, S.S., & Dhakulkar, B. (2012). Use of cloud computing in library and information science field. *International Journal of Digital Library Services, 2*(3).

Gutierrez, J., Villa-Medina, J. F., Nieto-Garibay, A., & Porta-Gandara, M. A. (2014). Automated Irrigation System Using a Wireless Sensor Network and GPRS Module", Instrumentation and Measurement. *IEEE Transactions on, 63*(1), 166–176.

Hashmi, M., Garcia, L., & Fontane, D. (1995). Spatial estimation of regional crop evapotranspiration. *Transactions of the ASAE. American Society of Agricultural Engineers, 38*(5), 1345–1351. doi:10.13031/2013.27957

Hori, Kawashima, & Yamazaki. (2011). Application of cloud computing to Agriculture and prospect to other fields. *Fijitsu Science Technology Journal, 46*(4), 446-454.

Hori, M., Kawashima, E., & Yamazaki, T. (2010). Application of cloud computing to agriculture and prospects in other fields. *Fujitsu Science and Technology Journal, 46*(4), 446–454.

Hou, Y. L. (2000). Theory and technological system of ecological balanced fertilization. *Acta Ecologica Sinica, 20*, 653–658.

Huang & Wang. (1996). The combination of GIS and ES and exploration for application. *Environment Remote Sensing, 11*(3).

Kebiao, M., & Zhihao, T. (2004). The Integration and Application of Spatial Data Mining And GIS. *Geomatics &Spatial Information Technology, 27*(1), 14–17.

Li. (1997). On Definition, Theory and Key Technics of the Integration of GPS, RS and GISb. *Journal of Remote Sensing, 18.*

Liping, C., Chunjiang, Z., & Xuexin, L. (2002). Design and Implementation of Intelligent Decision Support System for Precision Agriculture. *Transactions of CSAE*, 18(2),149-152.

Miao, X. K., Xia, K. J., & Wang, X. (2004). Study on intelligent decision making sustaining system of variable rate fertilization in precision agriculture. *Computer Application, 24*, 153–155.

Paul, P. K., & Ghose, M. K. (2012). Cloud Computing: Possibilities, Challenges, and opportunities with special reference to its emerging need in the academic and working area of information science. *International Conference on Modeling Optimisation and Computing*. Elsevier. doi:10.1016/j.proeng.2012.06.267

Qing, Z., & Linvill, D. (2002). Integrating crop models into GIS regional crop yield. *ASAE Annual International Meeting/CIGR XVth World Congress*, 28–31.

Qingquan, C., & Lin, L. (2003). The Developing Trend and Application of GIS on Agriculture. *Review of China Agricultural Science Technology* , 5, 22–26.

Qirui, Y. (2012). Kaas-based intelligent service model in agricultural expert system. *2nd International Conference on Consumer Electronics, Communications and Networks*. IEEE.

Ray, S., & Dadhwal, V. (2001). Estimation of crop evapotranspiration of irrigation command area using remote sensing and GIS. *Agricultural Water Management, 49*(3), 239–249. doi:10.1016/S0378-3774(00)00147-5

Sawashima, H., Hori, Y., Sunahara, H., & Oie, Y. (1997). Characteristics of UDP Packet Loss: Effect of TCP Traffic. In *Proceedings of INET 97: The Seventh Annual Conference of the Internet Society.*

Sun, B., Yan, H., Shi, J. P., Zhang, Y. P., & Zhang, B. N. (2006). Development and application of fertilization decision-making supporting systems based on ComGIS. *Transactions of the Chinese Society of Agricultural Engineering, 24*, 75–79.

Sun, Y., Tian, Z., Ye, J., Zhang, H., & Tang, S. (2013). UDP flow detection and analysis using dynamical timeout strategy based on sliding-window. *2013 IEEE Conference Anthology*, 1-4.

Waldhoff, G., Curdt, C., Hoffmeister, D., & Bareth, G. (2012). Analysis of multitemporal and multisensor sensing data for crop rotation mapping.*Proceedings of the XXII Congress of the ISPRS*. doi:10.5194/isprsannals-I-7-177-2012

Wang, Y., Song, J., Liu, X., Jiang, S., & Liu, Y. (2013). Plantation Monitoring System Based on Internet of Things, Green Computing and Communications (GreenCom). *IEEE and Internet of Things (iThings/CPSCom), IEEE International Conference on and IEEE Cyber, Physical and Social Computing*, 366-369.

Weiying, W. (2004). GIS Based Spatial Data Mining Techniques. *Journal of Shandong University of Science and Technology, 23*(4).

Wu, S., & Zhu, X. (2004). Application of a sliding window protocol in GPRS-based radio access networks. *Robotics and Vision Conference*, 787-791.

Wu, Zhang, Tang, & Liu. (2001). The System and Structure of Internet-based. *Geography and Territorial Research, 17*(4), 20-24.

Xiang, L., Baozhu Y., Tiancai, G., Chunjiang, Z., & Ping, C.L. (2003). Study on the Crop Management Information System Based on WebGIS and ES. *ACTA Agriculturae Borealisinica, 18*(20), 106.

Xinling, B. (1993). *Principle and method of geographic information system*. Beijing: Geological Publishing House.

Xu, W. F. T., Geng, Y., Bai, F., & Zhang, L. (2011). Design of environmental information monitoring system based on GPRS. *Awareness Science and Technology (iCAST), 3rd International Conference on, 469*, 27-30.

Compilation of References

Abdulgader, , Iismail, Zainal, & Idbeaa. (2015). Enhancement of AES Algorithm based on Chaotic Maps and Shift Operation for Image Encryption. *Journal of Theoretical and Applied Information Technology, 71*(1), 1–12.

Abed, F. S., & Mustafa, N. A. A. (2010). A proposed technique for information hiding based on DCT. *International Journal of Advancements in Computing Technology, 2*(5), 140–152. doi:10.4156/ijact.vol2.issue5.16

Aborisade, D. O. (2011). Novel fuzzy logic based edge detection technique. *International Journal of Advanced Science and Technology, 29*, 75–82.

Acharya, T., & Ray, A. K. (2005). *Image processing: principles and applications.* John Wiley & Sons. doi:10.1002/0471745790

Ahmadi, E., Azimifar, Z., Shams, M., Famouri, M., & Shafiee, M. J. (2015). Document image binarization using a discriminative structural classifier. *Pattern Recognition Letters, Elsevier, 63*, 36–42. doi:10.1016/j.patrec.2015.06.008

Ahmed, N., Natarajan, T., & Rao, K. R. (1974). Discrete Cosine Transform. *IEEE Transactions on Computers, 100*(1), 90–93. doi:10.1109/T-C.1974.223784

Ajay Kumar, S. M. (2010). A New Framework for Adaptive Multimodal Biometrics Management. *IEEE Transactions On Information Forensics And Security, 5*(1), 92–102. doi:10.1109/TIFS.2009.2031892

Ajay Kumar, S. S. (2011). Personal Identification Using Multibiometrics Rank-Level Fusion. *IEEE Transactions on Systems, Man and Cybernetics. Part C, Applications and Reviews, 41*(5), 743–752. doi:10.1109/TSMCC.2010.2089516

Akl, S. G., & Taylor, P. D. (1983). Cryptographic solution to a problem of access Control in a hierarchy. *ACM Transactions on Computer Systems, 1*(3), 239–248. doi:10.1145/357369.357372

Alahi, A., Ortiz, R., & Vandergheynst, P. (2012). *FREAK: Fast retina keypoint.* Paper presented at IEEE Conference on Computer Vision and Pattern Recognition (CVPR), Providence, RI. doi:10.1109/CVPR.2012.6247715

Ali, A. A., & Fawzi, A. N. (2010). A modified high capacity image steganography technique based on wavelet transform. *The International Arab Journal of Information Technology., 7*(4), 358–364.

AlMahafzah, H., Imran, M., & Sheshadri, H.S. (2012). *Multi-algorithm Feature Level.* Academic Press.

AlMahafzah, H., Imran, M., & Sheshadri, H. S. (2012). *Multi-algorithm Feature Level Fusion Using Finger Knuckle Print Biometric.* Springer-Verlag Berlin Heidelberg. doi:10.1007/978-3-642-35594-3_42

Al-Rajab, M., Hogg, D., & Ng, K. (2008). A comparative study on using Zernike velocity moments and hidden Markov models for hand gesture recognition. In *Articulated Motion and Deformable Objects* (pp. 319–327). Springer Berlin Heidelberg. doi:10.1007/978-3-540-70517-8_31

Amayeh, G., Kasaei, S., Bebis, G., Tavakkoli, A., & Veropoulos, K. (2007, February). Improvement of Zernike moment descriptors on affine transformed shapes. In *Signal Processing and Its Applications, 2007.ISSPA 2007. 9th International Symposium on* (pp. 1-4). IEEE. doi:10.1109/ISSPA.2007.4555333

Andreas Humm, J. H. (2009). Authentication, Combined Handwriting and Speech Modalities for User. *IEEE Transactions on Systems, Man, and Cybernetics. Part A, Systems and Humans*, *39*(1), 25–35. doi:10.1109/TSMCA.2008.2007978

Andreas, U., & Wild, P. (2009). Single-sensor multi-instance fingerprint and. *International Journal of Biometrics*, *1*(4), 442–462. doi:10.1504/IJBM.2009.027305

Antani, S., Gargi, U., Crandall, D., Gandhi, T., & Kasturi, R. (1999). Extraction of Text in Video. Technical Report of Department of Computer Science and Engineering, Penn State University, CSE-99-016.

Anuradha Kameswari, P., & Praveen Kumar, L. (2014). A Method for Recovering a Key in the Key Exchange Cryptosystem by Diophantine Equations. *International Journal of Computers and Applications*, *100*(14), 11–13. doi:10.5120/17592-8302

Atanassov, K. T. (1986). Intuitionistic fuzzy sets. *Fuzzy Sets and Systems*, *20*(1), 87–96. doi:10.1016/S0165-0114(86)80034-3

Avancha, S., Korolev, V., Joshi, A., Finin, T., & Yesha, Y. (2002). On Experiments with a Transport Protocol for Pervasive Computing Environments. *Computer Networks*, *40*(4), 515–535. doi:10.1016/S1389-1286(02)00294-3

Babler, W. J. (1991). *Embryologic development of epidermal ridges and their configurations. In Dermatoglyphics: Science in Transition* (pp. 95–112). New York: Wiley-Liss.

Background Models Challenge (BMC). (2012, November). *Asian Conference on Computer Vision*. Retrieved from http://bmc.iut-auvergne.com

Bae, Shi, & Tai. (2011). Graph Cuts for Curvature Based Image Denoising. *IEEE Transactions on Image Processing, 20*(5).

Bailey, K., & Curran, K. (2006). An evaluation of image based steganography methods using visual inspection and automated detection techniques. *Multimedia Tools and Applications*, *31*(8), 55–88. doi:10.1007/s11042-006-0008-4

Bakar, S. A., Hitam, M. S., Yussof, H. W., & Jawahir, W. N. (2013, January). Investigating the properties of Zernike moments for robust content based image retrieval. In *Computer Applications Technology (ICCAT), 2013 International Conference on* (pp. 1-6). IEEE. doi:10.1109/ICCAT.2013.6522011

Ballard, D. H., & Brown, C. M. (1982). *Computer vision, 1982*. Englewood Cliffs, NJ: Prenice-Hall.

Bansal, R., Arora, P., Gaur, M., Sehgal, P., & Bedi, P. (2009). Fingerprint image enhancement using type-2 fuzzy sets. In *Fuzzy Systems and Knowledge Discovery, 2009. FSKD'09. Sixth International Conference on* (Vol. 3, pp. 412–417). doi:10.1109/FSKD.2009.396

Barni, M. (2001). Improved Wavelet-Based Watermarking Through Pixel-Wise Masking. *IEEE Transactions on Image Processing, 10*(5), 783-791.

Barnich, O., & Van, M. (2011, June). Vibe: A universal background subtraction algorithm for video sequences. *IEEE Transactions on Image Processing*, *20*(6), 1709–1724. doi:10.1109/TIP.2010.2101613 PMID:21189241

Barni, M., Bartolini, F., Cappellini, V., & Piva, A. (1998). A DCT-domain system for robust image watermarking. *Signal Processing*, *66*(3), 357–372. doi:10.1016/S0165-1684(98)00015-2

Barreto, P. S., Kim, H. Y., & Rijmen, V. (2002). Toward secure public-key block wise fragile authentication watermarking. *IEE Proceedings. Vision Image and Signal Processing*, *149*(2), 57–62. doi:10.1049/ip-vis:20020168

Bartunek, Nilsson, Sallberg, & Claesson. (2013). Adaptive Fingerprint Image Enhancement with Emphasis on Pre-processing of Data. *IEEE Transactions on Image Processing, 22*(2).

Bascle, B., & Deriche, R. (1995). Region Tracking through Image Sequences.*Proc.Fifth Int'l Conf. Computer Vision*, 302-307. doi:10.1109/ICCV.1995.466925

Bauer & Schneider. (2009). *Analysis of time series of Landsat images*. Institute of Surveying, Remote Sensing and Land Information, University of Natural Resources and Applied Life Sciences (BOKU).

Bay, H., Ess, A., Tuytelaars, T., & Gool, L. V. (2008). Speeded-up robust features (SURF). *Computer Vision and Image Understanding, 110*(3), 346–359. doi:10.1016/j.cviu.2007.09.014

Bender, D. G., Morimoto, N., & Lu, A. (2010). Techniques for data hiding. *IBM Systems Journal, 35*(3 & 4), 313–336.

Bennet, D., & Perumal, D. S. A. (2011). *Fingerprint: DWT, SVD based enhancement and significant contrast for ridges and valleys using fuzzy measures.* arXiv Preprint arXiv:1106.5737

Bento, A., & Bento, R. (2011). Computing: A new phase in information technology management. Journal of Information Technology Management, 22(1).

Bérczes, A., Hajdu, L., Hirata-Kohno, N., Kovács, T., & Pethő, A. (2014). A key exchange protocol based on Diophantine equations and S-integers. *JSIAM Letters, 6*(0), 85–88. doi:10.14495/jsiaml.6.85

Bernard, Friboulet, Thévenaz, & Unser. (2009). Variational B-Spline Level-Set: A Linear Filtering Approach for Fast Deformable Model Evolution. *IEEE Transactions on Image Processing, 18*(6).

Bin, Y., &Jia-Xiong, P. (2002, October). Improvement and invariance analysis of Zernike moments using as a region-based shape descriptor. *Innull* (p. 120).IEEE.

Bin, M. R. (2008). *Vision based autonomous robot.* Malaysia: Universiti Teknologi Malaysia.

Birchfield, S. (1998). Elliptical Head Tracking Using Intensity Gradients and Color Histograms.*IEEE Conf. Computer Vision and Pattern Recognition*, 232-237. doi:10.1109/CVPR.1998.698614

Biswas, R., & Sil, J. (2012). An improved canny edge detection algorithm based on type-2 fuzzy sets. *Procedia Technology, 4*, 820–824. doi:10.1016/j.protcy.2012.05.134

Bo, Y., & Wang, H. (2011). The Application of Cloud Computing and The Internet of Things in Agriculture and Forestry. *International Joint Conference on Service Sciences.* IEEE Computer Society.

Boaz & Prabhakar. (2016). Extraction of Scene Text Information from Video, *International Journal of Image Graphics and Signal Processing, 1*, 15–26.

Bobick, A. F., & Stephen, I. S. (1999). Large occlusion stereo. *International Journal of Computer Vision, 33*(3), 181–200. doi:10.1023/A:1008150329890

Boland, M. V., & Murphy, R. F. (2001). A neural network classifier capable of recognizing the patterns of all major subcellular structures in fluorescence microscope images of HeLa cells. *Bioinformatics (Oxford, England), 17*(12), 1213–1223. doi:10.1093/bioinformatics/17.12.1213 PMID:11751230

Bouwmans, T. (2011, September). Recent Advanced Statistical Background Modeling forForeground Detection: A Systematic Survey. *Recent Patents on Computer Science, 4*(3), 147–176.

Bouziane, A., Chahir, Y., Molina, M., & Jouen, F. (2013). Unified framework for human behaviour recognition: An approach using 3D Zernike moments. *Neurocomputing, 100*, 107–116. doi:10.1016/j.neucom.2011.12.042

Brutzer, S., Hoferlin, B., & Heidemann, G. (2011). Evaluation of background subtraction techniques for video surveillance.*IEEE Conf. CVPR*, 1937–1944. doi:10.1109/CVPR.2011.5995508

Bustince, H., Kacprzyk, J., & Mohedano, V. (2000). Intuitionistic fuzzy generators application to intuitionistic fuzzy complementation. *Fuzzy Sets and Systems*, *114*(3), 485–504. doi:10.1016/S0165-0114(98)00279-6

Cai, M., Son, J., & Lyu, M. R. (2002). A new approach for video text detection. *Proceedings of International Conference on Image Processing*, 117-120.

Cai, J. R., Yuan, L. M., Liu, B., & Sun, L. (2014). Nondestructive gender identification of silkworm cocoons using X-ray imaging with multivariate data analysis. *Analytical Methods*, *6*(18), 7224–7233. doi:10.1039/C4AY00940A

Calonder, M., Lepetit, V., Strecha, C., & Fua, P. (2010). BRIEF: binary robust independent elementary features. In K. Daniilidis, P. Maragos, & N. Paragios (Eds.), *Computer Vision – ECCV 2010* (pp. 778–792). Berlin: Springer-Verlag; doi:10.1007/978-3-642-15561-1_56

Canterakis, N. (1999). 3D Zernike moments and Zernike affine invariants for 3D image analysis and recognition.*11th Scandinavian Conf. on Image Analysis*.

Cao, K., Liu, E., & Jain, A. K. (n.d.). *Segmentation and Enhancement of Latent Fingerprints : A Coarse to Fine Ridge Structure Dictionary*. Academic Press.

Caracciolo, L., De Luca, A., & Iannitti, S. (1999). Trajectory tracking control of a four-wheel differentially driven mobile robot. In *Proceedings of the 1999 IEEE Internatonal Conference on Robotics & Automation*. Detroit, MI: IEEE. doi:10.1109/ROBOT.1999.773994

Carmona-Poyato, A., Madrid-Cuevas, F. J., Medina-Carnicer, R., & Muñoz-Salinas, R. (2010). Polygonal approximation of digital planar curves through break point suppression. *Pattern Recognition*, *43*(1), 14–25. doi:10.1016/j.patcog.2009.06.010

Chadha, A., Mallik, S., & Johar, R. (2012). Comparative Study and Optimization of Feature-Extraction Techniques for Content based Image Retrieval. *International Journal of Computers and Applications*, *52*(20), 35–42. doi:10.5120/8320-1959

Chaira, T. (2004). *Image segmentation and color retrieval: a fuzzy and intuitionistic fuzzy set theoretic approach* (PhD Thesis). Indian Institute of Technology, Kharagpur, India.

Chaira, T. (2013). Contrast enhancement of medical images using Type II fuzzy set. In *Communications (NCC), 2013 National Conference on* (pp. 1–5). doi:10.1109/NCC.2013.6488016

Chaira, T., & Ray, A. K. (2003). Segmentation using fuzzy divergence. *Pattern Recognition Letters*, *24*(12), 1837–1844. doi:10.1016/S0167-8655(03)00007-2

Chaira, T., & Ray, A. K. (2014). Construction of fuzzy edge image using interval type II fuzzy set. *International Journal of Computational Intelligence Systems*, *7*(4), 686–695. doi:10.1080/18756891.2013.862356

Chakrabarti, S., & Samanta, D. (2015). A novel approach to Digital Image Steganography of key-based encrypted text. *IEEEInternational Conference on Electrical, Electronics, Signals, Communication and Optimization (EESCO)*, 1-6. doi:10.1109/EESCO.2015.7254009

Chakraborty, A. (1996). *Feature and module integration for image segmentation*. Academic Press.

Chamlawi, R., Khan, A., & Usman, I. (2010). Authentication and recovery of images using multiple watermarks. *Computers & Electrical Engineering*, *36*(3), 578–584. doi:10.1016/j.compeleceng.2009.12.003

Chan, C. K., & Cheng, L. (2004). Hiding data in images by simple LSB substitution. *Pattern Recognition Society*, *37*(3), 469–474.

Chan, C.-K., & Cheng, L. M. (2004). Hiding data in images by simple LSB substitution. *Pattern Recognition Society*, *37*(3), 469–474. doi:10.1016/j.patcog.2003.08.007

Chandel, B., & Jain, S. (2016). Video steganography: A survey. *IOSR Journal of Computer Engineering.*, *18*(1), 11–17.

Chang, C. C., & Chuang, J. C. (2002). An image intellectual property protection scheme for gray-level images using visual secret sharing strategy. *Pattern Recognition Letters*, *23*(8), 931–941. doi:10.1016/S0167-8655(02)00023-5

Chang, C. C., Chuang, J. C., & Chen, T. S. (2002). Recognition of image authenticity using significant DCT coefficients quantization. *INFORMATICA-LJUBLJANA*, *26*(4), 359–366.

Cheddad, A., Condell, J., Curran, K., & McKevitt, P. (2010). Digital image steganography: Survey and analysis of current methods. *Signal Processing*, *90*(3), 727–752. doi:10.1016/j.sigpro.2009.08.010

Chen, B., & Wornell, G. W. (1998). Digital watermarking and information embedding using dither modulation. In *Multimedia Signal Processing, 1998 IEEE Second Workshop on* (pp. 273-278). IEEE. doi:10.1109/MMSP.1998.738946

Chen, C., & Cheng, Y. (2010). *MatLab-based simulators for mobile robot simultaneous localization and mapping*. Paper presented at 3rd International Conference on Advanced Computer Theory and Engineering (ICACTE), Chengdu, China. doi:10.1109/ICACTE.2010.5579471

Chen, D., Luettin, J., & Shearer, K. (2000). *A Survey of Text Detection and Recognition in Images and Videos*. Institut-DalleMolledIntelligenceArtificielle Perceptive (IDIAP) Research Report, 00-38.

Chen, Zhao, Liu, & Du. (2002). Design and Implementation of Intelligent Decision Support System for Precision Agriculture. *Transactions of the Chinese Society. Agricultural Engineering*, *18*(3), 145–148.

Chen, D., Odobez, J. M., & Bourlard, H. (2004). Text detection and recognition in images and video frames. *Pattern Recognition, Elsevier*, *37*(3), 595–608. doi:10.1016/j.patcog.2003.06.001

Chen, D., Shearer, K., & Bourlard, H. (2001). Text enhancement with asymmetric filter for video OCR. *Proceedings of International Conference on Image Analysisand Processing*, 192-197.

Chen, H., Du, X., Liu, Z., & Yang, C. (2013). Color image encryption based on the affine transform and gyrator transform. *Optics and Lasers in Engineering*, *51*(6), 768–775. doi:10.1016/j.optlaseng.2013.01.016

Chen, H., Tsai, S., Schroth, G., Chen, D., Grzeszczuk, R., & Girod, B. (2011). Robust text detection in natural images with edge-enhanced maximally stable extremal regions. *Proceedings of International Conference on Image Processing (ICIP)*, 2609-2612. doi:10.1109/ICIP.2011.6116200

Chen, X., Yang, J., Zhang, J., & Waibel, A. (2004). Automatic detection and recognition of signs from natural scenes. *IEEE Transactions on Image Processing*, *13*(1), 87–99. doi:10.1109/TIP.2003.819223 PMID:15376960

Chen, X., & Yuille, A. (2004). Detecting and reading text in natural scenes. *Proceedings of IEEE Computer Society Conference on Computer Vision and Pattern Recognition (CVPR)*, 1, 366-373.

Cheung, G. K. M., Kanade, T., Bouguet, J. Y., & Holler, M. (2000). *Real time system for robust 3 D voxel reconstruction of human motions*. CVPR. doi:10.1109/CVPR.2000.854944

Cheung, S. C., & Kamath, C. (2004). *Robust techniques for background subtraction in urban traffic video*. SPIE Video Comm. Image Process. doi:10.1117/12.526886

Chitade & Katiyar. (2010). *Colour Based Image Segmentation using K-Means Clustering*. Department of Civil Engineering, Manit, Bhopal, Madhyapradesh.

Choi, Y., & Krishnapuram, R. (1997). A robust approach to image enhancement based on fuzzy logic. *Image Processing. IEEE Transactions on, 6*(6), 808–825.

Chowdary, V., Rao, N., & Sharma, P. (2003). GIS based decision support system for groundwater assessment in large irrigation project areas. *Agricultural Water Management, 62*(3), 229–252. doi:10.1016/S0378-3774(03)00144-6

Chui, M., Loffler, M., & Roberts, R. (2010). *The Internet of Things. McKinsey Quarterly.*

Chun-Lin, H. (2010). *A Tutorial of Wavelet Transform*. Academic Press.

Ciancio, A. (2011). *No-Reference Blur Assessment of Digital Pictures Based on Multifeature Classifiers. IEEE Transactions on Image Processing, 20(1).*

Civera, J., Grasa, O. G., Davison, A. J., & Montiel, J. M. M. (2010). 1-Point RANSAC for extended Kalman filtering: Application to real-time structure from motion and visual odometry. *Journal of Field Robotics, 27*(5), 609–631. doi:10.1002/rob.20345

Collins, R., & Liu, Y. (2000). Online Selection of Discriminative Tracking Feature. *IEEE Transactions on Pattern Analysis and Machine Intelligence, 27*(10), 1631–1643. doi:10.1109/TPAMI.2005.205 PMID:16237997

Color Space. (n.d.) Retrieved from http://www.compression.ru/download/articles/color_space/ch03.pdf

Comaniciu, D., Ramesh, V., Meer, P. (2003). Kernal Based Object Tracking. *IEEE Transaction on Pattern Analysis and Machine Intelligence, 25*(5), 564-577.

Comaniciu, D., Ramesh, V., & Meer, P. (2000). Real time tracking of non-rigid objects using mean shift.*IEEE Conference on Computer Vision and Pattern Recognition (CVPR '00), 2,* 142-149. doi:10.1109/CVPR.2000.854761

Corso, J., Darius, B., & Gregory, H. (2003). Direct plane tracking in stereo images for mobile navigation. *Proceedings of International Conference on Robotics and Automation, 1,* 875-880. doi:10.1109/ROBOT.2003.1241703

Cottenier, T., Elrad, T., & Prunicki, A. (2005). Contextual Aspect-Sensitive Services. T*he 4th International Conference on Aspect-Oriented Software Development (AOSD'05),* 84-92.

Cox, I. J., & Miller, M. L. (2002). The first 50 years of electronic watermarking. *EURASIP Journal on Advances in Signal Processing,* (2): 1–7.

Crandall, D., Antani, S., & Kasturi, R. (2003). Extraction of special effects caption text events from digital video. *International Journal on Document Analysis and Recognition, 5*(2-3), 138-157.

Cui & Li. (2011). Adaptive Multi wavelet-Based Watermarking Through JPW Masking. IEEE Transactions on Image Processing, 20(4).

Cura, E., Tepper, M., &Mejail, M. (2010). Content-based emblem retrieval using Zernike moments. In *Progress in Pattern Recognition, Image Analysis, Computer Vision, and Applications* (pp. 79-86). Springer Berlin Heidelberg.

Curran, K., & Bailey, K. (2003). An evaluation of image based steganography methods. *International Journal of Digital Evidence, 2*(2). Retrieved from http://www.ijde.org

D. A., N. H., & K. A. (2011). Performance of weighted sum- rule fusion scheme in multi-instance and multi-modal biometric systems. *World Applied Science journal, 12*(11), 2160-2167.

Das & Dutta. (2013). An approach of bitwise Private-key Encryption, technique based on Multiple Operators and numbers of 0 and 1 counted from binary representation of Plain Text's single character. *International Journal of Innovative Technology and Exploring Engineering,* 1-6.

Davies, E. R. (2004). *Machine vision: theory, algorithms, practicalities.* Elsevier.

Davison, A. J. (2003). Real-time simultaneous localisation and mapping with a single camera.*Proceedings of the Ninth IEEE International Conference on Computer Vision (ICCV'03).* doi:10.1109/ICCV.2003.1238654

Davison, A. J., Reid, I. D., Molton, N. D., & Stasse, O. (2007). MonoSLAM: Real-time single camera SLAM. *IEEE Transactions on Pattern Analysis and Machine Intelligence, 29*(6), 1052–1067. doi:10.1109/TPAMI.2007.1049 PMID:17431302

De San Bernabe, A., Martinez-de Dios, J.R., & Baturone, A.O. (2012). Entropy-aware cluster-based object tracking for camera wireless sensor networks. *IEEE/RSJ International Conference on Intelligent Robots and Systems, IROS'12.*

De San Bernabe, A., Martinez-de Dios, J. R., & Ollero, A. (2012). A WSN-based tool for urban and industrial firefighting. *Sensors (Basel, Switzerland), 12*(12), 15009–15035. doi:10.3390/s121115009 PMID:23202198

Deb, K. (2005). Practical Optimization Using Evolutionary Methods. KanGAL Report Number 2005008, Kanpur Genetic Algorithms Laboratory (KanGAL), Department of Mechanical Engineering, Indian Institute of Technology Kanpur.

Del Pilar, F., Guarnizo, J., & Benavides, G. (2014). Emulation system for a distribution center using mobile robot, controlled by artificial vision and fuzzy logic. *IEEE Latin America Transactions, 12*(4), 557–563. doi:10.1109/TLA.2014.6868855

Demirel, H., & Jafari, G. A. (2011). Image Resolution Enhancement by Using Discrete and Stationary Wavelet Decomposition. *IEEE Transactions on Image Processing, 20*(5), 1458–1460. doi:10.1109/TIP.2010.2087767 PMID:20959267

Denemark, T. D., Boroumand, M., & Fridrich, J. (2016). Steganalysis Features for Content-Adaptive JPEG Steganography. IEEE Transactions on Information Forensics and Security, 11(8), 1736-1746.

Desai P. and Rattan K.S. (2009). Indoor localization and surveillance using wireless sensor network and pantilt camera. *IEEE National Aerospace & Electronics Conference (NAECON),* 1–6.

Deshpande, A.S. Patil S.M. & Lathi R. (2008). A Multimodal Biometric Recognition System based on Fusion of Palmprint, Fingerprint and Face. *International Journal of Electronics and Computer Science Engineering, 3*(1), 1315-1320.

Dore, A., Cattoni, A. F., & Regazzoni, C. S. (2007). A particle filter based fusion framework for video-radio tracking in smartspaces.*IEEE Conf. on Advanced Video and Signal Based Surveillance, AVSS'07,* 99–104.

Dougherty, G. (2013). Pattern Recognition and Classification. Springer.

Dubey, P. (2006). Edge based text detection for multi-purpose application. *Proceedings of International Conference on Signal Processing,* 16-20. doi:10.1109/ICOSP.2006.346106

Dudani, S. A., Breeding, K. J., & McGhee, R. B. (1977). Aircraft identification by moment invariants. Computers. *IEEE Transactions on, 100*(1), 39–46.

Du, J. X., Wang, X. F., & Zhang, G. J. (2007). Leaf shape based plant species recognition. *Applied Mathematics and Computation, 185*(2), 883–893. doi:10.1016/j.amc.2006.07.072

Ehsanirad, A., & Sharath Kumar, Y. H. (2010). Leaf recognition for plant classification using GLCM and PCA methods. *Oriental Journal of Computer Science and Technology, 3*(1), 31–36.

Elamaran, V., & Praveen, A. (2012). Comparison of DCT and wavelets in image coding.*Proceedings of International Conference on Computer Communication and Informatics (ICCCI).* doi:10.1109/ICCCI.2012.6158923

Elashry, Faragallah, Abbas, El-Rabaie, & El-Samie. (2012). A New Method for Encrypting Images with Few DetailsUsing Rijndael and RC6 Block Ciphers in the Electronic Code Book Mode. *Information Security Journal: A Global Perspective, 21*(4), 193-205.

Elgammal, A., Harwood, D., & Davis, L. (2000). Non-parametric Model for Background Subtraction.*European Conf. Computer Vision*, 2, 751–767.

Elgammal, A., Harwood, D., & Davis, L. (2004). *Non-parametric model for background subtraction. IEEE Frame-Rate Workshop,* (Vol. 4). IEEE.

Elhoseny, Ahmed, Abbas, Kazemian, Faragallah, El-Rabaie, & El-Samie. (2015). Chaotic encryption of Images in the Fractional Fourier Transform domain using different modes of operation. Springer Verlag.

El-Khamy, S. E., Ghaleb, I., & El-Yamany, N. A. (2002). Fuzzy edge detection with minimum fuzzy entropy criterion. In *Electrotechnical Conference, 2002. MELECON 2002. 11th Mediterranean* (pp. 498–503). doi:10.1109/MELECON.2002.1014643

El-Khamy, S. E., Lotfy, M., & El-Yamany, N. (2000). A modified fuzzy Sobel edge detector. In *Radio Science Conference, 2000. 17th NRSC'2000. Seventeenth National* (pp. C32–1).

Ensafi, P., & Tizhoosh, H. R. (2005). Type-2 fuzzy image enhancement. In Image Analysis and Recognition (pp. 159–166). Springer. doi:10.1007/11559573_20

Epshtein, B., Eyal, O., & Yonatan, W. (2010). Detecting text in natural scenes with stroke width transform. *Proceedings of the IEEE Conference on Computer Vision and Pattern Recognition (CVPR)*, 2963-2970. doi:10.1109/CVPR.2010.5540041

Erbil, B., & Karaca, M. A. (2013). Emergency admissions due to swallowed foreign bodies in Adults. *World Journal of Gastroenterology, 19*(38), 6447–6452. doi:10.3748/wjg.v19.i38.6447 PMID:24151363

Ercan, A. O., Yang, D. B., El Gamal, A., & Guibas, L. J. (2006). Optimal placement and selection of camera network nodes fortarget localization. In Distributed computing in sensor systems. Springer.

Ercan, A. O., El Gamal, A., & Guibas, L. J. (2007). Object tracking inthe presence of occlusions via a camera network. *Int. Conf. on Information Processing in Sensor Networks, IPSN'07*, 509–518. doi:10.1145/1236360.1236425

Everything about the data compression. (n.d.) Retrieved from http://www.compression.ru/index_en.htm

Ezaki, N., Bulacu, M., & Schomaker, L. (2004). Text Detection from Natural Scene Images: Towards a System for Visually Impaired Persons. *Proceedings of International Conference on Pattern Recognition*, 2, 683-686. doi:10.1109/ICPR.2004.1334351

Fang, J., Liu, Gu, W., & Tang, Y. (2011). A method to improve the image enhancement result based on image fusion. *International Conference on Multimedia Technology (ICMT)*, 55-58.

Fan, J. (2011). *Structured Max-Margin Learning for Inter-Related Classifier Training and Multilabel Image Annotation. IEEE Transactions on Image Processing, 20(3).*

Fardousse, K., & Qjidaa, H. (2016). Handwritten motives image recognition using polygonal approximation and chaincode. *WSEAS Transactions on Systems and Control, 11*, 217–223.

Fausett, L. (1994). Fundamentals of Neural Networks. Prentice-Hall, Inc.

Fawcett, T. (2003). *ROC Graphs: Notes and Practical Considerations for Researchers.* Academic Press.

Fazli, S., Pour, H. M., & Bouzari, H. (2009). Particle Filter based Object Tracking with Sift and Color Feature. *Machine Vision, 2009. ICMV '09.Second International Conference*, 89 – 93.

Fei, C., Kundur, D., & Kwong, R. H. (2006). Analysis and design of secure watermark-based authentication systems. *IEEE Transactions on Information Forensics and Security, 1*(1), 43-55.

Feng, J., Zhou, J., Member, S., & Jain, A. K. (n.d.). *Orientation Field Estimation for Latent Fingerprint Enhancement.* Academic Press.

Fensholt, Sandholt, & Stisen. (2006). *Analysing NDVI for the African continent using the geostationary meteosat second generation SEVIRI sensor.* Compton Tucker at Institute of Geography, University of Copenhagen, University of Copenhagen.

Figuereido, A. B., Ferreira, B. M., & Matos, A. C. (2016). *Visión-based localization and positioning of an AUV.* Paper presented at OCEANS 2016 Conference, Shanghai, China. doi:10.1109/OCEANSAP.2016.7485384

Firoz, R., Ali, M. S., Khan, M. N. U., Hossain, M. K., Islam, M. K., & Shahinuzzaman, M. (2016). Medical Image Enhancement Using Morphological Transformation. *Journal of Data Analysis and Information Processing*, *4*(12), 1–12. doi:10.4236/jdaip.2016.41001

Fisher, R. A. (1936). The use of multiple meaures in taxonomic problems. *Annals of Eugenics*, *7*(2), 179–188. doi:10.1111/j.1469-1809.1936.tb02137.x

Flusser, J. (2006, February). Moment invariants in image analysis. In *Proceedings of world academy of science, engineering and technology* (Vol. 11, No. 2, pp. 196-201).

Folkers, A., & Samet, H. (2002). Content-based image retrieval using Fourier descriptors on a logo database. In *Pattern Recognition, 2002.Proceedings.16th International Conference on* (Vol. 3, pp. 521-524). IEEE. doi:10.1109/ICPR.2002.1047991

Foon, N. H., Pang, Y. H., Jin, A. T. B., & Ling, D. N. C. (2004, July). An efficient method for human face recognition using wavelet transform and Zernike moments. In *Computer Graphics, Imaging and Visualization, 2004.CGIV 2004. Proceedings. International Conference on* (pp. 65-69). IEEE.

Fossati, J. P., Galarza, A., Martín-Villate, A., Echeverría, J. M., & Fontán, L. (2015). Optimal scheduling of a microgrid with a fuzzy logic controlled storage system. *Electrical Power and Energy Systems.*, *68*, 61–70. doi:10.1016/j.ijepes.2014.12.032

Freeman, H. (1961). On the encoding of arbitrary geometric configurations. *IRE Transactions on Electronic Computers*, *EC-10*(2), 260–268. doi:10.1109/TEC.1961.5219197

Frischholz, R.W. (2000). BioID: A Multimodal Biometric Identification System. *IEEE Transaction*, 64-68.

Gandhi, T., Kasuturi, R., & Antani, S. (2000). Application of Planar Motion Segmentation for Scene Text Extraction. *Proceedings of International Conference on Pattern Recognition*, *1*, 445-449. doi:10.1109/ICPR.2000.905372

Gao & Jin. (1992). *Rice cultivation computer simulation and optimization decision system.* Beijing: China Agricultural Science Technology Publishing House.

Gauglitz, S., Höllerer, T., & Turk, M. (2011). Evaluation of interest point detectors and feature descriptors for visual tracking. *International Journal of Computer Vision*, *94*(3), 335–360. doi:10.1007/s11263-011-0431-5

Ghasemi, E., Shanbehzadeh, J., & ZahirAzami, B. (2011). A steganographic method based on Integer Wavelet Transform and Genetic Algorithm. *International Conference on Communications and Signal Processing (ICCSP)*, 42-45. doi:10.1109/ICCSP.2011.5739395

Gherghina. (2009). *Grid Services and Satellite Image Processing for urban and river bed changes assessment.* "Ovidius" University of Constantza.

Ghosal, S. (n.d.). *Zernike Moment-Based Subpixel Edge Detection.* Centre for Robotics &Mfgsys., University of Kentucky.

Ghosal, S., & Mehrotra, R. (1993). Segmentation of range images: An orthogonal moment-based integrated approach. *Robotics and Automation. IEEE Transactions on, 9*(4), 385–399.

Ghosal, S., & Mehrotra, R. (1994). Detection of composite edges. Image Processing. *IEEE Transactions on, 3*(1), 14–25.

Gil, A., Martínez, O., Ballesta, M., & Reinoso, O. (2010). A comparative evaluation of interest point detectors and local descriptors for visual slam. *Machine Vision and Applications, 21*(6), 905–920. doi:10.1007/s00138-009-0195-x

Gllavata, J., Ewerth, R., Stefi, T., & Freisleben, B. (2004). Unsupervised text segmentation using color and wavelet features. *Proceedings of International Conference on Image and Video Retrieval*, 216-224. doi:10.1007/978-3-540-27814-6_28

Goel, S., Rana, A., & Kaur, M. (2013). Comparison of image steganography techniques. *International Journal of Computers and Distributed Systems, 3*(1), 20–30. Retrieved from http://www.ijcdsonline.com

Gomez Lopera, J. F., Ilhami, N., Escamilla, P. L. L., Aroza, J. M., & Roldán, R. R. (1999). Improved entropic edge-detection. In *Image Analysis and Processing, 1999. Proceedings. International Conference on* (pp. 180–184). doi:10.1109/ICIAP.1999.797591

Gonzalez & Woods. (2009). *Digital Image Processing*. Pearson Education.

Gonzalez, R. C., & Wintz, P. (1977). *Digital image processing*. Academic Press.

Gonzalez, R. C., Woods, R. E., & Eddins, S. L. (2004). *Book*. Digital Image Processing Using Matlab.

Gonzalez, R. C., Woods, R. E., & Eddins, S. L. (2010). *Digital Image Processing Using Matlab* (2nd ed.). New Delhi: Tata McGraw Hill Education Private Limited.

Gorgan, Bacu, Stefanut, Rodila, & Mihon. (2009). *Grid based Satellite Image Processing Platform for Earth Observation Application Development*. Technical University of Cluj-Napoca.

Gosavi, N., Shinde, S.S., & Dhakulkar, B. (2012). Use of cloud computing in library and information science field. *International Journal of Digital Library Services, 2*(3).

Goshorn, R., Goshorn, J., Goshorn, D., & Aghajan, H. (2007). Architecture for cluster-based automated surveillance network for detecting and tracking multiple persons. *ACM/IEEE Int. Conf. on Distributed Smart Cameras, ICDSC'07*, 219–226. doi:10.1109/ICDSC.2007.4357527

Gray, R. M. (2011). *Entropy and information theory*. Springer. doi:10.1007/978-1-4419-7970-4

Greenberg, S., Aladjem, M., Kogan, D., & Dimitrov, I. (2000). Fingerprint image enhancement using filtering techniques. In *Pattern Recognition, 2000. Proceedings. 15th International Conference on* (Vol. 3, pp. 322–325). doi:10.1109/ICPR.2000.903550

Grumbach, S., Rigaux, P., & Segoufin, L. (1998, June). The DEDALE system for complex spatial queries. *SIGMOD Record, 27*(2), 213–224. doi:10.1145/276305.276324

Gutierrez, J., Villa-Medina, J. F., Nieto-Garibay, A., & Porta-Gandara, M. A. (2014). Automated Irrigation System Using a Wireless Sensor Network and GPRS Module", Instrumentation and Measurement. *IEEE Transactions on, 63*(1), 166–176.

Haddadnia, J., Faez, K., & Moallem, P. (2001). Neural network based face recognition with moment invariants. In *Image Processing, 2001. Proceedings. 2001 International Conference on* (Vol. 1, pp. 1018-1021). IEEE. doi:10.1109/ICIP.2001.959221

Hamid, N., Yahya, A., Ahmad, R. B., & Qershi, O. A. M. (2012). Image steganography techniques: An overview. *International Journal of Computer Science and Security, 6*(3).

Hanif, S. M., & Prevost, L. (2009). Text detection and localization in complex scene images using constrained adaboost algorithm. *Proceedings of the 10th International Conference on Document Analysis and Recognition, ICDAR, IEEE*, 1-5. doi:10.1109/ICDAR.2009.172

Hanmandlu, M., Jha, D., & Sharma, R. (2003). Color image enhancement by fuzzy intensification. *Pattern Recognition Letters, 24*(1), 81–87. doi:10.1016/S0167-8655(02)00191-5

Haouzia, A., & Noumeir, R. (2008). Methods for image authentication: A survey. *Multimedia Tools and Applications, 39*(1), 1–46. doi:10.1007/s11042-007-0154-3

Hardy, G. H., & Wright, E. M. (1979). *An introduction to the theory of numbers*. Oxford University Press.

Harris, C., & Stephens, M. (1988). A combined corner and edge detector. In *Proceedings of the Fourth Alvey Vision Conference*. Manchester, UK: Alvety Vision Club. doi:10.5244/C.2.23

Hase, H., Shinokawa, T., Yoneda, M., & Suen, C. Y. (2001). Character string extraction from color documents. *Pattern Recognition, Elsevier, 34*(7), 1349–1365. doi:10.1016/S0031-3203(00)00081-9

Hashad, A. I., Madani, A. S., & Wahdan, A. E. M. A. (2005). A robust steganography technique using discrete cosine transform insertion. *Enabling Technologies for the New Knowledge Society: ITI 3rd International Conference on Information and Communications Technology,* 255-264.

Hashad, A. I., Madani, A. S., Moneim, A. E., & Wahdan, A. (2005). A robust steganography technique using discrete cosine transform insertion. *Proceedings of Enabling Technologies for the New Knowledge Society: ITI 3rd International Conference on Information and Communications Technology* (pp.255-264). doi:10.1109/ITICT.2005.1609628

Hashmi, M., Garcia, L., & Fontane, D. (1995). Spatial estimation of regional crop evapotranspiration. *Transactions of the ASAE. American Society of Agricultural Engineers, 38*(5), 1345–1351. doi:10.13031/2013.27957

Hassanien, A. E., & Badr, A. (2003). A comparative study on digital mamography enhancement algorithms based on fuzzy theory. *Studies in Informatics and Control, 12*(1), 21–32.

Heikkila, M., & Pietikainen, M. (2006, April). A texture based method for modelling the background and detecting moving objects. *IEEE Transactions on Pattern Analysis and Machine Intelligence, 28*(4), 657–662. doi:10.1109/TPAMI.2006.68 PMID:16566514

Heikkila, M., Pietikainen, M., & Schmid, C. (2009, March). Description of interest regions with local binary patterns. *Pattern Recognition, 42*(3), 425–436. doi:10.1016/j.patcog.2008.08.014

Heinzelman, A. B. H., & Chandrakasan, W. (2000). Energy-efficient communication protocol for wireless microsensor networks.*Int. Conf. on System Sciences*. doi:10.1109/HICSS.2000.926982

Hemalatha P. A. (2013). Image Retrieval by Content Using Descriptors. *International Journal of Engineering Sciences & Research Technology, 2*(10), 1-7.

Hemalatha, S., Acharya, U. D., Renuka, A., & Kamath, P. R. (2012). A secure image steganography technique using Integer Wavelet Transform.*World Congress on Information and Communication Technologies (WICT)*, 755-758. doi:10.1109/WICT.2012.6409175

Hengartner, U., & Steenkiste, P. (n.d.). *Exploiting hierarchical identity-based encryption for access control to pervasive computing information, October, CMU-CS-04-172*. Retrieved from https://cs.uwaterloo.ca/~uhengart/publications/securecomm05.pdf

He, R., & Hu, B.-G. (2011). *Robust Principal Component Analysis Based on Maximum Correntropy Criterion. IEEE Transactions on Image Processing, 20(6)*.

Hirata-Kohno, N., & Petho, A. (2013). On a key exchange protocol based on Diophantine equations. *Infocommunications Journal, 5*(3), 17–21.

Ho, K. H. L., & Ohnishi, N. (1995). FEDGE—fuzzy edge detection by fuzzy categorization and classification of edges. In *Fuzzy Logic in Artificial Intelligence Towards Intelligent Systems* (pp. 182–196). Springer.

Holliman, M., & Memon, N. (2000). Counterfeiting attacks on oblivious block-wise independent invisible watermarking schemes. *IEEE Transactions on Image Processing, 9*(3), 432–441. doi:10.1109/83.826780 PMID:18255414

Holz, D., Nieuwenhuisen, M., Droeschel, D., Stückler, J., Berner, A., Li, J., Klein, R., & Behnke, S. (2014). Active recognition and manipulation for mobile robot bin picking. In F. Röhrbein, G. Veiga, & C. Natale (Eds.), Gearing up and accelerating cross-fertilization between academic and industrial robotics in Europe (pp. 133-153). Springer International Publishing.

Hongjun, L., & Xingyuan, W. (2010). Color image encryption based on one-time keys and robust chaotic maps. *Computers & Mathematics with Applications (Oxford, England), 59*(10), 3320–3327. doi:10.1016/j.camwa.2010.03.017

Hori, Kawashima, & Yamazaki. (2011). Application of cloud computing to Agriculture and prospect to other fields. *Fijitsu Science Technology Journal, 46*(4), 446-454.

Hori, M., Kawashima, E., & Yamazaki, T. (2010). Application of cloud computing to agriculture and prospects in other fields. *Fujitsu Science and Technology Journal, 46*(4), 446–454.

Hosny, K. M. (2007). Exact Legendre moment computation for gray level images. *Pattern Recognition, 40*(12), 3597–3605. doi:10.1016/j.patcog.2007.04.014

Hosny, K. M., & Hafez, M. A. (2012). An algorithm for fast computation of 3D Zernike moments for volumetric images. *Mathematical Problems in Engineering*.

Hou, Y. L. (2000). Theory and technological system of ecological balanced fertilization. *Acta Ecologica Sinica, 20*, 653–658.

Huang & Wang. (1996). The combination of GIS and ES and exploration for application. *Environment Remote Sensing, 11*(3).

Huang, Wan, & Shen. (2009). *An Object-Based Approach for Forest-Cover Change Detection using Multi-Temporal High-Resolution Remote Sensing Data*. School of Remote Sensing and Information Engineering, Wuhan University.

Huang, Zhang, Wu, & Li. (2010). *MODIS-NDVI-Based crop growth monitoring in China Agriculture Remote Sensing Monitoring System*. Grassland Ecosystem Observation and Research Station Institute of Agricultural Resources and Regional Planning of Chinese Academy of Agricultural Sciences.

Huang. S., (2011, Jan.). An Advanced Motion Detection Algorithm with Video Quality Analysis for Video Surveillance Systems. *IEEE Transaction on Circuit and Systems for Video Technology, 21*(1).

Huang, W., Lin, Z., Jianchao, Y., & Wang, J. (2013). Text localization in natural images using stroke feature transform and text covariance descriptors. *Proceedings of International Conference on Computer Vision ICCV), 1241-1248*. doi:10.1109/ICCV.2013.157

Hue, C., Le Cadre, J. P., & Perez, P. (2002, July). Tracking multiple objects with particle filtering. *IEEE Transactions on Aerospace and Electronic Systems, 38*(3), 791–812. doi:10.1109/TAES.2002.1039400

Hu, M. K. (1962). Visual pattern recognition by moment invariants. *Information Theory. IRE Transactions on, 8*(2), 179–187.

Hu, X., & Ahuja, N. (1994). Matching point features with ordered geometric, rigidity, and disparity constraints. *IEEE Transactions on Pattern Analysis and Machine Intelligence, 16*(10), 1041–1049. doi:10.1109/34.329004

Hyndman, R. J., & Athanasopoulos. (2015, May). *8.9 Seasonal ARIMA models*. Academic Press.

Hyunsoek, C., & Hyeyoung, P. (2014). *Gestures, A Multimodal User Authentication System Using Faces*. Hindawi Publishing Corporation.

Idbeaa T., Abdul Samad S., Husain H. (2016). A Secure and robust compressed domain video steganography for intra- and inter-frames using embedding-based byte differencing (EBBD) scheme. *PLoS One, 11*(3), 2. doi: 10.1371/journal.pone.0150732

Image Processing / Videocodecs/ Programming. (n.d.). Retrieved from http://www.hlevkin.com/TestImages/Boats.bmp

Iqbal, K., Xu-Cheng, Y., Hong-Wei, H., Sohail, A., & Hazrat, A. (2014). Bayesian network scores based text localization in scene images. *Proceedings of International Joint Conference on Neural Networks (IJCNN)*, 2218-2225. doi:10.1109/IJCNN.2014.6889731

Iscan, Z., Dokur, Z., & Ölmez, T. (2010). Tumor detection by using Zernike moments on segmented magnetic resonance brain images. *Expert Systems with Applications, 37*(3), 2540–2549. doi:10.1016/j.eswa.2009.08.003

Jadhav, D., Patil, M., Patil, A., & Phalak, L. (2013). A Novel Three Stage CBIR using Varying Higher-Order Zernike Moments and its Performance Analysis. *International Journal of Computers and Applications, 75*(3), 33–38. doi:10.5120/13093-0374

Jain, A. K., Duin, R. P. W., & Mao, J. (2000). Statistical Pattern Recognition: A Review. *IEEE Transactions on Pattern Analysis and Machine Intelligence, 22*(1), 4–37. doi:10.1109/34.824819

Jain, A. K., & Yu, B. (1998). Automatic Text Location in Images and Video Frames. *Pattern Recognition, Elsevier, 31*(12), 2055–2076. doi:10.1016/S0031-3203(98)00067-3

Jain, A. R., & Ross, A. (2004). Multibiometric systems. *Communications of the ACM, 47*(1), 34–40. doi:10.1145/962081.962102

Jain, A., Flynn, P., & Ross, A. A. (2007). *Handbook of biometrics*. Springer Science & Business Media.

Jain, K. (2004). Multimodal Biometrics: An Overview. *12th European Signal Processing Conference (EUSIPCO)*, 1221-1224.

Jantavong, J. (n.d.). *Chrominance and Luminance*. Retrieved from http://ladballbow.blogspot.com/2009_02_05_archive.html

Japan airports to install mobile biometric terminals to screen foreign passengers. (2015, September 8). Retrieved from http://www.airport-technology.com/news/newsjapan-airports-to-install-mobile-biometric-terminals-to-screen-foreign-passengers-4665642

Jasani, D., Patel, P., Patel, S., Ahir, B., Patel, K., & Dixit, M. (2015). Review of Shape and Texture Feature Extraction Techniques for Fruits. *International Journal of Computer Science and Information Technologies, 6*(6), 4851–4854.

Jayaram, B., Narayana, K., & Vetrivel, V. (2011). Fuzzy Inference System based Contrast Enhancement. In *EUSFLAT Conf.* (pp. 311–318).

Jeffrey, A. D., Corso, J. J., & Philip, D. (2010). Boosting with stereo features for building facade detection on mobile platforms. *Image Processing Workshop (WNYIPW)*,46-49.

Jimenez-Gonzalez Martınez-de Dios, J., De San Bernabe, A., & Ollero, A. (2011). WSN-based visual object tracking using extended information filters. *Int. Workshop on Networks of Cooperating Objects*, 11.

Jimenez-Gonzalez, A., Martínez-de Dios, J. R., & Ollero, A. (2015). An integrated testbed for cooperative perception with heterogeneous mobile and static sensors. *Sensors (Basel, Switzerland)*, *11*(12), 11516–11543. doi:10.3390/s111211516 PMID:22247679

Joseph, P., & Vishnukumar, S. (2015). A study on steganographic techniques.*Global Conference on Communication Technologies (GCCT), 206-210.* doi:10.1109/GCCT.2015.7342653

Jung, K., Kim, K.I., & Jain, A.K. (2004). Text information extraction in images and video: A survey. *Pattern Recognition, 37*(5), 977-997.

Jyothi, B., Latha, Y. M., Mohan, P. K., & Reddy, V. S. K. (2013). Medical Image Retrieval Using Moments. *International Journal of Application or Innovation in Engineering & Management, 2*(1), 195–200.

Kallel, Hégarat-Mascle, Hubert-Moy, & Ottlé. (2008). *Fusion of Vegetation Indices Using Continuous Belief Functions and Cautious-Adaptive*. Academic Press.

Kanhere, N. K., Pundlik, S. J., & Birchfield, S. T. (2005). Vehicle segmentation and tracking from a low-angle off-axis camera.*IEEE Conference on Computer Vision and pattern Recognition.* doi:10.1109/CVPR.2005.365

Kar-Ann Toh, S. M.-Y. (2004). Exploiting Global and Local Decisions for Multimodal Biometrics Verification. *IEEE Transactions on Signal Processing, 52*(10).

Karimi-Ashtiani, S., & Kuo, C.-C. J. (2008). A robust technique for latent fingerprint image segmentation and enhancement. In *Image Processing, 2008. ICIP 2008. 15th IEEE International Conference on* (pp. 1492–1495). doi:10.1109/ICIP.2008.4712049

Karthikeyan, C., Ramadoss, B., & Baskar, S. (2012). Segmentation Algorithm for CT Images using Morphological Operation and Artificial Neural Network. *International Journal of Signal Processing. Image Processing and Pattern Recognition, 5*(2), 115–122.

Kasawani, Norsaliza, & Hasmadi. (2010). *Analysis of Spectral Vegetation Indices Related to Soil-Line for Mapping Mangrove Forests Using Satellite Imagery*. University of Malaysia Terengganu.

Kassem, M. A. (2014). An Enhanced ATM Security System Using Multimodal Biometric Strategy. *International Journal of Electrical & Computer Sciences IJECS-IJENS, 14*(04), 9–16.

Kass, M., Witkin, A., & Terzopoulos, D. (1988). Snakes: Active contour models. *International Journal of Computer Vision, 1*(4), 321–331. doi:10.1007/BF00133570

Katharotiya, A., Patel, S., & Goyani, M. (2011). Comparative aalysis between DCT & DWT techniques of image compression. *Journal of Information Engineering and Applications, 1*(2), 9–16. http://www.iiste.org

Kaviani, F., Rashid, R. J., Shahmoradi, Z., & Gholamian, M. (2014). Detection of Foreign Bodies by Spiral Computed Tomography and Cone Beam Computed Tomography in Maxillofacial Regions. *Journal Dental Research and Dental Clinical Prospects, 8*(3), 166–171. PMID:25346836

Kavitha, R., & Murugan, A. (2007). Lossless steganography on AVI file using swapping algorithm.*Conference on Computational Intelligence and Multimedia Applications, 4,* 83-88. doi:10.1109/ICCIMA.2007.380

Kawaguchi, E., Maeta, M., Noda, H., & Nozaki, K. (2007). A model of digital contents access control system using steganographic information hiding scheme.*Proceedings of conference on Information Modelling and Knowledge Bases XVIII* (pp. 50-61).

Kayabol, & Zerubia. (2013). Unsupervised amplitude and texture classification of SAR images with multinomial latent model. *IEEE Transaction on Image Processing*.

Kebiao, M., & Zhihao, T. (2004). The Integration and Application of Spatial Data Mining And GIS. *Geomatics &Spatial Information Technology, 27*(1), 14–17.

Kekre, H. B., Thepade, S., Mukherjee, P., Kakaiya, M., Wadhwa, S., & Singh, S. (2010). Image Retrieval with Shape Features Extracted using Gradient Operators and Slope Magnitude Technique with BTC. *International Journal of Computers and Applications, 6*(8), 28–33. doi:10.5120/1094-1430

Ker, A. D. (2005). Steganalysis of LSB matching in grayscale images. *Signal Processing Letters, IEEE, 12*(6), 441–444. doi:10.1109/LSP.2005.847889

Khan, A. S., Fisal, N., Bakar, Z. A., Salawu, N., Maqbool, W., Ullah, R., & Safdar, H. (2014). Secure Authentication and Key Management Protocols for Mobile Multihop WiMAX Networks. *Indian Journal of Science and Technology, 7*(3), 282–295.

Khan, S. U., Chai, W. Y., See, C. S., & Khan, A. (2016). X-Ray Image Enhancement Using a Boundary Division Wiener Filter and Wavelet-Based Image Fusion Approach. *Journal of Information Process System, 12*(1), 35–45.

Khashan, O. A., & Zin, A. M. (2013). An Efficient Adaptive of Transparent Spatial Digital Image Encryption. *Procedia Technology, 11,* 288-297.

Khotanzad, A., & Hong, Y. H. (1990). Invariant image recognition by Zernike moments. *Pattern Analysis and Machine Intelligence. IEEE Transactions on, 12*(5), 489–497.

Kim, B.-G., Kim, H.-J., & Park, D.-J. (2002). New enhancement algorithm for fingerprint images. In *Pattern Recognition, 2002. Proceedings. 16th International Conference on* (Vol. 3, pp. 879–882).

Kim, H. K., Kim, J. D., Sim, D. G., & Oh, D. I. (2000). A modified Zernike moment shape descriptor invariant to translation, rotation and scale for similarity-based image retrieval. In *Multimedia and Expo, 2000.ICME 2000.2000 IEEE International Conference on* (Vol. 1, pp. 307-310). IEEE.

Kim, H. (1996). Efficient automatic text location method and content-based indexing and structuring of video database. *Journal of Visual Communication and Image Representation, 7*(4), 336–344. doi:10.1006/jvci.1996.0029

Kim, H. S., & Lee, H. K. (2003). Invariant image watermark using Zernike moments. *Circuits and Systems for Video Technology. IEEE Transactions on, 13*(8), 766–775.

Kim, H. S., & Lee, H. K. (2003). Invariant image watermark using Zernike moments. *IEEE Transactions on Circuits and Systems for Video Technology, 13*(8), 766–775. doi:10.1109/TCSVT.2003.815955

Kim, K., Keechul, J., & Kim, H. J. (2003). Texture-based approach for text detection in images using support vector machines and continuously adaptive mean shift algorithm. *IEEE Transactions on Pattern Analysis and Machine Intelligence, 25*(12), 1631–1639. doi:10.1109/TPAMI.2003.1251157

Klippenstein, J., & Zhang, H. (2009). *Performance evaluation of visual SLAM using several feature extractors.* Paper presented at IEEE/RSJ International Conference on Intelligent Robots and Systems (IROS), St. Louis, MO. doi:10.1109/IROS.2009.5354001

Koch, E., & Zhao, J. (1995). Towards robust and hidden image copyright labeling. In *IEEE Workshop on Nonlinear Signal and Image Processing* (pp. 452-455). NeosMarmaras, Greece: IEEE.

Kollnig, N. (1997). *Institutfür Algorithmen und Kognitive Systeme*. Retrieved from http://i21www.ira.uka.de/image_sequences

Kong, A., Zhang, D., & Kamel, M. (2009). A survey of Palmprint recognition. *Elsevier. Pattern Recognition, 42*(7), 1408–1418. doi:10.1016/j.patcog.2009.01.018

Kong, F.-H. (2009). Image Retrieval using both Color and Texture Features.*Proceedings of the Eighth International Conference on Machine Learning and Cybernetics, 4*, 12-15. doi:10.1109/ICMLC.2009.5212186

Konolige, K., Agrawal, M., Bolles, R. C., Cowan, C., Fischler, M., & Gerkey, B. (2008). *Outdoor mapping and navigation using stereo vision. In Experimental Robotics* (pp. 179–190). Berlin: Springer.

Kotkar & Gharde. (2013). Review of Various Image Contrast Enhancement Techniques. *International Journal of Innovative Research in Science, Engineering and Technology, 2*(7).

Krajník, T., Sváb, J., Pedre, S., Cizek, P., & Preucil, L. (2014). FPGA-based module for SURF extraction. *Machine Vision and Applications, 25*(3), 787–800. doi:10.1007/s00138-014-0599-0

Kulkarni, A. H., Rai, H. M., Jahagirdar, K. A., & Upparamani, P. S. (2013). A leaf recognition technique for plant classification using RBPNN and Zernike moments. *International Journal of Advanced Research in Computer and Communication Engineering, 2*(1), 984–988.

Kumar, V., & Kumar, D. (2010). Performance evaluation of DWT based image steganography. *IEEE 2nd International Advance Computing Conference (IACC),* 223-228.

Kumar, M. P., Goyal, S., Jawahar, C. V., & Narayanan, P. J. (2002). *Polygonal Approximation of Closed Curves across Multiple Views*. ICVGIP.

Kundur, D., Zhao, Y., & Campisi, P. (2004). A stenographic framework for dual authentication and compression of high resolution imagery. In *Circuits and Systems, 2004. ISCAS'04.Proceedings of the 2004 International Symposium on* (Vol. 2, pp. II-1). IEEE. doi:10.1109/ISCAS.2004.1329193

Kuralkar, P. (2012). Human Object Tracking using Background Subtraction and Shadow Removal Techniques. *International Journal of Advanced Research in Computer Science and Software Engineering, 2*(3).

Larose, D. T. (2014). *Discovering knowledge in data: an introduction to data mining*. John Wiley & Sons. doi:10.1002/9781118874059

Lassoued, I., Zagrouba, E., & Chahir, Y. (2011). An efficient approach for video action classification based on 3d Zernike moments. In *Future Information Technology* (pp. 196–205). Springer Berlin Heidelberg. doi:10.1007/978-3-642-22309-9_24

Latecki, L. J., & Lakämper, R. (1999). Convexity rule for shape decomposition based on discrete contour evolution. *Computer Vision and Image Understanding, 73*(3), 441–454. doi:10.1006/cviu.1998.0738

Lee, J. (2015, August 26). *ZKAccess releases multi-biometric access control device*. Retrieved from http://www.biometricupdate.com/201508/zkaccess-releases-multi-biometric-access-control-device

Lee, C. M., & Kankanhalli, A. (1995). Automatic Extraction of Characters in Complex Images. *International Journal of Pattern Recognition and Artificial Intelligence, 9*(1), 67–82. doi:10.1142/S0218001495000043

Lee, C. W., Jung, K., & Kim, H. (2003). Automatic text detection and removal in video sequences. *Pattern Recognition Letters, Elsevier, 24*(15), 2607–2623. doi:10.1016/S0167-8655(03)00105-3

Lee, K. H. (2006). *First course on fuzzy theory and applications* (Vol. 27). Springer.

Lee, S., & Kim, J. H. (2013). Integrating multiple character proposals for robust scene text extraction. *Image and Vision Computing, Elsevier, 31*(11), 823–840. doi:10.1016/j.imavis.2013.08.007

Lei & , Bian. (2010). Analysis of Spatiotemporal Difference of NDVI in an Arid Coal Mining Region using. *Remote Sensing*.

Lei, Y., & Jiafa, N. (2008). Subpixel Edge Detection Based on Morphological Theory. In *Proceedings of the world Congress on Engineering and Computer Science* (pp. 22-24).

Lemaitre, C., Smach, F., Miteran, J., Gauthier, J. P., & Mohamed, A. T. R. I. (2007). *A comparative study of Motion Descriptors and Zernike moments in color object recognition. In proceeding of International Multi-Conference on Systems, Signal and Devices*. Hammamet, Tunisia: IEEE.

Leutenegger, S., Chli, M., & Siegwart, R. Y. (2011). *BRISK: Binary robust invariant scalable keypoints*. Paper presented at IEEE International Conference on Computer Vision (ICCV), Barcelona, Spain. doi:10.1109/ICCV.2011.6126542

Li, Cheng, Yan, & Gong. (2010). *Monitoring System for Vegetable Greenhouses based on a Wireless Sensor Network*. National Library of Medicine.

Li, N., Liu, L., & Xu, D. (2008). Corner feature based object tracking using Adaptive Kalman Filter, Signal Processing. *ICSP 2008.9th International Conference*, 1432 – 1435.

Li, X., & Song, A. (2010, March). A new edge detection method using Gaussian-Zernike moment operator. In *Informatics in Control, Automation and Robotics (CAR), 2010 2nd International Asia Conference on* (Vol. 1, pp. 276-279). IEEE.

Li, Y., Chi, Z., & Feng, D. D. (2006, October). Leaf vein extraction using independent component analysis. In *Systems, Man and Cybernetics, 2006.SMC'06.IEEE International Conference on* (Vol. 5, pp. 3890-3894). IEEE. doi:10.1109/ICSMC.2006.384738

Li. (1997). On Definition, Theory and Key Technics of the Integration of GPS, RS and GISb. *Journal of Remote Sensing, 18*.

Liang Wang, H. N. (2004). Fusion of Static and Dynamic Body Biometrics for Gait Recognition. *IEEE Transactions on Circuits and Systems for Video Technology, 14*(2).

Liang, J., Doermann, D., & Li, H. (2005). Camera-based analysis of text and documents: A survey. *International Journal of Document Analysis and Recognition, 7*(2-3), 84–104. doi:10.1007/s10032-004-0138-z

Liao, S. X., & Pawlak, M. (1996). On image analysis by moments. *Pattern analysis and machine intelligence. IEEE Transactions on, 18*(3), 254–266.

Liao, S. X., & Pawlak, M. (1998). On the accuracy of Zernike moments for image analysis. *Pattern Analysis and Machine Intelligence. IEEE Transactions on, 20*(12), 1358–1364.

Li, C. T., Li, Y., & Wei, C. H. (2009). Protection of digital mammograms on PACSs using data hiding techniques. *International Journal of Digital Crime and Forensics, 1*(1), 75–88. doi:10.4018/jdcf.2009010105

Lienhart, R., & Wernicke, A. (2002). Localizing and segmenting text in images and videos. *IEEE Transactions on Circuits and Systems for Video Technology, 12*(4), 256–268. doi:10.1109/76.999203

Li, H., & Doermann, D. (2000). A Video Text Detection System Based on Automated Training. *Proceedings of International Conference on Pattern Recognition, 2*, 223-226. doi:10.1109/ICPR.2000.906053

Li, H., Doermann, D., & Kia, O. (2000). Automatic text detection and tracking in digital video. *IEEE Transactions on Image Processing, 9*(1), 147–156. doi:10.1109/83.817607 PMID:18255381

Li, L., Huang, W., Gu, I., & Tian, Q. (2003). Foreground object detection from videos containing complex background. *ACM International Conference on Multimedia*, 2-10. doi:10.1145/957013.957017

Lin, Xu, Y., Liang, X., & Lai. (2014, July). Complex Background Subtraction by pursuing Dynamic Spatio – Temporal Models. *IEEE Transaction on Image Processing, 23*(7), 3191-3201.

Lin, C. C., & Shiu, P. F. (2012). High capacity data hiding scheme for DCT-based images. *Journal of Information Hiding and Multimedia Signal Processing, 1*(3), 220–240.

Lin, C. H., Chang, C. C., & Lee, R. C. T. (1995). A new public-key cipher system based upon the Diophantine equations. *IEEE Transactions on Computers, 44*(1), 13–19. doi:10.1109/12.368013

Lin, C. Y., & Chang, S. F. (2001). SARI: self-authentication-and-recovery image watermarking system. In *Proceedings of the ninth ACM international conference on Multimedia* (pp. 628-629). ACM. doi:10.1145/500141.500266

Lin, Ch.-H., Chen, T.-H., & Wu, Ch.-S. (2013). A batch image encryption scheme based on chaining random grids. *Scientia Iranica D, 20*(3), 670–681.

Lin, H.-H. (2011). *Regularized Background Adaptation: A Novel Learning Rate Control Scheme for Gaussian Mixture Modeling. IEEE Transactions on Image Processing, 20(3).*

Liping, C., Chunjiang, Z., & Xuexin, L. (2002). Design and Implementation of Intelligent Decision Support System for Precision Agriculture. *Transactions of CSAE, 18*(2),149-152.

Li, S., Lee, M. C., & Pun, C. M. (2009). Complex Zernike moments features for shape-based image retrieval. *Systems, Man and Cybernetics, Part A: Systems and Humans. IEEE Transactions on, 39*(1), 227–237.

Liu, H., Rui, W., & Huang, J. (2007, September). Binary image authentication using Zernike moments. In *Image Processing, 2007.ICIP 2007.IEEE International Conference on* (Vol. 1, pp. I-385). IEEE. doi:10.1109/ICIP.2007.4378972

Liu, Y., Zhou, X., & Ma, W.-Y. (2004). Extracting Texture Features from Arbitrary-shaped Regions for Image Retrieval. *Multimedia and Expo 2004 IEEE International Conference, 3*(3), 1891-1894.

Liu, S., & Fu, C. (1998, September). Statistical change detection with moments under time varying illumination. *IEEE Transactions on Image Processing, 7*(9), 1258–1268. doi:10.1109/83.709658 PMID:18276338

Liu, X., & Samarabandu, J. (2005). An edge-based text region extraction algorithm for indoor mobile robot navigation. *Proceedings of International Conference on Mechatronics and Automation, 2*, 701-706.

Liu, X., & Samarabandu, J. (2006) Multiscale edge-based text extraction from complex images, *Proceedings of International Conference on Multimedia and Expo*, 1721-1724. doi:10.1109/ICME.2006.262882

Liu, Y.-F. (2011). *Inverse Halftoning Based on the Bayesian Theorem. IEEE Transactions on Image Processing, 20(4).*

Liu, Y., Lu, H., Xue, X. Y., & Tan, Y. P. (2004). Effective video text detection using line features, *Proceedings of International Conference on Control, Automation, Robotics and Vision*, 1528-1532.

Liu, Z. P. (2013). Linear discriminant analysis. In *Encyclopedia of Systems Biology* (pp. 1132–1133). Springer New York. doi:10.1007/978-1-4419-9863-7_395

Li, W., Xiao, C., & Liu, Y. (2013). Low-order auditory Zernike moment: A novel approach for robust music identification in the compressed domain. *EURASIP Journal on Advances in Signal Processing*, (1): 1–15.

Li, Y., Po, L. M., Xu, X., Feng, L., Yuan, F., Cheung, C. H., & Cheung, K. W. (2014). No-reference image quality assessment with shearlet transform and deep neural networks. *Neurocomputing, Elsevier, 154*, 94–109. doi:10.1016/j.neucom.2014.12.015

Loncaric, S. (1998). A survey of shape analysis techniques. *Pattern Recognition, 31*(8), 983–1001. doi:10.1016/S0031-2023(97)00122-2

Lowe, D. G. (2004). Distinctive image features from scale-invariant keypoints. *International Journal of Computer Vision, 60*(2), 91–110. doi:10.1023/B:VISI.0000029664.99615.94

Lu, S., Chen, T., Shangxuan, T., Joo-Hwee, L., & Chew-Lim, T. (2015). Scene text extraction based on edges and support vector regression. *International Journal on Document Analysis and Recognition*, 1-11.

Lyu, M. R., Song, J., & Cai, M. (2005). A comprehensive method for multilingual video text detection localization, and extraction. *IEEE Transactions on Circuits and Systems for Video Technology, 15*(2), 243–255. doi:10.1109/TCSVT.2004.841653

Ma, Wu, & Liu. (2010). *Remote Sensing Monitoring For Vegetation Change In Mining Area Based On Spot-VGT NDVI*. Institute for Geoinformatics & Digital Mine Research, Northeastern University.

MacCormick, J., & Blake, A. (2000). A Probabilistic Exclusion Principle for Tracking Multiple Objects. *International Journal of Computer Vision, 39*(1), 57–71. doi:10.1023/A:1008122218374

Mahalakshmi, J., & Kuppusamy, K. (2016). An efficient Image Encryption Method based on ImprovedCipher Block Chaining in Cloud Computing as a Security Service. *Aust. J. Basic & Appl. Sci., 10*(2), 297–306.

Mahesh, V. G., & Raj, A. N. J. (2015). Invariant face recognition using Zernike moments combined with feed forward neural network. *International Journal of Biometrics, 7*(3), 286–307. doi:10.1504/IJBM.2015.071950

Maltoni, D., Maio, D., Jain, A. K., & Prabhakar, S. (2009). Handbook of fingerprint recognition. Springer. doi:10.1007/978-1-84882-254-2

Manish Kumar, N., Mishra, D. C., & Sharma, R. K. (2014). Afirst approach on an RGB image encryption. *Optics and Lasers in Engineering, 52*, 27–34. doi:10.1016/j.optlaseng.2013.07.015

Manzanera, A. (2007). Σ-Δ Background Subtraction and the Zipf Law. *Pattern Recognition, Image. Analysis and Applications*, 42–51.

Mao, K., Zhu, Z., & Jiang, H. (2010). A fast fingerprint image enhancement method. In *Computational Science and Optimization (CSO), 2010 Third International Joint Conference on* (Vol. 1, pp. 222–226). doi:10.1109/CSO.2010.76

Marcialis, G. L., & Roli, F. (2004). Fingerprint Verification by Fusion of Optical and Capacitive Sensors. Pattern Recognition Letters, 11(25), 1315-1322.

Marcialis, G. L., & Roli, F. (2004). Fingerprint Verification by Fusion of Optical and Capacitive Sensors. *Pattern Recognition Letters, 25*(11), 1315–1322. doi:10.1016/j.patrec.2004.05.011

Marji, M., & Siy, P. (2004). Polygonal representation of digital planar curves through dominant point detection—a nonparametric algorithm. *Pattern Recognition, 37*(11), 2113–2130. doi:10.1016/j.patcog.2004.03.004

Marvel, L. M., Boncelet, C. G. Jr, & Retter, C. (1999). Spread Spectrum Steganography. *IEEE Transactions on Image Processing, 8*(8).

Masood, A. (2008a). Dominant point detection by reverse polygonization of digital curves. *Image and Vision Computing, 26*(5), 702–715. doi:10.1016/j.imavis.2007.08.006

Masood, A. (2008b). Optimized polygonal approximation by dominant point deletion. *Pattern Recognition, 41*(1), 227–239. doi:10.1016/j.patcog.2007.05.021

Masood, A., & Haq, S. A. (2007). A novel approach to polygonal approximation of digital curves. *Journal of Visual Communication and Image Representation, 18*(3), 264–274. doi:10.1016/j.jvcir.2006.12.002

Matas, J., Chum, O., Urban, M., & Pajdla, T. (2004). Robust wide-baseline stereo from maximally stable extremal regions. *Image and Vision Computing, 22*(10), 761–767. doi:10.1016/j.imavis.2004.02.006

Matsushita, Yang, Chen, Onda1, & Qiu. (2007). *Sensitivity of the Enhanced Vegetation Index (EVI) and Normalized Difference Vegetation Index (NDVI) to Topographic Effects: A Case Study in High-Density Cypress Forest.* Graduate School of Life and Environmental Sciences, University of Tsukuba.

McEwen, Puy, Thiran, Vandergheynst, Van De Ville, & Wiaux. (2013). Sparse image reconstruction on the sphere: Implications of a new sampling theorem. *IEEE Transactions on Image Processing, 22*(6).

Md. Maruf Monwar, S. M. (2009). Multimodal Biometric System Using Rank-Level Fusion Approach. *IEEE Transactions on Systems, Man, and Cybernetics. Part B, Cybernetics, 39*(4), 867–878. doi:10.1109/TSMCB.2008.2009071 PMID:19336340

Medeiros, H., Park, J., & Kak, A. (2007). A light-weight event-driven protocol for sensor clustering in wireless camera networks. *ACM/IEEE Int. Conf. on Distributed Smart Cameras, ICDSC'07*, 203–210. doi:10.1109/ICDSC.2007.4357525

Medeiros, H., Park, J., & Kak, A. (2011). Distributed object trackingusing a cluster-based kalman filter in wireless camera networks. *IEEE Journal of Selected Topics in Signal Processing, 2*(4), 448–463. doi:10.1109/JSTSP.2008.2001310

Melin, P., Gonzalez, C. I., Castro, J. R., Mendoza, O., & Castillo, O. (2014). Edge-detection method for image processing based on generalized type-2 fuzzy logic. *Fuzzy Systems. IEEE Transactions on, 22*(6), 1515–1525.

Menezes, A. J., Van Oorschot, P. C., & Vanstone, S. A. (1996). *Handbook of applied cryptography.* CRC Press. doi:10.1201/9781439821916

Miao, X. K., Xia, K. J., & Wang, X. (2004). Study on intelligent decision making sustaining system of variable rate fertilization in precision agriculture. *Computer Application, 24*, 153–155.

Mikolajczyk, K., Tuytelaars, T., Schmid, C., Zisserman, A., Matas, J., Schaffalitzky, F., & Gool, L. V. et al. (2005). A comparison of affine region detectors. *International Journal of Computer Vision, 65*(1-2), 43–72. doi:10.1007/s11263-005-3848-x

Millán, R. D., Dempere-Marco, L., Pozo, J. M., Cebral, J. R., & Frangi, A. F. (2007). Morphological characterization of intracranial aneurysms using 3-D moment invariants. *Medical Imaging. IEEE Transactions on, 26*(9), 1270–1282.

Mintzer, F. C., & Yeung, M. M. Y. (1999). *U.S. Patent No. 5,875,249.* Washington, DC: U.S. Patent and Trademark Office.

Mishra, M., Tiwari, G., & Yadav, A. K. (2014). Secret Communication using public key steganography. *IEEE International Conference on Recent Advances and Innovations in Engineering (ICRAIE-2014)*, 1-5.

Miyaki, T., Yamasaki, T., & Aizawa, K. (2007). Multi-sensor fusion tracking using visual information and wi-fi location estimation. *ACM/IEEE Int. Conf. on Distributed Smart Cameras, ICDSC'07*, 275–282.

Morkel, T., Eloff, J. H. P., & Olivier, M. S. (2005). An overview of image steganography. *Proceedings of the Fifth Annual Information Security South Africa Conference (ISSA).*

Mousa, A., & Hamad, A. (2006). Evaluation of the RC4 algorithm for data encryption. *International Journal on Computer Science and Applications, 3*(2), 44–56. Retrieved from http:// www.tmrfindia.org/ijcsa/V3I24.pdf

Muja, M., & Lowe, D. G. (2014). Scalable nearest neighbor algorithms for high dimensional data. *Pattern Analysis and Machine Intelligence. IEEE Transactions on, 36*(11), 2227–2240.

Mursi, M. F., Assassa, G. M., Aboalsamh, H. A., & Alghathbar, K. (2009). A DCT-based secure JPEG image authentication scheme. *World Academy of Science. Engineering and Technology, 53*, 682–687.

Natarajan & Shantharajah. (2016). An Effective Segmentation Pattern Using Multi-Class Independent Component Analysis on High Quality Color Texture Images. *Research Journal of Applied Sciences, Engineering and Technology, 12*(9), 926-932.

Natarajan, & Shantharajah. (2014). Image Denoising and Contrast Via Intensity Equalization Method. *International Review on Computers and Software, 9*(6).

Neumann, L., & Matas, J. (2010). A method for text localization and recognition in real-world images. *Proceedings of the 10th Asian Conference on Computer Vision*, 770-783.

Neumann, L., & Matas, J. (2011). Text localization in real-world images using efficiently pruned exhaustive search. *Proceedings of International Conference on Document Analysis and Recognition (ICDAR)*, 687-691. doi:10.1109/ICDAR.2011.144

Neumann, R., & Teisseron, G. (2002). Extraction of dominant points by estimation of the contour fluctuations. *Pattern Recognition, 35*(7), 1447–1462. doi:10.1016/S0031-3203(01)00145-5

Nguyen, Patel, Nasrabadi, & Chellappa. (2013). Design of Non-Linear Kernel Dictionaries for Object Recognition. *IEEE Transactions on Image Processing, 22*(12).

Niblack, C. W., Barber, R., Equitz, W., Flickner, M. D., Glasman, E. H., Petkovic, D., . . . Taubin, G. (1993, April). QBIC project: querying images by content, using color, texture, and shape. In *IS&T/SPIE's Symposium on Electronic Imaging: Science and Technology* (pp. 173-187). International Society for Optics and Photonics. doi:10.1117/12.143648

Noh, J. S., & Rhee, K. H. (2005). Palmprint identification algorithm using Hu invariant moments and Otsu binarization. In *Computer and Information Science, 2005. Fourth Annual ACIS International Conference on* (pp. 94-99). IEEE.

Novotni, M., & Klein, R. (2003, June). 3D Zernike descriptors for content based shape retrieval. In *Proceedings of the eighth ACM symposium on Solid modeling and applications* (pp. 216-225).ACM. doi:10.1145/781606.781639

Oikonomopoulos, A. (2011). *Spatiotemporal Localization and Categorization of Human Actions in Unsegmented Image Sequences. IEEE Transactions on Image Processing, 20(4).*

Ojala, T., Pietikainen, M., & Harwood, D. (1996, January). A Comparative study of texture measures with classification based on feature distribution. *Pattern Recognition, 29*(1), 51–59. doi:10.1016/0031-3203(95)00067-4

Ojala, T., Pietikainen, M., & Maenpaa, T. (2012, July). Multiresolution grayscale and rotation invariant texture classification with local binary patterns. *IEEE Transactions on Pattern Analysis and Machine Intelligence, 24*(7), 971–987. doi:10.1109/TPAMI.2002.1017623

Okumura, S. (2015). A public key cryptosystem based on Diophantine equations of degree increasing type. *Pacific Journal of Mathematics for Industry, 7*(1), 1. doi:10.1186/s40736-015-0014-4

Ollero, A. (2001). *Robótica: Manipuladores y robots móviles*. Barcelona: Marcombo S.A.

Onel, T., Ersoy, C., & Delic, H. (2009). Information content-based sensor selection and transmission power adjustment for collaborative target tracking. *IEEE Transactions on Mobile Computing, 8*(8), 1103–1116. doi:10.1109/TMC.2009.12

Panduranga, H. T., & Naveen Kumar, S. K. (2012). A Novel Image Encryption Technique using Multi- wave based carrier Image.*Procedia Engineering, 38*, 2998-3004. doi:10.1016/j.proeng.2012.06.350

Pang, Huang, Yan, Jiang, & Qin. (2011). Transferring Boosted Detectors Towards Viewpoint and Scene Adaptiveness. *IEEE Transactions on Image Processing, 20*(5).

Pan, Y., Hou, X., & Liu, C. (2011). A hybrid approach to detect and localize texts in natural scene images. *IEEE Transactions on Image Processing, 20*(3), 800–813. doi:10.1109/TIP.2010.2070803 PMID:20813645

Papakostas, G. A. (2014). *Over 50 Years of Image Moments and Moment Invariants*. Gate to Computer Sciece and Research. doi:10.15579/gcsr.vol1.ch1

Parameswaran, L., & Anbumani, K. (2008). Content-based watermarking for image authentication using independent component analysis. *Informatica, 32*(3).

Pareek & Patidar. (2014). Medical image protection using genetic algorithm operations. *Soft Computing*, 1-10.

Park, J. H., Park, C. H., Park, J. H., Lee, S. J., Lee, W. S., & Joo, Y. E. (2004). Review of 209 cases of foreign bodies in the upper gastrointestinal tract and clinical factors of successful endoscopic removal. *The Korean Journal of Gastroenterology, 4*(3), 226–233. PMID:15100486

Park, Y.-K., Kim, K.-O., Yang, J.-H., Lee, S.-H., & Jang, B.-I. (2013). Factors Associated with Development of Complications After Endoscopic Foreign Body Removal. *Saudi Journal of Gastroenterology, 19*(5), 230–234. doi:10.4103/1319-3767.118136 PMID:24045597

Paul, P. K., & Ghose, M. K. (2012). Cloud Computing: Possibilities, Challenges, and opportunities with special reference to its emerging need in the academic and working area of information science. *International Conference on Modeling Optimisation and Computing*. Elsevier. doi:10.1016/j.proeng.2012.06.267

Pavlidis, T., & Horowitz, S. L. (1974). Segmentation of plane curves. *IEEE Transactions on Computers, 23*(8), 860–870. doi:10.1109/T-C.1974.224041

Perez, P., Hue, C., Vermaak, J., & Gangnet, M. (2002). Color-Based Probabilistic Tracking.*European Conf. Computer Vision*, 661-675.

Performance Evaluation of Tracking and Surveillance (PETS). (2006, June). *Ninth IEEE International Workshop on Performance Evaluation of Tracking and Surveillance*. Retrieved from http://perception.i2r.a-star.edu.sg

Petcu, Zaharie, Gorgan, Pop, & Tudor. (2008). *MedioGrid: A Grid-based Platform for Satellite Image Processing*. Western University of Timisoara.

Petitcolas, F. (2015). *The Information Hiding Home page: Digital Watermarking & Steganography*. Retrieved from http://www.petitcolas.net/steganography/index.html

Piccardi, M. (2004). Background subtraction techniques: a review.*IEEE Int. Conf. Systems, Man and Cybernetics*, 3099–3104.

Pietikainen, M., Ojala, T., Scruggs, T., Bowyer, K. W., Jin, C., & Hoffman, K. (2000, January). Rotational invariant texture classification using feature distribution. *Pattern Recognition, 33*(1), 43–52. doi:10.1016/S0031-3203(99)00032-1

Pilet, J., Strecha, C., & Fua, P. (2008). *Making background subtraction robust to sudden illumination changes*. ECCV. doi:10.1007/978-3-540-88693-8_42

Pillai, J. S., & Padma, T. (2017). Semi Fragile Watermarking for Content based Image Authentication and Recovery in the DWT domain. *International Arab Journal of Internet Technologies*. (in press)

Pillai, J. S., & Padma, T. (2015). Secure Watermarking using Diophantine Equations for Authentication and Recovery. *Journal of Network and Information Security, 3*(2), 2–9.

Power, P., & Schoonees, J. (2002). Understand background mixture models for foreground segmentation. *Image and Vision Computing*, 267–271.

Prochdxka & Kolinovd. (2004). *Satellite Image Processing and Air Pollution Detection*. Prague Institute of Chemical Technology.

Prokop, R. J., & Reeves, A. P. (1992). A survey of moment-based techniques for unoccluded object representation and recognition. *CVGIP: Graphical Models and Image Processing, 54*(5), 438–460.

Provos, N., & Honeyman, P. (2003). Hide and seek: An introduction to steganography. *Security & Privacy. IEEE Journals & Magazines, 1*(3), 32–44.

Qader, H. A., Ramli, A. R., & Al-Haddad, S. (2007). Fingerprint Recognition Using Zernike Moments. *Int. Arab J. Inf. Technol., 4*(4), 372–376.

Qi, X., Xin, X., & Chang, R. (2009). Image authentication and tamper detection using two complementary watermarks. In *2009 16th IEEE International Conference on Image Processing (ICIP)* (pp. 4257-4260). IEEE.

Qin, S., & Li, R. (n.d.). *An efficient algorithm for edge detection using Robert-Zernike moments operator*. Academic Press.

Qing, Z., & Linvill, D. (2002). Integrating crop models into GIS regional crop yield. *ASAE Annual International Meeting/CIGR XVth World Congress*, 28–31.

Qingquan, C., & Lin, L. (2003). The Developing Trend and Application of GIS on Agriculture. *Review of China Agricultural Science Technology , 5*, 22–26.

Qirui, Y. (2012). Kaas-based intelligent service model in agricultural expert system. *2nd International Conference on Consumer Electronics, Communications and Networks*. IEEE.

Qiuting, W., & Bing, Y. (2008, December). 3D terrain matching algorithm and performance analysis based on 3D Zernike moments. In *Computer Science and Software Engineering, 2008 International Conference on* (Vol. 6, pp. 73-76). IEEE.

Quality of YUV-RGB conversion. (n.d.) Retrieved from http://discoverybiz.net/enu0/faq/faq_YUVbyBreeze_test_00.html

Raahat, , Raza, Umar, Hussain, Rasheed, & Rao. (2013). Coin Impaction at Upper end of Esophagus; Wait or Intervene. *Pakistan Journal of Otolaryngology, 29*(3), 77–79.

Radharani, S., & Valarmathi, M. L. (2012). content based hybrid DWT-DCT watermarking for image authentication in color images. *International Journal of Engineering Inventions, 1*(4), 32–38.

Radu, C., & Iulian, U. (n.d.). *DCT transform and wavelet transform in image compression: Applications*. Retrieved from http://www.etc.tuiasi.ro/sibm/old/DCT_Wavelet_Transform_engl_v6.PDF?

Ragab, Alla, & Noaman. (2015). Encryption Quality Analysis of the RCBC Block Cipher Compared with RC6 and RC5 Algorithms. In *International Bio-Metrics and Smart Government Summit, FTI Conference*.

Rahman, Balamurugan, & Mariappan. (2015). A Novel DNA Computing based Encryption and Decryption Algorithm. *Procedia Computer Science, 46*, 463 – 475.

Ramaiah, M., & Ray, B. K. (2015). Polygonal approximation of digital planar curve using local integral deviation. *International Journal of Computational Vision and Robotics, 5*(3), 302–319. doi:10.1504/IJCVR.2015.071333

Ramalingam, M., & Mat Isa, N. A. (2015). A Steganography Approach over Video Images to Improve Security. *Indian Journal of Science and Technology*, 8(1), 79–86. doi:10.17485/ijst/2015/v8i1/53100

Ramli, D. A., Rani, N. H. C., & Ishak, K. A. (2011). Performance of weighted sum- rule fusion scheme in multi-instance and multi-modal biometric systems. World Applied Science Journal, 11(12), 2160-2167.

Rani, J. S., & Devaraj, D. (2012). Face recognition using Krawtchouk moment. *Sadhana*, 37(4), 441–460. doi:10.1007/s12046-012-0090-4

Rasmussen, C., & Hager, G. (2001, June). Probabilistic Data Association Methods for Tracking Complex Visual Objects. *IEEE Transactions on Pattern Analysis and Machine Intelligence*, 23(6), 560–576. doi:10.1109/34.927458

Ray, I., Ray, I., & Narasimhamurthi, N. (2002). A cryptographic solution to implement access control in a hierarchy and more.*Proceedings of SACMAT'02*. doi:10.1145/507711.507723

Ray, S., & Dadhwal, V. (2001). Estimation of crop evapotranspiration of irrigation command area using remote sensing and GIS. *Agricultural Water Management*, 49(3), 239–249. doi:10.1016/S0378-3774(00)00147-5

Reddy, M. H. S., & Raja, K. B. (2010). High capacity and security steganograph using wavelet transform. *International Journal of Computer Science and Security*, 3(6), 462–472.

Robert Snelick, U. U. (2005). Large-Scale Evaluation of Multimodal Biometric Authentication Using State-of-the-Art Systems. *IEEE Transactions on Pattern Analysis and Machine Intelligence*, 27(3), 450–455. doi:10.1109/TPAMI.2005.57 PMID:15747798

Robert, E. (2015). Management of Ingested Foreign Bodies in Children: A Clinical Report of the NASPGHAN Endoscopy Committee. *Journal of Pediatric Gastroenterology and Nutrition*, 60(4), 562–574. doi:10.1097/MPG.0000000000000729 PMID:25611037

Rocha, A., & Goldenstein, S. (2008). Steganography and steganalysis in digital multimedia: Hype or hallelujah? *Research Initiative, Treatment Action*, 15(1), 83–110.

Roettger. (2006). *NDVI Based Vegetation Rendering*. Computer Graphics Group, University of Erlangen.

Ross, A. (2006). *Handbook of Multibiometrics*. New York: Springer.

Rosten, E., & Drummond, T. (2006). Machine learning for high-speed corner detection. In A. Leonardis, H. Bischof & A. Pinz (Eds.), Computer Vision – ECCV 2006 (pp. 430–443). Berlin: Springer-Verlag. doi: 34 doi:10.1007/11744023_34

Rosten, E., & Drummond, T. (2005). Fusing points and lines for high performance tracking. In *Proceedings of the Tenth IEEE International Conference on Computer Vision (ICCV'05)*. Beijing, China: IEEE. doi:10.1109/ICCV.2005.104

Russo, F., & Ramponi, G. (1994). Combined FIRE filters for image enhancement. In *Fuzzy Systems, 1994. IEEE World Congress on Computational Intelligence.,Proceedings of the Third IEEE Conference on* (pp. 260–264).

Russo, F. (1999). FIRE operators for image processing. *Fuzzy Sets and Systems*, 103(2), 265–275. doi:10.1016/S0165-0114(98)00226-7

Saabni, R., Asi, A., & El-Sana, J. (2014). Text line extraction for historical document images. *Pattern Recognition Letters, Elsevier*, 35, 23–33. doi:10.1016/j.patrec.2013.07.007

Sael, L., La, D., Li, B., Rustamov, R., & Kihara, D. (2008). Rapid comparison of properties on protein surface. Proteins. *Structure, Function, and Bioinformatics*, 73(1), 1–10. doi:10.1002/prot.22141

Sael, L., Li, B., La, D., Fang, Y., Ramani, K., Rustamov, R., & Kihara, D. (2008). Fast protein tertiary structure retrieval based on global surface shape similarity. Proteins. *Structure, Function, and Bioinformatics*, 72(4), 1259–1273. doi:10.1002/prot.22030 PMID:18361455

Safy, R. O. E., Zayed, H. H., & Dessouki, A. E. (2009). An adaptive steganographic technique based on integer wavelet transform.*Proceedings of International Conference on Networking and Media Convergence (ICNM 2009)* (pp.111-117). doi:10.1109/ICNM.2009.4907200

Saki, N., Nikakhlagh, S., Rahim, F., & Abshirini, H. (2009). Foreign body aspirations in Infancy: A 20-year experience. *International Journal of Medical Sciences*, 6(6), 322–328. doi:10.7150/ijms.6.322 PMID:19851473

Sakr, A. S., Ibrahem, H. M., Abdullkader, H. M., & Amin, M. (2012). A steganographic method based on DCT and new quantization technique.*22nd International Conference on Computer Theory and Applications (ICCTA)*, 187-191. doi:10.1109/ICCTA.2012.6523567

Sanfeliu, A., Andrade-Cetto, J., Barbosa, M., Bowden, R., Capitian, R., & Corominas, A. (2010). Decentralized sensor fusion for ubiquitous networking robotics in urban areas. *Sensors (Basel, Switzerland)*, 10(3), 2274–2314. doi:10.3390/s100302274 PMID:22294927

Sarkar, D. (1993). A simple algorithm for detection of significant vertices for polygonal approximation of chain-coded curves. *Pattern Recognition Letters*, 14(12), 959–964. doi:10.1016/0167-8655(93)90004-W

Sarvaiya, J., Patnaik, S., & Goklani, H. (2010). Image registration using NSCT and invariant moment.[IJIP]. *International Journal of Image Processing*, 4(2), 119.

Sato, T., Kanade, T., Hughes, E. K., & Smith, M. A. (1998). Video ocr for digital news archives. *Proceedings of Workshop on Content Based Access of Image and Video Databases*, 52-60.

Sato, Y. (1992). Piecewise linear approximation of plane curves by perimeter optimization. *Pattern Recognition*, 25(12), 1535–1543. doi:10.1016/0031-3203(92)90126-4

Sawashima, H., Hori, Y., Sunahara, H., & Oie, Y. (1997). Characteristics of UDP Packet Loss: Effect of TCP Traffic. In *Proceedings of INET 97: The Seventh Annual Conference of the Internet Society*.

Scassellati, B. M., Alexopoulos, S., & Flickner, M. D. (1994, April). Retrieving images by 2D shape: a comparison of computation methods with human perceptual judgments. In *IS&T/SPIE 1994 International Symposium on Electronic Imaging: Science and Technology* (pp. 2-14). International Society for Optics and Photonics.

Schmidt, A., & Kasinski, A. (2010). The visual SLAM system for a hexapod robot. In L. Bolc, R. Tadeusiewics, L. J. Chmielewski & K. Wojciechowski (Eds.), Computer Vision and Graphics (pp. 260-267). Berlin: Springer-Verlag. doi: 32 doi:10.1007/978-3-642-15907-7_32

Seki, M., Wada, T., Fujiwara, H., & Sumi, K. (2003). Background subtraction based on cooccurence of image variations. *IEEE Int. Conf. CVPR*, 65–72. doi:10.1109/CVPR.2003.1211453

Selvi, M., & George, A. (2013). FBFET: Fuzzy based fingerprint enhancement technique based on adaptive thresholding. In *Computing, Communications and Networking Technologies (ICCCNT), 2013 Fourth International Conference on* (pp. 1–5).

Senevirathna, E. N. W., &Jayaratne, L. (2015). Audio Music Monitoring: Analyzing Current Techniques for Song Recognition and Identification. *GSTF Journal on Computing (JoC)*, 4(3).

Sethi, I. K., & Jain, R. (1987). Finding trajectories of feature points in a monocular image sequence. *IEEE Transactions on Pattern Analysis and Machine Intelligence*, PAMI-9(1), 56–73. doi:10.1109/TPAMI.1987.4767872 PMID:21869377

Shahab, A., Shafait, F., & Dengel, A. (2011). ICDAR-2011 robust reading competition challenge 2: Reading text in scene images. *Proceedings of International Conference on Document Analysis and Recognition (ICDAR)*, 1491-1496. doi:10.1109/ICDAR.2011.296

Shaikh, M. M., Bahn, W., Lee, C., Kim, T., Lee, T., Kim, K., & Cho, D. (2011). *Mobile robot vision tracking using unscented kalman filter*. Paper presented at 2011 IEEE/SICE International Symposium on System Integration (SII), Kyoto, Japan. doi:10.1109/SII.2011.6147622

Shang, W., Yang, C., Liu, Y. & Wang, J. (2016). Design on a Composite Mobile System for Exploration Robot. *Shock and Vibration*. 10.1155/2016/6363071

Shao, Y., & Jin, Z. (2012). Trademark Image Retrieval Based on Improved Distance Measure of Moments. In Multimedia and Signal Processing (pp. 154-162). Springer Berlin Heidelberg. doi:10.1007/978-3-642-35286-7_20

Sheikh, Y., & Shah, M. (2005). Bayesian modeling of dynamic scenes for object detection. *IEEE Transactions on Pattern Analysis and Machine Intelligence*, 27(11), 1778–1792. doi:10.1109/TPAMI.2005.213 PMID:16285376

Shejul, A. A., & Kulkarni, U. L. (2010). A DWT Based Approach for Steganography using Biometrics. *International Conference on Data Storage and Data Engineering (DSDE)*, 39-43. doi:10.1109/DSDE.2010.10

Sherlock, B. G., Monro, D. M., & Millard, K. (1994). Fingerprint enhancement by directional Fourier filtering. In *Vision, Image and Signal Processing, IEE Proceedings-* (Vol. 141, pp. 87–94). doi:10.1049/ip-vis:19949924

Shi, J., & Tomasi, C. (1994). Good features to track. In *Proceedings of IEEE Computer Society Conference on Computer Vision and Pattern Recognition (CVPR'94)*. Seattle, WA: IEEE. doi:10.1109/CVPR.1994.323794

Shim, J. C., Dorai, C., & Bolle, R. (1998). Automatic Text Extraction from Video for Content-based Annotation and Retrieval. *Proceedings of International Conference on Pattern Recognition*, 1, 618-620.

Shivakumara, P., Huang, W., Phan, T. Q., & Tan, C. L. (2010). Accurate video text detection through classification of low and high contrast images. Pattern Recognition, 2165-2185.

Shivakumara, P., Kumar, N., Guru, D., & Tan, C. (2014). Separation of graphics (superimposed) and scene text in video frames. *Proceedings of the 11th IAPR International Workshop on Document Analysis Systems (DAS)*, 344-348. doi:10.1109/DAS.2014.20

Shivakumara, P., Phan, T. Q., & Tan, C. L. (2009). Video text detection based on filters and edge features. *Proceedings of International Conference on Multimedia and Expo*, 514-517. doi:10.1109/ICME.2009.5202546

Shivakumara, P., Phan, T. Q., & Tan, C. L. (2010). New wavelet and color features for text detection in video. *Proceedings of the 20th International Conference on Pattern Recognition (ICPR)*, 3996-3999. doi:10.1109/ICPR.2010.972

Shivakumara, P., Phan, T. Q., & Tan, C. L. (2011). A laplacian approach to multioriented text detection in video. *IEEE Transactions on Pattern Analysis and Machine Intelligence*, 33(2), 412–419. doi:10.1109/TPAMI.2010.166 PMID:20733217

Shi, Z., Liu, Z., Wu, X., & Xu, W. (2013). Feature selection for reliable data association in visual SLAM. *Machine Vision and Applications*, 24(4), 667–682. doi:10.1007/s00138-012-0440-6

Shlapentokh, A. (2007). *Hilbert's tenth problem: Diophantine classes and extensions to global fields* (Vol. 7). Cambridge University Press.

Silva, P. F., Marçal, A. R., & da Silva, R. M. A. (2013). Evaluation of features for leaf discrimination. In *Image Analysis and Recognition* (pp. 197–204). Springer Berlin Heidelberg. doi:10.1007/978-3-642-39094-4_23

Silva, R., García, J. R., Barrientos, V. R., Molina, M. A., Hernández, V. M., & Silva, G. (2007). State-of-the-art of the movable wheels robots. *Telématique: Revista Electrónica de Estudios Telemáticos, 6*(3), 1–14.

Singh, A., & Singh, H. (2015). An improved LSB based image steganography technique for RGB images. *IEEE International Conference on Electrical, Computer and Communication Technologies (ICECCT)*, 1-4. doi:10.1109/ICECCT.2015.7226122

SITA and AOptix partner to offer automated biometric systems. (2012, February 10). Retrieved from http://www.airport-technology.com/news/newssita-aoptix-partnership-to-offer-airport-automated-biometric-identity-solutions

Sivanandam, S. N., Sumathi, S., & Deepa, S. N. et al. (2007). *Introduction to fuzzy logic using MATLAB* (Vol. 1). Springer. doi:10.1007/978-3-540-35781-0

Skifstad, K., & Jain, R. (1989). Illumination independent change detection for real world image sequences. *Comp. Vision. Graphics, and Image Process., 46*(3), 387–399. doi:10.1016/0734-189X(89)90039-X

Sklansky, J., & Gonzalez, V. (1980). Fast polygonal approximation of digitized curves. *Pattern Recognition, 12*(5), 327–331. doi:10.1016/0031-3203(80)90031-X

Sloan, T., & Hernandez-Castro, J. (2015). Forensic analysis of video steganography tools. *PeerJ Computer Science, 1*(e7). Retrieved from https://doi.org/10.7717/peerj-cs.7

Smith, M. A., & Kanade, T. (1995). Video skimming for quick browsing based on audio and image characterization. Carnegie Mellon University.

Song, B., & Roy-Chowdhury, A. K. (2007). Stochastic adaptive tracking in a camera network. *IEEE Int. Conf. on Compute Vision*, 1–8. doi:10.1109/ICCV.2007.4408937

Sonka, M. et al. (2001). *Image processing analysis and computing vision*. Brooks/Cole.

Soto, C., Song, B., & Roy-Chowdhury, A. K. (2009). Distributed multi-target tracking in a self-configuring camera network. *IEEE Conf. on Computer Vision and Pattern Recognition, CVPR'09*, 1486–1493. doi:10.1109/CVPR.2009.5206773

Souheil Ben-Yacoub, Y. A. (1999). Fusion of Face and Speech Data for Person Identity Verification. *IEEE Transaction, 10*(5), 1065–1074. PMID:18252609

Srinivasan, B., Arunkumar, S., & Rajesh, K. (2015). A Novel Approach for Color Image Steganography Using NUBASI and Randomized. *Secret Sharing Algorithm. Indian Journal of Science and Technology, 8*(S7), 228–235. doi:10.17485/ijst/2015/v8iS7/64275

Stanescu, D., Borca, D., Groza, V., & Stratulat, M. (2008). A hybrid watermarking technique using singular value decomposition. In *ProceedingsIEEE International Workshop on Haptic Audio visual Environments and Games (HAVE 2008)* (pp. 166 – 170). doi:10.1109/HAVE.2008.4685318

Starks. (2004). *Interval and Fuzzy Methods in Remote Sensing and Satellite Image Processing*. University of Texas at El Paso.

Stauffer, C., & Grimson, W. (1999). Adaptive background mixture models for real-time tracking. *IEEE Conf. CVPR*, 2246-2252. doi:10.1109/CVPR.1999.784637

Sun, X., Chen, M., & Hauptmann, A. (2009, June). Action recognition via local descriptors and holistic features. In *Computer Vision and Pattern Recognition Workshops, 2009.CVPR Workshops 2009. IEEE Computer Society Conference on* (pp. 58-65). IEEE.

Sun, B., Yan, H., Shi, J. P., Zhang, Y. P., & Zhang, B. N. (2006). Development and application of fertilization decision-making supporting systems based on ComGIS. *Transactions of the Chinese Society of Agricultural Engineering, 24*, 75–79.

Sun, F., & Liu (2010). Selecting Cover for Image Steganography by Correlation Coefficient.*Second International Workshop on Education Technology and Computer Science (ETCS)*, 2, 159-162. doi:10.1109/ETCS.2010.33

Sun, Y., Tian, Z., Ye, J., Zhang, H., & Tang, S. (2013). UDP flow detection and analysis using dynamical timeout strategy based on sliding-window. *2013 IEEE Conference Anthology*, 1-4.

Sur, A., Shyam, D., Goel, D., & Mukherjee, J. (2012). An image steganographic algorithm based on spatial desynchronization. *Multimedia Tools and Applications*, *2012*(November). doi:10.1007/s11042-012-1261-3

Surendiran, B., & Vadivel, A. (2012). Mammogram mass classification using various geometric shape and margin features for early detection of breast cancer. *International Journal of Medical Engineering and Informatics*, *4*(1), 36–54. doi:10.1504/IJMEI.2012.045302

Szmidt, E., & Kacprzyk, J. (2001). Entropy for intuitionistic fuzzy sets. *Fuzzy Sets and Systems*, *118*(3), 467–477. doi:10.1016/S0165-0114(98)00402-3

Tahmasbi, A., Saki, F., & Shokouhi, S. B. (2011). Classification of benign and malignant masses based on Zernike moments. *Computers in Biology and Medicine*, *41*(8), 726–735. doi:10.1016/j.compbiomed.2011.06.009 PMID:21722886

Talati & Shah. (2014). Feature Extraction Technique using Shape Context Descriptor for Image Retrieval. *Indian Journal of Applied Research*, *4*(8), 1-2.

Tanaka, K., Nakamura, Y., & Matsui, K. (1991). Secret transmission method of character data in motion picture communication. In *Visual Communications,'91* (pp. 646–649). Boston, MA: International Society for Optics and Photonics. doi:10.1117/12.50295

Tang & Zhang. (2011). Secure Image Encryption without Size Limitation Using Arnold Transform and Random Strategies. *Journal of Multimedia, 6*(2).

Tang, X., Gao, X., Liu, J., & Zhang, H. (2002). A spatial-temporal approach for video caption detection and recognition. *IEEE Transactions on Neural Networks*, *13*(4), 961–971. doi:10.1109/TNN.2002.1021896 PMID:18244491

Taniar, D., & Rahayu, W. (2013). A taxonomy for nearest neighbour queries in spatial databases. *Journal of Computer and System Sciences*, *79*(7), 1017–1039. doi:10.1016/j.jcss.2013.01.017

Tao, C.-W., Thompson, W. E., & Taur, J. S. (1993). A fuzzy if-then approach to edge detection. In *Fuzzy Systems, 1993., Second IEEE International Conference on* (pp. 1356–1360). doi:10.1109/FUZZY.1993.327590

Taubin, G., & Cooper, D. B. (1991). *Object recognition based on moment (or algebraic) invariants*. IBM TJ Watson Research Center.

Taubin, G., & Cooper, D. B. (1991, September). Recognition and positioning of rigid objects using algebraic moment invariants. In *San Diego,'91* (pp. 175–186). San Diego, CA: International Society for Optics and Photonics. doi:10.1117/12.48423

Tayel, M., Gamal, A., & Shawky, H. (2016). A proposed implementation method of an audio steganography technique.*18th International Conference on Advanced Communication Technology (ICACT)*.

Teague, M. R. (1980). Image analysis via the general theory of moments. *JOSA*, *70*(8), 920–930. doi:10.1364/JOSA.70.000920

Teh, C. H., & Chin, R. T. (1988). On image analysis by the methods of moments. *Pattern Analysis and Machine Intelligence. IEEE Transactions on*, *10*(4), 496–513.

Thacker, P. G., & Lee, E. Y. (2016). Advances in Multidetector CT Diagnosis of Pediatric Pulmonary Thromboembolism. *Korean Journal of Radiology, 17*(2), 198–208. doi:10.3348/kjr.2016.17.2.198 PMID:26957904

Thrun S. Burgard W. Fox D. (2005). *Probabilistic robotics.* MIT Press.

Tian. (2013). A Review on Image Feature Extraction and Representation Technique. *International Journal of Multimedia and Ubiquitous Engineering, 8*(4), 385-396.

Tirpude, & Welekar. (2013). A Study of Brain Magnetic Resonance Image Segmentation Techniques. *International Journal of Advanced Research in Computer and Communication Engineering, 4*(3), 279–284.

Tizhoosh, H. R., & Fochem, M. (1995). Fuzzy histogram hyperbolization for image enhancement. *Proceedings EUFIT*, 95.

Toharia, P., Robles, O. D., Rodríguez, Á., & Pastor, L. (2007). *A study of Zernike invariants for content-based image retrieval. In Advances in Image and Video Technology* (pp. 944–957). Springer Berlin Heidelberg.

Torr, P., & Zisserman, A. (2000). MLESAC: A new robust estimator with application to estimating image geometry. *Computer Vision and Image Understanding, 78*(1), 138–156. doi:10.1006/cviu.1999.0832

Trier, Ø. D., Jain, A. K., & Taxt, T. (1996). Feature extraction methods for character recognition-a survey. *Pattern Recognition, 29*(4), 641–662. doi:10.1016/0031-3203(95)00118-2

Uhl, A., & Wild, P. (2009). Single-sensor multi-instance fingerprint. *International Journal of Biometrics, 4*(1), 442-462.

Uhl, A., & Wild, P. (2009). Single-sensor multi-instance fingerprint and. International. *Journal of Bioethics, 1*(4), 442–462.

Unay, D., Ekin, A., & Jasinschi, R. S. (2010, July). Local structured based region of interest retrieval in brain MR images. *IEEE Transactions on Information Technology in Biomedicine, 14*(4), 897–903. doi:10.1109/TITB.2009.2038152 PMID:20064763

Uyemura, M. C. (2005). Foreign Body Ingestion in Children. *American Academy of Family Physicians, 72*(2), 287–291. PMID:16050452

Valandar, M. Y., Ayubi, P., & Barani, M. J. (2015). High secure digital image steganography based on 3D chaotic map. *7th Conference on Information and Knowledge Technology (IKT)*, 1-6. doi:10.1109/IKT.2015.7288810

Van As,, A.B., duToit, N., Wallis, L., Stool, D., Chen, X., & Rode, H. (2003). Pediatric coin ingestion: A prospective study of coin location and symptoms- The South African experience with ingestion injury in children. *International Journal of Pediatric Otorhinolaryngology, 67*(1), 1–8. PMID:12560141

Vatsa, R. S. (2007). Feature based RDWT watermarking for multimodal biometric system. Academic Press.

Venkatraman, V., Chakravarthy, P., & Kihara, D. (2009). Application of 3D Zernike descriptors to shape-based ligand similarity searching. *J. Cheminformatics, 1*(1), 19. doi:10.1186/1758-2946-1-19 PMID:20150998

Venkatraman, V., Sael, L., & Kihara, D. (2009). Potential for protein surface shape analysis using spherical harmonics and 3D Zernike descriptors. *Cell Biochemistry and Biophysics, 54*(1-3), 23–32. doi:10.1007/s12013-009-9051-x PMID:19521674

Verma, N. (2011). Review of Steganographic Techniques. *International Conference and Workshop on Emerging Trends in Technology (ICWET–TCET)*, 990-993. doi:10.1145/1980022.1980237

Vincenzo Conti, C. M. (2010). A Frequency-based Approach for Features Fusion in Fingerprint and Iris Multimodal Biometric Identification Systems. *IEEE Transactions on Systems, Man and Cybernetics. Part C, Applications and Reviews, 40*(4), 384–395. doi:10.1109/TSMCC.2010.2045374

Vlachos, I. K., & Sergiadis, G. D. (2007). The role of entropy in intuitionistic fuzzy contrast enhancement. In *Foundations of Fuzzy Logic and Soft Computing* (pp. 104–113). Springer. doi:10.1007/978-3-540-72950-1_11

Vosters, L. P. J., Shan, C., & Gritti, T. (2010). Background subtraction under sudden illumination changes.*IEEE Conf. AVSS*, 384–391.

Vretos, N., Nikolaidis, N., & Pitas, I. (2011, September). 3D facial expression recognition using Zernike moments on depth images. In *Image Processing (ICIP), 2011 18th IEEE International Conference on* (pp. 773-776).IEEE.

Wadi & Zainal. (2013). Rapid Encryption Method Based on AES Algorithm for Grey Scale HD Image Encryption. *Procedia Technology, 11*(5), 1–5. doi:10.1016/j.protcy.2013.12.154

Waldhoff, G., Curdt, C., Hoffmeister, D., & Bareth, G. (2012). Analysis of multitemporal and multisensor sensing data for crop rotation mapping.*Proceedings of the XXII Congress of the ISPRS*. doi:10.5194/isprsannals-I-7-177-2012

Walton, S. (1995). Image authentication for a slippery new age. *Dr. Dobb's Journal of Software Tools for the Professional Programmer, 20*(4), 18–27.

Wang, Y., Song, J., Liu, X., Jiang, S., & Liu, Y. (2013). Plantation Monitoring System Based on Internet of Things, Green Computing and Communications (GreenCom). *IEEE and Internet of Things (iThings/CPSCom), IEEE International Conference on and IEEE Cyber, Physical and Social Computing*, 366-369.

Wang, H., & Wang, S. (2004). Cyber warfare: Steganography vs. Steganalysis. *Communications of the ACM, 47*(10).

Wang, L., & Zhao, G. (2010). A localization system for mobile robots based vision. In *Proceedings of the 8th World Congress on Intelligent Control and Automation*. Jinan, China: IEEE. doi:10.1109/WCICA.2010.5554159

Wang, Q. (2012). Transferring Visual Prior for Online Object Tracking. *IEEE Transactions on Image Processing*.

Wang, R., Sang, N., & Gao, C. (2015). Text detection approach based on confidence map and context information. *Neurocomputing, Elsevier, 157*, 153–165. doi:10.1016/j.neucom.2015.01.023

Wang, W. Z., Mottershead, J. E., Patki, A., & Patterson, E. A. (2010, August). Construction of shape features for the representation of full-field displacement/strain data. In Applied. *Mechanics of Materials, 24*, 365–370.

Wang, X. F., Huang, D. S., Du, J. X., Xu, H., & Heutte, L. (2008). Classification of plant leaf images with complicated background. *Applied Mathematics and Computation, 205*(2), 916–926. doi:10.1016/j.amc.2008.05.108

Wang, X., Song, Y., & Zhang, Y. (2013). Natural scene text detection with multi-channel connected component segmentation. *Proceedings of the 12th International Conference on Document Analysis and Recognition (ICDAR)*, 1375-1379. doi:10.1109/ICDAR.2013.278

Wei, F., Chou, S., & Lin, C. (2008). A region-based object tracking scheme using Adaboost-based feature selection. *IEEE International Symposium on Circuits and Systems*, 2753–2756.

Weiying, W. (2004). GIS Based Spatial Data Mining Techniques. *Journal of Shandong University of Science and Technology, 23*(4).

Wiliem, A., Madasu, V. K., Boles, W., &Yarlagadda, P. (2007). A face recognition approach using Zernike Moments for video surveillance. *Recent Advances in Security Technology, 341*.

Withey, D. J., & Koles, Z. J. (2007). Three Generations of Medical Image Segmentation, Methods and Available Software. *International Journal of Bioelectromagnetism, 9*(2), 67–68.

Wong, P. W. (1998). A public key watermark for image verification and authentication. In *Image Processing, 1998. ICIP 98. Proceedings. 1998 International Conference on* (Vol. 1, pp. 455-459). IEEE.

Woo, C. S., Du, J., & Pham, B. (2006). Geometric invariant domain for image watermarking. In *International Workshop on Digital Watermarking* (pp. 294-307). Springer Berlin Heidelberg. doi:10.1007/11922841_24

Woolfe, F. (2011). *Autofluorescence Removal by Non-Negative Matrix Factorization. IEEE Transactions on Image Processing, 20(4).*

Wren, C., Azarbayejani, A., Darrel, T., & Pentland, A. (1997). Pfinder, Real time tracking of the human body. *IEEE Transactions on Pattern Analysis and Machine Intelligence, 19*(7), 780–785. doi:10.1109/34.598236

Wu, C., Shi, Z., & Govindaraju, V. (2004). Fingerprint image enhancement method using directional median filter. In Defense and Security (pp. 66–75). doi:10.1117/12.542200

Wu, S., & Zhu, X. (2004). Application of a sliding window protocol in GPRS-based radio access networks. *Robotics and Vision Conference*, 787-791.

Wu, Zhang, Tang, & Liu. (2001). The System and Structure of Internet-based. *Geography and Territorial Research, 17*(4), 20-24.

Wu. (2011). A Linear Programming Approach for Optimal Contrast-Tone Mapping. *IEEE Transactions on Image Processing, 20*(5).

Wu, D.-C., & Tsai, W.-H. (2003). *A steganographic method for images by pixel-value differencing. In Pattern Recognition Letters 24* (pp. 1613–1626). Elsevier.

Wu, J. C., Hsieh, J. W., & Chen, Y. S. (2008). Morphology-based text line extraction. *Journal of Machine Vision and Applications, Springer, 19*(3), 195–207. doi:10.1007/s00138-007-0092-0

Wu, Q., Zhou, C., & Wang, C. (2006). Feature extraction and automatic recognition of plant leaf using artificial neural network. *Advances in Artificial Intelligence*, 3.

Wu, V., Manmatha, R., & Riseman, E. M. (1999). Text finder: An automatic system to detect and recognize text in images. *IEEE Transactions on Pattern Analysis and Machine Intelligence, 20*(11), 1224–1229. doi:10.1109/34.809116

Xiang, L., Baozhu Y., Tiancai, G., Chunjiang, Z., & Ping, C.L. (2003). Study on the Crop Management Information System Based on WebGIS and ES. *ACTA Agriculturae Borealisinica, 18*(20), 106.

Xiao-ying, X., & Hui-shu, Y. (2015). Imaging and differential diagnosis of pediatric spinal tuberculosis. *Radiology of Infectious Diseases, 1*(20), 78–82. doi:10.1016/j.jrid.2015.02.005

Xie, Zhao, Li, & Wang. (2010). *Calculating NDVI for Landsat7-ETM Data after atmospheric correction Using 6S Model.* Key Laboratory of West China's Environmental System.

Xing-yuan, W., Feng, C., & Tian, W. (2010). A new compound mode of confusion and diffusion for block encryption of image based on chaos. *Communications in Nonlinear Science and Numerical Simulation, 15*(9), 2479–2485. doi:10.1016/j.cnsns.2009.10.001

Xinling, B. (1993). *Principle and method of geographic information system.* Beijing: Geological Publishing House.

Xiong, Z., Ramchandran, K., Orchard, M. T., & Zhang, Y. Q. (1999). A comparative study of DCT- and Wavelet-Based image coding. *IEEE Transactions on Circuits and Systems for Video Technology, 9*(5), 692–695. doi:10.1109/76.780358

Xi, S. X., Hua, X. R., Chen, L. W., & Zhang, H. (2001):.A video text detection and recognition system. *Proceedings of International Conference on multimedia and expo*, 873-876.

Xu, W. F. T., Geng, Y., Bai, F., & Zhang, L. (2011). Design of environmental information monitoring system based on GPRS. *Awareness Science and Technology (iCAST), 3rd International Conference on, 469*, 27-30.

Xue, C., Chun, C., Zhu, M., & Chen, A. (2008). A Discriminative Feature-Based Mean-shift Algorithm for Object Tracking. *Knowledge Acquisition and Modeling Workshop, 2008. KAM Workshop 2008. IEEE International Symposium*, 217 – 220. doi:10.1109/KAMW.2008.4810464

Xue, G., Sun, J., & Song, L. (2010, July). Dynamic Background Subtraction Based On Spatial Extended Center-Symmetric Local Binary Pattern. *International Conference in Multimedia and Exposition*, 1050-1055. doi:10.1109/ICME.2010.5582601

Yang, W. (2015). Mutual dependency of features in multimodal biometric systems. Electronics Letters, 3(51), 234–235.

Yang, H. S., Lee, S. U., & Lee, K. M. (1998). Recognition of 2D object contours using starting-point-independent wavelet coefficient matching. *Journal of Visual Communication and Image Representation, 9*(2), 171–181. doi:10.1006/jvci.1998.0384

Yang, J., Liu, L., & Jiang, T. (2002). Improved method for extraction of fingerprint features. In *Second International Conference on Image and Graphics* (pp. 552–558). doi:10.1117/12.477196

Yas, A. (2008). Testing Image Encryptionby Output Feedback (OFB). *Journal of Computer Science, 4*(2), 125–128. doi:10.3844/jcssp.2008.125.128

Ye, W., & Gao, W., Wang, & Zeng, W. (2003). A robust text detection algorithm in images and video frames. *Proceedings of the Joint Conference of the 4th International Conference on Information, Communications and Signal Processing and 4th Pacific Rim Conference on Multimedia*, 802-806.

Ye, Q., Huang, Q., Gao, W., & Zhao, D. (2005). Fast and robust text detection in images and video frames. *Image and Vision Computing, Elsevier, 23*(6), 565–576. doi:10.1016/j.imavis.2005.01.004

Yi, C., & Tian, Y. (2011). Text string detection from natural scenes by structure based partition and grouping. *IEEE Transactions on Image Processing*, 2594–2605. PMID:21411405

Yi, C., & Tian, Y. (2012). Localizing text in scene images by boundary clustering, stroke segmentation, and string fragment classification. *IEEE Transactions on Image Processing, 21*(9), 4256–4268. doi:10.1109/TIP.2012.2199327 PMID:22614647

Yi, C., & Tian, Y. (2013). Text extraction from scene images by character appearance and structure modeling. *Computer Vision and Image Understanding, Elsevier, 117*(2), 182–194. doi:10.1016/j.cviu.2012.11.002 PMID:23316111

Yi, F. P., Hou, X., & Liu, C. L. (2009). Text localization in natural scene images based on conditional random field. *Proceedings of the 10th International Conference on Document Analysis and Recognition*, 6-10.

Yin, P. Y. (2003). Ant colony search algorithms for optimal polygonal approximation of plane curves. *Pattern Recognition, 36*(8), 1783–1797. doi:10.1016/S0031-3203(02)00321-7

Yin, X., Xuwang, Y., Huang, K., & Hong-Wei, H. (2014). Robust text detection in natural scene images. *IEEE Transactions on Pattern Analysis and Machine Intelligence, 36*(5), 970–983. doi:10.1109/TPAMI.2013.182 PMID:26353230

Yong Jian Chin, T. S. (2009). Integrating Palmprint and Fingerprint for Identity Verification. Third International Conference on Network and System Security. *IEEE Transaction*, 437-442.

Yoo, J.-C., & Ahn, C. W. (2012). Image matching using peak signal-to-noise ratio-based occlusion detection. *IEEE. Image Processing, IET, 6*(5), 483–495. doi:10.1049/iet-ipr.2011.0025

Yoon, S., Cao, K., Liu, E., & Jain, A. K. (2013). LFIQ: Latent fingerprint image quality. In *Biometrics: Theory, Applications and Systems (BTAS), 2013 IEEE Sixth International Conference on* (pp. 1–8).

Yoon, S., Feng, J., & Jain, A. K. (2011). Latent fingerprint enhancement via robust orientation field estimation. In *Biometrics (IJCB), 2011 International Joint Conference on* (pp. 1–8). doi:10.1109/IJCB.2011.6117482

Yoon, S., Liu, E., & Jain, A. K. (2015). On latent fingerprint image quality. In *Computational Forensics* (pp. 67–82). Springer. doi:10.1007/978-3-319-20125-2_7

Yosh, H. (2011). *The key exchange cryptosystem used with higher order Diophantine equations.* arXiv preprint arXiv:1103.3742

Youhao, Jihe, Shangyu, Ping, & Zihui. (2008). *Monitoring of Vegetation Changes Using Multi-temporal NDVI in Peripheral Regions around Minqin Oasis, Northwest China.* College of Resources Science and Technology.

Yuen, P. C. (1993). Dominant point matching algorithm. *Electronics Letters, 29*(23), 2023–2024. doi:10.1049/el:19931350

Zadeh, L. A. (1972). *A fuzzy-set-theoretic interpretation of linguistic hedges.* Academic Press.

Zadeh, L. A. (1965). Fuzzy sets. *Information and Control, 8*(3), 338–353. doi:10.1016/S0019-9958(65)90241-X

Zernike, F. (1934). Beugungstheorie des schneidenver-fahrens und seiner verbesserten form, der phasenkontrastmethode. *Physica, 1*(7-12), 689–704. doi:10.1016/S0031-8914(34)80259-5

Zhang, B., Gao, Y., Zhao, S., Liu, J. (2010, February). Local Derivative Pattern Versus Local Binary Pattern: Face Recognition With High-Order Local Pattern Descriptor. *IEEE Transaction on Image processing, 19*(2), 533-545.

Zhang, H., Zhao, K., Song, Y., & Jun, G. (2013). Text extraction from natural scene image: A survey. Neurocomputing, 310-323.

Zhang, B., Bai, L., & Zeng, X. (2010). A novel subpixel edge detection based on the Zernike moment. *Information Technology Journal, 9*(1), 41–47. doi:10.3923/itj.2010.41.47

Zhang, D., & Lu, G. (2001, June). A comparative study on shape retrieval using Fourier descriptors with different shape signatures. In *Proc. International Conference on Intelligent Multimedia and Distance Education (ICIMADE01).*

Zhang, D., & Lu, G. (2002). Shape-based image retrieval using generic Fourier descriptor. *Signal Processing Image Communication, 17*(10), 825–848. doi:10.1016/S0923-5965(02)00084-X

Zhang, D., & Lu, G. (2004). Review of shape representation and description techniques. *Pattern Recognition, 37*(1), 1–19. doi:10.1016/j.patcog.2003.07.008

Zhang, H., Liu, C., Yang, C., Ding, X., & Wang, K. Q. (2011). An improved scene text extraction method using conditional random field and optical character recognition. *Proceedings of International Conference on Document Analysis and Recognition (ICDAR)*, 708-712. doi:10.1109/ICDAR.2011.148

Zhang, S., Zhang, J., & Liu, Y. (2011). A Window-Based Adaptive Correspondence Search Algorithm Using Mean Shift and Disparity Estimation. *Proceedings of International Conference on Virtual Reality and Visualization (ICVRV)*, 319-322. doi:10.1109/ICVRV.2011.47

Zhang, W., & Cao, G. (2004). DCTC: Dynamic Convoy Tree-based Collaboration for target tracking in sensor networks. *IEEE Transactions on Wireless Communications, 3*(5), 1689–1701. doi:10.1109/TWC.2004.833443

Zhang, Y., Lai, J., & Yuen, P. C. (2015). Text string detection for loosely-constructed characters with arbitrary orientations. *Neurocomputing, Elsevier, 168,* 970–978. doi:10.1016/j.neucom.2015.05.028

Zhao, G., Barnard, M., & Pietikainen, M. (2009, November). Lipreading with local spatial temporal descriptor. *IEEE Transactions on Multimedia, 11*(7), 1254–1265. doi:10.1109/TMM.2009.2030637

Zhao, T., & Nevatia, R. (2004).Tracking Multiple Humans in Crowed Environment.*IEEE Computer Society Conference on Computer Vision and Pattern Recognition (CVPR'04),* 2, 406.

Zhao, Z., Fang, C., Lin, Z., & Wu, Y. (2015). A robust hybrid method for text detection in natural scenes by learning-based partial differential equations. *Neurocomputing, Elsevier, 168,* 23–34. doi:10.1016/j.neucom.2015.06.019

Zhong, Y., Kalle, K., & Jain, A. K. (1995). Locating Text In Complex Color Images. *Pattern Recognition, Elsevier, 28*(10), 1523–1535. doi:10.1016/0031-3203(95)00030-4

Zhong, Y., Zhang, H., & Jain, A. K. (2000). Automatic Caption Localization in Compressed Video. *IEEE Transactions on Pattern Analysis and Machine Intelligence, 22*(4), 385–392. doi:10.1109/34.845381

Zhou & Zhou. (2004). Agricultural Expert System application in cultural growth. *Agriculture Network Information, 11,* 32–35.

Zhou, Bao, & Chen. (2013). Image Encryption Using a New Parametric Switching Chaotic System. *Signal Processing, 93*(11), 3039-3052.

Zhou, G., Liu, Y., Meng, Q., & Zhang, Y. (2011). Detecting multilingual text in natural scene. *Proceedings of the 1st International Symposium on Access Spaces (ISAS),* 116-120. doi:10.1109/ISAS.2011.5960931

Zhu & Chen. (2009). *A Quantitative Evaluation of Image Segmentation Quality.* Clark University.

Zhu, Pan, Hu, Li, & Gong. (2004). *Estimating Net Primary Productivity of Terrestrial Vegetation Based on Remote Sensing: A Case Study in Inner Mongolia, China.* College of Resources Science and Technology, Key Laboratory of Environmental Change and Natural Disaster of Ministry of Education, Beijing Normal University.

Zhu, A., Wang, G., & Dong, Y. (2015). *Detecting natural scenes text via auto image partition, two-stage grouping and two-layer classification. In Pattern Recognition Letters.* Elsevier.

Zhuang, H. (2012). *Multichannel Pulse-Coupled-Neural-Network-Based Color Image Segmentation for Object Detection. IEEE Transactions on Industrial Electronics, 59(8).*

Zhu, P., & Chirlian, P. M. (1995). On critical point detection of digital shapes. *IEEE Transactions on Pattern Analysis and Machine Intelligence, 17*(8), 737–748. doi:10.1109/34.400564

Zulkifli, Z., Saad, P., & Mohtar, I. A. (2011, December). Plant leaf identification using moment invariants & general regression neural network. In *Hybrid Intelligent Systems (HIS), 2011 11th International Conference on* (pp. 430-435). IEEE. doi:10.1109/HIS.2011.6122144

About the Contributors

Arun Kumar Sangaiah received Master of Engineering (M.E) Degree in Computer Science and Engineering from Government College of Engineering, Tirunelveli, Anna University Chennai. He had received Doctor of Philosophy Degree in Computer Science and Engineering from VIT University, Vellore, Tamil Nadu, India. He is presently working as Associate Professor in School of Computing Science and Engineering, VIT University, India. His areas of interest include Software Engineering, Soft Computing, Wireless Networks, Bio-Informatics, and Embedded Systems. He has author of more than 50 publications in different journals and conference of National and International repute. His teaching areas include Software Engineering, Wireless Networks, Data and Computer Communications, Soft Computing, Programming Languages, and etc. His current research work include Global Software Development, Wireless Ad hoc and Sensor Networks, and Machine learning, He is active member for Compute Society of India. He has guided many research students and post-graduate students in the field of communication networks, ad hoc networks, database, and soft computing techniques.

* * *

Prabhakar C. J. received his Ph.D degree in Computer Science and Technology from Gulbarga University, Gulbarga, Karnataka, India in 2009. He is currently working as Assistant Professor in the department of Computer Science and M.C.A., in Kuvempu University, Karnataka, India. His research interests are pattern recognition, computer vision, machine vision and video processing.

Chantana Chantrapornchai obtained her Bachelor degree (Computer Science) from Thammasat University of Thailand in 1991. She graduated from Northeastern University at Boston, College of Computer Science, in 1993 and University of Notre Dame, Department of Computer Science and Engineering, in 1999, for her Master and Ph.D degrees respectively. Currently, she is an associated professor of Dept. of Computer Engineering, Faculty of Engineering, Kasetsart University, Thailand. Her research interests include: parallel computing, big data processing, semantic web, computer architecture and fuzzy logic.

Dejey Dharma received her B.E. and M.E. degrees in Computer Science and Engineering from Manonmaniam Sundaranar University, Tirunelveli, India, in 2003 and 2005, respectively. Later, she was with the Department of Computer Science and Engineering, Manonmaniam Sundaranar University, Tirunelveli, India, as a Junior Research Fellow under the UGC Research Grant. She completed her Ph.d in Computer Science and Engineering in 2011. She has been with the Department of Computer Science and Engineering, Regional Centre, Anna University: Tirunelveli Region as an Assistant Professor since 2010 and as the Head of the Department from 2011 to 2015. She is a member in IEEE, IET and IST. Her research interests include image and signal processing, watermarking, information hiding and multimedia security.

Jeyabharathi Duraipandy has completed her B.E degree in the department of computer science and Engineering from Jayaraj Annapackiam CSI College of Engineering, Nazareth, India, under Anna University Chennai in 2009. She has completed her M.E degree in the department of computer science and Engineering from Manonmaniam Sundaranar University, Tirunelveli, in 2013. She is currently pursuing her doctorate from Anna University: Tirunelveli Region. Tirunelveli, in the field of video processing. Her research interest include Image processing, Network security.

Naveen Jambhekar is a research scholar in computer science at s.g.b.amravati university (MS), He is having publications related to his research in various reputed conferences and journals. He also published a patent on his research work.

Alex Noel Joseph Raj received the B. E. degree in Electrical and Electronics Engineering from Madras University, India, in 2001, the M.E. degree in Applied Electronics from Anna University in 2005, and the Ph.D. degree in Engineering from the University of Warwick, UK, in 2009. He is currently a Professor at the School of Electronics Engineering, VIT University, Vellore, India. From 2009 to 2011, he worked as a Design Engineer at Valeport LTD UK. His research interests include signal, image and Sonar processing, Pattern Recognition and FPGA implementations.

Kuppusamy Krishnamoorthy is working as a Professor in the Department of Computer Science and Engineering, Alagappa University, Karaikudi, Tamilnadu, India. He received his Ph.D in Computer Science and Engineering from Alagappa University, Karaikudi, Tamilnadu in the year 2007. He has 27 years of teaching experience at PG level in the field of Computer Science. He has published many research papers in International & National Journals and presented in National and International conferences. His areas of research interests include Information/Network Security, Algorithms, Neural Networks, Fault Tolerant Computing, Software Engineering and Optimization Technique.

Adhiyaman M is a research scholar in School Advanced Sciences at VIT University, Vellore, Tamilnadu, India. He is currently doing Ph.D under the guidance of Dr.D.Ezhilmaran. His area of research is fuzzy image processing and biometrics.

Vasumathy M is a Ph.D Research Scholar in the School of Computing Science and Engineering at VIT University, Vellore, India. She received her Master's in Software Engineering from VIT University. She has industry experience of three years. Her area of specialization includes image processing and knowledge engineering. She has a research experience of two years as a junior research fellow for the sponsored projects funded by government of India.

Vijayalakshmi G. V. Mahesh received the B. E. degree in Electronics and Communication Engineering from Bangalore University, India, in 1999, the M.Tech. degree in Digital Communication and Networking from Visvesvaraya Technological University in 2005. At present she is pursuing her Ph.D degree in Image processing at VIT University, Vellore, India.

Balakrishnan Natarajan is working as an Associate Professor in Sona College of Technology, Tamilnadu, India. He has 16+ years of experience in academic field. His research area is Image Processing. He published his paper in various Journals and International Conferences. He is a life member of ISTE.

Jayashree S. Pillai earned her BE degree in Computer Science from Tamilnadu College of Engineering, India in 1992, M.Tech degree in Computer Science from M. S Ramaiah Institute of Technology, India in 2003 and is presently pursuing her research from Mother Teresa Women's University, India in the area of image authentication. She served as software engineer at Prom Systems Pvt. Ltd, Bangalore and presently working as Associate Professor, Department of MCA, Acharya Institute of Management & Sciences, Bangalore, India. She is a Life Member of ISTE and her research interests are in the fields of Computation, Networking and Security. She has over 20 national and international journal publications.

Jitdumrong Preechasuk is a Ph.D. student of Computer Engineering, Kasetsart University. He obtained his B.Sc. in Computer Science from Silpakorn University in 1997 and M.Sc. in Computer Science from Mahidol University in 2002. His research interests include pattern recognition, multimedia processing & content analysis and speech processing.

Swarnalatha Purushotham is an Associate Professor, in the School of Computing Science and Engineering, VIT University, at Vellore, India. She pursued her Ph.D degree in Image Processing and Intelligent Systems. She has published more than 50 papers in International Journals/International Conference Proceedings/National Conferences. She is having 14+ years of teaching experience. She is a member of IACSIT, CSI, ACM, IACSIT, IEEE (WIE), ACEEE. She is an Editorial board member/reviewer of International/ National Journals and Conferences. Her current research interest includes Image Processing, Remote Sensing, Artificial Intelligence and Software Engineering.She got Young Scientist Award VIFA,2015 in Research Field.

Mangayarkarasi Ramaiah is an Assistant Professor (SG) in the School of Information Technology and Engineering at VIT University, Vellore, India. She received her Masters in Engineering from Anna University. She has teaching experience of around ten years. Her area of specialisation includes computer vision, pattern recognition and computer graphics and she has published a number of research papers in international journals.

Bimal Kumar Ray received his PhD in Computer Science from Indian Statistical Institute, Kolkata, India. He received his Master degree in Applied Mathematics from Calcutta University and Bachelor degree in Mathematics from St. Xavier's College, Kolkata. His research interests are in computer graphics, computer vision and image processing. He has published a number of research papers in peer reviewed journals.

Shantharajah S. P. had served as an academia for 18+ years. Currently working as a Professor in VIT University, Vellore, India. He is a notable Research Supervisor. His specialization are Image Processing, Network Security and Intelligent Support Systems.

Gabriel Solar was born in Santiago, Chile. He received the Diploma of Electrical Engineering and the M.Sc. Eng. degree from Universidad de Santiago de Chile, Santiago, Chile in 2014.

Padma T received the Master's degree in Computer Applications from the University of Madras, India in 1992, M. Tech degree in Information Technology from AAU, India in 2004 and the MPhil and Ph. D degrees in Computer Science from Mother Teresa Women's University, India in 2003 and 2010 respectively. Currently she is working as Professor, Department of MCA, Sona College of Technology, Salem, India. Her research interests include Artificial Intelligence, Data Mining, Data Analytic and Knowledge Based Systems. Dr. Padma is a fellow of the Computer Society of India (CSI) and life member of the Indian Society for Technical Education (ISTE). She was the recipient of the Shayesta Akhtar Memorial National Award for the Best Women Engineering College Teacher of the ISTE for her contributions in 2015. Her Biography was included in the 2010 Edition of the Marquis Who's Who in the World, New Jersey, USA. She serves as Editor and Reviewer for a number of well-known National and International journals. She has over 30 publications in journals and chapters in books. She is serving as subject expert in the Board of studies of various institutions.

Mythili Thirugnanam is an Associate Professor in the School of Computing Science and Engineering at VIT University, Vellore, India. She received a Master's in Software Engineering from VIT University. She has been awarded doctorate in Computer Science and Engineering at VIT University in 2014. She has teaching experience of around 8 years. She has an research experience of 3 years in handling sponsored projects funded by Govt. of India. Her area of specialization includes Image Processing, Software Engineering and Knowledge Engineering. She has published five papers in international journals and presented around seven papers in various national and international conferences.

Ramkumar Thirunavukarasu had 16+ years of service in academic area. He is currently working as a Associate Professor in VIT University, Vellore, India. He is a Research Supervisor for scholars on the domain Image Processing, Data Mining and Big Data Analytics.

Claudio Urrea was born in Santiago, Chile. He received the M.Sc. Eng. and the Dr. degrees from Universidad de Santiago de Chile, Santiago, Chile in 1999, and 2003, respectively; and the Ph.D. degree from Institut National Polytechnique de Grenoble, France in 2003. Ph.D. Urrea is currently Professor at the Department of Electrical Engineering, Universidad de Santiago de Chile, from 1998. He has developed and implemented a Robotics Laboratory, where intelligent robotic systems are development and investigated. He is currently Director of the Doctorate in Engineering Sciences, Major in Automation, at the Universidad de Santiago de Chile.

Index

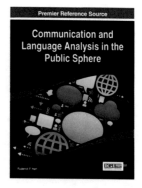

Stay Current on the Latest Emerging Research Developments

Become an IGI Global Reviewer for Authored Book Projects

Premier Reference Source

Solutions for High-Touch Communications in a High-Tech World

Premier Reference Source

Advanced Research on Biologically Inspired Cognitive Architectures

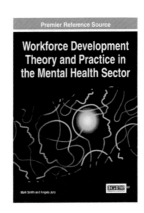

Premier Reference Source

Workforce Development Theory and Practice in the Mental Health Sector

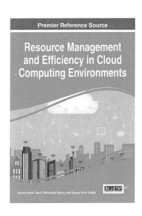

Premier Reference Source

Resource Management and Efficiency in Cloud Computing Environments

The overall success of an authored book project is dependent on quality and timely reviews.

In this competitive age of scholarly publishing, constructive and timely feedback significantly decreases the turnaround time of manuscripts from submission to acceptance, allowing the publication and discovery of progressive research at a much more expeditious rate. Several IGI Global authored book projects are currently seeking highly qualified experts in the field to fill vacancies on their respective editorial review boards:

Applications may be sent to:
development@igi-global.com

Applicants must have a doctorate (or an equivalent degree) as well as publishing and reviewing experience. Reviewers are asked to write reviews in a timely, collegial, and constructive manner. All reviewers will begin their role on an ad-hoc basis for a period of one year, and upon successful completion of this term can be considered for full editorial review board status, with the potential for a subsequent promotion to Associate Editor.

If you have a colleague that may be interested in this opportunity, we encourage you to share this information with them.

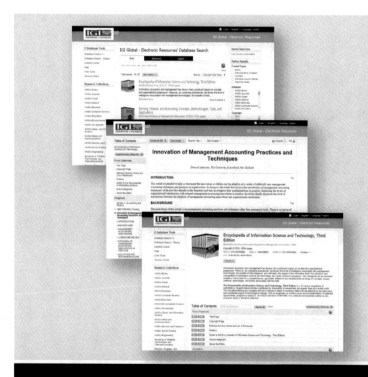